500 ALBUMS

You Won't Believe until You Hear them

I0224878

NEIL NIXON WITH THOM NIXON

Edited and scanned by Andrea Rider, Corinna Downes
Typeset by Jonathan Downes and Jessica Taylor
Cover photo by George Ward
This edition - layout by Peanutt for CFZ Communications
Using Microsoft Word 2000, Microsoft Publisher 2000, Adobe Photoshop CS.

First self published in Canada
Second edition by Gonzo Multimedia 2014

c/o Brooks City,
6th Floor New Baltic House,
65 Fenchurch Street,
London EC3M 4BE
Fax: +44 (0)191 5121104
Tel: +44 (0) 191 5849144
International Numbers:
Germany: Freephone 08000 825 699
USA: Freephone 18666 747 289

GONZO MEDIA GROUP

© Gonzo Multimedia MMXIV

All rights reserved. Without limiting the rights under copyright reserved above, no part of this publication may be reproduced, stored in or introduced into a retrieval system, or transmitted, in any form of by any means (electronic, mechanical, photocopying, recording or otherwise), without the prior written permission of both the copyright owners and the publishers of this book.

ISBN: 978-1-908728-46-3

For John Peel

Picture opposite courtesy of the John Peel Centre for the Creative Arts/*East Anglian Daily News*

Why This Book is Dedicated to John Peel

There are several people to whom we (as in Neil who was always likely to hog the dedication choice) could have dedicated this book. The point of the entries strewn over the following pages is to chart a series of strange, singular and hard to believe recordings that all, in their varied ways, celebrate the creative possibilities of the long playing recorded album. Finding and getting to know the contents of such works has been a lifelong quest for Neil. During this time a number of people have provided reality checks worthy of mention, and – almost – worthy of becoming dedicatees of the book. The kid at school who took Neil to task when he confessed to buying Rupie Edwards' "Ire Feelings (Skanga)" single with an incensed "what did you do that for?" The point of the rant being that spending any money on any reggae record was a no-no and the dependable Cumbrian values of "we don't bloody understand it and we don't want it here" should prevail. Then there was the sales assistant in Track Records in York serving Neil as he took Wild

Man Fischer's Pronounced Normal album up to the check out. "Oh, right" said the assistant "I told the boss we should get one of those in, I knew someone would buy it." The life spent finding and cherishing the sounds lined up and described in this book has held many such moments. The guess of both authors here – Neil and Thom – is that anyone motivated to read this book has had moments like those described above.

Without John Peel, all of our lives would have been infinitely poorer. You will see many mentions of plays by Peel of some of the records described in this book. You'll also see regular references to online repositories of information regarding unusual music and broadcasting operations covering the same material. Julian Cope's Head Heritage website, The All Music Guide, The Music for Maniacs web presence, radio operations like WFMU and BBC Radio Six Music and specific shows like Stuart Maconie's Freak Zone (on Six Music) have all – to a greater or lesser extent – been influenced by Peel's broadcasting career. At Peel's funeral his sometime colleague Paul Gambaccini suggested nobody to that point in history had actually listened to more records than Peel. This was no empty tribute, Gambaccini had an argument and evidence to support the claim. In an internet-connected world where most music remains available most of the time it is doubtful whether any radio DJ will ever be able to approach Peel's life-long level of influence in bringing sounds of all persuasions to the attention of a wide listening public. This book is aimed at those who remain insatiable in their search for sounds to enthral, amuse and open up the imagination. In other words those on the kind of journey to which John Peel dedicated most of his working life. The present authors give a heartfelt thanks for all the good work done by John Peel and a personal thanks to those at the John Peel Centre for the Creative Arts (www.johnpeelcentre.com) who provided us with a photograph and who continue to champion the cause of those seeking a break as creative artists.

Introduction, all round to ours...

As this book was being compiled a number of major news outlets reported the findings of a research project from the Rotman Research Institute, in Toronto. 19 volunteers were played 60 excerpts of music they hadn't previously heard. During the experience they were linked to a mock up online store and able to decide which music they would like to own. All of the above was monitored by MRI scanning, giving the researchers a map of brain activity linked to hearing new sounds. The work showed the brain's reward centres behaving in a similar way to the standard responses seen when a hungry person is presented with food. One of this book's authors (Neil) was particularly struck by the comments of Dr Valorie Salimpoor: "music is abstract: It's not like you are really hungry and you are about to get a piece of food and you are really excited about it because you are going to eat it - or the same thing applies to sex or money - that's when you would normally see [such brain] activity…what's cool is that you're anticipating and getting excited over something entirely abstract - and that's the next sound that is coming up."

So, at last, someone has begun to recognise, prove and explain the experience behind the writing of this book. Obviously we're biased but we're totally in agreement with the idea that it's "cool" to be anticipating the next sonic surprise. None of this proves we need abstract ideas as much as we need food, and it would be cruel to visit one of the world's worst trouble spots and open a conversation by asking what the locals were slammin' to at that moment. But, there is a commonality in our brains between the way we process the hunger for the basic needs, and way we process the hunger for those experiences that enrich our deeper understanding of life. Surely, that is cool.

Some people, (the term "sound hounds" appears occasionally in this book, but there are other – less complementary – alternatives), are insatiable when it comes to seeking out and appreciating music. That – more or less – is the premise of this book. We have lined up, described and put into context 500 "albums" in the expectation that those of you who can't help yourselves when it comes to finding and collecting music will benefit from these efforts in two ways. Firstly, you'll know you are not alone. Secondly, we hope that some of the work covering the following pages leads you to new discoveries, and makes your life slightly better as a result.

This is an all round to ours, session with the complication that you will have to locate the music and listen to it yourself. We'd better take a little time to tell you some of the thoughts that put this particular collection together. After which we'll let the entries, and the music you can discover, do the talking. By "album" we usually mean an album. A copyrighted, legitimately released, long playing collection of music. But sometimes we've taken liberties because things just felt right. We have tried to avoid too many compilations, but some just begged for inclusion. Similarly, we have chosen compilation albums for some artists – like The Legendary Stardust Cowboy - because their legitimately released original albums don't bring them alive as much as collections of their greatest work. Such liberties have been taken when it felt right to us to do so. So Aleister Crowley's "album" is very short by album standards, but then the most recent cuts on this collection date from 1914, and nobody really thought in terms of albums then. Lieutenant Pigeon's magnum opus – by contrast – calls itself a single but offers a more challenging listen and greater running time than many albums. There are bootlegs in this collection. We would always encourage our readers to support musicians (and there are loads of musicians mentioned in these pages who would be really grateful for your financial support) but in some cases the sounds on offer were never intended for release, and the bootlegs amount to the only way to buy them. In other cases the bootlegs are acts of creative compiling that present an artistic vision the original musicians would never have thought to present themselves. Frank Sinatra's Come Suck With Me is a clear case of the latter. To hear his twist record alongside his disco cut, nestling next to his abortive hippie phase and a duet with a dog is to appreciate that even "The Chairman of the Board" made desperate business decisions a few times. When we have presented such bootlegs we have limited them to collections you can buy legitimately. Indeed, the downloading options online mean you can source the original tracks from the original albums (Frank's disco foray lurks as a "bonus" cut in a 1990s box set BTW). Elsewhere we have made decisions to include non-musical albums and also agreed with the decisions of others about material that works best in a particular context. To truly get the majesty of Bob Anthony (cabaret singer and singing tutor who made a record teaching you his art), you have to do what an online compiler did and place his tuition album alongside his own long playing creative efforts. "Album" is a loose concept in this book. So, Johnny Cash reading the complete King James New Testament just belongs here, and so does the one collection by Beck presented on paper and subsequently recorded by others.

This book celebrates the album, but also chronicles an artwork that is declining in importance. The album is threatened by downloads, changing fashions amongst media consumers and the indifference of some musicians to recording with little chance of decent financial rewards. But it continues to be the focus of many musical careers and the lives of many who love their music. The death of the album, though much discussed, seems a long way off. Even if the changes in its current life mean it will never again achieve the importance it enjoyed in the final decades of the last century.

There are a few things to say about the choices here. Firstly, some of the most obvious and best-selling "out there" collections are conspicuous by their absence. When you get to the entries for Captain Beefheart and Hawkind this fact is discussed in some detail. Explained simply, the authors, and publishers, made some educated guesses about the likely buyers of the book and decided to avoid telling readers things they were likely to know very well. At the same time, we're conscious that some readers will already know and cherish every note of some cult classics that are included – Carla Bley's Escalator Over the Hill or Terry Reid's River being good examples. If we've just described you we hope that is taken as a complement and you will find a lot of other entries here to open your ears. Secondly, the focus here is on the kind of work that rock fans, and lovers of most other genres of popular music, are likely to cherish. But, we've cast the net very widely. In many cases we are making no apologies for a token inclusion. When you get to discussions of Sun Ra, Bernie Sizzey and many others it is made clear that almost any of their recordings would have met the entry requirements for inclusion. There are reasons for our final choices, but there are also good reasons for you to check out everything else they ever recorded. There are also some recordings here that plumb depths of tastelessness, take artistic statements into areas others would regard as needlessly depraved, and provide insights into comedy that doesn't make everyone laugh. Two of the albums included contain the sounds of people dying/being murdered (not fake dramatizations, but the real "Grim Reaper in attendance" deal). Peter Wyngarde's apparent joke about sexual assault on his only solo album hasn't amused many who have heard it since, and exactly what dimensions of listening pleasure are being addressed by inane novelties and dour instructional recordings involving everything from canine heartbeats to birds trilling along with opera tunes isn't always clear. Our point is to chart the places the long playing album has visited in its vast and varied life, and leave the decisions about "getting excited over something abstract" to the reader. Some of the material with the obvious power to offend identifies itself. What, exactly, do you expect to hear on Kunt and the Gang's Shannon Matthews - The Musical or Torsofuck's Erotic Diarrhoea Fantasy? Some such material is less obvious, but we've taken the trouble to warn those of delicate sensibilities before they read something they'd sooner not know about. We're not out to offend anyone, but to ignore the extremes of humour, documentary and art would have been dishonest in any search for albums you won't believe until you hear them. Similarly we're not out to mock the sincerity of people who poured their heart and soul into material that has since drawn ironic appreciation. The collection here is, what it is, a slew of strangeness in all its forms and much that is sublime and in need of wider recognition. What is sublime, what strange and what just plain silly is up to you. We presume only to find this stuff and describe it. Though once in a while we couldn't help ourselves and some opinions did stay on the page.* It was a hell of a ride researching and listening to the material that makes up this book, we've tried to stay objective, in circumstances that were always likely to make this hard.

With regard to the objectivity we have made every effort to check the pedantic things like spellings and dates of release (not always easy to find where some of the more obscure releases are concerned). You'll notice that once or twice a specific fact has eluded us, despite our efforts. When it comes to the basic details, like upper and lower case letters in song titles, this has proven even harder. There are plenty cases of spellings, upper and lower cases and other details changing with regard to the same track, compiled on different albums, by the same artist. We've generally gone with a reliable source we have found. But, many of them observe different rules to each other and some are determined to do it their own way (hence the artist nick nicely and the album title Tales of FiNiN).

With regard to "albums you won't believe until you hear them" we would say only that the extremes already mentioned were central to the inclusion of many albums. Elsewhere, a few albums cherished by the authors, or by die-hard fan bases, are included because they have become rallying points for long-running arguments about their under-valued achievements. When these albums appear they often do so with arguments drawn from the cases others have made on their behalf. We argue, for example, that The Twiggs would surely have achieved more in an internet age that would have taken their music to the world more readily than a small label printing 500 CDs could ever do. In making many arguments we have drawn material from obvious places – Amazon reviews, Wikipedia entries and the like. When we could credit the sources, we have done so. If it was you posing as a customer to review Neil Young's awesome Arc album, we offer respect because we couldn't improve on the words you wrote. Had you put your name there, we'd have offered respect and a name check. Collectively "albums you won't believe until you hear them" means we have compiled 500 recordings fit to challenge your beliefs on what is art, what is funny, what is clever and what other people get up to in the privacy of their own recording studios. We're confident that somewhere in here even the most addicted sound hound will encounter something they struggle to believe, until they've heard it.

Beyond that we hope you do what we would in the circumstances. Buy the music, search online in the most obvious places to find out more about it, find other music like it and never give up on seeking out sounds you can't believe, until you hear them. There are enough references to record labels, radio shows, web sites and the like to give you a start in this search. Many of these are already well known, but we include them to give due respect where it is due, and to point the way to others who haven't yet encountered the wonders that are Stuart Maconie's Freak Zone, WFMU, the Music for Maniacs web site etc. There's also Neil's Strange Fruit radio show available on Gonzo Multimedia and Miskin Radio, but it would be really cheesy to mention that. Our search doesn't end here, the material we search is beyond measure and – despite declining album sales – the work of those willing to put time and effort into creating sounds others struggle to imagine continues on a massive scale. All of these facts are life-affirming. So – in the humble opinion of the authors – are the works described in this book.

Neil Nixon: Thought up the idea for this book, though it was mainly a case of downloading the sort of things that have been going round in his head since he could first process a thought. You could regard the knowledge displayed here as an impressive achievement or a cry for help. Either way, he's unlikely to change his behaviour now. When not writing books he juggles a range of jobs, one of which involves

---

*This is a serious point. The entries here include opinions, some cited from other sources, most of them down to the authors of this book. They should be treated as such and not taken literally (especially if your work involves the legal representation of any person(s) whose work is discussed within these pages).

managing an undergraduate course in Professional Writing. A useful sideline of this course is the involvement with a community radio station – Miskin Radio – and the chance to present their alternative show, Strange Fruit, on which much of the music and many of the artists discussed in this book have been played. For those unwilling to chain themselves down for an online listening experience in a graveyard slot on radio Strange Fruit is also available on the web radio pages of Gonzo Multimedia (the people who publish this book). Neil has a website at www.neilnixon.com.

Thom Nixon: Grew up with his dad's music collection but has never been short of his own opinions. He had the good sense to make it to a good university at the first attempt and study a subject (Law with Politics) with the potential to give him a decent professional living. His collection of musical instruments, includes enough bass guitars to suggest he is serious about this aspect of his life, and he has qualifications along with photographs to prove he can play very well. He also accrued enough published journalism whilst a student to suggest this won't be his final book.

Those 500 Entries in Order (with a few titles shortened)

5,6,7,8s – Bomb the Rocks: Early Days Singles 1989-1996 – 2003
The Addicts – The Addicts Sing – 1963
Hasil Adkins – What the Hell Was I Thinking - 1998
Eden Ahbez – Eden's Island – 1960
Alarm Will Sound – Acoustica – 2005
Alberto y Lost Trios Paranoias - Mandrax Sunset Variations – 2001
A A Allen – Crying Demons -????
GG Allin – Brutality and Bloodshed for All – 1993
America – Hat Trick – 1973
Anal Cunt – It Just Gets Worse – 1999
Laurie Anderson – The Ugly One With the Jewels – 1995
And the Native Hipsters – There Goes Concorde – 2001
The Animated Egg – The Animated Egg – 1969
Bob Anthony - We'd Like To Teach You Sing/ Ile D'Amour – 1973-5
Aphex Twin - Selected Ambient Works II – 1994
Dorothy Ashby - The Rubaiyat of Dorothy Ashby - 1970
Ed Askew – For the World – 2013
Virginia Astley – From Gardens – 1983
Awesome Color – Awesome Color – 2006
Albert Ayler – Love Cry – 1968
Sibylle Baier – Colour Green – 2006
Moe Barbar - When the Eyes Cry – 1996
Barnes and Barnes – Voobaha – 1980
Louis and Bebe Barron – Forbidden Planet OST – 1957
Julianna Barwick – The Magic Place – 2011
William Basinski – The Disintegration Loops - 2012
Les Baxter – Jewels of the Sea – 1961
The Beach Boys – Holland – 1973
Beatles – At the Hollywood Bowl – 1977
Mark Bebbington – Piano Music by Ivor Gurney and Howard Ferguson – 2004
Beck – Song Reader – 2012
Captain Beefheart – Ice Cream for Crow – 1982
Chris Bell – I am the Cosmos – 1992 (1978)
Virginia Belmont's Famous Talking and Singing Birds – Same – 195?
Cathy Berberian – Beatles Arias – 1967
Steven Jesse Bernstein – Prison – 1992
Sir John Betjaman – Betjaman's Banana Blush – 1974
Vishwa Mohan Bhatt & Ry Cooder – A Meeting by the River – 1993
Black Box Recorder – The Facts of Life – 2000
Black Sweden – Gold – 2004

Carla Bley and Paul Haines – Escalator Over the Hill – 1971
Emit Bloch – Dictaphones vol.1 – 2010
Thomas Bloch – Music for the Glass Harmonica – 2001
Blowfly – The Weird World of Blowfly - 1971
Blue Cheer – Vincebus Eruptum – 1968
Boards of Canada – Music has the Right… - 1998
Marc Bolan and T.Rex – Bump 'n' Grind – 2004
Ross Bolleter – Crow Country – 1999
Pat Boone – In a Metal Mood – No More Mr Nice Guy – 1997
Barry Booth – Diversions – 1968
The Boredoms - Super æ – 1998
David Bowie – David Bowie – 1967
Donald Bradshaw-Leather – The Distance Between Us – 1972
Richard Brautigan – Listening to… - 1970
Broadcast – Ha Ha Sound – 2003
Garth Brookes – Chris Gaines – 1999
James Brown – Hell – 1974
Paul Buchanan – Mid Air – 2012
Tim Buckley – Lorca – 1970
Vashti Bunyan – Lookaftering – 2005
William Burroughs – Dead City Radio – 1990
Burzum – Daudi Baldrs – 1997
Kate Bush – Fifty Words for Snow – 2011
The Butthole Surfers – Locust Abortion… - 1987
Cabaret Voltaire – Red Mecca – 1981
Cantona – The Album – 1995
Caravan – In the Land of the Grey and Pink – 1971
Sebastian Cabot – Sebastian Cabot Actor/Bob Dylan Poet – 1967
Robert Calvert – Captain Lockheed and the Starfighters – 1974
Canya Phuckem and Howe - Sleeze Attack – 1980
The Cardboard Lung – Black Patch – 2008
Walter Carlos – Sonic Seasonings – 1972
Barbara Cartland – Album of Love Songs – 1978
Alberta Casey – San Diego Vokas – 1981?
Johnny Cash – Reads the Complete New Testament – 1990
Johnny Cash – The Mystery of Life - 1991
David Cassidy – The Higher – 1975
Bob Chance – It's Broken – 1980
Sheila Chandra and the Ganges Orchestra - This Sentence is True – Shakti 2001
Chinga Chavin – Country Porn – 1976
Richard Cheese – Aperitif for Destruction – 2005
Chimes of St. Dormition Monastery – Chimes of St. Dormition Monastery – 1991
Henri Chopin – Cantata for Two Farts and co – 1997
Keith Christmas – Fable of the Wings – 1970
Gene Clark – No Other – 1974
Del Close and John Brent – How to Speak Hip – 1959
C.O.B. - Moyshe McStiff and the Tartan Lancers – 1972
Miss Pat Collins – The Hip Hypnotist – 1968
Comets on Fire – Blue Cathedral – 2004
Connie Converse – How Lovely, How Sad – 2009
Alice Cooper – DaDa – 1983
Cosmic Rough Riders – Enjoy the Melodic Sunshine – 2000

Country 'N' Irish Accordion – 2003
The Creatures – Feast – 1983
Quentin Crisp – An Evening With Quentin Crisp – 1979
Criswell – The Legendary Criswell Predicts – 1970
Bing Crosby – Hey Jude Hey Bing – 1969
David Crosby – If I Could Only… - 1971
Sandra Cross – The MMs Bar Album – 2011
Aleister Crowley: 1910-1914 Black Magic - 2007
Culturecide: Tacky Souvenirs of Pre-Revolutionary America – 1986
Cut Chemist – Sound of the Police – 2010
Ivor Cutler – Dandruff – 1974
Dick Dale – Calling Up Spirits – 1996
Bette Davis – Two's Company – 1953
Deep Purple - Made in Japan – 1972
Derek and Clive – Ad Nauseam - 1978
The Dope King's Last Stand – The Dope King's Last Stand – 1977
Jon Downes and the Amphibians – The Case 1995
The Dragons – Bfi – 2007 (1970)
Dread Zeppelin – Un-Led-Ed – 1990
Keir Dullea – Keir Dullea – 1969
Edward S. Dumit - Say it Right – 1959
Duran Duran – Thank You 1995
Durutti Column – Someone Else's Party – 2003
Bob Dylan – Dylan – 1973
Bob Dylan – Bootleg Series Volume 10: Another Self Portrait – 2013
Easy Star All Stars – Dub Side of the Moon – 2003
The Electric Prunes – Mass in F Minor – 1968
Karen Elson – The Ghost who Walks – 2010
Preston Epps – Bongola – 2005
Roky Erickson and the Aliens – Roky Erickson and the Aliens – 1980
The Erotics – Erotica - The Rhythms of Love – 1961
Esquerita – The Definitive Edition – 2010
Stephen Ettinger – Canine Heart Sounds – 1970
Evolution so Far – The Armies of Bitterness – 2003
Explosions in the Sky – The Earth is not a Cold Dead Place – 2003
EyeSea – Blue Ten - 2014
Bill Fay – Life is People – 2012
Felt – Train Above the City – 1988
The Firesign Theatre – How can you be Two Places… - 1969
Wildman Fischer – An Evening – 1968
Wildman Fischer – The Fischer King – 1999
Five Starcle Men – Gomba Reject Ward – 2007
The Foghorn Requiem – The Foghorn Requiem – 2013
Fornicating Female Freaks – Fornicating Female Freaks - ?
Roddy Frame – Surf – 2002
Peter Frampton – Love Taker – 2000
Matthew Friedberger – Matricidal Sons of Bitches – 2012
Mark Fry – Dreaming With Alice – 1972
The Fugs – It Crawled into my Hand, Honest – 1968
Funkadelic – Maggot Brain – 1971
Funky Junction – Play a Tribute to Deep Purple – 1973

Billy Fury – The Sound of Fury – 1960
George Garabedian Players and the Awful Trumpet of Harry Arms - 1968
Charlotte Gainsbourg - IRM – 2010
Diamanda Galas – Plague Mass – 1991
Vincent Gallo – When – 2001
General Electric Silicone Products Department - Silicones – 1973
Bobbie Gentry – The Delta Sweete – Capitol 1968
Robin Gibb – Robin's Reign – 1969
Philip Glass – The Low Symphony – 1993
Benny Golson - Turn In, Turn On - 1967
The Great Kat – Beethoven on Speed - 1990
Grouper – Dragging a Dead Deer up a Hill – 2009
Arlo Guthrie – Alice's Restaurant – 1967
GWAR – Scumdogs of the Universe – 1990
Half Man Half Biscuit – Back Again in the DHSS – 1987
Claire Hamill – Voices – 1986
The Handless Organist – Truly a Miracle of God - ????
Rufus Harley with George Arvanitas Trio – From Philadelphia… - 2007
Harmony Rockets – Paralyzed Mind of the Archangel Void – 1997
Roy Harper – Lifemask – 1973
Richard Harris – A Tramp Shining – 1968
George Harrison – Electronic Sound – 1969
Alex Harvey – Presents the Loch Ness Monster – 1977
PJ Harvey – White Chalk – 2007
Nicky Haslam – Midnight Matinee – 2013
Donnie Hathaway – Extension of a Man – 1973
Hawkwind – It is the Business of the Future to be Dangerous – 1993
Hayseed Dixie – A Hot Piece of Grass – 2005
Murray Head – Say it ain't so – 1975
Jimi Hendrix – Woke up This Morning and Found Myself Dead – 1995
David Hentschel - Sta*rtling Music – 1975
Kristen Hersh – Hips and Makers – 1994
Steve Hillage – Rainbow Dome Music – 1979
Myrtle K. Hilo – The Singing Cab Driver – 1967
Alfred Hitchcock – Music to be Murdered by – 1958
Ake Hodell – 220 Volt Buddha – 1998 (1970-73)
Samuel J Hoffman – Waves in the Ether – 2004
Mark Hollis – Mark Hollis – 1998
David Holmes – This Films Crap Lets Slash the Seats – 1995
Julia Holter – Tragedy – 2011
Hoola Bandoola Band: Vem kan man lita på? – 1972
Paul Horn – Inside the Great Pyramid – 1976
Frankie Howerd – Get Your Titters Out – 2002
Engelbert Humperdinck - The Dance Album – 1998
Hundred Year Old Woman – Interview – 1978
William Hung – Inspiration – 2004
Laura Huxley – Recipies for Living and Loving - 1973
I, Brute Force – Confections of Love – 1967
Tony Iommi – Iommi – 2000
It's a Beautiful Day – Live at the Fillmore 68 - 2013
The Jacks – Vacant World – 1968

Millie Jackson – Get it Out'cha System – 1978
Jandek – Chair Beside a Window – 1982
Jandek – Worthless Recluse – 2001
Keith Jarrett – Koln Concert – 1975
Florence Foster Jenkins – Murder on the High Cs – 2003
Jóhann Jóhannsson - The Miner's Hymns – 2011
Elton John – Chartbusters go Pop – 1999
Daniel Johnston – Fear Yourself – 2003
Brian Jones – Presents the Master Musicians of Joujouka - 1971
Spike Jones and his City Slickers – Murdering the Classics – 1971
Janis Joplin – Love, Janis – 2001
Justified Ancients of Mu Mu – 1987… - 1987
Juxtavoices – Juxtanother Antichoir… 2010
Rodd Keith – I Died Today – 1996
Stan Kenton - City of Glass & This Modern World – 1953
Kerouac – Kicks Joy into Darkness – 1997
Kid Carpet – Ideas and Oh Dears – 2005
Kids of Widney High – Let's Get Busy - 1999
Klaus Kinski - Lieder und Balladen – 2003 (1959)
Basil Kirchin – Worlds Within Worlds – 1971
Basil Kirchin – Primitive London – 2010 (1965)
The Kominas – Wild Nights in Guantanamo Bay – 2008
Chief Kooffreh – Sweet Asian Girl – 2008
Leo Kottke – A Shout Toward Noon – 1986
David Koresh – Voice of Fire – 1995
KPM All Stars – Live at the Jazz Café – 2009
Kramer – The Guilt Trip – 1992
Kunt and the Gang – Shannon Matthews: The Musical – 2010
Catherine Lambert – Beltane: A Musical Fantasy – 1999
Barbara Lander – Music for Dancing and Mime – 1968
Fred Lane – From the One That Cut You – 1983
Langley Park Schools Music Project – Innocence and Despair – 2001
Lavender Country – Lavender Country – 1973
Sim Lawrence – Scandal - 2009
Timothy Leary – You Can be Anyone – 1970
D J Lebowitz – Beware of the Piano – 1988
Christopher Lee – Charlemagne: The Omens of Death – 2013
The Legendary Stardust Cowboy - For Sarah, Raquel and David - 2013
Tom Lehrer – In Concert – 1994
Leningrad Cowboys - We Cum From Brooklyn – 1992
John Lennon and Yoko Ono – Two Virgins – 1968
Sonny Lester – How to Strip for Your Husband – 1963
Pop Levi – The Return to Form Black Majick Party – 2007
Lieutenant Pigeon – Opus 400 – 2001
Lightning Bolt – Wonderful Rainbow – 2003
Liquor Ball – Fucks the Sky – 1992
Little Markie – It's a Whole New World – 1990s
Roddy Llewellyn – Roddy – 1978
Jon Lord – Concerto for Group and Orchestra – 2012
Lothar and the Hand People – Space Hymn - 1969
The Louvin Brothers – Satan is Real – 1959

Lydia Lunch – Smoke in the Shadows – 2004
Vera Lynn – In Nashville – 1977
Magnetic North – Orkney: A Symphony of the Magnetic North – 2011
Maharishi Mahesh Yogi – Maharishi Mahesh Yogi – 1967
Mahavishnu Orchestra – The Inner Mounting Flame – 1971
Man…or Astro-man? – Your Weight on the Moon – 1994
Charles Manson – Lie – 1970
John Martyn – Inside Out – 1973
Harpo Marx – Harpo at Work – 1958
Nigel Mazlyn Jones – Ship to Shore – 1976
Paddy McAloon – I Trawl – 2003
David McCallum – Open Channel D – 2006
John Lennon McCullagh – North South Divide – 2013
Dion McGregor – The Dream World of Dion McGregor - 1964
Medicine Head – Don't Stop the Dance – 2005
Joe Meek and the Blue Men – I Hear a New World – 1991 (1959)
Melt Banana – Squeak Squeak Creak – 1994
Melvins – Colossus of Destiny – 2001
Ethel Merman – The Ethel Merman Disco Album – 1979
Olivier Messiaen - Quartet for the End of Time – 1940-41
Mrs Miller – Greatest Hits – 1966
Steve Miller Band – Recall the Beginning, Journey From Eden – 1972
Kylie Minogue – Impossible Princess – 1997
Sugar Minott – Ghetto-ology – 1979
Robert Mitchum – Calypso – Is Like So – 1957
Miranda Sex Garden – Madra – 1991
The Modern Lovers – The Original Modern Lovers – 1981
The Monks – Black Monk Time – 1966
The Monkees – Head – 1968
Hugo Montenegro – Bongos and Brass – 1960
Archie Moore – Times Table with Soul and a Beat – 1964
John Moran – The Manson Family – 1992
Jack Mudurian – Repertoire – 1996
Os Mutantes: A Divina Comedia…– Polydor 1970
National Lampoon – Radio Dinner – 1972
Negativeland – Advertising Secrets – 1991
Michael Nesmith – The Prison – 1974
Neutral Milk Hotel – On Avery Island – 1996
nick nicely – Psychotropic – 2004
Nights of Love in Lesbos – Nights of Love in Lesbos – 1962
Jack Nitsche – St Giles Cripplegate – 1972
Ken Nordine – Word Jazz – 1957
Alex North – 2001 A Space Odyssey – 1993
Gary Numan – Pure – 2000
Laura Nyro – Angel in the Dark 2001
Dr. Obscenity – Suppressed Classics – 1978
Carroll O' Connor and Jean Stapleton – Side by Side – 1973
Des O' Connor – Sing a Favourite Country Song – 1973
Sister Irene O'Connor: Fire of God's Love…- 1976
Esther Ofarim – In London – 2009
of Arrowe Hill – Spring Heel Penny Dreadful - 2003

Mike Oldfield – Orchestral Tubular Bells – 1975
Mike Oldfield – Incantations – 1978
Olivia Tremor Control – Black Foliage – 1999
Yoko Ono – Approximately Infinite – 1973
William Onyeabor - Who is William Onyeabor? – 2013
Opeth – Watershed – 2008
Orchestral Manoeuvres in the Dark – Dazzle Ships – 1983
Daphne Oram – Oramics – 2007
John Oswald – Grayfolded – 1994/5
John Otway – Under the Covers and Over the Top – 1992
Lucia Pamela – Into Outer Space – 1969
Korla Pandit – The Grand Moghul Suite - 1951
PARC – Ghost Orchid – 1999
Parliament – Osmium – 1970
Harry Partch – Delusion of the Fury – 1999 (1969)
Ottilie Patterson - That Patterson Girl – 2007 (1955-1963)
Annette Peacock – I'm the One – 1972
Josh T. Pearson – Last of the Country Gentlemen – 2011
Penta Sales Corporation – Play it Safe Vol.4 – 1972
People's Temple Choir – He's Able – 19??
Linda Perhacs – Parallelograms – 1970
Perry and Kingsley - Kaleidoscopic Vibrations – 1967
Red Peters – I Laughed, I Cried… 1995
Plan 9 From Outer Space – OST – 1994
Sidney Poitier – Poitier Meets Plato – 1964
The Polyphonic Spree – The Beginning Stages of – 2002
The Portland Bike Ensemble/ The Levenshume Bicycle Orchestra - 2007
Portsmouth Sinfonia – Plays the Popular Classics – 1974
Elvis Presley – Having Fun…- 1974
Elvis Presley – Greatest Shit – 1983
Katie Price and Peter Andre – A Whole New World – 2006
Public Image Ltd. – Flowers of Romance – 1981
Quantum Dub Force – Assymetric – 2001
Quintessence – Indweller – 1972
Sun Ra – Cosmic Tones for Mental Therapy – 1967
Railway Children – Gentle Sound – 2002
Ramases – Space Hymns – 1971
Rancid Hell Spawn – Chainsaw Masochist – 1990
The Wit and Wisdom of Ronald Reagan – 1981
Lou Reed – Metal Machine – 1975
Adam Reichel – Gruene Reise – 1971
Terry Reid – River – 1973
The Residents – Commercial Album – 1980
Ambrose Reynolds – Greatest Hits – 1982
Boyd Rice – The Black Album – 1977
Buddy Rich – Sings Johnny Mercer – 1956
Andrew Ridgeley – Son of Albert – 1990
Billy Lee Riley – Classic Recordings 1956-1960 – 1990
Alasdair Robinson and Robin Robertson – Hirta Songs – 2013
Rock 'N' Roll Allstars – Red China Rocks – 1972
Rothko – A Continual Search for Origins – 2002

Demis Roussos – The Greek Side of my Mind/Fire and Ice – 1971
Ssgt. Barry Sadler – Ballads of the Green Berets – 1966
Saint Etienne – Finisterre – 2002
Alex Sanders – A Witch is Born – 1970
Hope Sandoval & Warm Inventions – Through the Devil Softly – 2009
Walter Schumann – Exploring the Unknown – 1955
Richard Scott and Rex Casswell – The Magnificence of Stereo – 1992
Screw Radio – Talk Radio Violence – 1995
Peter Sellers – Songs for Swinging Sellers – 1959
Peter Sellers and Spike Milligan – He's Innocent of Watergate - 1974
Sex Pistols – Carri On – 1978
SFT – Swift – 2002
The Shaggs – Philosophy of the World – 1969
William Shatner – The Transformed Man – 1968
William Shatner – Has Been - 2004
Gary Shearston – Dingo – 1974
Allan Sherman – My Son, the Nut – 1963
Judee Sill – Heart Food – 1973
The Simpsons – Sing the Blues – 1990
Frank Sinatra – Come Suck With Me – 2013
Bernie Sizzey – Hippie Heaven – 2013
Richard Skelton – Landings – 2009
Sleep – Dopesmoker – 2003
Sleepytime Gorilla Museum – Grand Opening and Closing – 2001
Sly and the Family Stone – Small Talk – 1974
Smithsonian Folkways – Man's Early Instruments – 2012
The Space Lady – The Space Lady's Greatest Hits – 2013
Sparklehorse – Vivadixie – 1995
Alexander Spence – Oar – 1969
Spock's Beard – V – 2000
Spooky Tooth with Pierre Henry - Ceremony – 1969
O.W. "Bud" Spriggs – What the Bible Says About Flying Saucers – 1966?
Vivian Stanshall – Sir Henry at Rawlinson End – 1978
The Stark Reality - Discovers Hoagy Carmichael's… - 1970
Meic Stevens – Outlander – 1970
Stinky Picnic – Peaceful and Quiet - 2012
Stockhausen – Helicopter Quartet – 2000
Strawberry Alarm Clock – Strawberries Mean Love – 1992
Styx – The Serpent is Rising – 1973
Yma Sumac – Voice of the Xtabay – 1950
Donna Summer – Back Off Boogaloo - 1999
Sunn 0))) – Flight of the Behemoth – 2002
Jimmy Swaggart – Color me a Story – 1980
Rachel Sweet – Fool Around – 1978
Margaret Leng Tan – Art of the Toy Piano – 1997
Tater Totz – Alien Sleestacks from Brazil – 1988
Aïcha Tachinwite - Aïcha Tachinwite – 2014
Creed Taylor – Panic…son of Shock – 1959
James Taylor – James Taylor – 1968
Shooby Taylor – Shooby Taylor: The Human Horn – 80's
Television Personalities – And Don't the Kids… 1981

This Heat – This Heat – 1979
Jens Thomas – Speed of Grace – 2012
Mollie Thompson – From Worlds Afar – 1966
Tracy Thorne – A Distant Shore – 1982
Throbbing Gristle – DoA – 1978
Tilted Tim – Fate Made a Mess…- 1992
Tiny Tim – God Bless Tiny Tim – 1968
Julie Tippetts and Martin Archer - Tales of FiNiN – 2011
Tonto's Expanding Headband – Zero Time – 1971
Jorge Torrens - Country Rican – 1976
Torsofuck – Erotic Diarrhoea – 2004
Tortoise and Bonnie Prince… - Brave and Bold – 2006
Tortura – Sounds of Pain and Pleasure – 1965
Trashmonk – Mona Lisa Overdrive - 1999
The Trashwomen – Spend the Night With… - 1993
Trek Bloopers – 197?
The Tremeloes – Master – 1970
Trio – Trio – 1981
The Troggs – Athens Andover – 1992
Thomas Truax – Sonic Dreamer – 2010
The Twiggs – 20,000 Leaves – 1994
Twiggy – Twiggy and the Girlfriends – 1972
Twink – Think Pink – 1970
The Two Petes – Live at the Montague Arms – 1981
Ultramarine – Every Man and Woman… - 1992
Stanley Unwin – Rotatey Diskers – 1961
Uriah Heep – Abominog – 1982
U.S. Girls – Gem - 2012
Utopia – Disco Jets – 2012 (1976?)
Dino Valente – Dino Valente – 1968
Van Der Graaf Generator – Pawn Hearts – 1971
The Velvet Illusions – The Velvet Illusions – 2011
Ana Vidovic – Guitar Recital – 2000
Vitamin String Quartet- The Gay Wedding Collection – 2008
Vulcan Freedom Fighters – Stardate Unknown – 2006
Scott Walker – Bish Bosch – 2012
John Waters – A John Waters Christmas – 2004
Jon Wayne – Texas Funeral – 1985
Eric Weber – Picking up Girls Made Easy – 1975
Scott Weiland – The Most Wonderful Time of the Year - 2011
Mae West – Mae West on the Air – 1985
When People Were Shorter – Bobby – 1989
Gregory Whitehead – Pressures of the Unspeakable – 1992
Williams Fairey Brass Band – Acid Brass – 1997
Robin Williamson – Myrrh – 1972
Wesley Willis – Greatest Hits Vol 3 – 2008
Murry Wilson – The Many Moods of – 1967
The Wind in the Willows – The Wind in the Willows – 1968
Paul Winter/Paul Halley – Whales Alive – 1987
Jah Wobble's Invaders of the Heart – The Celtic Poets – 1987
Bobby Womack – B.W. Goes C and W – 1976

The Wombles – Wombling Free – 1978
Chris Wood – Trespasser – 2009
Peter Wyngarde – Peter Wyngarde – 1970
Yes – Topographic Oceans – 1973
XXX Maniak – Harvesting the Cunt Nectar – 2004
Neil Young – Arc – 1991
Neil Young – Le Noise – 2010
Frank Zappa – Lumpy Gravy – 1968
Thalia Zedek - Liars and Prayers – 2008
The Zimmers – Lust for Life – 2008
Zola Jesus – Versions – 2013
John Zorn – The Bribe – 1998
ZZ Top – Rythmeen – 1996
Various Artists: African Scream Contest – 2008
Various Artists: The American Song-Poem Collection – 2003
Various Artists – Best of Louie Louie – 1990
Various Artists – C86 – 1986
Various Artists – Cambodian Psych Out – 2006
Various Artists – Come and Get it – 2010
Various Artists – Death Dealers – 1995
Various Artists – Dirty Fan Male – 2005
Various Artists – Elvis Impersonator Blues – 1995
Various Artists – Enjoy the Experience – 2013
Various Artists – Faith, A Message From the Spirits – 1996
Various Artists – Flappers, Vamps and Sweet Young Things – 1990
Various Artists – Flexi-Sex – 2003
Various Artists – The Girls are at it Again – 2009
Various Artists – Golden Throats: The Great Celebrity Sing Off – 1988
Various Artists – The Great Lost Elektra Singles Volume 1 - 2005
Various Artists – I Am The Center - 2013
Various Artists – Incredibly Strange Music Vol II – 1995
Various Artists – Las Vegas Grind 3 - 1999
Various Artists – Listen to the Banned – 1984
Various Artists – Mindexpanders Vol 1 – 2009
Various Artists – You Suffer, Napalm Death Tribute – 2011
Various Artists – The Pig's Big 78s – 2006
Various Artists – Polluting the Mainstream - 2012
Various Artists - The Rise and Fall of Paramount Records, Vol. 1 - 2013
Various Artists – The Rough Guide to Psychedelic Bollywood – 2013
Various Artists – Round the Gum Tree – 2004
Various Artists – Savage Pencil Presents – 1999
Various Artists – Savoy Wars – 1994
Various Artists – Scared to Get Happy – 2013
Various Artists – Songs in the Key of Z – 2002
Various Artists – Songs in the Key of Z Volume 2 – 2002
Various Artists – Stay Awake – 1988
Various Artists – Strong Love - 2012
Various Artists – Trojan X-Rated 2002
Various Artists – Trucker Hits 3: Hallo Trucker – 1990
Various Artists – Wavy Gravy – 2005
Various Artists – Yodelling Crazy – 1991

The 5,6,7,8s:
Bomb the Rocks: Early Days Singles 1989-1996
(Sweet Nothing, 2003)
What? Japanese she-riot of surf, punk, rockabilly and garage.

Massively popular in their native country and sporadically high-profile elsewhere (especially in the wake of their appearance in the first Kill Bill movie), The 5,6,7,8s spent their early years evolving from a quartet playing surf and rock 'n' roll covers into a broader band trawling trashy rock wherever they could find it and stamping their shiny stiletto heels over everything to knock it into a distinctive shape. Bomb the Rocks is well titled since the general twist here is that everything in the band's orbit is blown up with a solid bass, buried in impassioned (for which read: milking the tunes for effect not perfect pitch) vocals and electrified with shards of surf riffs and punky guitar chords. Originally the band lined up behind the vocals of Yoshiko "Ronnie" Fujiyama; who doubles on guitar. Ronnie and her sister Sachiko (guitar and vocals) are mainstays of a changing line-up and the sounds here vary with the production budget and members on hand. The later cuts featuring the muscular bass of Akiko Omo thud along with slightly more bottom. Culled from original E.P. releases Bomb the Rocks is a trash-tastic trawl of sounds. The band's early releases typically milked the E.P. format to bring variety to each release and the album lines up some great covers – none finer than their cover of The Ikettes "Woo Hoo" that made #28 in the UK singles charts after the Kill Bill appearance. Elsewhere "Three Cool Chicks" reworks the classic "Three Cool Cats" with enough 5,6,7,8s additions to make it their own. The same trick is repeatedly pulled when they cover classic surf guitar and trashy originals. The band make a decent fist of creating their own material in the same vein, including their own "The 5.6.7.8s," and rotate the lead vocals amongst the line up to avoid any one sound or style becoming too typecast.

The tonnage of pictures in the CD insert is also welcome. The pictures and music present the band as a glorious celebration of the brilliantly brainless and the limitless creativity that comes with low-fi originals. "Ronnie's resolute insistence on playing a Teisco guitar is another element of the sound and style of a band who have managed The Ramones' greatest trick of making short, in-your-face, trash into an art form; milking the myriad collisions of riotous indulgence and reverent revival to provide a compelling listen.

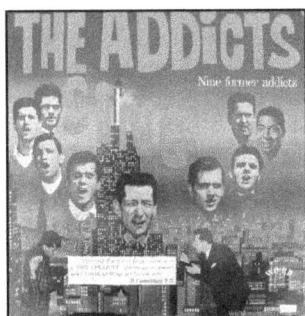

The Addicts:
The Addicts Sing
(Word, 1963)
What? Well-meaning wailing in a mainstream style from newly saved smack-heads and the like.

There's more nobility and less car-crash fascination about this collection than there is with most of the myriad of low-budget "miracle" musical efforts of the sixties, wherein the likes of the "The Handless Organist" and "The Braillettes" were obliged to parade their deformities as part of a package that presented their music as a triumph over cruel adversity. That – basically – is what is on offer here, but The Addicts Sing simply sounds like more of a triumph because it pitches itself, market wise, expertly into niche territory. These are Bronx boys gone wrong – by way of mental health issues, addictions and the like – and music is their salvation. As befitting the wisdom of addiction treatment programmes and self-help, then and now, the belief in a higher power is essential to their recovery, and the gospel performances here (classics and originals) are testament to that. Vocally, these boys aren't half bad, though they're not exactly The Beach Boys. But, the real killer here is the perfect location of the music halfway between standard gospel group and full-on doo-wop. A couple of cuts are more doo-wop than gospel and for most of the duration the "soul" on offer suggests strongly that the newly found faith in the Lord under-pinning this venture goes hand in hand with a love of late fifties doo-wop, and the boys are hitting on higher powers like The Platters too. It may not always be that spiritual. Frankly, for most of the album these boys sing like they want to impress girls. Consequently, they perform with a passion that is primal and spiritual at the same time, knocking out a version of a standard like "I Believe" that stands out from the – massive – collection of covers available. A curio for sure, and one worthy of investigation more for its history than massive musical merits, but – most certainly – a cut above much of its freak-show peers, and all the better for that.

Hasil Adkins:
What the Hell Was I Thinking?
(Fat Possum, 1998)
What? Psychobilly superstar on top form!

Adkins was a major player in "outsider music" long before anyone had seen fit to name such a thing. Adkins remained a perpetual outsider who lived nowhere other than West Virginia and ceaselessly contributed to his own myth, to the point even he hadn't a clue about the truth, "The Haze" was a fitting nickname. Adkins' work carved much of the furrow that would subsequently be labelled Pscychobilly. For all the apparent train-wreck qualities of his life, (his birth-date remained elusive, he claimed to have attended school for precisely four days and many feel he greatly exaggerated the vast tonnage of songs he claimed to have written), Adkins' peculiar genius was honed with a determined focus on a prize, and with the singularity of vision that marks out many gifted musicians. However, Adkins' rabid focus saw him developing a brand of low-fi, raucous and rapid country rock 'n' roll with rambling, frequently incoherent, lyrics and a regular focus on trash-culture subjects like flying saucers, fried chicken and vivid references to violence and serious injury.

The mystery on the amount of songs he wrote revolves around the similarities between many compositions and his less than faithful rendering of his own best known songs on stage. For sheer jaw-dropping curio value Poultry in Motion – an entire album of songs devoted to his love of chicken – is probably worth checking out, but the late period What the Hell Was I Thinking? is – arguably – the best place for a first timer to start. It's atypical because of the – occasionally – lucid lyrics and clear production, and in its sporadic ballads. In fact, "Beautiful Hills" is nerve-chillingly poignant, slow, sad and insightful and ranks with the very best of his prolific output. By this point – Adkins was somewhere around 60 when the album was released – his voice was a dark, and lived in element of his work. The borderline insanity of a track like "Up on Mars" (recounting a visit to the red planet) shows it to full effect.

Elsewhere there's enough breakneck chaos, shambolic rhythms, thrashing away at a barely tuned guitar and shameless diving into God and drink (though not on the same song) to satisfy the faithful, and reward anyone investigating the legend but sceptical the recorded work will match what they've read. "Stay With Me" is one of a number of cuts that hit the throttle, hang on for as long as possible and don't so much finish as simply shatter into their constituent parts. Bear in mind this is one of Adkins' most focussed and thoughtful efforts and All Music Guide still note it is: "music at the edge of sanity: potent, but only in very small doses."

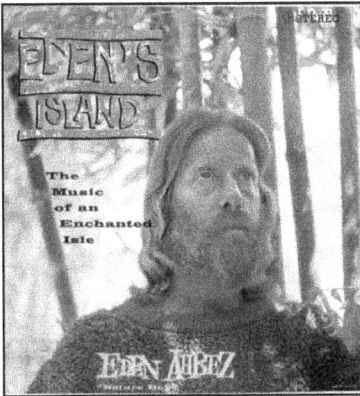

Eden Ahbez:
Eden's Island
(Del Fi Records, 1960)
What? "I had a little boat (I called it Life). Once I went out. And never came back…"

With all due apologies to aficionados of exotica – for whom the following story is known backwards - we should take some time to consider Eden Ahbez before we indulge in enjoying his master-work. Ahbez (1908 – 1985) was a true ground-breaker in musical terms who, ironically, supported himself for much of his life on the back of an MOR monster hit performed by Nat King Cole. Ahbez's "Nature Boy" topped the US charts for a few weeks in 1948, was covered by – amongst others – Frank Sinatra and (despite a lawsuit that resulted in Ahbez forfeiting $25,000) allowed him to continue a lifestyle and career that were truly unconventional by the standards of his time, or any other. Ahbez also penned a few other successful songs.

Shamelessly bohemian twenty years ahead of the hippie generation, Ahbez' life involved camping out with his family below the first L in the Hollywood sign, existing almost entirely on natural foods like fruits and nuts and combining a life-long study of mysticism with performing a blend of simplistic jazz: sparingly melodic, stripped-back instrumentally and suffused with sense of slight melancholy in its wistfully blissed-out imagery. In other words, peace and love, Man, but the sounds betray a knowledge of the harsher side of life.

In 1960 he committed this cult-classic to tape. Its poor sales and general low-profile have long been eclipsed by a steady long-tail in sales that have seen Eden's Island sporadically re-issued and re-appraised. This man for all musical seasons shows no sign of running out of influence. Eden's Island is a concept piece, if only because it follows a journey of the imagination, tells one story throughout and interjects musical interludes. Ahbez was pushing pensionable age by the time the hippie generation stumbled on the same concept of a self-contained paradise. But, his template is their vision too. Opening with "The Wanderer" (no! not that Dion song) Eden intones "Blow wind blow…to Eden's Island I must go" and spends the rest of the album getting there. For the most part he tells the story through slowly spoken beat-poetry, getting support from basic percussion, piano, flute and a sparingly twanged stand-up bass. He muses on the need for love and isolation, observes some of the flora and fauna on his mystic journey – there is an instrumental dedicated to the "Myna Bird" and a blissful evocation of the joys of eating bananas fresh from the tree: "Banana Boy" – and, of course, he makes it to the island. By which time he is observing a hippie paradise; "Eden has a sandy cove, Boys and girls fall in love they make fires on the shore, love is all they're living for." Bear in mind, he was recording this stuff in the wake of McCarthyist America, Doris Day was still a chart-topper and Elvis was in the army.

If Eden's Island has any real precedent it is probably the travel sketches and haiku poetry of the Japanese master poet Matsuo Basho (1554 – 1594), and his peers, all of whom lived by a code in which the notion of spiritual journeying, rejection of material wealth and the lack of any fixed line between life and art were central. Ahbez' album does nod towards popular stage musicals of its time (at least because the story and instrumental interludes have a narrative feel) but – this late in the day – it stands as an undisputed classic of the much-maligned concept album. So hopelessly out of step with its time, it will always be a cult classic, a bohemian Bat out of Hell.

Alarm Will Sound:
Acoustica: Alarm Will Sound Performs Aphex Twin
(Cantaloupe, 2005)
What? Organic re-imaginings of inspired electronica.

There isn't that much to say in this case, other than, in the humble opinions of the authors of this book the collaboration running to almost 70 minutes on this album works perfectly. Alarm Will Sound is a 20 piece chamber orchestra, their musical territory of choice takes in minimalist and experimental classical works and overlaps into the areas of ambient associated works that border modern classical. They bring a classical competence, an unfettered willingness to explore sounds, and a sense of performance to their work. This collection, is, in effect, a greatest hits package of Aphex Twin works to 2005, with Drukqs in particular being pillaged for suitable tracks. Richard D James and Selected Ambient Works Volume II are also rifled in search of material and Alarm Will Sound are at their best sequencing the varied works from each album to make a complete work that changes moods, subtly shifts its focus and showcases the compositional genius of a man more famous for providing ambient and mood changing music. The album is never better than the moments it segues from one Aphex album to another, for example, following "Meltphace 6" from Drukqs with "Blue Calx" from Selected Ambient Works Volume II with a confidence that suggests both pieces were always part of some greater whole.

This is acoustic music, performed by the very best musicians. The percussion tracks, in particular, manage the massively difficult job of imitating machines, and simultaneously sounding organic and inspired. The timing of each interjection, a blast of brass here, deep noted strings there, never slips from perfection and the production; a big sounding widescreen work that improves as the volume goes up, is another bonus. Ultimately, Acoustica works because it makes the completion of its demanding task, translating these works from one realm to another, sound inevitable.

Alberto y Lost Trios Paranoias:
Mandrax Sunset Variations
(Castle, 2001)
What? Decade's work for mirthful Manc head-cases.

Too damn clever for their own good, weighed down by an overabundance of talent and targets, Alberto y Lost Trios Paranoias came from Manchester but mocked the world. Or the world of rock, anyway. Mandrax Sunset collates much their seventies catalogue, presents it over two CDs and 40 tracks, and provides an alternative comedy commentary on the golden age of rock. Like most of the great rock comedians, the Albertos love the thing they mock, and play it like they mean it. It's just that their imagination takes strange turns all the time. When the relationship fails in the country song, "Old Trust", it's the singer's dog, also his best friend, who runs away with his wife, steals the car and even takes his best suit. Some of the song titles are a little over clever, suggesting a band tripping over puns when it came to writing lyrics: "Italians from Outer Space," "Teenager in Schtuck" and "A Fistful of Spaghetti" all deliver what you'd expect. "Invocation of the Fundamental Orifice of St. Agnes," by contrast, is more Firesign Theatre than a side-swipe at prog rock.

Like a lot of rock comedy, Mandrax Sunset Variations has dated because some of its subject matter has fallen a long way off the musical radar. Seriously, "Happy to be (on an Island Away From) Demis Roussos, was a damn good gag when the eccentrically attired Greek was a by-word for cod sophistication to UK audiences. The punk sideswipes, like "Anarchy in the UK," lack a little of the raw power of the genuine article, because, basically, this lot could play and they cared about knocking pomposity off its perch.

Their greatest hit, i.e. it scraped the British charts, "Heads Down no Nonesense Mindless Boogie," is here, and has aged well. It sounds like Status Quo in the days when the band packed a fair bit of distortion and buzz along with the riffs, and manages the double whammy of decent gag and nostalgia fest.

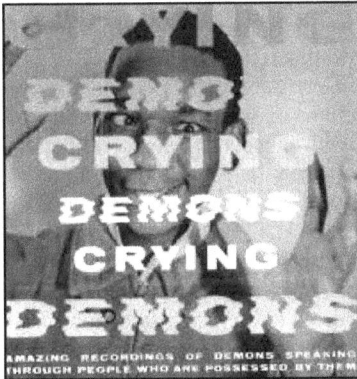

A A Allen:
Crying Demons
(Miracle Revival Recordings 19??)
What? Out demons out!

Asa Alonso Allen (1911-1970) was a religious pioneer who played a leading role in the vanguard of evangelical preachers embracing the media. One of the first notable television evangelists, he also enjoyed a prolific recording career and had the sense to vary the content of his releases. This long player features Allen in full flow, literally casting out demons. His melodious, slightly rough-edged, invocations gradually beat incarnate demons to a standstill. The preacher is a showman with an inventive and articulate turn to match every development in the action. He anchors his work with biblical readings but retorts to the demonic interjections with the skill of a top comedian taking on a determined heckler.

An online appreciation of Allen notes: "Brother Allen's style was bold and outgoing. He sometimes wore lavender suits with white patent leather boots. His television commercials declared, "See! Hear! Actual miracles happening before your very eyes! Cancer, tumours, goiters disappear. Crutches, braces, wheelchairs, stretchers discarded. Crossed eyes straightened. Caught by the camera as they actually occur in the healing line before thousands of witnesses."

Demons, then, were all in day's work, and an album's worth of material. Side one sees Allen cast out a particularly truculent spirit. The early exchanges have a parent/naughty child vibe:

> "Go back to Hell from whence you came!"
> "No I like it here."

But, as the possessed woman moans and suffers Allen ramps up the rhetoric with some sterling one-liners: "Thou stubborn devil of lust, I rebuke your foul voice." The moans and suffering get louder, someone in the congregation announces the departure of the demon and our previously possessed subject is able to talk to us after 18 minutes of Allen's close attention.

The second side is a rousing sermon with interviews and a range of demonic intonations. All Hell doesn't break loose, but we do get a slight glimpse into how such an event might sound. Years ahead of Christian television channels and private jet preachers, Allen is clearly hinting at the world of celebrant superstars on this release and even leads the singing at the end of the second side. Allen's current followers still agree on the man's influence and lingering potency, though complete agreement on when this album was released (most likely late fifties), is harder to reach.

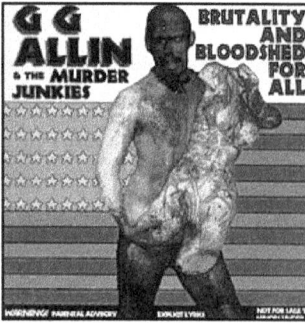

G G Allin and the Murder Junkies:
Brutality and Bloodshed for All
(Alive, 1993)
What? Growling punk monster is requiem for damage rock casualty.

Allin's demons drove him through one of the most brutal and unrepentant trails of destruction in rock. Punk and extreme hard rock were his styles of choice though his work also took in spoken word recordings. Prolific beyond all reason and typically recorded with a rotation of backing musicians and minimal budgets, Allin polarised almost every audience he encountered. Any defence of his work starts by taking his claim to be the last true rock 'n' roller at face value, and seeing every element of danger and destruction in his work as art. Allin polarised the most libertine fan. It's one thing to support extreme acts, another thing to pay ticket money when the things thrown from the stage include fresh shit and the performer's naked body. Allin gigs often ended after a few numbers, with acts of destruction aimed at the venue a regular feature. He treated fans and acquaintances in a similar way and regularly threatened suicide live on stage. A running annual event in the Allin calendar was a planned Halloween suicide at a live gig, he started these plans in 1989 but spent successive Halloweens in jail, unable to perform. He eventually died in front of fans, in June 1993, after a live gig ended in chaos and he wandered down local streets to a party, where he OD'd on heroin. Fans posed with his comatose body, unaware the ultimate monster was expiring in front of them. His catalogue includes much work with varied backing bands – the Scumfucs, Shitkickers, Southern Baptists, AIDS Brigade and Cedar Street Sluts – most of it low-fi. Brutality and Bloodshed is mainly full-on punk, with Allin growling like a bear. There are nods to hard rock with some choice grinding riffs and thumping drums. Tracks like "Anal Cunt," "Kill thy Father and thy Mother" and "I Kill Everything I Fuck" are core Allin works, and not that far from the truth. Allin avoided one scheduled onstage suicide through being arrested for extreme violence to a girlfriend. The psychiatric report presented in his defence noted alcohol dependence and a fermenting mix of personality disorder traits linking narcissism, masochism and borderline elements. On that basis, the endless variations on brutality, sex, threats and anti-authoritarian rants in his lyrics can be taken as sincere. Brutality and Bloodshed says it succinctly in "I'll Slice Your Fucking Throat": "If you're in my gang you better be real, no crossover, mainstream sellout deal." Ironically, this appears on Allin's most accessible album. Though, Brutality and Bloodshed's only real sop to selling out is its fatter sound and better production in comparison to much of the rabid, ranting and rapid release product that fills out his discography. This is the real deal, if you can take it. [*]

America:
Hat Trick
(Warner Brothers, 1973)
What? Alt-country cul-de-sac in a stellar MOR career.

A cursory glance at the early career of platinum selling country-rockers America suggests a fairly obvious conclusion with regard to this, their "difficult" third album. Their eponymous debut collection, and the single "Horse With no Name" both hit #1 in the USA, making instant stars of the precociously young trio who had honed their act in the UK, meeting because they were the sons of US service personnel stationed here. The hasty follow up Homecoming

---

[*] EDITOR'S NOTE: One of the perks of being the editor of a book like this is that I can cast my oar in occasionally, as - like Neil - I am an obsessive collector of trivia. For me the two pearls of my G.G.Allin collection are (probably) his most unpleasant song ever 'Expose yourself to Kids' and his surprisingly tasteful version of Warren Zevon's 'Carmelita', which is one of my favourite songs of all time. JD

marked their return to the USA, and offered "Ventura Highway" as its major hit; album and single duly went into the top ten. By contrast the #28 achieved by Hat Trick and fact that it spawned three singles with only "Muscrat Love" crawling into the charts at #67 suggests a crisis. The drafting in of George Martin as producer and a return to short, focussed, songs and a radio friendly sound ensured top five positions for Holiday (1974) and Hearts (1975), and a slew of new hit singles included "Sister Golden Hair" which also hit #1.

So Hat Trick appears as an aberration in a record of radio friendly, mass appeal, country rock. Oddly, this under-appreciated and oft-overlooked collection was the first America studio album to earn a silver disc in the UK. Hat Trick is the one America album that appears to sell to people who don't really like the band. It presents three singer/songwriters collected in one band, still in their early twenties and gifted with more time and money to make an album than they could have believed possible when they trooped into the Warner's UK offices clutching acoustic guitars and played their first album in its entirety. The "problem" – if such a thing can be said to exist here – is the sheer ambition of what Hat Trick attempts. Where most of the band's albums create a solid sound and allow the individual talents some wiggle room to meld it to their own songs Hat Trick takes every song where it wants to go, presenting a collection of sounds and visions more akin to the different elements that make up – for example – The Eagles' Hotel California. America also let their musical talents expand to fill the resulting space, Gerry Beckley plays superb piano in places, Dan Peek's love of country comes to the fore and Dewey Bunnell (already established as the best bet for hits on the back of "Horse With no Name" and "Ventura Highway") lets rip with some of the most ethereal and ambitious work being recorded by any country rockers at the time. Bunnell's "Wind Wave" mines a jazz groove and offers up a mouth-trumpet solo, his "Rainbow Song" combines a gentle melody with sudden uptemo bursts, "Molton Love" betrays the influence of the eclectic British folk artists he came to admire as a young man and "Green Monkey" is a rocker with Joe Walsh guesting on guitar. Bunnell, more than any other America, gives this album a sense of possibilities and new directions that place it amongst the most inventive offerings in folk-rock of the period. Touchstones at one end might be Neil Young and The Eagles but elsewhere Gerry Beckley's McCartneyesque paino doodlings and the influence of jazz/folk UK artists like John Martyn and Bill Fay on Bunnell's writing can be detected. Collectively it suggests the band had an ear on Stevie Wonder, not so much to steal his sound as to work outwards from their own style and create an album that stayed focussed but referenced every style it wanted. For an album that looks like a mishap in their big-selling career Hat Trick has an assurance and ambition about it that still sounds mightily unapologetic.

Alt-country, with its wilful incorporation of any suitable style and sound into a country-based style was a good quarter of a century down the line, but with Hat Trick, a band often slammed by critics for their predictability and blandness, anticipated an ambitious offshoot of their genre.

A.C.:
It Just Gets Worse
(Earache, 1999)
What? Grindcore grotesquery of the highest (i.e.; lowest) order.

If you're easily offended, most of the other 499 entries hereabouts may prove more palatable than this one. If you're wondering why the strict alphabetical sequence of entries appears broken here all you need to know is that A.C. (as they are on the packaging of this collection) are more commonly referred to as Anal Cunt. That much may – just about – be construed from the comic art on the cover in which some poor soul (clearly beaten to within an inch of life) is bolted into a guillotine whilst a slavering and be-quiffed male enjoys a last minute sexual experience, at her expense, before the blade falls.

A picture inside shows the action continuing after the blade has fallen and our decapitated victim has suffered an involuntary bowel-movement. A closer look at the band's logo of A and C shows the body parts after which they are named, an image of a child's pram burning appears on the front and back and, if you're so inclined you can read a list of the 39 songs (delivered inside 33 minutes) including the opener "I Became a Counsellor so I Could Tell Rape Victims They Asked for it." Later delights offer up: "I Convinced you to Beat Your Wife on a Daily Basis," "I Pushed Your Wife in Front of the Subway," "I Lit Your Baby on Fire," "I Snuck a Retard into a Sperm Bank," "Your Kid Committed Suicide Because you Suck," "Sweatshops are Cool" and "Domestic Violence is Really Really Funny." Sonically it's a breakneck blitzkrieg of guitar, bass and drums with (guitarist/vocalist) Seth Putnam's high-pitched death-growl out front ranting through the lyrics (which given the long titles and short songs often amount to little more than delivering the titles and a few other pithy abominations of narrative detail).

From which point on it's very much in the heads of the audience as to whether Anal Cunt are as funny as they think they are or just a bunch of idiot-dudes from Newton, Massachusetts getting away with it because they can. To put their in-your-face humour in context one track here was strongly restrained from its original. "Your Kid Committed Suicide..." started life under the title of: "Connor Clapton Committed Suicide Because His Father Sucks". It's macho, unrepentant and ultra-sick to the point that even the highly tolerant Earache label thought it expedient to censor some of the lyrics in the liner notes. Songs like "Body by Auschwitz" offer up lines like "You fat slob…here's the final solution to your flab" before the next thought is obscured by a massive sticker-print reading ANAL CUNT FUCKING OFFENSIVE. Full-on offence is hardly rare in grindcore and its offshoots, and the rabid rock-out assault offered up here is no faster, or more full-on than countless other bands, but Anal Cunt are amongst the originators of this level of extremity and they have spent years through break-ups and reformations standing precariously on the borderline of humour and social nuisance, occasionally creating albums that work their magic with a die-hard audience. One of the tracks here puts this lifestyle choice neatly into a song title: "Being Ignorant is Awesome." [*]

Laurie Anderson:
The Ugly One with the Jewels
(Warner Brothers, 1995)
What? Sublime travelogue delivered in effective less-is-more style.

Widely acclaimed as her best album since Big Science (1982) this lengthy collection collates a number of pieces devoted to travel, or ideas about travel. As with much of Anderson's work, the journeys remain as much inner-voyages as literal examples of being transported. "The Geographic North Pole" – for example – balances a knife-edge between plausibility and fanciful escape of the mind. It tells a story of Anderson hitch-hiking her way to the top of the earth, hopping a mail plane along the way, watching the northern lights and encountering those on the run from the mental horrors of Vietnam. The Ugly One with the Jewels eschews some of the more multifaceted musical ideas Anderson developed in the wake of her improbable hit "O' Superman" and returns to ambient, Enoesque backings; minimal but hugely evocative, sparing sound-effects, and a vocal style somewhere between spoken word and singing, usually presenting Anderson so close to the mic that her breathing and hesitations become part of the narrative.

The title track – which draws its name from a derogatory remark made about Anderson – is key to

---

[*] EDITOR'S NOTE: I am not going to do this every few pages (or at least I don't think that I am) but I could not let an entry on this band pass without mentioning their brilliantly awful 1998 album Picnic of Love, which consists of deliberately schmaltzy (and often out of tune) songs such as "I Respect Your Feelings as a Woman and a Human" and "Saving Ourselves for Marriage". Some things just *have* to be said. JD

understanding the entire album. Anderson visits her anthropologist brother and ends up having her hair braided, sees her reflection and feels ridiculous. The tribeswomen braiding her hair think otherwise and tell her she was ugly but now might find a husband. The dynamic of the story – within which Anderson manages to step easily inside and outside of her existence, seeing herself as others might – permeates the whole album. Unusually for Anderson this is an album with a simple idea behind it. The concept of the travelogue, and the constant sense of exploring a real world, and the world of experience (as would an anthropologist) give The Ugly One with the Jewels an anchor. They allow the listener to stay within the stories, and feel part of the whole experience. Anderson is a typically evasive and ceaselessly inventive companion, but she makes every effort to keep the sounds, and words accessible.

The Ugly One with the Jewels sets itself the difficult task of delivering a multi-layered concept, with the most minimal of musical tools. And, for the most part, it succeeds magnificently.

...native hipsters
there goes concorde again...

And The Native Hipsters:
There Goes Concorde Again
(Mechanically Reclaimed Music, 2001)
What? Low-fi bedroom experimentation of the highest order.

For a moment in 1980 And the Native Hipsters (ATNH) were something of an overnight sensation. In an era when cassette tapes were the nearest thing to file sharing and cheap electronic instruments had unleashed a generation of synth-pop and experimentation ATNH gathered John Peel plays and respectable sales for a 33 rpm EP boasting one bona-fide indie classic, "There Goes Concorde Again." Against the most minimal of backing Natalie Greenblatt delivered a razor sharp metallic vocal conveying frustration, incredulity, humour and something completely surreal. The track was a stand-out from a generation of musical acts who saw no dividing lines between bedrooms and recording studios, and frequently offered their wares for sale in exchange for small sums of money and stamped addressed envelopes via ads in the music press. The fertile imagination of their pop genius William Wilding suggested the band could go places and Rough Trade distribution, who handled many of Peel's picks at the time, were also involved. The closest musical touchstone at the time was – probably – the clanking rhythm and ice-cool Patti Palladin vocals of The Flying Lizards but ATNH often dispensed with rhythm instruments completely, timing themselves to the rhythms of conversations, lyrics or randomly, if at all.

True to their very singular version of a musical "career" the act duly took over twenty years to deliver an album titled after their almost-hit, which was already a "classic" on a Rough Trade compilation by the time this - the Hipster's second album - was released. There Goes Concorde Again, (the album) gathers 18 Hipster tracks from over 20 years of messing about with loops, studiously avoiding anything approaching a band-wagon and shamelessly exploring the possibilities of low-fi sounds and low cost instrumentation. As a long-playing listening experience it has all the other-wordly ambience of an art-installation and the fragmentary, fleeting pop genius of bands like the High Llamas, combined with the unrepentantly indie sensibilities of early eighties bedroom synth-pop.

Above all, There Goes Concorde explodes with ideas and a dark understated humour that allow it to deliver a previously unheard joke, after repeated listening. Wilding's pop visions are perfectly fronted by Natalie Greenblatt's vocals, combining the deep and dulcet delivery of Felicity Kendall with a permanent sense of underlying mental disturbance. The opener – "Mr Magic" – and the lost classic that gives the album its title are probably the standout tracks, but it's the haphazard glory, something akin to throwing a lighted match into an open box of fireworks, that gives this collection a riveting and random attraction. As Wilding describes it the album "has over 25 years of mash up and creativity all crammed into one wonderful riotous cascade." ATNH's low-key career continues at its own pace and other albums – of equal singularity and strangeness – are also available.

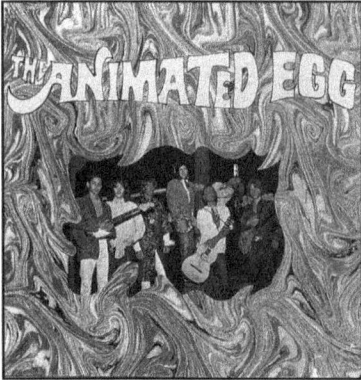

The Animated Egg:
The Animated Egg
(Alshire, 1969)
What? Infectious guitar-freakout from studio-only band.

All but anonymous at the time this album was released, The Animated Egg (band) appeared to be one of those cheap cash-in acts hell-bent on prising cash from gormless kids capable of mistaking them for the real thing. The release of their eponymous debut album on the UK's budget and Woolworth's friendly Marble Arch label only strengthened this image. In fact, the band were helmed by session supreme guitar wizard Jerry Cole, whose adept and flashingly brilliant chops appear on some of the most lauded cuts by the likes of The Beach Boys and Phil Spector. Cole was part of the legendary "Wrecking Crew" session mafia, a go-to outfit who could turn on the passion at will and make the sounds that spoke to the kids. Which is where The Animated Egg (the album) comes in. Ten slices of top-notch guitar-freakout with a solid rhythm section smacking away behind Cole's dexterous fret-wankery. Cole moves confidently from 6 to 12 strings and throws in fuzztones, blues licks and anything else from the trick bag to turn in a performance that belies the rapid recording process and limited budget. There are also fragmentary nods to other great music of the time, the lead guitar on "Sock it my Way" – for example – hinting at the descending phrase from Donovan's "Hurdy Gurdy Man." Jerry Cole also wrote the material here; most of it rejoicing in great throwaway titles like "Sure Listic," "Sippin' and Trippin'" and "I Said, She Said, Ah Cid." Whether Cole thought more of this than his many other gigs, from surf guitar instrumentals to regular slots in television show bands and some high-profile live work including a stint in Andy Williams' backing band and a place on stage with Elvis for the Aloha From Hawaii via Satellite show and album, isn't clear. But The Animated Egg has lasted longer than most cash-in crud of the period, gradually gaining a cult following on the basis of the unholy collision of an album clearly thrown together to mine a fleeting market and the presence on that album of some surprisingly good work. It's now widely accepted that – along with Cole – Billy Preston was a member of The Animated Egg. Cole's appearance on a series of "psychosploitation" instrumental works was recognised when other cuts, produced under other names, were added to the ten Animated Egg originals for the CD reissue.

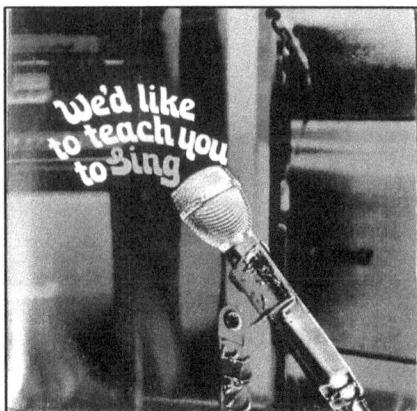

Bob Anthony:
We'd Like To Teach You Sing
(Eden, 1973)
Ile D'Amour
(Ile D'Amour, 1975)
What? But, do we all want to sing like Bob?

Anthony's album may be long gone from the shops but a thoughtful posting online of his masterclass in music making, alongside his own creative works, makes for a very interesting trawl. Bob's own tuition involves a slew of set exercises in areas like "Vibrato" and

"Vowels and Consonants." The longest track on side one, by some margin, involves "Finding Your Singing Range" wherein Bob coaches us through a musical backing that gets higher and higher. Listeners are invited to jump in when the right level/key is playing and explore their ability to work in a comfortable area. Side two is a series of backing tracks for the repetitive practice needed to take you to professional standard. All of it, sort of, bizarre in this stripped back format, and most of it potential mix-tape gold if your tastes extend to the sounds few others are ever likely to savour. Since the album is intended for regular practice, it's probably best not to moan too much about a running time little beyond the half hour mark. The "We'd" in the singing tuition, by the way, arises because an unnamed accomplice also features on the album. A certain David Noades turned the above into a particularly illuminating window on the world by investigating the professional genius of Bob Anthony and posting a consideration of his advice to others alongside Bob's own creative output. Online, this amounts to a twofer (with bonus single) to savour. Ile D'Amour is a particularly fine example of a phenomenon the UK produced to excellent standards in the 1970s. The locally manufactured, surprisingly lavish, album aimed at snagging tourist cash. Bob's concept piece wrings nuances of meaning and hitherto unimagined scenarios from the Channel Island of Jersey. Jersey may be BIG by Channel Island standards, but the island jewels in the sea base their tourist trade on their small scale and quaint charm. Bob doesn't see the limitations. Hell, we're only two tracks into the thing before caution is thrown to the English Channel winds and "The Jersey Polka" bounces into our ears, inviting us to: "Come on and dance the Jersey Polka, and make it a happy holiday." Bob doesn't explain whether failure to dance will result in some Wicker Man immolation for the hapless tourist as an unfeasibly ugly gaggle of local inbreeds bang drums to urge the flames higher. Probably not, Jersey isn't that kind of place. Bob varies styles, employs strings, and soon leaves behind the capital, St. Helier, to devote individual songs to a lighthouse, a valley (this one in a slightly maudlin country cut) and a castle. As we're running out of obvious visitor attractions we get to consider the particular delights of "Sunday on the Island" (bear in mind this is 1975, British shops are – by and large - closed on the Sabbath). "Sunday on the Island" is, predictably, an unapologetic invocation to let the local inhabitants sing and "give glory unto the Lord." Twelve tracks into the homage to his diminutive home Bob jerks the tears with "Au Revoir Ile D'amour." David Noades also posted both sides of a single by the Bobster.

Bob Andrews emerges as a cabaret stylist, much given to employing the vocal ticks and tricks promoted via his tuition album, (incidentally the album was a taster for a pricey course of lessons so Bob also emerges as a rabid entrepreneur with limitless talents). However, Ile D'Amour also presents styles so varied as to test Bob's own comfort range to destruction. He's a decent cabaret singer and balladeer, make no mistake. But the light-disco diversion on "Down to St. Helier" relies way too much on the double entendre of getting "down" to St. Helier and, in a moment probably unmatched in any other desperate disco shuffle, manages to rhyme "esplanade" with "got it made." This might have made some sense in Little England's cabaret vision of dance culture, circa 1975, but it's a high-camp embarrassment a few decades later.

The Aphex Twin:
Selected Ambient Works Volume 2
(Warp Records, 1994)
What? Out there, ethereal and more familiar than you might think.

Richard D James AKA The Aphex Twin has long been a feature of the stranger end of dance music and his soundscapes have also seen heavy rotation as backing tracks for all manner of television and film productions. His rampantly experimental approach to his craft has taken in stunts that push the whole concept of making music to the limits. He has, on occasion, produced a 'dance' track with beats so fast they obliterated the melody line and spun a sandpaper disc during a DJ set.

His stated method of working during the period in which this double disc collection was amassed was to fall out of bed, create the work in the same room and compile the final running order after listening back to the varied results.

Maybe so, but the one thing that sets apart this ethereal collection of 23 untitled works from much of the material produced in the mid-nineties ambient boom is the coherence it offers up. Apart from anything else the same production, same keyboard sounds and same absence of any driving rhythm mean everything here sounds like it belongs in the one collection.

Slowly turning melodies seep into each other, elliptical percussion echoes in the background and the soft edges of the synth sounds wrap the collected works in a soft audio fog, giving it a dream-like quality. As such, Selected Ambient Works Volume 2 lends itself to offering up new possibilities with every random play, and exists for all time in a curious borderland of experience, at once a focussed work of some genuine ambition and insight and at the same time a fleeting experience always just beyond the bounds of consciousness. Well, either that or it sounds gorgeous and gives you a sense of sharing a room with a loving companion, even when you are completely alone.

Dorothy Ashby:
The Rubaiyat of Dorothy Ashby
(Cadet Records, 1970)
What? Classical literary work + jazz harpist = an inspired mix.

The full subtitle of the album reads: "Original compositions inspired by the words of Omar Khayyam, arranged and conducted by Richard Evans." There are other talents involved, but this is the most determined effort made by Ashby to create a work of such singular vision that it transcends any easy categorisation. Ashby (1930-1986) was an accomplished multi-instrumentalist and singer who forsook touring to settle into the California session scene. The harp was her main instrument but wasn't in heavy demand for session work. One tactic Ashby eventually employed involved creating a series of unique albums, showcasing sounds and styles that broke new ground for harpists. As the Space Age Pop website notes: "Ashby's Cadet albums have come to be viewed as among the best early examples of acid jazz, and now fetch eye-watering prices among collectors. Breaks and rhythm tracks from the superb Richard Evans arrangements have become favorites for sampling and remix artists."

Of all these recordings The Rubaiyat is easily the strangest. Spiritual in both intent and impact, the album takes jazz into the abstract areas visited by the likes of John Coltrane and Pharoah Sanders but sounds like virtually nothing before or since. The sounds sampled by others since 1970 include the glissando harp from the opening "Myself When Young" and the percussion break in the following "For Some We Loved." By the end of the opening two tracks the listener has spent over nine minutes in the company of this collection of talent and both tracks have established a pattern of sudden swerves from one sound to another, "For Some We Loved" opens with a poem. From this point onwards the album rotates influences from eastern music, impressive and varied vocals from Ashby, and a masterful display of guiding the musical experiments by means of pulling every possible sound from the harp. The mixtures of instruments on each track, the arrangements, and the sheer conceit of creating a jazz work inspired by a work of classic literature from another culture make every passing moment both interesting and eclectic. But the real joy here is that so much of this music sets an agenda that hasn't occurred to many people, moves to its own territory and makes a compelling case over ten varied tracks. Ashby produced much more accessible collections. The Jazz Harpist, for example, is a much simpler blending of standard jazz with the twist of placing Ashby as the lead player. The Rubaiyat, by contrast, presents the uninitiated with a plunge into the deep end of Ashby's oeuvre. It makes some allowances for its otherness, notably by leaving the real diversion, "The Moving Finger" to the very end. With a chanted mantra: "The moving finger writes…" at the beginning, followed by a jazz groove with Ashby's harp briefly taking prominence, the string section and vibes take the piece towards proto-space rock territory before a fuzzed guitar arrives. In 1970 there were acid guzzling rock bands incapable of such perfect balancing on the borderlands of insanity and inspiration.

If the album makes few allowances for listeners unfamiliar with its varied sounds it does have two qualities that make it accessible. Firstly, Ashby's background gives the whole piece a staged and theatrical quality. "The Moving Finger," for example, begins and ends with her vocal. Secondly, Ashby's singing has a stagey quality and clear diction, so the listener engages with her personality, even when the music takes a few listens to reveal the varied sounds.

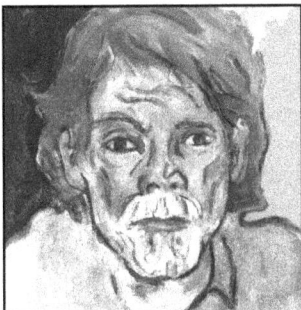

Ed Askew:
For the World
(Tin Angel, 2013)
What? Lived-in feel for vintage singer-songwriter's best work.

Askew recorded this collection after undertaking his first US tour, at the age of 71. With a 47 year career as a singer-songwriter behind him he had the material, and experience to focus his ideas to perfection and For the World benefits from the production skills of Black Swan Jerry DeCicca and a session crew including another Black Swan (Tyler Evans) and a smattering of talent that had rubbed shoulders with the likes of Tom Waits and Elvis Costello. Waits and Costello are a useful benchmark for Askew's lived-in vocals, reflective and direct lyrics and the slow tempos and melodies, effectively minimal and subtly hypnotic, pervading the album. Bill Fay's late career masterpiece Life is People stands really close comparison with Askew's work, the intimacy of the vocals and near-conversational pace and feel of the more intimate moments being a strong point of overlap. Chiming pub/barroom piano chords give most of For the World an understated muscularity and the slightly random and arty reference points of a song like "Gertrude Stein" make Askew's academic and art school background a feature of the work.

The pacing of individual songs and sequencing of the whole collection is deployed to provide moments of contrast. The cascade of piano notes on "Baby Come Home" ebbs into a hauntingly minimal, and stumble-paced, "Paper Horses" with a slow, echoing, banjo in the opening moments. Askew also manages to slip into a thin high register in his singing, a fragile element in a well deployed vocal armoury that takes the songs into occasional moments of reverie. A mature, mellow and effortless sense of life's passing informs the best moments. Songs like "Moon in Mind" present these qualities with a counterpoint of slight tempo changes.

A brusque harmonica, redolent of Askew's roots in the New York folk scene of the sixties, ensures the music ebbs and flows. For the World is one of those effortless gems that never loses its sense of intimacy, stays personal throughout, but still delivers a strong message to anyone willing to listen.

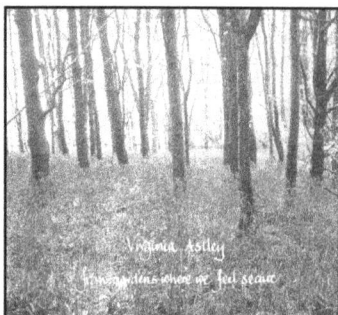

Virginia Astley:
From Gardens Where we Feel Secure
(Happy Valley,1983)
What? Ambient/conceptual work of fragile beauty, the nearest the eighties got to its own Tubular Bells..

It's doubtful if Astley or Rough Trade Records (who rapidly took over distribution and catalogue duties from Astley's own Happy Valley label) would welcome the Tubular Bells comparison, but for those who missed this album's brief sprint to #4 in the UK indie chart it's a good place to start. This is an album-length, self-contained masterwork that establishes its own terms and makes a case for you to join it. From Gardens... is a languid and dreamy album combining sampling technology, piano driven tone-poems, sparing studio effects and a plundering of English classical music to create a work of genuine beauty. The album charts an English landscape from dawn to dusk on an idyllic summer day. Astley's vocals add sounds, but not words to one track, woodwinds drive "Hiding in the Ha Ha." Elsewhere, chirping birds and church bells are amongst the field recordings woven into the musical tapestry. From Gardens… remained elusive for many years before a 2003 CD reissue but continues to cruise below the radar, probably for two reasons: firstly, Astley's headlong sprint into the past – as in reviving sensibilities for her work that drew on the English composers of the early twentieth century – was always likely to make it cultish. Secondly, From Gardens… suffers every time a book (like this) or a website rediscovers it because the descriptions inevitably focus on the idea behind it, and what you hear for fleeting seconds. Presented in words the album reads like a twee little indulgence from a middle-class musician. The whole point about From Gardens… is its strength, sense of purpose, adherence to its difficult task and ultimately the fact it pulls off its ambitious aims.

A few British musical acts have trawled historic ideas and used the latest technology to re-imagine them. Miranda Sex Garden – for example – opened their albums account with a collection of madrigals. Astley belongs in this company as much as she belongs with composers like Ivor Gurney. Somewhere between those two worlds From Gardens Where we Feel Secure indolently flexes its limbs, surveys the shimmering heat haze of a perfect English summer day, and decides there is no more beautiful place to be.

Awesome Color:
Awesome Color
(Ecstatic Peace, 2006)
What? The bastard children of The Stooges and Blue Cheer.

A New York power-trio with two members - Michael Troutman (Michael Awesome) and Allison Busch (Allison Awesome), originally from Michigan. The third member guitarist and vocalist Derek Stanton also adopted the Awesome surname and the band set about a five year (2005-2010) career pounding out a muscular, riff-heavy grind, fusing grunge influence, a smattering of Sonic Youth and their ilk and a shit-load of the incessant idiot/out there mantra-like rhythms that made the likes of The Stooges and the MC5 an electrifying live prospect.

None of the above does justice to the way this power-trio pushed enough originality into their sound to make the varied elements work perfectly from the start. Most tracks riff up to speed, weave around a steady pattern and drag in licks and quirks that bring the whole soup alive. The fuzzed out guitar lines are – at times - pure first wave acid rock and they send the sound searing into oblivion. The closer "Animal" spins the grove well beyond seven minutes and kicks up an audio obliteration of off-kilter psych and kraut-rock synth and drums monotony; building with vocal and guitar wails into something both blissfully enveloping and totally scary.

Awesome Color is wall-to-wall with similar sonic mash-ups, each jaggedly effective and each a diversion from the company it keeps on the album. "Hat Energy" presents a gleefully unhinged blast of sax, "See You Hear You" packs a stonking Iommi-esque riff. Gradually, Awesome Color reveal themselves as phenomenal talents, in-the-moment masters and an awesome power trio. The band's small discography boasts a trio of albums; this – their debut – is, arguably, the best of the bunch.

Albert Ayler:
Love Cry
(Impulse, 1968)
What? Cutting edge jazzer; turns out one of his sharpest releases.

Ayler (1936-1970) was already established as a leading blower of free jazz before the death of his friend John Coltrane in 1967. A loose and mournful record; Love Cry presents the interplay of Albert's sax and his brother Don's trumpet over a range of moods and some unlikely instrumentation. Alan Silva's bass plays some unusual parts (notably the inclusion of a tune up on the opening cut) and Call Cobbs' harpsichord, which throws in some psychedelic twists and light counter melodies to Ayler's powerful and raucous blasts. By contrast, the gentle and reflective "Love Flower" – penultimate track on the original vinyl release – touches on territory beloved of the more whimsical moments in psych-pop bands like The Music Emporium. Cobbs plays sparing and sporadic keyboard parts whilst Ayler's sax follows a melody akin to a soul ballad.

Ayler contributes some genuine vocals to "Love Cry" though the purpose of the Love Cry album is to provide an exploration of sounds, inner space and the frontiers of jazz. In that vein the entire album produces slices of changing sonic texture, surprisingly short for free jazz of the period; the lengthiest excursion here is the nine minute 48 second "Universal Indians." The first half dozen of the eight cuts are all short enough to be potential singles. Cuts like "Dancing Flowers" a meditation built around traded licks between Ayler and Cobbs (on a very "out there" harpsichord) did gain some radio play on stations more used to featuring the likes of the emerging psychedelic bands, but the strength of Love Cry is the strength of the small group of assembled musicians to take their moods and investigations into so many different places in little more than 35 minutes, and ask a serious question about exactly where jazz ends. Albert Ayler's concept of "energy music" pervades this collection. Almost all the tracks feature all the musicians improvising all the time; the sporadic changes in tempo and tone are part of the point.

The inescapable edginess of much of what follows is also – sadly – prescient. By the time of Love Cry's release Don Ayler was already into a period of mental health problems linked to drug use, a UFO sighting, and paranoid ideas about the future faced by himself and his brother. Albert's officially unexplained death a few years later was in all probability a suicide, at least partly brought about by his concerns over Don's problems (ironically, Don lived to 2007). It's tempting to try and hear these elements – notably the love and concern between the brothers – in the exchanges on Love Cry. But, whatever the emotional origins of the music, Love Cry is one of the finest ensemble albums of sixties free jazz, a career high for a master of the form and an album with a lasting influence on what followed.

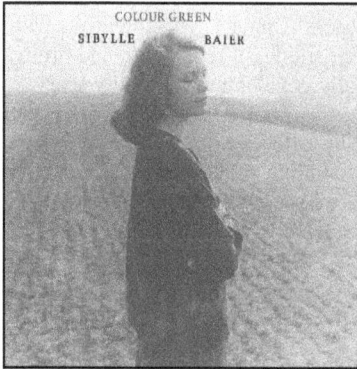

Sibylle Baier:
Colour Green
(Orange Twin Records, 2006)
What? Intimate encounter with the most reticent of folkies.

Another retro-unearthing of music never intended for release in the first place. Baier had long ditched any serious ambitions as musician or actress, though she had some success in both areas, when this collection, her first proper album, was released in 2006. Having moved from her native Germany to the USA, where she raised a family, Baier couldn't have been much more obscure. Orange Twin chanced upon the 14 tracks after Baier's son, Robby, compiled a CD from home recorded reel to reel tapes, to give to family and friends. J Mascis of Dinosaur Jr. was given a copy and his influence led to this release.

Colour Green has the timeless, intimate and lulling vibe of others rediscovered long after their original recordings, Vashti Bunyan and Linda Perhacs are both meaningful comparisons in terms of style and content. Baier's particular genius is to wrap her songs in the softest and most precise finger-picking (reminiscent of a gentle harpist) and unfold tales of intimate emotion, dwelling on the fragility of happiness and the massive emotional impact of life's minutest details. There were a few, none of whom appear to have left an online evidence trail, who were suspicious of a hoax. Such things have been attempted; check out the career of Ursula Bogner, alleged lost electronica genius who was nothing of the sort. But the slightly fuzzy analogue tones of Baier's guitar and vocal here have an authentic ring to them and simply feel like they were recorded between 1970 and 1973.

Nothing on Colour Green pushes itself beyond stiff walking pace and many of the reference points in the songs - from the "work" referred to in "Tonight" to the anonymous person addressed in "Girl" – remain obscure. Suggesting strongly this is music for her inner circle and, sometimes, for nobody other than herself. Elsewhere T.S. Elliot is referenced, albeit with a spelling mistake, in "Elliott" and another song concerns Baier's friend Wim Wenders, who directed her performance in Alice in the City. All of which gives the collection an agreeably arty edge. "Wim" and "Driving" trot along with some sense of urgency and the closing "Give me a Smile" stages a fitting finale when the string section arrives. But, fully ten of the songs here are gentle missives fragile enough to make late sixties Donovan sound aggressive.

Moe Barbari:
When the Eyes Cry
(Private Release, 1996)
What? Middle East meets middle of the road in compelling stalemate.

Barbari's self-released collection has accrued a certain amount of internet attention. Superficially it isn't a particularly revolutionary or challenging release, for the most part the man sings tuneful songs over a Roland keyboard and programmed beats. His voice has a carefully managed echo, suggestive of late period Elvis slow numbers, and his material is mainly intense ballads with most of the uptempo stuff holding back once it reaches a canter. So far: so predictable. The ironic praise of Pea Hix, posted online, begins to explain why Barbari has gathered a following: "It became an immediate smash hit with at least several of us!...Strained Iranian vocals and crappy Roland general midi synth arrangements. What's not to like?" The present authors would go slightly further, and seek to genuinely praise this collection. Where Barbari scores over a countless horde of home produced hokum is in the perfect balance of genuine emotion, reigned in for the sake of decency, but permanently threatening to erupt. The arrangements might be western but the lengthy chords, simple melody lines and slowly shifting patterns within the music are more suggestive of Middle Eastern drones. Barbari is certainly seeking to channel the western ballad elite, like Elvis, for some of the duration, but his surges of volume and stumbles off-key betray his emotional side, and a palpable sense of personal vulnerability behind the carefully managed facade. To hear his heavy accent and echo-shrouded voice working in English, but remaining elusive is akin to stumbling upon an argument between lovers, conducted in a foreign language. "Mother" runs almost six and a half minutes, two others amongst the ten cuts top five minutes. These virtual-epics of Barbari's craft show his work in its best light. He rages and suffers but, in keeping with a less demonstrative approach to emotion, he continues in this vein and the songs habitually avoid shuddering climactic finales. "To You With Love," which closes the proceedings, is an intimate and heartfelt peon to someone very dear, complete with an "Are You Lonesome Tonight" style spoken word passage.

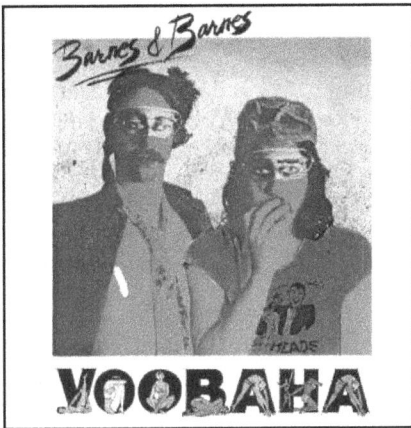

Barnes and Barnes:
Voobaha
(Rhino, 1980)
What? Great – sometimes grate – debut from oddball's oddballs.

Part Ziggy Stardust, part studio geeks and part parodists and comedians; fictional brothers Barnes and Barnes have carved a prankster path on the fringes of outsider music, comedy and electronica. This 1980 release is pretty-much a statement of the intentions they have subsequently followed. The early electronic production has an analogue recorded charm of its own but the songs here include several standouts for which the duo – fictional brothers Art and Artie Barnes – continue to be celebrated. Some of the humour is blatant attention-grabbing bad taste, and "Party In My Pants" and "Boogie Woogie Amputee" are pretty much what you'd imagine; decent pop, indecent thoughts. Though Barnes and Barnes continue to insist the "Amputee" track is a "misunderstood...celebration." The stand-out and most requested track when given a run out on Dr Demento's radio show, "Fish Heads," remains a high-point for strange, geeky eighties electronica. Basically a consideration of relating to dismembered fish heads rather than real people; it distils the outsider geek logic that informs much of the album in a deliriously offbeat celebration: "I took a fish head out to see a movie, didn't have to pay to get it in..." The Devo-esque "Please Please Me" suggests Barnes and Barnes noticed when Ohio's kings of the alternative covered the Stones' "Satisfaction" but that's about as derivative as the nerdily creative Barnes and Barnes get. Voobaha does bear the scars of a somewhat random assembly. Some songs are older than they sound. "I Hope She Dies" dates from 1973 (when the Barnes and Barnes were kids) and betrays some very juvenile thoughts. Elsewhere a handful of others drop in; notably Weird Al Yankovic who contributes accordion to "Gumby Jaws Lament," but these dilutions don't detract too badly from the creative vision of a pair who work best when delivering missives from their own world. A brief internet search on their unique logic might help in the understanding of all their work but Barnes and Barnes do have a habit of simply mugging the listener with an idea. The sleeve notes on the CD reissue – for example – cite "Linoleum" as a track featuring; "the best spuzzle percussion yet," it took the rest of the world a little longer to catch up on rhythmic possibilities of children's playthings. CD reissues have been exceptionally generous with adding bonus tracks to Voobaha's original 14 cuts.

EDITOR'S NOTE: Sci Fi buffs will remember Bill Mumy (Art Barnes) as the youngest of the children in *Lost in Space* as well as Lennier in *Babylon 5*

Louis and Bebe Barron:
Forbidden Planet OST
(GNP Crescendo, 1957)
What? Groundbreaking sci-fi film soundtrack; officially wasn't music in its day.

Credited in the original film as "Electronic tonalities" so as not to cause legal problems or offence, because the Barrons were not members of America's Musicians Union, this highly influential work had the odds stacked against it from the start. The electronic pioneer Barrons were married New York based studio geeks and pioneers in the use of early electronic devices like the ring modulator. As such, Charlotte May "Bebe" and Louis Barron broke new ground in many ways, their early sound experiments were more akin to scientific work than any conventional musical composition, not least because some of the sounds recorded came from circuits overloading and burning out. Once destroyed, a circuit couldn't be revived, meaning the recorded sounds could never be literally recreated. By experimenting and making a habit of recording every noise produced the couple built a stock of sound loops, the like of which hadn't previously been heard. They were initially hired to add a few minutes of additional sounds to the sci-fi film Forbidden Planet. Avant-garde composer Harry Partch was originally slated for the official soundtrack duties. The production team were so happy with the initial results from the Barrons that they were handed the entire movie score.

The resulting electronic tones, echoes, reverberating sounds and sudden bursts of noise were little short of revolutionary in their day. A preview audience broke into spontaneous applause when the combined sight and sound of the spaceship landing towards the start of the movie was first projected.

The soundtrack slowly became a classic album and continues to be widely available and loved around the world. To contemporary ears the old electronic and analogue sounds have a brittle and somewhat random quality of sound (understandable when you consider that some of what you hear is the sound of the musical machinery destroying itself as it gives birth to the sounds). But the sounds ebb and flow and – whether you have seen the movie or not – evoke a narrative arc with peaks and troughs of emotion, moments of high drama and, largely because the electronic sounds are presented in isolation without much sense of harmony or supporting instruments, a sense of movement. Forbidden Planet was so influential as a soundtrack that the Barrons, and many of their peers, concentrated efforts into the early sixties into producing similar sounds to meet a growing demand.

Juliana Barwick:
The Magic Place
(Asthmatic Kitty, 2011)
What? Sublime stillness in a slowly unfolding composition.

Juliana Barwick is one of the few performers combining a willingness to have the words "new age" associated with her music with the ability to produce compelling and original work. Barwick's stock-in trade is the production of music based on looping musical figures and layers of her voice. Touchstones are folk, choral music and the small branch of modern electronica that betrays classical roots. The end results have enough individuality to give Barwick a die-hard following and good reviews in the most eclectic of places. Her second album, released on the indie Asthmatic Kitty, garnered some radio play and enough respect to rank in a chart or two of 2011's best music.

It is a hugely personal work, dedicated to a tree on the Louisiana farm on which Barwick grew up and the cover artwork shows pictures of lush green trees against a rural background. Barwick explained in an interview that the "magic place" involved crawling inside a tree and the nine tracks on this album reflect that with a lush sound that envelopes the listener with a strong sense of place, using the built up loops of sound and drifting vocals to block out the surroundings. The sense of being in one place, with a strong presence and a feeling of safe space around you is the real point here. On a very simple level, this is music that resembles little else and makes no attempt to follow a trend, so the real world is banished in the act of conceiving this sound. The different tracks may also reflect the different spaces – described by Barwick as like rooms – in the original magic place.

Barwick herself is strongly present. Her vocals are built on loops and given the sound of a small choral group, but they are all her. Lyrics are forsaken in favour of a series of simple rising and falling intonations. It would be easy to damn this as – literally – tree hugging hippie dippy indulgence, but Barwick's music has that ability to draw from her innermost experiences and put itself out there, she has – for example – placed music in television commercials. For all its very personal beginnings, The Magic Place is a very accessible recording.

William Basinski:
The Disintegration Loops
(Temporary Residence, 2002)
What? Ambient drone work takes on life of its own as requiem for World Trade Centre, and meditation on temporary nature of beauty.

Basinski's near 75 minute meditative work of ambient drone resembles some of the other leaders in its esoteric field but also claims some unique interest because of the accidental nature of its creation. Basinski set out to transfer some analogue tapes – created in the 1980s – to digital format. The old tapes were showing their age and soon began depositing iron oxide on the tape heads, meaning the transferred music showed fragmentation, losing tones and melody. Crudely, the recordings were disintegrating in front of Basinski. Of all the works – indexed rather that titled – on offer, it is dlp4" that best demonstrates this. Based on a very basic combination of piano and string melody the simple tune breaks down into fragmentary snatches over 20 minutes. By the end of the piece periods of silence intrude, forming an unintended addition to the fragile beauty that is destroying itself before our ears.

The same process applies to all the pieces here. Because they were destroyed in the art of transfer they can't be recreated and the random nature of their destruction is forever worked into their sounds, and silences. Everything on offer in The Disintegration Loops is slow, meditative and dependent on the tonal qualities of a few instruments at most. The original recordings were drone-alike studies; the digital transfers throw in some blurring and distortion. The most abrupt and shocking moments arrive with the sudden silences caused by the dropping off of iron oxide from the original masters.

The collection has acquired a specific meaning because Basinski was working on the final sections of the project in his New York apartment with a view out to the World Trade Centre on the morning of 11

September 2001 when the buildings were attacked. Basinski has described sitting on the roof of the apartment block and listening to The Disintegration Loops as the twin towers collapsed. Basinski has also presented a video of The Disintegration Loops showing the final hour of daylight, looking at the same view, with the smouldering remains of the buildings. The original recordings were released on a series of four CDs starting in 2002. A 2012 reissue includes the four original CDs from their first release with two orchestral performances of the same music; one recorded on the tenth anniversary of the attack on the World Trade Centre.

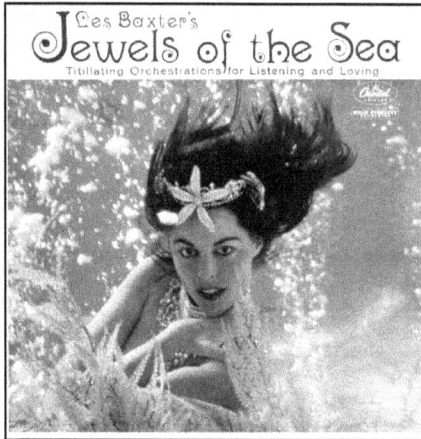

Les Baxter:
Jewels of the Sea
(Capitol, 1961)
What? Visionary exotica from prolific pioneer of loungecore.

Les Baxter's insanely prolific career didn't impress everyone – you can find online details of Nelson Riddle and Andre Previn's particular gripes with Les – but his vast output has found favour, and sampling, with a cult audience years after the fashion for the many sounds and styles he visited has waned. Baxter's stock-in trade involved creating melodic, listenable and unthreatening mood music that still retained the capacity to intrigue and surprise. Tinkling pianos, lush strings and skilful but restrained guitar lines run like a river through the vast quantity of orchestrated albums he created for Capitol Records in the fifties and sixties. Jewels of the Sea remains one of the most prized and sampled of these releases. The cover boasts a gorgeous depiction of a mermaid and has written promises offering Capitol's "Full Dimensional Stereo" (the separation of the instruments is a little primitive but in the early sixties the novelty of hearing different mixes from each speaker was a revolution) and "Titillating orchestrations for Listening and Loving" (note the capital letters on those later words). Baxter's take on any times in which he found himself was to grab at the best ideas, reinvent them in his own lush and mainstream style and bring enough of his signature flashes to the whole mix to make the results stand out from the crowd. It didn't hurt that he did most of this with the support of one of America's major record labels (moving over the years from RCA, to Capitol to Warner-Reprise), and with involvement from other major talents (which is where some of the less savoury arguments about who – exactly – should take the credit come in). A few years after the Capitol albums that produced Jewels of the Sea Baxter was leading a besuited and highly conservative folk group of Les Baxter's Balladeers in which a clean shaven David Crosby made a brief appearance. But that's another story.

Jewels of the Sea sets out to imagine a glossy magazine/Hollywood world of alluring mermaids, blue skies, azure seas and endless carefree days. Lingering string chords give way to gentle piano motifs, vague and sparingly employed electronic sounds intrude but nothing is allowed to usurp the sweetness of the string arrangements. Just at the moment the darker string-tones intrude the tension breaks with another lapse into sweet melody and the gentle piano sounds that can rescue any situation on one of Baxter's bigger selling albums.

To describe Baxter in such a way appears damning until you realise that what makes his work compelling and gives it longevity is – to some extent – what makes the better Beach Boys' ballads and most memorable moments in The Carpenters' career great. Albums like Jewels of the Sea know from the very start they're out there in a commercial market, but they believe deep down in the quality of what they're doing and in the power of music to move people and change moods. The intricacies of arrangements, harmonies and tempo matter to Les Baxter. It would be perverse and pointless to argue to what extent a collision of strings, vocal lines from a female choir, percussion and repeating patterns actually represents a "Dolphin" or "The Enchanted Sea" but it would be a hard hearted person who didn't get the attempt by one of Baxter's pocket symphonies to create a different reality and transport a listener to inhabit the imagined space.

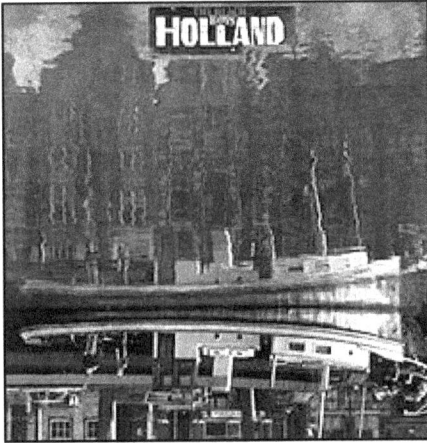

The Beach Boys:
Holland
(Reprise, 1973)
What? Three great EPs makes for flawed masterpiece of an album.

Since a fair percentage of a generation had gone to California to get their heads together it only seems fitting that the quintessentially Californian Beach Boys should decamp to a relatively old-cultured corner of Europe to attempt the same thing. The band's 19th studio album achieved moderate sales by the standards of their sixties hits, and subsequent seventies revival.

Holland is a crisis of identity and direction writ large, and a snapshot of a band digging deep and hoping hard, whilst their resident undisputed genius languishes in a cocaine coma, doodling with a rose tinted vision of childhood. To regard it as a finished album, or even the album the band imagined they were making when they decamped with their attendant families in 1972, is harsh. Indeed, so tangled and confused was the conception of Holland that early pressings of the sleeve wrongly credited the inclusion of the song "We Got Love" and a few, now highly valuable, pressings exist of an alternative running order featuring the lost track.

Holland's constituent parts continue to enthral Beach Boys' fans and any stray person happening upon the album, for two main reasons. Firstly, this is the strongest vision of the band they could have been if events had transpired differently. Secondly, the varied fragments on offer present tantalising glimpses of a creativity they would never attempt again. Holland opens with "Sail on Sailor" which credits five writers, including Brian Wilson, and was included at the insistence of Reprise Records who heard no obvious hit single in the first running order. Damn good Beach Boys, a decent song and serious attempt at a hit, also suggesting, spuriously, that Brian's demons were sufficiently under control to allow him to grind out more million sellers at will. "Steamboat," a soulful slow number originally intended as the opener, comes next. The brief song cycle that follows is the "California Saga," ironically, the major creative vision resulting from a lengthy stay in Holland was expressed in a convoluted suite exploring the love – particularly of Al Jardine and Mike Love – held for their home state. Robinson Jeffers' poem "Beaks of Eagles" is incorporated, offering a little off-the-shelf gravitas, and taking The Beach Boys as close to the pretentious end of progressive rock as they were ever likely to get.

"Trader" complete with a spoken "Hi" from Carl's three year old son Joshua, sets off the second side. Here, three songs recorded in Holland and "Leaving This Town" (recorded in California) present the band under the clear leadership of Carl Wilson, honing a blend of introspective country rock, not too far from the rapidly emerging sounds of a newer generation led by The Eagles. The playing is superb, the production accommodates layers of sound rather than a standard mix of a rock band and The Beach Boys emerge as a range of divergent talents. Brian doesn't write, or sing lead, anywhere on the side. Brian's main contribution was included on a bonus E.P. "Mount Vernon and Fairway (A Fairytale)" is exactly what it claims to be. A visionary audio drama based on young Brian's experiences of communing with magic via a transistor radio, all retold in a fiction that makes little effort to conceal the original truth. Brian's acrimonious split with the band revolved around his vision of "Mount Vernon…" as the centrepiece of a new album and their apparent disregard for the longest and most surreal piece he would ever contribute to a Beach Boys' recording. Brian voices the Pied Piper in the tale. The rough edges on his spoken voice are clear, and clearly suggestive of the tonnage of cocaine he had ingested in the run up to Holland.

Brian was back as undisputed main man a year later, mainly because the massive success of the oldies collection Endless Summer kick started a new phase for the band within which rapturous audience response to the hits allowed them to keep recording in a more familiar style, and dropping in a few new songs to each tour. Holland's relatively poor chart showing (US #37/ UK#20) didn't inspire many people to encourage the band to continue as a ground-breaking creative force. Had they done so the evidence here suggests Carl would have become the creative focus for an outfit capable of highly ambitious song writing, spellbinding vocal and instrumental passages and, probably, an able competitor for most of the country rock royalty. Whether this band could have produced its own Hotel California or a work as accomplished as Jackson Browne's The Pretender will never be known. Holland, probably more than Surf's Up, hints at how they might have developed. At the same time, it has the CSNY Déjà vu vibe of disparate talents, ably contributing on each other's songs but permanently threatening to fracture.

In that other world Brian may have been cast adrift as a solo artist in the mid-seventies and "Mount Vernon…" would only have been the start of the singular visions he could have brought to his recorded output. The sound and contents of those albums are, probably, beyond the comprehension of mere mortals. But, had he gone there, the results would undoubtedly have been mentioned in this book.

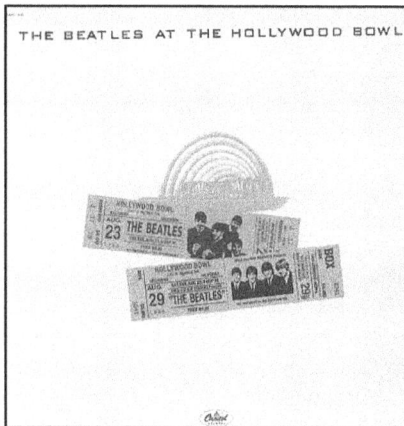

The Beatles:
At the Hollywood Bowl
(Parlophone, 1977)
What? A chronicle of madness and oft-overlooked fragment from the Fab Four.

Released years after the band's demise this fleeting collection – clocking in well under half an hour – is still an official Beatles' release. CD reissues have yet to take in most of the world but vinyl copies (the album topped the UK chart and hit #2 in the USA), and imported CDs do the rounds. If you have heard the original album and single versions of "Twist And Shout," "Can't Buy me Love" and "She Loves You" you'll have the general idea. Basically, this collection features rushed, lively and generally note-perfect renditions of songs already so familiar the massed audience could sing them in their sleep. Recorded twelve months apart, one performance from August 1964 and two from August 1965 were mixed, edited and generally tidied up by George Martin to make a listenable collection. The commercial and critical wisdom at the time was based on a lack of new Beatle product to release and Parlophone's wish to put a spoiler into an unauthorised live double album culled from the band's time in Hamburg.

Between tracks some of the stage banter refers to the band's most recent album, depending on the concert providing the track this is A Hard Day's Night or Help. Lennon thoughtfully helps out the howling fans, pointing out the band have made two films and: "One of them's in black and white and one of them's in colour." That quip precedes a scream drenched run-through of "Help" in which the band's amusement at what they are witnessing spills over into audible difficulty singing in time as Lennon suppresses a laugh. That, pretty much, is why you might want to hear At the Hollywood Bowl, because no band endured more madness than The Beatles and no fans were louder or crazier than their American following. Long before crowd hysteria was an orchestrated element in carefully planned rock shows, there was a naked and simple craziness that attended the performances of Elvis, The Beatles and a few others. And here it is revealed in all its raucous glory. The band might be dispensing with a Chuck Berry number within two minutes, but it makes little difference to the screaming fans, mainly girls. Any note, quip, shuffle of the feet or flick of the hair gets the same hairdryer moment and young lungs pump out a primal sound into the night air. The overall effect is like listening to snatches from the best-known catalogue in rock and pop whilst suffering the worst excesses of tinnitus. The one riveting question, which this album poses but fails to answer, is who – exactly – is watching who? Inside the well-rehearsed runs through the classic catalogue there are clear suggestions that The Beatles are as stunned watching their audience as the thousands massed at the Bowl are with the spectacle of their heroes in the flesh.

Truly, they don't make them – either shows or albums – like this anymore.

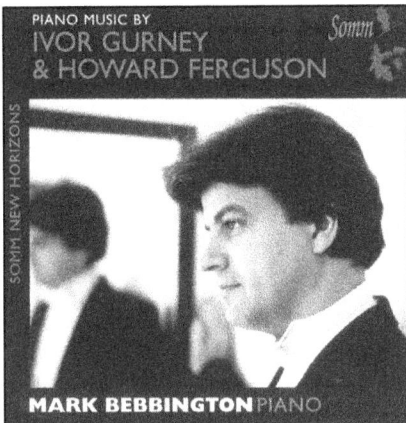

Mark Bebbington:
Piano Music by Ivor Gurney and Howard Ferguson
(Somm, 2004)
What? One of those classical collections that skirts ambient/Eno land.

This recording slipped out largely unnoticed but delivered a handful of spartan and meditative melodies previously unheard outside of the presence of their composer. The opening quartet of pieces being previously unpublished works by Ivor Gurney (1890-1937); best known as one of the better poets of World War One. Gurney is a curiously rock 'n' roll figure, albeit in ways he'd struggle to recognise. His phenomenal talent led many of his teachers to believe he'd eclipse the most promising young musicians of his generation, but Gurney's erratic behaviour worried those who knew him and he managed his first complete breakdown in 1913, by which point the word "unteachable" was often applied to him, genius or not. Three years in World War One, a shoulder wound and a serious gassing didn't exactly help his mental health, nor did his passionate and doomed love for a nurse who cared for him. His early symptoms suggest he had the condition that would today be diagnosed as bi-polar disorder. But, by 1922, things had become so bad his condition was diagnosed as "delusional insanity (systemised)" and the last 15 years of his life were spent in mental hospitals.

For all this, Gurney's output of poems and music was prodigious from his teens to his early thirties, much of his work reflecting a collision of his inner torment and his love for the countryside he'd known around his Gloucestershire home. His songs and poems remain the most often reissued works but this collection places 16 of his quietest and most intimate piano works alongside a dozen in a similar style by Howard Ferguson. The end results – particularly in the previously unpublished preludes – have the sparing tonal quality of the mid-seventies ambient works championed by the likes of Brian Eno. The lack of public performance of such works is perhaps the main reason he has been overlooked when others – like Eric Satie – have become cult figures amongst fans of ambient/new age sounds. Some of Gurney's passages are so lacking in central melody as to sound more like poems in sound with short bursts of chords chiming against each other. Shorn of words and arrangements, Gurney's work offers up the combination of internal melancholy and an unmistakably English and nostalgic streak, suggesting hope and a connection with beauty survive inside the pain. In a word: beautiful.

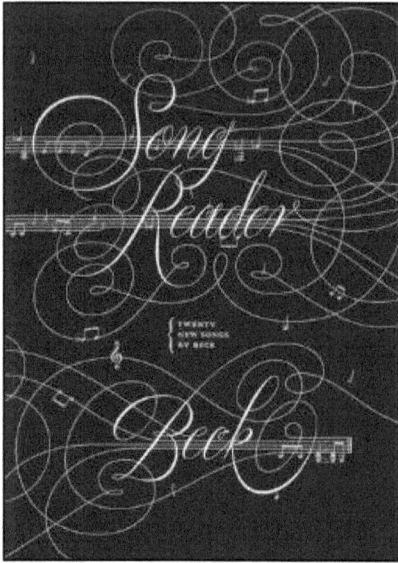

Beck:
Song Reader
(McSweeny's, 2012)

What? Cutting edge artist goes old school with a vengeance (doing it the way they did it a century before).

So, when is an album not an album? A good question given some of the short albums/ long singles/ posthumous collections, dotted throughout this book. Beck Hanson was never wired the same way as most of his peers. Song Reader is all the proof you need. It's not intended as an educational item, but it does deliver in that capacity. Over a century ago, with recorded sound in its infancy, there were only two realistic ways to make money in the music industry. You could turn up, perform and charge people to watch. Or you could publish your songs. To this day, the convoluted 100 page plus contracts of major artists reflect that history, and top-dollar wo/man-hours are sweated over negotiations for this live streaming option from a gig, or that festival billing (effectively all performance deals), and then there's "publishing." Songwriters write, every time a song is used their "publishing" rights mean they collect, even if it's from a backing track loaded into a Karaoke machine.

In the 21st century everyone steals music, shares it online etc. rendering the expensive business of recording an album much less profitable than before. But – hey – Beck has it sorted. If you haven't sussed it yet...he wrote this album and stuck it out...as a book! One hell of a book it is too. Original scripts for 20 previously unreleased songs, copious (as in 100 pages of) very engrossing art-work, and all produced by an American indie publisher with a justified rep for arty prose, cutting edge writers on the roster, and a terminally hip audience. You can hear this album, just not performed by Beck. www.songreader.net is your one-stop shop to the latest downloaded performances loud/soft, inspired/abysmal of Beck's vision. The album genuinely sounds different every day and the site, should you wish to check it out, almost obliges you to interact, either directly or via Facebook. This is a vision of the 21st century album as living, breathing event. The album as exponential, viral, cultural statement...well, either that or a massive mid-finger lifted in the face of anyone ripping his recorded tunes from file-sharing sites.

To Beck's credit, the eight years he spent developing the 20 tunes were well-spent. From the maudlin to the mounting they combine hooks, strong melodies, enough simplicity in their structure to allow the musically ham-fisted to have a bash, and enough subtlety to challenge those willing to explore the emotional possibilities. If you don't want to engage directly with the site, or Facebook options, there's always the likes of YouTube. A quick trawl in the course of writing this entry threw up some absolute winners. John Lewis' spirited solo banging piano attack on "Rough on Rats" appears an audience favourite, and having sampled 20 random run-throughs of Song Reader tunes, we'll admit a real fondness for Ori Rousso's decidedly indie take on "Old Shanghai." It packs enough of a sonic-nod to Beck to make it sound credible, a nice jump-cut video displaying admirable kookiness and a fleeting appearance of The Beatles. Beck – probably – approves, but the point at which these performances stop being his vision is hard to find. You could say this is just what he imagined. You could also say, this is the one album hereabouts that we all made.

You could also, buy the album of the same name – one track by Beck, the rest by a selection of artists (some well-known, others obscure) – that came out in 2014 and gave just a hint of the variety of interpretations this book has spawned.

Captain Beefheart:
Ice Cream For Crow
(Virgin, 1982)
What? Don brings up the dozen with an under-appreciated masterwork.

S'cuse the indulgence but this matters because – in a round about way – this first bit is about you. In the process of compiling this book Neil Nixon let it be known amongst friends, colleagues and Facebook contacts that he was in the market for any constructive suggestions for albums he might otherwise miss. A few well-meaning types who knew him, but not necessarily much about his involvement with music over the years, all did the same thing. They'd point out they knew someone at university/school/vaguely at work etc. This unnamed friend – always male – had "like, the wildest album you've ever heard, honest, it was mad…"

"Any idea what it was called?" Neil would ask.

"Oh, it's on the tip of my tongue."

"Describe the cover, I'll probably know it."

"Well, it had this man, but it was weird, I can't really describe it…look, I'll get in touch with him…"

Which they duly did, Neil could – more or less – predict where this was going, but it would have been rude to be so abrupt, and he might have been wrong. Those that got back, arrived with the same story. "That album, it's called: Trout Mask…"

We're assuming the above all made sense. Because when we started assembling the elements of this book we made the assumption that Trout Mask… was a non-starter simply because the likely buyers of the book would know and love it already. We made this assumption because on the evidence above, it is the one outsider classic that has been widely sampled and encountered by people who would otherwise ignore differently abled music in all its forms. If, by any chance, you find yourself in possession of this book but remain unfamiliar with Captain Beefheart's 1969 masterpiece Trout Mask Replica then ignore the remainder of this entry and investigate that album. Frankly, if any single release stands as a compelling argument for the importance and integrity of outsider music, in whatever form, then that recording is Trout Mask Replica. Rant over!

So, anyway, Beefheart's career spanned twelve studio albums, Ice Cream for Crow is the finale, and it's often overlooked when people discuss Beefheart's best work. Possessed of a darker, starker and altogether less psychedelic and jazzy vibe than the Captain's best known material, Ice Cream for Crow comprises 11 cuts put together specifically for the album and one: "Skeleton Makes Good," reworked from its original incarnation on the ill-fated (i.e. then mired in legal dispute) Bat Chain Puller. Beefheart's previously soaring and wide ranging voice is here presented more as a moaning blues growl shot-through with the wide-eyed rantings of a surreal preacher. The stripped back sound exposes his lyrics and sentiments in a vivid monochrome. All of which presents his bizarre flights of fancy as travelogues from a Beefheartian reality. Standout tracks include: "The Thousandth and Tenth Day of the Human Totem Pole" a gloriously insane bravado raconteur performance from Beefheart who tells a story of a human tower approaching three years duration. The whole flight of fancy proving all the more compelling because of the pulled punches, at times

Beefheart understates himself, making it clear that basic hygiene, the inability to exercise beyond flexing and changing position and the sheer boredom have long-since rendered the spectacle repulsive, for participants and observers: "The chatter wasn't too good, obviously the pole didn't like itself." As per usual with Beefheart, the totem pole story and most of the other offerings hereabouts simply are… There's little apology for bringing such outsider offerings into existence and little attempt to engage with more mainstream sensibilities. Indeed, it's the lack of any apology or any sense of dressing up the whole collection to impress any prevailing trend that makes Ice Cream for Crow both a very individual and very strong collection.

The title track produced a video banned by MTV on the grounds of its very weirdness and the lyrics of the same track give some indication of Beefheart's growing fascination with all things visual. "Ice Cream for Crow," as a phrase – quite literally – refers to contrasting monochrome colours, and the cover art combines a black and white picture of Beefheart with one of his own abstract paintings. "Cardboard Cutout Sundown" and "Ink Mathematics" also have a strong visual sense: "Moon to a flea, Ink mathematics, I breathe black and white, Day and night, Grey gymnastics." The darkly scatological beat-poem "'81' Poop Hatch" is a genuine hoot. Beefheart went on to devote the remainder of his working life to the visual arts. In this stark, honest and hugely characterful parting shot he left a work of complexity and imagination to rival anything – other than Trout Mask… - in his impressive canon.

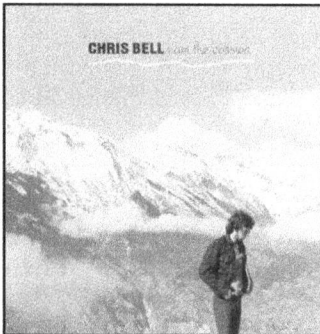

Chris Bell:
I am the Cosmos
(Rykodisc, 1992)
What? Big Star man's abortive solo album released over 13 years after his death. [*]

Big Star's classic incarnation were history before most of the music industry awoke to their true worth. When the UK music press belatedly used the double package of their first two albums as a vehicle to launch a true reappraisal of the band Chris Bell was living in the UK and recording the demos for this album. One single was released, featuring the title track of the album, and has duly become a highly valued collector's item. Bell died in a car crash at the end of December 1978 with the contents of I am the Cosmos completed in demo form. The tapes were finished and mixed to professional standard in the mid-eighties but didn't see final release until the early nineties, by which point the sound and work of the original band had become a rite of passage for most indie bands with any sense of their self-worth.

I am the Cosmos often sounds like Big Star. But its high art aspirations, spiritual ruminations and the underlying vulnerabilities beneath the romantic anger angle the collection away from genre defining power pop of prime period Big Star. The rising and falling cadence and the guitar-chord under the vocal highlighting of the message in a song like "Speed of Sound" is very Big Star, but fundamentally it is a frustrated lover's angry and circular outburst: "My love grows, And yours is gone, A lonely existence…"

All Music Guide stated: "this lone solo album is proof positive of his underappreciated pop mastery" and the present authors would add that I am the Cosmos amounts to a master class in channelling raw emotion through the prism of standard pop song structures. This may be Bell's demos made over after his death, but at heart it remains completely his album. The vocal performances and the sense of life unfolding in the moment and being poured into this collection mean that Bell remains in the room with the listener. In short, the original vision is so clear that knowing what to do to bring closure to the unfinished album can't have been that hard. At its most spiritual the album is genuine departure from anything in Bell's Big Star canon, where the band's concerns tended to be rooted in earthly pleasures Bell chances true spirituality on "Look Up." "You know we're all alone, Look up, look up

EDITOR'S NOTE: I also heartily recommend that you check out the sublime live version on 'Columbia' the 1993 live album by the reformed Big Star.

you'll see the sky, Look up, look up he's the life, Waiting to love you." I am the Cosmos gathers everything of value available in the original tapes and lines up two versions of the title track and three differing styles power pop/ country/acoustic demo of "You and Your Sister." This title track is "a luminous and fragile ballad almost otherworldly in its beauty" (All Music Guide). The untimely death and unfinished nature of the album makes I am the Cosmos a triumphant listen and a poignant pleasure. It is as good as you might suspect. It is pointless to speculate how much music of similar value Bell might have made, and how much of this could have been channelled through the sporadic reformations of Big Star. But, I am the Cosmos is, at least, a belated vindication of a massive talent.

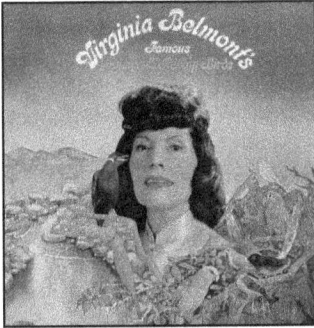

Virginia Belmont's Famous Singing & Talking Birds: Virginia Belmont's Famous Singing & Talking Birds (Virginia Belmont Enterprises, 195?)
What? She has birds, they are famous, they sing, they talk.

Another of those private eccentricities, chronicling a fame long since passed, that were made for online rediscovery. This is an animal act, strung out over two sides of an LP record and milked for every possible angle of peculiar charm. Ms Belmont is elegantly coiffured and made up on the garishly coloured cover. Her famous singing and talking birds are ready to trill and tweet in a variety of tailor made settings. Time and effort has gone into the training, in the case of the deceased "TV", Ms Belmont's Mynah Bird, we discover he was trained for six hours a day over an entire year. His life story is narrated by Virginia before TV begins to narrate his own story, he and Virginia both clearly convinced the other is the straight character in the act. As with many fifties novelty items Singing and Talking Birds feels obliged to present a different experience on each track. Precious, the Parakeet, provides a case study in teaching parrots to talk, elsewhere a chorus of canaries are singing "for your pleasure" a version of "On Wings of Song." The internet sites currently hosting downloads and discussions of this album are sketchy on information with regard to what happened to Ms Belmont and her birds after the release of the album, or its exact year of release. Virginia Belmont reveals details in the course of the recording about her shop containing birds and her live stage work featuring the feathered performers, once the tricks and talking are done the mainstay of the act is a series of popular selections of classical music over which the birds tweet and chirp their own particular embellishments. Fittingly, the proceedings close with a beautiful rendition of solo bird and operatic recording soaring into the sunset in a joint rendition of "Ave Maria."

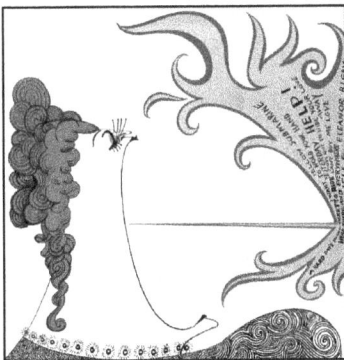

Cathy Berberian: Beatles Arias (Polydor/Philips/Fontana, 1967)
What? Listenable unlistenability, from a mezzo-soprano.

Berberian's website includes a quote from Los Angeles Times music critic Mark Swed stating: "What Berberian did was to make the unnatural natural...she seemingly encompassed the whole world of singing and song was only a start. She also extended vocal techniques dramatically and thus the dramatic potential of singing. And she did all this with a sense of grace, humor, immediacy and grandeur never before found in the same vocal package." In other words: however outlandish the eccentricities, Berberian (1925-1983) always maintained the ability to connect with an audience and present some semblance of sense to her musical endeavours. She remains – occasionally – bracketed with female freak-show fodder like Leona Anderson or Florence Foster Jenkins, but Berberian is better located with the likes of Diamanda Galas, for whom the vocal pyrotechnics become the major focus of a performance, and the backing music remains little more than an accompaniment. Berberian's best recordings – including this – also come with some over-arching sense that the entire sonic package will shine a new light on the material.

The late-sixties music industry was awash with Beatles' covers and individualistic performers. But, Berberian's efforts stood out, then and now, for their sense of purpose. Beatles Arias delivers – more or less – what you would expect. A dozen over-wrought attempts at tuneful Fab Four material within which Berberian hangs on every note, emoting with a sense of constant drama, and accentuating many of the minor cadences skipped over fleetingly in the originals. With a small chamber orchestra on hand, and forever located as minor players within the drama, it is Cathy's tour-de-force take on erstwhile lower-ranking Beatle ballads that makes the collection so compelling. "Here There and Everywhere" is slowed down to highlight the glorious highs and lows of the original tune at which point Berberbian belts out the words with a sense of high-drama and petulant demanding, masked by her perfect diction. "Girl" with its extended enunciation of the four letter title could have been written for Cathy's style.

The album keeps the tempos slower than the originals and Berberian attempts nothing rockier than "I Want to Hold Your Hand" or "Hard Day's Night." Having long been established as a singular delight amongst those in search of cultish and unusual sounds, Beatles Arias is generally regarded as the most eccentric choice in a canon within which Berberian covered much established classical work, along with pieces composed for her by the likes of Igor Stravinsky and John Cage. It is atypical of most of her recordings but gives some sense of her incredible vocal abilities, notably in terms of pitching, and sustaining an epic quality throughout a performance. It is questionable whether the conversational and confessional elements of "You've Got to Hide Your Love Away" fare well under such treatment and whether "Yellow Submarine" was ever ripe for such a cover, but elsewhere her makeovers of songs like "Michelle" and "Eleanor Rigby" do justice to Paul McCartney's beautiful melodies and songcraft.

Steven Jesse Bernstein:
Prison
(Sub Pop, 1992)
What? Dark beat poetry, dark jazzy/rock ambient backing.

Bernstein was always an edgy act, primarily a writer with an existence style wise somewhere in the middle ground between William Burroughs and Henry Rollins. Bernstein never heard the final release of his greatest work, having fatally stabbed himself in the throat whilst visiting friends; thereby beating his label-mate Kurt Cobain to Sub Pop suicide casedom by a little more than two years. Originally intended as a Sub Pop style attempt on Johnny Cash's Folsom Prison album, in which Bernstein would read to a live audience before the ensuing recordings would be treated with overdubs, this project eventually became much more studio centred when the prison visit produced little useful material.

Bernstein's notoriety made his time on Sub Pop memorable; he opened for acts like Nirvana, performed with a live rodent in his mouth and once pissed on a heckler. He had grunge attitude in spades and had managed to complete one track with Steve Fisk before his death. Prison has a compelling, brooding, and deeply dark aesthetic. Bernstein's vivid, free-form rambles – frequently moving in seconds from a random observation to the depths of self-examination and self-loathing that would eventually lead him to take his life – are allowed to roam to their own rhythms before Fisk wraps a musical backing around the results. The differing styles – generally referencing the darker end of modern jazz – give a sense of variety and breadth to the results and when a contemporary touch is required Fisk steps in with the doomy rock sounds that back "Party Balloons." If such a thing as a signature track exists it may well be "This Clouded Heart," a horrifically scathing look at sexual thoughts, told in the second person but leaking autobiography and offering up a bestial vision of humanity: "There is only one girl in the whole city and she is pregnant…You feel that everything you do is pornography." All of which comes with a percussion heavy blanket of jazz akin to early Quincy Jones in the throes of clinical depression.

The cascade of disturbing imagery ensures only repeated listening will give you familiarity with the whole piece. Fisk's musical landscapes take this on board with enough random licks and nuanced riffing to avoid becoming too familiar too soon. Bernstein's deep voice and obvious resignation to his depression make this an uneasy companion, all the more so since the only sensible way to fully comprehend Prison is to give it your full attention with headphones. It's debateable how long you would want Bernstein in your head, but also debatable whether this collection equals or betters the work of William Burroughs and Bill Laswell released around the same time.

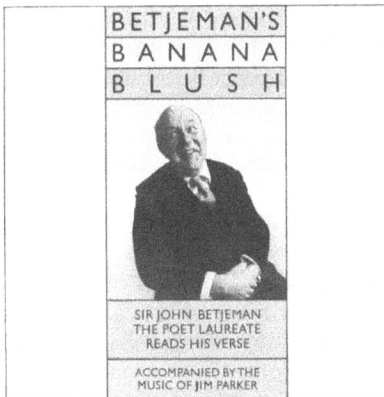

Sir John Betjaman:
Betjaman's Banana Blush
(Charisma,1974)
What? Pensioner prog, with well-played tubas and well-turned phrases.

The Charisma record label knew their prog in the mid-seventies and boasted Peter Gabriel era Genesis amongst their roster of acts. Charisma was – amongst other things – the home of a very English brand of popular music. The inspired signing of Betjaman, at that point the Poet Laureate, proved the point. The results drew fascination and generally good reviews, and earned a fair amount of late night Radio One play where Betjaman's poetry sat well with the complex prog-rock tales woven by a generation of wordsmiths young enough to be his grandchildren. The man was already pushing 70 when this, the first of a series of albums, was released.

Charisma paired him with musician and arranger Jim Parker for Banana Blush and the subsequent Late Flowering Love. Dripping brass band arrangements, deft piano chords, sweeping strings and clarinet, the albums are a requiem for an England already lost. A world of trains, trysts and tea-cakes, rural accents, good manners and – above all – a world in which people had time to stop and think.

Betjaman recites some classics, like "A Shropshire Lad" and several lesser known works, changing character and delivery, but always reliant on the band arrangements to give each piece life and texture. It may be poetry and musical arrangements, but few lead vocalists and backing bands of the period tackled such demanding material and came out sounding so solid. It may be whimsical, shamelessly nostalgic and unapologetically focussed on the concerns of an age long past, but that – frankly – is what makes this rich confection of sound and voice so unique.

Vishwa Mohan Bhatt & Ry Cooder:
A Meeting by the River
(Water Lily Acoustics, 1993)
What? Listening in on an affectionate conversation.

A jam session with four players; A Meeting by the River is simply explained but still offers depths and enchantment. Cooder's acoustic guitar and Bhatt's mohan vina (an instrument of his own making, played with a slide and halfway between a guitar and vichitra vina) trade licks out front, with percussion support from tabla player Sukhvinder Singh Namdhari and Cooder's son, Joachim, on dumbek. The promotional material produced at the time claims the lead pair met only half an hour before recording commenced but – for all the predicable looseness here – A Meeting by the River still presents satisfyingly complete conversations. Spread over four lengthy workouts - "A Meeting by the River," "Longing," "Ganges Delta Blues" and "Isa Lei" – the pair start by trading lead passages but soon settle into a mutual conversation of languorous and graceful sequences in which much of the pleasure comes from their listening to each other and responding. Cooder plays only slide so the sound remains very eastern with his free-flowing notes never jarring or buzzing. There is a distinct feeling that the track titles were added after the playback. Cooder's licks are bluesier in "Ganges Delta Blues" but this is far from a blues track. Each piece complements the other three and each track features all four musicians in – more or less – equal amounts; so the strongest musical feel here is of an ensemble in a small space simply playing for the love of their craft. It is possible – especially with headphones – to pick out each instrument but that is counter to a sound in which the blending of the two similar sounding lead players, is central to the spirit of a true fusion, and communication across cultures. The production manages enough separation on the four players to give a wide sound despite the lack of any amplified playing or overdubs.

A pedantic reading of the album could make an easy comparison between the Hindu tradition represented by the Ganges and Cooder's affinity with Mississippi Delta blues. So the points above ably describe what everyone brought to the session, not what they produced. Similarly, it is easy to try and contain the album with words like: beautiful, ethereal and sublime. But, the point of A Meeting by the River is to meld ideas and live instinctively. By common consent of professional and amateur reviews, it succeeds wonderfully in this aim.

Black Box Recorder:
The Facts of Life
(Nude, 2000)
What? Indie masterpiece by "malevolent scoundrels."

All Music Guide dubbed Black Box Recorder "malevolent scoundrels" and the present authors concur with the judgement. There isn't anything inherently evil about The Facts of Life, but as a window on the macabre lurking in the mundane few others have thought this way, let alone delivered a perfectly pitched expression of such a vision. The second, and highest charting (UK #37) album by a band at once steeped in the nuances of pop and also hell bent on destroying the social fabric and minutiae of life that make pop so damn important. Time and again the chillingly icy vocals of Sarah Nixey turn classic boy/girl scenarios into the kind of tableaux beloved of Kubrick or Hitchcock. "The Art of Driving," which opens the proceedings, being a case in point. Luke Haines and John Moore concoct a perfect hook-laden percussive pop-fest of a track over which Nixey and Haines trade chat up lines leaving you to speculate who will kill the other first. Most online reviews rightly highlight the title track as a sardonic wonder, at once a genuine hit and a searing expose of the darkness consistently threatening to rip the veneer off the top of life's supposedly simple pleasures. Elsewhere you just know Hell in a handcart is about to overrun you when "Straight Life" opens with the line: "It's a beautiful morning."

For British audiences, especially those living in the country's more traffic-congested areas, it's likely that "The English Motorway System" hits as hard as anything on offer here. A brittle piece of perfectly crafted pop in which the ice in Nixey's heart appears to get colder as the song progresses, "The English Motorway System" presents the nation's most used road network as "beautiful and strange," suggests it has been there "forever" and uses perfect scanning to craft the couplet: "a lorry jack-knifes on black ice and there's freezing fog in Northampton." Who else would attempt such songcraft, let alone make it sound effortless, elegant and utterly sinister? There are other purveyors of pop who use their intelligence to create works of beauty and celebration (see Saint Etienne in this book). Black Box Recorder are the hyper-intelligent kids who were given every material comfort, but deprived of proper nurturing. We should be glad they made albums, on this evidence they'd have been brilliant serial killers.

Black Sweden:
Gold
(EMI, 2004)
What? One joke, one album, but worth a punt.

A few entries hereabouts appear because we felt the need to cover some aspect of a huge phenomenon in the music industry. The Russian Church bells, canine heart beats and the rest are simply examples of incalculable tonnages of local releases, instructional records and/or other variants on finding a niche market and shifting a few cheaply produced units. We couldn't ignore the equally incalculable tonnage of mash-up recordings, most of them illegal. Danger Mouse's Grey Album brought the whole unlikely collision formula to a massive audience. It wasn't the first, and in this area there is no such thing as a best album. One person's laugh out loud funny is someone else's slack jawed response to sacrilege as a sacred canon of musical achievement is pillaged for unlikely sounds. A lot of mash-ups work for one song, (the Rick Astley/ Nirvana or Thomas the Tank Engine/Limp Bizkit mashes would never have sustained an album). So, in search of something legally buyable and in lieu of a handful of decent mashes, we give you Black Sweden. One mob who contrived an album's worth of a good idea and had the good sense to get out after firing their one good shot.

What you get for your money are ten classic metal tracks (well, nine and the tacky glam genius of "Ballroom Blitz"), all covered reverently by decent Swedish metal musicians and mashed with ABBA classics to create Satan's own take on most of ABBA Gold. The gags are obvious, but still funny. The mashers have the sense to recreate much of the original sound (the riffs and production sounds of the metal classics and the melody lines of the original ABBA hits). The ABBA choices take in the early and classic period. The metal choices cover the gamut from ZZ Top to Metallica and take in classic British stuff, and a Golden Earring riff mashed with "Ballroom Blitz" and "Dancing Queen." What's not to like? Black Sweden have a knack of making a mash work, Led Zeppelin's "Heartbreaker" crunches in only to morph into the wistful words and melody of

"Knowing Me, Knowing You" and, in a roundabout way, they've made an important point about romantic pain. There's no such thing as a best mash here. "Tush" mashed with "I Do I Do I Do I Do I Do" is great because growly blues and saccharine pop battle each other to a standstill, "Enter Sandman" mashing with "Take A Chance On Me" is a battle of noise versus melody, and so it goes. This is an accomplished and almost cerebral take on the art of mash, concocted by people accomplished in making and producing music. There are darker, dirtier and altogether more dangerous examples of the form out there in ever increasing amounts.

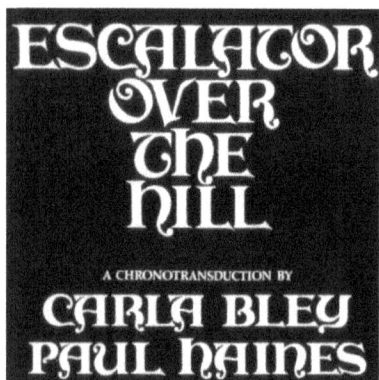

Carla Bley and Paul Haines:
Escalator Over the Hill
(JCOA, 1971)
What? A "chronotransduction"

A shorthand critical description of this monumental undertaking has often likened it to jazz's Sgt Pepper. Not accurate, but a good way for those unfamiliar with this hugely complex combination of jazz, opera, spoken word and Indian music to begin to navigate the two hours plus of listening originally packaged in a triple vinyl album with accompanying book. Considering it – years after the event – as one of 50 Great Moments in Jazz, The Guardian described it as: "a gargantuan, avant-cinematic, cross-genre venture."

Escalator Over the Hill is operatic but in the great tradition of some contemporary rock operas – Tommy, for one – it presents a central narrative and builds a story that can easily divert into character study and exploring a particular moment. Set in a hotel; the story involves two groups of musicians staying along with other guests. The musicians include Jack Bruce and John McLaughlin, both playing members of a rock group and Don Cherry who appears as part of an eastern music group. One of the hotel guests – "Ginger" – is played by a (then) little-known Linda Ronstadt. The set up allows for different styles of music to emerge and random noises, including speech, to become part of the narrative. The story is also moved forward with the words of Paul Haines which started life as poems sent to Carla Bley. Haines hadn't intended his work to become any kind of opera and hadn't written his words with any notion of their musicality. Bley's meditations on the words gradually led her to put keyboard passages (and eventually full-band accompaniment) to them, the result often being complex and convoluted passages of jazz that present a tense and uneasy vision of the run-down hotel housing most of the action.

Musically Sgt Pepper is a useful yardstick. Escalator… is unquestionably thematic, mind-blowingly adventurous when it needs to be, flashingly varied and also unafraid to be conventional and retro. It also sets out its terms confidently; in its scale and packaging and in the opening "Hotel Overture," over 13 minutes of free-flowing avant-jazz showcasing some of the main players and setting up Bley's keyboards as the central instrument to hold the remainder together. The sonic contrasts in the tracks are used to perfection; never more so than when the hard-blown and mordant brass section of "EOTH Theme" is thrown aside by the jazz rock of "Businessman." Escalator also scores because most of the main players step-up to the challenge and meet it. Linda Rondstadt turns in a performance in the torch ballad "Why" that hints at the work that would earn her platinum sales within half a decade. Jack Bruce's vocals are also assured and perfect for numbers like "Smalltown Argonist." Escalator… is still asking a lot of the listener; for starters you have to read the booklet and put in the work to totally understand what is happening in the vocal passages, and work harder still to interpret the musical passages and their relevance to the story. But, like Sgt Pepper, it offers that rite of passage to anyone willing to put in the work and rewards them with a recording of enough nuance and skill to be worthy of this attention.

Time hasn't been too kind to Escalator Over the Hill. Like Sgt Pepper, the scale and audacity of this work inspired wonderful and woeful work in almost equal amounts and Escalator's ground-breaking in 1971 is less evident because some of the work recorded in its wake normalises its innovations. But Escalator... is still celebrated for everything it achieved, the range of talent and quality of their collective achievements remain breathtaking and it remains a challenging listen that works only when given the listener's full attention. Then again; it's up to each listener how far they indulge the closing "... And It's Again." Originally equipped with a locked groove (i.e like the final fragment of Sgt Pepper it would repeat endlessly until the needle was lifted) after ten minutes, the CD release now offers up the track with almost 17 and a half minutes of the locked humming sound, which gradually fades.

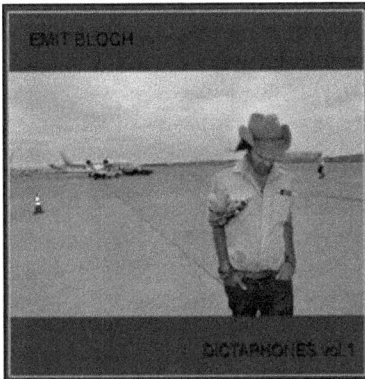

Emit Bloch:
Dictaphones vol. 1
(Lost Dogs/One Little Indian, 2010)
What? The future of the music industry...well; Steve Lamacq said something along those lines.

This spontaneous and animated collection caused a double stir on release. Firstly Bloch – who'd been around the business for a long time – nailed an opinionated, loose and rambling collection that evoked everything from Hasil Adkins' levels of infectiously direct songs to the endless verbal invention and interplay of chord structures and vocal inflections that made early Dylan so great. Bloch sings and drops into speech on songs like "Dorothy" telling tales peopled with an endless list of characters rubbing against each other, and in-the-moment life-events; all recounted with the skill of a good storyteller. But the other reason Dictaphones... grabbed attention is staring you in the face. The album was named after the Sony Dictaphone on which the entire performance – originally intended as demos – was recorded. Which is why DJ Steve Lamacq came to suggest the financially beleaguered music industry might learn something from the exercise.

The genius Bloch brings to this low-fi wonder is the ability to raise and lower his voice and adjust the attack on his bashing and strumming of the guitar to get the most from the very limited sound quality. The glowing reviews – of which there were many – went as far as to compare Dictaphones... to the early field recordings of Alan Lomax (who collected and chronicled American folk songs). Dictaphones... has the doggedness and assertion of legendary early blues recordings, and also some of the ramshackle stumbling along – complete with changes in timing and pace - heard on collections like Charles Manson's prison recordings. It's more country than blues (although it is easily in both camps) and as much in your face as in your ear. But, the bargain recording budget and character-ridden songs work time and time again to give Dictaphones... a personal magic that escapes the technical limitations. It should be noted here that the few bad reviews that beset the album often made their hatred of the sound quality the mainstay of their argument. When it works – which is most of the time – Dictaphones... does get its point across. High points include a rambling talking blues with harmonica cut "Married Creature" that imagines long-term married couples as existing in a world oblivious and aloof from the rest of society, refraining: "There's a creature called the couple that's been married too long."

At times the sound gives out completely, jarring harmonica wails overpower everything else for a second or two and Bloch's control of the level of his voice in the – one-take mono – mix does slip occasionally. But his country twang and choppy guitar push most of Dictaphones along at a pace that leaves the worst moments behind very quickly.

Thomas Bloch:
Music for the Glass Harmonica
Naxos 2001
What? Eighteenth Century Ambient Techno, with some banging modern tunes added.

Probably rivalling the Theremin as one of the strangest instruments, ever, the glass harmonica combines a spinning axle with glass bowls of varied sizes. Something like a high-tech version of the music making trick of running your finger round the rim of wineglass. The instrument dates back to the mid-eighteenth century but its fragility has always been its downfall. Easily breakable, possessed of a high-fluting tone rendering it a mixed blessing in the company of other instruments, and quiet enough to give it problems in filling a concert hall with sound; the glass harmonica belongs, if anywhere, in chamber music.

It's cruel to line the glass harmonica next its main rival, the piano. In comparison few composers penned works specifically for glass harmonica, few performers chained their careers to its fragile ways and few audiences paid good money to see the results. Thomas Bloch (b 1962) is one who set out to change that situation and the results packed onto a CD run well past the one hour mark and present an instrument whose time may, just, have come. The bulk of the collection shows the glass harmonica skilfully used in chamber pieces with some of the big names – Mozart, Beethoven – packed into the middle of the running order. In some chamber selections repetitive string figures provide a framework as the glass harmonica sings out with the strange high-end beauty of…well, John Hurt speaking in The Elephant Man isn't such a facile comparison. Elsewhere the instrument acquits itself well in tackling the shimmering stillness of a classic adagio or two.

The tinkling resonance and elegantly muffled tones of the solo glass harmonica interludes evoke everything from a half-remembered fairground organ to the kind of chilling stillness heard in a horror soundtrack just as the poor innocent girl with the wide eyes realises there is nothing but a wall behind her and nothing but pure knife-wielding evil in front. The notion that thousands would listen to this collection at a sitting seems fanciful. Ultimately, the variety of sounds and settings on offer make this a showcase for an instrument with a unique sound. A sound that exists somewhere between distinct melody and full-on soundscape. The notion that everyone from a dance DJ to a documentary maker might take the sounds and run with them, is a lot less fanciful, and the most encouraging aspect of all is that Bloch, when he isn't giving a virtuoso display of his talents, is also an accomplished composer. The closing track is his own "Sancta Maria" a wildly ambitious six minutes and 11 seconds, pitting the glass harmonica against a multi-tracked male soprano vocal.

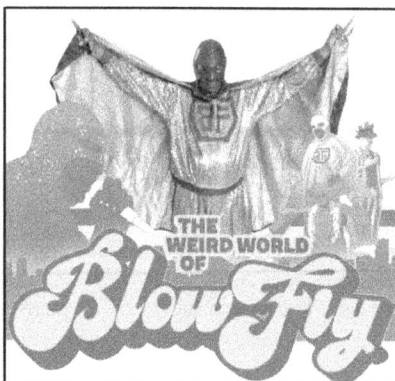

Blowfly:
The Weird World of Blowfly
(Weird World/Hot Productions, 1971)
What? Full-on filth storm; years ahead of gangsta rap.

Clarence Reid (aka Blowfly) enjoyed a 21st century rediscovery when the 2010 movie The Weird World of Blowfly hit cinema screens. Named after his first album; and celebrating a career in which Blowfly became best known for fiercely filthy parodies of soul and pop hits. The Weird World of Blowfly (as in the debut album) is – pretty much

– the manifesto for a career that saw Blowfly place recordings in the lower reaches of the US charts and achieve cult status despite being virtually ignored by radio stations with any sense of propriety. Blowfly's genius included an impressive set of production skills and a habit – as used here – of recording his tracks live in the studio, or in front of a small audience in a venue; allowing audience reaction to dictate some of the musical turns and ad libs. Blowfly is also a talented stand-up comedian with the stage presence to work off an audience, take the joke – just about – as far as it will go, and return without leaving his audience behind.

For all that, The Weird World of Blowfly isn't recommended for anyone of a prudish disposition or anyone for whom issues of political correctness are guiding principles. None of those notions appear to have troubled the audience who shriek and howl with laughter throughout The Weird World of Blowfly. Some of the things amusing them can be guessed at with titles like "My Baby Keeps Farting in my Face," "Shitting on the Dock of the Bay" and "It's a Faggots World." Those titles – near enough – give away the songs parodied; but those less obvious like "The Eating Song" (Blowfly's take on "Too Busy Thinking 'Bout my Baby") soon deliver a line like: "I'm saving my tongue for my baby" and the gags are obvious enough. On cuts like "Spermy Night in Georgia" it certainly sounds like the audience are gaining extra delight from hearing a portentous and upright ballad shredded and turned to filth; and the scatological humour of "Shitting on the Dock of the Bay" – wherein Blowfly watches turds rather than ships floating back and forth – is another complete reimagining of a classic. Elsewhere, the point appears to be to explore the intent of originals that restrained their sexual content in search of radio play. Blowfly's band are tight though this isn't about virtuoso playing or high-end production, and the seguing from one song to another during the performance hasn't done the collection too many favours as mix-tape or YouTube material.

Blowfly had several good recordings of R 'n' B originals under his belt when this – his first album as his own alter ego – was released. So, vocally he has the chops and stagecraft to deliver. Both of which also transfer to the original packaging, a major part of the experience for seventies audiences. Blowfly stands resplendent atop a trash can, attended by two – clearly naked – females and bedecked in a bizarre combo of monster mask, low-budget homemade Blowfly wings, a sweater with the "BF" legend clearly in sight and a tights/socks combi mocking superhero costumes. Somehow, the rubber chicken in one hand makes perfect sense in this context.

Blowfly cut enough decent material to warrant a CD retrospective and gain the patronage and collaboration of 2 Live Crew and Flea of the Red Hot Chilli Peppers. A fair tonnage of his material sits out there on the internet. Lots of which – like his Christmas single "Jingle Fucking Bells" – will either connect with you, or convince you he's not to your taste, within seconds. When Jello Biafra's Alternative Tentacles label issued Fahrenheit 69 (2005) Blowfly's rediscovery was complete. But this 1971 album is where it all started.

Blue Cheer:
Vincebus Eruptum
(Philips, 1968)
What? "…to do with large doses of LSD." Acid rock's finest hour: (okay, its finest 31` minutes and 54 seconds).

Widely recognised as one of the albums that made heavy metal inevitable, Vincebus Eruptum is easily explained, but much better experienced with the volume up. It works when you feel it, end of. Six slices of primal blues-rock roaring out of distorting amps and driven by Paul Whaley's Bonhamesque drumming Vincebus is a histrionic exercise in reining in the brutality just enough to make an album. The collection marked the long-playing debut of Blue Cheer who went on to make more music in this vein but never again captured the album chart position (US#11) or the zeitgeist moment marked by Vincebus Eruptum. The largest criticisms laid at the door of the album claim it as over-experimental, and less structured than its successors. Both fair points; but that is a why Vincebus Eruptum enjoys its cult status to this day. Opening with their top 20 cover of Eddie Cochran's "Summertime Blues" and the blues standard "Rock me Baby" Cheer leave it until the end of side one to unleash "Doctor Please" their first original and – near enough – the key to understanding the whole set. By the admission of bassist/ vocalist Dickie Peterson "Doctor Please" is a plea to a doctor to tell him whether he should, or shouldn't, take a particular drug. A single listen to Vincebus Eruptum will tell you which way the decision went. The ear-splitting sound, love of a bent string and resonating guitar chord, and that abandonment of everything else to revel in the moment pretty much lets you know that acid (as in LSD) worked for more than just the prog-noodling inner space explorers. It may have its roots in three chord tricks and twelve-bar blues but Vincebus Eruptum has its head in the stars and enjoys every mind-bending moment; up to and including a decent drum solo and bass break located in the middle of the closing "Second Time Around." "Kerrang!" (as in the sound of a lingering distorted guitar chord cranked up to hit the audience square in the chest), started with the likes of Vincebus Eruptum.

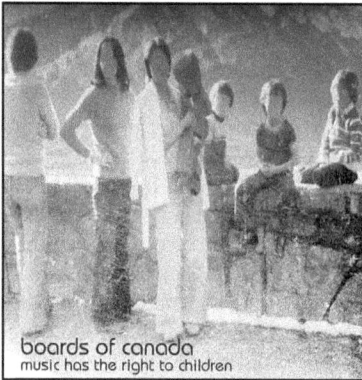

Boards of Canada:
Music has the Right to Children
(Warp, 1998)
What? Cutting-edge electronica from...the Scottish borders/ "[A] thing of wonder....The aural equivalent of old Super 8 movies..." (Q magazine).

boards of canada
music has the right to children

Like much of the company they keep in this book Boards of Canada defy easy description, achieve the most by ignoring the standard rules of achievement, and maintain a devoted cult following. Inspired – apparently - by nature films, some made by The National Film Board of Canada (hence the name), the duo produce music that apes the ambient and meditative dance structures of late nineties/21st century electronica but oozes the warm analogue resonance of much earlier electronic music. Music has the Right... features some cuts from earlier releases but – to all intents and purposes – is the duo's opening album and, pretty much, the manifesto for most of what has followed. Their craft is expertly displayed on tracks like the (occasionally compiled and sampled) "Aquarius" a slow, hypnotic dance beat shuffles along under a warm chord wash, and a treated but very human voice intones "Orange" a few times. Spot colour comes in the form of other voices intruding, childish laughter and random keyboard trills; the generally unpredictable nature of when and how each component will next appear, and the gradual ratcheting up of these appearances gives the piece some narrative. Music has the Right... boasts 17 pieces like this, the shortest a shade under one and half minutes, the longest a shade over six and a half minutes.

Themes in such an abstract work are hard to identify, but Boards of Canada clearly draw inspiration from nature (and if you live in the Scottish borders you probably live in a place that will bombard you with such inspiration). They also draw from childhood and a tangible sense of love for their work, which, in the end, is where Boards of Canada lord it over much of the competition. Forget sound effects, this is music that affects. The different meanings of the two words might be a regular feature of learning support worksheets, but Boards of Canada provide an object lesson in touching emotions rather than playing with the way something is experience. And, it is, more or less, all about the music. The band's profile has remained so low that it took years for music journalists to cotton on to the fact that Michael Sandison and Marcus Eoin are brothers. Granted, they played this down, just like they played down any conventional press and advertising for their works, but it matters – probably – because the intuitive and unspoken qualities of albums like Music has the Right... are the reason their works continue to be celebrated, whilst much else that made the initial wave of chill-out/Karma Lounge style compilations has slowly sunk into oblivion.

Marc Bolan and T.Rex:
Bump 'n' Grind
(Thunderwing Productions, 2004)
What? A rarity, a scraps and dog-ends collection that does demand a rethink of its subject.

The received wisdom where Marc Bolan and T.Rex was concerned had pretty much settled by the turn of the century. With a stack of great glam-rock singles in the catalogue and at least one classic album, Electric Warrior, to their name, the band were a good, but not truly-great fixture on the seventies scene. Fame had come so quickly that Bolan and his band toured the hits to hysterical screams and the Born to Boogie movie showed performances of riffing, pouting and strutting to perfection. The band could chug along and mug for the crowds, but underneath the glam and sparkle they appeared not to have broken beyond pub-rock levels of competence. Bolan's failure to crack America would be explained – by some – as a side-effect of fronting a band schooled in lengthy work-outs on simple chords and short of virtuoso skills.

T.Rex, great records, but they couldn't play, right? Well...sort of. Bolan's basic forays up and down the fret-board tend to compare poorly with the genuine guitar gods of his era, though his mid-seventies incarnation as the king of interstellar soul, complete with hints of funk in the backing band and "chicks" wailing in the background, did inspire one notable US fan, a certain PRINCE Rogers Nelson, to try a few of the same moves.

But most of Bump 'n' Grind presents a T.Rex nobody saw, and few suspected. Released in 2004 it was also a revelation to the die-hard Bolanites who'd suffered their way through the hours of half-cocked low-fi demos and studio jams on the Unchained series to grasp at the handful of genuine gems in the man's hitherto unreleased archive.

Bump 'n' Grind does have its less inspired moments, whether anyone needs 12 minutes of "Children of the Revolution" is debateable and "Christmas Bop" is as disposable as the title suggests. But the power of Bump 'n' Grind comes from two places. Firstly, this is a hit-strewn collection culled from the classic era, lining up "20th Century Boy," "The Groover," "Metal Guru" and "Telegram Sam" along with fan-favourites like "Jitterbug Love" and some of the best later hits like "Laser Love" and "The Soul of my Suit." Secondly, this is a hard-hitting band caught in action. Most of the album is live, but not in the manner of your standard live collection. Some of these cuts are working demos, shorn only of the final studio trickery and polish to make them fit for radio. Elsewhere the tracks catch the band rehearsing, for a recording, or a tour. And they catch them hot.

The odd flurry of lead guitar intrudes but mainly T.Rex get their heads down, slam hard with the beat and nail the grooves that gave the best of Bolan's music its classic power. And, they do rock, hard and well. The throwaway braggadocio nonsense of "The Groover" is more like a growled threat on the primal version that opens the collection, the surreal poetry of some of the other hits is beaten into place by crunching riffs, Steve Currie's bass pumping right on top of the drums and the sense of a band with their sleeves rolled up and the sweat popping. Bolan was one established name who suffered little at the hands of the punks and, on this showing, his influence on the safety-pinned contingent of late seventies rockers is obvious. It's more Pistols than Clash, more Adverts than Stranglers but Bump 'n' Grind shows that if T.Rex couldn't touch Led Zeppelin they could take on the likes of the MC5 and The Stooges without backing down.

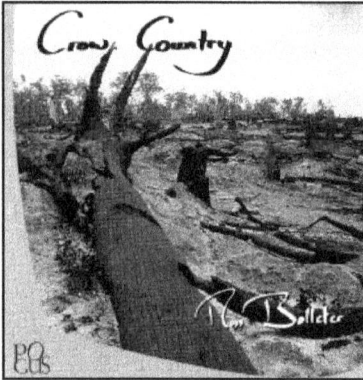

Ross Bolleter:
Crow Country
(Pogus, 1999)
What? Bolleter's the name; ruined pianos are the game.

It's doubtful whether an artist as individual and uncompromising as Ross Bolleter would recognise a simple kinship with many others. But, in this book, he may just be in the right company. Bolleter isn't easily summarised or accessed via any single work because each individual recording is more like a marker along the way of a journey so personal few others would ever contemplate such a trek. Briefly, Bolleter is a musician for whom none of the usual rules of performance, writing or career seem ever to have applied. His more mainstream activities occurred early in his musical life when improvised piano music with colleagues saw him performing in his native Australia. He went on to study composition in the sixties. His touchstones were always the edgy brigade like Stockhausen and Boulez, but Bolleter would soon take their uncompromising approach to a level at which he espoused composing anything and he chose as his main instrument the "ruined piano." That is, any piano that happened to have been ruined, preferably by the action of natural forces, like the weather, over time. Having established this working practice, Bolleter has carved himself a musical niche, earned radio play in places most musical acts don't touch and managed a few high(ish) profile residencies and appearances at the artier end of the spectrum.

By default each piano tends to come to him with its own peculiar problems and quirks, offering up a range of sounds no professional tuner could easily place within a perfect specimen. Bolleter's genius from this point onwards is to work with each instrument, explore its possibilities and improvise a sound-piece at once unique and timeless. His pieces in this context combine some musicality in the form of flurries of notes and snatches of melody suggested by the serviceable parts of the keyboard, along with rhythmic patterns tapped out on the casing, slow grinding drones achieved by scraping along the bare strings within the piano etc. The resulting music can achieve the stark and random beauty of nature at its most untamed and his work has often been linked with a sense of the elemental, not least because it is often the actions of nature in attempting to reclaim his instruments that have given each of his recorded and performed works their own identity.

It is pointless and – probably – wrong-headed to talk about any of his works being "accessible" but Crow Country is arguably one of the better places to start with Bolleter simply because it offers up collaborative pieces and – therefore – packs a greater range of sounds than his solo work. It does contain fleeting passages that verge on something recognisably classical or jazzy in intent. Recorded mainly on a piano abandoned in a remote sheep station, Crow Country compiles original works created in situ with a Bolleter composition for double bass played by Richard Lynn and the utterly bizarre "That Time (Simulplay II)," an experimental piece in which Bolleter and double bassist Ryszard Ratajczak improvise at the same time, for 27 minutes, on opposite sides of Australia, each completely unable to hear the other! By comparison, the accordion piece, "Labyrinth Tango" is fairly easy to assimilate and the closing "Piano Dreaming" presents Bolleter's playing on a ruined instrument in its most meditative and wistful dimension.

As an insight into the singular mind of a genuine outsider musical visionary Crow Country delivers enough moments of individuality to surprise and delight the most jaded musical palate. Chart positions and mainstream radio are likely to remain well off the Bolleter agenda.

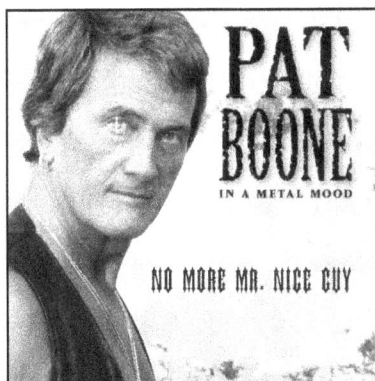

Pat Boone:
In a Metal Mood – No More Mr Nice Guy
(Hip-O, 1997)
What? Squeaky clean songster swings on Satan's tunes, rock elite drop by.

The jury is likely to remain out on permanent vacation in the debate over whether this stupendous car-crash of a musical concoction is a serious attempt to realign a moribund musical career, or a thinly disguised novelty cash-in. Either way, the facts themselves beggar belief, and the music manages to keep jaws slack and brains befuddled for most of the 53 minutes or so it takes to digest this strange delight.

The facts are; by 1997 Boone had become a byword for exemplary moral conduct and a poster-boy for middle of the road Christian values. His involvement with organisations like the Parents Music Resource Centre, a pro-God anti degeneracy pressure group campaigning against the social ills perpetrated by rock music, was typical of the man. He could pull a crowd but hadn't troubled the album charts since his White Christmas collection nudged the top 40 at the end of 1961. Having railed against ungodly elements in music for years, Boone stunned friends and enemies with In a Metal Mood.

Almost beyond satire, and years ahead of similar outings by the likes of Richard Cheese, Metal Mood collides stone-gone RAWK classics with the sounds of a big band and Boone crooning/intoning and almost talking his way through a catalogue of edgy delights. And he doesn't skimp on the scale of the standards tackled here. "Stairway to Heaven," "Smoke on the Water," "It's a Long Way to the Top (If you Wanna Rock 'n' Roll)" are all in attendance.

The newer (for the time) heroes are represented with a spirited take on "Enter Sandman" and Boone fearlessly tackles songs renowned for original versions fronted by manic metal frontmen. Ozzy Osbourne's "Crazy Train" and Ronnie James Dio's "Holy Diver" get the full treatment, the latter – incredibly – with the leather-lunged elf Dio helping old Pat out in the vocal department.

Speaking of high-profile guests; the session crew compiled bring this caper to completion boasts studio legends like Shelia E and Tom Scott. Dweezil Zappa is also on hand. But, the prize for sheer "WTF!!" unbelievability must go to Purple axeman Ritchie Blackmore spanking the plank one more time on a version of "Smoke on the Water" he – surely – never thought he'd hear.

Boone got a level of attention he hadn't enjoyed in years and his first placing on the Billboard album chart since that 1961 Christmas album. Cynics might suggest his people had taken a quick glance across the Atlantic and seen Rolf Harris wowing Glastonbury and Top of the Pops with his demolition of "Stairway to Heaven." However, the lengthy sleevenotes present a detailed argument of why Boone felt the need to produce this album and suggest – despite the cringe-worthy cover shot of a macho looking Pat in a leather waistcoat – he meant it.

He certainly didn't make a habit of it, returning to more familiar ground, and lower sales, with his work over the ensuing decade. His next US chart album: We Are Family (2006) was a run through of a series of R&B classics!

Barry Booth:
Diversions
(Pye, 1968)
What? Whimsical English charmful chamber-pop.

Virtually forgotten for decades, this little-heralded collection of brass-based pop backings and singularly out-of-step lyrics finally earned a low-key rediscovery in the 21st century. Booth's name was never high-profile but his pedigree includes significant arranging, musical direction and song-writing for a few of the great and good, including Roy Orbison. He was also involved in the British television industry during the 1960s and this brought him into the orbit of - record producer/ writer of Neighbours theme tune etc. - Tony Hatch. It also gave him a nodding acquaintance with Terry Jones and Michael Palin, emerging comedy talents of the time who would eventually become part of the Monty Python troupe.

All of the above matters because the collision of these unlikely talents is the best way for the uninitiated to begin to appreciate the strange delights offered by Diversions. Basically, Booth's talents involved arranging and concocting soundscapes, his appreciation of the dynamics of brass instruments being a particular strength. A selection of tunes were already well on the way but he needed lyrics. Enter Jones and Palin, comedy wordsmiths, ambitious graduates and grateful for any job on offer. Crucially, the pair – who co-operated to produce some of the best Python gags – worked alone. Jones' juvenilia-style scribblings offer up half a dozen stories with a sense of lonely-longing and the solitary pain of the terminally decent young man, always thwarted in love. By contrast, Palin's eight lyrics narrate a series of stories, often peopled with solitary, eccentric and very English characters. The opening "He's Very Good with his Hands" explores the skills of DIY enthusiasm and model-making, "Vera Lamonte" has an elegiac "Eleanor Rigby" quality as it tells the story of an "ordinary lady" with a dream of trampoline glory. Hatch's clear production owes little to the burgeoning psychedelic scene of its era, other than an attention to detail with the sound of all the instruments. The glue that holds the whole project together is Booth's presence, his limited but expressive and well-controlled voice is very English, terminally old-school and restrained throughout. It's also characterful to the point of suggesting those described in the songs, and the lovelorn quality of those Jones' lyrics, are all part of the singer's life. The same bizarre character inventions would go on to inform Monty Python but, in this context, Diversions teases out very few laughs, but does pathos by the bucketload.

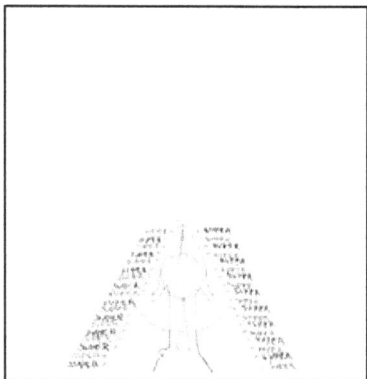

The Boredoms:
Super æ
(Warner (Japan)/Birdman (USA), 1998)
What? Alternative sounds on an epic scale; a post-rock masterpiece to make pretenders to the art weep.

Technically speaking it is; Super æ. But that title, along with the sounds on offer over a little less than 70 minutes, isn't designed to be easy. Super Ae and Super Are may appear in discussions of this album. The fifth outing by alternative/post-rock pioneers is, in all probability, the high-water mark of their career. By 1998 Japan's Boredoms were well-known to the point of being taken seriously by much of the mainstream rock press, and alternative enough to be awe-inspiring and influential in large amount. They didn't dip in the quality of their work but – from this point on – a sizeable chunk of the world set about trying to catch up with The Boredoms. The act, who started out with suicidal frenzy and levels of volume in their music, honed their style into a visitation of a few familiar musical locations, and pioneered post-rock by turning most established practice on its head. The usual post-rock tricks hold sway for much of the duration; song titles border the comical. Each of the seven titles here opens with the word "Super", the most accessible, short and catchy number – "Super Good" - still runs an ambitious six minutes and six seconds and closes (rather than opens) the proceedings, vocals and lead instruments are buried in the mix and drums and bass are elevated to places of prominence in a cacophony in which songs occasionally threaten to climb out of the general morass. Oh yes, and sporadic tricks are employed, like the rapid mixing across the channels on "Super Shine" that sends bursts of vocal and random sounds shooting from one ear to the other.

Beyond the above description it is – probably – pointless to ascribe any meanings to the whole affair beyond pointing out this is music very much about the journey. The real point is that this is possible and in the (1998) world of competing styles and free availability of all music the only sensible thing to do is collect and perform your own work in your own way. Super æ rises and falls, speeds and slows, amuses and amazes and sounds different depending on the moods in which you approach it. The scale and ambition of the whole piece were novel for the time in which it was produced. Bear in mind the Butthole Surfers were contemporaries and shared some of the same fans but their masterpiece, Locust Abortion Technician, runs less than half the length of Super æ. Like some of the great alternative releases – Trout Mask Replica for one - Super æ remains compelling because it sets out its own alternative agenda and achieves it with confidence; effectively making a case for others to follow. The history of post-rock – good and bad – was changed as a result.

David Bowie: David Bowie (Deram, 1967)
What? What if?

Hypothetical discussions about musical what ifs exist wherever sound hounds meet to drink and converse. The present book tries to avoid most of these but we'll make an exception here because the stakes are simply so high. David Bowie's original Deram album was released on the same day as Sgt. Pepper. The tapes he recorded for Deram and Philips have been recycled into so many compilations that it is easy for all but the most ardent Bowieites to lose sight of the original album. Let's get pedantic. David Bowie looks like this:

Side one:
1. "Uncle Arthur"   2:07
2. "Sell Me a Coat"   2:58
3. "Rubber Band"   2:17
4. "Love You Till Tuesday"   3:09
5. "There Is a Happy Land"   3:11
6. "We Are Hungry Men"   2:59
7. "When I Live My Dream"   3:22

Side two
1. "Little Bombardier"   3:23

2. "Silly Boy Blue" 4:36
3. "Come and Buy My Toys" 2:07
4. "Join the Gang" 2:17
5. "She's Got Medals" 2:23
6. "Maid of Bond Street" 1:43
7. "Please Mr. Gravedigger" 2:35

Those tracks exist in varied running orders on repackages, so it isn't that hard to hear the original album, even if you don't own it. Of these 14 cuts, one – "Rubber Band" – had already been released as a single the previous year, achieving no chart placing and another, "Love You Till Tuesday" would be unleashed as a single six weeks after the album's release, also achieving chart oblivion. "The Laughing Gnome" a chirpy piece of novelty nonsense, had been released in April. But that single and its B-side did not appear on David Bowie.

David Bowie presents the Thin White Duke's characteristic menagerie of character studies and surreal vignettes but sounds more like a quaint pop album, or the sound track to some mildly challenging and arty stage musical. Bowie's more compelling work has explored issues of madness and a seemingly endless search for identity. A harsh critique of David Bowie might suggest it is this process, done lite. What if, he'd achieved a decent hit single, or a significant commercial breakthrough with this stuff? What chance then of a headline appearance on Soul Train inside a decade, a trio of alienating and ground-breaking electronic albums or the Chic collaboration that marked a commercial high point in the early eighties?
David Bowie explores sexuality and gender identity in a quirky way, "She's Got Medals" presents a girl with the military success of a hard man as Bowie confesses himself bemused as to how she passed her army medical. It is also, quite literally, dramatic: "Please Mr. Gravedigger" is mainly a spoken word piece with Bowie's unaccompanied vocal forming part of the narration. David Bowie was released in the US, but it is a very British record (citing the "14-18 war," for example), and much of the material is very English and concerns itself with a lifestyle mainly enjoyed in "swinging London." It's also quite jokey and very free with lyrical puns. As the trendy-suited, floppy haired, would be pop star around town Bowie cut an arty and slightly fey figure, straddling the pop industry and the fringes of film and stage crowds.

It is not beyond the bounds of possibility that David Bowie could have launched a career of significant success. "Love You Till Tuesday" was unleashed in Britain's "summer of love," a technicolour whirl of musical experimentation, where Engelbert Humperdinck could still command the singles charts and a government act ensured the pirate radio stations would be outlawed by September. That act gifted the BBC a virtual monopoly of all the popular music radio that really mattered that they held until local commercial stations were allowed in by a new act in the mid-seventies. This world loved apparently wholesome pop stars with bright clothes, some quirky ideas and the ability to give a good three minutes on a television show (everything on David Bowie is short enough to fit on one side of a single). Between the release of David Bowie and Bowie's first hit in 1969 the British charts were a welcoming home for the likes of The Amen Corner and Dave Dee Dozy, Beaky, Mick and Titch. Bowie with a hit, like "Love You Till Tuesday," in 1967 would have been launched squarely at the same pop magazines, variety shows and teenage audiences that bought their product by the shed load. When he did finally hit the charts in 1969 it was because "Space Oddity" struck a chord, and found television use, in the coverage of the first Moon landings. The single had already tried, and stiffed, before then. So his first hit was, in effect, a novelty record. By the time that same single hit UK#1 in 1975 it was ready to appear alongside "Starman" and "Drive in Saturday" on a hit compilation presenting Bowie as an insatiable changeling with inexhaustible reserves of creativity. By then, the man was a world star.

Had some DJ, or quirk of fate brought him to widespread attention earlier he would still have possessed the same talents. But, the demand would have been for more of the same product. London's theatres and the kind of chirpy television shows fronted by Lulu or Cilla Black would have been the bookings of choice and it's likely that his publishers would have taken phone calls saying: "that lad can write a decent tune, could he see his way to penning a couple for Sandie Shaw?" In this reality David Bowie would have been the blueprint from which to develop the artist.

Donald Bradshaw-Leather:
The Distance Between Us
(Distance, 1972)
What? Nightmare-ridden masterwork; record collectors' gold!

One of the most sought after vinyl rarities is a mystery on almost every level. Along with the usual confusion in this area about who the artist might be, there's the perplexing question of exactly what is going on over the four sides of the original vinyl. Don Bradshaw-Leather is reportedly elusive and enigmatic and (allegedly) deceased. Rumours of him being either a member of Barclay James Harvest and/or an alter-ego of prog-rock maverick Robert John Godfrey appear spurious. His only album is just plain strange. A slowly unfolding, mainly instrumental, collection of four lengthy tracks, The Distance... distorts normal notions of melody and sound, offering up snatches of melody but building each track around subtly shifting sonic arrangements suggesting the man conceived the thing more like a classical piece. Any classical notions are undermined by the dark and very rock sounds and instruments, any notions that it's a rock album are undermined by the radio unfriendly long-impenetrable tracks, buried vocals and unnerving arrangements that come over more like early synth experiments, and any notions it belongs with the synth pioneers are undermined by the fact our man, or maniac, prefers organs to synths and has a pretty old-school rock notion of how they should sound. Strangely symphonic, rumbling like rolling rocks and meandering like the mind of a man obsessed but permanently unable to make his point, The Distance Between Us is perfectly titled because it continues to fascinate, whilst its secrets remain hidden. As perplexing and downright strange as anything recorded, anywhere, anytime, and not recommended for those of a nervous disposition.

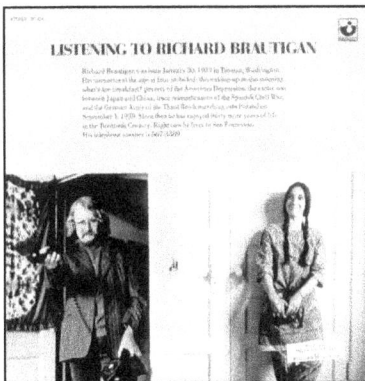

Richard Brautigan:
Listening to Richard Brautigan
(Harvest, 1970)
What? Beat banter from briefly best-selling American author.

Originally mooted as the third release on The Beatles Zapple label [*], Brautigan's album was conceived with help from bookshop proprietor and close McCartney friend, Barry Miles. Recorded in 1969; Listening to Richard Brautigan offers up readings including a short story, poetry and significant chapters from novels by Brautigan (1935-1984). In 1969 Brautigan was at his height as a resident poet amongst the San Francisco counter-culture and enjoyed a few rock-star traits, notably the trend for him to be photographed with young attractive female company on book covers. His soft mid-western accent and clear diction make Listening to... a very engaging experience. Brautigan's work, owes much to an earlier generation of beat writers, but also draws from the simple stylings of Ernest Hemingway and Brautigan's

EDITOR'S NOTE: A specialist imprint of Apple Corps, specialising in spoken word and avant garde material. Only two albums actually appeared on Zapple, one each by George Harrison and John and Yoko own rural roots to provide a concoction of gently surreal and whimsical observations. Brautigan's fondness for short narratives, (his early novels include surreal cascades of self-contained chapters, leaving the reader to piece together the narrative thread), and his use of apparently simple metaphors and similes lends itself well to providing a fast-moving and varied collection. The vivid scenery conjured in the sparse prose allows some of his work to leave the same impressions as song lyrics, revealing, repetitive and still allowing the audience to add something through their own imagination.

For all that, this is a spoken word album and the music of Brautigan's voice is only sporadically supported with sound effects. Two tracks comprise little more than actuality recordings made in situ as we share the author's "Life in San Francisco." It's not exactly hello trees/hello sky levels of tripped out bliss but there are only so many times you can listen to someone discussing getting in steaks as he makes coffee, or brushing his teeth. Obviously, those making the album were having a good time, these days those touching the shuffle button can avoid these moments. When it works best Listening to... takes into account the pros and cons of making an album. The poetic imagery of the two key book chapters – one on catching trout from Trout Fishing in America the other a gloriously alternative flight of fancy from A Confederate General From Big Sur involving counting the punctuation marks in the book of Ecclesiastes – are expertly chosen and "Love Poem," a one-line meditation read 18 consecutive times by 18 different readers (including Brautigan's young daughter, Ianthe) is a throwaway gem of a track.

Brautigan's critical and commercial star faded rapidly as the seventies drew on and his stock outside of the US has remained low ever since. The author committed suicide in 1984, an end that isn't remotely hinted at in the gentle beauty on offer here.

Broadcast:
Ha Ha Sound
(Warp, 2003)
What? Innovative act's finest release.

Broadcast never really sold in, so to note anything in a career focussed on being an alternative act as a "finest release" is probably against the spirit of everything they tried to do. Basically, Ha Ha Sound is a perfect start point for anyone unfamiliar with Broadcast. A pop group with an artful sensibility and a love of creativity for its own sake, Broadcast made the creation of pop songs their main medium of communication. Their resulting albums, and a few stop-gaps like the Pendulum EP, show a mixture of hugely effective pop and occasional experimental meanders. At worst, which is very rare, Broadcast could knock out an interesting but inconsequential instrumental diversion, showcasing production skills and some lively ideas. Pendulum has a couple of those. It also has the track "Pendulum" which features on this album. Ha Ha Sound makes a feature of different mixes for each track and different vibes for each piece. The band manage to play loosely, not something noted on their debut album The Noise Made by People. They also craft delicate melodies and Trish Keenan's vocals present different moods and characters to suit the variety. She is almost child-like, albeit with the kind of depths you might encounter in child from a horror movie, on "Colour me In." "Valerie" and "The Little Bell" also see Keenan presenting an innocent/waif-life quality but elsewhere her vocals are mixed back and given an android quality. Occasionally everything, including the lyric, is sacrificed to allow Broadcast simply to explore a sound. In this realm they belong with the eccentric production genius types – Spector, Meek, Brian Wilson, Saint Etienne – for whom a mash of symphonic ideas and pop structures is a one way ticket to another realm. To Broadcast's credit, they live comfortably in this company. Like a large number of its companions in this book Ha Ha Sound's main shortcoming is its ability to accomplish so much on one album. True appreciation of the work demands end to end listening repeated a few times, of all 14 tracks. This gradually brings the deft instrumental touches, inspired mixes and Keenan's brilliant performance into focus.

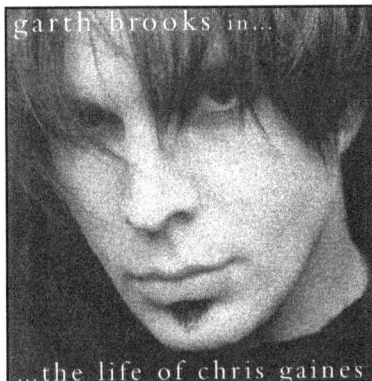

Garth Brookes:
Chris Gaines Greatest Hits/ In the Life of Chris Gaines
(Capitol, 1999)
What? Befuddling and bizarre alter-ego project.

The official line now the dust has settled says that Brookes – who for a sizeable chunk of the nineties was the one American artist capable of outselling Michael Jackson for months on end in the US market – released this album as a "Pre-soundtrack" to a movie called The Lamb. The thinking behind the project is still fairly clear to see. Brookes' multi-platinum sales and massive chart domination were achieved as a country artist. The music and artist remained massive in his native US but attempts to sell him to other lucrative territories – like the UK – weren't anywhere near as successful. Brookes and his management knew he had talent to burn, and some elements of his armoury were little used in his country career. His deft control of the upper register of his voice, his way with a pop hook-line and his soulful touch on an acoustic guitar had all been a fleeting feature of his high-profile career. The solution, aimed at gaining him respect across the board, increased foreign sales and achieving a major breakout from his country audience was to produce an album in his alter-ego of Chris Gaines, let the record sit there for a year or so and follow it with a movie in which Brookes played the fictional star and looked back on his career.

Brookes mega-fame ensured the Gaines project achieved some things instantly, the album hit #2 in the US charts and the beautiful pop-ballad "Lost in You" gave Brookes his only hit on the US pop charts. However, Brookes' popularity also proved a problem. Many die-hard fans were confused, the massive initial shipment of the album to US stores soon stalled in sales and the album was rapidly the subject of massive discounts giving it the unlikely history of being a massive hit and very public failure in very short order. Chris Gaines confused most audiences outside the US. At least in his home territory Brookes had appeared live on TV as his alter ego. The new identity, and the film project were rapidly dropped and music histories tend now to refer to the whole escapade as an "experiment."

In reality it is a superbly accomplished slice of adult pop/rock that delivers strongly on the items that appeared to matter most to its master-mind. "Lost in You" with its well-controlled high melody showcases a side of Brookes' singing that hits almost feminine levels of tenderness, the vocal is offset by a softly chopped acoustic guitar. "Driftin' Away" packs a similarly soulful punch and elsewhere the album hits on mainstream elements of rock and pop with sense of its own destiny. If this was the greatest hits of a mainstream artist he would have undoubtedly enjoyed a chart career and solid fan-base. Granted, Brookes had a few advantages, notably the deft knob-twiddling and pristine pop vision of producer Don Was, a man well-versed in mainstream sounds perched carefully on the edge of occasional irony. Listened to in short bursts, the performance and production here combine to do their jobs perfectly. "Driftin' Away" for example, slowly fades to make way for the muscularity of "Way of the Girl". Elsewhere a trio of rockers are scattered through the running order, ending with "Digging for Gold" which combines a lengthy, punch the air, chorus with a recurrent guitar figure right out of the Skynyrd songbook. Brookes even has the front to drop in "It Don't Matter to the Sun," a solid piece of straight country that would be at home on most Brookes' albums.

As with the sales, the strength here is also the main weakness. The album is so professional in its different styles and sounds that it offers little glimpse into what makes the fictional Chris Gaines an individual artist. Similarly, the songs may be anthemic and insightful, but the very general sentiments of the lyrics offer no real glimpse into Gaines' personality. As a pop songwriter he's up there with the likes of Diane Warren. As a personality, he eludes us. However, as a brave and ambitious release from an artist in a generally conservative corner of the music industry, Chris Gaines Greatest Hits is peerless.

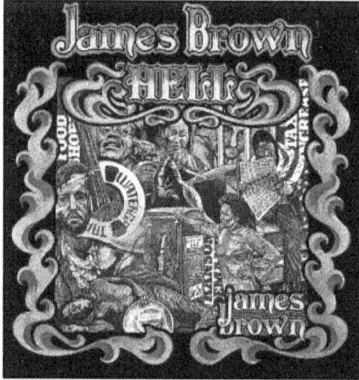

James Brown:
Hell
(Polydor, 1974)
What? Hellfire clearly burns with different coloured flames.

There's no argument about Brown's massive contribution to black music and MOBO (music of black origin). His sixties work – including the legendary Live at the Apollo – is as important as anything of its generation. Without Brown seventies soul would have been a totally different, probably more restrained and less adventurous, affair. Brown had a mixed seventies. His work showed the influence of the epic productions pioneered by the likes of Isaac Hayes and he did his own turn at a Blaxploitation soundtrack and referencing the right political issues. Brown's writing typically required a few musicians in the room, a jam and stops to decide what would be used. It was an approach that led itself to longer, more self-indulgent, tracks and allowed the man to become one of the most prolific artists of the seventies; never more so than in 1973-74 when his output included consecutive double albums. It has been argued elsewhere – like in Julian Cope's Copendium – that the first these – The Payback – is an inspired masterpiece.

Hell by contrast was well received by some but continues to baffle many. James Brown was never more scattergun or eclectic in his approach, and that is saying something because he always had those tendencies. Hell isn't exactly consistent, and isn't by any means a coherent statement. Different James Brown's turn up on different sides of the original vinyl and anyone revisiting the whole piece from beginning to end today is in for a change every twenty minutes or so.

The opening quartet is prime seventies Brown groove, effortlessly updating his sixties chops with meaty rhythms. Perfect for more sexually explicit times. "My Thang" and "Sayin' and Doin' It" really couldn't be anyone else. Flip the original first LP or leave the CD untouched into track five and things get decidedly weird. Tracks five to eight line up a reworking of "Please, Please, Please" – make that a full-on latin reworking of one of his greatest hits - before Brown attacks and demolishes three standards: "When the Saints go Marching in," "These Foolish Things Remind me of You" and "Stormy Monday."

Normal service – sort of – is restored on the next side, which includes a couple of majorly revised re-workings of earlier songs and some originals before the near 14 minute epic "Papa Don't Take no Mess" eats up all of the final side. After four sides the sense of "The Hardest Working Man in Showbusiness" grabbing at any convenient fragment to fill his album is fairly strong, and it's debatable whether Hell represents an identity crisis or over-reaching ambition. Brown got the fashion for lengthy grooves but often lacked the patience and love of studio trickery that allowed the likes of Isaac Hayes and Barry White to conceive their longest cuts as slowly building symphonies of soul. So, less here might well have been more in the long run. However, few soul albums of the period visit so many stations, take so many turns or offer up a tonnage of truly unique moments as readily as Hell.

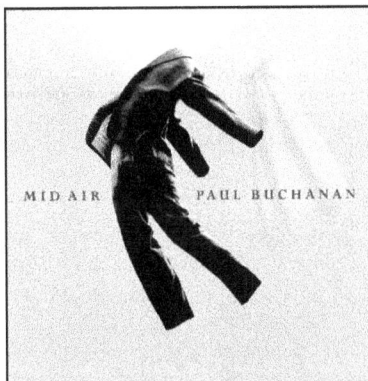

Paul Buchanan:
Mid Air
(Newsroom, 2012)
What? Solitary, stark and strangely effective solo effort from Blue Nilester.

Buchanan was a mainstay of The Blue Nile; studio-bound perfectionists who presented virtually no image as individuals and poured levels of care and attention into their albums (which emerged slowly and generally without fanfare). It is a measure of the band's low-profile that when Buchanan's self-released solo debut emerged in 2012 no reputable news source could state with certainty whether or not The Blue Nile had split up.

Mid Air is recognisably the voice and keyboard style that marked some of the most memorable Blue Nile moments, but the pace here is totally pedestrian, the vocals almost conversational and mantra-like, and the mood so introspective as to make the act of listening feel like intruding on private thoughts. Lyrically these are minor events, turned into short, highly effective fragments of thought and reflection and set – almost entirely – to solo keyboard. The stark chording of the keyboard with brief individual notes, very minimal strings and very little else suggests Buchanan is visiting the listener rather than performing. The most strident moments – "Buy a Motor Car" is supported by a few strings and has a rising section towards the middle when Buchanan borders on getting animated – are still so understated as to be best heard, alone, at home. Sometimes the home alone option is the only way to hear Mid Air. On songs like "My True Country" and the opening "Mid Air" Buchanan ends particular lines in a whisper at the very edges of audibility

As a demonstration in lone, melancholic, singer-songwriter work Mid Air is a masterclass in minimalism, and one of the best arguments for the less-is-more school of songcraft produced in the 21st century. The short running time of the album means the reliance on keyboard as the main musical backing doesn't cloy. Buchanan's deft skill as a lyricist means the individual stories behind the songs are accessible to the point of each providing some insight whilst still retaining an elusive, noir, quality in terms of what – exactly – is/was going on.

For Blue Nile devotees there is an inescapable, though ultimately futile, train of thought stemming from Mid Air in speculating how this material would have sounded with the full band in attendance.

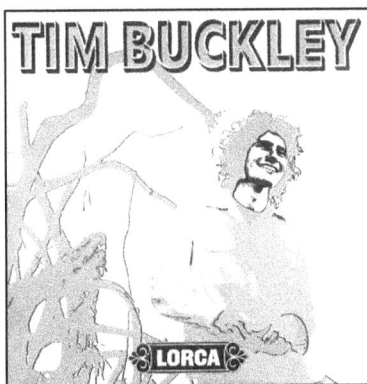

Tim Buckley:
Lorca
(Elektra, 1970)
What? Free-form folk rock of incredible ambition and very personal vision.

Buckley's fifth album, named after the Spanish poet Federico Garcia Lorca, ranks as the most ambitious and impenetrable work in his career. Widely regarded as "avant-garde" and "jazz influenced," Lorca might also be regarded in the same light as Dylan's Self Portrait or the uncompromising Lennonesque corners of The Beatles as an exercise in confronting his fan base, and fans of folk rock in general, with a watershed work. Time and again over the (almost) 40 minutes, Buckley takes the harder route, away from standard choruses, into new sections of a song that ride roughshod over any accepted notion of a middle eight, and frequently into vocal territory so extreme that his voice becomes another instrument rather than the means of purveying an easy to understand message. The lack of a standard rhythm section, chromatic scales in some of the songs and elliptical lyrics (when they are easily audible) gives Lorca the feel of an abstract expressionist work, very clear about its depth of emotion, but engrossing rather than explanatory when it comes to communicating anything.

"Anonymous Proposition," a truly outré love song that clocks in a shade under eight minutes and appears in movements rather than anything approaching standard verse/chorus form, shows just how far Buckley had moved from his earlier, more formulaic, songwriting. The opening title track simply hurls the constituent pieces of the album around with a ferocity and sense of abandon that almost turns song writing into performance art. Nothing here runs under six minutes, "Lorca" (the song) runs almost ten minutes and its appearance at the start of the running order seems deliberate. Anyone expecting standard singer/songwriter fodder is thrown off such a notion right away. Buckley's own comments on Lorca suggest he took a certain pride in its sheer outré reputation. He would never again enjoy such creative freedom, indeed his presence in the studio as the Elektra label was being sold was crucial to Lorca. The old, more tolerant, regime of Jac Holzman didn't have to worry about the sales figures on this and his new bosses were in no position to stop him.

If the discussion thus far suggests Lorca is simply an exercise in wilful disobedience to any standard practice that is to do the album an artistic injustice. The experimental end of folk, and the territory where it collides head on with jazz, took years to develop a coterie of artists this adventurous and this indulgent. Lorca is far less companionable than – say – John Martyn's Solid Air or One World, but it seeks to be as influential and as true to passions as it is to facts. The existence of a whole strand of similar work today is testimony to the lasting power of this album.

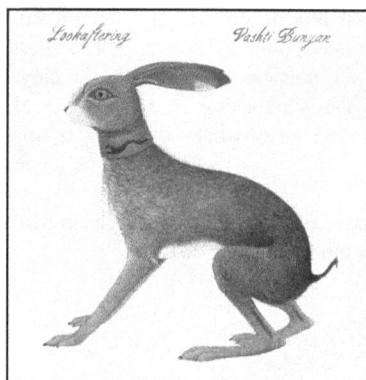

Vashti Bunyan:
Lookaftering
(Fat Cat, 2005)
What? That difficult second album; 35 years after the first, and sounding like part of the same session.

We can gloss over the background here really quickly. Bunyan recorded Just Another Diamond Day (1970) during a period when her confidantes included Donovan. The album saw her performing a gentle, pensive, and highly personal folk over the backing of a handful of string players; all within the capable production hands of Joe Boyd. The album did nothing commercially, Bunyan abandoned her musical career and gradually became a cult act with followers who also made their own – frequently gentle, pensive and personal folk based - records. After a 2000 CD reissue of Diamond Day Bunyan's was a name dropped in association with the likes of Devandra Banhart and Joanna Newsome.

Cue a return to work and a second album. The truly remarkable thing about Lookaftering is how much it sounds like Just Another Diamond Day. This time around Bunyan is aided and abetted by those she has inspired Otto Hauser, and Kevin Barker of Espers help out, along with Newsome and Banhart, and string arranger Robert Kirby – who was on board for Just Another Diamond Day – is back. So is the magic. Lyrically, she has moved on, but only in life experience. This is as much an affirmation of loving others, loving life and loving the moment as was Diamond Day. "Here Before" – a hymn of total and unconditional love to her children – is a case in point. She is a mother, she looks at her newborn and feels he has been "here before" and takes in the new reality with the philosophy that informed the first album. Lyrically Bunyan affirms her independence – notably on "Wayward" where she states she always wanted to be the one with: "a band of wayward children with their fathers left behind."

Sonically Lookaftering accepts the 21st century but uses the production possibilities to embellish what was always great about Vashti Bunyan. It's a clean, sparing, and gently crafted sound that usually allows Bunyan the space to gently pick her guitar and lean in so close to the mic that the gentle cadences of her voice are caught. She's marginally rougher edged than 35 years previously, but her phrasing, tone and the sheer love she can pour into these mild missives are still an aural embrace. And, the production treats every song like a child, dressing each appropriately and lavishing equal love on all 11 cuts. "If I Were" – for example – presents a combination of Fender Rhodes and Dulcimer that finds its perfect role backing Vashti. Elsewhere recorders, and that oh-so-expressive acoustic guitar work the same magic they worked in 1970. Lookaftering is a thing of beauty and – thankfully – it prompted a period of intense activity, including recording and live work.

William Burroughs:
Dead City Radio
(Island, 1990)
What? Acerbic and angular missives from beat master.

Cult authors and cult music might be a marriage made in many a bedroom by a devoted fan, but there has always been a problem of these creative geniuses producing work that appeals outside their usual medium. There are printed works of variable quality written by musicians just as there are recorded works by authors which will not withstand repeated listenings.

The combination of Burroughs, Island Records and his various companions here, tackles this problem directly, producing a work of genuine merit. Burroughs is presented in recordings made mainly in his home, and used as a (talking) lead vocalist over a variety of musical settings concocted by the likes of John Cale, Donald Fagen and Sonic Youth. Another master stroke is to build the album from snippets, effectively making it a best and the rest collection. So, the essence of Burroughs' best work rubs up alongside a few fleeting crowd pleasers and some genuine oddities (like a literal reading of "The Lord's Prayer"), all done with the kind of abstract, suggestive musical backing that confirms Burroughs as a permanently left-field figure.

The sequencing works well. The second track, the satirical "A Thanksgiving Prayer" ("Thanks for 'Kill a queer for Christ' stickers…"), is followed by a true greatest hit in a reading from The Naked Lunch. Burroughs' diction isn't always clear, so a few flashes of brilliance in the original writing are lost to mumbles and swamped by a musical passage that saves the tracks, but this combination also allows the more ambitious works to build some tonality and incorporate Burroughs' southern drawl.

The nine minute plus "Apocalypse" achieves this with some confidence, though whether the "bonus" track, a truly flat and generally tuneless rendering of "Ich bin von Kopf bis Fuß auf Liebe eingestellt" (Falling in Love Again), adds to the legend or just presents Burroughs as cranky for his own sake, is debateable.

Burzum:
Daudi Baldrs
(Misanthropy, 1997)
What? A voyage to the dark side.

The nineties Black Metal scene in Norway is well chronicled in the eminently readable Lords of Chaos. A major player in the most extreme goings on was Varg Vikernes, Burzum mainstay and a man with a vivid and dark vision he'd channelled into intense and chilling black metal albums. With churches burning and the competition to be the blackest of the Black Metallers also hotting up, something had to give. Burzum and their rivals Mayhem were the clear leaders in deeds of extremity, until Mayhem found themselves a member short, their lead guitarist - Euronymous - having been fatally stabbed, by Vikernes. Vikernes was convicted and imprisoned, he argued self-defence but his broad smile at the moment of receiving a 21 year sentence did little for his chances on appeal, even if it confirmed him as a Black Metal cult hero. He was also convicted in connection with arson at several churches.

Denied access to the usual tools of his trade – guitars and drums – Vikernes spent time in jail composing and recording two albums of an altogether different type; dubbed "Dark Ambient." The first of these releases; Daudi Baldrs, is – arguably – a masterpiece of disturbing musical ideas. It bears repeated, if uneasy, listening. Recorded mainly on a synthesiser, Daudi Baldrs is a concept piece, the title meaning "Baldr's death" and the storyline dealing with the legacy of Baldr, the second son of Odin in Norse mythology. Aurally the piece repeats simple, sometimes grating, notational patterns that hint at classical and dark-folk structures and hark back to melodic references from the middle ages. The lyrics, appearing in Norwegian, remain elusive to most listeners. The presence of a choir intoning the words works mainly as an added melodic device. For the most part, the work is instrumental.

The repetitive, unrepentantly dark and frequently intense clusters of notes give Daudi Baldrs the feel of the kind of chamber music that might just work in Hell. Still, the album remains both accessible and compelling. The same ideas and approach were subsequently used on Hliðskjálf . Now released and recording again, Vikernes continues his dark and highly individual musical journey. Burzum's first post-jail release, Belus, was a return to Black Metal ways, but packed an intro and outro that owed much to the music Vikernes made in jail.

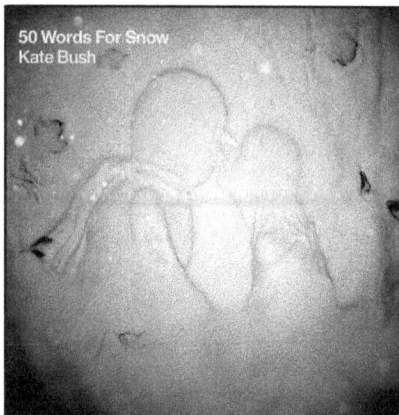

Kate Bush:
50 Words for Snow
Fish People/EMI 2011
What? First new release on own label is Bush at her best.

When cinema felt television encroaching on its audience in the late fifties it went widescreen and technicolour to provide an experience television couldn't match. When downloads provided a new threat, 3D propelled movies like Avatar and Gravity towards a market who could only experience the work in its intended, auditorium, setting. Kate Bush has gone in a similar direction with regard to her records. Having only done one tour, a short run around the UK in 1979, she compensated for the lack of live promotion with increasingly ambitious records. As downloads devastated record sales Bush cut down the productivity, concentrating on denser, more nuanced and longer running collections, lavishly packaged and strong in their celebration of the artistic possibilities of the long playing recorded work. In her 34th year as a professional musician 50 Words marked only her tenth studio album. When she, finally, began bucking this trend by announcing a series of dates in London in 2014 many, initially, wondered if the announcement was some kind of early April fool's joke.

Bush has long been a national treasure in the UK and valued cult artist elsewhere. 50 Words is a genuine album in all senses of the word, a perfectly sequenced collection with shifting moods and ideas, all contributing to an overall artistic vision. The collection is akin to a chamber work, repeating certain themes, like the use of spoken word, and a central motif linked to snow which is referenced in song titles, lyrics, sounds and a title track in which the different words are explored. Despite her lack of live work, Bush remains a very theatrical artist often prone to assembling the right cast and building the work on a set of dynamics. On 50 Words Bush's keyboards and Steve Gadd's expressive and sympathetic drumming anchor the sound. Much of it is very English and much of the Englishness comes from a notion of storytelling as a complex and subtle art. It doesn't sound Dickensian, but sometimes it just feels like that. The other lead vocals include Elton John in duet with Bush on "Snowed in at Wheeler Street." To some ears his familiar tones, apparently as Bush's love interest, or the ubiquitous voice of Stephen Fry taking the lead on the title track are distracting because each voice comes with its own baggage. Then again, if you are Kate Bush and your address book includes their numbers…

Distractions aside, 50 Words stands out in Bush's catalogue because everything that makes for a great album is writ large somewhere in this work. The music combines complexity with a deceptive simplicity on first hearing as the melodies entice you in. Lyrically the album drops reference points and narrative arcs capable of withstanding questions about their precise meaning. The whole fifty words for snow theme might be built on a myth, but it still has the ability to suggest varied meanings, and responses. Bush remains a consummate artist. Cliché or not, the studio is her real instrument and she continues to approach her music like a novelist of the pre-media age, expecting her audience to engage, meditate and live with her work. 50 Words is somewhere beyond being a mere collection of songs, and someway short of being a complete lifestyle choice. Few other artists still thought in those terms by 2011, but this is a territory Bush continues to make her own. [*]

The Butthole Surfers:
Locust Abortion Technician
(Touch and Go, 1987)
What? A collision of serious/sick, pscyh/punk, low-fi/ambitious production that works to perfection.

Running a touch over 32 and a half minutes. LAT isn't exactly an epic; but it is – arguably – the highest point of one of rock's most unholy alliances. The Butthole Surfers are perennial outsiders to rank with the best:Grateful Dead, Hawkwind, The Cure. Like those name-checked here, the band contains contradictions on almost every level and produces music that at its best is rich in explosive ideas and constantly threating to break

EDITOR'S NOTE: Many readers will be aware that I have a double life. Away from my Gonzoid activities I am the Director of the world's largest cryptozoological research organisation, and one of the songs on this album namechecks a friend of ours. Dipu Marek, who went with us into the Garo Hills of northern India some years ago appears in the song *Wild Man*. Ironically, I doubt whether it has snowed in the Garo Hills since the last ice age, but that is not really relevant.

apart as the uneasy co-existence of the elements erupts at random. Die-hard individualist punks with a taste for recreational drugs and a psychedelic acceptance of the most random elements, The Surfers have rotated band-members with gleeful abandon and still managed to sustain a career and hang on to their core personnel. They are – by turns – laugh out loud funny, threateningly sick, insanely talented songwriters and soundscape technicians capable of sourcing material from anywhere. In 1987 they put this skill to work crafting just over half an hour of music that spews forth so many ideas that listeners frequently over-estimate the running time. At a stretch it could be argued Locust Abortion Technician is Trout Mask Replica reimagined by hardcore punks. Well, maybe…

In reality LAT is a mini-masterpiece and something of a watershed work. Their initial brace of albums were experimental to the point that some dismissed the band as lacking focus. The following albums saw the band arrive in the studio with more fully formed songs. LAT straddles this divide with a backbone of insistent rockers like "Graveyard" and "Human Cannonball," throws in explosive freakouts like "U.S.S.A" and references any musical territory it sees fit to pillage. "The O-Men" is one case in point; a rapid-fire slice of novelty punk that tacks nonsense rockabilly vocals and a trash-culture sensibility over the hardcore backing, it throws in psychedelic Hendrix solo guitar, then rants along in a manner suggesting it's an epic, before petering out with a gentle fade just before the three and a half minute mark.

The sense of a drug-fuelled band partying their way through the whole process is palpable and this – in turn – leaves the listener permanently worrying that the album will go off the rails. If it does fall from the sublime it is probably in the only non-original cut: "Kuntz" may be a really clever cut-up of Asian music samples and Butthole production flourishes but it's also probably more valued for the sledgehammer subtlety of its blatant double-entendre than any credentials it boasts as world music. Fortunately, the glorious proto-grunge sludge-rocker "Graveyard" storms in to save the day and the Surfers see out their master-work with confidence and inspiration with the darkly psychedelic "22 Going on 23."

Uneven, impossible to categorise and timeless, Locust Abortion Technician remains inspirational and challenging in equal amounts.

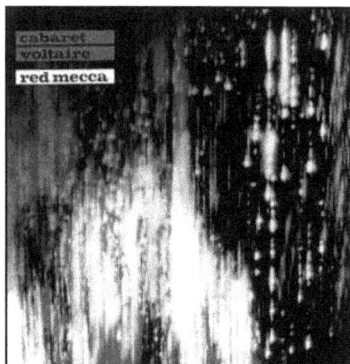

Cabaret Voltaire:
Red Mecca
Rough Trade 1981
What? Analogue synths drive industrial/post-punk watershed work.

Sheffield's Cabaret Voltaire (named after a 1920s nightclub frequented by Dadaist artists) were already well established performance artists and musicians when punk and the post-punk industrial wave of musicians hit their native Sheffield. Their intelligence and familiarity with electronic sound gave them a head-start on a slightly younger generation still learning their craft. By the late seventies Cabaret Voltaire were combining their sound experiments with samples and music that managed to challenge pop music norms and make cultural comments into the bargain. Well, either that or their native cunning and natural skill allowed them to put together sounds so compelling that John Peel and a generation of music journalists couldn't help but notice.

1981's Red Mecca is the culmination of the first phase of their existence and the parting shot of founder member Chris Watson (pushing 30 by the time the album was released). Red Mecca is lyrically obscure, favouring vocalising as part of a mix that is also rich in guitar, analogue synth (though notably less than on the band's earlier releases), along with samples of radio. There are random other sounds imported and nods to reggae influences, psychedelic echo and delay and a host of twists along the way. So, it's an uncomfortable and frequently perplexing listen that manages to communicate concerns (both personal and political). Red Mecca frequently presents music that allows what tune there is to be constantly attacked by the individual instrumental sounds (using them more as blasts of competing sound than comrades in presenting a coherent melody) and cuts these into bite size pieces so most of the tracks are short enough to be singles. The ten and half minute monster of "A Thousand Ways" is the one lengthy noise-excursion that apes the nihilist noodlings of some of their competitors of the time but Red Mecca remains as uncompromising as the darkest work of its era. The only real allowances it makes to explaining itself literally are in the looped – darkly trippy – grooves of "A Touch of Evil" – which both opens and closes the album – and in the staccato vocals of Stephen Mallinder who often keeps things so short and focussed that his contributions work more as chants to urge the tracks forward than lyrical statements.

Red Mecca is an uncompromisingly abstract assault on your ears, a work about paranoia and the possibilities of sound; as much a travelogue as a focussed text.

Sebastian Cabot:
Sebastian Cabot Actor/Bob Dylan Poet
(MGM, 1967)
What? Golden throat meets greatest of Dylan's early catalogue…what could go wrong?

Two cuts from this album appear on the iconic first edition of the Golden Throats series. Cabot (1918-1977) was an English born actor who achieved notable fame in Hollywood and on US television, but to a certain group of music fans he has long been the focus of bemusement, a view based on the ironic appreciation of an album of Dylan covers, the like of which few others would have dared attempt. The title – pretty much – says what you need to know. Dylan's poetry, Cabot's clear and slightly gruff diction…what could go wrong?

By common consent – Sebastian Cabot Actor… is one of those rare items that is so wrong it becomes profoundly right. Cabot hits on a high proportion of protest songs – including "Who Killed Davy Moore?," "Blowin' in the Wind" and "The Times They are a Changin,'" and few notable love related tunes: "It Ain't me Babe" and "Tomorrow is a Long Time" both feature. He also makes a determined stab at "Like a Rolling Stone." He's backed by musical arrangements that throw in strings and a few pop/rock sounds, forming a portentous and serious background against which Cabot can treat Bob's words as meaningful missives of significance. That may well be what Dylan intended, but Cabot's laboured diction is a far cry from Bob's sneer. His treating of Dylan's rock 'n' roll and blues inspired patter like a Shakespearean sonnet is the main reason this album acquired cult status in the first place, and the reason it continues to line up with William Shatner's The Transformed Man and a fistful of other long playing thespian audio curiosities as a genuine jaw dropper. Where Shatner hams it up a treat in his attempts to inhabit texts, including "Mr Tambourine Man," Cabot attempts to drag Dylan into unfamiliar audio territory and interpret him for a middle-American audience as familiar with Cabot's star turns on television as they are with the intricacies of Dylan album tracks. So, it's best imagined as a battle fought over every line as Cabot takes his turn at covering the iconic songs and Dylan's original meanings are tested (sometimes to destruction). A post on WMFU's blog notes: "We're back here at ringside for the thrilling conclusion to this bizarre audio-matchup…Cunning actor and car-fancier Sebastian 'Killer' Cabot pits his able tongue and massive bulk against the barbed and velvet-covered pen of youth favorite Bob Dylan, light and lean but full of fight."

We concur. The battle is fought out over 12 rounds: "Who Killed Davy Moore?," "It Ain't Me Babe,"

"Boots Of Spanish Leather," "Don't Think Twice, It's All Right," "Tomorrow is a Long Time," "Blowin' In The Wind," "Seven Curses," "All I Really Want To Do," "The Times They Are A-Changin'," "Quit Your Lowdown Ways," "Like A Rolling Stone" and "And Mostly They Sing." Irving Spence's musical arrangements provide the venue and at no point do Cabot and Dylan ever appear to be in the same place in terms of what they intend. The final result of the "audio-matchup" battle is in the ear of the beholder. To Cabot's credit he treats political statements with genuine gravitas and also scores points for selecting a few lesser known cuts that don't jar so badly in the mind, because the Dylan originals are far from ubiquitous. Dylan's scoring blows come in rapid flurries with the cynical, ambiguous and attitude-riven turns of phrase in the love songs; Cabot's mature and rugged diction rides roughshod over these gems with all the artfulness of a man re-assembling a broken vase whilst wearing boxing gloves.

Sebastian Cabot, Actor remains one of those car-crash releases that will forever remain timelessly strange, and beyond parody.

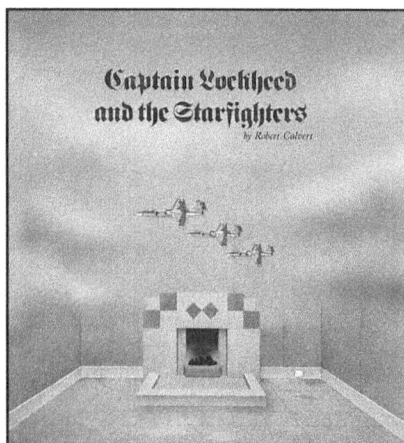

Robert Calvert:
Captain Lockheed and the Starfighters
(United Artists, 1974)
What? Concept album which is literally about crashing dreams.

Captain Lockheed and the Starfighters may just be the work Robert Calvert (1945-1988) was put on this planet to create. Afflicted by bi-polar disorder and acknowledged (even by those who couldn't cope with working alongside him) as a brilliant talent, Calvert's highest profile days were spent in Hawkwind, and his most intense and elaborate solo works were cut in the mid-seventies. The perfect fusion of his own ambivalent world vision and a subject for a concept album occurs in Captain Lockheed... which concerns itself with the ongoing disaster that resulted from the mass sale of Lockheed Starfighter aircraft to the Luftwaffe. The high-performance fighters looked deadly enough in air displays and mock battles but by their retirement in the mid-eighties well over 250 of the planes had been lost to accidents, with a massive knock on cost in lives and hard cash.

The grimly funny and frequently surreal story lends itself perfectly to a large concept work in which Calvert's space rocking style of music is interspersed with spoken word tracks and a fair amount of comedy. The presence of (an uncredited) Brian Eno, most of his former Hawkwind colleagues, some Pink Fairies and Arthur Brown also gives some insight into the range of sounds on offer, and Vivian Stanshall steals the spoken word interludes much in the way he steals attention as MC on Mike Oldfield's Tubular Bells.

Given the quality of the humour and music it's possible to enjoy the whole (chancy) ride on its entertainment value alone. But the spoken word segments include actual recordings concerning the state of Germany's air force in the late fifties, the opinions of pilots subsequently charged with flying the "Widomaker," and the off-the-wall opinions of the mechanics faced with fixing the flying death traps.

Musically Captain Lockheed... is less strident than the thumping space rock of Hawkwind – though their quieter moments of their early seventies Calvert incarnation are a good yardstick – and conceptually the complex story does trip over itself to the point that only a listener's rapt attention will unpick it. Those who love the album and inflict it on others – often urging them to: "listen to this bit" – achieve their affection through lengthy exposure and familiarity. That dynamic tells you all you need to know about why it didn't chart. Captain Lockheed... finds its peers amongst The Firesign Theatre and The Fugs in its complexity; with the added bonus of having a plot as complex and furiously twisted as a good Goon Show, and being able to prove the whole thing is rooted in provable fact. It's prescient too, the Starfighters went on crashing long after Calvert's album was released.

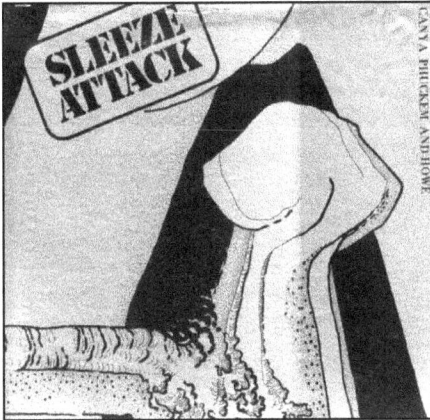

Canya Phuckem and Howe:
Sleeze Attack
(More Best Productions, 1980)
What? Puerile punk with a smattering of power pop.

At glorifytheturd.com there's a reverent appraisal of the delights offered by this album including the following thoughts: "anybody can grind this sort of thing out, but when you can throw it out with a degree of seriousness and enthusiasm, it tends to push it to a higher level...pretty entertaining stuff without a dud in the bunch."

In other words, this will not change your life, but it may well make you smirk. Shamelessly sex-obsessed and clever enough to focus each song on a specific aspect of coming (or cumming) together, we get a beginners guide to gay male behaviour. Fisting and – ahem – water sports, make an appearance and one song (available to hear online as of this writing), "Left Pocket, Right Pocket" is genuinely perplexing. Seriously, is this gay people talking in code to their own or is the whole thing a smokescreen to ensnare the kind of know-alls who pretend to get non-existent gags? The production betrays the lack of budget, but the playing and singing covers the gamut from punk to a decent pastiche of tuneful "British Invasion" pop. However loud the guitars and off-key the singing, the diction (should that be dickion?) is clear enough to ram the message home. All of the above is achieved with a consummate sense of balance between celebrating gay culture, implicitly campaigning for an understanding of this culture, and grabbing every double entendre and half-decent gag that presents itself. They may want to have their cake and eat it too, but Canya Phuckem have put the work in to produce a product fit for support from the most worthy campaigner and sniggers from the most puerile drive by fan. Song titles like: "This Guy's the Limit," "A Night at the Orgy" and "Woof Woof, Oink Oink" deliver what you'd expect. Doubtless those responsible would even chuckle at the difficulty of locating this entry in an alphabetical list. Is it under C for Canya, like M for Molly Hatchett, or do we treat Phuckem as the family name like C for Alice Cooper?

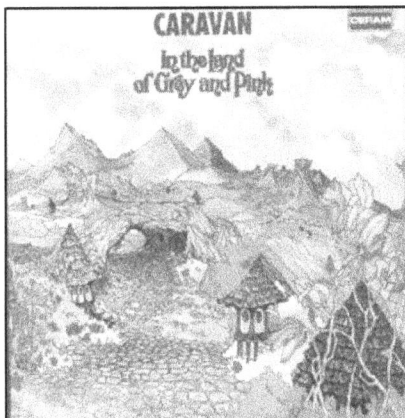

Caravan:
In the Land of the Grey and Pink
(Deram, 1971)
What? Whimsical English Prog-delight.

It's fitting to note that this slow-selling, never-charted collision of prog-jazz-semi-classical and pop finally gained a gold record decades after its initial release. Generally regarded as the creative peak of the leading lights of Britain's "Canterbury Scene," In the Land of the Grey and Pink is a glimpse into a gentle, idyllic and very English take on psychedelia. One of the most English of cities, Canterbury was home to a generation of musicians who combined technical proficiency with a very lyrical approach to their craft and bands like the Wilde Flowers (note the literary reference in the name), provided the training ground for future members of Soft Machine, Caravan and a few other outfits.

Three albums into their account Caravan collided gentle hippie whimsy and ambitious musical ideas to produce a view into a world that has proven highly appealing ever since. The opening "Golf Girl" is the ultimate middle-class nerdy-boy love song. Our protagonist meets his golf girl as she sells tea at the golf course, during the ensuing rain of golf balls she protects him. Bear in mind, chest-beating RAWK! of the Robert Plant variety was already shifting shed loads of albums by this time. Notably, this track had a mid-eighties revival when Nigel Planer, in the guise of his Young Ones TV character: Neil the hippie, covered it on Neil's Heavy Concept Album. The album's closer, all 22 minutes and 40 seconds of "Nine Feet Underground" is a patchwork composition of vivid lyrical fragments and virtuoso musical chops that will see you through a hefty joint, or a satisfying sexual experience from foreplay to sparking up a post coital fag... you get the idea.

And, where Grey and Pink, is concerned, that is probably it. If the reliable year on year sales, that took the album from the vinyl to CD era and beyond tell us anything they suggest a steady trickle of people find and cherish this collection, their numbers expanding slightly every year. In a word: "students." Along with Leonard Cohen, Bob Dylan and Mike Oldfield's Tubular Bells, this album played gently away as first joints were smoked, first bodily fluids were exchanged and, a couple of years later, late night hours were spent scribbling away in a desperate attempt to salvage a decent level of degree after two enjoyable but unproductive years at university. Few melodic rock records have ever proven as companionable, or steadily attractive to succeeding generations. Add to that the notion that this mythical Land of Grey and Pink is a very English idyll. As depicted on the cover it seems a vision of Middle Earth much given to languid and philosophical days, and little concerned with life-threatening quests in search of anything truly dangerous. A paradise of the mind: almost within reach and quite possibly accessed via five tracks of classic prog-rock.

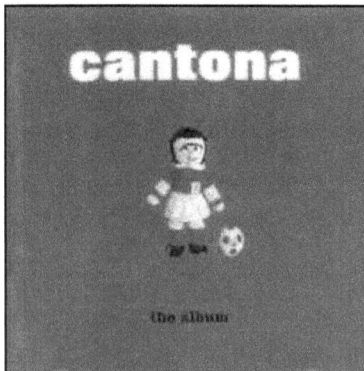

Various Artists:
Cantona:
The Album
(Exotica, 1995)
What? "We'll drink, a drink, a drink, to Eric the king, the king, the king..."

Your perception of this album and its subject depends very much on your interest in football (or, if you're reading this in some part of the world that equates the word "football" with a brand of licensed brutality that involves mainly carrying a long-ball and colliding with opponents: "soccer"). Apologies if you already know this but: French-born Cantona (b. 1966) is one of the most enigmatic, gifted and impenetrable figures ever to become famous as a football hero. Under-appreciated by his national team, possibly because the old adage of there being no "I" in team, was applied, Cantona found adulation and news headlines in Britain. His tenure at Manchester United (1992-1997) saw him captain one of the world's biggest clubs in his final season, feature in notable cup wins and play a significant part in winning four league titles in five campaigns. It also remains memorable for an eight month ban from football and conviction for assault that resulted after Cantona launched himself into the crowd to attack an opposing fan who taunted him after a sending off. If you've never seen the 1995 incident it remains a massive YouTube favourite and any combination of Cantona + Kung Fu Kick typed into a search engine should find it in seconds.

And there's an album. Cantona is one of a series of football compilations produced by the British Exotica label. Their Bend It compilations collected low-fi abominations, spirited and frequently tuneless cash-ins and a few genuine gems. Cantona is different if only because it packs a narrative. The featured acts include; The K-Stand and Captain Sensible, cult heroes, maybe but presented here as players in a great narrative as England's newly founded Premier League begins to flex its financial muscle and Cantona emerges as phenomenally gifted football magician, producing tricks that take him to national hero status in front of millions of television viewers. For the non football fan the moments of snatched commentary in which Cantona's gifts reduce experienced commentators to catch-up merchants spouting clichés like "Brilliant!" tell you all you need to know about why he mattered. News coverage of the fall-out surrounding his foray into the crowd, and his subsequent re-emergence as a major player in club success are teased out in sampled snatches of media coverage, and the music on offer includes inspired and, less-than-inspired novelty items. When we need gravitas it arrives in the form of George Best (arguably the one Manchester United star who may be considered more naturally gifted than Eric the King) and Alex Ferguson, the one managerial talent capable of taming and directing the mighty Cantona.

Cantona: The Album is occasionally tuneless, somewhat repetitive and does betray a sense of grabbing at any audio artefact that might add to the mix, but it's also a recording of history as it happened and a tribute to a true legend of his era. Cantona the man remains mystic and elusive as he floats above the fan-praise here like some minor deity. And that – pretty much – is the point of compiling everything on this album.

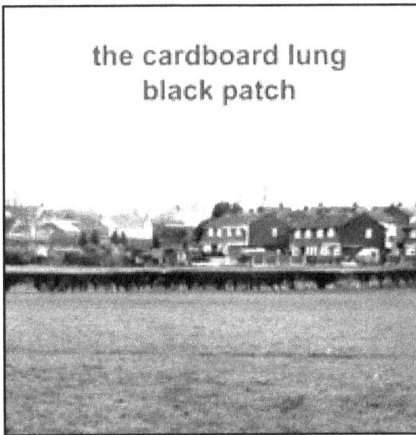

the cardboard lung
black patch

The Cardboard Lung:
Black Patch
(Earth Monkey Productions, 2008)
What? Dark ambient, glitch and beyond.

To be brutally honest the world isn't exactly short of dark-ambient, glitch techno any combination thereof or – indeed – any variation that takes either of the above and hurls it towards any other variant of computer generated sound or sample. Still reading this entry? Well, then, it might be worth making a brief case for the work of John Kenneth Hall – visual artist, man about community educational projects and occasional musician. Ironically one of the major strengths Hall – AKA The Cardboard Lung – brings to his craft is the fact he isn't primarily a musician. Black Patch isn't exceptionally long, isn't out to grab your senses and scramble them and doesn't do more than most dark ambient works. It samples dialogue, plays insistent and mildly disturbing tricks on your senses with slow rhythmic assaults and sporadic bursts of speed and noise, and also manages a cinematic quality hinting at a range of dark and disturbing images.

Hall – a man whose talents have gone from film composition to an ambitious arts project linked to football (as in soccer if you're American) in the community – is an adept if unspeaking MC, guiding the mood music through the chambers of the subconscious. Hall describes himself on one website as a "rennaisance underachiever" a shorthand reference – perhaps – to way his low-key work often references high-art principles. "The Cuckoo" on this collection being a good example, sampling a beautiful English folk song before crumbing into minimalist and mournful glitch-techno. "Fox Dream" is another collision of sample (this time sound from nature) and a disturbing techno excursion though the two chord backing, slow shuffling, drum track. The voices at the edge of perception exercise of "Watershed" shows The Cardboard Lung taking on standard ambient/glitch territory and getting the sense of analogue warmth from digital sound that eludes many in this area.

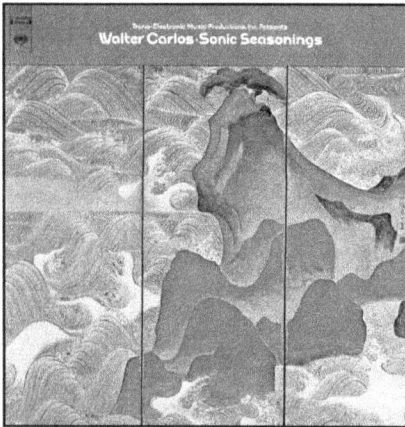

Walter Carlos:
Sonic Seasonings
(CBS, 1972)
What? V sign to Vivaldi from early synth pioneer. *

If casual music fans know anything about Carlos it's probably one of two facts. Either, the history of high-profile compositions including the soundtracks for the movies A Clockwork Orange (1971) and Tron (1982), or the fact that Walter Carlos – who made this album – has lived as Wendy Carlos, complete with gender realignment surgery, for most of her adult life.

These footnote facts that still appear occasionally in dad-rock magazines and the like obscure a cutting edge career in which Carlos won massive praise and major awards for an early reworking of classical music in Switched on Bach (1968) before producing this 86 minute masterwork of sound effects and envelope pushing on analogue synth in 1972. Sonic Seasonings can't help but be compared to Vivaldi's Four Seasons, the concepts are similar, though sonically both works are poles apart.

The basic idea here is to use (then) modern recording techniques to gather high-quality clips of natural phenomena (crashing waves and the like) and mix these prominently into stereophonic soundscapes in which slowly evolving melodies played on electronic instruments evoke the moods of the different seasons.

Each piece: Spring, Summer, Fall, Winter, takes up one side of the original vinyl. A lavish CD reissue includes out-takes, taking the original running time well over 130 minutes.

Sonic Seasonings anticipates early ambient music and has passages that resemble Brian Eno's early solo work – notably on the highly understated opening to the Winter section – but fundamentally this is conceived in the way of major classical works, with recurrent themes, a sense of the different sounds – natural and man-made – working alongside each other like a tone poem, and strident sections that demand to be listened to.

Sonically, it shows its age and its public appearances in the present age are more along the lines of individual pieces, or snatches of pieces, appearing in the most eclectic and out-of-step corners of internet radio. But Sonic Seasonings is something of a high water mark for ambition amongst the first generation of electronic keyboard wizards, and one of the most coherent and successful concept albums of its era.

---

* EDITOR'S NOTE: I have been a little bit self indulgent here by including the covers to two different issues of the Carlos album, but as a sometime record sleeve designer myself I am amused at the synchronistic happenstance which made the original design such a doddle to redesign after Mr Carlos had carried out his own redesign and become Ms Carlos. Such little pieces of coincidence make me happy. However as my old friend and mentor Tony 'Doc' Shiels is fond of shouting at me "There's no such thing as a bloody coincidence you Saxon bollocks!"

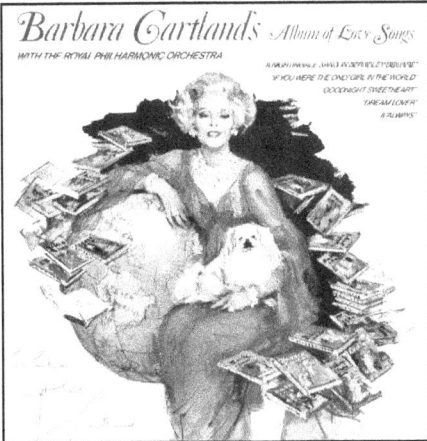

Dame Barbara Cartland:
Album of Love Songs
(State, 1978)
What? Dotty old dame goes defiantly old school in her dotage.

Cartland (1901-2000) was a prodigious purveyor of romantic fiction, initially considered risqué, she soon settled into a groove of high morality and historic romance, allowing the virginal nature of her typecast heroines to appear more plausible. Debate continues as to whether the massive sales figures claimed for her output have any remote link to the actual truth, and Cartland was already something of a caricature before her death. Anyone watching Matt Lucas in drag artfully dictating romantic drivel whilst draped on a chaise longue in Little Britain is looking at the popular image Cartland had towards the end of her life.

Cartland was always capable of generating media interest, so the fact this late seventies long player is virtually unknown in the twenty first century might, just, suggest that even she realised what an inescapable stinker it is. Given the constituent parts, something useful could have emerged. The Mike Samms Singers (with a credible pedigree) provide the backing vocals, The Royal Philharmonic Orchestra are the backing band and Magnet Records (with a track record of astute signings, pop success and well-aimed novelty items) are hosting the party. The whole arrangement sets up a lush wall of sound for Cartland to artfully front her vision of morally scrupulous, old school, love. Seriously, it's great until she opens her mouth. The Dame's dull vocals, limited range, wavering power and off key warbling mangle standards like "Goodnight Sweetheart" and "A Nightingale Sang in Berkely Square" and the one allowance made to her cloth eared crooning involves an abundance of spoken word introductions, reducing the collection to something akin to a disastrous drag act besotted with his/her own thoughts on the songs. The truth of these little asides appears dubious, for example, Ms Cartland claims she did once fall in love in Berkely Square and a nightingale did sing as it happened. It may be that the spoken word pieces were allowed simply because any available bucket in which she might have carried a tune was otherwise engaged as the musically competent backing crew queued up for collective chunder in response to the horrors unfolding before their ears.

This truly is a twelve track torture beyond satire and, almost, beyond belief. An ill-starred irony-less venture that exists in a terrifying twilight zone somewhere between Roddy Llewllyn's one and only album and Ethel Merman's disco diversion. The CD reissue has yet to appear.

Alberta Casey:
San Diego Vokas
(?, 1981?)
What? Alternative take on pop standards and stage standards.

A masterclass in a high pop/popular operatic reworking of the uber middle of the road catalogue. Currently an online cult favourite. Casey tackles material from the stage and some pop standards including "Yesterday" and "Bridge Over Troubled Water." She is backed by a flowery and note perfect pianist. Elsewhere we get enough in the way of other instruments to keep the arrangements interesting enough to sustain the album, and sympathetic enough to allow her ostentatious warbling to soar and sweep around the melody line. It is restrained, respectful to the vision of the various composers, and totally predictable in the context of low key/privately funded albums of well-known material. Casey's belated cult status revolves around one, hitherto unmentioned, aspect of this release.

All the lyrics are sung in Esperanto, the well-meaning linguistic experiment that sought to unite the population of the planet in one single spoken tongue. So, Paul Simon's classic "Ponto Trans Akvo Storma" is track two and if you want to check out Lennon and McCartney's most covered song, you should find one of the internet homes of this album and aim for track five: "Kredis Mi." The present authors would respectfully suggest the best performance, allowing Ms Casey to act as well as sing, and truly inhabit the material, is probably "Venu La Klaun" ("Send in the Clowns). It is nothing like Judy Collins' hit version, but in a world of very personal interpretations of this song, nobody else sounds like Alberta Casey.[*]

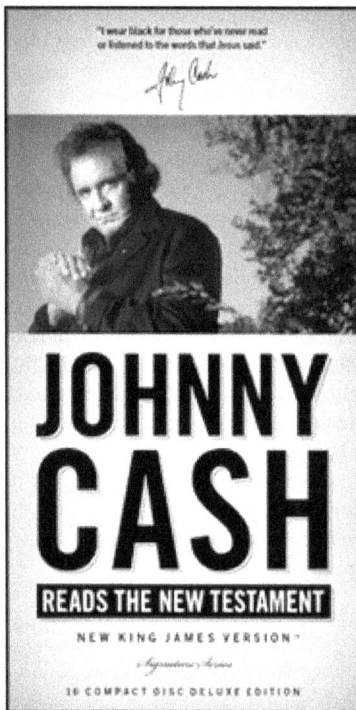

Johnny Cash:
Johnny Cash Reads the Complete New Testament
(Thomas Nelson, 1990)
What? The Man in Black recounts to story of the Son of Man.

Running around 19 hours and delivering exactly what it promises on the cover, this complete, unabridged reading of the King James' version of the New Testament was originally offered on 14 cassettes, retailing around the $50 dollar mark in 1990. Cash's warm baritone, and slow and steady delivery gives a folksy and honest feel to the greatest story ever told.

But, it is unaccompanied, and that is a long time in anyone's company; even the totally committed, convivial and companionable Cash.

Subsequent CD and DVD reissues have kept the work in print, the latter also offering some visual extras including a slide show. Cash is an excellent narrator offering a clear diction without much attempt to disguise his original accent, and achieving the whole thing through a slow, deliberate and accomplished telling of a story he clearly feels personally.

As a personal act of faith in a career low-point, the recording of the work had a meaning to Cash that intrudes on his telling of the story and makes for a personal and intimate feeling.

YouTube, and a few other online sources, still offer copies of the original television commercial with Cash, in black tie, laconically talking about his motivation to record the New Testament before a rapid fire sales voice takes over, offering a $10 reduction on the usual retail price.

---

* Bizarrely it was one release we couldn't find a cover image for.

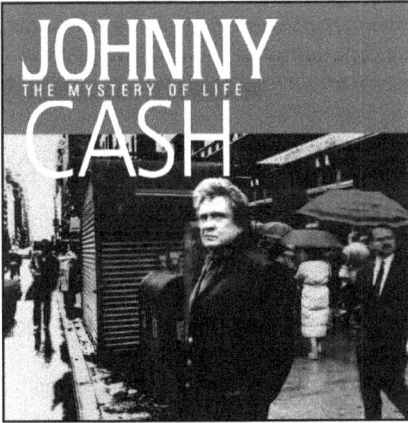

Johnny Cash:
The Mystery of Life
(Mercury, 1991)
What? What if…?

A few of the entries in this book amount to great "what if…?" moments in well-chronicled careers. What if…for example: America's Hat Trick had spawned a top ten hit single, would the band have followed its more esoteric path towards their own version of Hotel California? What if…Johnny Cash and the Mercury Label had gelled well enough to reinvent him successfully? Cash's stay on the label ranks as the sorriest stop in a history of labels that all got greatness from him, and presented their own version of Cash. Sun's early recordings are rightly regarded as classics and Cash's tenure at Columbia lasted long enough for a number of great recordings and re-inventions, including his live prison recordings. The relative failure of Mystery of Life marked the end of a short stint at Mercury before the American Recordings series with Rick Rubin re-invented and re-launched Cash to a hugely successful final series of albums.

In the mid-eighties Cash and Columbia were getting on badly and when a self-parody song: "Chicken In Black" (in which Cash's brain is placed in the head of a chicken) proved more popular than his serious material Cash was convinced to jump ship to Mercury. Cash's genius was essentially simple, and he never lost the touch of presenting the situation of the ordinary man with the extra-ordinary challenge, so his public appeal always remained. Getting the right production and right songs to update that image and keep Cash selling records was the challenge. In 1987 Mercury set about presenting a more rock sounding Cash, making the guitars a little harsher, gathering material that played on his maturity, but also presented him as insightful on the problems of a new generation. Chart-wise it didn't work and by the final throw of the dice: Mystery of Life, there was resignation on both sides. According to Cash's (1997) biography, Mercury pressed a mere 500 copies of this album.

Mystery of Life is well short of a classic and the original ten tracks include re-workings of earlier songs – "Hey Porter" and "Wanted Man" – elsewhere this is Cash presented as was John Wayne in True Grit: old, wise and apparently out of touch (the cover features a blurred shot of Cash on a street; the singer is presented in black and white, the busy street in vivid poster colours, the passers-by apparently indifferent to Cash's presence). Like True Grit Wayne, Cash is offering his wisdom with a sense of gravity and isn't above being able to laugh at himself and his history. But, he is serious about what he knows. There are no apologies for putting God centrally in the lyrics and the song shared with Tom T. Hall – "I'll go Somewhere and Sing my Songs Again" – is an affirmation of faith in the magic of music. Had Mercury succeeded in placing Cash as an elder statesman, drawing on his rock 'n' roll roots, channelling a simple but slightly updated version of his best country music and pushing God further up the lyrical agenda, it is likely the end of his career would have still been high profile; but hugely different to the re-invention master-minded by Rick Rubin. Mercury's best-shot at this and – probably – the best song he cut for them in four albums was the single taken from this album. "Goin' by the Book" is a non-original but Cash is all over it to the point it is his song and his message. With a chugging guitar, rock style solo and a clear ear on the mainstream radio territory then welcoming back the likes of John Fogerty "Goin' by the Book" is an apocalyptic vision of the end-times about to engulf us. The Book of Revelation condensed to a little under three and a half minutes and delivered with the brusque baritone of an unapologetic evangelist willing to save us, but unwilling to compromise. Buried in a patchy album produced at the end of a tetchy stint on the label that got the least from him, the handful of gems here have yet to force a re-evaluation of the least regarded period of a great career. But

"Goin' by the Book" – for one – had the potential to take him somewhere else before the end. And, it would have been a journey some would have welcomed.

David Cassidy:
The Higher They Climb The Harder They Fall
(RCA, 1975)
What? Concept work from little-regarded seventies popster occasionally hits the highest heights.

Cassidy continues to cut a strange figure in music history. The case against him lines up some powerful evidence: lead singer with the blatantly manufactured Partridge Family, a pop version of the all-American single parent family and purveyors of a stupendous stream of slushy ballads and needless rehashes of pop standards. Cassidy's hugely successful solo career started with the same fodder, before diversifying into competent if hardly earth shattering rockers, and some self-penned material. The case in favour of Cassidy also musters some credible evidence, an Emmy nominated actor (though not for The Partridge Family), a respected and honoured stage performer and – at his height – holder of the record of the most active members of a fan club at one time, (bigger even than Elvis at his height). He briefly craved serious standing as a rock musician and – once his pop career had been buried – made a strong attempt to achieve it on the back of three albums with RCA Records. This, the first of the trio, remains a genuine pop/rock curio. A concept album, apparently charting the rise and fall of a pop star, its allusions to Cassidy's career are obvious. To its credit The Higher They Climb… has a narrative that is easy to follow and packs some banging tunes. The backing band include a couple of Beach Boys and a stack of mid-seventies country rock names, in other words those usually seen hanging in the bands of Joe Walsh and Jackson Browne. Their participation was assured since most of these people knew and respected DC, and shared his ambitions. When it works, the album works surprisingly well, opening with 'When I'm a Rock 'N' Roll Star' a self-penned Cassidy composition. It also packs a trio of pop/ rock standards: "Be-Bop-A-Lula," "I Write the Songs," and "Darlin'" into the first side of the old vinyl release, as Cassidy charts the rise of his semi-autobiographical self before introducing a trio of Bee Gees' style cod-disco numbers on the second side, broken up with an ultra-strange spoken word track and a gentle country rocker.

To Cassidy's credit, he sings and plays it like he means every second, and strives like hell for credibility. But, that's also the problem. The spoken word "Massacre at the Park Bench" features a tramp and a washed up pop star debating life's cruelties, the tramp having discovered a sob story in the paper about the fall of 'Da......iddy' (there being a hole in the middle of the column.) It doesn't take a genius to figure out the moral from this point on, revealing the strange balance of the concept album. It's almost as if Homer's Odyssey has been reworked by the makers of glossy seventies pop magazines.

Whatever the intention, the critical backlash was ferocious, generally spun into variations on the theme of: "the harder he tries the more he flops." Cassidy's music career was finally revived to some effect with less serious adult pop, placing him somewhere between the schmaltz of Barry Manilow and the sexy cool of George Michael, in the mid-eighties. For fans of items like The Turtles' Battle of the Bands or Todd Rundgren's Faithful, collections in which the artist changes personality and sound from track to track, Cassidy's odd, obscure and terminally ambitious mid-seventies effort has proven a fruitful little find.

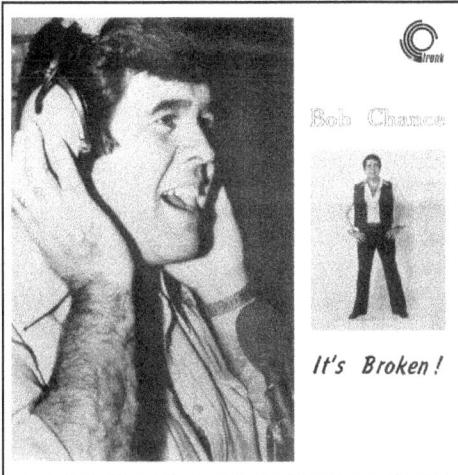

Bob Chance:
It's Broken
(Morrhythm Records, 1980)
Homemade hokum of the highest order.

Basically, another of those languishing in the gutter and dreaming of the stars efforts from an under-appreciated auto-didactic genius; subsequently re-discovered, re-evaluated and revived online. Chance's 1980 album earned a 2012 reissue on Trunk Records, including a vinyl release. In the 32 years since its original unleashment the seven tracks and little more than half an hour of music on offer gradually earned the kind of cult following that breeds interest. Of all the praises heaped on Chance's mangled menagerie of styles DJ Shadow's pithy trio of words: "hairy forearm disco" may well be the best place to start. It's Broken remains riveting largely because each nugget and nuance of musical intent makes plain its aim but often spends its duration hinting at something else entirely. The album wears its tinny production and moments of limited musical ability well because the lyrical flourishes, blasts of solo instrumentation and Chance's middle-of-the-road/man of the people vocalisations give it the kind of hokey, hominess that has left listeners loving his efforts, even when they're also laughing at the quantity of musical cheese on offer.

Chance clearly fancied himself as a pop star in a very mainstream sense. "Brown Skinned Girl" and "Honey Lips" which open the proceedings are hook laden toe tappers, the first an up-tempo peon to a dark skinned woman, the second a sugary sax-drenched slice of young-innocent-love ballad that wears its fifties roots on its sleeve. Cuts five and six – "I See Her" and "Colors" - repeat the formula touching on a style of gleeful and unrepentant sunshine pop that makes The Osmonds sound muscular by comparison. It's well into Archies and Spanky and our Gang territory. Settled around the scarier moments of the album these pop gems give some credence to Johnny Trunk's assessment of It's Broken as "a touch of Giorgio Morodor, a bit of The Beach Boys and a sprinkle of Glen Campbell as a serial killer."

The disco moments cascade out of the speakers in the extended workouts of the title track, a bizarre exercise in down the line disco beats, minimal vocals and a lengthy slabs of instrumentation including a competent guitar solo mixed with mystifying restraint. The closing "Jungle Talk" is entirely instrumental, presenting a choppy near-dance percussion and layered instrumentation all noodling away in a collision of cod-disco, cheesy light entertainment and production genius. The Tarzan call that erupts well inside the final minute of "Jungle Talk" is – probably – the moment you know you're listening to Chance's unique talent and not some random demo lifted from a cassette in Todd Rundgren's car. And then there's "The Van Man," a cautionary tale warning against the activities of a roving sexual predator; apparently sincere despite its cheerful tempo and catchy hook. The song earned a place in the celebrated 365 Project's online repository of audio strangeness. Given the competition from the rest of Bob's output "The Van Man" had to be special to make the 365 cut and it does, indeed, deliver the show-stopping moment to anchor this album. Having described the sleazy modus operandi of the title character, Chance focuses on the action taking place in the van and delivers a killer line: "Oh no, the adult toy!!" in a voice both horrified at the sexual predation and still aiming for the wholesome musical middle-ground of The Carpenters. Whether his original hand-written lyrics had a double exclamation mark isn't clear, we think it's justified for a moment so far beyond satire it marks It's Broken out as an undisputed member of the outsider music club, and a singular delight which – like many of its bedfellows in this book – defies imitation.

Sheila Chandra and the Ganges Orchestra: This Sentence is True (The Previous Sentence is False)
(Shakti, 2001)
What? Fullest flowering of a slew of experimental vocal works.

Best known as the vocalist of Pop/Asian band Monsoon, Chandra gradually moved from overtly commercial music to a unique, experimental and frequently spell-binding series of works concentrating on solo vocal and occasional drone accompaniment. Cutting three albums for Peter Gabriel's Real World label she developed this approach into a minimalist mix she could perform as a solo artist, with backing tapes where necessary. This Sentence is True takes things a stage further with The Ganges Orchestra providing the instrumental agility and inventive qualities to respond to Chandra in a series of pieces that exist somewhere in the vicinity of ambient works, experimental songs and tone poetry. Chandra's voice is used in a range of settings. She talks (with heavy treatment on her words) on "Not a Word in the Sky" whilst the orchestra hold a slowly shifting pattern around her vocal. "Sentence," by contrast, has an obvious debt to religious intoning and Chandra's Asian roots. "Abonechronedrone 7" has Chandra and the orchestra providing a defining work in her journey into drone experiment and varying vocal styles. Running for over 15 and a half minutes this is an iridescent meditation within which the various sounds interweave and slowly shift to hypnotic effect. "True," by contrast, explores a more traditional form of religious devotional singing and the opening "This" is heading into the more experimental end of synth-pop, albeit with Chandra intoning and providing a lead melody rather than attempting to sing in a traditional style before an Asian flavour takes over in the backing.

As a start in exploring the canon of a truly experimental and uncompromising talent This Sentence… is probably the best demonstration of the range and diversity of what Chandra has achieved on her unique journey.

Chinga Chavin:
Country Porn
(Country Porn Music, 1976)
What? Full-on seventies cheese, political incorrectness the way it used to be!

Not so much in your face as sitting on it, Chinga Chavin's most celebrated work turns in the aural equivalent of the big-breasted brainless-scripted seventies porn-cheese that now enjoys cult appreciation on the back of its collision of inept talent and incredible ambition. Porn was innocent, in its own way, back then. Pun-strewn, cheeky and not greatly given to depicting sex the way real, or really perverted, people actually did it.

Chavin's take on his country lyrics stakes out the same territory and packs titles to kill for: "Talkin' Matamoros First Piece O' Ass Blues," "Cum Stains on my Pillow," "Sit, Sit, Sit (on my Face)" and "Dry Humping in the Back of a Fifty-Five Ford" tell you pretty much all you need to know. You will find country music buffs who take this whole caper to task on the basis that the playing is far from brilliant. That's hardly the point. Sure, it's straight down the line Merle Haggard style simplicity with clear lyrics, horns, pedal steel and strings entering and leaving on cue, and yer man Chavin out front shooting from the hip and intoning the whole message with a straight faced, no none-sense air. Then again, he lets rip with an impressive take on a ranting southern preacher on "Cum Unto Jesus (A Sacred Tune)."

Not for the po-faced, or lovers of intense and deadly serious country music, and unless you get lucky it is possible that the current asking price for the 1992 CD reissue will also wipe the smile off your face. But, if you can hunt it down, Country Porn still packs a hefty load.

Richard Cheese:
Aperitif for Destruction
(Surfdog, 2005)
What? Loungecore reimaginings of hardcore sounds

If you're unfamiliar with the undisputed genius of Richard Cheese (Dick Cheese: geddit?) then a couple of sentences here will explain everything. Cheese's stock-in trade involves cocktail jazz reworkings of hardcore anthems and rock standards; occasionally amended for added comic effect.

His vocals are assured. He carries the cheery nightclub singer comic persona to perfection and most of his tunes present his performances against a tight cocktail jazz backing alternatively swinging and holding back. Cheese albums mix and match the new and old to perfection and Aperitif for Destruction is arguably the best mix and match job in the Cheese catalogue.

Sixteen stonkers line up as follows: "Me So Horny," "People Equals Shit," "Welcome to the Jungle," "Brass Monkey," " Let's Get It Started (i.e. a re-working of "Let's Get Retarded"). " Man in the Box," "Been Caught Stealing," "The Girl Is Mine," "You Oughta Know," "Enter Sandman," " Sunday Bloody Sunday," " We Are the World," " Do Me," "American Idiot," "Add It Up," and "Somebody Told Me." It might be the same joke from beginning to end but Cheese's timing is perfect so each song offers some twist on the original performance that suggests he listened hard and put in the effort to make his version memorable.

For the most part Cheese's ability to amuse without offending the original fans holds up though his version of Nirvana's "Rape Me" (featured on another album: The Sunny Side of the Moon) does announce the song as "one for the ladies."

Aperitif for Destruction opens with one of Cheese's best performances; his take on Slipknot's "People Equals Shit" is done in a cheery and accessible manner and you'll know a few seconds into Cheese's swinging delivery of "Come on, motherfuckers, yeah yeah…" whether it's your kind of joke, or not.

The one anomaly here – Michael Jackson/Paul McCartney's "The Girl is Mine" – fits in well when you realise the staged – "I'm her forever lover" – argument at the end is carried out between Cheese and (apparently) Professor Stephen Hawking.

Chimes of St. Dormition Monastery:
Chimes of St. Dormition Monastery
(?, 1991)
What? Ermm…very appealing.

We are not seriously suggesting that everyone motivated to wander these pages in search of audio thrills actually tracks down and digests every note of this 12 track tour of the varied peals and solitary sounds of a the bells in a specific Russian Monastery, as recorded in 1991. However, we are using the album to make two important points about all such recordings. Firstly, the world is awash with strange and sincerely meant recordings of any and every noise you might ever desire to hear. There's an obvious appeal (okay, we promise, no more of those puns!) for church bell recordings because lovers of the sound know and appreciate the variations from one belfry to another. A number of such recordings have done sterling work, selling to this specialist market and generating the cash to sustain the very bells featured on the recordings. The second point worth making is that the many field recordings, within which one church, one nature reserve etc. is captured in various guises and edited into some semblance of a varied long playing recording, have long been a staple of thrift/charity store bins. Some of those consuming them have employed sampling equipment to rework the original sounds into guises their original owners couldn't have imagined. To ignore the existence of this market in a book that aims to chart eclectic albums in all their forms, would have been an injustice. Even a cursory Google will show you a plethora of places online offering mp3 samples and knowledgeable comment with regard to church bells, each with their own story. The particular obscure eastern bloc gem discussed here is an object lesson in varying moods and textures, the mournful "Chime on Carrying-Out the Cross" being a particular highlight and proof, if it were needed, that an instrumental featuring only bells in a belfry can still hold a narrative. There's another story regarding the way this album made it to the authors of this book after being donated by an individual who had acquired whilst on a trip from Kent to Russia, a trip he undertook to facilitate a deal whereby people in Dartford would liaise with those in Russia so the English could teach the Russians a thing or two about refrigeration! But, that's one for another book.

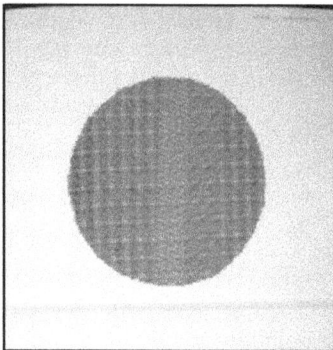

Henri Chopin:
Cantata for Two Farts and co
(Radiotaxi, 1997)
What? Concrete poetry master; compiled.

Excuse the indulgence here but many years ago now one of the authors of this book (Neil) found himself on a few occasions in the company of an unassuming Frenchman. He was convivial but said little and the encounters passed quickly. It was years later, reading the hyperbole in a mail-order catalogue of outsider music that Chopin's works came to Neil's attention, were duly bought and have been treasured since. Chopin's complex history includes losing two brothers to the German army during the war and a career spent immersed in a dizzying welter of avant-garde activities; organising, creating and working in writing, graphic design, film and a range of other media. In 2008 Chopin's obituaries focussed on the concrete poetry for which he was most famed and four of his best and most celebrated works make up this hard-to-find album (the whole collection is – however – easily sourced on ubuweb).

Chopin's work frequently started with sounds disregarded by all others: involuntary vocalisations, the smallest sounds made by the human body, the playful noises generated by manipulating the throat... His work also took on board the increasing sophistication of tape-recorders with delay, echo, mixing and the like and frequently wore its radical political intentions as a badge of honour. "Cantata For Two Farts and Juan Carlos 1" which opens this collection is a good example "marked primarily by a series of derisions and percussions" and fairly blatant in its disdain for Spain's political history, the sounds pop and spit in the speakers as the piece develops. It is physical performance if only because the listener can never escape being reminded that the main sounds come from one human voice. "Throat Power" – a 1974 work that remains amongst Chopin's best-known – opens the second side and spends a little over ten minutes exploring a range of sounds made with the human throat and tape effects, including bursts of feedback.

Cantata for Two Farts is as good a sampler for Chopin as you are likely to find. The will to explore previously unmapped territories of sound and create works of visceral strength and artistic endeavour is really the point. Studio trickery in the present age can easily replicate the sounds Chopin developed through painful trial and error and – whilst he may well shudder at the comparison – some of the wonder on show for your ears puts Chopin in similar territory to other mavericks like Spike Jones; their shared purpose being a cinema of sound and work to challenge mainstream opinions and stand strongly on its own merits. Then again, Chopin sounds nothing like Spike Jones.

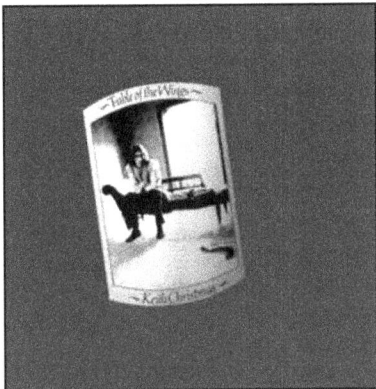

Keith Christmas:
Fable of the Wings
(Polydor, 1970)
What? Most complex early offering from British Psych folkie.

There are enough of the right names on Keith Christmas' CV to make his general absence from round ups of "best ever" folk and roots from the seventies something of a mystery. Christmas plays on Bowie's Space Oddity album and his touring schedule behind his first three albums Stimulus (1969), Fable of the Wings (1970) and Pigmy (1971) included opening slots for – amongst others - The Who, King Crimson, Frank Zappa, Ten Years After and Roxy Music. Christmas' style shifted during this period and Fable of the Wings is easily the most complex and demanding of his early releases. There is enough attention paid to arrangements, production and simply letting the songs breathe to allow Fable of the Wings to stumble sporadically into jazz and progressive territory. Christmas' control and strength in his high pitched vocal holds everything together, and his varied lyrical targets give Fable of the Wings a sense of purpose and depth. "Kent Lullaby" is a reflective and intense alternative to Neil Young's "Ohio" and its gothic splashes of organ give it a suitable funereal quality. The opening "Waiting for the Wind to Rise" has Christmas' holding his own against jazzy flashes of piano, bass and drums and delivering a trademark rapid and muscular acoustic guitar over an epic lyric. Typically this gives way to a gentle folk number "The Fawn" with a simpler focus. Lyrically Christmas was never the most direct, and his opaque and lengthy explorations don't sit easily with the work of his peers. Never as self-consciously arty as Dylan or as polemic or searingly honest as the singer-songwriter crowd Christmas is – if anything – more like indie and 21st century roots songwriters in his elliptical and complex lyrics. You often get the gist of the stories but key facts – like exactly who he is singing about – remain obscure. Christmas also has a sharp wit and some of his songwriting – though not a huge amount here – is informed with touches of humour. "Robin Head" – which recasts Robin Hood and his gang as out and out stoners - from Brighter Day (1974) remains something of a cult favourite. By contrast, Christmas' wit on Fable of the Wings is more a case of some rapid and barbed broadsides. His acoustic guitar work on "The Fawn" and "Fable of the Wings" is exemplary and the musicianship throughout is of a high standard, one of the reasons – maybe – why the album boasts only seven cuts and the majority tail off into some element of lively jamming.

Gene Clark:
No Other
(Asylum, 1974)
What? "Cosmic country rock."

No Other is a perennial performer in those lists drawn up by music writers about "best of" this or "most overlooked" of those. Electra Asylum spent years nurturing talents – like Judee Sill – capable of drawing on widescreen vision of the United States. The label achieved a fusion of sorts with regard to a vision of American national myths and contemporary country rock with The Eagles' Desperado (1973) and Hotel California (1976). No Other exists somewhere between the pair of these. It looks backwards both in terms of referencing country music, and mourning the loss of a natural environment: "have you seen the, The changing rivers, Now they wait, Their turn to die…"(from "The Silver Raven"). It also draws enough from soul and rock to anticipate the blurring of country rock boundaries that would occur massively in the wake of Hotel California.

No Other digs as deep as the reflective ruminations of Asylum contemporaries like Jackson Browne but frequently wears its intelligence and spiritual seeking very lightly. The title track, "The Strength of Strings" and "The Silver Raven" in particular flow by on effortless tunes that sugar the soul searching in lines like: "When the stream of changing days, Turns round in so many ways, Then the pilot of the mind, Must find the right direction" (From "No Other"). The individual tracks veer into light soul, old-style country licks and all the standard reference points of country rock but – as the liner notes in the CD reissue consider – this is frequently in the territory Gram Parsons aspired to visit. A realm he termed "cosmic country rock." At the culmination of the original album "Lady of the North" takes a haikuesque journey from living in the moment to linking individual experience with the elements, throwing in the odd metaphor along the way. Clarke – probably – produces the best lead vocal performance of his career on this cornucopia of country rock brilliance and the shit-hot session crew assembled – including the likes of Joe Lala, Craig Doerge, Lee Sklar and Russ Kunkle – all rise to the challenge, making No Other an embarrassment of riches. Of Clark's former Byrd-mates only Chris Hillman is on hand; Hillman's mandolin on "From a Silver Phial" is a minor highlight on a collection bulging with good playing. The obvious problem that held this collection back from widespread appreciation is its ability to vary the sound and style from song to song such that it never sounds less than excellent, but it doesn't easily tick any one stylistic box. No Other is a solo album in the true sense of the word; a collection of observations, insights and attempts to achieve a perfect fusion of feeling and musical form from song to song. All of which contribute to an insight into a complex and highly creative artist at the peak of his powers.

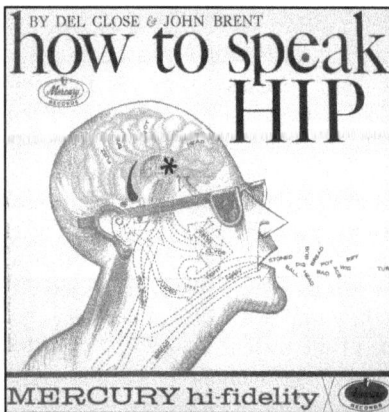

Del Close and John Brent:
How to Speak Hip
(Mercury, 1959)
What? Linguaphone's lost opportunity turns to comedy gold.

Like much good comedy How to Speak Hip takes a decent joke, milks it to perfection and gets out before outstaying its welcome. The joke here is that How to Speak Hip treats the language of the hipster jazz fan as a foreign tongue and the album sets about explaining this as it would any foreign language exploring "The twilight world of the hipster." Two sides of the original LP break down the basic vocabulary, explore its use and – by side two – offer up three "Field Trip" tracks in which the language student is out there exploring the hipster world. Geets Romo (John Brent) is our guide and opens the lesson by castigating anyone who bought the album from a standard record store for their uncool behaviour. The joke works well for two reasons: firstly, the album genuinely does a good job of getting inside hipster culture, exploring the meanings of words and explaining the values of the scene. Secondly, the interplay between Close and Brent is well-timed and has the natural conversational rhythms of two people doing the job for real. As a satire on the business of teaching a language How to Speak Hip is flawless. In its best satiric moments about jazz, it is inspired. "Cool" explores the concept and Geets Romo is challenged about the fact hipsters claim to be so relaxed but operate a complicated code of rules. Romo responds with: "If you break the rules of hip; you get put down…" before exploring the whole business of social exclusion and comparing it unfavourably to going to jail. Elsewhere the insider knowledge that explores the varied uses of the word "dig" and discusses the conversational riff is also brilliant.

It isn't until the three field trip tracks on side two that the album needs to resort to standard sit-com gags and sound effects. The field trips are – apparently – recorded with a microphone concealed in a false beard; but in Romo's first encounter with a hipster friend the microphone gets spotted, a hipster wanders into traffic (cue screeching brakes as he remains too cool to acknowledge the danger) and the obvious "let's go somewhere where we can talk" (cue door opening and sudden loud jazz music). How to Speak Hip rides some of the obvious gags well and is all the stronger because the major comedy talent on show here - (Del Close had an incredible and influential career and boasted everyone from the comedians coming up on Saturday Night Live to Frank Zappa as friends and colleagues) – takes the role of straight man and plays it to perfection.

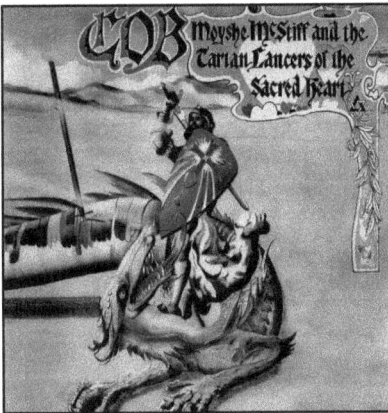

C.O.B. (Clive's Original Band): Moyshe McStiff and the Tartan Lancers of the Sacred Heart
(Folk Mill, 1972)
What? Prime acid folk with a backward glance and blissful vibe.

The Guardian's blog chronicling the 101 strangest records on Spotify says: "utter genius, an album so pure in intent it will sound like a camomile tea and cannabis scented English late summer's day for the rest of time. Delivering the perfect balance of sunset-enraptured hippie-folk idealism and LSD-stained experimentalism." The album represented the second, and by far most ambitious, long playing work by the band, and something of an about face for Palmer. Palmer was involved in the early Incredible String Band before decamping when financial success became a reality. He sought a bohemian purity and music created for its own value. The hippie vibe on Moyshe McStiff permeates everything from the overblown and epic knights and dragon cover to the mix of instruments and the sound of each track. It is a study in perfection and being true to an artistic vision. The vibe may be blissful but the individual musicians, and Ralph McTell's production, present a case study in getting it all right. A mark of a wonderful album is the impossibility of finding a way that any song or any sound could have been improved. The crafting of Moyshe McStiff shows one inspired touch after another, an expressive banjo pushing forward "Pretty Kerry" or the exposed vocal of "Solomon's Song" perfectly capturing the character telling the story. The slow and effortless beauty of "Eleven Willows" makes the song sound like an epic, despite it clocking in short of two and half minutes. The album has long been regarded as a touchstone for folk rock gold. It is heresy to suggest anything is wrong with this album but its innate genius may well be its shortcoming. Each song sounds different to the others, nobody really sounds like C.O.B. and anyone attempting to cover these songs or equal this album is asking for trouble. If you come a cropper combining drones and banjo on the same album and the world will never forget. C.O.B.'s strongest supporters are those who know, and love, their acid folk. As a rite of passage Moyshe McStiff and the Tartan Lancers of the Sacred Heart is the sonic equivalent of that first sip of a fine malt whisky. Those convinced, find a delight fit to be savoured for years to come.

Miss Pat Collins:
The Hip Hypnotist
(Warner Brothers, 1968)
What? Kitsch classic of highest order!

The hitherto unmapped twilight world between Timothy Leary and Eartha Kitt is explored over two sides of vinyl in an album that continues to defy satire, or categorisation. The concept is clear enough, a hypnotist for a hip generation, offering an alternative to psychedelic drugs or eastern religion. Indeed, Miss Collins lays it bare in the opening seconds: "Let's turn on, by that I mean the power of the mind...how to have a great self-image, without the use of anything else," this from the opening 13 minute epic exploring a trance like state of self-hypnosis, positive thinking and creative visualization. This opening cut, "Turn on" comes with a loose, hip jazz, backing mixed well behind Collins' instructions. Collins has enough echo on her voice to provide a vaguely trippy feel and if she stumbles over the lines, occasionally sounding hesitant, it only adds to the ramble/rapping quality suggested by the jazz. So far, so good. The identity crisis arrives with storm force once the singing starts. "Imagination" (the second track) is, just about, in tune with "Turn on" but by the third cut Collins is giving it a tinkling piano, high drama, old trouper take on "I Only Have Eyes For You." There's a brief spoken ramble introducing the song, making a vague connection with the vibe of "Turn on," but, in the opinion of the present authors at least, she's fooling nobody. "I'll See you in my Dreams" follows, by which point it's more hip-operation than hip territory, but just when all hope appears gone a high-camp cavort through "I Think I'm Going out of my Head" puts a truly transcendental quality back into the tack. And, we salute the ham-handed slinkiness that sees "You Stepped out of a Dream" as the correct closer. This is kitsch of a remarkable resilience, capable of surviving decades without any dimming of its original lustre. The Hip Hypnotist is so sure of its unique combination of appealing to an intuitive and hip market, whilst simultaneously beating them over the head with a massive stick so they get the marginal relevance of show tunes to the general message of self-help, we feel sure it will be hunted down and loved by sound hounds for many years to come.

Comets on Fire:
Blue Cathedral
(Sub Pop, 2004)
What? Difficult third album makes a virtue of achieving a difficult goal.

For all its out-there, alternative, self-indulgent chic this outré epic packs the riveting tension of many famed outsider classics, like Hawkwind's Space Ritual or The Boredoms' Super æ, in presenting fleeting seconds of randomly assembled sounds, forever threatening to disappear into its own indulgence and still emerging over its full-length as a supreme achievement of ambition and well-honed talent. Its predecessor – Field Recordings From the Sun – was an unrepentant psychedelic attack seeking to take no prisoners. A fleeting exposure to the heavy guitar riffs and vocal delays of "Whisky River" might suggest we're back in the same territory. But with additional members, liberal sax breaks and – shock, horror! – delicate moments of melody, Blue Cathedral is WAY more than that. As All Music Guide put it: "One of the most captivating things… is how it weds the band's garagey MC5 meets Hawkwind attack with a more textural, spacious approach that includes keyboards up front much of the time -- as in organs and pianos adding some Ummagumma-Atom Heart Mother-ish Pink Floyd sounds to the cauldron."

First half-decade Floyd are a touchstone, especially when a track like "Pussy Foot the Duke" wanders into wistful territory without suggesting for one second it is also wandering anywhere near the mainstream. Blue Cathedral references sonic territory more usually inhabited by the biggest selling prog artists but seldom sounds like a sell-out. For starters a gem like "Organs" runs well short of two minutes whilst the closing blunderbuss, "Blue Tomb," is a tad over ten minutes. They certainly weren't out to do radio programmers any favours with either of those. The drenching of much of the sound in echoplex (in other words delays and looping) also makes for an uncompromising state of affairs, even when the music segues into the dreamy territory visited in the middle of "Wild Whisky," with its blissed guitar and Atom Heart/Meddle… Floyd vibe. The fact that two of the eight tracks on offer name-check whisky may also be a sign that nobody involved sought a soft option. Blue Cathedral ranks with Steven Jesse Berstein's Prison as a challenging but ultimately very accessible Sub Pop triumph.

Connie Converse:
How Sad, How Lovely
(CD Baby, 2009)
What? Fifties folk songs manage collide the winsome and worthy in a compelling collection.

Rediscovery of lost tapes has been a feature of outsider and obscure music for years. The internet has allowed long forgotten artistes of every hue to revive careers or, in some cases, belatedly start them. Whether any of this was ever known to Elizabeth Eaton "Connie" Converse, remains a mystery. 17 of her recordings finally saw a public release in 2009, over 35 years after a depressed Connie, troubled by ill health, had written letters to those closest to her, packed her belongings into a her Volkswagon Beetle and vanished from their lives. Her fate remains unknown and she would have been well into her mid- eighties if she ever encountered a CD copy of her recordings.

Born in 1924, Connie was one of Pete Seeger's generation of folkies and, briefly, recorded and performed in New York in the 1950s. Her minimal finger picking, spartan recordings and clear diction make for work, both traditional and revolutionary in the most understated way. Connie's concerns are happiness in the moment, traditional joys and an understanding of the needs of others. The title track of How Sad, How Lovely perfectly captures Connie at her best, a naturally deep voice with an effortless ascent into a slightly reedy high register floats above the basic accompaniment and on tracks like "Honeybee" Connie Betrays her bookish background and natural gifts as a storyteller (she also produces a melody with an eerie anticipation of the Velvet's "Femme Fatale").

The digital makeover was applied to two collections of tapes. Tracks culled from recordings held by Connie's brother and from a mid-fifties series of songs recorded in the kitchen of Gene Deitch, comprise the cuts on How Lovely, How Sad. Converse spent happy years working as Managing Editor for The Journal of Conflict Resolution and her songs frequently seep into a deep thinking, caring but slightly aloof academic view of life. If there is a signature personal statement anywhere on the album it may well come at the start of "We Lived Alone." "We lived alone, my house and I, we had the earth, we had the sky, I had a lamp against the dark and I was happy as a lark"

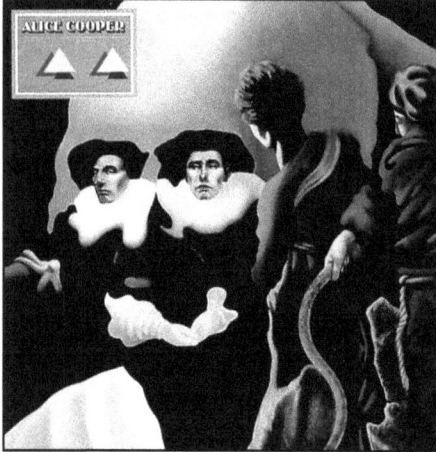

Alice Cooper:
DaDa
(Warner Brothers, 1983)
What? Somnambulant slog through major identity crisis, dressed up as art!

By his own admission Cooper can't recall making this album. Indeed, the entire eighties period from Flush the Fashion (1980) to here is a blur. Substance abuse and its attendant damage to Cooper's life meant this collection marked a three year break before his re-emergence with a solid hard rock sound on Constrictor (1986) and a true second coming when hits like "Poison" revived his career with a vengeance. The befuddling and inconsistent phase in the early eighties is perhaps best summed up in the words of sometime editor of Tribal Scream, Neil Waters: "Alice Cooper's Italian housewife period." Early eighties Cooper combined glamour and gaudiness in his appeal, frequently shot from the hip lyrically, organised things well in terms of laying on plenty of the right musical trappings and then vented sudden and, occasionally, incomprehensible passions. Never more so than on DaDa.

WTF Da Da is about, if – indeed – it is about anything, remains a mystery. In the unlikely event that Alice recovers his memory of making it, perhaps, all will be revealed. His most pertinent comment to date is to state he regards DaDa as his scariest album. Given that it is musically one of his more restrained and theatrical efforts, the scariness must relate to the lyrical content. DaDa's lyrics may have been written by an intoxicated Alice, but the individual songs make sense and contain some standard Cooper reference points and predictably acerbic couplets. "I Love America" (the only single released from the album) is an ironic appreciation of the land of free: "I love that mountain with those big heads/ I love Velveeta slapped on Wonder Bread" and "I love the bomb. Hot dogs and mustard/ I love my girl but I sure don't trust her." But Cooper's trademark dark comedy is here swathed in a near-subterranean sensibility wherein the man himself appears to be caught in the act of watching events unfold and prey to a menagerie of alternative personalities intruding on his consciousness – scary indeed. The watching is sometimes quite literal, Cooper's autobiography includes a story about the real life cocktail waitress who inspired "Scarlet and Sheba."

The album opens with a sound-scape title track fashioned by producer Bob Ezrin and the – relatively – long running times of the individual tracks allow Ezrin to repeat his epic production flurries throughout. Cooper typically nails the scenario in the opening lines of a song before allowing a character to tell another twisted and calamitous tale. "Former Lee Warner" opens with: "In an upstairs room – under lock and key/ Is my brother – former Lee" and the next track "No Man's Land" the opening couplet runs: "I got a job in Atlanta in a mall playing Santa/ Not because of any talent but because I was the only one the suit would fit."

The one inescapable theme under-pinning all of this is a sense of identity being a fluid and frequently elusive thing. If there's a key thought anywhere in the words Alice can't recall writing it may just be in "No Man's Land": "If only I could feel me...Sometimes I gotta play me/ It's really hard to stay me." Elsewhere there is one positively chilling vignette in "Pass the Gun Around", a nihilistic vision of purposeless life which touts senseless violence as a fitting solution to the endless ennui: "Pass the gun around/ And throw me in the river – let me float away."

Despite the extensive list of personnel who had something to do with the album this is really Cooper, Ezrin and guitarist supreme/producer/arranger Dick Wagner. And – no pun intended – Wagner lets rip at the appropriate moments to give this collection a truly Wagnerian feel. His guitar embellishments on "No Man's Land" and "Pass the Gun Around" in particular adding theatricality to the sound and taking the mood in the directions Cooper's words demand, but Cooper himself – apparently – can't be bothered to express.

DaDa – for the most part – exists in some sonic middle ground between classic seventies period Cooper and Bowie's more confused efforts of the mid-eighties. It is by no means an easy listen, either for you, or Alice Cooper. Chart wise it tanked almost everywhere, and its attendant single fared no better.

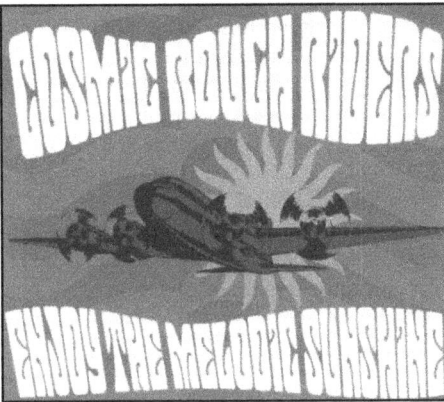

Cosmic Rough Riders: Enjoy the Melodic Sunshine (Poptones, 2000)

What? Blissed out psyche-pop from the golden period of the turn of the century and the hotbed of trippy psych that is Scotland.

Technically speaking this is a compilation; culled from tracks recorded on a shoestring budget and cut in a community studio in Glasgow. The original albums Deliverance (1999) and Panorama (2000) gave the band an audience and critical support way beyond the imaginings of most bands working in such limited circumstances. A one-off licensing deal with Alan McGee's newly formed Poptones label took this album to the UK charts, helped the band onto Top of the Pops and heralded the highest profile and most lucrative period of their career to date.

Basically, this is muscular but blissful psych-pop; conceived in a city more noted for hard-as-nails rock shouters. In the world of the Cosmic Rough Riders Jefferson Airplane, Country Joe, CSNY and – above all – The Byrds are the manifesto, bliss is in the moment and music is a saviour. That, crudely, is the power of this album. Enjoy the Melodic Sunshine is so gloriously in love with its own beliefs it infects listeners with its improbably inventive riffs, effortless harmonies and unstoppably cheerful vibes. "Revolution in the Summertime" is – arguably – the key to the whole concept, opening with the line "We'll have a revolution in the summertime."

There's no negotiation; it will happen, and the sight of the band performing the song, their first UK top 40 entry, on Top of the Pops underlined the point. Enjoy the Melodic Sunshine scores because it packs an album's worth of such gems onto a single disc, never lets the quality slip and – for almost the entire duration – suspends the listeners' disbelief regarding exactly when and where it was recorded. Twenty second bursts from this album would sit effortlessly alongside 20 second burst of the best Californian pscyh-pop from the founders of the form.

There are moments when the limited budget and turn of the century elements do intrude, but these are fleeting and it is a credit to the band and those helping them that Enjoy the Melodic Sunshine gets so close to perfection in bringing the feeling of a more innocent and optimistic time.

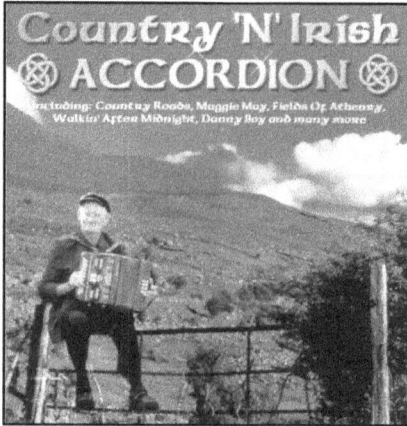

Country 'n' Irish Accordion
(Delta Music, 2003)
What? Lively, tuneful relentless grin-fest of cascading notes and familiar tunes.

We're not for one second claiming this comfy collection as a ground-breaker or – indeed – as exceptional in any notable critical way. Simply as an example of a strange musical phenomena that has passed much of the world by. Country 'n' Irish is a generic term applying itself to an Irish offshoot of country music that might best be described as a fundamentalist approach to the basic values. Where the songs have lyrics (not the case here) great value is placed on statements pledging unshakable allegiance to your place of birth, spouse and the values that make a family a strong unit. Musical experimentation remains at the most moderate levels (perhaps by including a harp on an otherwise country set up of bass, drums, guitar and vocal) and the whole scene has supported several successful performers; some of whom have exported. A brief look online at a television show like Kilkenny Country will tell you all you need to know.

This collection, by contrast, emphasises the musicality and delivers what it promises. Every mix presents a fistful of familiar tunes, blended into a medley, supported by a steady and mightily simple rhythm and moving along swiftly enough to depart before familiarity breeds contempt. This album is by a budget label in the UK but much Country 'n' Irish continues to sell physical CDs at profitable prices and this little hard-core market remains resilient, mocking the impact of downloads and shifting fashion trends.

Country 'n' Irish Accordion name-checks no performer (although much Country 'n' Irish depends on the loyal following of particular acts) and it presents less variety than many collections in this area. However, as an insight into a sound and mentality you might mistakenly think consigned to history, this collection (sounding like the 1950s but released in the 21st century) suggests the music has staying power. Country comes no simpler, but that is the point here. Some medleys blend familiar folk tunes – "Botany Bay/ A Place in the Choir/ The Irish Rover/ Farewell to Carlingford/ Lowlands Low" – and others blend more up to date (but still pretty old) standards – "Walkin' After Midnight/ I Fall to Pieces/ Crazy/ Someday You'll Want me to Want You/ Have You Ever Been Lonely?"

The Creatures: Feast
(Wonderland (Polydor), 1983)
What? Percussive pandemonium rites from Siouxsie and Budgie.

The Banshees took a brief hiatus on 1983 and Steve Severin (the band's guitar genius) sidled away to work on The Glove's Blue Sunshine with Robert Smith. Having previously turned out a charting EP Siouxsie and Budgie (already an item and eventually to marry) set about recording a full album under their moniker: The Creatures. History records they settled on Hawaii as the venue for the sessions mainly because they stuck a pin in a map of the world. Whatever, forever after the album has been associated with descriptions of humidity, sexual tension and notions of a psychedelic beach party. For the most part the album offers up layered percussion, endless echo and reverb to the point of distorting the sources of the original sounds; allowing most of the tracks to transmute into a dense percussive feast with Siouxsie's reverberating and metallic vocals wandering the jungle of sounds. The "tunes" are mainly teased out from Siouxsie's intonations and the more melodic bashes on Budgie's assorted percussion. A local (i.e. Hawaiian) choir also drop in. The opening "Morning Dawning" features the sampled sound of the sea but rapidly sets out the agenda for what is to follow. Siouxsie stretches her larynx to wail over the top of a bed of sounds including that choir, wind chimes and a steady thumping bass drum at the end of every verse. Perversely it is that solid beat that makes this most like a song, and less like some pagan ritual, and sets up a dynamic in which the percussion isn't so much driving the "songs" as providing a structure for the array of sounds – a horn here, synth there, smashing glass, handclaps, whistles…but never a sniff of guitar – all of which leaves Siouxsie free to incant, intone, wail, groan and act as something between a lead singer and a high priestess over-seeing a bamboozling ritualistic rite which never seeks to make its purpose clear. Well, either that or they legged it to Hawaii and – without too much record company interference – set about letting their joint imaginations run riot.

Songs stop and start without the usual signals and the moods vary, the original side one of the vinyl album closes with "Dancing on Glass" an explosive riot of percussion and – ermm – breaking glass, with one of Siouxsie's edgiest vocals and a comic/gothic lyric. "Gecko" follows, a slow and sublime track at complete odds with the song that precedes it, Siouxsie half-speaks/half sings a simple tale of a Gecko's progress through the undergrowth whilst Budgie teases character and melody from a marimba, and the pair are surrounded by sampled animal sounds. The same stunning volte-face of styles continues, perhaps most effectively towards the middle of side two with "Festival of Colours," featuring the Lamalani Hula Academy Hawaiian Chanters layering a beautiful vocal harmony. Siouxsie joins in – apparently mimicking them – before diverging into singing in English. Whistles and sirens go off around the vocals and the track gradually fades, as it arrived, before the skeletal and scary "Miss the Girl" obliterates the peaceful mood with minimalist precision; lining up dabs of synthesizer, percussion and Siouxsie's voice on a short, sharp story of a hit-and-run accident. It's the least sensual, least Hawaiian and most atypical cut on a very varied album that stood apart from most of what was released in 1983. So, fittingly, it was selected as Feast's only single and duly repaid the faith by charting one place outside the top 20.

Champions would subsequently –and with some evidence - claim Feast as years ahead of its time, presenting it as a slice of unfettered World Music or a cross-over between minimal classicists like Steve Reich and the mainstream. Well, maybe, but the evidence that The Creatures were that forward looking is minimal. Feast has the feel of boundless creativity caught in the moment and produced by the members of a band – singer and percussionist – usually less involved in crafting the overall sound. It's random, explosive, infuriatingly inconsistent, but still an album that surprises so long after the event and refuses to sound dated. Feast is notoriously hard to buy legally and affordably but The Bestiary compilation that mops up the early – and highest charting – efforts of The Creatures, including music described here, is a good alternative.

Quentin Crisp:
An Evening with Quentin Crisp
(DRG, 1979)
What? A tour of one the stately homos of England.

Crisp's greatest performance was his life. Born so far ahead of political correctness and gay rights; Crisp's response to discovering himself both effeminate and homosexual in the fiercely straight London of the 1920s was to work initially as a rent boy and then establish a career as a model for life drawing and painting classes for Art students. This story – from changing his name to Quentin Crisp, via the modelling to the emergence of a character full of Wildean witticisms and attitudes that set him apart from gay rights campaigners as much as they set him apart from any moral majority – formed the basis of a television drama: The Naked Civil Servant. After which things were never the same. Crisp combined occasional acting – notably playing Queen Elizabeth I in a film adaptation of Virginia Woolf's Orlando – with live work and a willingness to pick up the phone to anyone, accept any dinner invitation and regale his host (whom he expected to pay) with a virtuoso performance of anecdotes and witty retorts to questions.

That – more or less – is what you get in An Evening With… recorded live in New York (Crisp's later life saw him reside in New York and London at different times) the first of the two vinyl albums comprises a monologue on Crisp's life; tried and tested stories that have worked countless times around dinner tables and on stage, and some asides or recent observations pertaining to current (1979) events. Since Crisp's take is personal the material hasn't greatly dated. His acerbic and individual views on the process of simply being yourself remain insightful: "we'd all like to have friends, but if it means you've got to listen; the price is ridiculous." It's at such moments that Crisp - the intractable opponent of clubbable gay rights campaigners, uniting under slogans and aims - truly emerges. Delivered in a mannered, world weary, studiedly camp and artfully enunciated voice: An Evening with Quentin Crisp is a bare performance made substantial by the complexity of some thoughts, and Crisp's gradual teasing out of the way his celebrity works to sustain him. Talking about the people who seek him out as company he observes that wayward and wild young women at odds with their parents form part of this group and imagines the moment when a girl – driving her family to despair – is accused of treating the family home like a hotel, only to respond: "You don't know the half of it Mother; I've met Quentin Crisp!" The second and slightly longer vinyl album comprises "the frightening half of the programme" wherein Crisp answers questions written by his audience during the first half of the show. There are moments of seriousness here, notably in the opening minutes when Crisp discusses how his inescapable role as a social outsider helped to develop his personality. He is forever comfortably within reach of an anecdote, witticism or philosophical insight. He rails against conformity and remains hell-bent on promoting individual happiness as the only reliable happiness. One question relating to Crisp's opinion of The Queen's style prompts the riposte: "it can't be natural for the fifth richest woman in the world to adopt a deliberately middle class image" before he celebrates the flagrant pomp of previous generations and decides: "If I were part of the royal family I would be wearing my crown at breakfast."

The fierce intelligence and unrepentant individuality of a performance running to almost an hour and fifty minutes (plus a 35 minute interview between Crisp and Morgan Fisher on the 2008 CD reissue) is the main attraction. It also overcomes the thin laughter from the small venue and the age of the original recording. Crisp worked in an age before mobile phones and the internet – both innovations that would have enhanced his ability to perform his life – but his notion of self-created celebrity is still relevant in the 21st century and comes across in this recording.

Criswell:
The Legendary Criswell Predicts Your Incredible Future
(Horoscope, 1970)
What? Days of future passed.

Criswell, aka Jeron Criswell King, (1907-1982), was a crowd pleasing prediction artist. Famed for the overblown delivery of his visions, the wild inaccuracy of his work and appearances in resplendent celluloid rubbish of the highest order. It is Criswell who speaks the first words in Plan Nine from Outer Space (1959), famed as the worst movie ever made. The self-same shtick: "we are all interested in the future for that is where you and I will spend the rest of our lives" opens this long playing stream of consciousness. As the willardswormholes website notes: "Criswell was hysterical, not only for his inane predictions, but also for his awful writing and sideshow delivery. These tapes…feature 42 minutes…of Criswell going on about everything from aliens to education pills to odor TV…it's a hootenanny as Cris prophesizes everything from 'brain transplant by vending machine' to 'men decorating their genitals'…a classic drug party album of the early 70s,"

All of the above is achieved with Criswell alone at the microphone and his mellifluous vocal cadences rising to rapid-fire raptures during the most surreal passages.

If Russ Meyer imagined the Book of Revelation Criswell would undoubtedly have appeared, and in that reality his predictions of:

- Embalming by radar
- "Riot, rape and revelry" becoming the new 3 Rs
- UFOs landing at the White House on 6 May 1991
- LSD, speed, marijuana changing your sex

And

- Scientists revealing pigs once had wings, and are growing them again.

might have some validity.

To be fair to Criswell, this is about entertainment and he throws in the odd obvious joke, like working to a decent level of gravitas before predicting that nudist funeral processions will end at the police station. He is accurate about the future, (he's speaking in the 1960s and the album came out in 1970), ubiquity of vending machines in providing food for the workforce. He is spot on with regard to the possibility of cremated ashes being loaded into warheads of rockets for deployment in space. But, Criswell is a scattergun psychic with an Old Testament vision of the end times, which are all boiling seas, cataclysmic disasters and a select few faced with continuing the human story on some other world. But, there is hope because being "one with God" means you are always in the majority. Whether the "drug party" crowds enjoying this album, have ditched their bongs and followed Criswell's urging to get right with God isn't explained online.

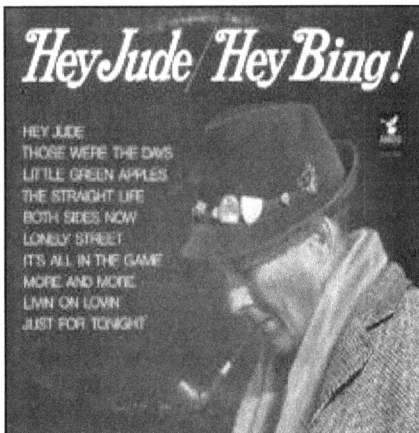

Bing Crosby with The Jimmy Bowen Orchestra and Chorus
Hey Jude / Hey Bing!
(Springboard, 1969)
What? Some of the right ingredients, very few of the right ideas.

The end of the sixties/early seventies period saw a plethora of pop-tastic ageing celebs throwing themselves on the random mercies and talents of recording studios. There was a general fear that anyone not at least capable of showing affinity with the exploding pop culture would be left behind with the dinosaurs within a few years. Most of the results show uninspired oldsters turning in passable if passionless collections of songs by the usual suspects (Lennon/McCartney, Dylan etc.). A few sublimely strange collections – like William Shatner's The Transformed Man - stand out for their willingness to push the envelope on performance, and then there are the perplexing efforts, like this. By common – and Bing's – consent this ten track collection is far from his finest work. The album title screams desperation. But, broken down into its varied parts there's no reason to think it should sound so slipshod and directionless. For starters, Jimmy Bowen's string arrangements are massive, ultra-sweet and clearly intended to do for Bing what Richard Perry was beginning to do for the likes of Tiny Tim, creating a lush listening experience and (as a welcome fringe benefit) bloating the running time of each number to reduce the amount of original songs required. The selection of material shows some intelligence. "Hey Jude" is a slow ballad with a strong sense of story behind it, so it's certainly in Bing's comfort zone. So too are most of the country and pop tunes attempted.

However, the end results are lacklustre to the point the album remains hard to track down, and mp3 copies have drawn complaining reviews about the wrong running speeds (possibly because the complainants are mistaking low-grade bootlegs for legitimate releases). Hey Jude Hey Bing! has been deemed ripe for rediscovery only by lovers of the camp, kitsch and absurd. That ironic appreciation relies mainly on the car-crash qualities of the track that gives the album its name. Crosby's sense of distance from the emotion of the lyric leaves his performance of "Hey Jude" sounding like a run-through to check the levels, and he ends the whole thing by ignoring the anthemic "Nah-nah" chorus in favour of his own trademark "Pom-pom…" It's obvious what they were thinking, not so obvious why they chose to let the results stand once they'd heard them. A few tracks are well chosen and thrown away, notably "Little Green Apples" which sounds like something Bing would have cut twenty years earlier but doesn't begin to catch fire on this rendition. Ironically, with nine largely uninspired tracks already come and gone, the closer – "Those Were the Days" – finally begins to deliver on the promise. A massive UK hit for Mary Hopkin, this old Russian song with English lyrics has a deep nostalgia that Bing – then 66 years old – can grasp and turn to his advantage. It may be too little too late by the time you get to there, but it does deliver some insight into what this album could have been. Ultimately Hey Jude Hey Bing! stumbles through three quarters of its running order with a disjointed sense of everyone in the room pulling punches and not enough engagement between the constituent parts to provide the living legend Crosby with a fitting addition to his oeuvre. Add one calamity and one fleetingly sublime take that shows another side to that displayed by a young female British hit maker and you have one of Crosby's oddest outings. Ironically (again) Bing and Count Basie cut an album of semi-hip material (including "Gentle on my Mind," "Snowbird" and "Everything is Beautiful") a few years later that did suggest the Old Groaner could cut it with this type of material.

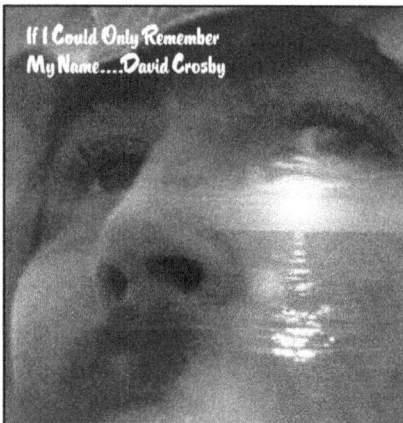

David Crosby:
If I Could Only Remember my Name
(Atlantic, 1971)
What? Stoned immaculate!

Derided by – amongst others – The Rolling Stone Record Guide for its rambling hippie excesses and distanced from current day listeners for the same reasons, David Crosby's first solo outing is still a singular creation and a touchstone for a truly different and more innocent time. Time has been fairly kind to Crosby's creation; even Rolling Stone appear to have revised their savage criticism. Today If I Could Only… stands as a curio partly because of the stellar line-up on show and Crosby's all inclusive approach to sharing the work load. The fading in and out of tracks and the fact that some of the most compelling moments are – basically – jams with improvised scat vocals gives the whole piece the feel of a stoner jam in the noblest tradition of seeking after truth and beauty. That's no derision to the songwriting.

If I Could Only… has grown in critical standing over the years because the licks and grooves give it a warmth and – for all the radical politics – a cosiness that most other skin-up sounds can't touch. If I Could Only… defies critical logic in delivering its best moments in the most incoherent moments. So, for example "What Are Their Names?" basically a rant about those running the USA and a threat to "drive right over" and "give them a piece of my mind" suffers badly from its black and white political naivety and lack of anything other than general anger. By contrast, "Song With No Words (Tree With No Leaves)"; a glorious near-six-minute groove with vocal sounds rather than words and "Traction in the Rain" a blissful meditation that borders on making sense both invert the traditional values of song-writing and win the battle. Crosby is at his best when the sublime melodies and sense of flying above everything carry the message and everything else – including lyrics – is reduced to part of the furniture. So, it's spiritual, but not religious, raging but blissful, and a solo album that only works because it's infused with a sense of community. Above all, it's in the moment with little sense that sales, or critical opinion matter. The momentary nature is best demonstrated on the beautiful closing track. "I'd Swear There Was Someone Here" is patched together from Crosby's vocalising for harmony during the sessions, forming a beautiful motet of sighs and snatches of song. Specifically, it means nothing but it says everything about the spiritual state Crosby is approaching on the better moments here.

Sandra Cross:
The MMs Bar
(Trunk Records, 2011)
What? "Bacon rolls, toasted sandwiches, bottle of pop….." But, is it art?

Sandra Cross, the artist who recorded this material during 2006 and 2007 isn't listed in big letters on the packaging as the creative vision behind this caper. Trunk Records simply unleashed the MMs Bar with the old school British Rail Inter-city logo against a plain white background. The contents of this limited edition remain jaw-droppingly simple as a compiled long-playing recorded work, but they are strangely effective.

Basically, Ms Cross travelled on Midland Mainline (MMs) making many journeys between Leicester and London over the two year period. She recorded the buffet car announcements, compiling a series in which the same basic information was conveyed at different times during the journeys, by different staff, with different presentational styles. As Trunk Records own site states: "There was no consistency as to when the announcements would start, sometimes at the beginning of a journey, sometimes they pipe up several minutes after the train had started. You'll hear that recordings have a wide fluctuation in quality based on a wide variety of voice, tone and delivery. Simply shunted together like old rail yard stock, these basic recordings represent a strangely engaging set of monologues all based on the same exciting menus and occasional safety information".

And that, more or less, is the attraction and interest that sustains the MMs bar through around half an hour of variations on the same basic performance. The staff's personal interpretations of the duty to impart information make the collection characterful, strangely comforting and very human. It is also part of history since the MMs bar has since been replaced by a trolley service. Whether it is art, in any traditional sense, or – indeed – an enlightening or entertaining listening experience is hugely debatable. The vinyl and CD copies are both in limited editions, giving the release a collectable and curious quality. The recording quality is variable but combines clarity on the main spoken passages with enough background noise to give the collection a low-fi charm. You wouldn't use it to show off your new stereo, and it packs a little too much background noise to be comfortable listening on loud headphones, but, like the original announcements themselves, it does blend comfortably into the background whilst your main attention is elsewhere.

Aleister Crowley:
1910-1914 Black Magic Recordings
(Cleopatra, 2007)
What? "Wickedest man in the world sounds… well, middle class and slightly cute.

Purveyor of black "Majick" adventurer, mystic, heroin addict and voracious sex-machine, Crowley was more rock 'n' roll than most of the self-styled head-cases who aspire to such a mantle today. He styled himself "The Beast" but others labelled him the world's most "wicked" man. Over a century after he stalked polite society like a combination of the Grim Reaper and Jim Morrison we still have his work. The man was something of a rock star, keen to embrace cutting edge technology and use it to promote his works and impress whatever passed for a "hot chick" in Edwardian times. Crowley recorded spoken word rambles, rants and mystical intonations onto wax cylinders, and the results have been made available in various packaging, by various labels, for many years now. Be warned, this entire "album" clocks in a mite under 22 minutes, includes some chants duplicated in English and Enochian (a little used occult language), and packs sound quality that leaves present day low-fi sounding crystal clear. But it certainly is yer man Crowley and some of this material is the stuff of legend. So, the cult continues and each succeeding generation takes an interest. What you get for your money is a well-spoken, sometimes ponderous, slew of rising and falling chants, fleeting references to current events, well the sinking of the Titanic was a big deal when Crowley was kicking around, and some majick rituals likely to remain incomprehensible to anyone without a working knowledge of Enochian. One label releasing the collection said: "The Beast speaks from the grave on this special collection of wax cylinder recordings packaged with full biographical liner notes…

Contains creepy intonations of black magic rituals."

Strangely, from this distance, his public school education and a certain gentle bonhomie leak out of the speakers. Crowley comes over as part mystic, part deranged genius and – frankly – fairly cuddly into the bargain.

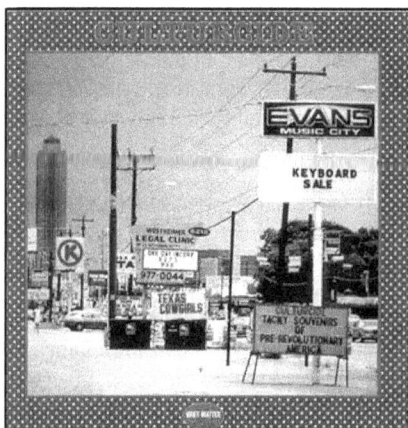

Culturcide:
Tacky Souvenirs of Pre-Revolutionary America
(No label, 1986, reissued by Grey Matter)
What? Classic rock?! These guys don't give a shit.

Culturecide are a great idea although it's questionable whether listening to this album strengthens the cause. Technically speaking, it's not an official release although tracking down some copy via a mail order list or dealer at a record fair hasn't proven too difficult in the past and the "everyone is an artist" right-on sensibilities underlying Culturecide's work have made the internet an ideal home for their oeuvre.

Culturecide state in their liner notes that: "Vandalism is the last resort of the voiceless" before copying the works of household names onto a CD and burying their celebrated tracks under a welter of fuzzed out guitar, overlaid vocal snatches and other attempts to mock the rich and famous. The copying is quite literal.

This CD includes the original versions of some celebrated hits, Culturecide simply chip in to accompany the songs as they see fit. So - for example - the track "Bruce" buries the Springsteen hit "Dancing in the Dark" under power chords from a Woolworths guitar and changes the lyrics with the subtlety of a bull rhino on speed. The Boss sings "There's something happening somewhere." Culturecide burst in with the retort "But Bruce Springsteen ain't it." That sums up the general idea.

The targets of Culturecide's wrath are all in the big league. Bowie, McCartney, Stevie Wonder and others lay down the backing for the most unlikely collaborations of their careers. Culturecide don't disappoint as they add lyrics and sounds that start at disrespectful and end up somewhere on the wrong side of the law. The messy result makes for memorable listening.

If your sensibilities lead you to see classic rock as a high-point of popular culture your brain will probably go with the original and the overall effect will be like finding yourself pinned up against a wall by an insistent nutcase with a point to prove. If, on the other hand, the experimental and bizarre grabs you…you'll find laughs and inspiration here.

Cut Chemist:
Sound of the Police
(A Stable Sound, 2010)
What? Mastermix.44axz

DJ, mixer, some-time actor, Cut Chemist released his first proper album, in the late nineties and his first studio album: The Audience's Listening in 2006. His highest profile appearances include playing a Chemistry teacher in the movie Juno, but the basic genius that allows him to select, mix and blend a perfect programme has never deserted the man.

Released in 2010, Sound of the Police mixes Latin and Hip-hop beats. Latin and African Jazz, and pours the ensuing blend over two tracks, both around the 20 minute mark. As a comment on, and tribute to, the good, old fashioned, two-sided, forty odd minute vinyl album Sound of the Police is an effortless romp through great sounds, great beats, snatches of the most random elements, and the sense of the master mixer in charge and creating in the moment. One turntable, one mixer and one loop pedal allowed Cut Chemist to concoct the whole mix live, and that is the secret to the erupting energy and invention of Sound of the Police.

Benchmarks include the likes of DJ Shadow – with whom Cut Chemist has toured – but Sound of the Police is an altogether jazzier affair than Shadow's best and it retains the capacity to move off in its own directions, with perfect timing. Witness the drum break around 13 minutes into the first cut, and the gradual emergence into a soundscape subtly altered from the grooves that preceded the break.

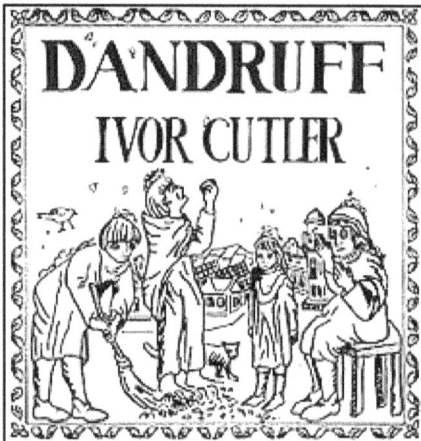

Ivor Cutler:
Dandruff
(Virgin, 1974)
What? "Never knowingly understood."

It is unlikely the world will ever agree on whether Cutler (1923-2006) was a genuine eccentric, a wilfully obtuse performer who traded on a unique style or simply an oddball who couldn't help himself. John Peel supported him with sessions and radio play, Cutler made an appearance as the bus conductor in The Beatles Magical Mystery Tour and after cutting an album for EMI with George Martin at the controls he enjoyed recording deals with a handful of the coolest British labels: Virgin, Rough Trade and Creation. Dandruff – which opened his account with Virgin – is arguably the definitive Ivor Cutler album. The usual tricks and traits are on offer in its 45 (generally very) short tracks. Very simple poems, and songs, spoken word vignettes (generally autobiographical), and a thematic link in the clear influence of Cutler's childhood in Scotland. Dandruff is the earliest Cutler album to feature snippets from the ongoing series "Life in a Scotch Sitting Room" and also features performances from Cutler's long-term collaborator Phyllis King. Cutler's trademark eccentric humour – often with a straight faced telling of some improbable tale in which a clear taboo is downplayed in favour of horror at some minor transgression of manners – is displayed gloriously in fragments like "Dad's Lapse" (wherein his father – having been outed for having sex with a polar bear - stalls for time by arguing about the location of the act) and "Three Sisters" (the recounting of favoured locations for sex of three sisters all still living at home with their parents. The sister telling the story has cold wet sex with her boyfriend on the path from their house to the outside toilet. It is uncomfortable but her parents avoid visiting the toilet during these episodes so the couple have the path to themselves).

Cutler never had anything as crass as a greatest hit but the fifth track "I Believe in Bugs" – a jaunty calypso inspired piece in praise of insects – saw live action throughout the remainder of his career, and typically went down very well. Dandruff is minimal to the point of making singer-songwriters with one instrument sound lavish. When Cutler accompanies himself on the harmonium it is typically with a few simple chords, held for a long time as his voice soars above the sound. Most spoken word tracks use no backing at all and only the "Life in a Scotch Sitting Room" pieces get near three minutes of running time; many tracks clock in well short of 30 seconds. Cutler typically communicated in phrase-length "Cutlerisms;" "Never Knowingly Understood" being a particular favourite. Much of the work here has that quality, existing at the very edge of comprehensibility, and presenting stories and ideas that would fit into a Postit note.

Dick Dale:
Calling Up Spirits
(Beggars Banquet, 1996)
What? Superb and spiritual ear-splitting surfathon!

Surf guitar never really went away but its revival in the mid-nineties marked a high-point for a sound side-lined since the Beatles and their peers stormed America. Surf pioneer Dick Dale rode the new wave as convincingly as he'd instigated the first one and garnered some strange nuggets of attention. When Dale's band cut a BBC session for John Peel there were complaints from others in the building about the noise. Bear in mind, this building was used to take-no-prisoners punk bands and the uncompromising likes of The Fall turning up to nail some tracks. As a rule, their noise levels were survivable. Dale – already within sight of his seventh decade – had more attitude than most of them.

Where others play surf guitar the same thing is something of a spiritual calling for Dale. It's an exceptional surf guitar album that includes the following in the sleeve notes: "I must tell you there was a time, that there was life, that was free from disease, free from illness, free from taxes, free from greed. Untrust was unheard of: they had only happiness, harmony and caring for their children with open hearts. Yes, they killed, but only to eat. Then the white man came…I reach out to the spirits of the indigenous ones that were here first and call up their spirits." It is this philosophy that sets Dale apart from nineties surfers like The Trashwomen (also chronicled in this book) for whom the revival was an excuse to get down, low-fi, and dirty.

Dale's mission here extends to taking the lead vocal on "Window" – which expands the message of the sleeve-note above and fades out with a didgeridoo – and to a storming cover of Jimi Hendrix' "Third Stone From the Sun" (which opens with Dale saying: "Jimi, I'm still here; wish you were." But for the most part Calling Up Spirits is surf guitarist as shaman/original. The sound is immense, some tracks start or end with the rhythm section shuffling about whilst Dale's guitar speaks out front. The tempos elsewhere – like the explosive opening on "Nitrus" – are frenetic, and the mix of the sound is muscular and clear with enough power in the drums to separate out the kit so the cymbals rattle in your ears and the tom-toms – when required – explode in the centre of your head. Dale's rattling and round lead guitar notes are his voice for most of the 13 cuts and yet none of the message of spiritual purity and a man communing with a spiritual realm is lost.

Bette Davis:
in Two's Company
(RCA, 1953)
What? "Bette had four notes to her voice, all of them bad." Vernon Duke

Official histories, and online retailers attempting to sell this album (which had a vinyl reissue in 1975 and CD release in the 21st century) will inform you that Two's Company – a musical and comedy sketch revue view – ran for 90 performances on Broadway and was cancelled when Bette Davis' health gave out and audiences (intent on seeing the living legend) stopped buying tickets because she was the show. True enough, but like Madonna's turn in the London stage in an Arthur Miller play there was a gulf of light-years between the star-struck punters and the critical reaction. Finding a critic with any musical credibility willing to praise Davis' chops as a singer has remained very hard. The fact that the quote at the head of this entry was produced by someone who loved and admired Bette Davis says everything. For all this, Davis' sporadic recording career continued over many years, contained clear attempts to produce hits, including some novelty items, and continues to excite sound-hounds with a taste for the truly different. In this context Two's Company is the one most hunted and prized items.

This is a full cast recording, so Bette is simply the star turn. But she takes the first solo lead vocal and fronts five of the 19 cuts; "Turn me Loose on Broadway," "Purple Rose," "Roll Along Sadie," "Just Like a Man" and the "Finale." From the opening notes of the first the listener is confronted with perfect diction and the kind of honking, grating flat voice that Billy Connolly (albeit referring to himself) once described as "like a goose farting in the fog." Florence Foster Jenkins and/or Mrs Miller (both featured elsewhere in this book) are useful reference points. Bette isn't as bad as them. But, she shares an apparent lack of awareness with regard to her limitations with Jenkins and a calamitous ability to destroy musical nuance and lyrical deftness with her grating warble such that her vocal numbers become exercises in audience survival, and bring comedy of an unintended kind to the show. These are indeed show tunes, with a big band in support and stories to tell. But, to put this work in context the (highly recommended) tome on celebrity songsters Hollywood Hi Fi by George Gimarc and Pat Reeder features this recording as the first entry, highlighting; "Bette's off-key hollering" and stating; "It appears that turning Bette Davis loose on Broadway was roughly equivalent to turning a cougar loose on a hamster!" They effortlessly trawl other critical opinion, like New York Times critic Walter Kerr, who notes: "It's a lot like listening to Beethoven's Fifth played on a pocket comb. You marvel it can be done at all. And five minutes is just about enough of it." Davis' own solos here amount to over five minutes, when you add the songs in which her vocals front those of the ensemble she's way outstayed her welcome.

Deep Purple:
Made in Japan
(Purple, 1972)
What? Byword for bludgeoning behemoth rock, isn't what it's made out to be.

Purple were hot to the point of inducing meltdown in 1972, topping their home chart with the sublime Machine Head, an assured collection combining instantly classic metal riffs and a production confident enough to earn the collection copious airplay in America's rapidly expanding FM radio network. With Japan – the world's second largest market for records – surrendering before the Purple juggernaut and buying every ticket for a tour, the next step was to gather the best live moments, pack them onto a double album, and unleash the thunderous results to clean up at Christmas. Made in Japan duly did the business, becoming both an instant and enduring classic of seventies metal. So, with all due apologies to the millions already initiated, it's time to make a case for its inclusion here.

It might pack blazing Ritchie Blackmore fretwork, shelf-shattering Ian Gillan screams and explosive re-workings of over half of Machine Head, but to label this a heavy metal album is to miss almost half of what is truly great about Made in Japan. Sure "Smoke on the Water" rocks out and the opening "Highway Star" is fit to run-over slow moving listeners, but Made in Japan also captures a virtuoso line-up yet to be convinced that full-on in-your-face metal is a meal ticket for life. Purple had started life on the fringes of psychedelic rock, stumbled into furious acid-rock on stage and even flirted with the infamous classical monstrosity Concerto for Group and Orchestra before crunching riffology started to swell the coffers. Live in Japan in 1972, their varied roots and disparate talents were all called into action to fill an evening. Laid bare across the original seven tracks of Made in Japan Purple are more akin to a travelling masterclass than the godfathers of the Metallica generation. Without warning "Space Truckin'" segues unapologetically into the lilting melody from Gustav Holst's "Jupiter." On the same track Jon Lord's classical keyboard wash colliding with Ian Paice's jazz drumming makes for a mash up that would still be daring in the 21st century. Other moments of indulgence and excess almost beggar belief by today's standards. Paice's drum solo – taking up most of "The Mule" – is brilliant and utterly pointless in equal measure, whilst Gillan's showpieces of perfectly matching improvised riffs from Blackmore's guitar on "Lazy" and screaming like a wounded banshee before announcing "Oh my soul, I love you baby" at the end of "Child in Time" are moments even Spinal Tap wouldn't have dared.

Made in Japan has the random firepower of early Libyan rebels fighting Gadaffi. You are never in doubt about the punches it packs, but where they'll land and what damage they'll do is hard to predict. The welcome avoidance of overdubs to clean up the messier moments, the fluffed lyrics and the elliptical stage banter, like asking the road crew to make: "everything louder than everything else," are also part of the warmth and appeal of an album that cost around $3000 to make and was only intended for Japanese release. Four decades and a few platinum discs later, this remains a good 'un.

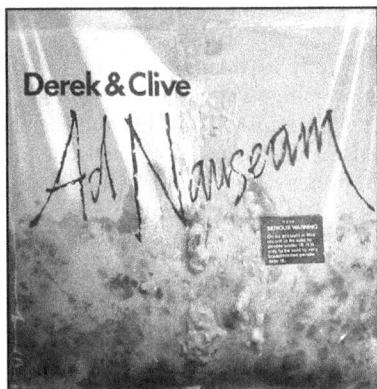

Derek and Clive:
Ad Nauseam
(Virgin, 1978)
What? Comedy duo's Let It Be.

When Rolling Stone described Let It Be as "a cardboard tombstone" they weren't deaf to the merit of songs like "The Long and Winding Road" or "Across the Universe." They were, however, mindful of the way the variable quality control betrayed a band in break up and the variable contributions of each talent to the particular tracks meant even the best moments were hollow triumphs. Cook and Moore's first two Derek and Clive albums were ramshackle and drunken affairs, sporadically brilliant and worthy of their cult status. Ad Nauseam marked a change in approach, more focussed, and boasting the longest and most surreal of their recorded duets. It also presented a personal vitriol and animosity directed from Cook to Moore that saw Moore depart during the recordings, never to return. Ad Nauseam shows the Derek and Clive masks slipping visibly. The original characters had a nominal back story as toilet cleaners and stuck mainly to their London accents. Ad Nauseam has a higher proportion of sketch based spoken word, Cook refers to Moore as "Dudley" during a vicious, and very funny, attack on British television legend Bruce Forsyth. Some of the sketches are character based, and better timed and focussed than anything on the first two albums. "Horse Racing" presents a field of runners with names like The Prick, Big Tits, Vagina and Arseole and milks the ensuing possibilities of their positions: "The Prick might just have got up in the last few strides, but I wouldn't like to put my money on it." "The Horn" is the longest and most ambitious audio sketch the pair ever attempted. Its jokes about British Prime Minister James Callaghan "that oily heap of shit" and even Margaret Thatcher and the recently deceased Pope might have dated, but the darkly comic musings on being sexually excited by everything other than your own wife are still disturbingly funny.

All of the above and many other moments of triumph come with two health warnings. Firstly, this is politically incorrect and vicious comedy to a degree that can easily give offence, much of it beyond broadcast and acceptability to this day. They are ahead of the curve in the jokes about the most vacuous celebrity television shows (the projected "Celebrity Saviours" involves crucifying famous nonentities for general entertainment). Incidentally, the "Horse Racing" track is also well ahead of the curve with its closing gag about "topless darts." Within a couple of decades British television would be screening it for real. Less easily digested these days is the misogynistic rant when Dolly, the wife of Cook/Clive, is so tardy in taking a picture of his snot trailing from the wall that he loses any chance of appearing in the Guinness Book of Records, he, therefore, decides to kick her repeatedly and intimately to become the world's best in that department. The second warning comes with sadness to fans of the duo. In the free-form and open ended duets Cook repeatedly jumps on Moore's comedic interjections, snuffs out potential ideas and hogs the narrative arc with a dominance that makes for some discomfort. He's funny, the ideas are good, but so are those he is blocking. The best moments allow the pair to work together, the snippet "Street Music" has Cook ranting punk lyrics over Moore's volatile piano only for Cook to slip into a posh-boy voice and demand his work is sent off for polishing to be made into a hit. So, they still had it, but the gloves were off. This cardboard tombstone is sporadically great comedy, and also a chronicle of a fracturing partnership.

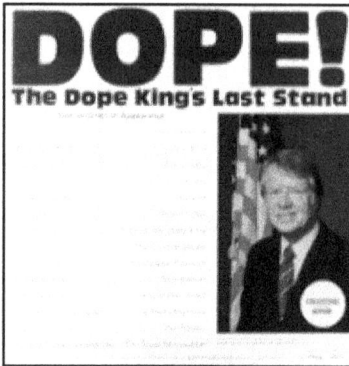

The Dope King's Last Stand:
The Dope King's Last Stand
(Cornucopia, 1977)
What? An audio drama of almost indescribable strangeness, starring Jimmy Carter!

Explaining the basics of this – mainly – dramatic/spoken word concoction is easy enough. A late seventies vintage cautionary tale designed to deter drug-taking amongst impressionable youngsters, The Dope King's Last Stand stumbles along like a surreal episode of Scooby Doo with Blaxploitation pretensions. Good battles evil, inane and – occasionally – inventive sound effects/cod-soul licks provide the scenery. The surreal narrative is cemented with a guest list of almost implausible fame and diversity. Muhammad Ali provided a similar turn on another album, a tour-de-force recording wherein he and "his gang" may be found battling tooth decay.

But Jimmy Carter was incumbent president of the USA when this bewildering blusterthon was unleashed, and that is far out. Any 21st century animated movie, and even the Muppets, would struggle to gather a vault of voice-talent to rival, amongst others: Lily Tomlin (who narrates), Arlo Guthrie, Pat Boone, Billie Jean King, Hoyt Axton and Frank Sinatra. The cack-handed dynamics of the narrative are predictable enough; good kid goes wrong, damn near poops his pants in fear, gets lecture on rights and wrongs, mobs up the good guys and wins out after the predictable showdown. So too the clunking informative messages and sound-bites as we answer those vital questions like: "What is a peddler?" and drop in the life-saving nuggets of information: "A pill head is someone who uses barbiturates."

Whether everyone in the stellar array of talent thought they were making the same album is debateable. This is barely a decade after Arlo Guthrie's dope-soaked Alice's Restaurant and the question of whether he's the only one packing a wry smile as he delivers his part has continued to tax the sound-hounds who have hunted down and cherished this bizarre bestiary of cameos. By contrast, the squeaky clean Pat Boone may well have believed this would make a difference to youngsters.

The Dope King's Last Stand certainly straddles the invisible line between well-meaning public information and Airplane-alike satire. Each blatant gag is supported by stereotyped names and sound effects that leave their subtlety at the door. As side one closes we hear "Fat Cat" on the phone, his mumbling evil being preceded by the strident opening to Beethoven's Fifth. It's doubtful whether Monty Python or The Firesign Theatre would have deployed the sonic sledgehammer as thickly as that.

The curious collision of plot, celebrities and sounds long ago made this collection a prized curio. No CD reissue looks likely but there have been mp3 files available online for years, making it clear that Chris Beyond's online comment: "This is an album that uses psychedilia to sell the idea of getting kids off drugs" is a fair summary of the consistent dramatic tension that – just about – makes this a compelling listen as well as an undisputed audio car crash of the highest order.

"Welcome drug-users to the rich man's high, cocaine. It's our luxury flight, and we'll experience a high in cocaine-energy. Cocaine is addictive at times; so our landing may be rough due to nosebleeds, destroyed membranes, high blood pressure, a few passengers may even die. But then, the trip is such fun." Classic!

Jon Downes and the Amphibians From Outer Space:
The Case
(Own Label, 1995)

What? "I don't want to learn about gender roles from Schrödinger's cat, Sexual indeterminancy's really where it's at."

A true English Renaissance Man of the margins, Jon(athon) Downes is – depending on the day of the week – a leading Cryptozoologist, author, anarchist, mental-health advocate and underground rock star. That'll do for starters, check out his Wikipedia page (which is way longer than this entry). Downes spent four years running a fan-club for Steve Harley in the early nineties and the wordy missives, complex series of hook lines, rambling narratives and treble heavy acoustic guitar chops of classic-period Harley are probably a good way into this personal and occasionally impenetrable box of delights. Throw in a bunch of prog-rock tricks and season the whole dish with fleeting references to everything from English history to the lesser trodden myths of the paranormal, and you have an album unlike much else unleashed in 1995. Elsewhere the country went mad for a Britpop chart battle for the #1 spot and Robson and Jerome outsold everyone, cementing the reputation and Svengali-pop-visionary genius of Simon Cowell. Down in deepest Devon Downes' poured out the most ambitious album of his career. Recorded over 14 months, it kicked aside earlier efforts that betrayed their hasty creation and Portastudio birth pangs.

Fittingly, Downes responded with lyrical visions fit to withstand repeated listenings and recruited a band capable of taking over when his own considerable multi-instrumental talents ran out of road. It's seldom simple, frequently self-indulgent (notably on the closing "English Heritage" with its final section entitled "Land of Dopes and Tories"). The one thing missing from The Case is any coherent sense that he is making a case for any agenda we could all follow. Indeed, it makes more sense if we assume Downes himself is "The Case." But, hell, when this insane conglomeration takes flight, it takes popular music into territory so little trodden that the ride alone is memorable. Never more so than the explosive opener "Invocation of my Daemon Brother," from which comes the pithy lyrical couplet at the head of this entry. "Daemon Brother" packs a killer hook, a blood-chilling cameo from Tony "Doc" Shiels; monster hunting legend/incurable mentalist (depending on your point of view). It also makes clear that Downes will spend the rest of the album exploring a darker side of his inner life as much as any checkable fact. And he doesn't disappoint. For the train-spotters and insatiable Googlers there are stops at paranormal legends "The Mad Gasser of Mattoon," beat writing references "Naked Lunch (There ain't no such thing as a...)" and extreme political activism "I'm on Fire" (not the Pointer Sisters dance classic or the Springsteen love-song but an exploration of self-immolation by flame). For all its worthiness and ceaseless trawling of counter-cultural fragments The Case is best experienced as a vision into the darkest recesses of the Downsian soul. He relives overwhelming teenage lust "Better Than Dying" and pours out his heart to his hero Harley "Letter to Stephen," wherein he sings: "Some things you did were wonderful, some things you did were shite, but if it wasn't for you I wouldn't be standing on stage tonight." Classic!

Shortcomings; well, for all the ambition and multi-instrumental talent on show there is still a limited production sound that fails to do justice to some of the better licks. Albums this complex demand major studios, Downes' fan-base renders that notion impossible. James Farebrother's stunning piano licks sometimes get flattened at the edges of the sound. There's also the problem of firing off the corking big-shot of "Daemon Brother" at the start meaning the remainder of the album never quite hits the heights effortlessly charted in the opening seven minutes. Plusses, hell, loads: a lyric sheet that makes for entertainment simply from reading it, enough side-swipes and obscure references to leave a listener thinking "now I get it" on the sixth or seventh run through, the glorious and honeyed vocals of Natalie Beard and Lisa Peach, wrapping themselves round Downes' rough-edged rantings with enough sexual chemistry to add an extra dimension to some of the songs and – above all – the gargantuan and insistent presence of Downes' presiding over the whole circus like a demented and slightly dishevelled ring-master[*].

The Dragons:
Bfi
(Ninja Tune, 2007)
What? Uh-oh, "best album you never heard," alert. Hang on; this is brilliant!

The world and his reissue label continue to assault us all with claims about unreleased masterpieces and woefully overlooked works of genius. Few such items – however – boast the back-story and pedigree of Bfi. It's widely accepted that Ninja Tune's first reaction on hearing the recording they'd just been offered was to suspect a scam. One track – "Food for my Soul" - from this 1970 recording had made it to a long-forgotten compilation and on tracking down the band Ninja Tune were stunned get a complete album of well-produced Californian psych-rock, suggesting – as a one commentator has put it – "something of a missing link between the Doors and Steely Dan." Far too good to be true, right?

Well, no. The Dragons are three brothers and whilst they never made it, one of their number became a household name. It's just that Daryl Dragon – AKA "The Captain" of Captain and Tenille fame – wouldn't have been doing his M-O-R audience of the late seventies any favours to revisit works like the terminally trippy "Sunset Scenery" complete with its Manzarak organ chords and eastward-looking drum solo. Bfi – meaning; apparently, "Blue Force Intelligence" – throws forth an album's worth of such pscyh-rock, most of it conveniently contained in radio friendly running times and much of it setting off in some clear direction with the intent of evoking a mood, making a point and doing what a great pop song can do. At which point layers of clavinet, organ, drums and vocals are added to give each track its own sense of identity.

Throw in lyrics that reference every west coast psychobabbling bit of cod-philosophy on offer and a production sound fit to rank with the great Brian Wilson himself and you have the blueprint for something so monumental Ninja Tune were right to be suspicious of a latter day scam. But, Bfi is most certainly the real deal and it made its full debut 37 years too late for The Dragons to get their due recognition. To be fair to those who passed on it in 1970 it is probably more Electric Prunes than The Doors, and the uneasy tension between music with one ear on hit singles and one on the trippier end of west coast psychedelia doesn't always work to perfection. But blissed-out sunshine pop joys like "Amplified Emotions" are – if anything – stronger songs today than they were when first offered up for release.

To be totally pedantic – and fair to Captain and Tenille devotees – it should be noted that the sleevenotes credit Doug and Dennis Dragon as the mainstays of the band, listing Daryl (The Captain) atop those credited as "Additional musicians."

---

* EDITOR'S NOTE: My dear fellow, I am totally overwhelmed, thank you.. JD

Dread Zeppelin:
Un-Led-Ed
(I.R.S/Capitol, 1990)
What? File under Zeppelin; in a reggae style!

S'cuse the brief indulgence but one of those behind this book (Neil) is still capable of pinning unsuspecting people to the wall and ranting passionately about the mind-blowing night he caught the tour in support of this album. Dread Zeppelin stand with the likes of Spinal Tap, Hayseed Dixie and Spike Jones amongst the best musical gags of all time. Dread Zeppelin's first album collides an overweight Elvis impersonator, (Tortelvis), with a white reggae band boasting phenomenal musical chops and commands this unholy combination to rip the piss out of the greatest pomposities in the Led Zeppelin catalogue. What would be madness in lesser hands is here concocted into an explosion in which the best gags are also the most breathtaking musical moments. Un-Led-Ed asks a lot of your musical knowledge but frequently throws in a comedy aside or a musical trick that cuts through disbelief to assault your funny bone. The band went on to develop the formula – a la Hayseed Dixie – into original material and massacring other acts. But, Un-Led-Ed remains the signature album because it takes on and trashes most of the music that locates the Zep legend.

Reggae cuffings are duly dished out to: "Black Dog," "Heartbreaker (At the End of Lonely Street)," "Living Loving Maid (She's Just a Woman)," "Your Time Is Gonna Come," "Bring It on Home," "Whole Lotta Love," "Black Mountain Side," "I Can't Quit You Baby," "Immigrant Song" and "Moby Dick" with maximum mirth and minimum mercy. "Stairway to Heaven" sidled up to be slaughtered on Dread Zep's sophomore effort 5,000,000. The sound is alive with deft musical flicks; Tortelvis' kingly inflections capture Vegas-era Elvis in all his nuanced glory. On stage Tortelvis would typically work up the crowd to perform Elvis' signature Vegas-era "claw" hand gesture. The percussion is exemplary and every Dreadster is allowed to step up to prominence in the mix. All take their turn and all shine. The comic timing is seldom less than brilliant and the resolute power of the music seldom slacks. Like the best musical gags this is affectionate in the throes of attacking, and it hits all the harder because it is so authoritative. Once the shock value has worn off Un-Led-Ed – and for that matter most of the Dread Zeppelin catalogue – is a glorious advert for its own conceit. All Music Guide describe this album as "a gag-infested tour de force where almost every dubious musical moment is safeguarded by a healthy dose of humor -- and vice versa." We concur and so – apparently – does Robert Plant!

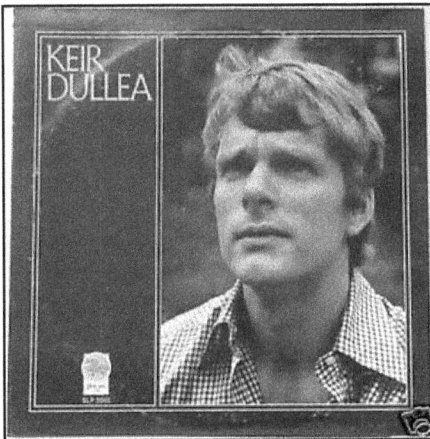

Keir Dullea:
Keir Dullea
(Platypus, 169)
What? From odyssey to oddity (with no relation to Bowie).

Keir Dullea's estimable acting career hit its highest public profile when the man starred in Stanley Kubrick's 2001 A Space Odyssey. A glance at his career credits shows him as a talent consistently in work; and all the more creditable for devoting so much time to (generally well received) stage performances. As a rule his one and only album doesn't receive major retrospective coverage when his career is discussed. It does warrant a page in the highly recommended book Hollywood Hi.Fi wherein George Gimarc and Pat Reeder describe Dullea's voice as "thinner than the atmosphere on Mars…his pitch wavers so wildly that his attempts to reach and hold notes resemble…recordings of the Apollo chimps being subjected to extreme G-forces." Had the people behind this book encountered the elusive Apollo Chimps in Agony album we could comment on the accuracy of that observation.

To be fair to Dullea, and the production crew behind his eponymous album, everyone seems aware of this. The man is frequently given the option of intoning over the lightest of light folk-rock-cum-ballady backings with sporadic instrumental licks, some harmonies and a few other random sounds being added to liven up the mix. In the smartest production move of the whole collection "A Cup of Coffee and you" is performed in a faux twenties jazz style with extended and tinny trumpet solo and Dullea sounding as if he's crooning through a megaphone; thereby masking any vocal thinness.

Other reality checks worth considering are that Platypus records – who released this – aren't exactly famous for signing the biggest acts, and a fawning website devoted to all things Keir spends much of the paragraph devoted to the album discussing the songs he could have recorded (like Simon and Garfunkel covers).

Keir Dullea is tree-hugging light hippie folk with a message – specifically in "Mother Earth" when Keir sings: "Mother Earth don't cry we love you." He generally shies away from anything already covered and claimed as a major vocal triumph by another singer, but does perform "Butterflies are Free" (as in the title track from a play in which he performed on stage – the same play that was turned into a movie vehicle for Goldie Hawn). As an insight into the kind of thesp-cum-recording-artist product that filled release schedules at the time Keir Dullea is something of an historic artefact (nothing sounds like this these days because Autotune and a range of other studio trickery has been developed to save the world from such sounds). Oddly, we'd depart from the comments of Gimarc and Reeder above (who are generally spot-on in their assessments) on the grounds that Keir Dullea has the feel of something honest and companionable and doesn't smack of the kind of desperation that saw some actors – like Leonard Nimoy – packing albums with copious renderings of high-profile tunes, originally performed by sizeable talents. Frankly, for all the vocal limitations and evidence of turning in the whole album at a budget price, you get the feeling Keir means this – particularly the global consciousness and be nice to your fellow man stuff - and wants us to share the love.

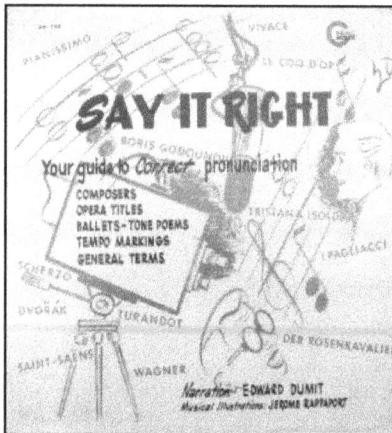

Edward S. Dumit:
Say it Right
(Grayhill, 1959)
What? A litany of classical legends, performed with perfect diction.

Self-help seldom sounded so perfect. Over 15 tracks of highly varying length (five seconds to 12 minutes and 54 seconds), Dumit pronounces the names of classical composers, titles of famous works, the names of musicians and musical terms (the latter with a few illustrations on piano). Dumit's diction is perfect, the intention is to acquaint an American audience with the correct pronunciation of "Bach" and many lesser known names. The results can be akin to listening to a litany from some barely comprehensible creed. Bear in mind, the "Harpists" (track eight), or "Operatic and Orchestral Groups" (track 14), were known to a select few in the late fifties USA, many of them are now lost to most popular memory. History's loss is the sound hound's gain if only because the conceit of this piece now betrays a lot about the time and culture into which the album was launched. Shamelessly high-brow, Dumit's diction dictates no prisoners will be taken and the results make for a very singular listen. Say it Right may instruct less as time, and the internet, take their toll on the need for this information presented in this way. But, as mix tape material of a truly unique shade, Say it Right is virtually peerless.

Duran Duran:
Thank You
(Capitol/Parlophone, 1995)
What? Durannies pay tribute to their inspirations; critics show befuddlement.

Duran Duran are by no means the only big sellers to devote an entire album to thanking those that influenced them by collecting and covering a long-player's worth of their tunes. The eighties pop behemoths always trod a fine line between ephemeral glam and big big grooves and – like many of their ilk – set about trying to prove themselves as serious contenders once a new generation of pretty boys had replaced them on the covers of teen mags.

By 1995 the Durannies were a decade past their pop pomp, still mining credible sales of albums and concert tickets, but doing so against massive critical indifference. In one sense, where Thank You is concerned, they didn't have that much to lose. The jaw dropper for fans and critics alike came in the selections, and styles, poured over the running order. Their big eighties pop sound suggested some roots in disco and soul and their bright pop videos suggested the British band had plenty of T.Rex and other glam stars in their record collections.

Indeed Duran offshoot The Power Station covered T.Rex's "Get it On." What Thank You suggests is this band always saw themselves as down with the cutting edge rebels and visionaries. Grandmaster Melle Mel's "White Lines" kicks off the collection, before we run through Sly and the Family Stone, Lou Reed, Elvis Costello, Bob Dylan, Public Enemy…you get the picture. And whether those at Q Magazine who listed this as amongst the worst albums ever made bothered to venture further into the covers of the The Doors, Iggy Pop and Led Zeppelin is debateable. There's no doubt J D Considine of Rolling Stone ventured that far because his comments make it clear: "[S]ome of the ideas at play here are stunningly wrongheaded, like the easy-listening arrangement given Elvis Costello's "Watching the Detectives" or the version of Zeppelin's "Thank You" that sounds like the band is covering Chris DeBurgh. But it takes a certain demented genius to recognize Iggy Pop's "Success" as the Gary Glitter tune it was meant to be or to redo "911 Is a Joke" so it sounds more like Beck than like Public Enemy."

The album hit the top 20 on both sides of the Atlantic, though its durability in sales past the first few weeks proved limited. In truth, it was never likely to be a critical favourite. Rolling Stone certainly have a point; some of these cuts aren't covers so much as reinventions. Sometimes the thinking process behind the project does suggest they shut any considered advice from the A&R department well outside the studio.

However, in the time since Thank You first muscled its way out of the speakers, a stack of other acts have taken a similar route, tackling the holiest popular music relics in very strange styles. Thank You is unlikely to garner universal respect, but these days it doesn't look quite as lonely as it did on first release.

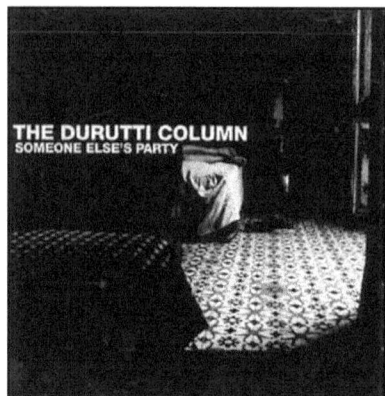

Durutti Column:
Someone Else's Party
(Artful, 2003)
What? A requiem.

Vini Reilly – who to all intents and purposes is The Durutti Column – has carved such a personal niche in music since the late seventies that any attempt to categorise his work borders on pointless. Racked initially with punk and new wave Reilly's stock-in trade of chiming guitar over rhythm track, with guest vocalists interspersed with his own gruff singing (usually well back in the mix) has filled a steady succession of albums. The running joke in the 24 Hour Party People movie that chronicled the life of Tony Wilson and Factory Records was that Wilson, and pretty much only Wilson, got him. In reality lots of people get The Durutti Column but figuring out who they are isn't always easy. Radio plays have been as varied as Radio One, Radio Three's Late Junction and all manner of obscure college and indie stations in the USA. The band remain punk in their approach and ethic, determinedly independent and alternative, but classical, jazz and rock stylings creep into their guitar and drum sounds. Their popularity is at its highest in unlikely territories, like Portugal. A moment in the 24 Hour Party People movie sees Reilly playing to an empty Hacienda club. That is harsh, and unsubstantiated, but the point is clear…live audiences in the UK have tended to be small in number and very respectful in their approach.

Someone Else's Party is downbeat and reflective and – arguably – the greatest expression of the singular Reilly genius, if only because it shows beyond all question that his music remains a very personal channel for his emotions and insights. The central focus of the album is the death of his mother and some tracks deal directly with the event "Requiem for my Mother" and "Somebody's Party" stand out in this respect, both following on from "Spanish Lament" in which an operatic vocal is added to the Durutti sound. Elsewhere looped sounds and a slow dance rhythm are combined to make the backing for "Woman." For all its funereal sensibilities and the heavy preponderance of black throughout the packaging Someone Else's Party is cathartic and loving along with the grief. It is personal to a very intense degree, but also accessible and compelling. It's also something of a vindication of Reilly's own comments on his work. Discussing The Durutti Column he once said: "whatever music it is, bad, good, indifferent, stupid, boring, whatever, – it's truthful. At the time, it's the truth, and it's honest. There's no attempt to portray an image or a career or anything. It's what it is. And truth can be painful. It's about losses close to me, and about my own depression, but it's cathartic. But you have to be truthful. If you're not true in what you do, if you're creative, then you should forget it. All I've ever tried to do is be truthful."

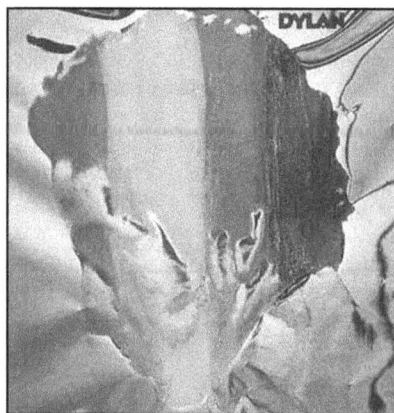

Bob Dylan:
Dylan
(Columbia, 1973)
What? A bitter kiss-off to a departed cash cow.

Almost all of Bob Dylan's high-profile career has been carried out within the CBS stable. The label was described as a national treasure when acquired by Sony in the 1990s. A fair point, the Japanese electronics giant had just acquired one of the most American of labels, including the best-known works of Michael Jackson, Bruce Springsteen and Bob Dylan. They also acquired this album, which in the two decades since they've seen no need to release on CD for the US domestic market. Various versions do CD business outside the USA under the title A Fool Such as I. Unluckily, or not, this is generally counted as Dylan's thirteenth studio album. Critically it remains little regarded, commercially it bucked a trend by charting more significantly in the US (#17) than it did in the UK where it failed to trouble the top 30. Dylan didn't compile or record this as an album, Columbia gifted it to the world when Dylan decided to sign for their rival Asylum. Dylan isn't exactly awful, and any keen-eared fan with some familiarity with Dylan's catalogue could soon tell from the simple backing and general quality of sound on most tracks that most of the recordings come from sessions around the time of New Morning. Two of the nine cuts started life as contenders for Dylan's most eclectic and inconsistent collection Self Portrait. None are Dylan originals though one of the traditional material songs – "Mary Ann" – is credited as a Dylan arrangement. Elsewhere Bob covers Joni Mitchell's "Big Yellow Taxi" and provides a five and a half-minute interpretation of "Mr Bojangles."

The derision for the album in 1973 came mainly from the way it added little to the Dylan legend, instead presenting the man as all too human. Some of his eighties albums and a lot of the gigs on his "Never Ending Tour" would also present this side to the man before – fifteen studio albums later – Good as I Been to You saw him presenting an entire long-player of traditional songs and covers. So, gradually, this side of Dylan emerged. Because Dylan sits uncomfortably before the sparky and sporadically brilliant Planet Waves (his only Asylum studio effort) and also before the unquestionably brilliant Blood on the Tracks and Desire, which marked his return to CBS, it was quickly dismissed in its own time. Since when, a number of Dylan completists and the generally curious have delved into its 35 minute running time to discover it isn't exactly a bad album but it most certainly isn't a great one and/or any kind of unrecognised visionary classic. Played over a few times Dylan has the spirited but provisional quality of Let it Be Beatles or the Beach Boys' Pet Sounds Sessions. At best it's an insight into the way he sounded back then, when he wasn't convinced anyone else would ever hear it. At worst, it's a blatant swipe at a man who'd just jumped ship in search of a more understanding record company.

Bob Dylan:
The Bootleg Series, Volume 10: Another Self Portrait (1969-1971)
(Columbia, 2013)
What? Dylan's Let It Be Naked?

So Dylan represented a rag bag collection of the most dire and desperate dregs in the Dylan barrel of the time. The man recovered, the legend was duly embellished and by the 21st century enough words had been written, and history recorded, to put that period in its place. Dylan himself had discussed his Self Portrait (1970) album as a blatant attempt to confound those who saw him as a leader or prophet. Indeed; Greil Marcus' Rolling Stone review of the original Self Portrait famously opened with the words; "What is this shit?"

When the monumental reissue and reappraisal of Dylan's tapes – The Bootleg Series – finally got around to the Self Portrait period it produced one of those rare bootleg/lost tapes collections that genuinely rewrote a small piece of history. The killer twists here are twofold. Firstly, this collection culls its material from a two year period in which Dylan wrote and recorded a significant number of original songs (thereby escaping the wilful avoidance of massive statements and stand taking that marked Self Portrait as Dylan's most befuddling work to that point). Secondly, Another Self Portrait revisits the original recordings and finds some unissued work still in its skeletal state, and strips extraneous overdubs from other work. What remains is an album that sounds coherent – if only because so many of the 35 tracks are low key, provisional, acoustic and under-rehearsed – and also presents an artist grappling with his position and slowly solving an identity crisis.

Let's be clear, a lot of what's here is rehearsal and first take stuff that isn't exactly radio friendly or anthemic. But it is an attempt to find and define Dylan between 1969 and 1971, and it makes a few monumental statements along the way. Firstly, some of the major cover versions are gone: "The Boxer," "Early Morning Rain," "Blue Moon" and "Let It be me" are all conspicuous absentees. Secondly, in the interests of coherence some of the songs from the period are presented in different versions. A defining move in this regard is an intimate and slightly insecure take of "I Threw it all Away" significantly less hymnal and reverberating than the – generally celebrated – cut on Nashville Skyline.

Where Dylan's albums of the period did make statements – even if Self Portrait was saying: "leave me alone I've got nothing to say to you, I'm just trying to figure things out" – the evidence from cuts here like "Little Sadie" and "In Search of Little Sadie" is that Dylan had some fun in the studio, messed around with licks, and sounds, and ideas, and generally drew on the things he relied on to make him feel good. Another Self Portrait presents enough of these moments to suggest the tortured soul image of the man at the time isn't the complete picture. Both "Sadie" tracks amount to Dylan and guitarist/multi-instrumentalist David Bromberg working their way through an idea and clearly relishing the opportunities to just play with a song.

Where the reliance on Nashville sessions and old-school country structures throughout the period from Nashville Skyline to Planet Waves suggested to many that Dylan had deserted any relevance to a young audience Another Self Portrait suggests it was more a case of Dylan being honest with himself about the music he grew up with and searching for a simple structure in that music to re-emerge as a sincere and insightful artist. In that regard the presence of "New Morning" and "When I Paint my Masterpiece" towards the end of this collection mark the successful end of a journey within which fragments like "All The Tired Horses" and "Sign on the Window" – pleasant as they are – represent signposts along the way.

Whether even his most ardent fans will want to listen repeatedly to Another Self Portrait is debateable, and whether repeated exposure this late in the day to Dylan covering Tom Paxton's "Annie's Gonna Sing her Song" adds even a footnote to our understanding of the man is very questionable. But as a vision of a major artist in search of his soul; and a vindication of subsequent decisions to head – generally successfully - towards country and covers albums of work that inspired him – Another Self Portrait is way more substantial than most artists' collections of out-takes and cast-offs.

Easy Star All Stars:
Dub Side of the Moon
(Easy Star, 2003)
What? What it says on the tin…but way better than you might imagine.

Superficially this looks so contrived it shouldn't work. Easy Star records get their best production crew into the studio, line up a few singers (some notable reggae names/some relative unknowns) and set about re-imagining one of the best-selling albums of all time. Some cynicism at the time of release anticipated a novelty advert for the abilities of the various talents featured on the album…but it's so much better than that. Dub Side of the Moon works for two reasons: firstly, Floyd's classic is so strong and so varied that it offers the studio crew helming the whole affair a perfect opportunity to throw in every trick in their armoury without any one sound outstaying its welcome. Secondly, the different sounding and very distinct parts of the album are carefully allocated to the right vocal and instrumental talents; a real strength being the rhythm sections brought in to give life to the lengthy samples/ambient and instrumental passages from the Floyd original. Dub Side of the Moon may be a little inconsistent (the jokey cuckoo clock and cockerel noises that precede "Time" jar a little) but it is honest in covering the original and strong because of the irreverence that creeps in. Having started badly "Time" is a tour-de-force in which Corey Harris and Ranking Joe set about the description/observation lyrics about life ticking away as a jaunty conversation, bringing humour to the most fateful of Floyd lyrics and pitting strong baritone vocal against machine-gun rap to explore the tension in the song. Dub Side of the Moon slightly overplays the curio angle by checking in at most of the major reggae styles – dancehall, roots, jungle, lovers – but redeems itself on a massive scale by making the strengths of each style count in covering the diverse material on offer. The presence of heavyweight vocal talent – Corey Harris and Frankie Paul – ensures that Dub Side of the Moon out-performs the original in this area. Frankie Paul's cover of "Us and Them" gets a strong vocal grip on a song notable for the aloofness and resignation in the original performance.

It would be trite to put the successful crossover between original and re-working down to the link both works have to ganga, but Dub Side of the Moon certainly takes on and runs with the notions of madness and multiple meanings that pervade the Floyd's original work. Both original and cover album function in a world of raised consciousness and myriad possibilities. Floyd may have got the sales; but Easy Star All Stars corner a few unexpected laughs and a lot good vibes without compromising (too much) the artistic vision of The Dark Side of the Moon.

The Electric Prunes:
Mass in F Minor
(Reprise, 1968)
What? Psychedelia meets high church; with mixed results.

The Electric Prunes scored one massive psychedelic hit, "I Had Too Much to Dream Last Night," but didn't hold the momentum; largely because their line-up and working arrangements were never quite as solid as those of other; hard gigging bands. By the time of their dissolution a few years after their formation there were no original members still in the line-up. Where the Prunes outdid most of the competition was their adept use of the studio and the talent that could be pulled into the ranks. Mass in F Minor shows both to perfection. Written and arranged by David Axelrod and produced by Dave Hassinger this is basically a hugely ambitious piece built around imagining a high church mass as a work of psychedelic rock. In bursts of a few seconds it may have more in common with the cod-psychedelia imagined by film composers, or the studio created works of guitar freakout presented by the likes of The Animated Egg. In reality Mass in F Minor sits somewhere between these pieces and the early self-conscious experiments like Deep Purple's Concerto for Group and Orchestra. Like the film work/session musician psych it visits the predictable reference points (explosive guitar, jazzy organ freakouts etc.) and like Purple and the early experiments with rock band and orchestra there is a sense of band and classical elements taking turns as much as working in harmony. For all that, David Axelrod's composition and overseeing of the piece does bring about moments of effective blending and Mass in F Minor falls well short of the disaster it could have been.

It delivers what the title suggests; a Latin mass forms the entire vocal, with male lead vocals and choirs taking their turn. The Electric Prunes rock band drive forward the faster portions of the six part mass and a brass section wade in with strident chords. The star of the whole performance is the work itself. Bursts of lead guitar here, unsupported choral passages there and that ever lurking brass all take their turn, and particular sections showcase the talent on offer. The Electric Prunes spend a few minutes mining a psych-jazzy groove to good effect on the fifth track, "Benedictus." Mass in F Minor has long been able to take its place whenever serious and lengthy rock magazine articles begin to discuss the most unusual, strangest, one-off, "out-there" works. It sounds its age and yet sounds magnificent, given the quality of production and lack of much else out there remotely like it. There is that rock mass featuring Spooky Tooth, also chronicled in this book, but these strange sounding concoctions have always been a rarity.

The one genuinely well-known number here – the opening "Kyrie Eleison" appeared on the soundtrack album to Easy Rider – is atypical in its peaceful vocal and gently floating melody. Much of Mass in F Minor is more muscular, more stridently psychedelic and –basically – more "rock."

Karen Elson:
The Ghost who Walks
(XL, 2010)
What? Varied and triumphant debut from Mrs Jack White.

The musical output of a model married to a noted rock musician sounds like a recipe for a self-indulgent disaster of epic fail proportions. The Ghost Who Walks is the complete antithesis of that. Elson had a musical background sufficient to suggest her debut solo release would pack some merit. But this particular concoction of folk, indie, country and a few other random elements is an inventive, characterful and darkly comic triumph worthy of more recognition than its fleeting chart rise, #16 in the UK Indie list, suggests. It isn't an easy listen, but, once admitted, it engages and compels because the collection is so much more than the sum of its elegantly realised parts. A track like "Garden" is a case in point, opening with gentle and atmospheric waves before the drums push the ease aside and Elson arrives to deliver a sweeping, epic and emotive vocal, dragging the backing along in its wake as it asks "why does love fade into darkness." Where "Garden" attempts something mainstream and radio friendly there's a Nick Cavesque gloom surrounding "Stolen Roses" (a murder ballad of a notably English persuasion). The majority of the album is credited to Elson as sole composer, most of the remainder sees her with a co-composing credit and none of the songs on offer would embarrass a professional songwriter or singer. The fact she enjoys a career as a top model and an improbable beauty may, just, bias those prone to jealousy away from The Ghost Who Walks. That's their loss.

Preston Epps:
Bongola
(Active, 2008)
What? Bongo, bongo, bongo.

Californian Preston Epps ranks as one of popular music's less heralded virtuoso performers. A situation easily understood when you realise the talented percussionist's main instrument is the bongo drums. His highest profile came with the hit "Bongo Rock" in 1959 (US Billboard #14). Despite another hit "Bongo, Bongo, Bongo" the following year and the brief chart appearance of the album Bongo, Bongo, Bongo Epps' chart days were over by the end of 1960. Epps' mainstream career extended to three albums, and sterling attempts to gain radio play and achieve more hits by diversifying the basic bongo sound into any fashionable genre that might usefully renew interest. His old recordings eventually became the kind of curios fit to appear in the margins of popular music radio. A number of American stations, and BBC Radio One in the person of John Peel played Epps. CD compilations duly followed. This is the most comprehensive and generous of the collections available, containing the hits and more. The more ambitious cuts like "Bongos in Pastel" (a tender and introspective jazz number). "Bongo in the Congo" and "Jungle Drums" have attempt at novelty hit written all over them and the likes of "Bongo Hop" are attempts at teen-beat chart fodder. Spread over 19 cuts, some amazingly long considering the instrumental basis in the bongo drums, it is likely Epps' abilities will outstay their welcome for all but the most committed of sound-hounds. But, as an insight into just how many ideas you can generate around one unlikely instrument, and as a look into Epps' enormous talent, this collection is in there with the best exotica on the market. It also boasts two genuine rarities in which Epps works with producer Jack Nitzsche one of which – the 12 and a half minute enormity of "Call of the Jungle" – is basically a concept piece, moving from sound to sound with the Epps' bongos as our constant companion.

Roky Erickson and the Aliens:
Roky Erickson and the Aliens
(CBS, 1980)
What? "I-I-I…think of demons"

Erickson's most celebrated work appears in the catalogue of the 13th Floor Elevators, fearless Texan psychedelic voyagers who had the misfortune to live within striking distance of a police service who took zero-tolerance as an instruction to perform maximum intolerance. Online biographies chronicle in more detail than we need to how Erickson copped an insanity plea in response to being caught in possession of one joint, and how the resulting incarceration, well-beyond three years, saw him treated with extreme measures to cure his "Schizophrenia." We need only concern ourselves here with the fact that the Roky who re-emerged in 1973 was a pale shadow of his former self and brought with him a music referencing the early rock 'n' roll he'd grown up with, the psychedelic garage rock he'd made in the Elevators, and a view of the world seemingly shaped by low-budget horror movies and Roky's – understandable – paranoia.

Since when Roky's career has seen low-budget albums, rehashing and compiling of his solo cuts, and a stop-start stumble through decades of cult stardom and criminally cruel deals. The 21st century finally saw a reversal of his financial fortunes. Roky's solo cult standing needed no reversal because – occasionally – he got enough of his demons down on tape. Probably never more so than the brief collision with major label interest in the late seventies/early eighties. Roky Erickson and the Aliens features recordings available elsewhere, but the CBS release is significant if only because it marked a decent pressing of material recorded on a workable studio budget.

This is transcendental trash-rock of the highest order. The single "The Creature with the Atom Brain" samples the Z list horror movie of the same name and "Don't Shake me Lucifer" is a piece of throwaway horror rock made all the more compelling because Roky's warbling tenor gets far enough inside the lyrics to make them believable. Roky's vocal performance is central to the appeal of cuts like "I Walked with a Zombie," another reference to a low-budget old movie in which the bulk of the lyrics involve repeating the title, but Roky's growing discomfort turns the mantra into a story. "Two Headed Dog" – "Two-headed dog, two-headed dog; I've been working in the Kremline(!) with a two- headed dog" – has the thick psyched distorted guitars of prime period 13 Floor Elevators. The collection also packs two excellent slow numbers: "Night of the Vampire" and "Stand for the Fire Demon," suggesting there was serious thought given to varying and sequencing the album.

It's inescapable that in listening to solo Roky you are listening to a man confused, in-pain and – on some later recordings – in the hands of those keen to milk him for money and reward him with nothing. This 1980 release at least has the excuse that Erickson's creative energies are high, his focus is clear, even when it is paranoid, his voice is in fine form and the backing musicians and production crew are capable of doing justice to his ideas.

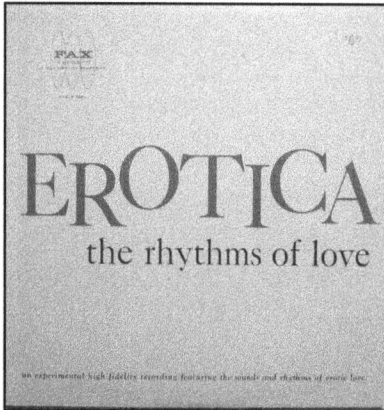

The Erotics:
Erotica – The Rhythms of Love
(Fax Records, 1961)
What? Bongo-tastic shag-fest!

Long lauded as one of the strangest one-offs of its era Erotica has proven a hard record to pin down. The scarcity of information on exact recording date or the identity of those involved hasn't stopped web sites devoted to the strangest sounds – like Waxidermy or the Confederacy of the Wrong blogspot – exploding into florid print about a simple but highly effective recording. Getting copies in the present era is also fairly easy since specialist reissue outlets, like the UK's Trunk Records, have made it available. Fax Records (so named well ahead of the invention of the fax machine) were based in Hollywood and released product on the margins of popularity. Their stock-in trade included adult humour, which is where this belongs.

Erotica comprises two lengthy tracks – each one side of the original vinyl – in which a couple pound away relentlessly at their bed springs, Spartan but enthusiastic musical accompaniment is provided by some energetically spanked bongo drums. The anonymous man and woman involved gasp, sigh and suggest incredible athleticism and ferocious sexual staying power. It's a noisy, banging and solidly squeaking shag-fest of an album, end of! There is a narrative – of sorts – with the start of side one including sounds of waking up and some mumbled comments. But, for the most part, Erotica is exactly as described above. The bongo playing, and sexual sounds, speed up, slow down, suggest a little about the story but – basically – suggest sex. A true oddity, rightfully celebrated as such, and widely enough available in the present day, should you be so inclined.

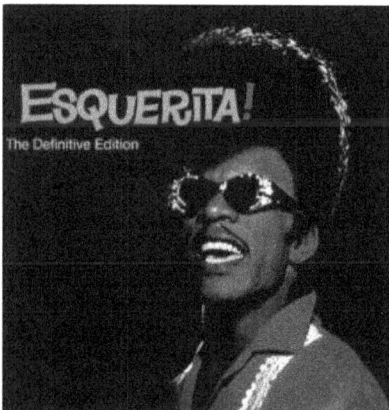

Esquerita:
The Definitive Edition
(Hoodoo, 2010)
What? Rock 'n' roll original, captured in his pomp.

Esquerita, aka Eskew Reader, born Steven Quincy Reeder Jr, whose stage name is sometimes pronounced "excreta," is an elusive and legendary figure. He died of AIDS, aged 51, in 1986, before CD reissues or his handful of high profile fans (like Clashster/BAD mainstay Mick Jones) got the chance to revive a career that was always on the margins. A loose cannon even by the standards of rock 'n' roll eccentricity, Esquerita probably never produced the work to do justice to a personality widely acknowledged as forceful. The best known photograph of the man adorns the front of this collection, and a few others of his work: massive pompador hair, shades, huge grin and garish shirt. The high-camp appearance and a full-on performance style, in which Esquirta attacks the lyrics as much as singing them, remain a trademark of his work. The obvious comparison, with Little Richard, remains an issue of debate amongst rock 'n' roll fanatics. Some claim Richard lifted Esquerita's act. Richard certainly got to the recording studio first, got a better sound, recorded genuine hits and turned the whole shtick into a trademark bundle that made his name. And, frankly, Richard is deservedly a legend.

Definitive Edition (culled entirely from tracks cut for Capitol singles and one album between 1958 and 1959) is a distillation of the very best Esquerita managed in staking his claim to be an original. Richard might have stolen the chart thunder, and nailed a harder production, but Esquerita, probably, shades it in terms of channelling genuine lunatic charm. "Esquerita And The Voola" is a classic piece of knockabout nonsense, little more than an insistent set of sounds with Esquerita whooping a basic tune over the top. It is a track that has seen duty on compilations where low budget desperation and madness are celebrated, like Roots of Trash and Garage. Several other cuts border on this level of strangeness, and following Esquerita's logic isn't always easy. Even a standard rock 'n' roll cut like "Laid Off" leaves the listener with the thought that anyone employing the man might soon start looking for reasons to terminate the arrangement. There isn't anything specifically threatening about the Esquerita, but 21 tracks played end to end soon begin to leave you with the notion that his mind followed its own rules.

Esquerita's work here is the best and most consistent he ever produced. The tracks compiled on this collection include the complete Capitol album, the only genuine album (as opposed to collections of singles and other tracks), he ever recorded. The sound isn't always as big, or as crazy, as his act requires, and the performances stagger between serious attempts to nail a radio friendly rock 'n' roll hit and cuts where Esquerita unleashes his peculiar genius and everyone else tries manfully to respond. So, this is a glimpse into a legend and a sense of what might have been. In another reality sales and management would have taken him to a bigger market, and the man himself would have restrained his more wayward tendencies sufficiently to carve out a sustainable niche of eccentricity. He would, possibly, have landed somewhere in a gleefully colourful middle ground between Captain Beefheart, James Brown and Little Richard. In that reality, the world would have been a slightly better place.

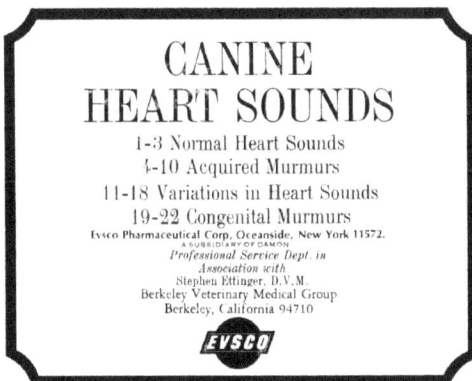

CANINE HEART SOUNDS

1-3 Normal Heart Sounds
4-10 Acquired Murmurs
11-18 Variations in Heart Sounds
19-22 Congenital Murmurs

Evsco Pharmaceutical Corp, Oceanside, New York 11572.
A SUBSIDIARY OF DAMON
Professional Service Dept. in
Association with
Stephen Ettinger, D.V.M.
Berkeley Veterinary Medical Group
Berkeley, California 94710

EVSCO

Stephen Ettinger, D.V.M.:
Canine Heart Sounds
(EVSCO Pharmaceutical Corp, 1970)
What? The best and worst beats, available on one handy long playing record.

There really isn't that much to say about this entry. 7" and 12" works, financed by drug companies, were a long time feature in the recording industry before cassettes, video and the internet killed them off. Many such items subsequently turned up in junk/thrift/second hand stores where the curious were sometimes motivated to chance a few coins in return for a very unique listening experience. If you're listening to the winning arguments regarding "which patients need a diuretic?" it probably helps if you have a clue what, exactly, a diuretic is, a fact that explains why Neil Nixon seldom listened to that particular single purchased for five pence from a Carlisle junk shop.

All of the above probably explains why Canine Heart Sounds accrued just enough of a cult following to insinuate itself at #93 (3 April 2007) on the second 365 Days Project, where, as of this writing, its 22 tracks continue to exist for your – ahem – listening pleasure. The rest is very predictable. With clear diction and just a hint of his original local accent, Stephen Ettinger provides an insightful and erudite master class in discerning the good and bad beats inside the chest of a dog. You don't need any skilled knowledge to start with, and the road map is clear from the sleeve. The tour opens with the normal sounds of a canine heart, visits acquired murmurs, considers variations in canine cardio tones and finishes with the darker, congenital failures (probably best to skip everything from track 18 onwards if you really love dogs). Each separate variation on the theme of thumping is preceded by directions in understanding what we are about to hear. Once explained, the evidence is easy to understand and Ettinger strikes just the right note of informed expert and understanding instructor. Mix tape gold, but only if your taste for mash ups veers well away from work with any sense of mass appeal, and also an insight into a market that flourished for the best part of two decades.

EVOLUTION SO FAR / THE ARMIES OF BITTERNESS

Evolution so Far:
The Armies of Bitterness
(Nh-N/Road2Ruin, 2003)
What? Articulate anti-Desert Storm punk rant from unlikely territory.

The Armies of Bitterness straddles the punk/rock borderline, revs up repeatedly to fury, rattles the traps and rips solos from the guitars as the righteous anger about the wrong-headed invasion of Iraq boils over most of the album. When it isn't directly sideswiping the war – "War intentions to control black gold/America lies to act" from "Baghdad Recall." – The Armies of Bitterness sinks into general anger and bitterness; "Reason stinks and drowns in contradictions/ I just keep on feeling lower and lower" from "What the Fuck are You Laughing at?" Evolution so Far rock hard, manage a lead vocal that holds the line and hits the edge of screaming most of the time, and throw in enough sporadic samples and musical flashes to hold the attention over the whole album. As American radio became fearful of anti-war messages to the point of blocking radio play for The Dixie Chicks, albums like The Armies of Bitterness were thin on the ground. It took Neil Young and Living With War (2006) to make a major stand, but that was long after Iraq had fallen and the factional fighting of the post "mission accomplished" period was well underway. Evolution so Far – by contrast – had little to lose by venting their fury as the troops were poised to go in. This anti-war rhetoric and hard-edged sounds were coming out of Italy. This self-released musical missile was recorded in Tavernago and eventually got enough distribution to see copies trickling across Europe and into the USA where the gallows humour of "Don't Worry and Love the Bomb" and the raging polemics of tracks like "Fear of a Right Planet" found some respect and appreciation.

Explosions in the Sky:
The Earth is not a Cold Dead Place
(Temporary Residence, 2003)
What? Post-rock, incendiary and alive, which might explain the title.

Experimental Texas instrumental post-rockists Explosions in the Sky have carved out a career largely away from radio play, fashion and anything approaching a standard career structure. Lacking lyrics and vocal sounds, and frequently lining up as a drum kit and three guitars (though bass is occasionally in the mix), the band specialise in soundscapes and combine a rock sound with an approach to composition more akin to film or classical music. The end result is music that swirls, roars, grates, shimmers and sparks with energy. Despite the lack of traditional songs there is often a sense of story to Explosions' pieces, slow meditative beginnings grow in volume and pace to shuddering cadenzas of guitar and drums as rhythm and lead playing collide.

The band's oeuvre has slowly gained them a loyal following. Eight years and five albums into their career All of a Sudden I Miss Everyone finally brought them chart recognition on both sides of the Atlantic. But The Earth... remains a fan favourite and was one of the albums featured in heavy rotation in the final days of John Peel's Radio One show. Key to the album's enduring appeal is "Your Hand in Mine." The full eight minute wonder from the album was edited and adapted for inclusion in the Soundtrack to the movie Friday Night Lights. This move presented the band's atmospheric and compelling sounds to a wide audience, generating the interest that put future recordings in the charts. The cataclysmic finale to the same track appeared in television adverts for Reliant Energy.

Michael Moore added a snatch of "The Only Moment We Were Alone" to the soundtrack of Capitalism: A Love Story. And so it goes.

Like Sigur Ros it is likely that Explosions in the Sky will always be better known from snatches and samples of their work presented behind images, but heard end to end over the five tracks of The Earth..., their changing moods, melodic inventions and permanently restless sound plays like a vivid and visual series of vignettes in the mind of a listener. The band persistently fascinate, surprise and change moods and, for all their forward looking qualities, they continue to celebrate the possibilities of the good old album. All their albums, and particularly this one, appear perfectly sequenced with each track informing those before and after, and the album packaging always shows care and attention. The vinyl version of The Earth...has the music pressed onto three sides and etchings of birds on the remaining side.

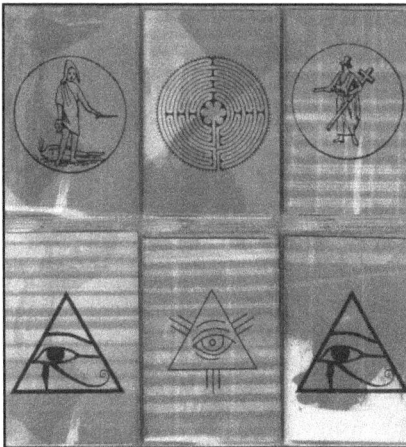

EyeSea:
Blue Ten
(Blue Tapes, 2014)
What? Acapella death metal.

What's not to love here? Ten tortured slabs of death metal vocalising, punctuated by silences and pushed forward by surging growls and sudden bursts of anger. Released exclusively on a cassette only label operating in the twenty first century and emblazoned with hand crafted artwork. Seriously, you'd think people still cared about making music and pushing the limits of artistry. In another reality each of the tracks here would be the national anthem of a separate country and there'd be moshing in response at every Olympic medal ceremony. We can only wish...

Eye Sea sets out to be an exploration and celebration of the sound of the human voice. Blue Tape's write up states: "Even without the quasi-occult connotations, DM vox are a brutal and particularly effective instrument, though not as blunt and crass as some may believe - there's a swarm of textures and tonal variations in even the most straightforward death growl." The present authors agree to the point of ripping and pasting that statement and saluting a short album that rejoices in using the same title, "Stück," for each song, separating them only with individual numbers. A unique listen, mixtape gold and a collection that stands comparison with anything else in these pages.

Bill Fay:
Life is People
(Dead Oceans, 2012)
What? Masterful and mature late-period collection.

Fay's presence in the singer-songwriter scene of late sixties/early seventies UK resulted in a small collection of work, largely ignored at the time, that gradually became cultish. Albums like Time of the Last Persecution brought jazz influences into Fay's, mainly acoustic, songs and displayed a melancholy, empathic and deeply thoughtful side to his lyrics. These releases marked the high-point of a career that made most low-profile acts look positively gregarious. But, Fay finally got widespread critical acclaim and some notice in his home country when the American indie Dead Oceans saw fit to get him into the studio for this – largely self-penned – collection of musings and recounting. Like late period Dylan and Johnny Cash, Fay intones as much as sings, using his lived in and occasionally cracked voice to set a mood of intimacy. The minimal arrangements, sometimes down to a single instrument, are produced with warm echo to give the feel of listening in a room with Fay almost within touching distance. The intimacy is strengthened by songs that wear their wisdom lightly, eschewing clever metaphors for straightforward observation. On "The Never Ending Happening," basically a song about life, Fay suggests "just to be a part of it" is "astonishing" and intones the whole thought over little more than a piano. He lets the final line hang and plays out the simple piano figure as a solo violin comes in to play a melody to the end. The pace picks up occasionally and there's a nod to fashions that have come since Fay's first foray into the music business, notably in a beautiful cover of Wilco's "Jesus Etc." but Fay has that late-period Johnny Cash ability to bring enough character to someone else's song to make it feel completely like his own. Life is People is a caring, humane, and very companionable work that repays repeated listening.

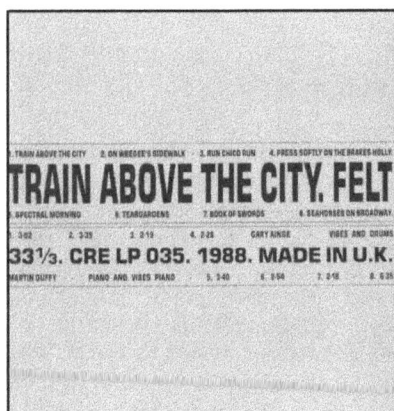

Felt:
Train Above the City
(Creation, 1988)
What? When is an Album not an Album?

We could start with the good news: Lawrence Hayward, generally known as "Lawrence," remains one of the most dependable creative forces in indie/alternative music. His work with Felt, Denim and Go Kart Mozart is testament to a creative talent apparently able to reinvent itself at will. So far, so good. As the mainstay of Felt, Lawrence's sparky lyrics and distinctive guitar gave an identity to their records that…

Well, anyway. The reason this album sticks out is that – with eight highly regarded albums to Felt's credit – the "band" took a creative body swerve that would've ruined lesser reputations. Train Above the City comprises 27 minutes and 25 seconds of pleasant, noodling, piano/vibe heavy cocktail jazz. Musically Felt – on this outing – are keyboard player Martin Duffy and drummer/percussionist Gary Ainge. Of the eight tracks on offer, only one – "Seahorses on Broadway" – is remotely lengthy (clocking in at an epic 6 minutes and 38 seconds). Lawrence's creative contribution to the whole caper amounts to precisely 25 words. Quite literally giving names to all the tracks:

"Train Above the City," "On Weegee's Sidewalk," "Run Chico Run,"

"Press Softly on the Brakes Holly," "Spectral Morning," "Teargardens,"

"Book of Swords," and the aforementioned "Seahorses on Broadway." Granted, the titles hint at inventive juxtaposition of images, along with elegiac and insider tales of great character. The kind of stuff Lawrence brought to Felt's earlier albums and has continued to develop since. But – FFS! – he doesn't sing, perform or produce a note of this. As an exercise in the alternative it's hard to top Train Above the City. Its more charitable critics have alluded to situationist art (i.e. the kind of statement that involves putting the audience into a situation to the point they realize their predicament is – sort of – the point). Well, maybe. It's hard to believe a major label, or massive band could have pulled this off.

Once you're through the shock of how different this sounds to anything else Felt ever did. It is – kind of – pleasant in a tinkling, unchallenging, nicely in the background sort of way.

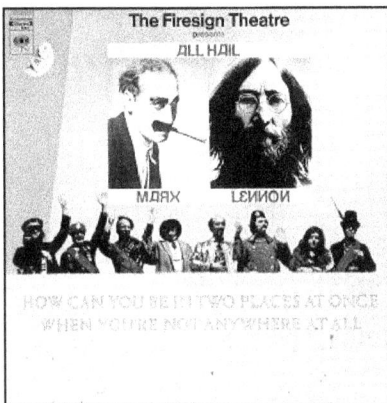

The Firesign Theatre:
How Can You Be in Two Places at Once When You're Not Anywhere at All
(Columbia, 1969)
What? Head humour heads off to infinity.

Time hasn't been too kind to The Firesign Theatre. The LA based comedy troupe hit their heights early on, since when their particular brand of genius has been bypassed by time and technology. The four Firesigners (so called because all have Zodiac fire signs) have proven resilient and able to adapt, but their early recordings (improbably on the major Columbia label) still elicit the most critical respect. Basically, The Firesign Theatre produced recorded comedy involving dense narratives, surreal plot twists, multi-layered jokes and enough audio trickery to make their best works worthy of repeated plays. In the 21st century there are two obvious downsides to any rediscovery of their early genius. Firstly, their early albums demand devoted listening; any attempt to play them in the background and/or dip in for a few minutes, is largely pointless. The rules involve: long attention spans, headphones, volume well up, closed eyes and treating the whole production like you would a well-loved book. Secondly, their magpie-like marauding of all elements of popular culture in search of jokes has dated. Newbie fans simply have to trust that some of the jokes and diversions, like the occasional straying into radio adverts and the like, are superb parodies of contemporary American culture of the time.

Basically, these guys grew up in post-war USA, and their style suggests that from their earliest conscious moments they were critical of mass commercialism, tuned into radio and its infinite possibilities of mental scenery, and possessed of imaginations so explosive that real life would always seem dull. For British, and all lands once-owned by the British, listeners, The Goons (as in the radio shows produced by The Goons) are an obvious touchstone. Another way into the Firesign universe might be to imagine what might have happened if Monty Python had relocated to hippie-central west coast USA. Where the Pythons considered albums a diversion from the televisual work the Firesigns treated the form as the perfect repository for a brand of surreal humour that found a turned-on, semi-stoned audience willing to go with the journeys on offer.

If you're still reading then – frankly – any of their early Columbia albums is probably worth a punt. This, the second such creation, offers up cover pictures of Groucho Marx and John Lennon, (Marx and Lenin, geddit?!), which gives you a good idea of the general philosophy on offer. How Can you be… serves up just short of an hour of surreal sonic adventure. It's just about comprehensible when we meet the car salesman at the start of side one but, once we are near to the sale of a car, a demonstration of the in-car audio system takes us into sonic trickery and the laws of physics begin to dissolve. The new owner finds road signs talking to him. Realities – literally – change as the car's climate control system transports us all into a tropical paradise and…(bear in mind, we've hardly started yet). The twists come thick and fast, sketch-style highpoints of the action involve one character enlisting in the army and an advert for a dope dealership (touching on two counter-culture staples of the late-sixties) and once Nick Danger (a pulp detective character owing a lot to Raymond Chandler) appears we're well into classic Firesign territory. By this point, with the images and ideas cascading like a monumental acid trip, it's also very clear that America, and that country's view of itself, is the main subject of the comedy, a point made perfectly towards the end of the proceedings with a gag in which America decides to surrender after the attack on Pearl Harbour. Early Firesign, and this bizarre outing in particular, remains one hell of a ride, and an audio experience like very little else. The Firesign Theatre – who lost one of their quartet, Peter Bergman, in 2012 – continue to work on in their hugely inventive way.

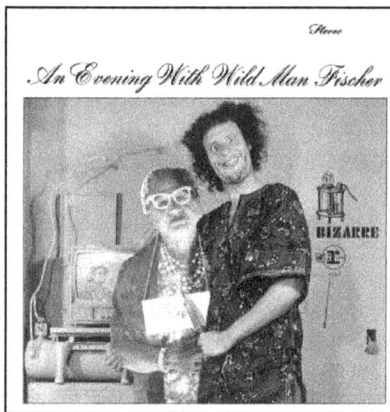

Wild Man Fischer:
An Evening With Wild Man Fischer
(Bizarre, 1968)
What? Legendary lunatic outing.

Twice committed as a paranoid schizophrenic before being "discovered" hitting on passers-by for change and rewarding them with some free form rant of a nursery rhyme, Larry "Wild Man/ Wildman" Fischer's arrival in music was typical of the man. There was a certain insane logic to his style. Apart from anything else his approach to pedestrians, followed by a song, gave him the excuse that he was a busker and not a mugger. From this point onwards, lunacy, shot through with a small thread of logic, marked his entire career.

The cover picture of an insanely grinning Larry holding a large carving knife to the throat of a middle aged woman suggests that the "evening" of the title might be, erm, memorable. The discovery of a label round the poor woman's neck proclaiming her to be "Larry's Mother" confirms our suspicions, and the knowledge that this is a double album makes matters worse.

Production credits are handled by Frank Zappa. Zappa's band, along with a handful of assorted luminaries, also handle backing tracks and some of the vocal performing. For the most part Zappa's jazzy sound-scapes featuring looped live recordings of Larry do add some atmosphere but they also suggest the album is a vehicle for Zappa to show off this prize curiosity and his own production skills. Side two features Larry's basic busking style and "songs" like "I'm Working For the Federal Bureau of Narcotics" in which Larry veers from a full-throated bellow to a hysterical whoop without ever coming close to singing. "The Leaves Are Falling" trades mainly on grunts and whistles, and other compositions struggle to get above Sesame Street levels of literacy.

The closing side features the harrowing "Wild Man Fischer Story" with Larry's history retold complete with hysterical impressions of his mother and screaming confessions about being "Committed to the mental institution." In the face of such competition the hopeful "Why I Am Normal" is, frankly, unconvincing. Fischer states that his mind is "one of a kind" and that fact, at least, isn't in dispute on this evidence.

Rightfully cited as a true outsider classic, An Evening with Wild Man Fischer was out of print for years and is one of the handful of albums never likely to be reissued on CD, though it is now downloadable. It remains a virtually peerless wander through a brief reality in which genuine lunacy (as in certifiable paranoid schizophrenia) was cool to the point of being the basis for the launch of a musical career. Fischer's wild mood swings and Californian hippie culture rub shoulders agreeably. But, Larry Fischer's ongoing collision with the Zappa clan got personal, he blaming them for unfair treatment and exploitation, their counter-arguments revolving around the fact he genuinely scared them. With Frank's death his work passed into the hands of his widow and children the personal issues -apparently – outlasted Fischer, who died in 2011. There are old vinyl copies circulating and whilst it would never the intention of those behind this book to encourage illegal music buying, you can find CD copies of An Evening With Wild Man Fischer if you want them badly enough.

Wild Man Fischer:
The Fischer King
(Rhino Handmade, 1999)
What? Outsider music gold.

As the entry above attests, Larry "Wildman" Fischer was a singular and uncontainable talent. His entire career was blighted by paranoid schizophrenia and the complications it brought to every area of his life. It is – then – to the eternal credit of Rhino Records and in particular to the Barnes and Barnes production team that the recordings on this generous double CD exist. After parting company with Frank Zappa, Fischer recorded almost every significant note of his wayward, stop-start musical career for the Rhino label. The bulk of the work appears on the albums Wildmania (1977), Pronounced Normal (1981) and Nothing Scary (1984). These appear in sequence and in their entirety on The Fischer King along with other hard-to-find treasures like the original "Rhino Records" single that launched the label in the mid-seventies and the gloriously spirited "It's a Hard Business" in which Fischer duets with Rosemary Clooney. All this with copious sleeve notes and a poster of the Mona Lisa modified to look like Larry, what's not to like?

The Fischer King opened the account of the Rhino Handmade label; a specialist operation for collectors that has gone on to release complete session recordings from key albums, and other treasures that would otherwise have remained impossible to get. In the case of The Fischer King this lavishing of attention is something of a saintly act given that the unmanageable Fischer had staged one of the least successful marketing campaigns in music industry history when he took to visiting Rhino Records – as in the same shop he'd praised on a single – approaching queuing customers and ripping records from their hands, before replacing them with copies of his own albums. The misguided charm offensive resulted in copious complaints, no sales of Fischer product and the eventual banning of the man from the shop he lauded in song.

His trio of Rhino albums give shape to The Fischer King. Larry is wayward, sparky, clearly coming from the back of left-field with regard to some of his lyrics and permanently packing the ability to be scary and in need of love. The Wildmania cuts include solo vocal items, live recordings out of doors and some skeletal rock numbers of which a loose and vocally ragged take on Frank Sinatra's "Young at Heart" is something of a stand out. Lyrically it isn't always pleasant, Fischer acts out his autobiography (again) making it plain there are family members who find it hard to be with him and a line from "I'm the Meany" about a girlfriend shocks when he sings: "She told me she was pregnant, so I hit her in the stomach." It isn't exactly easy listening. There's hilarity, invention and even a passable impersonation (though not by Larry) of George Harrison. Pronounced Normal and Nothing Scary are helmed by Barnes and Barnes and feature Larry supported by electronic backing along with the usual guitar/bass/drums. The rapping title track of Pronounced Normal is a corker; from the second Larry belts out "Certified wrong…" at the start you know you're in for a bumpy and compelling ride. "Watch Out for the Sharks" (a sideswipe at those who have wronged him) is another barbed gem. Nothing Scary is a bumper 34 track helping of Fischer on form in which "Derailroaded" is yet another insistent rap about life's misfortunes, "Oh God Please Send me a Kid to Love" is heartfelt and chilling in equal measure and the band America each contribute a song, both of them fragile gems that bring out a sense of Larry's vulnerability. Gerry Beckley plays most of the instruments on his "All I Think About is You" and Dewey Bunnell's "The Rain Song" would easily have graced any of America's best-selling albums.

The Fischer King was released in a limited edition of 1000. The original Rhino albums have all enjoyed CD reissues, albeit with no sign of the bonus tracks that pack out The Fischer King. A few other, download only, Fischer cuts appear on the odds and ends collection, Lost and Found Pep.

Five Starcle Men:
Gomba Reject Ward Japan
(Lost Frog, 2007)
What? Beefheart's children.

The liner notes on the download site state: "This FSM history album (spanning 1992-1998) for study by government demons and cartoons for Japanese kid of audience is not gay. But this is a gay press release for the University Press and Disney CGI." Their record company kindly provided us with the following biography: "These kids were involved in alien drug torture and deadly cartoon culture governments. They loved performing their little hit "Pizza Hut Families Rule" which often led to their being kicked off stage by the police or various forces that didn't like the song. Using modern cultural, pharmacological, and other technologies, these young suburban punks constructed highly aestheticized, delusional realities for themselves and their viewers, often resulting in a dangerous sense of political and intellectual ability. Original Members: Glen Hobbs, Luke McGowan. Location: Lancaster, California, USA."

Now we've cleared that up, this elusive and enigmatic band present 28 cuts of dazzlingly demented outsider strangeness. Most of which mine the Beefheartean realm of impossible time signatures and its counter-intuitive element of the least together instrumental sounds, like apparently random guitar noises, being the glue that holds the "songs" together. There is more spoken word, less blues and more conventional, just, vocal sounds than on classic Beefheart. But, Trout Mask Replica mashed with the most surreal alternative rock of the nineties and beyond, is the basic sound here. Not that anyone could accuse Five Starcle Men of being derivative, or lacking their own ideas. The real strength of Gomba Reject Ward is its self-contained sense of authority. This works, because it works. Like The Residents, these inveterate experimenters with sound create worlds within worlds, populate everything with characters and vivid scenery and produce a soundtrack of ceaseless invention and fearless creativity.

Seriously, it is that good. Whether it means anything is totally beside the point. Tracks like "Only Kids of Nothing Star" with its refrain of "there is no such thing as Devil worship…there is no such place as Hell" could be read as critiques on narrow, fundamentalist, thinking. But to look for such literal meanings in this festival of abstractions is to miss the main attraction. This is an album that makes a manifesto of outsiderdom and pulls no punches. "Ten Foot Barbie" sounds like the nightmare promised by its title and, by contrast, "Mummy on Drugs" is just over 100 seconds of genuine knockabout hilarity. Every track here works in its own perverse way, the gamut of strangeness covered through the 28 cuts establishes Five Starcle Men amongst the envelope pushing greats and even the Music for Maniacs blogsite has got itself into a froth about how out there this collection is: "Every sound is warped beyond recognition, lyrics range from unintelligible jabbering to surreal nonsense, samples and tapes loop themselves into delirium, unnatural rhythms pound away, all adding up to a mind-melting experience." Praise comes no finer.

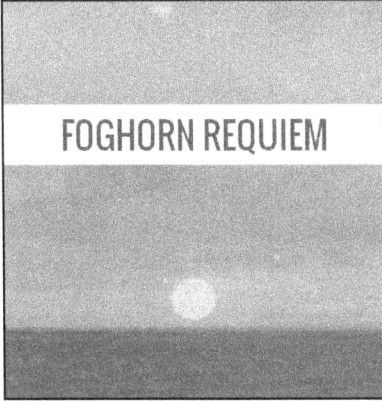

FOGHORN REQUIEM

The Foghorn Requiem:
The Foghorn Requiem
(www.foghornrequiem.org, 2013)
What? One-off gig by three brass bands, 50 ships and – ermm – one massive foghorn housed at a coastal lighthouse.

On June 22nd 2013 a one-off live performance marked the premiere of a piece designed to commemorate the disappearance of the foghorn from the British coast. A subsequent tour is unlikely; for starters any participating venue would need to provide a number of brass bands, a stretch of coast sufficient to house a large audience, a lighthouse complete with foghorn and enough seaborne vessels to provide a range of foghorn sounds on demand. Participation on the day was open to anyone willing to contribute a seaborne vessel. More than 50 ships eventually gathered on the – typically cold and seldom calm - North Sea, playing their part in an ambitious work.

The Foghorn Requiem has few close living relatives in terms of its sound and intention, though Jóhann Jóhannsson's The Miner's Hymns isn't too far away. Both works rely for the major tonal qualities on the warmth and slow stridence of a huge brass band sound to provide an elegy for something all but disappeared from life, (in Jóhannsson's case working miners in the county of Durham), and rely very much on context to give the full meaning to their sounds. Jóhannsson's work originally appeared in-situ with films of mine workers but The Foghorn Requiem was always intended as a one-off live event, conceived by artists Lise Autogena and Joshua Portway in collaboration with composer Orlando Gough. Gough – Oxford educated and no stranger to unique commissions – provided the score for the brass bands. Autogena and Portway conceived the event and put work into all aspects from publicity to a website with helpful directions to the venue, Souter Lighthouse near South Shields. Sound recordings made on the day were subsequently made available via the website.

The open-air location and lingering notes in the original brass band score make the work effortlessly sad. The notes – even the massive sound of the foghorn – rapidly die in the big sky and open landscape as they travel on, over the sea, to infinity, leaving the listener behind in an instant. The epic scale of the British network of coastal foghorns, and the inevitable decline of this once proud and enviable achievement in the face of 21st century computer driven technology, under-pin the epic scale of the work. A situation made slightly more poignant because the new technology allowed precise ship-to-shore communications, producing the correct timing of sea-borne foghorn contributions to the requiem. This was never a piece about tunes to captivate you and haunt your consciousness, although eye-witnesses and reporters discussed being struck by the sheer physicality of The Foghorn Requiem as the massive coastal horn roared in close proximity to the audience. Similarly, the sheer quality of three bands - the Felling Band, the Westoe Band and the NASUWT Riverside Band – and the level of sound generated by their 65 musicians was moving and awe-inspiring on the day.

The website for the event spoke of the last chance to hear the "majestic honk" of the coastal foghorn. But, a "majestic honk" is a fraction of what the coastal foghorn achieves in this context. As with The Miner's Hymns this is a work in which the recordings available only hint at the true impact of the complete work in its original location. Unlike The Miners Hymns this is a changing recording; available from fragments gathered as they were sent by participants and audience and an original "official" recording made by the instigators on the day.

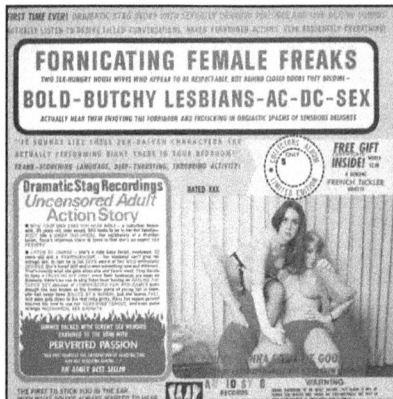

Fornicating Female Freaks: Fornicating Female Freaks – Audio Stag Records
What? Mutton dressed as ham! "Two lonely bitches on the loose for the weekend"

Not recommended for those easily offended, or closely wedded to notions of political correctness. In fact, if we've just described you it's probably best to skip this entry. Seriously, you'll hate this album. This is a notorious slice of vinyl sexploitatuion of dubious origin and (current) widespread availability online. Trunk Records in the UK have seen fit to make this sleazefest legally available; others have simply pirated its moaning and screaming, offering them up for free.

Who – exactly – you are listening to, when this was recorded and whether the two scantily clad women on the cover have any direct link to the two women going down on, up inside and generally all over each other for most of the recording is also unclear. No matter, it's a simple idea and it has long outlived the obvious cheap cash-in concept that spawned it.

Two American housewives find themselves briefly deserted by husbands they don't totally trust or love; they resolve to spend the weekend together and the bulk of the two sides of vinyl offers up an audio porn-fest with sound effects, vivid descriptions and orgasms aplenty. Rainer (the older and more experienced, self-proclaimed "35 year old hag") initiates Joanne (young, innocent, ripe for educating and pissed off because her husband has been made a vice president of his company and hasn't touched her sexually in a month) into an inventive orgy of lesbian lust and experimentation. That – basically – is the plot. Like any decent porno the set-up is dispensed with undue haste to allow the bulk of the running time to involve ripping off clothes, dragging in any useful domestic item (like the squirty cream) and pepper the action with as many gratuitous appearances of "cunt," "fucking" and "motherfucker" as the scriptwriters can dream up. The descriptions provided as Rainer (mainly) and Joanne (a little) comment on the action gives Fornicating Female Freaks some narrative momentum, so when Rainer sees Joanne spread out on the bed with "pale white skin, flowing black hair spread out on the scarlet…" there's the imagery to keep the porn scenes alive.

Fornicating Female Freaks has earned cult notoriety on the back of two continuous marks of quality. The performances are pure porn. The dramatic acting is hammy to the point of self-parody, especially from the deeper voiced Rainer who brings perfect clear diction to her lines. The porn acting pulls every tinge and touch from the performance of orgasmic frenzy and the balance of essential and intensely performed sex versus obligatory and moderately performed set up continues for the duration. The sound effects, squelching, squirting and general rhythmic accompaniments to sex are also top-notch. And then there's the dialogue; Fornicating Female Freaks is a full-on fuck-festive fusillade of fulminating sex talk: "That was a motherfucker of a soul kiss; you damn near sucked my assole up into my mouth… suck baby, you little bitch, suck, put your finger up my…" And when Rainer decides to make "The biggest juiciest ice cream sundae" she doesn't whip it up in a dish.

Cheap, nasty, politically incorrect and hopelessly stranded in time it may be. But Fornicating Female Freaks is – depending on your taste – timeless titillation or matchless comedy.

Roddy Frame: Surf – Redemption 2002
What? Starkly beautiful break-up album.

Frame is best known as the singer/songwriter and mainstay of Aztec Camera, folky tinged indie-pop emperors from Glasgow. Several of his eighties hits like "Good Morning Britain" still see regular radio action. Camera's die-hard fans knew there was a more personal and intimate side to Frame, songs like "Down the Dip" from the first album had hinted at this and Camera's parting-shot, Frestonia (1995), had shown a maturity and complexity that made for repeated listening, if not hit singles.

However, nothing in his catalogue before or since, has approached the stark sound and sense of intimacy of Surf. Offering up the shortest running time of any Frame long-player, Surf's reliance on acoustic guitar, the recording in Frame's front-room, and its repeated exploration of the intimacies of a recently failed relationship all make it feel longer than it is. The title track with its lingering tender-affection for the love he has lost is – arguably – almost too honest. Elsewhere, the sense of a mind slowly turning over past events and coming to terms with loss is slightly easier to take, though reviews at the time suggested playing the collection back to back was a trying experience. Sonically there is little escape from limited tracks, acoustic guitar with overdubs and Frame's frequently quiet and conversational vocals. There are no big sounds or instantly hummable choruses here. But there is a coherent work that delivers a sense of focus and its own stark vision, similar in that regard to Bruce Springsteen's raw emotion on Nebraska, but looking inward to the writer's heart. Similar also to the self-examining of Bon Iver's For Emma, Forever Ago – but more accessible with its lyrics and meanings.

Peter Frampton:
Love Taker
(Bianco, 2000)
What? Piss taker?

The dishonourable habit of dragging recordings from the vaults and rehashing them as something they were never intended to be for the purpose of sales should be marked at least once in this book. There are some albums hereabouts – like Felt's Train Above the City – where the link between the main creative force of an act and the music purporting to represent said act is a little tenuous. Lawrence and Felt – at least – knew what they were doing. There isn't much evidence that Peter Frampton sanctioned or approved this album. Love Taker is a bizarre curio in the disreputable dreg pile of desperate discs.

For starters, this isn't a solo Frampton release, but he is involved. Love Taker's convoluted history starts in the seventies where all of the material started life on the album Grits and Cornbread by big-voiced and highly hopeful Nanette Workman. Her backing band includes some notable names: Johnny Hallyday (yeah, really, him!), Bobby Keyes and Jim Price. Backing vocalists Madeline Bell, Doris Troy and Lisa Strike are also on hand and Frampton does contribute some vocals and guitar. One of the cuts "All I Wanna be is by Your Side" is a Frampton original – albeit lacking the original brackets on his title - which first saw release on his debut solo set Wind of Change (1972), around the time Love Taker was recorded. Nanette Workman's solo set stiffed and the tapes have subsequently been reheated to order in an attempt to get some sales out of a spirited recording. The same set has traded under the name Pacific Freight a couple of times, firstly being credited to The Heavy Metal Boys and later credited to Frampton "and Friends." Love Taker is simply another roll of the desperate dice. Lacking a couple of the numbers – "Billy" and "P.S. Get Lost" - that closed the original Nanette Workman album Love Taker clocks in just over the half hour mark, offers up seven cuts and does rock out in a range of seventies styles. In addition to covering Frampton, Nanette turns in a decent cover of The Stones' "Loving Cup." Love Taker's title track is composed by Gary Wright and Nanette Workman contributes some originals. For the most part it's classy blues-rock. Workman's voice does sterling work to direct it all, and Love Taker visits country and rock 'n' roll to some useful purpose. Taken on its own merits it is a solid set and it started a respected if less than stellar solo career for Nanette Workman. Online reviews are – to say the least – mixed. Frampton fans slating it as a total rip-off, Workman's supporters recognising it for what it is and chiming in with comments like the following from Mark "OneCoolRockin'Daddy" Austin: "Start with a heavy dose of Janis, mix in a li'l Ruby Jones/Ruby Starr (Black Oak Arkansas), some Joy Of Cooking, and then for integrity, Ann Wilson and eventually Melissa Etheridge & anyone sounding like her…you've got one healthy supply of some of Workman's finest work in her career."

Austin, has a point, but so does everyone who ever complained that the music business is a cynical hell-hole willing to squeeze the last tepid drops from a briefly hot recording. Obviously, any opinion offered here is personal and we respect the rights of the owners of recorded works to release their wares as they see fit. Love Taker is a decent listen, packs decent material and includes decent performances. Elsewhere in the music industry there is a depressing tonnage of out-takes, sub-standard live cuts and abortive attempts to create magic that were subsequently mis-sold, misrepresented, and widely mistaken for genuine product by punters who probably still wake up in cold sweats thinking of their exposure to abysmal audio and their parting with vast sums of cash to own copies of these putrid performances.

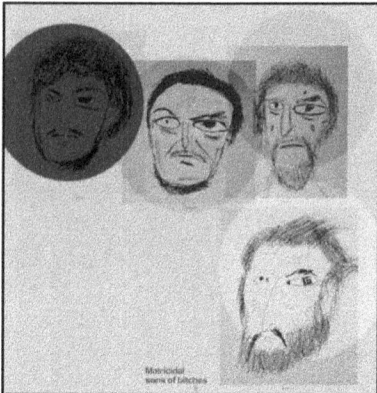

Matthew Friedberger:
Matricidal Sons of Bitches
(Thrill Jockey, 2012)
What? Musical visionary of Fiery Furnaces lets imagination run wild on soundtrack to imaginary movie.

A complete and utter indulgence that is likely only to make complete sense to its creator, Matricidal Sons of Bitches is never-the-less a major stop along the road of a varied and hugely prolific solo journey for the male half of The Fiery Furnaces. With sister Eleanor Matthew Friedberger has achieved most of his profile as a member of the indie rock band. A hiatus in their career allowed both siblings to download solo ideas. Matthew's output dwarfed his sister's and included a series of "Solos," albums focussed on exploring the possibilities of working with a single instrument – including guitar, piano, double bass and harp. Matricidal Sons of Bitches aspires to explore sound in a different direction.

This is sonic narrative, a soundtrack to an imaginary horror movie, running almost movie-length and separated into four parts which – even on the CD edition – are identified as: Side One, Side Two….

Sonically the old-school instrumentation: chiming and aged piano, organ, general rumbling and scraping generated on acoustic instruments etc. puts the whole piece into a retro-chic horror mood in which the lengthy slow passages are – presumably – the accompaniment to the sections of movie we spend with the characters whilst they aren't being threatened. Much of the tension builds with repetitive chord patterns, sudden stops as the broody themes return to take over, and the simple but effective trick of turning up the volume. There are words, but not many, and the packaging is the most useful narrative guide. If offers up exposition that weaves a confusing narrative: "So Jeff had to murder his or her Zombie twin to save herself himself or to save the un-zombied parts of the zombie twin or the zombie bits of the non-zombie…" Similarly the guide to the four sides doesn't specify a running order but does list titles included on each side.

The onus is on the listener to take the guidance, take the music, and imagine. For the most part the music on offer builds on Friedberger's ability with a solo instrument. He presents a number of mournful refrains, favours acoustic instruments and relatively simple arrangements, but shows willing to throw them aside with rapid fire busts of electric sound including standard keyboard/bass/electronic percussion moments that reference the sonic signature of a whole breed of low-budget gore-fest movies.

Like the work of others collated here – William Schumann, David Holmes – this does demand the listener gives it an effort. Matricidal Sons of Bitches simply isn't background music or a notably easy listen despite its atmospheric and gentle passages. As an advert for Friedberger's abilities as a sound-track composer it works superbly. As mix-tape material it's also fairly effective.

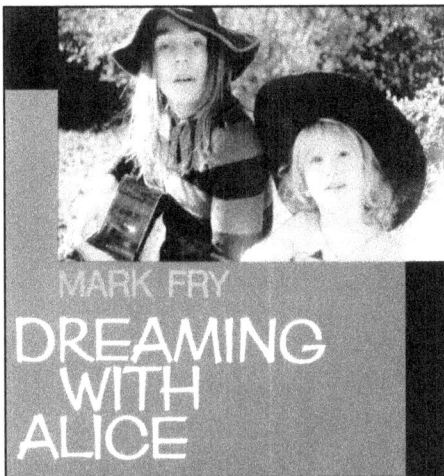

Mark Fry:
Dreaming With Alice
(IT Dischia/ RCA, 1972)
What? Allged "lost classic" alert…hang on; it's beautiful.

Latterly rediscovered, re-released and played in places like Stuart Maconie's Freak Zone, this long-lost seventies gem is finally finding the belated appreciation enjoyed by the likes of Vashti Bunyan. Bunyan, or Donovan pre rock band backing, are a useful yardstick for a wistful wonder of a collection that eschews standard percussion, strips the instrumentation to the bare essentials needed to surround Fry's mellow vocals, and gives the impression of intimacy and sharing. By common consent some of the above was achieved out of necessity. Il Dischia were an autonomous Italian offshoot of RCA, a nurturing but cash strapped crew who obliged Fry to cut this collection in a basement which – quite simply – didn't allow for big percussion in the form of a drum kit. The strategy used to fill the two sides in such limited circumstances leaves Dreaming With Alice pulling every psych-folk stroke time and again. "The Witch" and "Mandolin Man" noodle and improvise their way onwards and upwards before finally locating themselves somewhere comfortably in inner space. The presence of vocal echo, generally blurring on the edges of Fry's diction, sporadic flute, sitar and bongos all keep the psych-folk vibe to the fore and a master-stroke in this department is the splicing of the lengthy title track into segments which crop up from the start of the album, and separate most of the other tracks. Like the instrumental interludes on James Taylor's eponymous debut on Apple, it's effective, thoughtful and suggestive of an over-arching theme. "Dreaming With Alice" – as in the whole song – actually clocks in a shade short of seven minutes, but only the final fragment on the album, one short of the final track, runs over a minute. By this point Dreaming With Alice has proven its worth with a series of songs that make a virtue of the simple beauty of chord changes, vocal inflections and the adroit adjustment of a level here, or a backing instrument there. Having put you in the presence of a perfectly arranged collection, that teeters permanently on the edge of Alice in Wonderland/ gentle soul spilling itself lyrical territory, Dreaming With Alice delivers a killer finale with a revisit to "Song For Wilde" – the fourth track on side one – re-titling it "Rehtorb Ym No Hcram" and delivering the whole two and half minutes backwards. Kim Fowley – in the guise of Napoleon XIV – did the same thing, presenting a B-side to his hit that amounted to the a-side in reverse, but on Dreaming With Alice this is less a stunt and more an affirmation of the dream we've just shared. The original "Song For Wilde" is a love song to Fry's little brother, pictured on the cover, and is driven slowly forward by somnambulant finger-picking and slowly shifting chord pattern, so backwards it is a familiar web of gentle sound.

Acid folk was seldom more enticing.

The Fugs: It Crawled into my Hand, Honest – Reprise 1968
What? Funny ho-ho and funny strange.

Comedy, protest and the thick scent of marijuana collide to perfection in the best moments of The Fugs' catalogue. Time hasn't been kind to their comedy. Most of their early targets are long dead or highly irrelevant (as in the case of the Vietnam War) to much current thinking. But history has exposed their anarchic and often inspired recordings for the surreal flights of comic fancy they often are. Their second outing, It Crawled... is arguably the pick of the bunch. Close enough to their angry/anarchic origins to still have their early energy in abundance, and helmed with enough of a budget from Reprise Records to provide the troupe with the soundscapes to do justice to their ambitious ideas. The Fugs' closest relatives are probably The Firesign Theatre, both acts seeing the long-playing album as the perfect vehicle for comedy and counter-culture to co-exist, and trusting in their audience to put in the effort to unpick the most complex jokes. The Fugs resemble Monty Python in their willingness to present sketch and song length pieces, but offer up more of an insider take when it comes to music, satirizing, self-satirizing and clearly in love with some of the material they maul. All of the above intellectualizing blurs the fact that It Crawled... is that rare comedy classic that can amuse and inform in equal measure. The opening "Crystal Liaison" being a case in point; a blissful piece of psychedelia that cops all the – then – current sounds and still manages a massive broadside at the Electric Prunes' "Kyrie Eleison." The second side opens with equal force, the redneck satire "Johnny Pissoff Meets the Red Angel" being – arguably – the best thing on It Crawled... whilst the fragmentary "Marijuana" – basically a hymn to the herb presented in a high church style vocal arrangement – shows the kind of explosive comedy genius the Fugs armoury had at its high-point. Elsewhere little gems like "National Haiku Contest" are buried between towers of wordy comedy, obliging the listener to unpick them with concentration and headphones. Formed by poets Ed Sanders and Tuli Kupferberg in New York in the mid-sixties, The Fugs always had the capacity to be wordy, dense and wilfully obscure. Today, their most indulgent moments are more nostalgic than inspirational but It Crawled... offers enough of the biting satire and surreal riffing on a theme to stand up well so long after the event.

Funkadelic: Maggot Brain – Westbound 1971
What? Out there – musically speaking – but generally in the mix when the best/most influential funk is considered.

Maggot Brain is a monster more than one sense of the word. Massively influential on funk, disco and just about every major trend of "black" seventies music, bookended by two extended workouts – "Maggot Brain" and "Wars of Armageddon" – and an album that can barely contain the ideas and aspirations for itself within the 37 minutes allocated. Funkadelic remain a by-word for ground-breaking in musical styles, and this is the first full stirring of the manifesto that applied in their best days. The third album by the band and the final outing credited to their original line up, Maggot Brain is in your face as soon as it is in your ears. A spoken word intro stating: "Mother Earth is pregnant for the third time, for y'all have knocked her up" announces the opening instrumental cut which meanders and plays tricks from speaker to speaker, setting up a range of restrained sounds which will feature in what is to come. Once the groove of "Hit it or Quit it" hits hard, the pace quickens, Funkadelic start to reference the Sly Stone, Hendrix and James Brown roots that have brought them here and Maggot Brain is upon us for what will be one hell of a ride.

It is all over the place in terms of style but the closing freak-out of "Wars of Armageddon" – which samples everything from a mooing cow, to a crying baby and airport announcements - is a perfect finale. Eddie Hazel's lead guitar has gone everywhere from the lengthy forays of the title track to bursts of blues, rock and elegant licks behind the soulful vocals. George Clinton's bass has driven massive, and sweet grooves and the band have checked in everywhere from sex and fun to serious social issues. "You and Your Folks, Me and My Folks" was still a cutting edge comment on inter-racial relationships in 1971. The strength of a band who could follow "You and Your Folks…" with "Super Stupid" – a groove so gleefully simple it is an articulate argument for pure fun – is the strength of a band completely in charge of their mission. "Super Stupid" pits furious soloing, a brief punky riff and that massive bass into a mix that assaults any idea of dividing lines between musical genres, makes its case and swiftly departs.

Maggot Brain continues to matter because the power of what Funkadelic achieve time and time again here has eluded many of those with similar pretensions ever since. In that sense Maggot Brain is important because it channels the spirit of the handful of barrier breaking musicians who had explored this territory before – notably Hendrix and Sly Stone – and foresees everything from the best things disco and soul would offer to the way Lenny Kravitz and his ilk would distil, perfect and popularise some of the elements fused here.

Funky Junction:
Play a Tribute to Deep Purple
(Stereo Gold Award, 1973)
What? Not much like a tribute, not that much like Deep Purple either.

Knocked out as a supermarket budget-price slice of hard rock for the kids, Funky Junction Play a Tribute to Deep Purple has become belatedly collectible because the one-off quintet who recorded this album-for-cash were made up of Thin Lizzy (in their 1972 entirety of Phil Lynott, Eric Bell and Brian Downy), supplemented by Irish vocalist Benny White and keyboardist Dave Lennox (who performed Purple covers with their band Elmer Fudd). Only five of the nine tracks on offer are genuine Purple songs and one of these – "Hush" – a big American hit in 1968, dates from the pre-Mark II Purple line up who recorded the originals of "Fireball," "Strange Kind of Woman," "Speed King" and "Black Night."

It might be collector's gold for Lizzy completists (many of whom hadn't a clue about the members of Funky Junction until long after vinyl copies had ceased to sell), but this collection screams "budget" pretty loudly. The front cover is simply repeated as the back picture, laid over a yellow background and placed on top of a track list (which is presented in the wrong order). The band pictured rocking out on the front cover aren't Deep Purple and definitely aren't Funky Junction (who never played a gig and completed their career after "two or three hours" of rehearsal followed by knocking this album out in a day). In fact, internet pages devoted to the album claim the cover stars to be a largely forgotten bunch of seventies hard rockers called Hard Stuff.

The quartet of non-Purple cuts that make up the album include the kind of party tricks and favoured jamming fodder that were second nature to the participants. Lizzy guitarist Eric Bell let's rip on "Dan," (imagine Jimi Hendrix having a stab at "Danny Boy") and Dave Lennox gets his keyboard moment in "Rising Sun" (a moody jam-along of "House of the Rising Sun"). All the non Purple songs are credited to Leo Muller (who was the main mover in getting this collection recorded and released).

Given the thrown together nature of the affair the production sound is passable if somewhat one dimensional. The set was cut in the London's De Lane Lea Studios that boasted Purple cuts "Flight of the Rat" and "Hard Lovin' Man" from In Rock. The big sound and incendiary licks of prime period Purple are in short supply. Benny White acquits himself manfully in the nigh-on impossible role of mimicking Ian Gillan at his best and for all its Purple-lite hollowness Funky Junction Play a Tribute to Deep Purple stands one good listen for those who were there, or thereabouts at the time. If you can't track it down anywhere (the world still awaits a CD reissue) you could always try hunting a vinyl copy of a German release called "The Rock Machine Play the Best of Deep Purple," it's exactly the same album as this. [*]

Billy Fury:
The Sound of Fury
(Decca, 1960)
What? Decent rock 'n' roll album written and recorded in Britain shocker!!

Billy Fury (1940–1983) achieved some impressive career statistics – clocking up over 330 weeks in British charts from 1959 to 1983 and managing a lengthy series of hit albums and singles. However, in terms of lasting achievement The Sound of Fury may well be the most impressive achievement of all. A ten track 10" album, The Sound of Fury aped the leading American acts, like Elvis, with an echo-laden but essentially simple rock 'n' roll backing and plenty of space in the mix for the singer to tell his stories. Fury offers a selection of vocal tics and range of intonations and a series of love/swagger/lifestyle stories in the songs presenting him as – by turns – tough, aloof and just a shade vulnerable. Fury's classic cheekbones, general good looks and wistful but strong expression on the front cover are also winning touches. But the real break-through – placing him ahead of most contemporary American acts – is the song-writing. Fury wrote every cut himself, most of them credited to Wilbur Wilberforce. The secret to the rockin' set is partly the presence of a solid band. The same musicians play over the whole album and Joe Brown's lead and rhythm guitar is a particular stand out, belying the speed at which the whole collection was cut and the quality of British studio recording at the time.

The opening "That's Love" – credited to Fury's writing – was the big hit from the album but the tough but tender sentiments of "Turn my Back on You" and "Since You've Been Gone" are also up there with the best song-writing and performances of the era and the way the collection clatters by, sounding like a polished set from a damn good rock 'n' roll band with a confident singer out front, is the real attraction. Subsequent reissues have tended to surround The Sound of Fury with a welter of bonus material.

---

[*] EDITOR'S NOTE: There is a possibility that there *may* be a second album which was credited to *Funky Junction* in the mid 1970s, although I am quite prepared to accept that it may be a figment of my over addled imagination. . I actually owned the album described above, and when I was about fifteen I remember seeing another album by the same band, this time singing songs of Ike and Tina Turner, for sale in Woolworths in Bideford High Street. I had no money so didn't buy it, and have never seen it again. I also can find no trace of the record online. However there is a completely different band with the same name who do cover versions (including of Tina Turner), but they are all younger than me, so would appear to have nothing to do with the case. If any reader can help with this mystery please write to me c/o Gonzo Multimedia.

The George Garabedian Players and the Awful Trumpet of Harry Arms:
Hooray for Hollywood
(?, 1968)
What? Pfffttt! For Hollywood.

This one-shot novelty from the sixties is scarce to the point of extinction on the original vinyl. Enough copies have been snaffled in second hand shops over the years to ensure a certain cult status and mp3 files of the individual cuts now appear on a range of music sites and blogs. All of which means, the music is known, but any person or website purporting to give you the original facts of its production shouldn't be trusted completely. The claim, via more reputable sites like the WFMU blog, suggests that George Garabedian was a record executive with access to the best session players. That much is, provably, true. Garabedian is credited on other, more mainstream releases from the burgeoning brass scene of the sixties and beyond.

The USP on this release, Harry Arms' "awful trumpet" is harder to prove. There's a story that Arms was "a third-month trumpet student with no idea of how to tune his instrument." He certainly sounds like such a creature, but it's beside the point now whether his paint peeling lead lines present him as a victim of a cruel joke. Acts like Spike Jones and his City Slickers turned apparent incompetence into a fine art of fun-making, and Arms has that quality consistently.

The concept is simple, a lively brass ensemble set about the material that Herb Albert and others were turning into sales gold. Two sides of tuneful and lively standards are lined up and played with skill, and Arms is the wild card in the bunch. Out of tune, out of time and exposed in the full glare of the mix. He throws brass chords off key and crashes and burns repeatedly as the arrangements call for an accomplished soloist. The fact he is slaughtering the likes of "Spanish Flea" and "Hooray for Hollywood" – i.e. massive tunes, wholly dependent on a combination of strong tempo and precise hitting of notes – only makes things worse. If you sample just one cut online we would suggest it is the near flatulent obliteration of Jimmy Webb's "Up Up and Away." Arms' lead line wavers, belches and scrapes its way along. The mirth comes thick and fast because Arms' never lets the tension drop. He's so close, but so far away, from getting it right and the big "hold 'em" notes are comedy gold.

Charlotte Gainsbourg:
IRM
(Electra, 2010)
What? Post-traumatic master class of processing inner darkness through performance.

Gainsbourg records as she acts, fulfilling roles and appearing at her best when another person is present to direct and guide the work. In the case of IRM that person is Beck (who writes and produces) and their collaboration digs into a darkness that does credit to both artists. Gainsbourg brings a sense of theatricality that extends the lyrics and ideas into a series of studies of character. She may, on occasion, be acting her way through a song, but the character she plays clearly draws from herself. Beck's songs, soundscapes and incessant generation of new moods give Gainsbourg the quality of material to make her means of performance work perfectly. Gainsbourg had suffered a traumatic head injury, sufficient to threaten her life, in the run up to this recording. That she escaped with her mobility and memories in shape was little short of miraculous and this experience is relived in the title track: "Hold still and press the button, looking through a glass onion, following the x-ray eye, from the cortex to the medulla." The track incorporates the sounds of an MRI scanner (IRM is the same terminology in a French acronym).

The confident move from this to something as gleefully effervescent as "In the End" is a mark of the abilities of both songwriter and performer. "Trick Pony" is another standout, the kind of edgy and resourceful production Beck can pull out in his sleep with Gainsbourg effortlessly cool and swaggering her way through the vocal. The variety and quality of the more demanding material here allows the pair to throw the simplest of riffs into a track like "Trick Pony" and still leave the album sounding like a perfect sequence of varied moods, all contributing to a masterclass in making a collection of real merit.

Diamanda Galas: Plague Mass – (Mute 1991)
What? Gargantuan life/death theme conveyed with virtuoso vocal pyrotechnics.

Galas doesn't do anything by halves, with a track record of being arrested for her beliefs she has regularly taken protests on issues like AIDS to the doorsteps of those opposed to her views. As a rule her music explores big life/death issues and a great many offshoots, setting agendas to make lesser talents flinch and building complex works around her incredible vocal range.

Plague Mass is – arguably – the perfect fusion of all of these elements. Culled from a performance in the Cathedral of Saint John the Divine in New York; the sound is cathedral/cavernous, the vibe spine-chilling, and the results generally sufficient to silence any casual conversation in rooms where Plague Mass is played.

The blatant statements about AIDS and criticism of authorities – including those in charge of the venue for this performance – erupt from "Let Us Praise the Masters of Slow Death" but Plague Mass works its complex magic because in-your-face references to "pussy licking" and "genocide" here lie side-by-side with the vocal gymnastics that propel an epic like the 11 minute 44 second "This is the Law of the Plague."

The backing is frequently little more than slapping and stark percussion (never more effective than when building suddenly into a cacophony). Galas achieves ranges of tone and flights of jazzy riffage with her voice, which moves in a split second from intoning and singing to vocalising rapid-fire sequences of notes. Treated with echo and driven forward by a mentality bordering madness on "Sono L'Antichristo," Galas' performance presents her voice as an instrument to rival any other. Crank up the headphones to let the wandering voice inhabit your brain, turn down the lights, and for three minutes you taste madness in the raw.

Over the duration it is that raw-edged tension between the changes and facets of Plague Mass and the fact that so much of it is delivered with one human voice that makes for a challenging, frightening and matchless work.

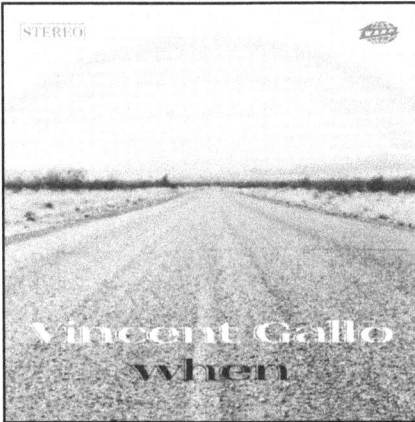

Vincent Gallo:
When
(Warp, 2001)
What? Moody and mellow full-length solo debut from actor, director and alternative polymath.

Gallo remains much better known for acting, writing and directing movies than for a music career that has seen membership of several bands, helming soundtracks to movies and involvement in a range of other projects. When and Warp records are a perfect fit. The label that launched The Aphex Twin appears a fitting home for music that is inescapably alternative, influenced by dance and still very much in its own world. Half of When's ten tracks are instrumental within which we find instruments in stark isolation, stop-start beginnings and a slow, brooding, moodiness to offset the simplicity. Nothing here is hard to access, most of what's on offer is hard to grasp. The five vocal cuts sound like Gallo cut them with the levels very high and his lips almost brushing the mic. He sings gently, thoughtfully and with a conversational tone to the point that in songs like "Honey Bunny" some lines fall away, almost, into conversation. Solo instrumental breaks offer up the simplest melodies with the shifting but very sparing layers of keyboard and guitar underneath bringing in some counterpoint, though Gallo is frequently happy to let the message be carried when every instrument but one stops, the songs simply fade etc.

There are nods to the most introspective ends of indie and alternative rock and enough sense of the ambient production sounds that made Warp one of the hottest labels for dance music with cross over potential. When blends all of these elements behind the strong sense of Gallo's personality and Gallo's thoughts, producing a vulnerable, intimate, apparently simple, but haunting collection that sounds – sometimes – like home demos tidied up, but still works its charm in an effortless way.

General Electric Silicone Products Department:
Got To Investigate Silicones
(Own Label, 1973)
What? If you only sample one industrial product musical show in your lifetime...

The internet has sparked a mini-revival of interest in industrial product musicals and related items. In their sixties and seventies pomp these shows were frequently the highlight of lavish corporate events wherein sales forces, employees and any other persons involved in an area of work, were force fed the corporate message and sent out, suitably charged, to maximise sales and sooth shareholder anxieties. For years the varied results of this work could be found languishing in thrift store bins (this was mainly a US phenomenon). A handful of hardened collectors would avail themselves of the random delights on offer.

By common consent, this gem (ho ho) ranks with the very best. B.C. Sterrett of The Lost Media Archive, praising it as: "the Holy Grail of industrial/product musicals." A back to back listen is akin to attending a massive religious festival in a country gone completely, obsessively, mad. The standard of work, quality of production, variety of tunes and performances on offer is amazing. Did we mention that the ceaseless ingenuity in spinning out the basic message is awesome? C'mon Buddy, get with it, Silicone is a miracle and YOU are the messenger!

The first message to hit home is that so much focus and effort went into praising the qualities of silicone (bear in mind this is pre computing/pre Silicone valley). We are treated to a genuine, original, show orchestra overture. Then "We've Got a Story to Tell" introduces the abundant and highly able cast before suggesting their subject would lend itself to everything from an operetta to a situation comedy. It punts luscious lyrical gems like: "I got a way to show the Silicone romance: tap out the message with a tip-top tap dance" into the limitless cheese on offer and heralds half a dozen tuneful, varied and wholly on message delights exploring the miracle product. Just before the short "Finale" a beautifully vamped ballad "Sand" really pushes the envelope on mature sexiness, or as much of that quality as Silicone can muster. Assuming you're male, tied to the mortgage and the sales targets, and hell bent on climbing the career ladder this is – presumably - the moment when the show takes the message from your head to somewhere between your legs and gives you the whole body experience of getting onside to sell, sell, SELL!!

Mp3 copies are – as of this writing – not too hard to track down online. Be warned, should this masterpiece whet your appetite for other such product, there are alternatives also available, many of which are nowhere near as accomplished, varied and inventive as this.

Bobbie Gentry:
The Delta Sweete
(Capitol, 1968)
What? Master work from long retired country chanteuse.

This late sixties second long-player from self-taught and self-reliant chart star has all the hallmarks of a true cult classic, but few of the long-tail sales. It sounds nothing like Richard Harris' A Tramp Shining or Robin Gibb's Robin's Reign, but might usefully be compared to those two steady sellers, and established cult favourites, for several reasons. Firstly, The Delta Sweete hangs together with an overarching sense of each song being part of a greater whole. Care is taken in the sequencing and the way one piece fades to another. Secondly, the skilful blending extends to the gradual teasing out of themes. Gentry may have her roots in country balladry but she has the intelligence and confidence to apply skilful touches when and wherever required. It is her playing the attention grabbing guitar riff that opens a creditable cover of Mose Allison's "Parchmant Farm" and her lyrics that skilfully pun on her surname in the opening "Okolona River Bottom Band."

Another comparison to Gibb, Harris and a few other cult classics is the combination of grandeur in production, and a consistent sense of songs and artist pushing against the limits of any one genre of music. Delta Sweete may be steeped in country and sure of its down home roots, but when it wants to be blue Gentry takes on "Big Boss Man" and does it determinedly her way (a brazen act in an era when Elvis turned in a fine version of the same song). The problem in describing such a collection is that any such account is permanently in danger of listing a series of triumphs and using the collective sum of the parts to argue the merits of the album. Delta Sweete works at a higher level than this because it marks three notable high points on one record. Firstly, Gentry plays and sings to such a degree that her talent is always there to be celebrated. Secondly, she claims a range of material, both originals and covers, and uses this to channel performances that celebrate her abilities and move the listener through a series of emotions. Finally, she sequences these gems to deliver an album that, quite simply, works as a complete piece and withstands repeated listening without losing its lustre.

Robin Gibb:
Robin's Reign
(Polydor, 1969)
What? Fleeting moment of monarchy makes for pop gem.

Robin Gibb was the mystical/freakish Bee Gee and the only one to formally leave the band for a solo career. A brief but bitter spat regarding the favouring of Barry's "First of May" over Robin's "Lamplight" as a single A' side prompted the massive solo hit "Saved by the Bell" (included here) and the recording of a deliberate stab at establishing a solo career and solo sound.

There are other solo Bee Gee outings (more by Robin than anyone else) but nothing other than Robin's Reign that starts with the intention of never returning to the band. For the most part this is pure pop music, a thicker instrumentation than the band built around Robin's sharp, expressive and nasal vocal lines, and a definite attempt to call in at a few productive pop stations in the hope of establishing the kingdom for Robin's reign. As such, Robin's Reign is great in parts (though few fanatical lovers of the album can agree on the best ones) and forever interesting and ambitious.

Scott Walker's solo efforts around the same period are one useful yardstick in terms of production. The massive sound of the opener "August, October" drags in a full string section and still finds space in the production for a mandolin, whilst "Lord Bless All" – from the second side of the original album – puts Robin's vocals into a cavernous sound and surrounds them with a doomy church organ.

Elsewhere Robin's Reign makes a determined grab at a level of detail, social realism and strong heart-rending emotion that the Bee Gees typically eschew. Both sides close on such cuts: "Mother and Jack" – which ends side one – deals with eviction and "Most of My Life" – which closes the original album – clocks in over five minutes and pulls off the apparent simplicity/deep inner life/ pathos trick of The Smiths at their most sincere. All of it slowly sung over a standard pop-with-strings backing and supported by a gently descending melody.

There are stabs at atypical and never repeated experiments; "Worst Girl In This Town" is the nearest thing to a straight Bee Gees number, albeit with Robin on all the vocal harmonies, and "Farmer Ferdinand Hudson" is the kind of cheery pop-psyche-out perfected by The Monkees.

Most of the other solo Bee Gees efforts mine the same groove of sounding like spin-offs from brand Bee Gee and adding an extended glimpse of the individual skill of Robin or Barry. Robin's Reign – by contrast – is a collection of sixties pop styles and wilful experiments to find both the inner Robin Gibb and a strong solo identity. He returned – of course – to the band and died feted and wealthy, but he never wandered this far out creatively until his classical work Titanic Requiem; first performed as he lay dying and unable to attend the concert in 2012.

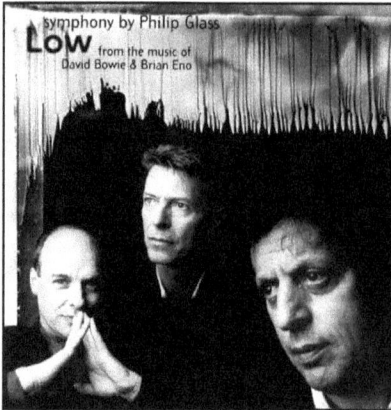

Philip Glass:
Symphony # 1 (The Low Symphony)
(Point Music, 1993)
What? Rock/classical collision that works to perfection.

The world was awash with various orchestral massacres of classic rock works long before Philip Glass began work on a classical re-imagining of the first of David Bowie's "Berlin Trilogy" albums. The original Low packs one-side almost completely instrumental in nature, slow in tempo and starkly introspective. Glass addresses himself to the slow melodies, repetitive themes and tonal dynamics of these tracks to produce a 42 minute orchestral work, set in three parts and built firmly on the major melodic pieces on Low's "dark" side. The symphony offers up its three movements under the titles "Subterraneans," "Some Are" and "Warszawa" and anyone familiar with the original work is likely to feel at home immediately on hearing the first and last movement. "Some Are" – based on a Low outtake – is a perfect complement to the opening and closing pieces.

As one of the most influential and forward thinking composers of his generation Glass had every right here to take the same licence with reality that Salvador Dali would have allowed himself with Low's cover. But, the really striking element about The Low Symphony, (actually the subtitle but the name almost everyone applies to this work), is how reverent and restrained it is. Glass's main stylistic approach involves sticking closely to the opening sounds of each original track, recreating the tonal dynamics - originally presented with keyboards, guitars, sax and percussion – with the differing sounds of an orchestra and then expanding the melodic themes in the middle of each movement to move the music into typical Glass territory of minimalist and slowly unfolding melody, all heavily reliant on the sounds of individual instruments. In all, 20 orchestral instruments (including trumpets and trombones) take or share a brief lead role, a separate string section, harp, piano and assorted percussion also play their part. The varied instruments – arriving and departing as readily as individual instruments on a rock album – give The Low Symphony a modern feel and constantly reference the original sound crafted in Berlin by Bowie, Eno and Visconti. The first recorded version to be released in 1993 incorporated the ideas – though not the performances – of those who had been there at the original recording. NOT something subsequent recordings have done. Glass went on to compose a Heroes symphony.

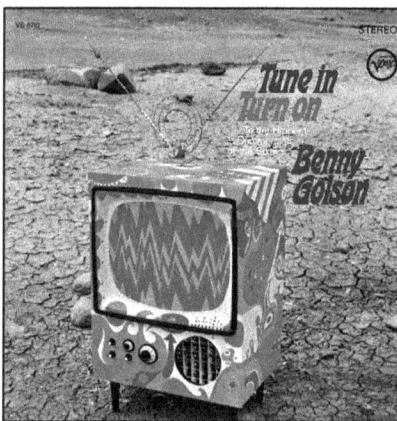

Benny Golson:
Turn In, Turn On to the Hippest Commercials of the Sixties
(Verve, 1967)
What? Crazy! But not always in the way the makers intended.

Musically this album walks a thin line between self-parody and stupendous inspiration. The idea is simple enough, a hip jazz reworking of classic 1960s American television commercials. Sometimes the short meanders from standard commercial melody line into instrumental flurries and brief experimentation work exceptionally well. Sometimes the silk-purse-from-sow's-ear efforts betray the brainlessness of the originals. "The Swinger" may look promising as a title in the running order, but – for anyone under 50 – we should point out this was the brand name of an instant camera produced by the Polaroid Corporation. The track of this title struggles manfully to make magic from a tune never designed for such heights. That, crudely, is the charm of this bizarre collection of a dozen, radio friendly, nuggets.

Anyone old enough to recall the original adverts is bound to think of the music in that context, though the album emphasises the point for anyone too young in this regard by leaving original vocal tracks on some recordings. The theme music for The Magnificent Seven might also be a distraction for anyone not brought up in the USA, where the music is instantly recognisable as the sound behind a series of Malboro cigarette adverts. Nobody is seriously going to argue that top end musical merits of this highly mixed collection. But, it packs a curious charm and the CD packaging recreates the original cover art, complete with old style bulky television set painted in psychedelic colours.

The Great Kat:
Beethoven on Speed
(Roadracer/Intercord, 1990)
What? Rock/classical collision that works to perfection. (Hang on, didn't we just say that about Philip Glass and Bowie?)

Katherine Thomas was born in Swindon, Wiltshire, raised in New York, trained as a classical violinist and employed in this capacity. The Great Kat (basically a foul-mouthed metal dominatrix alter-ego) took possession of her body decades ago, since when guitar-shred (basically rocket fuelled metal soloing of incredible durability and dexterity) has been her calling card of choice. Kat long ago ditched proper albums in favour of hit and run EP collections wherein she trashes the greatest hits of a specific composer. If you're up for sampling one of those we'd recommend Rossini's Rape with its wham-bam wallop through the "William Tell Overture." However, for the full bag of tricks Kat has yet to better Beethoven on Speed. The work stands as a manifesto for the career that followed it. At once a ludicrously ambitious weaving of classical sensibilities, concept album notions of thematic links and RAWK-writ-large sonic assault, Beethoven on Speed shreds the great one's works with gleeful irreverence. We could find no detail of how many devotees of classical originals have encountered Kat's caper and gagged in response. No matter, her machinations piss off enough metal and rock devotees, like the "vtelenie" who's Amazon review was headed "OMG" and included the observation: "it is pure masturbation of non artistic virtuosity." Debateable, IOHO.

The whole point with Kat's music is to stick it to anyone who can't stand the pace and fury. Beethoven on Speed sticks it solidly and steadily with each new trick unleashed before the last one went stale. Each side of the original vinyl claims itself as an opus (i.e. Kat's creative vision of the compiled pieces) and the greatest hits are duly trashed. As a measure of her love of theatricality the signature 5th Symphony is rifled through and sent reeling inside the opening two minutes of the album, after which Kat's occasional vocals intrude on tracks like "Worshipping Bodies," her violin virtuosity erupts on "Sex and Violins" (great violin-shred but if you want to have sex whilst listening, take your clothes off first, the track is done in one minute and 28 seconds), visits worlds beyond Beethoven, notably with a Paganini shred on side two before ending the whole caper with the perfect collision of attitude and arrogance in the 25 seconds of "For Geniuses Only."

This is novelty, shameless genius and surprisingly effective hard metal in one package. Far too tricksy for lovers of pure metal (or classical) music and funny in the jaw-drop Jackass tradition that obliges you to get on board with the whole idea before the joke makes any real sense. But Kat's Beethoven does allow the great man, and The Great Kat, to emerge with reputations well and truly intact.

Grouper:
Dragging a Dead Deer up a Hill
(Type, 2009)
What? Minimal ethereal wonder, made from the simplest ingredients.

Liz Harris, AKA Grouper has carved a niche of a career based on simple melodic structures, barely discernable vocals and albums with a dream-like presence in the room. Dragging a Dead Deer…marked something of a departure in its dispensing with the fuzzed out guitar sound that had made her first releases sound a little like the Jesus and Mary Chain. More determinedly acoustic, and more ready to use Liz's assured and strong vocals as the lead line on the melody, Dragging a Dead Deer…opens on a wind/fuzz effect but soon veers into basic keyboards, lots of acoustic guitar and a sound both heavily muffled and epically wide. Obvious touchstones are the Cocteau Twins for its other-worldly and dream-like qualities or Bon Iver for the in-the-room acoustic sense and the bittersweet melodies. It's only the odd track – like "A Cover Over" – on which the vocals are clear, elsewhere "Wind and Snow" is an atmospheric instrumental gem. Some of the simplest musical tricks work wonderfully; the production on "Travelling Through a Sea" is so minimal that the scratching of Harris' fingers on the strings of her acoustic guitar forms an extra element to the melody and floats above the sea of sound as the only treble heavy element in the mix. The sound palette is taken from both inside and outside the studio, and the overall effect is like being in a twilight wood, or far enough away from other people that nature – with its different rhythms and sense of time – is setting the tempo.

Fundamental to the fragile magic of the whole creation is the slow flowing of one track into another, the changes, from far away vocals offering no clear sound-bites, to songs you can follow, from a one simple melody to another, from a vocal track to an instrumental, all make for an album that sounds like a complete work rather than a selection of the best takes from a series of sessions. Dragging a Dead Deer… is an elusive companion, offering up secrets sparingly, but it is a warm presence in the room, and one that repays the time and effort you need to put into a good friendship.

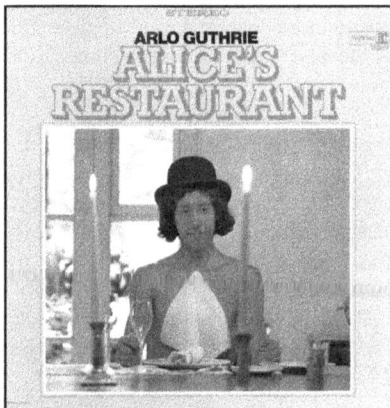

Arlo Guthrie:
Alice's Restaurant
(Reprise, 1967)
What? Known for one track. Under-rated as a collection.

Most albums don't share a title track and story-line with a movie, so it would be hard to describe Alice's Restaurant as any kind of under-achievement. Its presence in record stores – especially outside the US – and the amount of critical discussion lavished on an album that was once, almost, a rite of passage, has diminished over the years, but the collection still gets discussed as a classic. Alice's Restaurant is known mainly for the side-long 18 minute plus epic title track: "Alice's Restaurant Masacree". It is a sardonic and autobiographical slice of narrative brilliance in which Guthrie recounts a tale of hanging with amiable hippies, a few borderline-legal clandestine activities and his – eventual – disqualification from the draft to fight in Vietnam because he was a convicted litterbug. This tale is woven into a gentle polemic inviting anyone so inclined to rise up and resist the draft by singing the chorus: "You can get anything you want at Alice's restaurant." It may be stoner humour of a particular vintage, but like the most apt and acerbic observations of Bill Hicks it is authoritative because it strikes at the heart of hypocrisy and uses intelligence to fight dogma. It also has the warmth and spontaneity of a good live recording in front of a clearly appreciative audience.

The other side of the vinyl album presents a half dozen of the songs that had – by 1967 – helped Guthrie to establish himself as a cherished and capable presence on the folk circuit. More a sampler for his abilities than a statement of a particular position; these songs present a range of moods and styles with understated confidence. Most of the songs are excellent. Collectively they are an argument for Guthrie's abilities being the equal – at that time certainly – of many of his contemporaries. There is throwaway, hippie, humour; particularly in the surreal ramble of "The Motorcycle Song" with its chorus: "I don't want a pickle, I just want to ride on my motor-cycle (pronounced sick-el)…I don't wanna die, Just want to ride on my motor-cycle." An agreeable piece of jugband style nonsense – "Ring-Around-a-Rosy Rag" – also raises a smirk on Alice's Restaurant but the introspective cuts on the song side, particularly "The Chilling of the Evening" – which packs the kind of accessible emotional heft of Jimmy Webb's best ordinary-guy-with-deep-thoughts songs – present Guthrie as a contemporary songwriter with the ability to interpret his own material to great effect. Alice's Restaurant and its immediate aftermath represented a commercial high-point but Guthrie's stock has fallen to the point that many younger listeners don't pick him up along with the other late-sixties touchstones. On this evidence, that's a shame.

GWAR:
Scumdogs of the Universe
(Metal Blade, 1990)
What? The perfect gore-metal pantomime.

Taken seriously this cacophony of grinding riffs, epic vocal harmonies and lyrical gross-out is a disturbing and deranged tirade of the darkest thoughts. GWAR pleasure themselves with envelope pushing, but the tell-tale signs of tongues well in the cheek are never far away. The soaring choruses, emphasising the gags, the hideously over-the-top image and the relentless mining of the borderlands of chunder/chortle in the lyrics make Scumdogs of the Universe that rare animal that satirizes and simultaneously pisses on the competition. GWAR bring intelligence and passion to the party, channelling it into corking observations like: "Maggots are falling like rain!/Putrid pus-pools vomit bubonic plague/The bowels of the beast reek of puke/How to describe such vileness on the page/World maggot waits for the end of the age!" ("Maggots") Armageddon might be upon us, but we're too busy punching the air to give a shit.

Scumdogs of the Universe allows various GWAR's to step up to the mic, altering the sound a little to give each the right space and production to showcase his vocal style. It incorporates a few samples and restrains the indie production and rapid-fire attack of their earlier work to bring in soaring hair-metal guitars and showcase the lyrics. Each song presents a perfect vignette of sick idea and slick delivery. For example, "Slaughterama" gathers laughs from the notion of a game show in which GWAR slaughter followers of other fashions – hippies and skinheads.

In keeping with classic pantomime horror values each character is developed. Sleazy P. Martini gets his turn to shine in the self-explanatory "Sexecutioner." Elsewhere horror lore is invoked with expertise when

"Horror of Yig" calls in somewhere in H.P. Lovecraft territory and we have the obligatory easy to understand/hard to forget RAWK anthem in "Sick of You" (subsequently to see years of service as a show-closer for the band). Dissected on the page like this Scumdogs of the Universe can seem a cynical exercise in building a metal legend. In your ears it is a different experience. GWAR have the visual strength of Kiss, the story-telling inventiveness of Alice Cooper and – whilst it might seem a crass comparison – Scumdogs of the Universe has the Bat out of Hell quality to kick your prejudices about the music into touch for long enough drag you into its smirking and sick world.

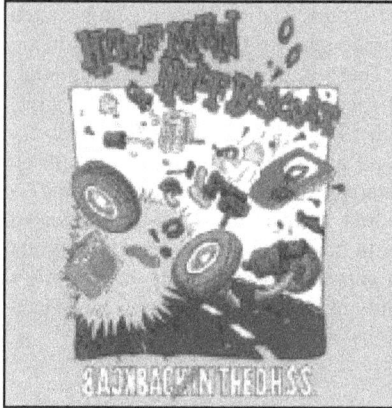

Half Man Half Biscuit:
Back Again in the DHSS
(Probe Plus, 1987)
What? Prime period alternative indie-pop from mirthful masters.

The band's second, and highest charting (#59), UK album is the only posthumous collection on the Half Man Half Biscuit (HMHB) canon. Described by John Peel as a "national treasure" HMHB purveyed a mirthful and scratchy blend of alternative pop, chock full of hook lines, random cultural references and allusions to the mundane and magnificent in British culture. Their main weaknesses, a lack of willingness to tone down the gags in search of radio play and a wilful trawling of any and every obscure cultural reference point in search of material, are also the major strengths of a band who reformed in 1990 and have continued to push out a steady stream of humour laced with hook lines from their – apparently – inexhaustible well ever since.

As with many acts in this book, any album in the differently abled catalogue of these titans of trash culture might prove a useful starting point to the uninitiated. Oddly, this collection is the nearest thing to a non-album the band ever produced, being culled from a range of sources, including Peel sessions, in the wake of their brief split. No matter, it belongs here because – in 1987 – HMHB were leaders in a world in which photocopied fanzines were cutting edge and a generation of bedroom media barons had begun reinventing their obsessions in search of a manifesto, or merely a few laughs. HMHB were there ahead of most of the competition and deftly engineered a blend of assured satire and forceful guitar-band attack that turned most of their tunes into stop and listen moments as soon as Peel first played them. Back Again... packs plenty of these corkers, including: "The Best Things in Life" (a hymn to the joys of staying in that references ball point pens and cosmonaut Yuri Gargarin), "Rod Hull is Alive Why?" (an insane blast of animosity aimed at a popular television entertainer…who has since died, and considering why minor talents flourish and major ones die), "Dickie Davies Eyes" (a fairly obvious rip-off of a major hit wherein the singer's girlfriend has eyes like a famous television sports presenter) and the 7" single mix of "The Trumpton Riots" (combining anti-Thatcher politics with a popular children's television show and referencing Basque separatism and CS Gas).

To write up the myriad references on any HMHB long player is to do an injustice to a band who pioneered a style of comic raconteur lead vocals over standard guitar band antics, the former providing a seemingly innate ability to collide the obscure reference points to forge new insights, the latter betraying a love of classic British bands and enough invention around standard verse/chorus structures to do justice to HMHB's ceaseless explorations in search of subject matter. When it works – which it does brilliantly almost everywhere on Back Again... - it is positively life-affirming. As "Dickie Davies Eyes" follows a baffling journey, comparing the shape of a football commentator's head to the London Planetarium and still finding space to consider prog rock album cover artist Roger Dean, and advertising for the Cadbury's Flake chocolate bar, you begin to understand John Peel's viewpoint.

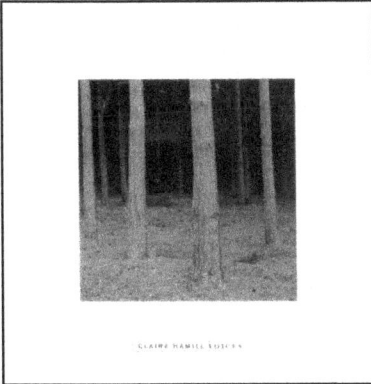

Claire Hamill:
Voices
(Coda, 1986)
What? Hello trees, hello sky. No seriously, hello trees, hello sky.

Claire Hamill is one of those musicians who has tried most things, once. An under-appreciated singer/songwriter of the early 70s folk rock boom, she drifted through a series of reinventions including a spell as a muscular voiced would-be diva in the eighties and an interesting, if ill-advised, stint as the voice of durable British rock stalwarts Wishbone Ash. Like a few others who'd existed on the fringes of massive success Hamill found herself marooned by eighties fashions and went for a full-scale reinvention. The resulting album, Voices, was entirely her own work and – in retrospect – was an almost prophetic work in terms of future developments. An ethereal collection of eighties keyboards, steady rhythmic backing and layer upon layer of intoned vocals, Voices is a concept piece, dividing its ten tracks between evocations of the four seasons of the year. Sitting down and listening intently to the whole collection is – probably – not the point. But, Voices certainly had something at the time, and continues to reach people long after its release. First and foremost, it was an almost inspirational work in the context of the developing areas of television at the time. When Channel 4 decided to devote early morning slots to a series of films of the landscape, dubbed: "The Art of Landscape," Voices and Hamill's subsequent recording in a similar style of Pachobel's "Canon" provided much of the soundtrack as trees and sky filled the screen. As incidental music for television Voices proved something of a watershed, spawning imitations and prompting viewers to phone and write asking where they could buy the music. These were pre-internet days when such information wasn't readily available.

Musically Voices does now sound its age. The keyboard backings are unmistakably the first wave digital machines of the eighties, but in snatches the album sounds, by turns, pseudo classical, like out-takes from a Cocteau Twins' recording of the same period and – probably most significant of all – like the blueprint for the sound that would briefly take Enya to world-wide hits and massive album sales.

The Handless Organist (Rev Alberta Baker):
Truly A Miracle Of God
(Cyclical Records?)

Long the subject of online fascination on the basis of what is indisputably one of the most memorable album covers in the history of recorded sound. Basically, the down-market design throws in some simple lettering outlining title and artist name, devoting the rest of the front of the cover to a black and white photograph of Ms Baker in action on the organ, with the photograph making clear the extent of her severe physical deformity. Technically speaking she isn't handless, but she is lacking proper hands. She is also lacking the lengthy arms and fully developed wrists to manipulate the residual hands she does have. Add to that the fact that these residual hands are facing at around 90 degrees to the rest of her arms and you can – perhaps – spare yourself the need to study the picture.

Truly A Miracle... is a celebrated example – and arguably the most infamous case – of a number of "miracle" releases from the fifties and sixties in the USA, all of them using the music presented as proof of something miraculous and a triumph of talent over physical adversity. Other acts – notably – The Braillettes, were not necessarily held back musically by their handicaps (it's not as if lack of sight greatly held back the likes of Stevie Wonder). But in the case of the Handless Organist the ability to hit specific keys on the keyboard, or follow a musical score written for someone with ten perfect digits is blatantly a problem. So is the availability of a major studio in which to record and any significant budget for production.

Truly A Miracle… offers, then, what you might expect. There are gospel standards: like "Jesus Use Me" and "The Lord is my Shepherd," ten original instrumentals and a combination of Ms Baker's occasionally tuneless voice (she has more control over the volume of her vocals – which range from restrained to a resonant bellow – than she does over hitting the full range of notes in a vocal score). For the freak show loving contingent of listeners, (apologies for harping on about this but it is truly where the present day audience for this collection are located), Truly a Miracle… delivers exactly what you would expect. The organ playing manages flurries of melody but frequently betrays a basic-chording approach wherein Alberta employs what limited mobility her appendages offer to impressive effect. In that context, at least, the album does present something bordering on the miraculous, it's also fairly generous with its offer of a shade over 50 minutes of music.

Rufus Harley With George Arvanitas Trio: From Philadelphia to Paris
(Blue Cat, 2007)
What? Blue-note bagpipe time!

Rufus Harley (1936-2006) and George Arvanitas were already deceased when this CD reissue of a 1988 original album hit the shelves and online listings. Harley's reputation – as the hip jazz saxophonist who made the bagpipes his own and made jazz bagpipes more than a curio – was intact at the time of his death. His career from 1964 saw him adopting the pipes, specifically the tall and large Great Highland Bagpipe, as his main solo instrument in jazz. He boasted a CV of some repute with a quartet of albums delivered to Atlantic starting with Bagpipe Blues in 1965, followed by lengthy spells as a sideman for – amongst others – Sonny Rollins. A documentary of Rollins in action at Ronnie Scott's London Club in the seventies shows Harley truly letting rip on the pipes; eyes closed, sweat pouring, drones over his right shoulder (most pipers tip them over the left) and audience rapt as he solos.

His session work included appearing on Laurie Anderson's Big Science album. He was also something of a curio and made sporadic film appearances as well as turning up on television favourites like What's My Line? For true lovers of Harley's unique take on jazz it's likely nothing less than the limited edition Rhino Handmade release Courage which compiles his Atlantic recordings will do. For those who need an in-at-the-deep-end introduction to the man this rambling and incendiary collection is probably the best starting point. Harley got more intense and more adept at mining the sonic possibilities of the pipes as his career progressed so this later period session is an insight into the territory he reached. His USP also led some to ignore his fine abilities on the saxophone. From Philadelphia to Paris presents the pair of lead instruments, occasionally alternated from track to track but heavier on bagpipes over the duration.

Harley remains out front as a lively trio push the tracks forward, take respectful solos and generally miss few tricks in providing counter-points to Harley's album long exploration of great melodies, and unlikely combinations of tone. A couple of showpieces push the curiosity envelope: "Scotland the Brave" is pretty much what you'd expect, the most-stirring of Scottish tunes on the most-stirring of Scottish instruments whilst a fluid and muscular jazz trio fill in all the gaps. It's the same trick with Harley leading a series of solos as the quartet roam around the melody of "Greensleeves." The pipes are central and loud to both. If you can't stand the heat from this brace there probably isn't much point in continuing to explore the other eight cuts, although, they do present the kind of surprises and discoveries that slowly emerged over Harley's career. "Home Coming" has the pipes out front but uses the tones and a slow trickle of notes to present music veering into M-O-R territory and – just about – touching on exotica/lounge for a few bars. That isn't case with "Moon River" wherein Harley's strident pipes grip a timeless melody, strangle and twist it, wringing a different degree of soul from the standard to anything previously attempted on record. There are some vibrant trio + lead tunes here that showcase Harley's considerable sax playing: "Sem la" and "Out Free" being the kind of accomplished live workout Rufus could knock out at will at the height of his powers.

Author Ken Kesey – no stranger to an altered state of awareness or a challenging idea – once said that the art of artistic leading didn't involve pointing the way, it involved going somewhere and making a case. Harley's ever-inventive pipes, and the sense the stripped back setting in which even the supporting musicians are in at the deep end for the duration, is – arguably – the most accessible case he ever made for one of the most eclectic and inventive careers in jazz.

Harmony Rockets:
Paralyzed Mind of the Archangel Void
(Big Cat, 1997)
What? Mercury Rev do a Mogwai

A single live performance running 41 minutes and 42 seconds. Paralyzed Mind... features Mercury Rev in the guise of their alter-ego Harmony Rockets and is – for this period of their career – astonishingly restrained and meditative. Rev gradually emerged as a band capable of creating breathtaking moments of ethereal beauty, something they achieve within Paralyzed Mind... The band's stock-in trade at the time was more a case of ear-splitting assaults on their audience and the profuse use of noise as an element of performance, both live and on CD.

Paralyzed Mind... by contrast celebrates analogue recording – the sleeve notes explaining the role of "a hand-held Arrivax Tandbert 183 analogue cassette recorder" in capturing the original performance. The piece unfolds with drone-effects, random bursts of instrumental flare-ups with guitar, trumpet and keyboard in evidence and standard percussion totally absent. The bulk of any rhythm comes from the pulsed bass tones that prevail throughout and random rhythmic eruptions, as drums are hit and other banging noises appear, soon vanish. Jonathan Donahue's sporadic vocals stay far enough in the background to leave most of the focus on the slowly unfolding melody and persistent drone.

As All Music Guide notes: "Donahue's vocals float in and out of the mix like random messages intercepted from another galaxy." This is a piece that sets out to establish its own reality and succeeds on its own terms. As a missing link between the confrontational experiments of early Mercury Rev and the delicate beauty of their later and better selling work, Paralyzed Mind of the Archangel Heart is also an under-appreciated work.

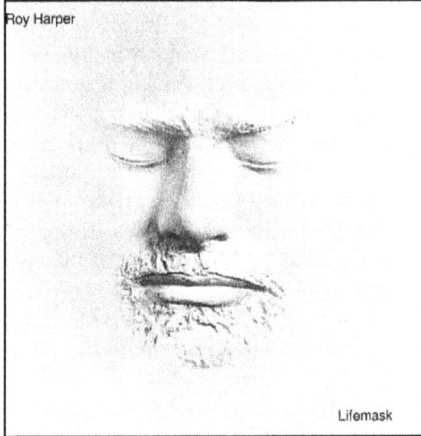

Roy Harper:
Lifemask
(Harvest, 1973)
What? One side of psych-folk last will and testament. One side of general Harperish songcraft.

Harper's singular and self-focussed song-writing, along with his vocal prowess and ceaseless creative invention have long endeared him to peers including sometime collaborators Jimmy Page and Pink Floyd.

The man is more widely known for being lauded by Zep in song ("Hats off to (Roy) Harper") and for his appearance on Floyd's Wish You Were Here album. That second high-profile moment wouldn't have arrived at all if the serious lung condition that laid him low before Lifemask had gone the whole way and seen him off this mortal coil. Which is – sort of – why Lifemask lines up in this book instead of the many varied and ambitious other albums that pepper the Harper catalogue. By common consent it isn't his best, it's also something of an oddity in that a goodly chunk of the five side one cuts had already seen a public airing in the movie Made, wherein Harper played a psych-folkie in a typically downbeat indie Brit-flick.

But, we digress. Lifemask is an accomplished addition in a lifetime's work of occasionally under-rated splendours.

It also contains the most avant-cut in an avant career. "The Lord's Prayer" fades out within touching distance of 23 minutes. A lumbering, portentous meditation on Harper's close shave with the Grim Reaper, "The Lord's Prayer" gives up its secrets sparingly, doesn't offer a hook or melodic burst worth the epithet "catchy" and spends a lot of its time – apparently - trying to decide if Harper is talking to himself or us. For that reason alone it is highly recommended to anyone poring through this book in search of downloads like no other downloads. Harper's peculiar brand of psych-progressive-folk hit its zenith in the seventies with his work for the Harvest label and the most focussed and accomplished example of his craft is arguably Lifemask's predecessor Stormcock (1971) but Lifemask presents five first-side tracks of accessible and slightly simpler folk material than Stormcock which manage to sound coherent despite being culled from a lengthy period of recording.

"South Africa" a love song dripping emotion that references the political situation in minority rule South Africa, packs a plaintive melody and holds up years after the event because it is a damn good love song as well as a sleight of hand polemic. "Highway Blues" a solid crowd rouser with a tasteful dash of synthesiser is also a stand out. Jimmy Page crops up adding guitar to "Bank of the Dead" on side one and his licks, and sonic intelligence are also in evidence on "The Lord's Prayer." And, over the duration, Lifemask presents enough lyrical depth, lick invention and musical backbone to withstand repeated plays.

End-to-end it is never a comfortable experience, because "The Lord's Prayer" – which was all of side two of the original release - sits there like a high church mass waiting to ambush the listener and hijack any other mental commitments. So, Lifemask works best when approached as the separate sides it was intended to be on vinyl or cassette.

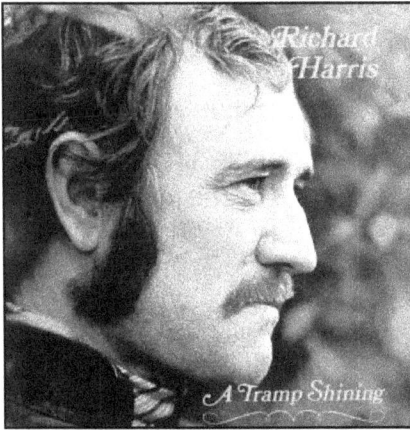

Richard Harris:
A Tramp Shining
(Dunhill, 1968)
What? Quality pop and ballad masterpiece, widely misunderstood.

To the generation who put "McArthur Park" at #2 on the Billboard singles charts and placed this album at #4 in the US albums list A Tramp Shining is likely to remain a vivid memory. The album impressed so many people with its lush production, superb performance from Harris, and Jimmy Webb's songs that it earned a Grammy nomination for Album of the Year. So, apologies if you were there and know all of this, but A Tramp Shining remains misunderstood by many. The baroque bluster of "McArthur Park" is simply the key to a range of more subtle delights and unknown gems. The seven minute plus epic might have been a "Bohemian Rhapsody" for the late sixties but it is unrepresentative of how most of A Tramp Shining works. "McArthur Park" has it all, in spades, rising to a level of histrionics at which Webb's widescreen production and towering ambition as a lyricist along with Harris' thespian chops combine to stop time. It is also, by a considerable degree, the longest piece on the album.

To their credit the pair don't try and spin that trick out over the length of the album. Webb came from working with The Fifth Dimension and hired a high-class session crew including Larry Knetchel (keyboardist with Bread) and percussionist Hal Blaine, all of whom are rightly credited for their "invaluable assistance" on the liner notes. At the time the results weren't regarded as hip or happening, simply as an incredible curio that, briefly, gained a massive following. In retrospect the album presents a brand of pop, tinged with soul and a sense of late sixties hip show tunes. The Fifth Dimension's blend of soulful/sunshine pop is a useful yardstick for most of A Tramp Shining. But vocally it is a world away from Fifth Dimension harmonies and high points. Harris' vocal performance combines a highly competent attempt to hold the notes through his vocal range, with an actor's innate sense of dramatizing the moments he can't convey on range and power alone.

When it works, which is most of the time, it works superbly. Webb has the sense to produce each song with the right touches to bring out the narrative. The melancholy vibe of "In the Final Hours" is evoked perfectly by pitting Harris' sympathetic performance against a beautifully realised backing chorus of female voices (thoughtfully kept in the background as a counterpoint rather than full contrast to Harris). One reason a song as complex and, frankly, brilliant as "If you Must Leave my Life" hasn't become a massive hit for another artist is that Harris' navigation of the space between the memorable beat and lavish orchestra is a consummate lesson in performance, you'd need to be very brave to try and improve on this. If there are drawbacks these largely revolve around the sheer richness and diversity of what is on offer.

A Tramp Shining is an overwhelming listen from end to end and often requires a few runs through to locate itself in your life with some degree of comfort. At worst the two major players are simply going for the highest levels of achievement so often that a listener loses sight of any notion of these songs or performances being drawn from real life. At best, A Tramp Shining is a theatrical blend of the best elements of late sixties popular music using musical interludes, a classical sense of arrangement and an embarrassment of talent to produce a collection capable of capturing a listener for the duration. Every arrangement, accompaniment and vocal performance offers something of value and the moods and melodies are sequenced effectively. The pair reprised many of the same tricks on The Yard Went on Forever and a CD compilation offering both albums remains widely available.

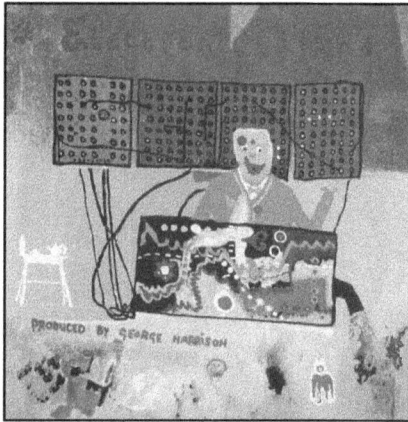

George Harrison:
Electronic Sound
(Zapple, 1969)
What? "There are a lot of people around, making a lot of noise; here's some more." (Statement credited to Arthur Wax on packaging of original album)

The cover remark, printed above, suggests something of Harrison's own feelings about this project. Electronic Sound is an experiment, released on an avant-garde and experimental offshoot of The Beatles' own label. You can research online to follow the bitter battle between Bernie Krause and Harrison about the authorship of the music contained here. There's also another entertaining diversion concerning the two pieces – each originally one side of the vinyl – comprising Electronic Sound: "Under the Mersey Wall" (almost 19 minutes of two Moogs playing off against each other), and "No Time or Space" (just over 25 minutes of varied Moog-generated sounds with background chords and music). On the original US pressing of the album the titles were wrongly ascribed so the largest market for music on earth still contains many people who confuse title and music (despite a subsequent CD release correcting the error).

Electronic Sound is a self-indulgent, meandering foray into the (then) cutting edge sound capabilities of the Moog synthesizer. In 1969 this was out there in ways that appear tame to present day ears. Melodies are forsaken in favour of tones, repetitive figures recur randomly and the music often explores sound and spontaneity for its own sake. Bernie Krause's argument concerned the "composition" of "No Time or Space" which he claimed was recorded as he demonstrated the Moog machine to Harrison. It certainly sounds like a tricksy advert for the top-end musical hardware, opening with sounds akin to gunshots and – at different points - arousing sonic associations with the wind, birdsong and industrial machinery.

At the time of release this composition was regarded as the more memorable and significant of the two pieces. Its favouring of momentary attention-grabbing over the lengthy development of a key theme sounds more dated now. Music technology long-ago rendered the sounds here as passé. So, "No Time…" might better be regarded today as a fairly bald snapshot of musical history in the making. In the late sixties only the best regarded musicians, with the best tools, could do this!

By contrast the shorter "Mersey Wall" piece; with Harrison noodling away in his Esher bungalow, pre-empts the early experiments by the likes of Tangerine Dream. It is a long way from the angsty bedroom electro noodling and geekish enjoyment of playing with toys that under-pinned Britain's explosion of synth pop in the eighties, but Harrison does veer into this territory and his ear for chord changes and deceptively inviting tunes holds up over the whole piece. "Mersey Wall" isn't an easy fit with any of the electronic music that followed in its wake. Too distinctive to qualify as ambient, too loose to qualify as classically influenced electronica and too mature to be any precursor of synth pop.

It also flogs one idea to exhaustion as two Moogs play off against each other and Harrison employs the inventive use of over-dubbing to highlight the duel. But, "Mersey Wall" is a strangely timeless piece that holds up well decades later, and shows a side of Harrison's musicality that seldom appeared in recorded works afterwards.

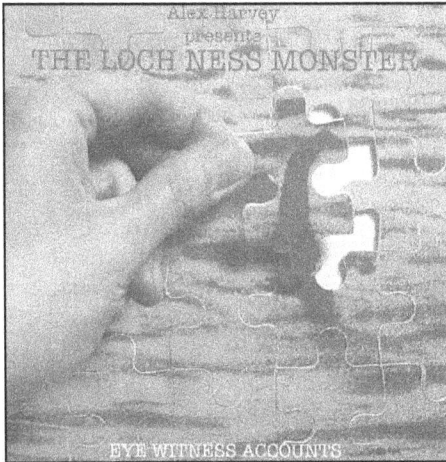

Alex Harvey:
Presents the Loch Ness Monster
(K-Tel, 1977/Voiceprint, 2009)
What? Monstrous indulgence, two Scots legends on one album.

The Sensational Alex Harvey Band earned a reputation and some significant 1970s record sales with a brand of psychopathic glam, mining a furrow somewhere between early Bowie, mid-period Mott the Hoople and embryonic punk. In 1977 they temporarily parted company for a deserved rest, the four musicians in the band (minus Alex) recording their own album whilst their leader set about a very personal project that continues to astound people. Basically, Alex decamped from Glasgow to Invermoriston, tape recorder in hand (this was the mid-seventies after all), and proceeded to interview the locals about their – alleged – legendary neighbour. Sometimes cited online as a "radio documentary" this project was always intended as an album, but Harvey's musical performance appears after over forty minutes of interviews and is limited to 40 seconds of strumming, whistling and singing an otherwise unavailable song called "I Love Monsters." Mostly, he asks a few leading questions about the monster, briefly introduces the interviewees, prompts debate on the monster's existence, gets to interview eyewitnesses, experts and locals and generally explores a mystery. Actor Richard O'Brien also appears, acting as a master of ceremonies with announcements. None of this is done with obvious comedy, or mockery. Indeed, the local residents emerge as a cosmopolitan and very articulate lot. They include a German-born nurse and Sam Job, who started his life in Africa. To all intents and purposes this is a serious investigation into a genuine mystery. But…it's also an insight into the strange world of Alex Harvey. With Harvey it shares an unrepentantly Scottish character, a sense that the rest of the world has to know this stuff and the belief that the surreal and mundane exist quite happily side-by-side in the most unsuspecting places. If Harvey's career was stymied by one thing it was a blunt refusal to compromise his creative vision for the sake of hits. For all the engagement with the locals here, the whole shebang stands as testimony to a man who could only do it his way. The 2009 reissue puts the CD in a small book with original photographs and handwritten notes.

P J Harvey:
White Chalk
(Island, 2007)
What? Stark, occasionally somnambulant, offering.

Harvey's seventh studio offering is the strangest and most singular in a career that has seen every album marking a distinct shift from its relatives. Peaking at UK#11 and US#65 White Chalk hardly needs the present book to inform the world of its presence but, for those unfamiliar with Harvey's work, it does have a strong claim to be a perplexing and slightly strange work. Harvey took up piano, near enough from scratch, to write and record White Chalk. There's an obvious parallel with Neil Young's abandonment of lead guitar in the wake of the deaths of Danny Whitten and Bruce Berry and, the stark chording and slow chunky deliberation of much of his resulting Tonight's the Night. But, White Chalk combines a slower set of tempos, and starkly stripped back sound with a series of introspective and enigmatic lyrics that place it closer to Joni Mitchell's Blue for its narrative breadth and enigmatic intent. When it is stark, it is really stark. "When Under Ether" includes lines about being "waist down undressed" on a bed, a "lady beside me, holding my hand" and then delivers: "Something's inside me, Unborn and unblessed, Disappears in the ether, This world to the next."

Harvey remains characteristically elliptical on what any of it means. The obvious interpretation of the experience of an abortion from the mother's point of view has taxed many of those motivated to discuss her lyrics online. Harvey remains adamant that her lyrics are "non-specific." White Chalk emphasises this with a series of brief, (the entire album falls well short of 35 minutes and only "To Talk to you" goes up to four minutes), missives and characteristic open endings. If there is a key to any message it may be in the title track, Harvey noting: "White chalk hills are all I've known…And I know these chalk hills will rot my bones, Dorset's cliffs meet at the sea." Harvey presents herself ruminating, feeling pain, connecting to the landscape she has always known and just giving in to the experience. Above all, the album seems like a set of indirect responses to moods and events, like abstract sketches.

White Chalk keeps its arrangements simple, eschews a rhythm track on some cuts, lets the steady piano chords form a base for Harvey to sing in a high register, often well above her normal territory, and inhabits a room like a confused but compelling companion. In a career of singular collections this remains the most unusual and enigmatic of all Harvey's albums

Nicky Haslam:
Midnight Matinee
(Cherry Red, 2013)
What? Celeb-fest of seventies excess proportions: a Transformed Man for the 21st century.

There are a number of albums produced by celebrities and music industry figures that are generally celebrated as records that must have been fun to make; not necessarily a great listening experience. Keith Moon's Two Sides of the Moon (1975) being one such animal. With the music industry bricking itself over the future profitability of recorded music in the 21st century, such jovial and eccentric celeb fests and novelty items were generally assumed to be a feature of the past. What Cherry Red Records thought they were doing unleashing this strangeness on the market in 2013 is anyone's guess. Nothing remotely like it had been issued in years and a few radio shows and critics could barely contain their amazement.

Celebrated interior designer and socialite Nicholas Ponsonby "Nicky" Haslam was fast approaching his 74th birthday when his first album came out. Ably supported by a truly eclectic cast of celebrity mates, and gathering material from his own preferences rather than anything supplied by a focus group or marketing expert, Haslam's album is a true throwback to the days when the likes of Roddy Llewellyn could get a recording contract. It is also one of the most unusual creations of the 21st century British music industry. If it doesn't readily appear on lists of the all-time strangest albums it's simply because – by 2013 - many compilers of such lists had assumed the world had long since given up on making the likes of Midnight Matinee.

Sonically this is a late-night, predominantly jazzy, never likely to rock out, session. There are some rumbling, dark bass, minimal piano chords, well played solo jazz horns here and there, and a 21st century feel to a production that uses mainly 20th century styles of playing and singing. Some tracks amount to spoken word with samples. The choice of material says everything about the Haslam's mindset and absolutely nothing about the market for music in 2013. Cover versions begin with the opening "Total Control" – as in the song originally by US new wavers The Motels – but soon divert into material from film musicals, covering Marlene Dietrich, readings from literature including Andy Warhol, James Joyce and Tracy Emin's writing, and a Guy Chambers song. Haslam can intone and carry a story. It would be cruel to compare his performance to proper singers, and that may be the reason that he has assembled one of the strangest casts of collaborators of any 21st century album. Seriously, where else – other than maybe a production involving The Muppets – would the credits list Cilla Black, Brian Ferry, Rupert Everett, Helena Bonham Carter (who duets with Haslam on Guy Chambers' "Last Man Standing"), Bob Geldof and Tracy Emin? If you count samples you can also add Sophia Loren to the collaborators.

Haslam is both executive producer and performer, happy to sit out a track if he can get Geldof to read Raymond Chandler and drag in a sample of Sophia Loren's warbling. Haslam's socialite accent, and limited range does begin to drag on numbers like Irving Berlin's "How Deep is the Ocean," which require real interpretation to drag every ounce of meaning out. But, he's never far from being rescued by a celebrity mate taking a verse, or a sample appearing from a classic movie.

If Midnight Matinee has musical relatives; they are the strange creatures born of actors intruding into the recording studio in the sixties and seventies. Truly, Midnight Matinee is strange on a Shatneresque level, and all the better for it.

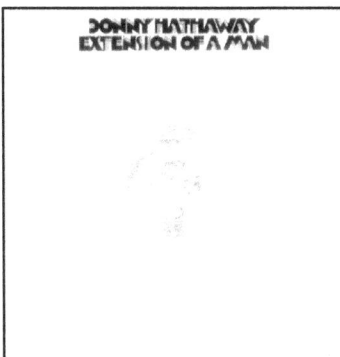

Donnie Hathaway:
Extension of a Man
(Atco, 1973)
What? Occasionally an over-extension of man. One of the quintessential flawed masterpieces.

Two years after What's Going On and in the same calendar year as ambitious efforts of black music like Isaac Hayes' Black Moses, Donnie Hathaway (1945-1979) produced his most aspirational and far reaching work. Extension of a Man doesn't wear its social values as effortlessly as Marvin Gaye's work and its attempts to hit a range of musical bases outside standard soul aren't as naturally felt as Isaac Hayes. But, this is still an album of minor triumphs and some significant achievement. What might have happened – perhaps – if Stevie Wonder had been more introverted and hadn't met the electro wizards behind Tonto's Expanding Headband.

Extension of a Man opens with a brace of the most ambitious tracks Hathaway ever attempted. The orchestral overture "I Love the Lord; He Heard My Cry (Parts I & II)" takes up the opening five and a half minutes before Hathaway produces one of his most heartfelt vocals on the slow and sonorous "Someday We'll All Be Free." The depth of his vocal performance makes the refrain: "take it from me, someday we'll all be free" sound believable. If the rest of the album doesn't live up to the sublime ten minutes that open it, Extension of a Man is still standing shoulder to shoulder with works like Innervisions that came out in the same year. The musicianship is exemplary, the arrangements are all intended to take the ideas exactly where they should go and the styles and moods vary over the duration to provide a portrait of an artist at the top of his game. The excursions can be surprising, and a little showy; especially on "Valdez in the Country" a jazz fusion jam with Hathaway throwing some inspired licks over the backing.

Hathaway's slender canon includes another very ambitious release – Everything is Everything (1970) – which is altogether more coherent, and a slightly easier listen. Extension of a Man is prone to over-reaching. Hathaway's natural reticence and the twists of the depressive illness that would eventually contribute to his suicide mean this level of ambition doesn't sit too naturally with his character. But for lovers of the flawed masterpiece, and those under-rated albums that repeatedly crop up in conversation for the most dedicated music fans, Extension of a Man is indispensable.

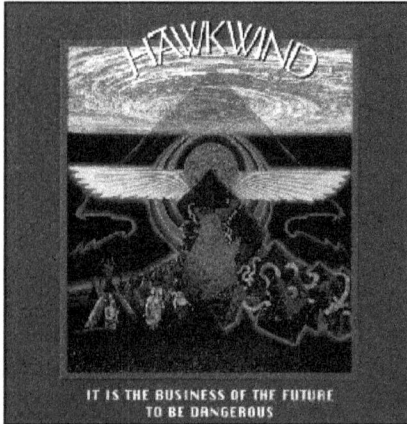

IT IS THE BUSINESS OF THE FUTURE
TO BE DANGEROUS

Hawkwind:
It is the Business of the Future to be Dangerous
(Essential, 1993)
What? Typical Hawkwind, do everything a band shouldn't do, and come back winners.

Firstly, a brief aside along the lines of the discussion that opens the Captain Beefheart entry hereabouts. We're making the assumption that many of those motivated to buy a book like this will already have some familiarity with Hawkwind, and the band's greatest works. Specifically, we're making the assumption that it would be redundant to inform you of why Hawkwind's double album Space Ritual Alive is an utter masterpiece of space rock, so assuredly out there and so ragingly alive with ideas that its life force belongs in the existence of every sentient being on this planet. Rant over! If you've avoided it…it's probably a more pressing concern than checking out It is the Business….

Before we get to It is the Business…it is also worth a brief consideration of the cardinal rules broken on this, Hawkwind's 18th studio album. Rule one: Don't pillage your old catalogue, rework it and claim to be going somewhere new. Rule two: it is okay to turn up and guest with those who claim you inspired them, but under no circumstances try and get down with the kids by taking the youngsters on at their own game.

It is the Business… sees a Hawkwind functioning as a trio and diving headlong into the sounds and styles of acts like The Orb and Eat Static. Ambient/rave/dance territory which drew some of its original sounds from classic Hawkwind albums. The second cut – "Space is Their Palestine" – with its insistent Arabian melody and chiming spot-colour percussive sounds clocks in a shade under 12 minutes and wouldn't have been out of place on Eat Static's studio efforts of the period. Chunks of It is the Business… were already familiar to Hawkwind's audience. "Letting in the Past" is based on an eight year old track "Looking in the Future" from Church of Hawkwind and "The Camera That Could Lie" reworks a reggae groove that had previously been part of the band's live set and had appeared on the live album Palace Springs (1991). Even the album's title – which was lifted in the first place – had appeared in the Space Ritual sleeve notes.

For all the above, It is the Business… - which notched a single week at #75 on the UK charts – achieves what most bands couldn't in the circumstances. It is up there with the dance/ambient/techno material of its day. Hawkwind always relied on massive grooves, albeit with thumping bass and monumental waves of space-rock keyboards, but the three piece line-up here – basically mainstay Dave Brock and a rhythm section – slow down the pace, leave the sound as wide and fat as usual, fill much of the space with rumbling bass and percussion, and loop a few effects into the mix. Once the blues-based and echoing guitar fills are added, it still sounds like Hawkwind, and the occasional – as in very little indeed – vocals also serve to remind us who we're listening to. Hawkwind make a good fist of trippy dance numbers like "Let Barking Dogs Lie" and hit the ambient spot with excursions like the beautiful "Wave Upon Wave" but it's their ability to keep inventing within these parameters that makes the whole show so convincing. They can keep it short and pithy – "3 or 4

Erections in the Course of a Night" – whilst veering into the world of Porcupine Tree and their ilk, and follow that with the solid groove of "Techno Tropic Zone Exists" (which has declaimed vocals referencing a work like "Sonic Attack" from Space Ritual Alive).

The one clanger is a spirited cover of the Stones' "Gimme Shelter," originally produced as part of a charity project. Hawkwind do it justice but for anyone who has heard the improbable but – frankly – stunning single A' side ripping through the song with Samantha Fox on vocals, this album version – with La Fox replaced by Hawkwind drummer Richard Chadwick – isn't in the same league.

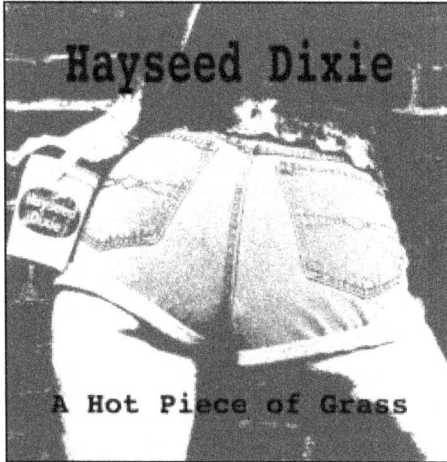

Hayseed Dixie:
A Hot Piece of Grass
(Cooking Vinyl, 2005)
What? Bluegrass bludgeoning of beloved behemoths.

Hayseed Dixie are that rarity, a comedy outfit who have taken the joke and run with it to produce creativity and work of genuine lasting merit. The genre of "Rockgrass" is credited to the band who were briefly named AC/Dixie (before Sony's lawyers intervened) but the name and genre are a fair insight into an American band who take standard rock, keep the attitude and reimagine it all as hot and bothered bluegrass. Endless inventions on shuffle rhythms, insanely fast flurries on acoustic guitar, mandolin and banjo, and the ever present southern twang in the vocals are the basic building blocks of their style. The band have made a trio of majorly smart decisions along the way to cement a solid cult following. Firstly, they've gone with the joke, running wherever the laughs and audience take them. Secondly, their superb musicianship is only enhanced when they choose to record in Nashville with analogue equipment. Thirdly, they've never been afraid to take off in their own musical direction – however briefly – even when covering the classics; "Whole Lotta Love" on this collection qualifies the "every inch of my love" line with a reference to centimetres, in case you're listening in "the UK." A look at their history reveals the band opened their account with a covers album of AC/DC songs, and went on to appear on major festival bills and achieve undreamt of success in Scandinavia such that they have recorded one album in Norwegian. So there is progression and no such thing as a "typical" album in their catalogue. Truly a long strange trip.

A Hot Piece of Grass is – arguably – the best way in for the curious. Almost half a decade into their career Hayseed Dixie had broken out of AC/DC covers and begun to flex their musical muscles such that guitar solos were at a minimum because these guys could make a mandolin or banjo speak. Hot Piece... lines up some well-chosen covers: "War Pigs" and "Whole Lotta Love" are amongst the classic rockers. Elsewhere Hayseed Dixie tackle tracks by Franz Ferdinand, Outkast and The Reverend Horton Heat ("Marijuana") and there are enough Hayseed Dixie originals to make a statement of intent for a future in which they have gone on to write and record their own stuff, developing their own crowd pleasers. The originals give coherence to the whole collection, making it clear these guys are a band and not just a comedy act treading out the same old joke. And, just at the point you have registered all of the above, Dixie deliver an absolute killer. A breakneck demolition of the "Duelling Banjos" track from the Deliverance soundtrack. Dixie push pickin' to the limit, parading dexterity and skill, colliding the breathtaking and hilarious, and focussing their whole philosophy into a fleeting tour-de-force. If that doesn't win you over to their catalogue, nothing will.

Murray Head:
Say it ain't so
(A & M, 1975)
What? Big in Europe songster's great underrated work.

Murray Head's recording, stage and film/television career has kept him in consistent work. So, the relative failure of this collection in the main music markets of the US and UK was probably more of an annoyance than any great lasting trauma. The hit single, "Someone's Rocking my Dreamboat," was a reverent cover of an old standard but the rest of Say it ain't so is a combination of listenable adult oriented singer-songwriter material with a lush production and attention to detail that make it a superior example of the form. In 1975 it lacked the sense of urgency to appeal to any hot market. Sounding too restrained and mainstream for the edgier, confessional, troubadour market, too Radio Two in intention to hit home with fans of superior – Abbaesque – pop and nowhere near accessible enough to spawn more hit singles. Though, on the last point, the title track certainly had some the potential to be a minor hit. Head managed to achieve and retain a serious following in territories like France where the tradition of the mature balladeer was always a strong player on television and radio. Over the years the singer, and this particular album, have picked up a following including some notable champions, like Guy Garvey. Most of Say it Ain't so betrays Head's roots on stage. Each song attempts the self-contained-gem manoeuvre of offering up its own particular combination of instruments, a vivid lyric and some theatrical twists in Head's clear diction and shifts of mood. Basically, he tells stories. When it works, it works impressively. The third cut, "Boats Away," starts in a low key fashion, builds to an emotional crescendo in which Head holds his diction as his voice soars, segues into a dreamy wind instrumental break and returns to a vague calypso outro, occasionally availing itself of a massive wall of backing vocals. The tonnage of backing singers and embarrassing coterie of able session musicians is a mixed blessing. Everything here sounds pristine and every instruction relayed from the control room was probably actioned on the first take but, at its worst, Say it Ain't so, is simply buried in accomplished licks and inspired cameo turns. Somewhere inside "She's Such A Drag" a shoot from the hip missive is trying to break out. But, the guitar licks are striking rather than scary, Head's histrionics at the end would enthral rather than terrify theatre goers and the odd listener who chanced on this in 1975 might well have considered that the Stones, or Terry Reid, would have done it way better. Say it Ain't so simply oozes good material, and, retrospectively, shows itself as a prime slice of quality adult pop, fit for a market that didn't really find recognition until a decade and a half after this album first appeared. Elbow, amongst others, bear the hallmarks of having listened to such work. Thankfully, it climbed to a cult status and has earned sporadic CD reissues.

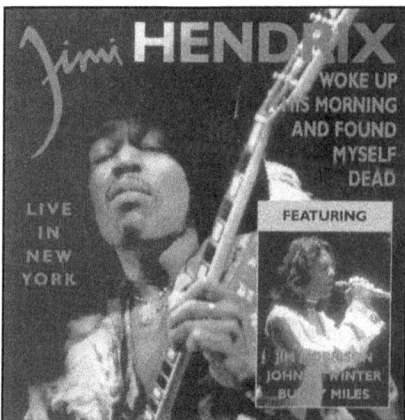

Jimi Hendrix:
Woke up This Morning and Found Myself Dead
(Action Replay, 1995)
What? A genuine superstar jam, unfortunately.

Amidst a veritable sea of varying quality posthumous "Hendrix" product this collection rightfully earns a place of some notoriety. Its origins are far from honourable. Culled from two track tapes of live jams which, according to most sources discussing the origins of the album, were stolen from Hendrix's apartment, Woke up

This Morning… is one of a number of collections all offering variations on the same recordings. Depending on availability, price and the rest anyone intent on owning this material might also search Bleeding Heart or The Scene Club and find some variant on the same material.

These are 1968 jams from a New York club that catch Hendrix in transition, post Experience, pre Band of Gypsies and willing to experiment. The other personnel on stage include Jim Morrison (spectacularly drunk, contributing obscenities and nowhere near as engaged as the others), Buddy Miles and Johnny Winter (possibly, see below). The stellar line up and the fact Hendrix leads performances of songs including "Tomorrow Never Knows," "Sunshine of Your Love" and an impressive take on Elmore James' "Bleeding Heart" are the main points of interest. Having said this, the Cream and Beatles "covers" are only stumbles into recognisable snippets. Basically, these are messy and sporadic jams and the titles of some tracks are simply invented by those releasing the work. "Bleeding Heart" is, however, a recognisable stab at a slow blues seldom covered by other artists. But, be warned, this does little to add to any of the legends on show. Buddy Miles is laying down a jazz groove before Hendrix is totally committed to that direction, Winter and Hendrix are respectful to each other and fiery on cue, but neither sets the speakers on fire. Morrison is, basically, off his face. The woeful original sound quality has had some attention but its laser etched releases from the mid-nineties onwards only highlight the lack of any meaningful production of the original tapes, which Hendrix would probably have been horrified to think were out there in this form.

Beyond this, two points are clear. Firstly, the truth of exactly who is involved here will never be known. Johnny Winter denies he is on the recordings, but his name appears on packaging for various releases. It may well be Rick Derringer on the second lead guitar. Secondly, the detailed discussions available online do make intelligent comments on the performances, possible participants and where – exactly – these recordings sit in terms of charting Hendrix' development as an artist. All very enigmatic and interesting. Whether actually listening to poor quality recordings of rambling jams increases anyone's appreciation of the legends on show here is another question entirely.

David Hentschel: Sta*rtling Music (Ring O' Records, 1975)
What? Bizarre Beatle-related revival

Recording engineer David Hentschel was personally known to George Harrison and Ringo Starr, having worked on significant solo recordings by the pair. He also had a CV that boasted work on albums like Elton John's Goodbye Yellow Brick Road when – in 1975 – he released this strange album. The idea is clear enough, but the thinking behind the whole endeavour still leaves Beatle aficionados scratching their heads.

Ringo Starr's biographers have long noted his changeable nature when it comes to projects. Ringo's early to mid-seventies work marked the commercial and critical high point of his solo career, But, by the middle of the decade, his fortunes in both areas were starting to plummet. Around this time he formed and fronted his own label, Ring O' Records. The talent roster was never notably thick and only power-rock singer Graham Bonnet went on to significant success. Ring O's album account opened with Star*tling Music, the only long player the label ever risked in the US market. Star*tling Music features Hentschel on synthesiser, reworking in its entirety, as an instrumental collection, Ringo's best-selling Ringo album. That is: the same tracks, the same running order, but just the tunes and sound effects.

Released in 1973 Ringo is, by common consent, Starr's best solo outing. It came within a whisker of topping the US chart, hit the top ten in the UK and made it all the way to #1 in Australia. Full of characterful songs, performed superbly in Ringo's lugubrious vocal style and – crucially for sales – marking the first time since the break up of the Fab Four that all The Beatles had appeared together on the same record, Ringo remains a gem. However, its best qualities include the stellar guest list. Marc Bolan, Billy Preston and Harry Nilsson are amongst the vast assembly of talent. Richard Perry's production wraps Ringo's voice in a warm and soft aural blanket and the lyrics – some by Starr – have character and a sense of their own identity. One standout, John Lennon's "I'm the Greatest," has a glorious self-depreciating humour when intoned by Starr.

 So the tunes might be familiar, and the keyboard sounds that form the vast bulk of the album might be cutting edge for the time, but the wisdom of taking an album that belonged to Ringo and reworking it as an instrumental showcase for a production/keyboard talent isn't so clear. Other than Ringo snapping his fingers behind the tune of "Step Lightly," the one bona-fide star on show is Phil Collins, respected drummer with Genesis in 1975, but a full half-decade short of his first solo album. Ringo's label produced no major selling records and was quietly put to bed little more than three years after it started operations, Hentschel went on to work with a who's who of rock royalty. Despite an army of Beatle obsessives willing to buy merchandise in the twenty first century Star*tling Music has yet to see a CD reissue.

Kristin Hersh:
Hips and Makers
(4AD, 1994)
What? Alt rock Blue?

As a rule we wouldn't take a review from the artist's own website at face value, but Hersh's site is honest and descriptive. Stating, amongst other things: "like a family, it's happy on the surface, intriguing when explored," and adding some pointers: "Hips and Makers infuses the singer/songwriter tradition with a jolt of complexity and authority… favors the taut, stream of consciousness lyrics [Hersh] whittled down to the bone with the [Throwing Muses]…allow[s] peeks into a world where clotheslines, bee stings, and the occasional ghost aren't unusual." The genius of the collection revolves around three elements. Firstly, Hersh and her acoustic guitar are central, everything is built around them. Her ability to speed up, slow down, raise and lower the power, and helm the whole piece as a personal performance is never compromised. Secondly, Lenny Kaye's production is sympathetic to the above, adding touches without fuss to complement Hersh's performances. Finally, the lyrics are elliptical, occasionally confusing and bring a late-century sensibility to the intimate performance. It is useful that Hersh's own website makes it clear that the ghost is to be taken literally.

If Hips and Makers has one obvious problem it is shooting the best shot, "Your Ghost," at the very start. Michael Stipe's second vocal sets up a dynamic the album never develops. But, that is a minor criticism. What follows is a personal, intimate and sympathetically sequenced collection to showcase Hersh as a genuine solo artist. She is shorn of the support of her band, but able to provide variety and a composite picture of her concerns. Hips and Makers is never better than when the acoustic ramble of "Sparky" gives way to the strident "Houdini Blues," two tracks with complementary sounds, leading to an emotional crescendo, and perfectly sequenced. This strength as an album extends to the later tracks building, via strident chords and a big vocal sound, to work like the end of a live set, before the title track provides a conclusion, of sorts.

In this context Joni Mitchell's Blue is a meaningful comparison. The stripped back acoustic sound, with minor changes of arrangement from track to track, enables a complex and intimate set of works to build an overall picture. Hersh emerges as a deep, occasionally reticent, narrator with the ability to love others completely, as evidenced in the moments she considers motherhood. Like other artists drawing on this material, for example Kate Bush, she will only let us see as much as she wants us to see. But that act of selection, and painting the vivid pictures, remains compelling throughout.

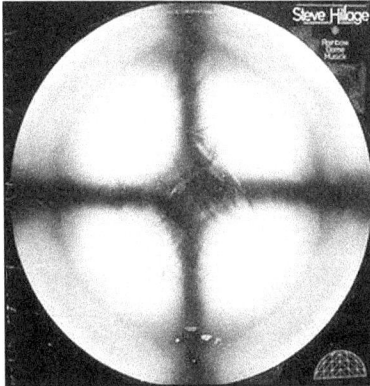

Steve Hillage:
Rainbow Dome Music
(Virgin, 1979)
What? Installation music that became avant-garde institution.

Originally composed and conceived as the installation music for the Rainbow Dome at the London's festival of Mind-Body-Spirit in 1979 this 43 minute and 45 second slice of ambient and alternative music managed to locate itself outside most prog fashions and inspire a new generation of ambient and chill merchants, like The Orb's Dr. Alex Patterson. All Music Guide note of Rainbow Dome Music: "too avant-garde to be classified as a new age album and too sleek sounding to fit into any progressive rock subgenres, but no matter how it's categorized, it's an excellent example of Steve Hillage's adeptness and vast musical background." In fact, Hillage may be the name on the front but half of Rainbow Dome Music is composed by his long-term partner: Miquette Giraudy. Her contributions on a range of keyboard instruments, programming and Tibetan bells anticipate the significant and similar role she would play when the couple formed ambient and dance act System 7. Giraudy composed the longer of the two pieces here: "Garden of Paradise," Hillage contributed "Four Ever Rainbow" and their skills complement each other perfectly. Where Hillage favours layered guitars, glissando guitar and more rhythm, Giraudy's piece is a delicate and floating weave of layered keyboard. Each brings their respective strengths to the other's compositions, giving Rainbow Dome Music a sense of coherence.

The piece also uses sampled sounds and does make an early sprint for the much derided genre of new age music. In reality, All Music Guide have it right in that Rainbow Dome Music exists on the fringes of prog, ambient and a range of other genres but locates itself firmly outside of most music produced in its own time, and since. Its closest living relatives are Hillage's own glissando guitar experiments on albums like L and the more reflective moments of his time with Gong. So, Rainbow Dome Music is progressive in as much as it represents massive progress for Hillage in comparison to his earlier work, and also in its clear influence on subsequent acts like The Orb. Hillage met The Orb's Alex Patterson because Patterson – in the role of DJ – was playing Rainbow Dome Music as chill out music to a rave crowd.

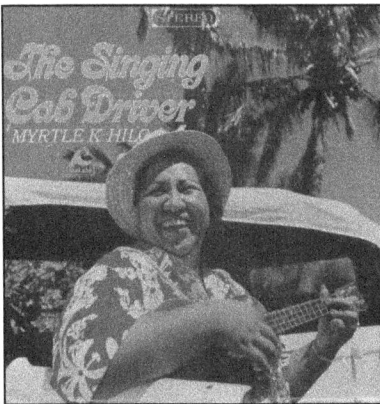

Myrtle K. Hilo:
The Singing Cab Driver
(Makaha, 1967)
What? Low fi + high spirits = classic exotica.

This novelty classic was rescued from obscurity as outsider music and the rediscovery of novelty in all its forms took hold in the later years of the last century. Amongst other things Myrtle K. Hilo's efforts were compiled onto Incredibly Strange Music Volume II in 1995 and her 1967 vinyl album duly received a laser-etched reissue, since when its peculiar delights have charmed a new generation of listeners. It's fairly simple, over a tuneful and at times muscular backing of the usual Hawaiian instruments the amply proportioned and big-hearted Myrtle strums her ukulele and lets rip with a big and surprisingly deep voice on a series of local tunes and standards, reworked into Hawaiian style and – as with "A Lover's Prayer" – occasionally festooned with some new Hawaiian lyrics. The production is functional rather than great and the one-sound-fits-all approach of most budget recordings of the period does few favours to Myrtle as she speeds up, slows down, and tries to vary the mood. It doesn't help matters that the one dimensional production is cluttered at times because Myrtle appears to have invited every friend capable of making a decent musical noise to help at the party. But, the belated appreciation directed at this disc isn't all ironic. It's an infectious collection with a very "up" mood that breaks out of its time and escapes the notion of novelty for novelty's sake. The intention – made clear in the sleeve notes – is to recreate a local party rather than a tourist experience of Hawaii, and get that friendly atmosphere because: "These are fun songs mostly and Myrtle has fun singing them." Locally written songs like "Manuela's Girl" and "Ma'ane'i Mai Oe" rub shoulders with standards like "I'll Remember You" and the album throws in a low-key leaving song in the shape of "Sweet Someone." And, she really was a cab driver in Hawaii.

Alfred Hitchcock:
Music to be Murdered by
(Imperial, 1958)
What? "Mood music in a jugular vein."

The concept here may rival the crassest novelty cash-ins but the results are strangely effective; pretty much in line with the strangely effective movies made by the master of the macabre. Hitchcock plays the role of a ghoulish MC introducing orchestral arrangements of standards well-chosen for their relevance to the whole concept. He devilishly deadpans his way through titles like "I'll Never Smile Again," "Body and Soul" and "The Hour of Parting" bringing in some gruesome bon-mot to spin each tune into the twilight zone.

The semi-psychotic set up involves Hitchcock opening each track with a straight-faced statement before the orchestral arrangements of Jeff Alexander drag the original tune into terror-inducing territory. Considering the constituent parts of the caper are little more than ballad and theme tunes, and Hitchcock's morbid humour, Music to be Murdered by is a triumph of technique over content. The arrangements vary the sonic palette and mood, but keep it slow, mordant and funereal. The odd flourish like the ghostly female voice on "Suspicion" or the heavy-footed brass chords on "Lover Come Back to Me" show Alexander's care and attention to the project. Hitchcock wades in with a few twists, turns and grisly gags.

"Lover Come Back to Me" is dedicated to a particular married couple but Hitchcock declares himself unsure of whether the husband will be listening in "the Precinct" having murdered his wife. Hitchcock's well-enunciated words and unwavering love of the ghoulish give Music to be Murdered by that psychopathic sense of calm in the middle of a massacre. The stated intention of the album is to provide a musical backdrop to the act of murder, they might be kidding but the jokes are fairly good. At the outset Hitchcock states: "This record is long playing, although you may not be." As we head into the closing "The Hour of Parting" he adds: "If you haven't been murdered I can only say: better luck next time." Music to be Murdered by also forms part of a budget-twofer along with Ghost Stories for Young People (1962).

Åke Hodell:
220 Volt Buddha
(Alga Marghen, 1998)
What? Electronic experimentation from master of the art.

Hodell (1919 – 2000) was a polymath and inter-textual artist. At varying points he worked as a fighter pilot, poet, author, sound composer, and visual artist. Like Henri Chopin, and others of the same generation, his work typically took a strong polemical stance (Hodell was a committed pacifist for much of his life). Hodell's works remain available via sites like ubuweb and sound recordings, some of which combine his works with those of others. The 220 Volt Buddha album combines the titular masterwork with two pieces of a similar intent: "Kerberos (Hellhound)" and "Orphic Revelations - Electronic Purgatorium V"

To hear the full four-channel concert version of 220 Volt Buddha is to get an insight into why this elliptical, artful, and occasionally playful, 21 minute piece gave permission to everyone from Tangerine Dream to This Heat to follow innovative paths. Mostly electronic and experimental, Buddha still references organic sounds and the mystical power of music (the latter with a recurrent motif of a mindfully struck gong). A puttering series of electronic rhythms permeate the piece. 220 Volt Buddha reaches its end after a journey that offers a lengthy narrative and drags the listener on an eccentric and captivating trek. It is all abstract. Phrases like "intense whirl" and "strange magic" get close to the original intent. The piece accompanied an artwork, which can be glimpsed online or savoured on the cover of the album, by Hodell's fellow Swedes: At the Gates, called With Fear I Kiss the Burning Darkness.

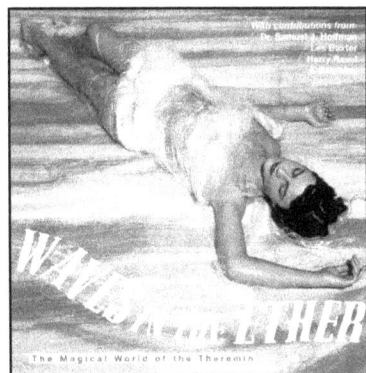

Dr Samuel J. Hoffman:
Waves in the Ether
(Rev-Ola, 2004)
What? Space rock; before we had "rock," or space travel

The story of Dr Samuel J Hoffman would make a good movie. It would also be an appropriate subject, since the man's best known recorded sounds appeared over a few decades in movie soundtracks. A qualified podiatrist and highly skilled violinist, the good doctor combined medical practice and moonlighting as a musician under the name of Hal Hope before a series of fortunate events launched an intriguing recording career. He acquired a Theremin – an electronic instrument, played by moving of the hands in the air near its two antennae – in settlement of a debt from another musician. Having moved to Los Angeles he continued the night-time gigs. He incorporated the Theremin in his stage act, and registered with the local Musicians Union. As the only player of the instrument listed with the local union branch, and someone seen regularly by movie folk out for the evening, he soon started working on movie soundtracks. The eerie soundtrack to Alfred Hitchcock's 'Spellbound' (1945) was the break he needed. There were concert standard players of the instrument far more accomplished at the time but Hoffman had the ability to generate the perfect sounds to accompany the on-screen action, and soon developed an expertise in using simple melodies and surprising changes of tone to conjure up images and moods, emotions and...other worlds.

As the space race between the USA and USSR gathered pace strange, opportunist merchandise appeared. Amongst the more substantial items was Music Out Of The Moon, a slowly wailing and surprisingly tuneful collection by Hoffman. The album remains the best-selling Theremin led long-player of all time. Other recordings followed, along with soundtracks like the original of The Day The Earth Stood Still. Hoffman's live appearances included the Hollywood Bowl and he was frequently interviewed about his musical achievements. The fad for his solo recordings eventually passed but he remains a cultish figure and Rev-Ola's recent collection includes the whole of Music Out Of The Moon. Hoffman died in 1967, 18 months too soon to realise that one fan of his, a man so keen he took a taped copy of his masterwork on a very notable journey, was Neil Armstrong.

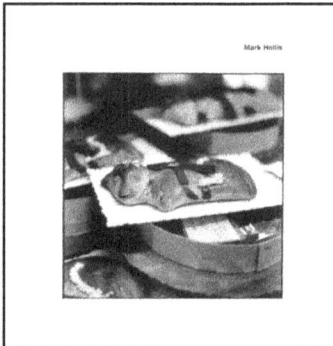

Mark Hollis:
Mark Hollis
(Polydor, 1998)
What? Breathtaking – though often impenetrable – tour-de-force from former Talk Talk frontman.

The only solo album by the former Talk Talk frontman Mark Hollis is something of a yardstick for the borderlands of alternative music, and a regular item on shows like Stuart Maconie's Freak Zone (and Neil Nixon's Strange Fruit) where the presenters pride themselves on sorting out the enduring gems of obscurity from the incalculable tonnage of records that simply failed to sell.

Over meandering melody lines and slow tempos a minimal and deftly arranged sound ebbs and flows as Hollis times his vocals to go with the waves of the music, using his voice like an instrument, expressing himself through lingering notes and changes in volume. All of which makes for compelling – if not always easy – listening, and makes the lyrics hard to decipher. Allmusic have cited the collection as: "quite possibly the most quiet and intimate record ever made".

Frankly, it isn't, but along with any other pretenders to such an accolade Mark Hollis pulls all the right sonic moves. It draws some blatant influences from the experimental ends of classical and jazz and assumes any complex lyrical message will be deciphered by a listener, closely involved with the album and be willing to do the thinking to figure it out.

To that end the signature piece, (given the album's influences piece is probably as fitting as "song" to describe the individual tracks), here is probably the longest: "A Life (1895 - 1915)".

A work in honour of Roland Leighton, war poet, war casualty and fiancé of author and feminist Vera Brittain. In Hollis' hands this is an exploration – through the story of one man – of major themes regarding the high-expectations and self-worth of Empire era Britain, and the way dashed dreams and disillusionment set in as the slaughter of the Great War took hold. Hollis explores his theme in swings of mood, tempo and sound.

Hugely ambitious, intensely personal and designed entirely for listening (Hollis publicly stated at the time he had no intention of playing the music live), Mark Hollis is an uncompromising collection, demanding undivided attention and repeated listens, but the evidence of its continued hold on a hard-core fan-base suggests it repays such attention.

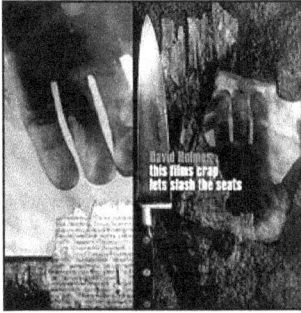

David Holmes:
This Film's Crap Let's Slash the Seats
(Go Discs, 1995)
What? Movie soundtrack masterclass and mix-tape magic.

Okay, for the pedants amongst you we know the title that appears on the front of the packaging is: This Films Crap Lets Slash the Seats but most sources that seek to say anything about this album have seen fit to add the proper punctuation; so we will. Amongst the online material and book entries devoted to this album there is a standard – and wholly correct argument – that it is best-judged as a dry run for the career Holmes subsequently enjoyed composing memorable and highly effective film scores. But taken on its own merits This Film's Crap... is like a best of collection from nineties noir. It also harks back to the fifties fashion for instrumental albums with narrative elements. It doesn't sound much like the work of Creed Taylor or William Schumann but it takes the vibe of their best efforts and reworks it for a nineties, techno, generation. You know this isn't a normal album from the slow, slow burn of the opening "No Man's Land." Bells fade into footsteps which fades into nearly thirteen minutes of a slowly developing insistent melody that disturbs as it draws you in. Moods change, Holmes' compositional abilities visit every evocative corner of edgy embellishment and unstable situation he can squeeze into the running time, and several tracks emerge that would be welcomed by the best film directors. Sarah Cracknell's self-possession on the vocal for the noir-jazz ballad "Gone" is a particular highlight and it is no surprise that a US release of This Film's Crap... which offered a bonus CD of B-sides and remixes featured a trio of varied re-imaginings of "Gone." Steve Hillage also puts in an appearance, adding a distinctive guitar figure to "Inspired by Leyburn" – a John Barryesque concoction and easily the most self-consciously retro piece on offer. Dialogue intrudes; the instrumental pieces typically go on at length, and sudden changes of pace or mood arrive with little warning as they would if you were listening to a film soundtrack. This Film's Crap isn't always an easy or convivial companion. The experience of listening to great soundtrack music which never appeared on a soundtrack can be disconcerting. But the quality seldom slips below excellent and Holmes' ability to blend the right amount of melody and atmospheric touch remains almost flawless throughout.

Julia Holter:
Tragedy
(Leaving Records, 2011)
What? Accessible avant effort from prolific US polymath.

Julia Holter's work remains impossible to categorise, jumping from mainstream pop sounds into avant-garde and electronica – often within a few seconds. A lazy description might suggest she bears some sonic resemblance to Big Science period Laurie Anderson made over for the 21st century. Commercial and categorising music sites tend to provide some linkage between Holter and other talents on the margins of popular music; like Julianna Barwick or Grouper.

Tragedy marked her first album release after a period contributing to compilations and other musical projects (including one presenting phonetic interpretations of songs originally recorded in languages other than English). At its most accessible Tragedy has a catchy pop feel. "Godess Eyes" has an insistent hook, a sense of sweet frustration and even merited a decent video that stood up well next to the indie promos of its period.

But the six track album as a whole demands much more; the layered electronics of "Try To Make Yourself a Work of Art" give this one – the opening cut – a really complex vibe, made more so by vocals at the limit of intelligibility and a slightly ominous spoken word passage. It comes across as both experimental and indie but still drags a gothic sensibility into the mix and slows in an instant to segue into the icy and Spartan wastes of "The Fallen Age." Tragedy repeatedly plays these mood tricks and doesn't lend itself to casual listening. A darkened room, headphones and – possibly – a really good wine might just make for the best engagement with an accomplished and subtle work that has the depth to repay very close attention from the listener.

Hoola Bandoola Band:
Vem kan man lita på?
MNW 1972
What? Socialist Swedish prog from the anti-ABBA

European prog in the form of Italy's PFM, Greece's Aphrodite's Child and a few other notables gradually made inroads into the mass market. Sweden, one of the most liberal and progressive societies in Europe during the seventies, foisted the pop monster that was ABBA on the world, but didn't succeed in exporting The Hoola Bandoola Band, one of its most strident and ambitious prog/protest outfits. Vem kan man lita på? (which translates most accurately as "who can you rely on?") is the band's second outing and their first as a fully-fledged mouthpiece for socialist values. The title track sounds like the bouncier end of protest folk, and the other lyrical detours take in classic prog/psych territory, notably on "Keops Pyramid" a sprawling, near seven minute epic, which pits a simple vocal melody and short riff against washes of acoustic guitar and keyboard to build an insistent message before seguing into a CSNY style harmony and allowing the guitar licks to get a little edgier. Footage exists on YouTube of the band playing "Keops Pyramid" much in the manner of classic jam footage of Jefferson Airplane/CSNY around the time. "Maya" hits similar sonic territory but betrays a backward looking vibe with hints of late sixties psych-pop and eastern drums. The closing "Rocksamba" is, pretty much, what the title suggests and manages, in a vague manner, to kindle the curious psych-exotica vibe of the likes of Os Mutantes.

Massively popular in their own land, Hoola Bandoola went on to push the sonic envelope in a truly progressive manner by recording with a balalaika orchestra. Their reformations were always major events in the Swedish music world, especially so when they snagged a support slot with Bob Dylan in 1996. The death of key member Björn Afzelius left the band in a limbo akin to a Garcia-less Grateful Dead.

A strong affinity with the nuances of the Swedish language is probably essential for anyone aiming to get the very best from listening to The Hoola Bandoola Band. But, for those intent on hunting down rare prog in all its myriad forms, this work comes highly recommended.

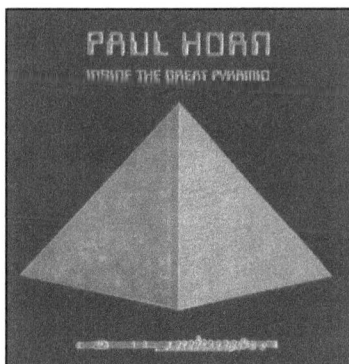

Paul Horn:
Inside the Great Pyramid
(Epic, 1976)
What? A user's guide to inner space and/or seamless self-indulgence of the highest order.

Horn kept some distinguished company, notably hanging with The Beatles in Rishikesh, and cutting a very unique swathe through the music industry. Categorising his singular career is largely pointless given that Horn is one of those musicians who starts by being true to himself. His best known recordings are – arguably – those that also fit best into this book, though most of his work is intended to challenge/stretch/inspire. The "Inside" albums, an occasional, ongoing, series that started when Horn snuck a tape machine into the Taj Mahal in 1968, revolve around slow-moving, echoing sounds recorded in locations of spiritual importance. When the Taj Mahal album (1969) proved a slow but insistent seller Epic Records proved amenable to a sequel and Horn prepared to record inside The Great Pyramid. Much reading on the history and significance of the pyramid, and consulting with experts, preceded the recording and Horn's own account of the mystic experience is central to the mythology of the album. Just before the recording he reported: "I heard what seemed like chanting voices far away, very clear and very real, but so distant I couldn't make out a specific melody. They sounded like whispered chants from thousands of years ago, or like strings inside a piano sympathetically resonating quietly after you finish playing a note on the flute. They were beautiful tones and seemed to envelop me and the whole room. There was nothing spooky about this. I felt warm and comfortable." His companion experienced the same thing. Soon after Horn began a series of recordings, moving from chamber to chamber.

The resulting work features slowly meditative passages, sometimes little more than clusters of notes echoing and being joined by more sounds as Horn builds up a chord, one note at a time, interacting with the location. It's ethereal, mystic and mystifying but it is more focussed than the Taj Mahal outing if only because Horn arrived with some pre-conceived ideas and – at some level – remained aware he was there to cut an album. A close contemporary of Brian Eno's first forays into ambient music, and a pre-curser by some years of the countless meandering melodies released as "new age" albums of the eighties, Inside the Great Pyramid still has a stillness and sense of peace that few recordings can match. It also has echoes of a time long past and a spiritual sensibility – once fashionable – that took a pounding a decade later.

Frankie Howerd:
Get Your Titters Out
(Hallmark, 2002)
What? Funny ho-ho/funny strange car-crash of a compilation.

As a rule Howerd fans don't rate this collection and it should be noted that the 2002 release isn't the only instance of this unholy grab-bag of old and less-old Frankie being thrown onto the same disc to generate a few sales; it is simply the most readily available edition. Howerd (1917-1992) was a British comedian best-known for a self-depreciating double-entendre laced raconteur style of performance. Since his death in 1992 Howerd's private life has also been the subject of much public interest. A rapacious homosexual who spent many weekends with his psychiatrist taking LSD in an attempt to "cure" his tendencies, Howerd never-the-less was noted for bouts of promiscuity and tried very hard (sometimes successfully) to "turn" straight men. Howerd's prodigious talents struggled to find a steady home to the point that comedy writer Barry Cryer described his career as "a series of comebacks." As a rule Frankie didn't make albums but music was a regular part of his career. Oddities in his music-related career include a version of the Jane Birkin Serge Gainsbourg hit "Je T'aime" recorded with June Whitfield. Frankie also appeared in the infamous Sgt. Peppers' Lonely Hearts Club Band movie alongside the Bee Gees and Peter Frampton. A late-career revival saw Frankie's act going down a storm in British universities, by then a hotbed of understanding for different modes of sexual alignment and also receptive to "alternative" comedy of all kinds. The new audience prompted a revival of sorts in Frankie's recording career and Get Your Titters Out puts some of these recordings alongside a slew of Frankie's set pieces from much earlier. Frankly, it's a bizarre concoction, as much off the wall as side-splitting.

The older material here isn't quite what it appears: "Song and Dance Man" has enough additional noise to suggest the master tapes were unavailable to the compilers and "Three Little Fishes" – pretty much his greatest hit – is a later and inferior version of the well-known original. The addition of good bit of sketch comedy with Margaret Rutherford on "Nymphs and Shepherds" is a real throwback to his best old-period work. But the real stunners on this compilation are the lavish helpings of down-with-the-kids late period Frankie. "Get Your Titters Out" puts dance grooves – better than Jive Bunny but referencing that ilk – under a classic double-entendre Frankie-rap (let it all hang out…get your titters out…once they're out it'll be hard to get them back in again etc.) with references to Vanilla Ice (who actually was hot around this time) and "the mic." Frankly, Frankie doesn't sound convincing dropping the names and modern lingo and "On No Missus" and "Nay, Nay and Thrice Nay" take it a stage further by sampling standard stage patter and putting the grooves underneath. "Frankie's Grooving" (of which there are two versions on offer) is comedy DJ fodder in which Frankie banters with a DJ, takes on the decks and sees his initial fear dissipate as he and the audience go with the groove. This material spends most of its length pitting Frankie's old school double-entendres "I think I've pulled a muscle" with the language and sounds of the young 'uns.

A handful of records compiled in this book amount to ill-judged bandwagon jumping but Get Your Titters Out isn't Frankie Howerd's Hey Jude/ Hey Bing so much as a rag-bag that – accidentally – tells the story of a man who spent most of his career inside an identity crisis

Engelbert Humperdinck: The Dance Album (Interhit Records, 1998)
What? More retrofit than Reload.

To place this collection in context Tom Jones had re-invented himself with strong, dance-flavoured, hits and was about to unleash the monster selling Reload when Engelbert's Dance Album hit the racks (there were still plenty proper record shops in 1998). In another coincidence both acts were managed by their young and in-touch sons (Scott Dorsey – Engelbert's third son – eventually took charge of all his touring commitments in 2010). The Dance Album is a stab at street cred from a middle aged crooner. To be fair to Engelbert he had already done disco rather well. Tracks like "You are There," from 1977's Miracle album, pushed the livelier end of his balladry into light dance grooves. A signature move in these early forays in disco involved allowing his ability to hold a note to function as the top end of the melody line. The total lack of serious chart action at that time probably owed more to changing fashions than any failings on Engelbert's part.

Engelbert's chart action in the nineties was minimal. No albums in the US charts and only one: Love Unchained (complete with cover photograph astride a powerful motorbike), had hit the UK charts (#16) before The Dance Album briefly arrested the rot with a climb to UK#48. It sure as hell isn't Reload, and some of its belated fame involves the kind of appreciation the original makers didn't plan. The idea is clear enough, rework a few classics – "Release Me," "Man Without Love" and "Last Waltz" are amongst the more familiar items – and throw in some new sounds, from a cool production team. Mix in a tonnage of hip dance sounds and await the flocking of the faithful and newly converted. The main problem here is the resulting dog's breakfast of familiar tunes duffed up in unfamiliar styles, and the inescapable sense that the collisions involved have thrown out more scrap metal than gold. On first listen it appears daring, but the pulled punches soon reduce the collection to a meander along a familiar road. Tom Jones, by contrast, had staked out new ground and taken on a younger crowd with some confidence.

Engelbert's sashays into salsa and some other light Latin grooves mean his original ballads like "After the Lovin'" emerge as recognisable, but the uncomfortable blend of his warm and effortlessly tender voice with syncopated beats often destroys the original soul. The braver sorties take Engelbert into questionable "bonus track" territory where the tepid "Spanglish Mix" of "Spanish Eyes" amounts to the kind of culinary delight you might get pouring HP Sauce on Doritos or mixing two flavours of bargain cheese.

It isn't all bad, but an end to end listen of The Dance Album may well explain why the revival of his chart fortunes remained minor, and Engelbert's future assaults on the top ten of the UK album chart were mounted with hits compilations done in his old style. The best thing, by far, about The Dance Album is Engelbert's sheer professionalism. He gives the vocal lines everything he can in terms of emotion, and the effortlessly classy croon remains intact, even when ham fists are layering keyboards and mechanical beats all over the mix. That battle is fought out in all its gruesome splendour with a bizarre remake of "The Last Waltz" where the kind of needless noodling a clueless teenager might generate on the dance setting of his downloaded music programme is let loose in Engelbert's very best work. For four and a half minutes Engelbert is dragged into the same camp calamity that is celebrated by lovers of Ethel Merman's Disco Album.

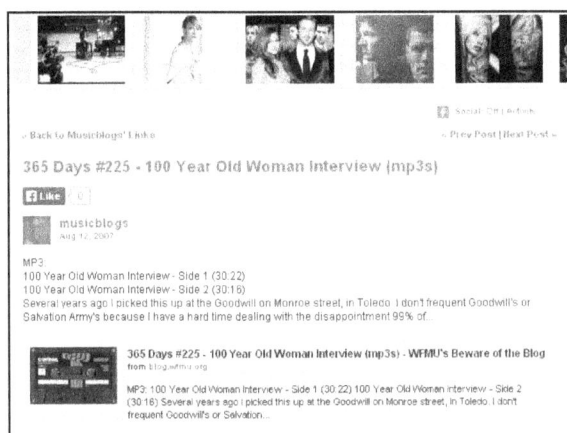

Hundred Year Old Woman: Interview
(Cassette turned to mp3, 1978)
What? Audio artefact = online enigma.

The internet is crawling with random sounds recorded in situations never properly logged or described. This C60 length interview sounds like it formed part of a history project. A young woman interviews a 100 year old woman. The tape was discovered in a charity store in Toledo. The unnamed subject of the interview recalls a world in which her father wouldn't let her drive with the horses on Sunday because the horses "needed their day of rest too." The subject of the interview is still independent enough to be able to comment on her investments, though she now lives in a home and her sight and hearing are failing. She has also lost a good deal of weight. The little noises of encouragement made by the interviewer, plus the interviewer's growing infatuation and admiration for her subject, give the recording an unfolding narrative. The conclusion involves the interviewer stating she has to "write it up" and her teachers seem "pretty interested" in the story.

Most of the action, recalled by the subject, presents a story of day to day events as told by someone who was already an adult when the twentieth century dawned. A few random noises of the microphone moving or a clock chiming punctuate the recording. The curt observations and pragmatic take on life of the subject in which the dustbowl was characterised by "a lot of dirt blowing" and the depression occurred when "nobody had any money" puts a human take on history. So too the facts of our subject's life, she clearly understands a lot about the stock market, and inherited land by outliving her siblings.

Despite this, she turned down the one chance she was offered to fly in an aircraft. Most of the story is delivered with clear diction and clear recall, only a few details, like the year in which the subject had a serious hospital operation, are forgotten. The whole interview, in two parts, now sits at #225 on the 365 Days Project of 2007.

William Hung:
Inspiration
(Koch International, 2004)
What? Karaoke king's finest hour.

This 200,000 selling (#24 on US Billboard chart, # 1 on the indie version of the same) first album by William Hung may be well known inside the US. In other territories it is a different story. Hung turned in a spirited – if hardly stunning – audition for American Idol which won the hearts of the viewing public and led, eventually, to a recording deal in which Hung produced vocal performances to Karaoke backing tracks. The usual laughing at/ genuinely celebrating debate applies where Hung is concerned. Though, by common consent, it is agreed he enjoyed his pop career (which effectively ended in 2011 when he went to work as a technical crime analyst).

Hung covers a series of standards and cultish pop on Inspiration. Ricky Martin's "She Bangs" (Hung's audition piece for American Idol and a single release) is the second track in the running order, which works its way down to include "I Believe I Can Fly," "Hotel California," "Can you Feel the Love Tonight," "Rocket Man" and "Y.M.C.A." Technically speaking everything from Hung's pitching to his phrasing is a triumph of enthusiasm over pedantic perfection – the missed notes at the end of "I Believe I Can Fly" being amongst the biggest clangers on the album. Songs of complex meaning, like "Hotel California," and of technical difficulty, like "Can you Feel the Love Tonight" (wherein Hung falls really flat on the soaring opening line of the chorus), are the real nub of the album.

To some this is social callousness writ large. Hung can't hold a tune and his diction - arguably - belongs in Karaoke bars, not burned over 12 songs and three personal messages on a CD. But this isn't the "savant-garde" freak-show splendour of Wesley Willis or Wild Man Fischer, because there is no doubt Hung was fit to make his own decisions. On the positive side he got to appear on major television shows and at major sports events. He was genuinely a pop star with decent (if fleeting) record sales. He even comments on this in his final personal message, stating: "it's great to be myself and have people respect me for who I am," following it – fittingly – with a spirited assault on "Y.M.C.A" in which his enjoyment of his pop star life spills over as he briefly cracks up laughing as he sings.

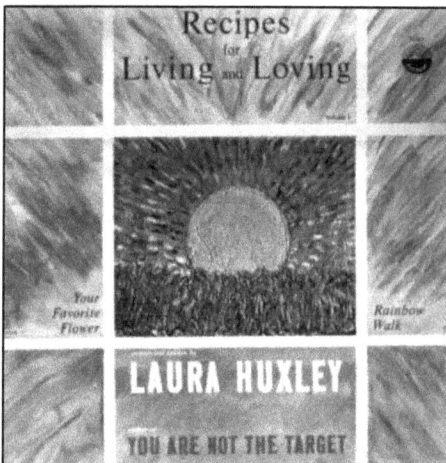

Laura Huxley:
Recipes for Living and Loving
(Everest, 1973)
What? Self-help with a side order of strangeness.

Huxley (1911-2007) is probably best known as the wife of author Aldous Huxley, but, this slice of audio strangeness deserves, (in the humble opinion of the present authors, at least), to be better known. Effectively two meditations, each spread over one side of the original vinyl, this is a meander through a creative and differently abled vision of life. Huxley's heavy, and heavily accentuated, European tones, (born in Turin, her education took in Paris and Berlin amongst other destinations), walk a thin line between a comedy caricature of a European accent and the genuine article. Her work as a counsellor, musician, film-maker and general free thinker/expresser finds its perfect focus in the vivid journeys on the album. From the opening minutes of side one when you are invited to look at our favourite flower: "the way your favourite flower looks at you" you know you are in a land of "hello trees, hello sky" beauty wherein all is one and we become our inner nature. Cynics should reach for the bucket at this point because the second side is a guided meditation through nature scenes and bonding with our own inner nature. After the trees, water features and wildlife are sighted we ramble into inner space. By way of visualising subtly changing shades of colour, we enjoy a superbly balanced stroll through psychedelic ideas and psychological depths. This second side is designed as a guide to falling asleep. The beautiful and sparing strings that gently intrude around the quarter hour mark present themselves as the perfect accompaniment to deep, restful and dream-laden sleep.

The old school eccentricity some find in this recording has long placed it in the land of audio curiosity alongside some of the more obvious freaky items listed in this book. That, seemingly, was never the intention of Mrs Huxley. But, her mannered accent and reliance on a classical style of music set this album well apart from the synthesized keyboards and cod-ambient compositions of much "new age" music. So Recipes for Living and Loving tends to receive a varied, ironic, amazed and indulgent love in return for its efforts to reach out to us all.

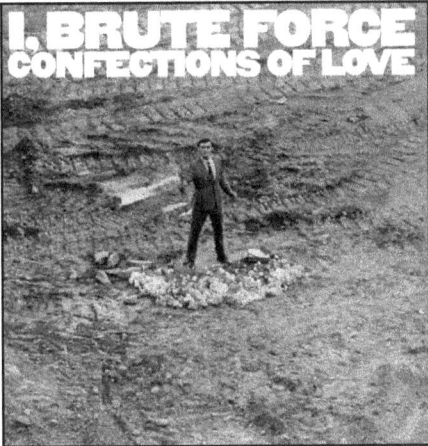

I, Brute Force:
Confections of Love
(Columbia, 1967)
What? MOR + LSD = Funny

Virtually unknown outside the USA (and largely unknown within it) Stephen Friedland who has recorded (mainly) as Brute Force and, on this debut release, as I, Brute Force has boasted the great and the good in his fan base: John Lennon, Jello Biafra, point made. Confections of Love is a truly strange delight, akin – as in Forrest Gump's explanation of such – to a chocolate box, because: "You never know what you're gonna get." The continuing cultish appeal of the collection relies on two divergent strands of sixties music approaching each other at terminal velocity, and the scattered remnants of the ensuing collision leaving strong traces of the two original vehicles. On one side Friedland is a singular talent as a songwriter with a world view both strongly askance and vividly enabled. He sees song subjects where others see nebulous ideas and thoughts to be dismissed. On the other side we have die-hard white-bread middle-America elevator (aka lift) friendly MOR production values and an aversion verging on allergy where standard rock instrumentation or attitude is concerned. So, as Jello Biafra has described it: this is an album packing "Forceful uptempo crooners." Imagine if Richard Cheese wrote his own stuff and never once took the piss…that's the vibe.

The front cover picture of Stephen/Brute Force stood in a square-as-square-can-be polyester suit holding out a bunch of flowers is bad enough, worse when you clock the fact the large expanse of land surrounding him is clearly a landfill site. We're in there with the low-concept of burning tyres and cheap-tack ghoulish suits that made The Louvin Brothers' album cover excursion to Hell such a toe curler. But, Brute Force follows on with the MOR/tacky/don't give a shit cos this is my party vibe to deliver songs the like of which never occurred to Frank Sinatra. "To Sit on a Sandwhich" and "Tapeworm of Love" are the titles that stand out from the original 11 cuts on the album but it's the convoluted observations on life that make Confections of Love the connoisseurs' jaw-dropper of choice. Some of the cuts betray the same opaque but insightful logic beloved of those collectors of song-poems written by the public and recorded on a shoe-string budget. "Brute's Circus Metaphor" trawls this territory, clearly seeing the machinations of skilful performances for an audience as a metaphor for human affection. "The Sad Sad World of Mothers and Fathers" is another missive from a marginal viewpoint, made all the stranger by its big production. An Amazon review by Elastic Rock notes: "a very stagy number that wouldn't seem out of place in an off-off-Broadway show...on acid." We concur completely.

Musically the album visits the same territory and offers hope to the hopelessly stranded MOR crooners of the sixties: BIG orchestrations, BIG drums, horns-a-plenty and the occasional sonic body swerve, like the ill-advised move into cod-acid-folk vocal style: "No Olympian Height." Stephen/Brute Force is a nasal singer though not – exactly – in the chillingly effective Gene Pitney mode, and the occasional inclusion of a sound effect more at home on a rock album also clouds the question of who – exactly – was supposed to listen to this. It's MOR for sure, but hardly romantic, or comfortable, and definitely so far into its own world view that any comedy impact is a spin-off rather than the main point. As quirky as the quirkiest moments in the catalogue of Jonathan Richman and his ilk, Confections of Love was reissued on CD with bonus cuts (including the infamous "King of Fuh" released on the Apple label).

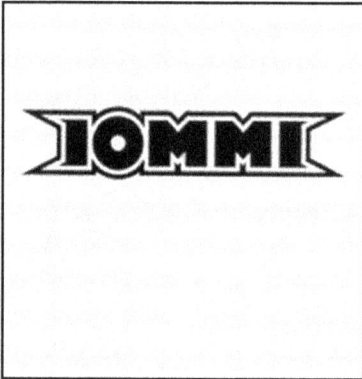

Toni Iommi:
Iommi
(Priority, 2000)
What? First solo outing proper from Sabs' axeman.

Ozzy Osbourne calls Iommi "the master of the heavy metal riff" and three decades after The Sabs' eponymous debut Iommi finally had his solo debut to showcase the skills. There had been near-solo excursions along the way, especially Sabbath's The Seventh Star which is credited to Iommi and Black Sabbath and features a line-up few would recognise as genuine Sabs. Iommi is a genuine attempt to capture what the great man does best. Set up a riff-based song, make a big rock sound and prepare the stage for the singer (preferably Ozzy) to give the whole thing a story. For all its formulaic set up, (Iommi co-writes everything here, every song has a different high-profile vocalist, everything is solid metal with a hint of old school and the sound is BIG), this album does manage to breathe life into the clunky concept described above. It made little inroad into the marketplace where a US chart position of #129 was its peak; though five years after release Rock Hard magazine saw fit to place it 451st amongst the 500 Greatest Rock and Heavy Metal Albums of All Time.

With its massive sound, rotating star vocalists, the sense that everything (bar the simple and seldom flashy bass) is turned up high, and brief searing solos Iommi is aiming for the US market and – specifically – US rock radio. On that score it is perfect product. Nothing distorts, but not much goes quiet either, and the songs give the vocalists space to be themselves. If the vocalists are variable Iommi is majestic in roaring away, ripping out those big chords and pushing enough variations on that trademark big round Duane Eddy meets The Devil tone to remind you he is in charge; and he still sounds like Black Sabbath. Vocally the performances are standard rock, big voices, lyrics (mainly) exploring some declaration or disaster, and most of the performers giving a good – if predictable – account of themselves. Standout performances include Skunk Anansie's Skin, who takes "Meat" from a borderline ambient beginning into massive rock anthem territory, gradually ramping up the emotion to righteous anger. Ozzy does a turn on "Who's Fooling Who" and enough names – Dave Grohl, Billy Corgan, Ian Astbury - turn up to hang with the guitar legend and give Iommi a sense of A-list importance.

A few meetings fall flat, Pantera's Philip Anselmo has the dubious honour of vocalist on "Time is Mine" one of the slower numbers and a track so steeped in that big, round, first-five-years-of-Sabbath, guitar tone that only Ozzy's most manic performance will do. Anselmo sounds – sadly – too sane to pull it off. Similarly, the two bookend tracks "Laughing Man (In the Devil Mask)" featuring Henry Rollins and "Into the Night," in which Billy Idol gets a run out, don't quite do the business. Rollins simply lacks the vocal range to drag the tune out of incessant repetition and Idol is playing with the big boys here but still thinking a bit clichéd/small with his lyrics: "Come back to Hell it's warm inside/ I sleep through the day coz I'm into the night."

As a master-class in deploying the best tools in the classic metal armoury Iommi is the choice of Iommi's small canon of non-Sabs works. At times he steps up with sublime moments that simply ooze class. Improbably, he throws in some deft guitar fills at the end of "Into the Night" that damn near save the whole thing from Idol's posturing. Iommi doesn't risk de-railing itself in self-indulgence, holds the flashy pyrotechnics at bay and lacks the madness of Sabbath's edgy first decade (which much of the metal hordes can only look upon and weep), and – for fully half its running time – it delivers massively in presenting Iommi, the man, as a performer worthy of his legend.

It's a Beautiful Day:
Live at the Fillmore '68
(Weinerworld, 2013)
What? Burnin' bay area live set, from band not famed for burnin'

It's a Beautiful Day hung out in the same San Francisco bay area music scene as The Jefferson Airplane and Quicksilver Messenger Service. The band's opening studio albums, It's a Beautiful Day and Marrying Maiden presented a gentle and complex music, drawn from jazz and the free improvisation of the best bay area jammers. The production showed finesse and attention to detail and the arrangements were a credit to the band's mastermind, violinist/vocalist David LaFlamme. The incendiary rock power in evidence on, for example, early Quicksilver Messenger Service work wasn't a feature of LaFlamme and co in the studio. It's a Beautiful Day became a byword for the more restrained end of the San Francisco hippie boom, released a live album and wandered on in a stop-start career into the present century.

It would be fair to say that the scheduling of this belated live album didn't send waves of anticipation through the music press. But, this captures the band at their live high-point where their incredible playing and ability to spark off each other made their live shows an overwhelming experience. A lot of the best moments on the longer workouts involve playing soft, suddenly exploding into rapid bursts of instrumental fury and using the fast/slow loud/quiet dynamic to keep breathing life into the extended workouts. Everything from Val Fuentes' drums to the LaFlamme's asides on the violin is miked and mixed to perfection, making this set a real find in a sea of substandard reissues. Above all, this makes clear that the studio productions and the line taken by their opening brace of studio albums was a deliberate reining in of a ferocious power this band could channel at will. This is – more or less – the material that established their sound and made their first studio album the definitive work in the eyes of critics. But, as an unexpected insight into a few lost treasures that might lurk out there Fillmore 68 shows that some of the least promising finds, can turn into unexpected riches.

As an aside to all this, It's a Beautiful Day came agonisingly close to sharing this explosive live power with the world. When bay area promoter Bill Graham was involved in negotiations to put The Grateful Dead on the bill of the Woodstock festival he drove a bargain obliging the festival organisers to take one of his other bands. Having listened to a tape of Santana and one of It's a Beautiful Day, Woodstock co-creator Michael Lang couldn't decide because he loved both. A coin was duly flipped and came down in favour of Santana. The festival appearance, inclusion in the documentary movie and appearance on its soundtrack helped start a stellar career for them. Had the coin fallen the other way Live at the Fillmore is an insight into how It's a Beautiful Day would have sounded in the same circumstances.

The Jacks:
Vacant World
(Express, 1968)
What? Narcissistic Nipponese psyche of a very strange hue.

The Jacks' first incarnation produced two albums. By common consent one is a classic and one a major letdown. So, lack of consistency, the generally low expectations of any great breakthrough coming from Japan at the time, and the band's own rapid demise have reduced this strange slice of sixties psych to a footnote in popular music. Undeservedly so, because Vacant World is a sonic experience of high-strangeness, and one of a handful of albums from the period that redefined the rules, even as they were being made. It's a wildly inconsistent collection, and probably does itself few favours from an odd sequencing that places the two longish, doom-laden, nihilistic numbers in the opening trio. The sense of this gesture revolves around "Marianne" – the opener, and only cut on here over five minutes – being a hit single in Japan, and the title track being another of their "hits" because it was well-known by fans. As the sleeve-notes for the reissued album note: the "dark, morbid and melancholic images" generated in Jacks' lyrics were at odds with the pop of the times. So were the instruments lined up on the varied tracks of Vacant World. The title track being a case in point, juxtaposing echoing fuzzed guitar with acoustic flute. Around half the album basks in a mood of minimal jazzy psyche with doomy vocals (all in Japanese; another departure from the custom of Japanese bands at the time), fuzzed guitars and restrained percussion. The middle passage of the album speeds up and produces a rockier psyche, albeit with a sonic sense at odds with late sixties US/UK efforts in the same style. The closing "500 Miles from the Sky" is a shade under three minutes of light psyche backing a spoken word poem. Being fluent in Japanese would help in an understanding of what The Jacks are on about, but the soundscapes and titles betray some of what is happening and, to western ears, it is the strange and singular take on the emerging sounds of psychedelia that make Vacant World such a singular delight.

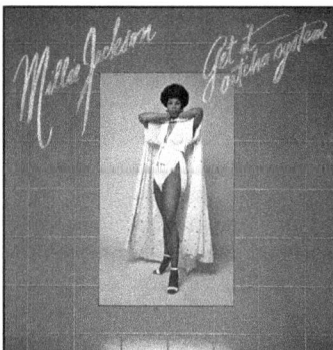

Millie Jackson:
Get it Out'cha System
(Spring 1978)
What? Soulful, sassy and scatological. Go Millie!!

Jackson's feisty rants and impassioned takes on sexual politics always ran the risk of alienating as many listeners as they drew in. Despite a lot of her material being unsuitable for radio and some of the jokes making the faint of heart gag, just a little, she posted three gold albums in the US charts during the seventies of which this was the last. Drawn from some covers – like an inspired interpretation of Dolly Parton's "Here You Come Again" - that drag the originals into her territory, and some of her own material, Get it Out'cha System also sees Millie rapping up a storm. The third track – "Logs and Thangs" – is as good a rap as she ever committed to album; a verbal whipping to any man stupid enough to deny her the respect she truly deserves. It puts the thinnest veils on the metaphors, warning any cheating lover he might find "a different log in the fireplace" if he leaves her alone too long, and enthusing about the "nice logs" available locally…'nuff said.

When she lets the band kick in fully, and the arrangements surround her, Millie's voice is up to a heart-touching hugely soulful interpretation on the right material. The raw sex of and "Logs and Thangs" works its way into the pained opening of "Put Something Down on it" and gradually ratchets up into an insistent groove. But it's the trio of ballads: "Why Say You're Sorry," "He Wants to Hear the Woe," and "I Just Wanna Be With You" that make up the middle of the second side on the original vinyl, and pour like treacle from the speakers, that add an extra dimension here. If Get it Out'cha System has a serious fault it is simply that it does so many things, so well, inside nine tracks that – despite the asides and comments that link some tracks - it is more a series of brilliant performances than a coherent album.

Jandek:
Chair Beside a Window
(Corwood, 1982)
What? The easiest way into one of the greatest outsiders?

Jandek is an outsider's outsider. For over thirty years albums have been independently issued under the Jandek name; a person – obviously the same individual who appears on many album covers – has been performing as Jandek since 2004, but that doesn't – necessarily – explain everything. According to one school of thought Jandek is Sterling R. Smith, his prolific and intense output amounts to an emotional diary, unpolluted by standard notions of commerciality in music and responding to his own life-events. In this scenario it is also considered possible that the greatest periods of output and bursts of creativity amount to manically productive phases in his life. Another school of thought suggests the Jandek name fronts an artistic collective (hence the productivity levels and divergent sounds).

Jandek lore and speculation is – frankly – part of the fun so we would recommend you get surfing, get involved and get listening (assuming the works have eluded you thus far). Jandek albums cover a range of sounds from avant-garde voice experiments to a very basic folk-blues (sometimes with bass and drums backing). Chair Beside a Window is about as accessible as the song-based works get. Jandek's work rides along on a wave of riffing and raking guitar playing, redolent of the earliest blues recordings, frequently sounding out of tune, but always perfectly out of tune when it veers into this territory. In one of the very few interviews ever given Jandek has claimed to play guitar to personally devised open tunings. Chair Beside a Window sounds like a good example of the form. For the most part these are echoing vocal, sharp guitar, intensely emotional broadsides, varying the pace and subject matter and – unusually for Jandek – sharing a lead vocal. "Nancy Sings" brings a beautiful performance from "Nancy" and takes the dishevelled and dissonant noise (briefly) into a skeletal acid-folk of slow, shimmering beauty. The couplet of "if you reach into the air/rain will come to kiss your hair" from "Nancy Sings" highlights Jandek's ability with a simple lyric. By the following "No Break" Nancy and Jandek have moved into the rambling, ranting, stream-of-dark-consciousness that marks much of his early folk, blues output.

For those unfamiliar with the approach that marked the first few years of Jandek albums, this is akin to the Melvins gate-crashing a Bon Iver session. Chair Beside a Window touches the main landmarks of Jandek's early work. "Mostly all From you" is a basic blues with echoes of early masters like Leadbelly, "Down in a

Mirror" and "You Think you Know how to Score" are caustic epistles of emotional disturbance, clearly heartfelt and stronger on the emotions than the specifics of the situations described. The independent ethic and sense of downloading raw emotion extends here – as it does with most Jandek releases – into a sequencing that appears quite literal, when he feels blues, he plays blues and lines up the bluesiest tracks as if they represent one outpouring on a single day. Some albums (see below) show more contrivance and some sense of overdubbing and planning. Chair Beside a Window – by contrast – follows "Mostly all From you" with "The Times" and "Blue Blister" which trawl the trouble with no pause for breath; providing the uncompromising rawness for which Jandek is appreciated by a fanbase including members of Death Cab for Cutie, Sonic Youth and Pearl Jam.

Jandek:
Worthless Recluse
(Corwood, 2001)
What? The hard way into one of the greatest outsiders?

Worthless Recluse is amongst the least penetrable and least musical of Jandek's releases (and that is saying something). The monumental title track clocks in at 17 minutes and ten seconds. A wordy acapella wonder with silences that borders concrete poetry and sets the tone for the whole album. For the most part Jandek intones (as in he doesn't exactly talk and doesn't exactly sing). The shorter pieces have a lyrical structure akin to songs, and typical Jandek themes apply. There are barbed assaults on those causing him discomfort which deliver lyrics suitable for a folk blues song. "You Won't Get up" offers: "I'm gonna do it/ I'm gonna knock you out…I'm gonna beat you down/ You won't get up." Jandek is – typically – unclear about who he is ranting at, but the message certainly sounds personal and sincere. Most Jandek albums throw in some wild card or unexpected twist.

Here it is a beautifully crafted love song, albeit one presented in the same style as everything else here. So, he doesn't actually sing it. This love song - "The Stars Spell Your Name." – has a dark side, but also brings the kind of straight, clichéd, pop wordplay Jandek appears able to deliver at will: "In the labyrinth and scramble/In the smooth and flowing dust…Where the dance is something I can't do/Through all these things it comes again/Some quiet thrill that/I love you."

Worthless Recluse works its way through these moods. The album is close and conversational, with silences which prove unnerving on first hearing, before gradually emerging as thoughtful pauses in the complex messages. This is an album so intimate as to be too close for comfort. Especially so on the longer and more involved material. The epic title track is near enough a multi-faceted wallow in self-loathing, and a crisis of confidence. The ten minute plus twosome of "In the Cave" and "Out of the Cave" is a lengthy narrative. An elliptical but clearly cautionary tale: "But who wants to go down fast?/I just want to stay alive/ We were into the cave/ Playin'with fire all day/It cost a lot."

Like some other acts mentioned in this book – Zappa, Sun Ra, Daniel Johnston etc. – Jandek's entire oeuvre could be broken down album by album, with most of it passing muster for inclusion in this book. At his most accessible he is certainly "different." At his least accessible, he is near enough "unique." Worthless Recluse belongs with his more unique offerings.

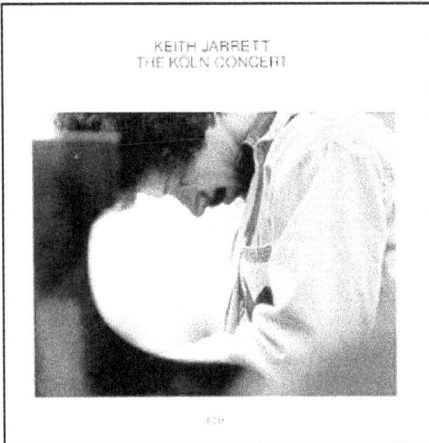

Keith Jarrett:
Köln Concert
(ECM, 1975)
What? A touchstone work of inspirational music.

This 66 minutes of solo piano and, very occasional, slaps on the body of the instrument and vocalising from Keith Jarrett remains the biggest selling jazz work performed entirely on a solo instrument. In an age of wall-to-wall piracy it's unlikely to lose this title. But solo jazz instrumental works are marginal sellers at best and there are relatively minor works in the collections of most rock legends that have wiped the floor sales-wise with this master-class in staying in the moment. You can easily find information online about the marginality of everything on offer here. Jarrett pocketed money for a rail ticket and travelled uncomfortably by car to Cologne where the size and quality of the piano on which he was expected to perform left him ready to pull the gig. Things were resolved, after a fashion, and the spell-binding performance of fluid invention, repeated melodic diversions and bursting passages of strong rhythm that resulted has now become a classic recording. Generations of listeners, and Jarrett's fellow musicians, remain awestruck at the timing of each new turn, and the meditative quality of his playing. There are no titles; each part of the performance comes with a number, corresponding to its place on the original vinyl album. The whole show was improvised and played out in two extended pieces, the first – a 26 minute wonder of alternating moods with the occasional appearance of a hypnotic riff – formed side one of the original album. The much longer second piece was divided into three, including a final section, running a fraction under seven minutes, restating some of the earlier themes and tailing off into a borderline-ambient final coda.

Jarrett is mainly regarded as a jazz pianist but the power of this album lies in the way the tired and fractious musician managed to dig deep into his own soul to heal himself, publicly, with a performance of emotion. Technically the show may have been rooted in jazz, but in a very profound sense this is a spiritual and soulful work that has the pace of a deeply felt conversation. On that level Köln Concert reaches the heights of the most moving classical works, providing that emotional eloquence without words or clear focus that allows listeners to find a personal meaning and feel intense involvement.

Florence Foster Jenkins & Co:
Murder on the High Cs
(Naxos, 2003)
What? A true opera grate.

Foster Jenkins may be celebrated as something of a one-trick pony, but it is one hell of a trick and her mastery of her own little niche in opera history continues to attract new fans to a catalogue that dates back to the early part of the twentieth century. Her story and style are inseparable. The daughter of wealth with one failed marriage behind her, Foster Jenkins longed for a singing career, despite open discouragement from her family and first husband. Inheritance money from her father in 1909 and mother in 1928 turned around the trajectory of her life, her father's death funded singing lessons which led to the start of her performing career. Her mother's death gave her freedom of choice and money which bankrolled the recordings, all of which came from the repertoire she had performed in Philadelphia and New York. In total she cut nine operatic arias and also recorded one lengthy interview. All the music is now compiled on one CD, along with the work of a few other notable peers. But, it is Foster Jenkins' 'singing' that makes Murder on the High Cs such a celebrated collection.

For all the lessons and live work even a cursory listen to her oeuvre makes one thing very clear. Foster Jenkins was musically hopeless. She struggled to hold a tune, her pitching was poor, her timing – arguably – worse. All of her shortcomings terminally under-mined her attempts to convey the deep-emotion of the arias she recorded. For all their early twentieth century low-fidelity limitations her recorded works establish these musical facts beyond all argument. The existence of the recordings has been the key to her immortality. Succeeding generations have sought out and treasured the work of the woman who murdered Mozart and slaughtered Strauss. Her album is riveting for both the wrong, and right, reasons.

Foster Jenkins could hold it together for a few bars and a casual listen sometimes betrays little of what is to come. Foster Jenkins tends to lose it at the moments of high drama, bringing unintended hilarity to desperately serious opera works. More serious students of music have studied and treasured her works for wholly different reasons. Her timing and sense of drama are so fluid that a careful listen reveals the sterling work of her accompanying pianists, generally reduced to busking and altering their approach in the moment, to hold the whole effort together. Bear in mind, these are recordings made well before the Second World War, overdub wasn't even a word and magnetic recording tape was a scientific pipe dream.

In the days of Autotune alterations and digital remastering naked incompetence on the scale provided by Murder on the High Cs is needless. So, on top of her unique take on a selection of noted arias, this compilation of vanity recordings is also something of an insight into the times in which it was recorded.

Jóhann Jóhannsson: The Miner's Hymns (Fat Cat, 2011)
What? Intense, poignant, elegiac and deeply-magnificent, with a passing nod to Arthur Scargill.

Commissioned by Durham County Council, The Miner's Hymns is a work for brass band and cathedral organ, initially premiered in Durham Cathedral. Initially created to accompany a film culled from national archives like the BFI and BBC collections, the music is intended to provide a powerful backdrop to pictures of miners and mining communities, tracing the history of mining in County Durham. The thinking behind the commissioning of a work for brass band and cathedral organ involved linking the film images on the screen to the tradition of colliery bands. The official statement at the time stated: "Focusing on the Durham coalfield in the North East of the UK, the film is structured around a series of activities including touching on the terrible hardship of pit work, the role of Trade Unions in organising and fighting for workers' rights, and the pitched battles with police during the 1984 strike as Thatcher's government sounded the death knell for the industry. Immaculately edited, the film serves as a 'kind of requiem for a disappearing industry but also a celebration of the culture, life and struggle of coal miners... The titles of the individual sections of the soundtrack are slogans taken from the trade union banners that are an iconic part of the Miners' Gala.'"

The revelation of the performance and the subsequent CD release is how well the music stands up on its own. Shorn of pictures The Miner's Hymns is a dark and brooding presence in the room, slowly shifting through powerful chord changes with – for the most part – a minimal melody, the whole piece works more like a massive poem in sound. The piece is continually evoking moods, exploring themes and bleeding a raw emotion with a sense of stoicism and strength. In short, it is magnificent and deeply emotional. The opening "They Being Dead Yet Speaketh" and "An Injury to one is the Concern of All" set the mood, the instruments sounding like a strong community, murmuring their way through sweeps of chords, before a series of bright brass figures announce the arrival of "Freedom From Want and Fear," introducing the first melody led piece long after the start. The pattern, and balance is established and The Miner's Hymns never lets the quality of its vision slip. The official website noted: "Jóhann expertly demonstrates how a single body of instruments can be used to create chilling, stirring and powerfully evocative music of genuine beauty."

Technically speaking this seemingly uncommercial and obscure release is something of a breakthrough record, having earned plays on BBC Six Music's Stuart Maconie's Freakzone amongst others, and become a word-of-mouth success. Whilst the CD itself can't do justice to the experience of hearing the music live, in the glorious acoustics of a cathedral whilst the film plays, the generous packaging does include a few stills from the film and a photograph taken as the work was performed live.

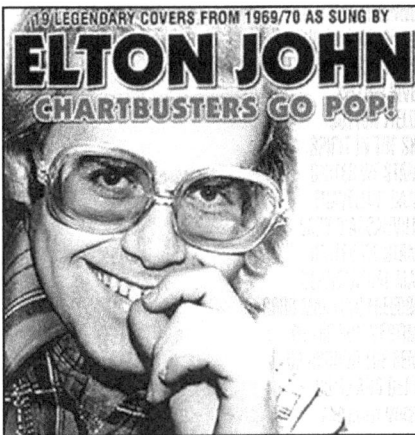

Elton John:
Chartbusters go Pop!
(Delta, 1999)
What? Apprenticeship of rock's Liberace.

Elton John's record sales put him up amongst the popular music elite, his songs remain ubiquitous staples of mainstream radio and his position as one of the most enduring and loved writer/performers in popular music history appears almost unassailable. Chartbusters go Pop! is a minor insight into one element that contributed to the current legend. As a jobbing wannabe in the music industry Elton spent the turn of the 60s/70s decade working at a range of jobs. With Bernie Taupin he was a salaried minimum wage songwriter, he had his own burgeoning career as a writer performer, and he had session work. In the final area he played on the records of several studio bands, brought together to make pop singles. He also contributed to a series of Top of the Pops albums (hastily recorded cover-version collections of 12 recent hits, stuck out at budget price, sold in industrial quantities through outlets like Woolworths and highly popular amongst children). These Top of the Pops collections sold so well that they frequently topped the UK charts. Eventually the rules on qualification for the album chart were changed to exclude them.

As the extensive sleeve-notes on this collection make clear, there is a certain irony in being able to hear the trademark piano playing and early vocal style of Elton as he tackles the work of the Beach Boys ("Cottonfields"), Stevie Wonder ("Signed, Sealed…") and the Hollies ("I Can't Tell the Bottom from the Top"). Within a couple of years Elton would be seen fit to be named in the same breath as these acts, by the end of the same decade he would have outsold most of them. More ironic still is the fact that because Elton John was one of the go-to piano players for London session work, and because his work-rate was such that he'd take sessions all over the place, he played on the records of studio bands and the likes of The Hollies, and then played on some of the same songs again when the Top of the Pops albums covered them.

Chartbusters go Pop! offers up 19 bouncy pop hits, basic British chart-fodder of the period. Listen hard and the radio-friendly vocal style of Elton John and his strong, solid ivory bashing is easy to pick out. The production is quick, effective and a little basic, a few of the tracks sound tinny in comparison to the originals. "Spirit in the Sky" being – arguably – the palest imitation on show. But, there's an adage amongst athletes that 10,000 hours of practice will produce muscle memory likely to improve performance. Musically, the equivalent might be right here. For Elton John in the late sixties living and breathing current pop music in this way was – literally – a means of paying the rent. Maybe, he learned enough during these sessions to pay mortgages on several palatial properties!

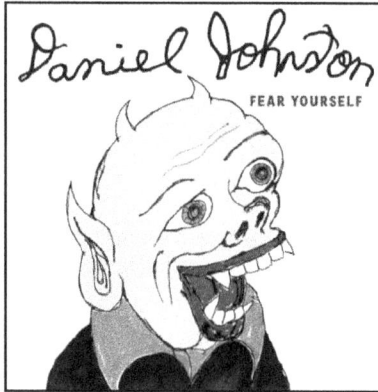

Daniel Johnston:
Fear Yourself
(Gammon, 2003)
What? Link up with Mark Linkous makes for highly individual record in notable career.

As with a few acts featured in this book, we're making some assumptions in writing this entry. Mainly, we're assuming many readers will be familiar with the troubled life and prolific career of Daniel Johnston. Specifically, we're assuming you may be familiar with the fact that Johnston's recording career has gone hand-in-hand with a lifelong affliction with mental illness to such a degree that strong delusions and behaviour likely to harm himself and others has marked Johnston's adult life. His early work from the 1980s onwards is marked by low-cost production and the most basic musical tools appearing on his albums. By the 21st century this situation had changed, Johnston remained inside his comfort zone of revelatory, vivid and indie-school song-writing but the production values of his output increased. Some of his work became radio-friendly, much of it managed musical backings that took his ideas, and the moods he set, supporting them with flashes of inspiration that finally did justice to a talent many had come to admire. If you're unfamiliar with Johnston, the feature length documentary The Devil and Daniel Johnston (2005) is the perfect primer.

The combination of Johnston and his long-time fan Mark (Sparklehorse) Linkous was always likely to be intriguing. Critical reactions were mixed but we'd argue this is a real grower of an album, frequently marked by a combination of Johnston's best observations on life and Linkous' sonic sensibilities. Fear Yourself is certainly an inconsistent and varied collection; sporadically austere and forever in search of something it struggles to find. There's a vibe akin to the starkest early seventies Neil Young moments on a cut like "Love Enchanted" as a tinny piano plays Johnston sings: "I was lost in the discount bin, listening to the tired philosophers who never quite made it," later in the same song he sees the face of Death staring back at him. All of this presented over a descending and basic melody that would have been at home on an early Sparklehorse album. For all Johnston's torment, such lyrical moments are atypical of his work, but count as signature pieces on Fear Yourself. For that reason alone the album is worth a listen. Linkous clearly has a take on Johnston and he sets out to present the Johnston who has inspired Sparklehorse. By contrast, to "Love Enchanted" the closing "Living it for the Moment" is a rough-edged and insistent rocker with some self-depreciating humour and a cheerfully ragged guitar solo. It is also a song that doesn't much end as fall apart in the best Hasil Adkins tradition. The sound is marked with instruments and vocals distorting at the edges and occasionally vanishing from earshot as they do. Johnston's voice is given space in the centre of the mix and often exposed with no echo to come over as isolated and alone. Johnston's surrounding instruments serve to protect him. Linkous has the sense as arranger to vary the sounds and moods in line with Johnston's lyrics. The sequencing also works superbly, slowly moving between moods. So "Must" – a slow-turning, introspective but ultimately hopeful ballad – follows "Love Enchanted." Linkous stamps his mark from the start with an outstanding sleight of hand in the opening seconds as he opens "Now" with a basic four-track mix, making it sound like the earliest and most uncompromising of blues recordings before the song explodes without warning into a widescreen 21st century mix. The effects and overdubs ebb and flow around most of the songs, frequently sliding away into a fade after Johnston has left the stage.

"The Power of Love" – an unrequited and effectively simple peon to an unattainable muse – and "Wish" – a hauntingly simple stroll in the same territory – capture a vulnerability few performers can communicate so well. Fear Yourself achieves its goal of carving out a niche mid-way between Linkous and Johnston; drawing on the best of both and producing a work of lasting depth and considerable merit.

Brian Jones/The Master Musicians of Joujouka:
Brian Jones Presents the Pipes of Pan at Joujouka
(Rolling Stones Records, 1971)
What? Ground breaking world music recording, and release.

Categorising this album, and making any significant sense of it, has confounded critics since it was first released on vinyl in 1971. Brian Jones visited the annual music festival at Joujouka in Morrocco and on, 29 July 1968, recorded live performances. A couple of years after Jones drowned the recordings were released on the label of his former band. The original album offered no track details, simply presenting elongated instrumental pieces edited together on each side. Subsequent CD reissues have divided these into six tracks, from the opening "55" which runs less than a minute, to the lengthy "Your Eyes are Like a Cup of Tea," which amounts to the closing 18 minutes of the album. The resulting pieces are all meditative, trance-like and dependent on drone effects and highly repetitive patterns. The original intention of the work was to present an insight into the Rights of Pan festival and its musical performances, some of which could last for hours.

Jones' release features solo instrumental moments, chants, male and female vocals and moments of forceful energy along with quiet, reflective passages. Lacking significant sleeve notes, it isn't even clear if the main solo instruments are flutes. The Master Musicians of Joujouka as presented here are not a performing outfit so much as the varied performers at an annual festival, though the name has since become a brand to the extent that they have their own presence online and their own listing on the All Music Guide. It seems fair, at this remove in time, to credit this album to Jones. It might mark the first flowering of the Master Musicians' recording career and a benchmark for early world music, but Jones presents this sketchily annotated collection as an audio documentary. It is, essentially, his argument that something is going on in this music that his peers could usefully recognise. Jones didn't live long enough to see a generation of seventies synth pioneers take the ambient/drone ideas into new directions or the advent of world music, but his album contributed mightily to all of this.

Spike Jones and his City Slickers:
Spike Jones is Murdering the Classics
(RCA, 1971)
What? Murder can be fun!

Firstly, an important point, if you're a newbie to Jones' work and can't hunt down this classic compilation there is so much Spike out there on so many compilations, so many of which have a smattering of his best, that it is worth diving in when the opportunity presents itself. Even if you find yourself presented with second-string Spike Jones you're still sampling comedy gold. Jones (1911-1965) and his like-minded City Slickers made a career of massacring popular standards with a combination of utter contempt for anything profound and an explosive imagination with regard to sourcing musical sounds. Having reduced a once beloved song to a ravaged corpse Jones and his gang would sometimes mock the putrid remains by throwing in some musical import from a great work and delivering it with consummate musical skill.

This book champions original albums and Jones made several of those. But his stock-in trade was savaging individual songs and his compilations work like good sketch comedy. Jones' demolitions of pop songs in the pre-video era became so ubiquitous that singers considered it a mark of their achievement when the City Slickers finally got round to destroying their work. Jones' relationship to the standards wrecked in his recordings is akin to the Marx Brothers relationship to department stores in The Big Store or Monty Python's relationship to lumberjacking in their famous sketch. The songs are the excuse to get started. From then on it's pure Spike Jones. The anarchy here is the real point. Like any great anarchic comedians Jones and his crew present one thing and practice another. Jones was a strict bandleader who conceived and rehearsed performances to the point that everything from the ludicrously loud check on his jacket to the perfectly timed gunshots worked to perfection. It worked superbly live, made great television and in the days before the pop video Jones' comedy classics ranked as the most visual music available. Rant over!

Most Jones' compilations are good. Some – like this one – are widely acclaimed as great. Murdering the Classics includes a dozen mirthful massacres, opening with "The William Tell Overture" re-imagined as racing commentary. "Dance of the Hours" pulls a similar stunt and "Ill Barkio" reworks classic opera by allowing dog yelps to compete with an opera singer. Jones' raids on the great and good were generally short and brutal but "Nutcracker Suite" here clocks in at almost seven minutes and the closing "Carmen" runs well past 12 minutes; both reliant on Jones' habit of bringing everything to a grinding halt and dragging in some random musical moment to set off in another direction. You'll find as many belches, gunshots, cowbells and car horns as most Spike Jones' albums but ultimately Murdering the Classics is a winner for its perfect comedy vision, translated into perfectly timed gags that just work. It's there in "The Jones Laughing Record" basically a series of outbreaks of laughter punctuated by portions of "Flight of the Bumblebee." It's a basic gag, (it's never made clear why the people are laughing but the similarity of the "Bumblebee" sections to a well-tuned fart is probably a clue). In lesser hands this joke would fall flat. Spike's timing is immaculate and only the City Slickers would have thrown in a gratuitous and stunningly played trombone solo. Music has never been short of satirists, many of them possessing more basic talent than the targets of their humour, but, as All Music Guide puts it: "the simple fact remains that Spike Jones & His City Slickers did it better than anyone before or since."

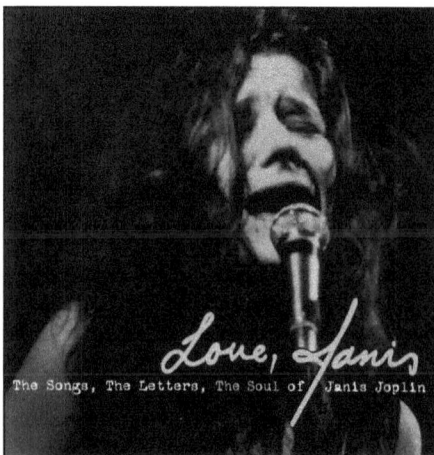

The Songs, The Letters, The Soul of Janis Joplin

Janis Joplin:
Love, Janis
(Sony, 2001)
What? The heart and soul of a blues legend.

Released on the back of a stage show and masterminded by Joplin's sister, Laura, Love, Janis is an ambitious and ruthlessly exposing attempt to present the essence of a performer who has become a byword for the live-fast/die young brand of "27 Club" rockers. The concept is simple enough, a series of Joplin's performances are presented chronologically and interspersed with readings of personal letters mailed to her family throughout her career. Each letter is dated and the frequency of the letters – some coming close together, the later ones betraying the hard work and hard living and apologising for not writing more – tell part of the story. Actress Catherine Curtin does a rasping, tired and emotional turn as the attention seeking star, by turns reverting to her child-like expressions of love for her family and wallowing in the adoration and attention she gets as a fully-fledged rock star. The performances are not always the known and celebrated hit versions but they are well chosen to tell the story of Janis' changing fortunes and moods. A live take of Big Brother and the Holding Company's "Ball and Chain" catches the band at the height of their ramshackle and chaotic glory. Joplin's ability to seize the moment and manifest herself more as a force of nature than a traditional front-woman is well established here, and later letters discussing money provide a perfect frame for the throwaway gem of "Mercedes Benz."

The distance from the tired and self-indulgent early composition "What Good Can Drinkin' Do" to the grim humour and more complex notions of the later songs is – pretty much – the whole point of Love, Janis. If Joplin is celebrated as much as an interpreter of other's work as she is as a songwriter then Love, Janis at least makes a serious point about what she brought to the songs in terms of her own complex personality. It suggests why she didn't so much perform her greatest shows and studio sessions as get inside the songs and inhabit them. It is by no means an easy listen and almost half of the tracks are her letters, but Love, Janis is as much rock biography as essential collection.

The Justified Ancients of Mu Mu: 1987 (What the Fuck Is Going On?) (The Sound of Mu(sic), 1987)

What? Hip-hop pioneers' original long-playing effort, long deleted and likely to stay so whilst musicians have lawyers.

Bill Drummond and Jimmy Cauty are best remembered as the KLF and for a series of high profile actions including once setting fire to a million pounds. The extent to which this – their first long-playing effort – is genuinely intended as ground-breaking hip-hop and the extent to which it is situationist art, fully intended to self-destruct, has been debated since the cutting edge collection was first unleashed. Unlike most early hip-hop 1987... is unmistakably British and white. It also makes no attempt to hide the high-profile samples that under-pin most of the musical efforts. Apparently a comment on the world in which it found itself, 1987...samples conversations, noises and other random elements which are positioned in opposition to copious samples of copyrighted music some of it – like Abba's "Dancing Queen," Led Zeppelin's "Whole Lotta Love" and Dave Brubeck's "Take Five" – being so ubiquitous and so blatantly used on the album that it is a positive incitement to a lawsuit. The nearest thing to a narrative thread running through the collection is a series of samples commenting on the vacuous nature of popular culture – the BBC's Top of the Pops show is sampled on side two as it goes through the chart rundown, making it clear just how many old songs were reappearing as late eighties hits – and after a shout from Drummond of "Fuck this, let's have the JAMS!" "All You Need is Love (106 bpm) begins.

The JAMS make a regular habit of mashing highly regarded music with samples of television theme songs, basic and clunking electronic rhythm tracks and simple keyboard melodies. 1987... comes over as angrily and blatantly in your face as other early hip-hop, but the targets aren't the police or rival players so much as the crass stupidity of mass culture and the public who consume it. The message being it's all shit, nothing means more than anything else and change demands anger and taking control. The best example of this philosophy in action "Next" closes the collection. It offers up a truly eclectic sample selection including Stevie Wonder's "Superstition", Scott Walker's "Next" from Scott 2, the Fall's "Totally Wired," Wild Man Fischer's "Merry Go Round," Julie Andrews' "The Lonely Goatherd" and The JAMS own reworking of the main melody line from The Stranglers' "No More Heroes."

Predictably, lawyers got involved. In the end it was Abba, who weren't greatly amused to hear their "Dancing Queen" riff fading into the dry quacking of a duck as it took up the same melody line in "The Queen and I." Remaining copies of 1987 were ordered to be destroyed, rendering surviving copies instantly collectable. The JAMS responded with an edited version of the album, removing samples and replacing them with long bursts of silence; the resulting album contained so little recorded material the British chart compilers reclassified it as a single. "All You Need is Love" and "Don't Take Five" (with the Brubeck sample) are available – officially on the career spanning The History of the Jams.

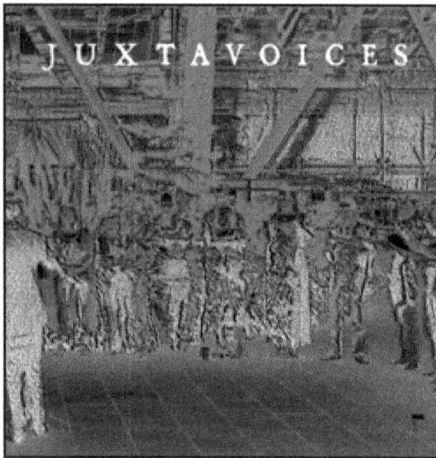

Juxtavoices:
Juxtanother Antichoir From Sheffield (Discus, 2010)
What? If The Smiths had been high-church Catholics, and hired Diamanda Galas as producer.

S'cuse the anecdote…when Neil Nixon took delivery of this album for use on his Strange Fruit radio show he gave it a blast in his kitchen.

With his wife out at her yoga class Neil set about preparing food with Juxtavoices cranked up good and loud. Despite the presence of fresh tuna fish both the cats in the house soon exited the kitchen at high speed. When Neil informed Martin Archer – one of the genius minds behind Juxtavoices and head honcho of Discus Records – of this fact, Martin replied: "That's nothing, you should see what we do to live audiences." This is well weird shit, and yet it's so much more than that.

For starters, this is music that knows its roots inside out but seeks only to use them as a palette from which to build its own identity. That quality, and the self-aware sensibility that knows this music is making an important point, whilst also convincing others of its nutcase credentials might, just, make Juxtavoices a Smiths amongst choirs. Vocally, Juxtanother… takes the dynamics of a traditional choir, employs high and low registers, harmonies, and soloists against a wall of backing singers and then creates the kind of elongated intensities best known in Diamanda Galas's catalogue.

The self-mocking title of the album, and cuts like "Nine Entries from the Encylopaedia of Natural Sexual Relations" (wherein Juxtavoices come over like a bunch of stir-crazy Gregorians perving over the reproduction of plants) suggest some of this work is enjoyed for its sheer otherness, and should not be taken too seriously.

With the nine cuts varying from four to 14 minutes and styles varying from well-modulated conversations to fully fledged choral workouts Juxtanother… is a choirmaster's feature length nightmare of ecstasy, flavoured with gritty northern humour. Part experimentation for its own sake, and part fearless exploration of the unfettered possibilities presented by massed voices, it is out there enough for fearless listeners to marvel at the extremes reached on one album, but not recommended for cherished pets.

Rodd Keith:
I Died Today
(Tzadik, 1996)
What? Nightmares of Ecstacy.

It's a touch hypocritical to put a book together on the strangest listening experiences out there and then start a written review by suggesting you don't read the story, but just check out the sounds. But, that's probably the best thing to do here. What matters for the writing element is to fill in the details the audio tracks can't supply. Rodd Keith (1937-1974) spent a sizeable chunk of his working life in the low-paid thankless drudgery of turning "song poems" into finished recordings. This branch of vanity recording involved professional studios offering to turn amateur lyrics and vague notions of creating "a country song," "a ballad" or similar into finished work. For all his invisibility during his lifetime and the derision with which most of the music industry regarded the whole craft of song poem recording, Keith is now rightfully hailed as a major talent in that thankless field.

His skill was to weave a musical arrangement and workable vocal around the clunkiest of lyrical howlers and the most insane concepts in song ideas. When the handful of sound hounds who had been filtering the divine from the dross by picking up song poem 7"s in junk shops finally began to communicate, Keith – who died in the mid-seventies and didn't even begin to sniff the cult status he subsequently enjoyed – was finally recognised for his incredible talent and ceaseless inventiveness. Elsewhere in this book The American Song Poem Collection – a best of collection trawled from across the whole industry – is discussed. Rodd Keith is central to that compilation. I Died Today is one of a small number of compilation albums devoted exclusively to the man's work.

Keith played all manner of keyboard instruments, accordion and sax as well as picking up any other useful source of sound, and contributing lead vocals to many of the tracks he worked on. Like The American Song Poem Collection, I Died Today draws strength from the variety of sounds he produced and his ability to provide an arrangement for the least rhythmic of lyrics. It is a showcase for the varied and resplendently off kilter ideas that kept his industry in cash. By lining them up to avoid repetition of the same thing I Died Today presents a parade of the demented, desperate and deluded and celebrates Keith's incredible ability to drag victory from the jaws of defeat. Anyone working their way through the collection at one go might usefully ask two questions: 1 – WTF would I do with these lyrics? And: 2 – what chance did any of these lyricists have without Rodd Keith?

Highlights – if that's an appropriate word here – include revisionist history in "General Custer's," the predictable religious righteousness of "Real Americans," a slew of cornball attempts at novelty hits and inventing crazes of which "The Music Man from Mars" – which Keith imagines verging on a Chipmonk/ Pinky and Perky vibe – and a halfway decent production of a ballad "Don't Throw My Love Away" which clearly has one ear on Elvis' re-emergence as a mature artist. "I Died Today" is one of those truly unique efforts – like "Beat of the Traps" on The American Song Poem Collection – that resembles little else in popular music, other than an inspired creation by Rodd Keith in the face of a lyric others would have ripped up and forgotten.

I Died Today is more a dipper than wall-to-wall listen and is tailor made mix-tape gold. But, along with the subsequent Ecstacy To Frenzy and Saucers in the Sky, it is a fitting tribute to the extraordinary talent of Rodd Keith.

Stan Kenton:
City of Glass & This Modern World
(GNP, 1953)
What? Album's length of highlights of highly unusual collaboration between atonal composition and sublime big band arrangements.

History often tells a story suggesting in the aftermath of the horrors of World War Two America hauled itself to a comfortable standard of living and contented style of politics. Hip jazz and rock 'n' roll might have threatened the cosiness of the domestic agenda, but much of the most dangerous sounds came from Europe. This album makes a strident case against such simplicities. Kenton and composer/arranger Bob Graettinger combined over six years in the recording and performance of a series of atonal and massively challenging works that left audiences indifferent and critics dumbfounded. The two sides of this original vinyl album present side long suites that get to the heart of their collective vision. "City of Glass" and "This Modern World," push the sonic envelope into an area somewhere between experimental classical work and big band jazz. The jazz instruments, occasionally, present harmonies and the odd ensemble passage breaks out, but everything is subsumed within a mighty sound and each mighty sound wraps itself around a complete suite. Graettinger remains mindful of a vision in which the rapidly moving patterns in jazz become a metaphor for the bustle and movement of a modern city, but his crashing strings and mighty chords in "City of Glass" present an unfeeling world in which the massive urban sprawl sounds like an all-consuming monster. Solo instruments appear jittery and vulnerable in this landscape. "This Modern World" takes the concept further, bringing in some slow passages, discordant and disturbing noises and a selection of solo instruments. The effect is akin to watching separate lives acted out in pain and loneliness. "This Modern World" is, marginally, more celebratory and empathic, but the whole album still packs a vibe as warm and welcoming as Metallica at their most strident. Kenton's crew acquit themselves with incredible skill and spend most of the duration sounding nothing like The Stan Kenton Orchestra. This album followed an earlier 10" release of "City of Glass," by the mid-nineties a multi CD package was available, presenting the collected works of Kenton and Graettinger.

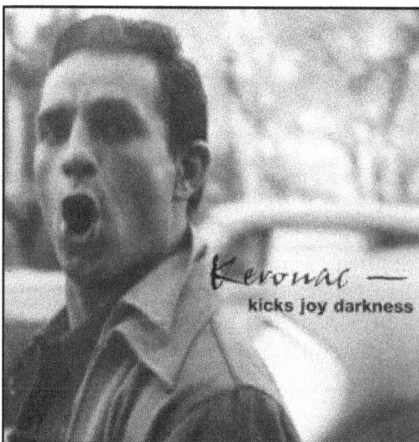

Kerouac:
Kicks Joy into Darkness
(Rykodisc, 1997)
What? The write stuff by the right artists.

Technically speaking this could have been listed with the various artists' compilations. Kerouac was long dead before this compilation was unleashed. The beat giant recorded his own albums. Collections like Blues and Haikus, presenting Kerouac's performance of his own words with jazz accompaniment, have become cultish. This collection is part document (Kerouac is sampled and presented), part documentary (Kerouac's work is supported by extensive liner notes) and a large part response to Kerouac's influence. Johnny Depp, Michael Stipe, Jeff Buckley, Stephen Tyler and Patti Smith are amongst those turning up to put music to Jack's words, read fragments and channel the spirit of the most musical of writers.

Predictably, this is – by turns – a combustible, contrary, wounded, wasted and confusing collection within which Kerouac's rhythmic prose and free-form word-play forms the nearest thing to a continuous thread. Highlights – if the word is even appropriate here – include some of the least promising cuts from the list. Richard Lewis reads "America's New Trinity of Love" in which Kerouac astutely dwells on the triumvirate of Presley, Dean and Brando. Alan Ginsberg reads nine of ten pieces from an unpublished poem. Morphine open the album convincingly with "Kerouac" – one of two original responses – and near enough steal the show there and then. Kerouac himself sings – high-pitched jazz scatting – on Robert Hunter's spoken performance of a section from Visions of Cody, offsetting the description of Neal Cassady: "who walks as fast as he can go on the balls of his feet...Something about his tigerish out-jutted raw facebone could be given a woe-down melancholy..." Kerouac is also sampled against electronic beats by Joe Strummer on "MacDougal Street Blues."

Kicks Joy into Darkness is a hard and inconsistent listen back to back, though the liner notes and listener concentration do turn it into an insight into a major talent. As mix-tape material it is unbeatable. A trio of (then) surviving beats – William Burroughs, Lawrence Ferlinghetti and Alan Ginsberg – reveal one dimension of Kerouac, the tonnage of musical talent – which also includes Eddie Veddor, Warren Zevon and John Cale – all filter the man and his influence through their own styles. Some tracks simply explode with surprises. Juliana Hatfield throws childishness and comedy into "Silly Goofball Pomes," the most playful pieces Kerouac wrote: "The Dachshund is a snake full of Love... The Abominable Snowman is not abominable at all, he doesn't hurt anybody…" and she almost steals the album in the process. The sequencing also works well. Hatfield signs off with a jaunty and playful "The end" before John Cale's resonant Welsh accent and a slowly turning string section lead us into "The Moon."

Whether this captures Kerouac, or even amounts to a fitting tribute, isn't really the point. Kicks Joy into Darkness explores the man and his work, acknowledges his influence and locates his tradition in the work of the varied and capable cast collected to pay tribute to the man.

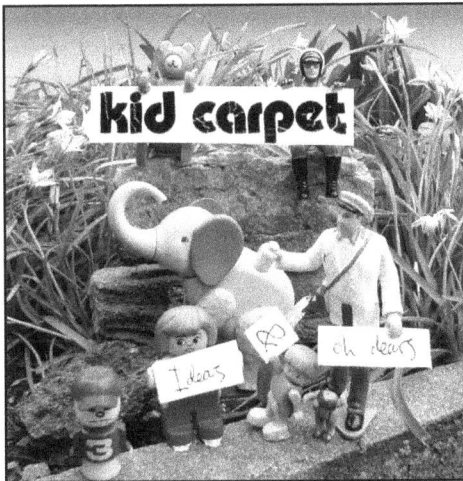

Kid Carpet:
Ideas and Oh Dears
(Tired and Lonesome, 2005)
What? The shit-hop manifesto/ KC is the sunshine man.

Bristolian Ed Patrick – AKA Kid Carpet – has been described musically as a purveyor of 'kiddy disco punk' and 'shit-hop.' If you imagine Kid Rock locked forever inside a large branch of the Early Learning Centre you're getting close to his style and vision. Basically, Carpet rocks and raps out on equipment better known as the top-end toys of imaginative children. Korg keyboards and Gibson guitars would be wasting their time sponsoring the man who sticks with Casio and Fisher-Price. Ideas and Oh Dears opened Carpet's albums account alongside the release of one of its tracks – "Your Love" – as a single. Musically, KC borrows freely from all over the canon of popular music, frequently for the purposes of lampooning and abusing the originals. The fleeting fragment "1 Trick Pony" that nicks Chesney Hawkes' "One and Only" and intones "I am a one-trick pony" is typical of an element of his work that forms one big running joke. Elsewhere everything from "If I Had a Hammer" to ABC's "Poison Arrow" are reworked to pithy perfection.

The one quality that raises Ideas… from the level of low-fi genius that might be funny played around a pub table to something akin to a demented and engrossing manifesto is Carpet's ability to mix and match the myriad ideas to create something that does, genuinely, smack of a creative vision. The man has supported – amongst others – Badly Drawn Boy and the comparison stands up well. Like BDB, Kid Carpet is determinedly indie, determinedly low-fi, determinedly out of step with anything approaching a movement and still compelling in his own individual way. In terms of big ideas there are two themes running like juggernauts through Ideas… and most of the albums that follow. Firstly, the low-fi assault of kiddie equipment reduces the whole notion of rock/hip-hop and every other style fleetingly sampled to the same level and – by implication – mocks those who would argue otherwise. Everything is up for grabs, we should assume nothing is worthy of respect simply because of the genre it inhabits. Carpet's fragmentary takes on banging tunes rehashed through his array of toys is proof of the point. Secondly, KC's own explosive imagination fires the whole collection with a random glory that leaves you wondering if the next thing to assault you will be a good joke or a deft one-liner suggesting he has the chops to make music with straight-faced seriousity if the wants. Some of the tunes – notably "Your Love," and "Green and Pleasant Land" – do have enough pop sensibility to suggest the man could crank out single hits if he chose. But the strong Bristolian flavour (which includes sampling details from a carpet retail outlet in the town), and KC's hopeless addiction to playing with ideas mean he'll never completely buy in to the mainstream. For as long as he can get away with sampling Tamagotchi toys and channelling his guitar heroics through instruments designed as Christmas presents for bright seven year olds Kid Carpet will keep 'em comin' like Ideas and Oh Dears.

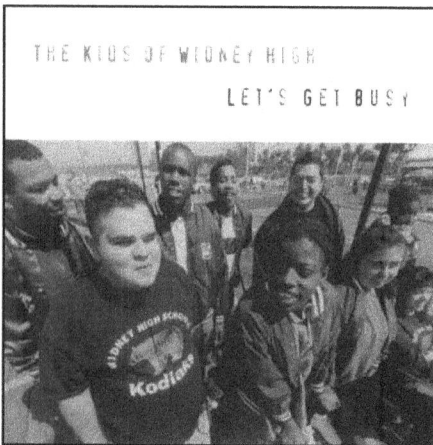

Kids of Widney High:
Let's Get Busy
(Ipecac, 1999)
What? Taking on and besting the challenge.

The music industry has a lengthy and frequently uncomfortable history of turning life's challenges into product with novelty value at best. A short surf of the internet, especially on sites devoted to the worst in album cover art, will show you evidence of album releases by the likes of The Handless Organist or The Braillettes…'nuff said. The Kids of Widney High are a noble exception to a freak show tradition. The concept here is to allow mentally and physically challenged kids to find expression through popular music and surround them with enough production power and musical skill to produce work that does justice to their dreams. The band – with changing personnel – has been in existence for over a quarter of a century, making their sporadic album releases more like yearbooks than an end in themselves. Indeed, the Widney High brand has evolved to the point of different groups (one of graduates, one of current students) now trading under the respected moniker. LA venues continue to host their gigs and their live work has included opening for other respected acts, like Melvins.

1999's Let's Get Busy is almost all original material. The exception is Otis Redding's "Respect" reworked in Widney High style. A fitting cover because sixties soul, with strong rock influence, is the start point for the distinctive Widney High musical style. The sound is big, different lead vocalists take turns and a big choral sound on the backing vocals blends the voices of the small group. Choruses are typically handled by the whole bunch. The school offers a song-writing class and the material here shows evidence of being worked up to present adolescent troubles "Facts About Life," street-swagger "Every Girl's my Girlfriend" and honest vulnerability "Help me to Find my Way Home."

The massive backing, drums, bass, guitar, keyboards, skilful horns, and well-placed guitar licks, wraps the kids in a hugely listenable sound. All making for tuneful listening even when the vocals miss the note. As a feel-good project of high-ambition Let's Get Busy is an absolute triumph. It breathes the identity and concerns of the Kids of

Widney High and tramples the usual platitudes about sincerity and honesty in music right into the ground. Few commercially released albums would dare be this honest and open. Many of the songs stand up to repeated listening, and treated in this way, reveal witty asides, smart performances and the good-vibe of the group. "Cowboy Brown" – for example – makes reference to a cat, only for one of the voices to come in with a "meow" timed to comic perfection.

Klaus Kinski: Lieder und Balladen (Deutsche Grammophon, 2003)
What? Brecht, interpreted by iconic actor on top form.

Originally recorded in the town hall, Vienna, on 9 April 1959, these recordings of Brecht's ballads and songs remained unissued during Kinski's lifetime because custodians of Brecht's estate were unhappy with Kinski's variations on the master's work. The entire recording is in German (so an affinity with that language would greatly enhance your understanding of the work and your general listening pleasure). For English speakers, however, there is still much to be gained from a performance in which Kinski lives inside the characters and situations and acts out Brecht's words whilst the guitar accompaniment acts more as incidental music than any guide to a melody. On the longer works – like "The Barbarian" – Kinski's intimate performance is so well recorded that the breaths and sighs of his character become part of the story, and we live the dramatic ups and downs with him. It is telling that a large auditorium, sold out, barely intrudes on a live performance that was clearly spell-binding to everyone witnessing the event. The voluminous acoustics add a sense of loneliness and natural echo in those moments when Kinski's vocals roar and rage. Brecht's words were often employed in presenting loner characters and dramatic situations in which life crushes the individual and despair prompts self-destructive, but understandable, acts. On record few interpreters have got so far inside this mentality as Kinski. The original German texts allow for long, drawn out consonants – ably delivered by Kinski – to further enhance the sense of brooding and circular thoughts in the characters. On "Ballad of the Woman and the Soldier" Kinski is so far inside the female reality (with furtive whispers and rapid delivery) as to carry the story as well as any other on the album. This is far from a reverent revue of great writing and it is easy to see why some purists would take exception to a noted actor turning one man's texts into a one-man-show. But, as a listening experience, even for those unable to follow the German words, Lieder und Balladen is an astonishing, draining and compelling journey in sound.

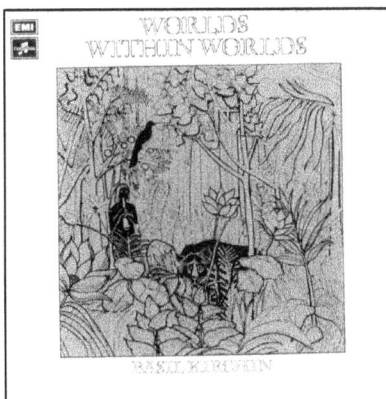

Basil Kirchin: Worlds Within Worlds (EMI/Columbia, 1971)
What? Ground-breaking early experimental recordings.

Kirchin (1927-2005) was so far ahead of the game that history has often ignored his accomplishments and credited the likes of Brian Eno with inventing ambient music. It might have been different had he avoided an accident when his possessions were dumped in Sydney harbour in the late fifties. The loss that day included recordings from his time at the Ramakrishna Temple in India and his work with The Kirchin Band. Having returned to the UK in 1961 he set about rebuilding an archive of alternative and experimental work and specialised in recording and treating sounds – including birdsong and the voices of autistic children. The first significant release in a career he would subsequently devote to avant-garde and experimental sound work was the poor-selling Worlds Within Worlds.

Comprising two side-long pieces – "Part 1: Integration (Non-racial)" and "Part II: The Human Element" - Worlds Within Worlds sounds at different moments like floating and occasionally intense free jazz, and at other times like the random samples of wildlife and ambient sounds Kirchin was undertaking on a regular basis. There are slowly developing themes. Similar sounds appear minutes away from each other, giving both individual sides, and also the whole album, some claim to working like a tone poem. Stylistically it resembles very little else around at the time. Though, Terry Riley's A Rainbow in Curved Air might be claimed as some distant relative if only because both albums are clearly intended to explore a complementary series of sounds, work within the standard length of a vinyl album and immerse the listener in an auditory adventure designed to challenge conventional notions of how music works. Apart from anything else, each appeals as much to the sub-conscious as the conscious mind. Like Riley, Kirchin works with an ensemble of musicians, in this case a jazz sextet, so the piece has the feel of work on the very fringes of modern jazz. But the sounds of animals and birds always give it its own distinctive identity. In recent years the UK repository of much strange and ground-breaking work – Trunk Records – has set about a substantial release programme of Kirchin's works.

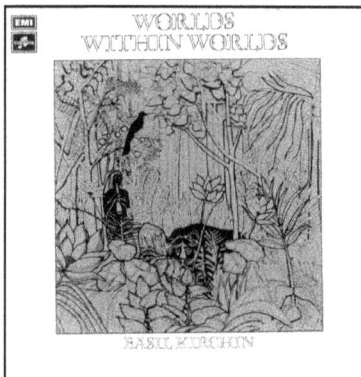

Basil Kirchin:
Primitive London
(Trunk Records, 2010)
What? Ground-breaking early non experimental recordings.

Kirchin recorded and released a few soundtracks during his life but this ten track sidle through sounds produced to accompany a documentary on the sleazy side of Britain's capital city didn't see a bespoke release until Trunk Records did the honours in 2010. Primitive London marks Kirchin's film score debut, comprises six tracks with the title "Primitive London" (#1-#6) and four more titled "The Freelance" (#1-#4). For those intent on easing their way into Kirchin's visionary and dense soundscapes Primitive London is both an accessible first point of call and a challenging companion. Kirchin is clearly trying to satisfy a film audience, his creative ideas are bursting, but remain secondary to the requirement for this sound to narrate the lives of the characters on screen. Primitive London frequently hurls atmospheric and abstract jazz at your ears, abruptly alters tempos and sound quality, and still manages passages of rapid intensity that feel like live improvisations in a club. Elsewhere a few deft touches as the sound slows begin to show the material that went on to influence ambient masters like Brian Eno. Kirchin had already mastered the dynamics of film sound. Sudden discordant whirls are genuinely frightening, the scrape and crash of a cymbal is suggestive of lurking danger on screen and recurrent motifs, insanely catchy from first hearing, appear and re-appear like characters in a crowded urban scene. A close listen betrays some cut-price tricks of the trade deployed with effective results, castanets recorded with heavy echo double as dripping water. The building blocks of Kirchin's most ambitious experiments are already here. The drones and other eastern influences are hinted at. There are also Kirchin's love of jazz horns, hand-twanged bass strings and his favoured moments of free-form abstraction erupting from the cacophony to comment eloquently and steer the listener's understanding. A measure of the assurance in this early example of Kirchin's composing for screen is the fact it received plaudits and positive responses, despite the fact that many making such comments have never seen the original movie.

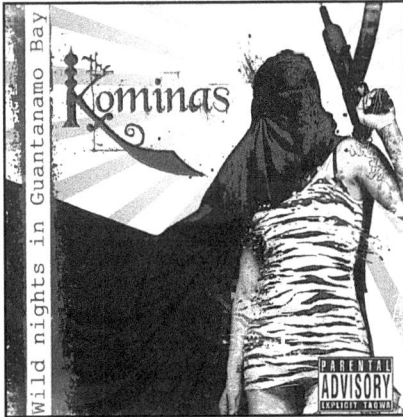

The Kominas:
Wild Nights in Guantanamo Bay
(Self released, 2008)
What? Like the best rebellion, this comes with intelligence and humour.

The Kominas present Pakistani-American Desi punk rock with intelligence, humour, attitude and some banging tunes. What sounds like an unlikely collision of elements is easily understood after you hear the opening cut: "Sharia Law in the U.S.A." This starts with street sounds from Pakistan and morphs without apology into "Anarchy in the UK." If that isn't mind numbing enough "I Want a Handjob" has another take on in your face culture clash and "Suicide Bomb the GAP" pushes the polemic into your thoughts and groin with a cracking funk groove, scratching, samples and a superb vocal. None of the excursions into musical styles, either mentioned above or featured elsewhere on the album, ever lose sight of the punk attitude. When The Kominas want guitar abrasion and guttural vocals, they can call on them. This is dangerous music, especially when cuts like "Rumi Was a Homo" risk fundamentalist wrath, even though they seek understanding and the odd wry smile. Whether "douchebag," as applied to a person, has a literal translation outside of English, isn't made clear on "Rudi Was a Homo" but the song is quirky enough to get its message over either way.

The Kominas are as accomplished as any satirists, with a love of music that extends to the core of their being. Their collision of cultures and concoction of styles is permanently asking a lot of listeners. But that, probably, is a good thing.

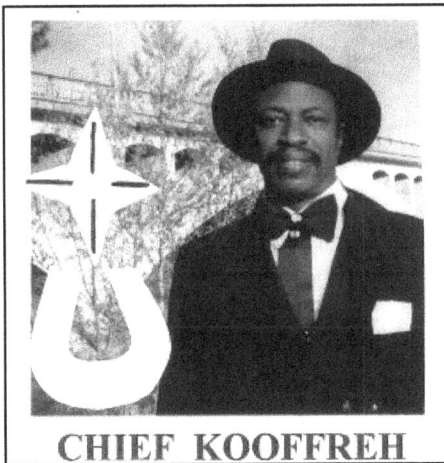

Chief Kooffreh:
Sweet Asian Girl
(Self released, 2008)
What? The kind of "star" for whom Spotify was invented.

Kooffreh exists well beyond satire and well beyond the norms of rap. His furious output of self-released product is easily explained when two strands of his peculiar genius are taken into account. Firstly, the man has a fondness bordering on obsession with variants on the basic drum track/repetitive phrase/minimal additions formula, and appears to be averse to overdubs on many cuts. Secondly, the stack of self-released albums currently available often rotate the same beats, and – frequently – the same tracks as other releases. There are few acts for whom a simple scan of an album tracklist would amount to the perfect introduction for the uninitiated, but Kooffreh wears his mighty heart on his sleeve. Sweet Asian Girl lines up: "Viagra Will Cancer Your Balls," " A Soldier's Christmas," "The Tragedy and Fall of Lindsay Lohan," "Broken Love Promises Shame On You," "The Tribute to Shakira, Gwen Stefanie, Jennifer Lopez," "Sweet Asian Girl," "America's Tribute to Bruce Springsteen (Boss Born in USA),"

"Women Power," "Do Not Marry That Bitch," "Miley Cyrus, Vanity Fair, Daddy Soft Porn," "Valentine's

Day Everyday for You," "Part Time Prostitutes Many (Your Neighbours)," "Mother's Day" and "Kiss the Pussy Cat." To take in the track list is to realise that Kooffreh's strongest concerns are a black and white morality and the tragic falls from the path of righteousness experienced by others (especially young and good looking female celebrities).

Missing from this album, but well worth investigating on YouTube, are the Chief's touching tribute to the late Princess Diana and his one song/two tributes covering Lady Gaga and Beyonce, which bigs up their humanitarian work and pours love on the goodly pair by way of repeating the chorus of "Twinkle Twinkle Little Star." The Beyonce/GaGa love fest also runs an impressive nine minutes and nine seconds and samples the sound of a barking dog when things threaten to drag. American based but possessed of a noticeable African accent, and with a fondness for a dress sense somewhere between preacher and gangster, Kooffreh is a robust one-off with a massive body of work. The Guardian's blog on "The 101 Strangest Records on Spotify" notes: "You have to prepare yourself for what you're about to hear, because these records feel more like outsider art than anything else." A fair point, if Kooffreh has relatives in the music industry then, surely, those people are the likes of Shooby Taylor, Wild Man Fischer, Wesley Willis and The Space Lady. Acts who couldn't have sold in if their lives depended on it.

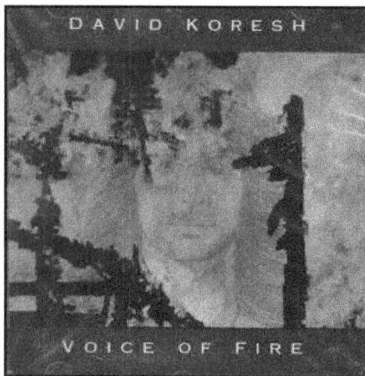

David Koresh:
Voice of Fire
(Junior's Motel, 1995)
What? Another low-fi cultish collection from a messianic figure.

Koresh's posthumous cult status is more positive than that of notorious killers and criminals, like Charles Manson. If you are unfamiliar with the demise of Koresh and his Branch Davidian sect in the burning remains of their compound in Waco, Texas, then the internet is still awash with footage, conspiracy theories and messages from those who see Koresh as sinned against rather than sinner. Koresh played decent guitar and wrote some catchy songs, singing them in a reedy but well-controlled voice. Some of his work – at demo quality – appears online, two songs and a sermon of around one hour in length are collected onto Voice of Fire. Musically, Koresh possesses a mainstream quality that eludes some of those – like Manson – with whom he is inevitably linked. His guitar mastery extends to a love of big-sounding chords, the ability to pick out individual strings on the instrument and bring agreeable harmonies to the guitar accompaniment. He has an affinity with AOR sounds of the late eighties/early nineties. The sound quality here – and on the other recordings available online – leaves something to be desired. But, on this evidence, anyone wandering into a bar in the early nineties wouldn't have been surprised to see someone of Koresh's appearance, ability and style, on stage. He clearly had the chops to write well-structured songs, and the lyrical touch to hold big ideas in simple lines, leaving the listener to read deeper meanings into the song's suggestions.

That – more or less – is where his conversational and sonorous delivery of the lengthy sermon sets off as well. Like any recorded sermon, it only works if the listener has some affinity with the good/evil underpinnings and follows the preacher's notions with regard to the revealed truth of the Lord. This isn't the ranting and paranoid finale of Jim Jones or the wild-eyed strangeness of Charles Manson's social commentary. Koresh sounds approachable and walks a pleasant and accessible line with regard to the honesty of his southern accent and the clear diction of his best thoughts. He is, at times, a hesitant speaker and generally at pains to make the more complex elements of his message clear to his audience. Voice of Fire is mainly cherished as an insight into the man behind a major news event. In that context, the sound quality is less important than the glimpse it gives into a man with a strong message, but – apparently – little malice and none of the ranting fury of the more infamous cult leaders who have been recorded and sold on album.

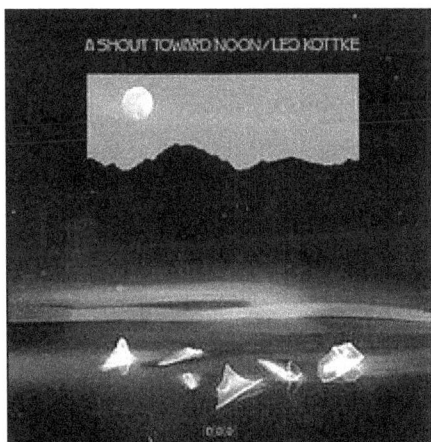

Leo Kottke:
A Shout Toward Noon
(Private Music, 1986)
What? The right album...for all the wrong reasons.

If you look at the ingredients that make this thoughtful and evocative recording they don't promise much. Kottke is an awesome guitarist, hailed by his contemporaries as one of the best finger-picking modern acoustic players of his generation. But in the early eighties the metal picks and aggressive style that had been the calling card of his well-received albums on Capitol and Chrysalis led to problems. Tendonitis in his hands obliged a rest, a rethink and training in a more classical style. Whilst the world wasn't exactly going mad for his works Kottke had become a popular live act with critical respect, tours outside his native US and steady record sales. But in three years he did little high profile work other than record soundtracks, sign to a label best known for new age and jazz recordings and practice his new style. His new work clearly made a stab for the – then – vaguely trendy new age crowd. Any of his regular fan base perusing the packaging for A Shout Toward Noon would probably have been disappointed to discover a synthesiser player credited alongside Kottke and a cellist.

But what might have looked like a virtuoso in reduced circumstances shamelessly leaping onto a passing bandwagon soon revealed itself to be a masterwork of real magic. A Shout…is entirely instrumental, kicking off with "Little Beaver" a typical fast-picking Kottke gem, it soon slows into soulful flowing melodies which hint at classical and new age but always retain Kottke's trademarks of expressive phrasing and clear tones. The other instruments wrap themselves around Kottke's guitar, ten of the twelve tunes are Kottke originals and the whole thing drips with understated beauty. At times it is very sparse, the lilting echo of a faint guitar figure in "Echoing Gilewitz" or the long slow unfolding of the melody of "The Ice Field" being cases in point. But its most fragile moments are also, often, its strongest statements. A return to live work obliged Kottke to bring back the faster tunes, dry-witted stories and vocal numbers that had always been the mainstay of his act, and these – too – are seldom less than superb. But this album, as a stand-alone surprise that repays repeated listening and haunts any room in which it plays, remains a very unique fixture in his impressive catalogue.

KPM All Stars:
Live at the Jazz Café
(Alan Hawkshaw, 2009)
What? TV themes played live and loud.

London's Meltdown musical festival has long prided itself on eclectic and bizarre events, some work, some are best left as scribbled ideas. But the gig recorded for posterity in this limited edition release counts as one of the triumphs of Meltdown's shamelessly permissive policy of programming. Jarvis Cocker curated the 2006 festival and at his behest the organisers collected a group of musicians and composers involved in the original library music recordings that formed the collections of music from which television themes and incidental sounds were often selected. Whilst "library" or "programme" music had long been a cult item for die-hard collectors, like Cocker, the notion of gathering the under-valued performers and devoting an entire evening to their greatest hits hadn't seriously forced itself on anyone before Cocker decided Meltdown merited the historic gig.

By 2006 their style and sound was a dead art, a generation of computer literate musicians and the free availability of their mp3 files had long since done away with session players on hourly rates grinding this stuff out to tight deadlines before the results were pressed onto LP records, left to lie in record libraries to be poured over by producers in search of exactly the right sound for their new programme. For this reason the triumphant gig is both a greatest hits show and a requiem for a generation and an art now lost to progress. What you get for your money are tracks you can already hum in your sleep, played live with passion in front of an audience ready to greet each nugget with the unconditional love crowds usually reserve for the moment when Metallica unleash the opening notes of "Enter Sandman" or Deep Purple let rip with that riff.

The themes from Grange Hill, Dave Allen at Large and Grandstand leap out from the pack, along with incidental masterpieces like the 30 second melody that accompanies the countdown on Countdown. So many short snippets and so much audience enthusiasm infuses this collection with the feeling that every listener to the album was actually there, an illusion only strengthened if you are old enough to count most of this music as the soundtrack to significant part of your life. If it makes a serious point beyond this Live at the Jazz Café probably proves to many that these tunes were as much a part of growing up as the rock and pop they heard on the radio and that those responsible for this music were every bit as creative as their more famous peers when it came to writing a killer melody or insistent hook line.

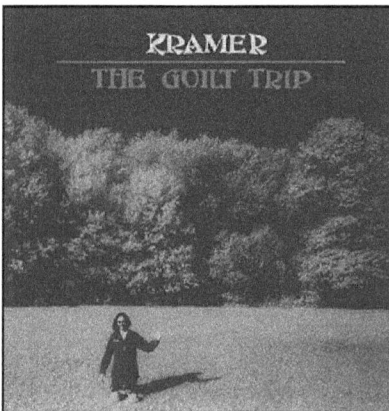

Kramer:
The Guilt Trip
Shimmy-Disc 1992
What? Most ambitious album release from terminally ambitious artist.

Mark Kramer (aka Kramer) has an alternative music CV to put most of his peers to shame. His involvement with record production, studio ownership and one-off projects in areas like live magic shows is testament to a restless spirit and insatiable urge to take his musical ideas and apply them wherever he might best ambush another audience. He has been a mainstay or member of New York Gong, Shockabilly, Bongwater and Dogbowl and his touring work has seen him involved with the Butthole Surfers, The Fugs and Half Japanese, amongst others. There have also been – at times - on-going collaborations with John Zorn and Debbie Harry. And then there's his Shimmy-Disc record label, production of Low, GWAR and Galaxie 500… You get the general idea.

The nearest he has come to channelling this Renaissance Man quality into one of his own releases is the two hour plus rock opera The Guilt Trip. Left to his own devices in his own Noise New Jersey studio, Kramer crafted a combination of noise and intricacies of narrative that works best when given complete attention from the listener. Kramer was born in 1958, making him old enough to have engaged with the early rock operas, and it is the concept albums of The Kinks, The Beatles and their ilk that inspire the lengthy vision here, whilst the sonics of Led Zeppelin and Kramer's generation of psychedelic guitar bands are referenced in the sound. For all its narrative arcs and offshoots The Guilt Trip offers the casual visitor an embarrassment of delights. Insistent rockers like the second disc's "God Will Send You" clip along with catchy lyrics and reverberating guitar solos and three tracks later "I Love You" plunges into a gorgeously tentative acoustic guitar intro before a performance and lyric worthy of paisley-period Donovan transports the journey into a patchouli soaked landscape of infinite possibilities.

There are lyrical revelations, stories and much dwelling on experience and the passing moment but the samples, layered guitars and endless playing with loops tell another story. A cynical view – which we wouldn't encourage for one second – might see The Guilt Trip as the best advert possible for Mark Kramer's production skills. The album is most certainly such an advert but – in all probability – it makes more sense as a love letter from Kramer to his muse. In other words, to music itself. Making sense of such an impressive but impenetrable piece will always be a subjective exercise. But if there are keys here they are in apparently throwaway pieces like "Hello Music" which start with an idea and some samples, morph into vibe and melody and celebrate the moment as they create it. Kramer is in love with catchy choruses, the sound of his own riffs and the power of this psych-rich tapestry to bring bliss to the most jaded sensibility. Like The Residents, he's incessantly stumbling on the next distraction and blending it into an on-going journey in sound. But Kramer's touchstones are guitar bands, that brief era in the late sixties when these sounds were – apparently – changing the world, and the belief that combinations of guitars, well-crafted vocal lines and lyrics still retain an unearthly power.

The Guilt Trip is well-named, if only because it is a colossal indulgence on the part of producer/performer Kramer. But it is an indulgence that pays off massively for those prepared to live with the album and let it take over an afternoon of their time.

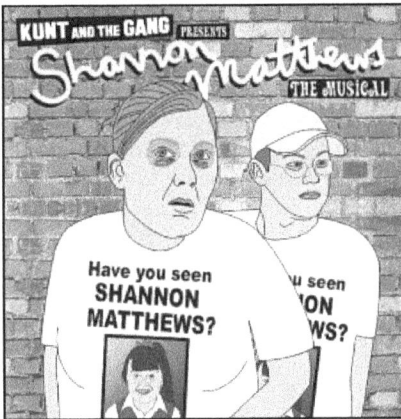

Kunt and the Gang:
Shannon Matthews – The Musical
(Club Tuppence, 2010)
What? Shameless Scumfest is Kunties' best.

First of all a warning. If you're easily offended there are 499 other entries in this book, most of which don't trawl the territory turned over in this musical masterwork. And if you're reading this outside the UK, you might want to go online and acquaint yourself with the details of the "kidnapping" of Shannon Matthews. Still reading? Right, if the work of the gloriously monikered Kuntsters has escaped your attention, a brief catch-up might help. South Essex's comedy finest have mined a fur-tile furrow of minge-gags, cuss-laden song titles and pure puerility that has rewarded them with two of the most memorably titled entries into the UK's top 75 – "Fucksticks" and "Use My Arsehole As A Cunt" – and sell-out shows in the kind of compact and bijou venues that host cabaret and comedy. This, pretty much, is where KATG belong. Musically, they wear their synth-infested Basildon roots as a badge of honour and crank out hook-laden pop ditties with a seemingly innate ability to find nuance and new invention on the age-old themes of toilet humour, human genitalia and the margins of acceptability. A signature song, if such a thing exists in their catalogue, may well be "Sexy Kids," which involves the ghost of (posthumously disgraced, child-abusing, media personality) Jimmy Savile visiting the Kuntsters in a dream to put his side of the story: "It was sexy kids, sexy kids, made Jimmy Savile do what he did." You get the general idea. Charlie Brooker is quoted on their website commenting on their style: "Life-affirmingly puerile stuff, set to one of the most infectious and upbeat melodies imaginable." The present authors agree wholeheartedly, though seldom play KATG CDs in the car when travelling with friends. Faced with the challenge of inflicting the Kuntsters on his radio audience Neil Nixon was pretty much limited to "Teach Your Kids to Smoke" (a radical rethinking of social policy which advocates tackling overcrowding by shortening life expectancy via a fairly obvious method). This, incidentally, can be found on the gloriously titled Hurry up and Suck me off Before I get Famous.

But, if this lot have a signature album out there (i.e. an ambitious piece of creative work that distils and contains the very best of their capabilities) it is this scum-fest of songs and spoken words. Surely, some of it is obvious. Shannon Matthews the Musical does pretty much what it says on the front cover. Spread over 29 tracks, Shannon… presents itself like a stage musical, with a sung overture of "Shannon, Shannon" opening the proceedings and a selection of characters turning up, telling their stories and singing their way into your memory, if not your heart. The narrative stays close to the real case (and for those of you unfamiliar with the whole caper, this involved a fairly feckless attempt to fake the kidnapping of a nine-year-old Yorkshire lass, the aim of which was to get attention and money). But, the Kuntsters can't resist the odd stumble sideways when an obvious gag presents itself. Witness the appearance of a copper whose second name is World, PC World (geddit?) It's tasteless, but probably truer to life than some of the salubrious headlines that attended the real events and – at heart – it has some sympathy for Britain's least sympathetic family. Karen Matthews (cack-handed criminal mastermind) and Craig Meehan (her partner packing a few dodgy pictures on his PC) were pilloried by the press, the Kuntsters see them as terminally damaged and curiously suited to each other.

Given that stage performances of the whole piece were unlikely to run for years in London's west end it's also fair to say that this "musical" was designed, first and foremost, to make sense on CD. So the narrative of Inspector Radgit is central to unfolding the story and allowing in a series of side-swipe gags (starting with the suggestion that dead and disgraced Coronation Street character Len Fairclough might be "noncing from beyond the grave"). From which point on songs, scenes and sick-sick jokes tumble over each other for 70 minutes, all reliant on relentless invention around the theme of a family so feckless they stole a criminal idea from an episode of Shameless*. If your taste, is for the tasteless, this one is definitely worth the trouble of tracking down.

*Bearing in mind that it's accepted fact that the kidnapping of Shannon Matthews owed something to a faked kidnap in an episode of the bleak comedy/drama Shameless, it's also worth noting that as Shameless played out its final episodes in 2013 one of the very last storylines – sort of – provided a response to this real life event. Another cack-handed attempt to fake a kidnap allowed for a moment in which the character of Shane Maguire openly discussed the pointlessness and low success chances of faking a kidnap.

Catherine Lambert:
Beltane: A Musical Fantasy
(ATMA, 1999)
What? Ethereal, pseudo-classical epic based on early Bolan.

During an edition of The Record Producers on BBC Radio One Tony Visconti – who twiddled the knobs that turned Bolan and Bowie into household names - recounted a conversation he'd once had. Questioned by an ultra-serious type Visconti had found himself defending Marc Bolan. His companion had pointed out you could play pretty much everything in the T.Rex catalogue on around eight guitar chords.

Visconti's reply was something along the lines of: "Yes, but Marc Bolan has sold nearly 40 million records, how many more guitar chords does he need?"

The point being that Bolan and his various incarnations of Tyrannosaurus Rex and T.Rex was about ideas, communication and opening up the visions inside his head. On one side Bolan's influence runs and runs. Nirvana's Nevermind era sound and Slash's appropriation of his sound, one of his songs on Guns 'n Roses Spaghetti Incident and Bolan's image from the front of The Slider, leave Bolan's rock credibility intact. His early pixiefied hippie-folk has fared less well. But this curio does take Bolan's vision into a world where Slash wouldn't feel at home.

Employing an ensemble mainly comprising cello, recorder, harpsichord, organ, and classical guitar, and taking in ethereal voices, Caroline Lambert's "Musical Fantasy" welds selections from the first four Tyrannosaurus Rex albums into a unified work, with a baroque slant. Bolan never finished his projected thematic work The Children of Rarn but Beltane also revisits the fragments he did record and uses them to bookend the whole piece. It reads as one of the most bizarre classical works imaginable but, once heard, shimmers with a strange beauty and delicate sense of magic Bolan himself may well have admired.

The female lead vocal chimes well with the classic Victorian painting of a fairy on the cover and takes the sound of the work well away from Bolan's bleating and frequently hard to decipher vocals on the original cuts. The simplicity of his musical structures may have brought critics, including the one arguing with Tony Visconti, down on Bolan but it is arguably the making of Beltane. The whole point of a musical fantasy is to explore and embellish and it makes sense, therefore, to start with something more akin to a sketch or blueprint than a complicated work. Catherine Lambert's fills, meditations and excursions from Bolan's original melodies bring enough colour and originality to Beltane to give it an identity of its own.

Barbara Lander:
Music for Dancing and Mime
(Discourses, 1968)
What? Tunbridge Wells ballet matron, so straight she's – like – "out there"

A few labels – notably the UK's Trunk Records – have made it their business to track down and revive the sounds that once saw action in school classrooms as the inspiration for drama and dance classes. Dance mats and online directions for sessions weren't even conceived of in the sixties and seventies, indeed most of this work pre-dates VHS tapes. Along with major players, like the BBC, a handful of entrepreneurial, eccentric and downright strange chancers also strayed into this territory with their own visionary works. The word "visionary" used in this context should come with a health warning. These artists clearly had visions, though how clearly they communicated them isn't always clear.

This late sixties double album was the brainchild of dancer, teacher and musician Barbara Lander. In comparison to some of the eccentric work in the same genre it packs a very clear idea of what it aims to achieve. Spread over the four sides Barbara gives direction, generally by way of a short descriptive command such as: "Plant growing from a seed to maturity, then withering or drooping." At this point the classical tones of a precisely played piano intrude with original music. The point is clearly for impressionable youngsters to respond to the commands with improvised dance or mime as they become a plant, a tree, the wind…

Barbara's cut-glass English tones (she was based in Tunbridge Wells) and the piano segments which frequently hint at popular classical greats like Chopin and Debussy set up a collision between the essentially free-form nature of the responses and the strict nature of the instructions. Used at the time for well-behaved young ladies, the album was doubtless the soundtrack to well-executed pirouettes and flowing arm movements. Heard in the internet age it is a curio of colossal proportions. At once a throwback to an age few can now imagine, and also so shamelessly straight it is almost satirical. The people behind this book would never want to openly encourage illegal behaviour but, an adult and very alternative change from a game of Twister might involve an evening with this album, and some illicit substances!

Fred Lane & Ron Pate's Debonaires
From the One That Cut You
(Say Day Brew, 1983/ Shimmydisc, 1989)
What? Situationist art disguised as song craft.

Reverend Fred Lane is more commonly encountered these days trading as visual artist T.R. (Tim) Reed. A native of Tuscaloosa, Alabama he launched a brace of albums that have continued to stop conversations ever since. Of the two it is From the One That Cut You that – probably – shades the attention as the more singular and successful effort at crafting a musical approach based on standard American popular forms and free-form Dadaist lyrics. Lane sounds nothing like I, Brute Force but his appeal is similar in its presentation of two opposing strands that collide and reassemble themselves into a whole unlike anything else in popular music. Lane's development of a stage and front cover persona - extreme long-sight glasses that blew up his eyes, trimmed and oiled goatee, and randomly slapped sticking plasters over his face and head – added to the effect. On stage he sported a black Tuxedo and boxer shorts. The detail could easily get lost to his audience. Ron Pate's fictitious name is a nod to a radical concept – Pataphysics – developed by playwright Alfred Jarry. Musically, however, the big band backing and Lane's borderline insanity/stream of consciousness wordplay centre the album and allow for excursions into gleefully moronic country and other offshoots of great American sounds. The eight titles alone are a feast of furtive fun and creative possibility, up there with the top titular talents of Rancid Hell Spawn and their ilk: "Fun In The Fundus," "Danger Is My Beer," "I Talk To My Haircut," "From The One That Cut You," "Rubber Room," "Mystic Tune," "Oatmeal," and "Meat Clamp Conduit."

The title track is a down-home maudlin country song with sublime steel guitar in which Fred – almost – holds it together as he re-states his love for the woman he left "mad and spurting." The anger management issues and sense of self-loathing constantly threaten to overwhelm the song. "I Talk to my Haircut" is a punchy big-band romp-a-long – not a million miles from Richard Cheese – in which Lane's irrational love of his looks is celebrated but the surreal wordplay has the whole sanity issue under question from the start. The notion of a standout track in such singular company is misplaced but "Rubber Room," a mini-loungecore/exotica epic at almost seven minutes exploring borderline psychosis in the context of a boring life, may just be the one that deserves the accolade. Lane's jokes are – fittingly – razor sharp, although not always in the best taste. Ron Pate and his crew have the musical chops to back them. Lane has long since disappeared into a respected career as a visual artist. This most image strewn set of songs is likely to serve for all time as his greatest musical achievement.

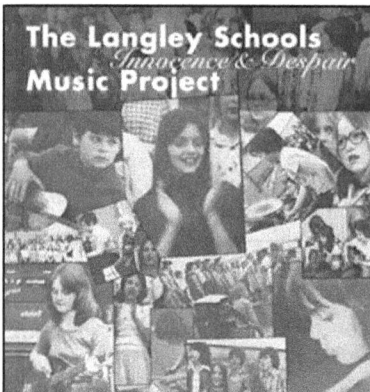

The Langley Park Schools Music Project:
The Langley Park Schools Music Project
(Bar/None Records, 2001)
What? Music lessons were never this way when I was at school!

An innovative and intoxicating music project undertaken in two Canadian schools (collectively known as the Langley Park Schools) between 1976 and 1977. The 21 tracks on this CD (compiled from two original vinyl albums released at the time) feature precociously young performers, recorded in school gyms and let loose on the classics of pop and rock up to the mid-seventies. It is, pretty much, what you'd imagine with young voices tackling the most meaningful pop fodder from the likes of the Beach Boys ("Good Vibrations" "God Only Knows" and "I Get Around" and others are here) along with the very biggest acts of the era in which the albums were cut. Fleetwood Mac's "Rhiannon" is covered along with "Venus and Mars/Rock Show" and "Band on the Run" from Wings (the Wings Over America tour was news during the period). Music teacher and project-supremo Hans Fenger succinctly explains the charm of the work: "I knew virtually nothing about conventional music education, and didn't know how to teach singing. Above all, I knew nothing of what children's music was supposed to be. But the kids had a grasp of what they liked: emotion, drama, and making music as a group. Whether the results were good, bad, in tune or out was no big deal -- they had élan. This was not the way music was traditionally taught. But then I never liked conventional 'children's music,'" which is where this collection scores with outsider music lovers to this day. It's never better than when the mythology and contemplative philosophy of The Eagles' "Desperado" is reimagined with a solo lead vocal from a youngster that fails on the most demanding notes, struggles to pronounce let alone understand the most complicated words, and still comes over sounding like a plaintive and emotional statement of great importance. This collection also shines a light on the music of its era because, at a time when rock and pop was falling hopelessly in love with the growing studio trickery, it was an act of genius to strip back songs which had relied on lush production, to expose their basic core. Richard Carpenter and David Bowie have both expressed praise and wonderment at the achievements of this project in covering their hits. You could damn this collection with words like "charming" and diss it for the predictably one-dimensional and echoing production and the over-reliance on young voices and acoustic piano to carry these classic songs, but that is to miss the magic by a mile. The Langley Parks Schools Music Project works because it is about emotion and drama. There are 18 tracks to prove the claims of the "innocence and despair" in the title of the compilation, collectively they suggest that Hans Fenger had a brilliant idea. A later British release added two more songs.

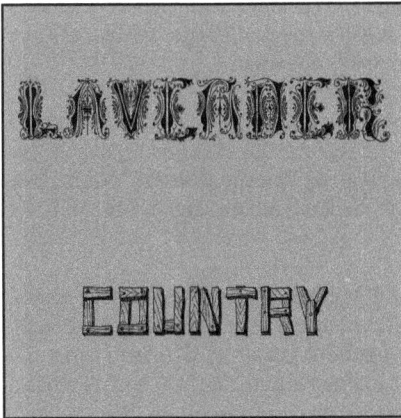

Lavender Country:
Lavender Country
(Paradise of Batchelors, 2014/Private Release, 1973)
What? Come out singin'!

The title of the album pretty much says all you need to know. Released to virtually no fanfare in 1973, Lavender Country is now widely recognised as the first openly gay long-playing country music release. Like Chinga Chavin's Country Porn, released around the same time, Lavender Country is a head on collision between the innately conservative structures and sounds of country music and the ultra-liberal message contained within its lyrics. Patrick Haggerty, who helmed the whole project, assembled a bunch of like-minded musicians, including guitarist Robert Hammerstrom (who was straight) and one lesbian member, fiddler Eve Morris, who throws in some of the more memorable musical licks. The original 1000 vinyl copies were funded and released by Gay Community Social Services of Seattle, and the recording betrays its limited budget. Musically it is straight (no pun intended) country, visiting the usual stations, fast ones, slower ones, maudlin ones, thoughtful ones etc. Lavender Country has a predictable sound but that makes the lyrics all the more of a focus and that is where it scores mightily.

The opening "Come out Singin'" is pretty much what you'd expect, as is "Back in the Closet Again" but several of the songs have a well-studied mash up of confrontational attitude and creative mischief. None more so than the gloriously titled "Cryin' These Cocksucking Tears." The title alone makes it the stand out cut for anyone looking to sample Lavender Country, but, for all its in your face sexual reality it's a skilfully woven meditation on some stark realities. Haggerty said in an interview: "[it's] not even a song that's about sex…It's about the rigid sex roles that men were educated and trained to assume and how that role was oppressive to women and to us, and how it needed to go. It's a pretty overtly political song." Which, ultimately, is where Lavender Country carves its unique niche. We get conventional country tunes, typical stories of struggle and heartbreak and an intention, a mile wide, to get the message across. Country music was always good at communicating the story of the little guy with the big dilemma. It's just that – until 1973 – nobody had attempted to theme those stories around gay rights and create an entire album's worth of such nuggets. Original vinyl copies are ultra-rare, but the 2014 CD reissue is widely available.

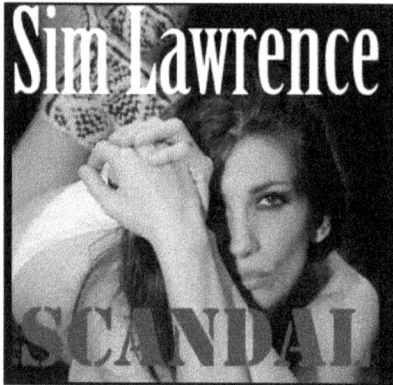

Sim Lawrence:
Scandal
(Download from simlawrence.com, 2009)
What? Hell hath no fury…

Breakup albums have often become a critical high-point of a noted career. Especially in the case of male performers noted for elusive lyrics. The uncompromising emotional honesty of a break up has shown the performer in a strangely naked (metaphorically at least) light. But with all due respect to classic works like John Martyn's Grace and Danger, Phil Collins Face Value, Bob Dylan's Blood on the Tracks (which may according to his autobiography be based on short stories by Chekhov), Peter Hamill's Over or Bon Iver's For Emma; Forever Ago these guys didn't get close to first-timer Sim Lawrence. In fact the only man close is probably Marvin Gaye with Here My Dear an album chronicling his break up, the proceeds from which were, legally speaking, part of his divorce settlement. Maybe, when it comes to walking the post break up walk, it takes a woman.

Maybe it takes one like Sim Lawrence. In 2009 40 year old Sim faced the end of her marriage to surgeon Hans Desmarowitz. The tabloids made much of the messy end, running reports that Hans had 'stalked' his secretary (a former model), whilst Sim was quoted as slating her love rival as: "a complete flirt." Left alone with their two children Sim didn't do the dutiful dignified silence. She made an album, and promoted it via national press stories.

Scandal comprises ten slices of adult dance-pop, varying the styles and delivering a hefty emotional punch. Musically, the album's low key origins are betrayed by some limitations in the sound, but it's no slouch. Think early 21st century Kylie melodies, the lived-in but essentially youthful vocals of Gloria Estefan and the odd rock/shouty Carol (T'Pau) Decker moment when the pain really starts to bite, and you have the basic sound. "Sorry" stumbles into a bluesy melody, "Come Closer" is a sparky piece of disco-pop that wouldn't disgrace an album by the great Minogue herself etc. etc.

The real interest came with two elements of the whole caper. Lyrically, Scandal told it the way Sim saw it. "The whole world is looking at you," she sings on the title track, showing – maybe - a solid grasp of a tactical master-plan including album and tabloid stories. Madonna and Lady Gaga do master-plans linking music and life events, but the arrival of a spurned Truro housewife in their company was news in 2009. And when Sim lets rip, she really lets rip. A trio of tracks include the word "explicit" in brackets, warning of lyrical firecrackers like: "Everyone thinks you're such a nice fella…you're a devil to me…a fucking bottom-dweller." ("The Secretary"). Go Sim!!

And the lyrics weren't the worst kiss-off. The track touted as a single – "Shake Me" – offered an added incentive for buyers. Every download came with the chance to be part of a truly unique raffle, the prize, illustrated in tempting detail on one page of simlawrence.com, being the former marital home; a sumptuous and well-appointed four bedroom property overlooking Truro. In the end New Zealander Chris Dawson had to be content with a cash alternative. Sales of "Shake Me" failed to reach the required minimum to put the house into play as a prize. The real winner though, has to be Sim. For style, spunkiness and maintaining a sense of self-worth fit to inspire any woman scorned.

Timothy Leary:
You Can Be Anyone This Time Around
(Rykodisc, 1992/ Get Back, 2004)
What? Turn on, tune in, try and make sense of this lot!

'The name of the game is to feel good…and the function of government should be to put itself out of business.' (From 'Live and Let Live').

Leary followed a standard academic career, gaining a prestigious teaching post at Harvard University until he was sacked in 1963. The wish of his bosses to rid themselves of the man was probably linked to his increasingly outspoken rants in favour of taking LSD. From this point Leary followed a stunningly shambolic career. Part-shaman, part professor without a post, part troublemaker and scourge of US law enforcement. Leary was the man who coined the phrase 'Turn on, tune in and drop out,' a mantra perfect for the hippie generation. As he hung out with the bands, rapped to the crowds and generally tried to put into words what the whole chaotic and blissful explosion was about, it seemed natural that Leary should release an album. The small sales and rapid deletion of his 1970 effort only served to give the release a cult appeal as time passed, and CD reissues have kept it available long after the man's ashes were blasted into space to descend as twinkling testaments to his trend-setting heyday.

Clocking in at a little over half an hour You Can Be Anyone…is more a curiosity than a classic. But, there are random ideas and shocks aplenty for those willing to shut out distractions and don the headphones. Years ahead of samples Leary got in there with an eclectic mix of snatched sounds on the title track. Sampling The Beatles, beat poet Alan Ginsberg and the sounds of birds Leary raps and rambles in a barely believable rant, suggesting you can be anything you want in a new incarnation. Since the possibilities include everything from athletic success to having sex with the universe whilst sporting a ten foot erection, we're not exactly in the realms of standard motivational speaking at this point. And, s'cuse the pedantry but…a ten foot phallus may be humungous by human standards but that's a little – ahem – limited when directed at the immeasurable cosmos, surely.

Another strange element is the jam session on the opening track. Snatches of Leary wisdom, mainly glib press-conference patter, are looped into a lengthy track whilst a chugging rock backing is provided by a super-group featuring Stephen Stills on lead guitar and Jimi Hendrix on bass. The trio of tracks closes with 'What Do You Turn On When You Turn On?' Another rambling bliss-trip with jazzy percussion and piano in the background. It packs all the pristine focus of mid-period Yes lyrics, or any speech of more than two minutes by David Beckham. There are probably drug casualties still staggering around claiming this album as a manifesto for a better world, many others regard it as a strange and often silly concoction, but love it for those very reasons.

D J Lebowitz:
Beware of the Piano
(Fowl, 1988)
What? Punky pianothon.

An album often discussed in strange music circles but seldom heard. The legend and reality of this record differ, but it remains a seriously strange recording. Lebowitz' repertoire includes 2000 numbers, many of them hardcore punk classics. Stuff loved by nihilists and noise-addicts. He has peddled his barroom piano versions of these tunes, amply supplemented by many of his own compositions in the same style, since the mid-eighties. His debut long-playing release collected the best of the early-days version of his set and the use of his ivory-rattling take on The Dead Kennedys' 'Holiday in Cambodia' in a UK compilation – Beautiful Happiness - mistakenly led many to believe his whole oeuvre relied on reworking punk classics, not so. Granted, this album also contains a glorious take of The Ramones' "Judy is a Punk" but elsewhere compositions like "Because of my Hemorroids" are Lebowitz originals. As an act there is an inescapably freakish quality to Lebowitz' work, something made all the stronger because of his love of instrumentals and songs built around trite song titles and references to taboo items, like Haemorrhoids. But the compelling qualities start with Lebowitz' ear for a torrent of a tune and continue into his phenomenal skill on the keys. The Dead Kennedys and Ramones covers here are both prime examples of the form. "Holiday in Cambodia" storms along with DJ running his hand up the keyboard to pile crescendo on crescendo and pumping a mean left-hand into the action to bring out the thumping rhythms of the original. At such moments DJ's approach to his craft turns standard piano playing on its head. He reduces the instrument to a noise machine, more akin to a guitar feeding back, before snatching seconds of sublime melody out of the ensuing chaos. Predictably the major concert halls have yet to call and his performances continue mainly in the bars of his native USA. The CD reissue of this legendary collection – often mooted – has yet to appear.

Christopher Lee:
Charlemagne: the Omens of Death
(Charlemagne Productions, 2013)
What? Metal juggernaut, recorded on lead vocalist's 91st birthday.

Lee has been a fairly prolific lead vocalist, in his own style, but his late-life sprint for the deeper and darker end of metal still took many by surprise. Charlemagne: By the Sword and the Cross (2010), opened this particular sub-account in an eclectic career. Metal, for sure, but occasionally restrained and symphonic. Omens of Death, by contrast, is a roaring monster much of it, apparently, conceived because the nonagenarian actor had loved previous excursions into such territory, like his narration on a Manowar record. His summary of the affair as "rather exciting" might not have chimed with the slang of the usual Kerrang crowd, but the album is a beast of a set with Lee taking the role of the main character and also his ghost. Lee's lead vocals showcase a moderate vocal range with impressive control and timing, he talks, sings and intones his way through the major vocal parts as the rocking riffs combine old school metal chops with punishing swathes of ringing guitar. Ritchie Faulkner, sometime Judas Priest axeman, concocts the riffs and late period Priest are a useful comparison for the results. Hedras Ramos, who also contributes guitar, takes the chops into Iron Maiden territory at times, but that works too.

Omens of Death charts a narrative arc covering the final days of the great conqueror of Europe, slowing and meditating when it needs to and revving up at full throttle when blood and battles overtake the story. "Massacre of the Saxons" which appears midway through the album, is a particular highlight. When darkness and death overtake the great one towards the end "The Devil's Advocate" and "Judgement Day" bring in a reverent production and suitably dour twists to the riffage and rhythm track. By this point the listener is well over the novelty of having a classic actor fronting a mighty metal sound. Omens of Death is old school in its concept album construction and packs an early nineties vibe in the tonnage of death on show. It also offers a 21st century production of equally epic proportions to that enjoyed by those old school bands, like Judas Priest, with an ear on newer sounds.

It may look like a curiosity described on a page. But Omens of Death sounds strong, compelling and, in its own way, glorious.

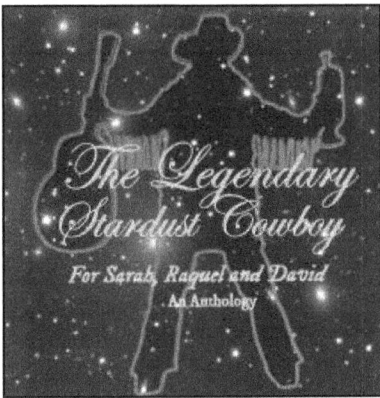

The Legendary Stardust Cowboy:
For Sarah, Raquel and David: An Anthology
(Cherry Red 2013)
What? A musical force of nature, captured and compiled.

The great haiku poet Basho was known to advise his students to: "learn all the rules, and forget them." An adage that roughly translates as be true to your muse, even if that truth takes you away from the way others plan and do things. The authors of this book have made every effort to celebrate albums, as in original albums, recorded and released at a set time. Sometimes, to do so is to do a great injustice to a matchless talent. And, in the case of true outsiders – Wild Man Fischer's Fischer King and the present entry – we'll observe these rules, and forget them.

The Legendary Stardust Cowboy has carved out a decades long career of musical outsiderdom, generally existing somewhere in the realms of rocka/psychobilly but capable of flashes of everything from standard balladry to avant-garde noise assault. All of the above comes with a central core of confidence suggestive of the fact that the Ledge's most extreme moments are the result of highly intelligent conception and an approach to music that revels in the disposability of the popular form. The Ledge has the capacity to use this disposability to drag the whole event somewhere into Dadaist notions of art. You still reading? Then, we can't recommend this career spanning twofer collection highly enough.

The one, and only, significant problem here is the firing of the main shot, "Paralysed," in its correct chronological order, right at the start. "Paralysed" is prime rockabilly/ novelty insanity of the highest order, with a bus loony on acid screaming vocal, shambolic drumming and off kilter guitar playing that observe the perfect rhythmic approach simply because they seem to be inventing their own timing from moment to moment. 41 tracks follow this classic, and fail to match it, but the two CDs amount to a differently abled musical manifesto that asks serious questions about the pomposity of rock's most portentous moments, (add a touch of real insanity to "Riders on the Storm" and the pain of being "thrown" into this world, along with possible vacuity of Jim Morrison's beat poetry is suddenly seen from a new angle). Fittingly the two CDs come dressed as 45rpm singles and, in the spirit of learning the rules and forgetting them, we would humbly suggest this collection is best enjoyed a few tracks at a time. The bulk of The Ledge's best material works on the borderlands of novelty/avant-garde. The first CD comes rich in his best rockabilly and related cuts. "I Took a Trip on a Gemini Spacecraft" (covered by Bowie on the Heathen album!) is acid rockabilly of a truly individual hue and "Standing in a Trashcan (Thinking of You)" would be one of the scariest love songs ever, if it wasn't almost as funny as "Paralysed."

Intellectually The Ledge makes sterling efforts to dwell and express himself in the true language of Hicksville, though when he provides a perfect simultaneously mocking and celebratory cover of "Ghost Riders" or a lyric at once as accessible and elliptical as "Radar" he easily stumbles into the same realms as Alice Cooper. The Ledge doesn't make up the character of The Legendary Stardust Cowboy, he becomes the beast. For Sarah, Raquel and David should be a companion rather than a one-off listen, because The Ledge is a multi-faceted act, much greater than the sum of the 42 cuts on offer here, and much more diverse than you might realise if you limit yourself to an amused snort at his nutcase vocals or a blast of toy trumpet. The dedicatees of the album Raquel (Welch), Sarah (Ferguson) and David (Bowie), could hardly be a more eclectic crew. Bowie's love of The Ledge extends – by Bowie's own admission – to a reverent nicking of the "Stardust" name for his own celebrated (Ziggy) creation. And, that, pretty much gives the uninitiated an entry point into this differently abled, under-appreciated genius of the outsider realm. The two CDs here do something to make the case that The Ledge is a Hicksville Bowie intent on standing his ground and pandering only to the audience that takes the trouble to find him. We may be biased but...that journey is worth the effort.

Tom Lehrer: In Concert (Decca, 1994)
What? Stupendous, seminal, satirist at the height of his powers.

Lehrer's satirical songs and sporadic live appearances have been celebrated by a die-hard band of the devoted for decades. Don't be fooled by the release date of the album, this is a UK compilation chock-full of recordings from his heyday in the 1950s and 1960s. Lehrer (b. 1928) ranks amongst the best mathematicians of his generation and a glance at his presence online betrays a schizophrenic existence in which cutting-edge Mathematics in America's finest universities went hand in hand for a couple of decades with a night-club act/ television career based on solo performances of piano-accompanied satirical gems, revealing a deeply-dark sense of humour and razor-sharp incisiveness directed at political subjects. Put crudely, a particular tradition that now boasts Randy Newman and Tim Minchin would look very different if Lehrer hadn't left his ivory tower for nightclub gigs and self-released albums in the early days. In Concert culls a generous and highly representative selection of the best works, which Lehrer typically recorded live. It's very US-centric in its observations on life in academia, Mexico's role as a haven for fugitives etc. But, there isn't that much lost to translation and Lehrer's gag-fest comes so fast and furiously that this is that rare gem amongst comedy albums, a whole disc that bears repeated listening. Lehrer's real skills involve taking highbrow humour (like "Oedipus Rex" concerning incest) and presenting it so cleverly and swiftly that the laughs precede the stomach-churning thoughts, and we're all in on the gag.

Lehrer was geek-chic before the concept existed, offering a clear diction that leaves his recordings well outside the rock/singer-songwriter genre. His style, singing and playing, owes more to stage musicals and the kind of live revue comedy shows that have all but disappeared in the internet age. But, was he ever funny? Some of these songs have survived half a century for no other reason than they are amongst the best musical comedy produced anywhere on earth at the time, and the gags still stand up today. Lehrer's reticence about live performing and producing new material makes Kate Bush look like Lindsey Lohan by contrast, and his career has – as a result – become, quite literally, the stuff of legend. It is widely believed, but wholly untrue, that he packed in writing and performing when the award of the Nobel Peace Prize to (alleged war criminal) Henry Kissenger convinced him that his satire couldn't top real life.

In reality, he has limited his use of the abundant talent on show here because Mathematics has been his real calling. But the work he has put out there remains available, and like very little else you'll ever hear.

Leningrad Cowboys: We Cum From Brooklyn (Plutonium, 1992)
What? Rockapolkabilly prog, or something close.

A joke with very long legs and a comedy/cult curio to rank with the very best: (Dread Zeppelin, Spinal Tap etc.) Leningrad Cowboys' origins in Finland (where their original style of Russian polka and rockabilly made sense as a surreal comment on the decline of the Soviet empire), and their subsequent cult status on the back of the Leningrad Cowboys Go America (1989) movie, eventually set the scene for the working band that cut this album, amongst their fairly impressive output. Cum From Brooklyn is as good an introduction as any to the band because its combination of live and studio cuts, originals and covers, and studied professionalism up against wilfully shambolic outings is an insight to most of what they do wonderfully. "Sauna" is skilfully played blistering, break-neck punk with a horn section, feedback barely held in check and all done before an adoring audience with no overdubs. It fades into the wave of balalaikas opening "Katjusha," with a polka beat and comedy vocal in a manner only Leningrad Cowboys could present as normal. Once those cuts are finished we're still not halfway through. Having kept a straight face in covering "Those Were the Days" as the opening cut, the band end the festivities with the double sixties whammy of "These Boots" and "Back in the USSR." Their default settings involve polka, punk, rockabilly (they cover the classic "The Way I Walk") and traditional Russian and Scandinavian sounds. All of the above is generally played by a band numbering around ten individuals, all of whom manage to maintain focus despite the mayhem of mixed styles. When it works, which is most of the time on Cum From Brooklyn, this is music that makes its own rules. It's great because it is hilarious and hilarious because it is great.

Like other freaksome collisions (Dread Zeppelin, Hayseed Dixie) Leningrad Cowboys long ago escaped the original joke and channelled the resulting self-belief into music of incessant invention. The worst moments here, like "Monkey Hat," are those in which the band can manage an entire half minute sounding like they care about selling massive amounts of records and standing shoulder to shoulder with radio friendly acts. Usually some catchy lick on an unfamiliar instrument or an agreeably insane vocal tick will rescue the situation. When it doesn't, the next track usually obliges by heading off unstoppably into a musical mash of Leningrad Cowboys' own making. The band don't so much progress as stop, examine, explore and move on, so any album credited to Leningrad Cowboys will deliver some musical surprises. Cum From Brooklyn is the starter pack. For the fearless there is always Zombies Paradise with a fair smattering of speed metal and industrial music, "Manic Monday" is amongst the familiar items beaten to pulp on that one.

John Lennon and Yoko Ono: Unfinished Music No.1: Two Virgins (Apple,1968)

What? "What we're saying is make your own music. This is Unfinished Music." John Lennon

One of the most controversial releases of its day and a recording all the more significant for marking one of the most prominent sprints from mainstream into avant-garde of any high profile musician, ever. Two Virgins turns conventional musical practice (certainly by the standards of The Beatles and 1968) on its head, elevating pre-prepared tape loops to the main element of continuity, and using standard musical instruments as sporadic accompaniment, stopping them abruptly to move on to other instruments. Lennon had a stock of pre-prepared loops and was experimenting with musique concrete before inviting Yoko Ono over for the session that brought Two Virgins into existence. Some of Lennon's experiments made it to "Revolution 9" on the White Album but Two Virgins marks the point at which he turned the "Revolution 9" idea into an end in itself, and used his more usual approach to embellish his new direction. The music has a provisional and rambling quality, frequently veering off into conversation; though this conversation is not mixed high enough to provide a strong focus away from the music. In 1968 Yoko's vocal experiments were new to the point of proving completely unfamiliar to The Beatles' audience. But, they work in the context of a work that remains experimental throughout. Lennon's tapes are effective and his use of echo, delay and repetitive musical sounds via the tape loops anticipates the work of samplers and all manner of avant-garde musicians to follow.

Two Virgins is the loosest and least focussed of the three Unfinished Music collaborations between John and Yoko. The subsequent Wedding Album and Life With the Lions took similar ideas and ran off in slightly different directions. Neither had the shock value of Two Virgins; its notoriety strengthened by the full frontal nude and back shots of John and Yoko on the cover. Years after the event Two Virgins still retains that provisional quality and underlines Lennon's statement that this truly is music created in the moment, about possibilities and existing as much to inspire others to the same behaviour as to make any one statement.

As a measure of the departure this represented at the time, and the scale of confusion about where popular music ended, it is worth noting a positive review in Melody Maker for the 1969 Wedding Album. This album is a more focussed version of the early Two Virgins experiments. For example; the first side of Wedding Album features John and Yoko's heartbeats over 25 minutes as each calls out to the other with voices indicating a variety of moods from terror to love. A review pressing of the single album was sent out with each side of the album pressed on a separate vinyl disc. The sides of each vinyl disc not used for Wedding Album material were pressed with a continual test signal (i.e. a single continuous tone). You've probably guessed the rest. Melody Maker – amongst others – made the mistake of thinking everything they heard to be part of the album, believed they heard slight variation in the tone, and raved thus: "This oscillation produces an almost subliminal uneven 'beat' which maintains interest."

Lennon responded with a telegram marking: "The first time a critic topped the artist" and wishing reviewer Richard Williams "love and peace."

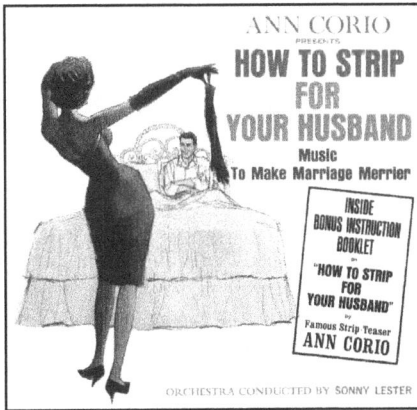

Sonny Lester:
How to Strip for Your Husband
(Roulette, 1963)
What? Cheerful cheeseathon from a different world.

An album long loved by exotica hounds and hated by anyone with strongly feminist ideas. How to Strip for Your Husband hovers in a netherland wherein it is loved for ironic reasons, hated for the reason it existed in the first place and generally never appreciated in the way it was intended to be. The concept here is simple enough. A series of short and punchy Latin-tinged instrumental tracks supplied by Sonny Lester are intended as the backdrop to bedroom antics that start with a housewife performing a range of disrobing dances. In a world where Playboy magazine was the hot new domestic must-have and men still ruled, the notion that a woman should be an angel socially and a whore in the bedroom – just about – had a high-point. With burlesque legend Ann Corio providing instructions – which came with the original album – a series of grinding big band tunes offer up the likes of: "Seduction of the Virgin Princess," "Blues to Strip By" and "Lonely Little G-String." Most of the music is original material – albeit clearly influenced by standard stripper tunes – and the odd incursion from somewhere else – Irving Berlin's "Easter Parade" and "A Pretty Girl is Like a Melody" – is brought into the sonic fold. Musically, these are tunes that elongate individual notes, often with a blast of brass, thumping bass drum or grinding sax; all the better to slowly rotate your hips, gently pat your bottom or perform a slut-drop artfully enough to indicate class. Sonically, this is a bold, brassy and BIG sound with just a hint of lounge jazz.

For all of the above, this is a novelty item, and such appreciation as it enjoys now puts it in the company of lounge and exotica genius performers like Les Baxter or Esquivel. How to Strip… shipped enough business to prompt the obvious follow up; More How to Strip… a slower, subtler work with more imported music. Both albums are now available on a single CD with Corio's original written commentary, including the nugget: "Nothing looks better on a woman than anatomy!"

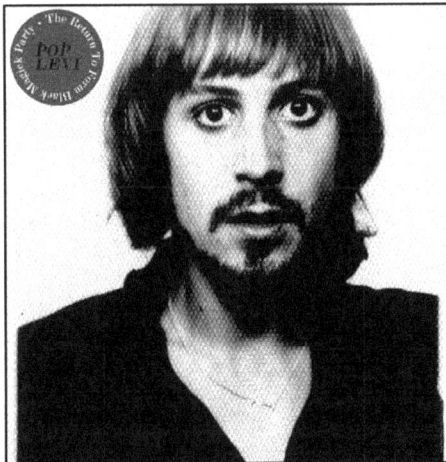

Pop Levi:
The Return to Form Black Majick Party
(Counter Records, 2007)
What? Under-rated pop-polymath on fine form.

Gloriously beyond categorisation, ambitious beyond all reason and fleetingly brilliant, The Return to Form Black Majick Party (TRTFBMP) is one of those concoctions that approaches the fence between insanity and genius, sets fire to that fence and turns round with a shrug. Jonathan Pop Levi makes films, plays enough instruments to be able to form his own band in a studio and tackles production duties. He's also to be found on YouTube in clips more akin to art student pranks where he screams on public transport and plays the role of a glam rock star convincingly. Musically his influences leap from the speakers with eclectic abandon, though a useful touchstone for the sense of a maverick genius overseeing the whole caper might be Joe Meek, Phil Spector, or Prince without the nods to classic soul.

The explosion of ideas crammed into this album make psychedelia a good place to start making sense of it. Though, the effortless pop-genius, glam-elfin-figure and the recurrence of swaggering rock-n-roll underpinnings make T.Rexstacy era Marc Bolan another useful comparison. The insistent strut of a cut like "Blue Honey," combined with the full-on sexuality of its video is pure Bolan in influence, though the album also packs moments of overwhelming emotional intensity, notably "From The Day You Were Born," which drips beauty and celebrates the birth of Levi's daughter. "From The Day…" comes across as a tearing of the veil between performer and audience…the twist being that Levi had no daughter when he recorded it.

The strength and weakness of this album is the sheer weight of ambition and artistry. Performers from Frank Zappa and Madonna to Lady Gaga have long recognised the usefulness of creating an artifice and then milking the tension between the fantasy world and reality, inviting the audience into the fantasy. If Pop Levi miscalculated this on his first long-player it was only in the way he threw in every idea – good and bad. He may well make more accessible and successful music, but few records at the time TRTFBMP hit the shelves pushed themselves so hard to achieve. Even when it is frustrating and impenetrable, TRTFBMP still grabs you.

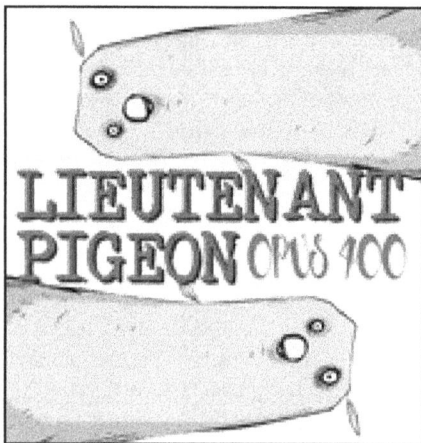

Lieutenant Pigeon:
Opus 400
(Makepeace Music, 2001)
What? Tales from Topographic Puddles

Best known by far as purveyors of the ragtime tinged novelty hit "Mouldy Old Dough," an infectious chunka-chunka pub-piano item that took up residence on top of the UK singles list for a month in late 1972, Pigeon were – in reality – a slightly more complicated musical item than they appeared. Their Lieutenant Pigeon recordings were novelty items. The band clocked up another top twenty hit with "Desperate Dan" in early 1973 and took the Irish ballad "I'll Take You Home Again Kathleen" into the Australian top three the following year.

Television audiences were stunned to discover the twin piano attack fronting the band featured the amply proportioned Hilda Woodward *, 57 year old mother of Rob Woodward, the other piano player. Mother and son pumped pianos before the spell binding sonic assault was topped off with young Rob's periodic blasts on the penny whistle. The growling tones of drummer Nigel Fletcher, usually intoning little more than variations on the title of a song, completed the Pigeon style. Serious music fans took little notice and the band's sales power soon waned. Though a handful of the more astute "pop-pickers" of the day were aware that Pigeon's personnel also provided most of Stavely Makepeace, a credible and collectible pop-outfit who provided catchy piano-led pop in a very British style.

When Pigeon finally went into semi-retirement the musical mainstays – Rob Woodward and Nigel Fletcher – went into producing jingles, and other sound-backing for the growing commercial radio sector.

But nothing in their history prepared the way for Opus 400. Indeed the 35 minute composition almost defies categorisation, even in the company of the strange in this book. Lyrically it starts off somewhere in batshit crazy territory and just keeps going. "Fat cats and Irishmen are so profound" being one incomprehensible couplet in a sprawling array of random references that takes in cod hippie philosophy, fantasy references,

* EDITOR'S NOTE: She died, aged 85, in 1999

economist Milton Friedman, morris dancing and sampled words from hymn tunes. Musically the piece shifts styles like a tweaked radio dial. Witness the cutting from dance beats, to pub piano, to edgy strings somewhere between the two to three minute mark. For all that, it still manages to hold together some sense of direction and pace. Pigeon claim the work as a "single" though it is longer than some of the albums collected in this book and easily as complex and bizarre. Imagine Topographic Oceans period Yes let loose in a radio jingle factory whilst members of the BBC Radiophonic Workshop oversee the proceedings. Whilst it is hard to escape the notion that the whole concept was carefully conceived as a raving masterwork of novelty-rock it is also hard to deny that, in the company of the other recordings listed here, this kicks outsider-music ass as hard as the best of them.

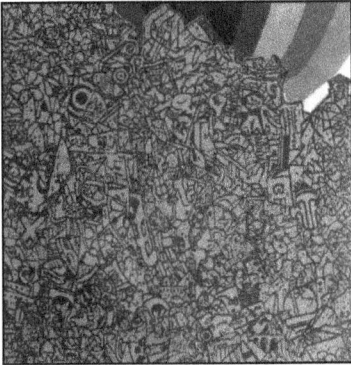

Lightning Bolt:
Wonderful Rainbow
(Load, 2003)
What? A differently abled delight in a sea of drone dross.

There's not much the book you're currently reading and 1001 Albums You Must Hear Before You Die would agree on. But we are as one with regard to Lightning Bolt's third outing. Ten slabs of extreme noise-attack barely held together by riffs that appear to come and go on a whim, and the most basic melodies. This is rapid, free-form noisenik indulgence of the highest order. Wonderful Rainbow crawls from the same slime as countless hordes of self-indulgent would-be artists (most of them long-forgotten) and makes a clear case for its own artistic integrity such that it gets cited alongside the great and the good in 1001 Albums... So, it is special. Rant over.

As with other terminally marginal acts – like Melvins – Lightning Bolt have their foibles and history; including a preference for playing in the middle of the floor surrounded by their audience and a track record that includes being deported from Japan for work permit irregularities. To all intents and purposes the band is duo Brian Chippendale (drums/vocals) and Brian Gibson (bass guitar). Others have come and gone but the Lightning Bolt sound remains. On Wonderful Rainbow it sets up its usual relentless, earsplitting, thrash of rhythm instruments that sound disturbing and frenetic over a few seconds but gradually reveal that the band's claims to be influenced by the likes of Philip Glass and Sun Ra have some foundation. Like early thrash pioneers, such as Napalm Death, this is music that moves the drums to the centre and features them as a lead instrument, chopping, changing and flying briefly off into excursions whilst the relentless wall of drone behind roars on. Lyrically the album, (and the band's work in general), favours interjections, shouts and a sense of the childish. When the drone and feedback breaks down on Wonderful Rainbow it sometimes gives way to some distorted but gleefully playful vocal break. Lyrically the band are generally inaudible but – as with the best of thrash metal and its myriad offshoots – the lyrics are clever, or wilfully moronic in a clever way, and generally known to the hard-core fans.

Lightning Bolt's skill, never better demonstrated than it is here, is to rein in this mixture to the point that it – just about – remains coherent. A sense of musicianship shines through the general assault, all aided by a thinner than usual sound on the drums that allows the percussive assault to sail over the top of the wall of noise. The notion that someone would reverently sit down to listen to this remains unlikely. However this collision of sonic attacks and the odd gem like "Crown of Storms," in which a song keeps threatening to break out, has inspired others to push the envelope. In its knife-edged wander between unlistenable surface and deeper ideas this is a near-perfect manifesto for the disaffected everywhere.

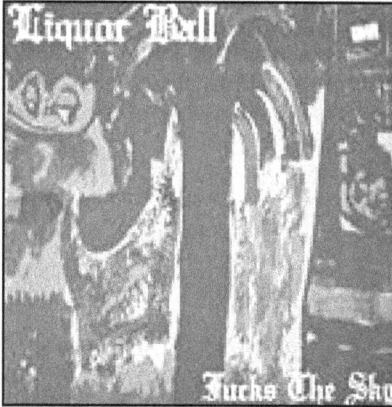

Liquor Ball:
Fucks the Sky
(Blackjack, 1992)
What? Guitar-growl, fuzzed-out-feedback-ridden full-on-fuckin' ear-assualt.

The big rock histories tend to ignore the footnotes, so the "rock" sounds of the early nineties were grunge, metal and their offshoots, right? Well, the little-remembered and barely discernable Liquor Ball might beg to differ on that score. Not greatly given to tarnishing their message with anything as simple as track titles, and so obscure that only Grady Runyan's name tends to appear on the odd site still sussed enough to list Liquor Ball's personnel, this is an act and sound that says as much about the early nineties as some of the more celebrated sound-stylists of the time. Touchstones in terms of sound would be the death-growl vocals of early thrash and black metal and the relentless riffing of the less inspired grungers. Liquor Ball offer up an insight into a group of low-profile early nineties acts who took the slacker antics and nihilistic posturing of the music press cover stars of the time and mashed it into a sonic assault that expected little radio play or attention. Basically, Fucks the Sky rants and rambles over eight tracks, led by a thin growling vocal, riffing that – just about – keeps the steady threat of feedback at bay, minimal lead guitar lines that loop and pack the slacker grace of early Dinosaur Jr. and a solid rhythm section that sets the pace with sudden stops and starts. Since the track titles don't exist and the lyrics offer little guidance, the stops and starts are the best guide to the starting and finishing of songs. For fleeting moments it sounds like the more accessible end of thrash metal, or the more desperate end of grunge, but Fucks the Sky works because – basically – it always sounds like itself. It comes over as little more than one almighty session focussed only on Liquor Ball venting their fury and throwing in a few random samples. But, this is music that still has a sense of its own self-worth and refuses to compromise to any fashion trend. If ever there was a single anthem for lonely bedroom angst it is side one's closer in which the thudding leaden assault of the music backs a vocal that repeats the word "Why?" to such a pointless degree, that it makes a point. Which – just about – is where Liquor Ball score over everyone else. Fucks the Sky is a work so wilfully brainless it packs its own perverse twist on genius.

Little Markie:
It's a Whole New World
(Bootleg, 1990s)
What? Inner child, projected outwards to praise the Lord.

The career of Mark Fox, AKA Little Markie, AKA L'il Markie is easily located online, and we'd highly recommend a brief session acquainting yourself with his live performances and recorded works. These can be found on YouTube and several other easily accessed sites. We're deeply indebted to the 365 Days Project, specifically the #47 blog entry for 2007 which makes a collection of Markie's work available in one place. The basic building blocks of a truly singular act are easily explained, but seeing and hearing is the only thing that matters in this case. Mark Fox is a preacher with a unique talent. He channels his inner child by means of a highly strangulated, soft round the edges, voice. And, he retains the capacity to slip from his tuneful adult singing into the puppet-like Little Markie tone in the passing of a single musical beat. If you're British, imagine Keith Harris and Orville. But, when Mark Fox is onstage there is no puppet. Suzanne Baumann found a home burned CD of the best of Markie's work in a thrift store and those tracks currently reside on the 365 blog. The backings are schmaltzy nineties echoes of perfect restrained beats, gentle trills of melody from keyboard and lush washes of electronic chords. It can get lively when necessary. All this provides a perfect backdrop for clear intonations and heartfelt words from Mark/Markie. Along with religious work of a mainstream bent, like "Shalom," Whole New World provides some inventive childish fun and jaunty sing-a-longs with works like "King of the Jungle," with its call and response pattern: "Who is the king of the Jungle?...J-E-S-U-S, he is the king of me." You get the picture. In a world of endless re-inventions on the theme of characterful evangelism Little Markie has come further than most in gathering a cult following on both sides of the religious divide. One YouTube clip characterises the rotund and mullet ridden Mark displaying his art onstage as an "epic fail." On the other hand, it's doubtful whether anyone presented with the man live in a church would forget the performance and it's highly doubtful whether any young child in that church could sit bored through another manifestation of Little/L'il Markie. To the current authors the standouts in this particular collection are the opening "Big House" a mainstream rocker allowing Markie full reign to enthuse about the fun, especially "football!!" in the big, metaphorical, dwelling the Lord allows him. We'd also recommend a rockin' take on "The Lord's Prayer" that soundly kicks the butt of Sir Cliff's "Millenium Prayer." This skirts a truly strange line with Little Marky's voice blending in and out of Mark's adult tones, and ends in a rowdy punkathon of thump thump beats and Little Marky's gleeful shouts. Whatever your stance on the existence of a Christian God, this is AWESOME!

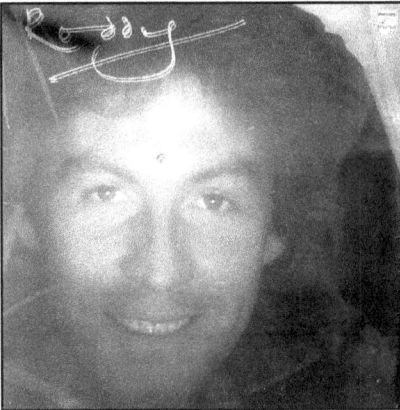

Roddy Llewellyn:
Roddy
(Philips, 1978)
What? Croontastic curio with aristocratic credentials.

The soft focus photo and handwritten title that adorn the cover of Roddy present a staid and classically handsome combination suggesting – rightly – this is an album of easy listening/ ballad standards. That it came about at all probably owes something to Roddy's (as in the man not the album) notoriety at the time. Roddy is more widely recognised today as a famous garden designer and should he decide on a more formal introduction he has every right to announce himself as Sir Roderic Victor Llewellyn, 5th Baronet. Granted, when he made the album his father – an Olympic show jumping medallist – was the baronet and Roderick only succeeded to the title on the death of his elder brother, Dai, in 2009. But we digress…

Roddy's prolific press appearances in the late seventies and early eighties coincided with an eight year relationship he had with Princess Margaret, younger sister of Queen Elizabeth II. Within the upper echelons of society Roddy's ability with a tune became public knowledge, as did his fondness for the kind of middle-of-the-road standards that were already fossilized by the mid-seventies. Philips Records eventually saw an opportunity to make an unusual record and Roddy is most certainly that animal. If Roddy has a close relative from the period it may well be The Ethel Merman Disco Album. Like Ethel, Roddy is trapped hopelessly out of time and found giving his best shot to a series of songs already well known in other incarnations. Like Ethel, Roddy's efforts are – occasionally - supported by sounds that resemble disco and given some semblance of danceability. And, like Ethel, Roddy ends up creating a record that finds its most avid supporters well away from the dance floor.

Wrapped in occasional lush strings, and the most restrained of productions, Roddy's public school and oh-so-English pipes bring an – ahem – different interpretation to material previously handled by the greats including "When I Fall in Love," "Everybody Wants to Find a Bluebird" and "Who's Got the Last Laugh Now." Sprinkled sparingly amongst the standards are some – then – contemporary numbers from the fringes of folk-rock, notably Keith Carradine's "I'm Easy" which nestles in the middle of the second side (there are only two-sided copies available; Roddy currently awaits CD rediscovery). Perhaps "I'm Easy" is the best entry into what Roddy does uniquely well. There's very little pretence anywhere on this album that the scenes and situations originally associated with the songs covered were a major inspiration in Roddy's takes on the same material. "I'm Easy" started life as the gentle and understated free love anthem that gives an insight into Keith Carradine's character in the gentle and understated free love drama that is Robert Altman's movie Nashville. Roddy reimagines it as a lush and erudite missive, perhaps best experienced in plush surroundings as an Englishman delivers the kind of tongue-tied heart-melter of a speech best exemplified by Hugh Grant waffling on to Andie McDowell about David Cassidy in Four Weddings and a Funeral. Or, to put it another way, Roddy, the album, takes these tunes and presents them very much as if they were written to describe the life of Roddy, the man. Which, after all, is exactly the quality we celebrate in the best interpreters of song. Nobody is suggesting for a second that Roddy Llewellyn should be considered in the same bracket as Billie Holliday but if Roddy has musical merits warranting more than ironic appreciation and a certain tacky fascination as a prime slice of exotica, it succeeds because it refuses to be embarrassed and/or apologise for its adherence to old ways. It's not trying to change the world and it's not pretending it's down with the kids (who were mad for punk and slammin' disco at the time). As the man himself scrawls on the back cover: "We all had a lot of fun recording the album, hope you enjoy it too!"

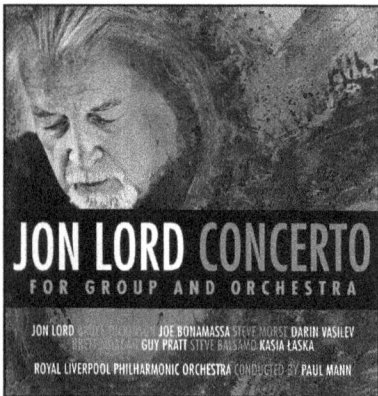

Jon Lord:
Concerto for Group and Orchestra
(Ear Music, 2012)
What? The original finally gets its best performance.

Jon Lord was an ever present member of the first four line ups of Deep Purple and came back on board for their 1984 reunion. He established a keyboard sound that influenced prog and hard rock players around the world. He was also central to the first full performance and full-length recorded work combining a rock band and symphony orchestra in one purpose made composition. The Concerto for Group and Orchestra was – (pub quiz fact alert!) – the first full length album to feature the legendary Mark II Purple crew of Blackmore, Gillan, Glover, Lord and Paice. It has sparked almost every possible critical reaction from utter derision to absolute rapture and remains a genre changing piece; cited when everything from the worst prog excesses to Metallica's performance with an orchestra are discussed. There are three recorded versions of the piece: the original (1969 US/ 1970 UK) album and 1999 remake are both live performances but as Lord battled terminal illness the only studio recording of the work was made in Abbey Road.

The Royal Liverpool Philharmonic Orchestra perform along with a host of senior rock names – Lord, Bruce Dickinson, Joe Bonamassa, Steve Morse etc. – in a recording that squeezes the gradations from a complex work and gets close to doing justice to Lord's original vision. Both live versions are lively and great fun but this mix, and recording, takes time to get a few of the details right to the composer's satisfaction. Lord lived long enough to approve the mix, but not long enough to see the CD with its lavish sleevenotes released.

Concerto for Group... was always conceived as a ground-breaking sound experiment and its narrative over the three movements is a dialogue between the sounds of a (heavy) rock band and a full orchestra. During the "First movement (Moderato - Allegro)" Lord always intended the group and orchestra should appear as the audience might expect them to be: "antagonists." A slow beginning draws on early twentieth century British orchestral music (conjuring Vaughn Williams in the lingering near-silence of the opening and Holst soon thereafter). It is thrown aside as the group explode into the movement, before each fights the other to the end. The second movement sees the pair working together with moments of fusion – notably the brief but important vocal section – but the group clearly sit on top of the orchestra, embellishing and adding but riding the main theme delivered by the strings and brass. The final section is tightly knit, cohesive and – in the great prog/heavy metal tradition of the time – stops for an almighty drum solo (here called the drum cadenza).

The studio sound allows the subtleties – notably in moments when percussive breaks build from the orchestra, or individual instruments begin a theme that gradually takes over – to be fully appreciated. The individual rock instruments are also produced to get the best from each player's own style. Lord's sixties influenced organ sound brushes against the later crunching metal guitar tones of Darin Vasilev in the first movement. The one thing that went down badly on this version with some of the greatest admirers of the work was the presence of three guitarists, each allocated a different movement and each sounding different to the others.

Concerto for Group… always was a lumbering beast of a work. Mighty, demanding of attention and prone to inhabiting the space between your ears to the exclusion of anything else. Never background music and never really done justice when heard as a recorded live performance; Lord's work got its chance to shine at the end of the man's life. He cared enough to make this happen, which is a measure of how much he believed in it.

Lothar and the Hand People:
Space Hymn
(Capitol, 1969)
What? Psychedelic soup of varied musical styles.

Posting an online appreciation of this collection on Julian Cope's Head Heritage site the gloriously named venus willendorf does an admirable job of nailing the particular charm of the second and final album outing of these psych masters. "psychedelic, but in an eccentric grown-up kind of way…its politeness belies a certain sonic subversion. Imagine a bunch of cerebral junior west-coast music professors, circa 1968, hanging out with the kids on campus and deciding to get weird." The best and worst qualities of Space Hymn are contained within that observation. At worst, Lothar and the Hand People (great name, great story of their name, it's online if you're that bothered), simply stray into sonic territory to experiment. A clunking and strangely soulless take on Martha Reeves and the Vandellas' "Heatwave" is easily the low point here. It doesn't sound like they intended to satirise the song so it's probably an ill-advised stab at the kind of mash up Vanilla Fudge and Blue Cheer successfully achieved with bludgeoning covers of classics, whereby the original was dragged into their sonic territory and duly beaten into submission. Lothar and the Hand People are far better at writing decent originals, producing work with a psychedelic angle and then subtly achieving the perfect arrangement. Fully half of this album is great psych pop/rock with skilful use of a Theramin, decent playing, and a real sense of an accomplished bunch in love with their work. If it occasionally betrays a kind of 10cc/ Steely Dan cerebral and studied quality then it delivers mightily by standing up to repeated playing and offering a varied collection of individual charms. It visits pop, rock and briefly touches down in a psych country vein that Lothar and the Hand People nail with aplomb. An early B-side around the time of their first album, "Rose Coloured Glasses" is a hugely under-rated psych-folk delight, but isn't available on the original Space Hymn. "Wedding Night For Those Who Love," an instrumental that sticks the mysterious Lothar out front, is one stand out track. But the piece that sets this album well apart from most identikit stabs at the same territory by hopeful bands in fashionable trousers is the title track. "Space Hymn" is a trippy tumult of psychedelic sounds. A perfectly pitched spoken word intro offers an exploration of inner space for those willing to surrender their consciousness. Once we've counted backwards from five we are tipped into a swirling world of sound and a slab of seminal psychedelic weirdness so skilfully woven that it's a celebration and satire in one, and all the better for that. That one track remains the most ambitious, and most successful, single work in the Lothar canon. If the world refused to wake up to their genius, at least the final cut on their final album left them with a moral victory. Confusingly, the complete Capital Records catalogue of Lothar and the Hand People was unleashed on a double CD, also rejoicing in the title of Space Hymn, this twofer offers their first album and stray tracks including the aforementioned "Rose Coloured Glasses."

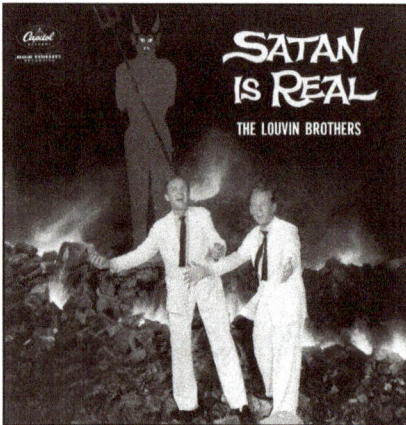

The Louvin Brothers:
Satan is Real
(Capitol, 1959)
What? Baptist brimstone…with great harmonies.

The Louvin Brothers' brand of fundamentalist Baptist religiousity, solid country and western playing and superb harmony singing proved exceptionally popular from the mid-fifties until the duo split, acrimoniously, in 1963. Over the years Satan is Real has gained a strong cult following; much of which has a minimal link to the music it contains. There are famously kitsch elements to the cover, which sports a picture of the brothers clad in pure white, standing amidst the fires of Hell (a close glance reveals the bursts of flame to be coming from kerosene soaked tyres) whilst a low-budget Lucifer (12 feet tall and made of plywood) glowers in the background. The uncompromising lyrical messages with regard to good and evil have also come in for some ironic appreciation. Will Ferrell's one man Broadway show: You're Welcome America: A Final Night with George W Bush employed the title track as a comment on Bush's beliefs. Ira Louvin's Baptist faith went hand in hand with a hard-drinking and womanising lifestyle that saw him display frequent anger management problems, including smashing his mandolin when he couldn't tune it. Ira did well to survive into his fourth marriage because his third wife – Faye – made a determined attempt to shoot him dead after he'd tried to strangle her with a telephone cord. Ironically, Ira and his fourth wife died in a head-on smash caused by a drunken driver. At the time of his death Ira was facing charges of driving under the influence. Charlie Louvin – by contrast – lived a virtuous life and died, aged 83, in 2011.

So, The Louvin Brothers packed a chemistry as explosive as the Everlys or Gallaghers and poured this into music of passion and uncompromising faith. Satan is Real is the clearest expression of their best work. An album so strongly principled its greatest songs have lived to be remade by the cream of subsequent generations. Johnny Cash, The Byrds and Emmylou Harris have all reworked tracks from this album. It offers a sound sporting the classic brotherly trick of each taking a separate area of the music before combining in the most spellbinding moments. Over 11 tracks and a little more than half an hour the brothers invoke God's presence, present evil and the existence of Satan as a stone-gone certainty and ask the kind of rhetorical questions posed by the most animated of preachers: "Are you Afraid to Die" (note: the title is generally written without the question mark).

Central to the message and meaning of the album is the title track. This opens the proceedings and features as much spoken preaching as singing, and "The Christian Life" which affirms the value of faith, even if it costs friendships. Ira takes mandolin duties and sings the higher register. Charlie's guitar playing is to the fore and his lower register singing drives the songs along. The two harmonise on choruses and blend their playing – often backed by a basic bass line and shuffling drums mixed well down in the sound. As tight, sincere, fine fifties country Satan is Real still stands up. The moralising in the songs was old school, even when it was released. But, the stories of "The Kneeling Drunkard's Plea" and "The Drunkard's Doom" have the dramatic, vivid and unsparing quality of Hank Williams' best work. Johnny Cash covered "The Kneeling Drunkard's Plea."

It would be a brave act that would release such fundamental statements and black and white opinions into the mass market today. But, Satan is Real is championed to this day by some listeners because of the courage of the convictions contained in the lyrics. It also displays the love/hate tension of brother acts. Ira playing the Liam Gallagher role of possessing the only voice capable of getting to just the right notes and inflections to turn good songs into great performances, and Charlie putting enough work into the sound to ensure the record works as intended. They couldn't live with each other and couldn't make music this good once they split.

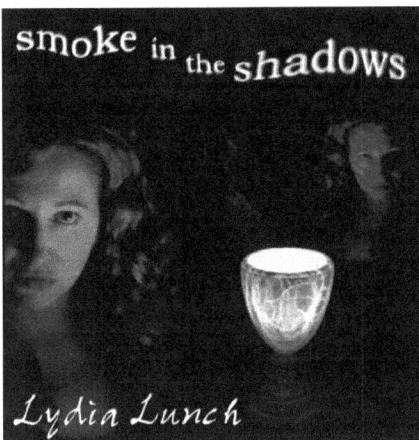

Lydia Lunch:
Smoke in the Shadows
(Breakin, 2004)
What? As dark as a pop album can usefully get.

Lunch had carved out a notable avant-garde career including noise assault music, experimental vocal works and the kind of female empowerment work that positively scares chauvinists. So, when her fifth solo album steered her directly into a dark pop groove she came not to sell out, but to claim catchy songs, sultry arrangements and sexually charged female vocals for her kind. Not to praise pop, but to bury it. Over 13 tracks of varied sounds and styles Lunch and standard song formats battle each other to a standstill. On balance, she probably takes the fight. Lunch had been in this territory before, and her work in no wave punksters Teenage Jesus and the Jerks showed an ability to front a band and deliver a vocal. But, Smoke in the Shadows is arguably the standout in the more accessible area of her canon.

The sense of sex, (as in real desire, the performer literally channelling a mixture of hard lust and harder won experience), hangs over the whole collection like a fug in a badly aired room. Lunch's lived in and growling delivery references the sex kitten and sultry sirens of this territory, like Eartha Kitt and Lauren Bacall. The sense of her acting is palpable. The sense she knows what she is doing is stronger. "Touch my Evil" has the kind of unstinting insistence, delving into the madness that Alice Cooper frequently courts in his darker works. It rambles over a rapid and cluttered jazzy groove, forcing the attention onto Lunch, who remains the most focussed part of the piece, whilst her words are nihilistic and threatening. "Smoke in the Shadows" is like the dark and more damaged sister of half the cuts on Madonna's Erotica collection and "Trick Baby" is an attitude ridden rant barely managing to contain itself inside a simple groove. It's also a good illustration of how the well-paced singing of the word "motherfucker" synchs to perfection with a catchy bassline.

The entire album sets out to explore this territory with enough variation and attention to song craft to work as genuine collection of listenable songs. The end results carve out a strange middle ground somewhere between Madonna's sexually charged dance pop and other works of unrepentant she-power like The Teaches of Peaches.

Vera Lynn:
Vera Lynn in Nashville
(EMI, 1977)
What? UK national treasure meets US national institution. We'll call it a draw.

Vera Lynn – subsequently Dame Vera Lynn – was already a national treasure in 1977. As the "forces' sweetheart" of World War Two her natural beauty and inspirational songs had helped Britain face the worst and emerge victorious. The problem with a young national treasure is managing the rest of their career. Lynn survived the post-war years quite well, posting a #1 UK single in 1954 but declining in sales once rock 'n' roll had taken hold. In Nashville emerged twenty years after her final UK hit single and did nothing to reverse the fortunes, despite promotion in a television special. This is country and western as imagined in middle-England. Restrained strings, careful song choices and a mid-Atlantic accent that appears afraid of a genuine country twang. Lynn's intonation is – ahem – variable; clearly leaning strongly on Connie Francis phrasing for "Whose Sorry Now?" but elsewhere staying close to her own generally perfect diction. You'll find online reviews praising the clear annunciation.

From the off-white trouser suite on the cover (against a background of country style wooden fencing) via the varied song choices (offering: "By the Time I Get to Phoenix" and "Make the World Go Away") to the presence of a few handy names like Pete Drake, The Jordanaires and arranger Bergen White this is an album that screams compromise. As such it retains the same kitsch appeal as Bing Crosby's Hey Jude/ Hey Bing and – like Bing – remains highly elusive and sporadically collectible in its original form. You won't find many full-blown country albums boasting talent on this scale that sound less country. In fact, the live performances viewable online have Vera backed by British television orchestra supremo Geoff Love. A man who knew how to get the best sound for the old-schoolers like Vera Lynn, but wasn't greatly noted for his down-home chops.

A couple of post-scripts are worth considering. Lynn's sales were steady rather than spectacular and – national treasure or not – EMI parted company with her after this outing. Her singles sales never worried the charts again but in 2009 – when the world and his dog had got so used to stealing music that the entire retail industry linked to recorded music teetered on the brink – Vera's generation of record buyers came through big time by placing a Very Best of… collection back at #1 in the British charts.

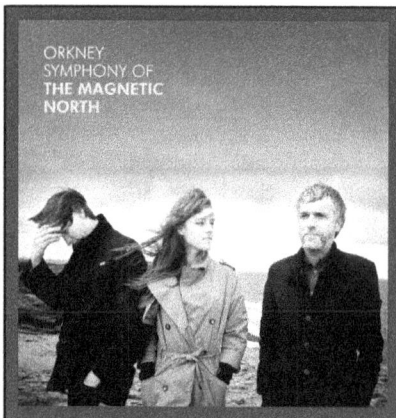

Magnetic North:
Orkney: A Symphony of the Magnetic North
(Full Time Hobby, 2011)
What? Song cycle, with spiritual slant.

An album, apparently, conceived (no pun intended) when Orcadian musician Erland Cooper was visited in a dream by the spirit of Betty Corrigall, an Orcadian girl who killed herself in the eighteenth century after being cast out by her village after becoming pregnant to a visiting sailor. Thankfully, the Orkney Isles appear more welcoming and open minded these days, which is – more or less – the point here. A song cycle conceived with the intention of accompanying a journey to the isles and performed by

Cooper, his sometime bandmate Simon Tong and Hannah Peel (a highly accomplished solo artist and arranger in her own right). The "symphony" checks in at the places you might expect, its more rapturous moments easily bring to mind the dreaded "ethereal" label for all such music. The acoustic instruments, notably the guitars and violin, soar and resonate with a sense of being truly engaged in the moment and the vocals, from resounding male harmonies to Peel's elegant timbre, are skilfully varied and ably deployed. Symphony of the Magnetic North joined a market packed with rustic/sincere/roots product. But, the recording does itself a massive favour by taking as its starting conceit the notion that this album is to be listened to from end to end whilst travelling to the Orkneys. There is little testimonial evidence available suggesting listening here prompted or accompanied many such physical journeys but, mentally, this is truly a topographic work. The presence of lengthy instrumental passages and tracks like "Warbeth" which present their vocals sparingly, allows the work to linger in a room, accompany other activities and slowly work its magic. The varied sounds, from solo vocal to string arrangements to a creditable blast of feedback guitar in "Ward Hill," allow it to withstand repeated plays. Peel's presence in this work is particularly important, with her high register, inhabiting the space with a lulling pleasance and power. At worst the whole symphony notion may appear a little too contrived and overblown, but each track and each moment works so well within the sequence that the album touches on the dreaded notions of concept piece and still emerges as a winner in such a context.

Maharishi Mahesh Yogi:
Maharishi Mahesh Yogi
(Liberty, 1967)
What? "The stream of life is a wave on the ocean of love"

The fleeting high-profile fame accorded to spiritual leader Maharishi Mahesh Yogi and his brief dalliance with The Beatles all brought about the circumstances within which this lengthy lecture-cum-meditation could be unleashed to record buyers, find shelf-space in the hippest sales outlets and find an audience that continue to cherish it to the present day. The scarcity of vinyl copies, and copies of the CD reissue, also give it a curio value. Cut to the needs of a vinyl album, this eponymous release is made up of two spoken word pieces – "Love" and "The Untapped Source of Power That Lies Within" – both delivered in a mantric monotone. The pace remains slow, the vowel sounds in words like "soothe" are milked for added blissed-out value and the eastern flavour is enhanced with meandering sitar sounds resonating and gently intoning around the Maharishi – who is mixed into the centre of the stereo sound.

The style and – frankly – the conceit of a release that set out to change lives was so easy to parody that a stack of comedians took aim and sent up the Maharishi's gentle delivery and peaceful message. Chance encounters with this straight faced spiritual purity so long after the event can still bring about unintended mirth. The lengthy spoken word pieces on each side don't do themselves any favours in the present day by demanding your full attention for their entire playing time to make complete sense. These meditations seek to deepen understandings and bring about deeper levels of spirituality. But, it takes attention to follow an observation like: "love of God is abstract in its infancy" through the examples of the love of mothers for their children to a final conclusion about the way the love of God overtakes other forms of love. Similarly, it is easy to dismiss references to the light of the dawn pushing back the darkness of the night as little more than cod-philosophy. It's also true – probably – that the Maharishi did himself few long-term favours – even with Beatles' fans – by throwing in a phrase like: "here, there and everywhere" halfway through side one.

The mantra-like pace and layered arguments on offer here give the listener some insight into why the Maharishi's support slots for The Beach Boys are currently ranked alongside Jimi Hendrix opening for The Monkees when support act disasters are discussed by sound-hounds. All of the above explains why Maharishi Mahesh Yogi ranks as a listening experience unlike most others in this book, or available from any sales outlet you are likely to visit. Those behind the release and the Maharishi's many disciples – then and now – continue to regard the work, the man, and his message as integral to their understanding of all aspects of life. The album has changed lives on a level few others collated in this book can claim.

Mahavishnu Orchestra: The Inner Mounting Flame (CBS/ Columbia, 1971)
What? Cutting edge jazz fusion, that still cuts.

An undisputed supergroup, the nucleus of which had met during the recording of a Miles Davies album, Mahavishnu Orchestra unleashed two ground-breaking and incendiary albums before the split of the original line up. Helmed by guitarist John McLaughlin, who wrote this album and its successor Birds of Fire (1973), the group pioneered a brand of jazz fusion incorporating the fluid melodies and complex production of artists like Carla Bley with a hugely ambitious and elegiac ability that hinted at classical influence, and dragged in fleeting moments of what would now be considered world music. Central to McLaughlin's vision was the notion of a band all capable of taking lead instrumental duties, even drummer Billy Cobham took his share, driving "Vengeful Fury" on this album with moments of Bonhamesque power and the dexterity of Buddy Rich. Also central to McLaughlin's vision was the presence of violin as a significant lead instrument. The concept of the group drew from spiritual roots and, from the Mahavishnu name to the intention behind each piece on this instrumental album, that intent is writ large over eight tracks and a shade beyond 45 minutes.

Jazz fusion may have taken twists and turns since 1971 that have left The Inner Mounting Flame behind. But, this and its successor still find few peers because the power, passion, and scale of achievement written into the original grooves defies any attempt to improve on the work. At worst the jazz fusion community became a haven for shameless self-indulgence and incessant noodling to little useful purpose. But early Mahavishnu set a standard that gave credibility to their little, (rock/jazz/anything else that fits), corner. There is a user-friendly attempt to vary the moods from track to track and sequence a running order that never allows any virtuoso to hog the stage. There's also, fleetingly, some chummy humour when "The Dance of Maya" grabs itself a standard blues grind and throws in a touch of barroom piano before vanishing at warp speed into the ether. If McLaughlin is credited as sole composer there's still enough influence from the others to suggest this is a band effort. For every McLaughlin showcase of fret fury (his trademark twin neck six and twelve string guitar allowed him to vary his contributions in each track), there are spaces when each of the five dominates a lengthy passage. Jan Hammer's keyboard and Rick Laird's bass swim along amiably in "Dawn" and subtly steal the piece from the lead instruments. When they all want to show off, like in the rapid fire closer "Awakening," the indulgence is forgivable in the face of the results. Above all, the sounds, tones and textures combine time and again to focus the changing moods. Fittingly, you'll hear samples of this album in the work of other respected acts including Massive Attack and David Sylvian.

Cynics would point out, with many justifying examples, that any band of instrumental virtuosos claiming spiritual credentials for their ambitious works are likely to split in acrimony amidst arguments about who composed what, and how much individual credit (and hard cash) is due to each member. This line up of

Mahavishnu Orchestra stand convicted on all counts. These five musicians gave us two albums, the first presented to stunned reviews hit #89 on the Billboard chart and set out the manifesto. The second flew to #15. The chart positions and ongoing respect for this early work continue to bear witness to the power and influence captured on record in the early seventies.

Man…or Astro-man?:
Your Weight on the Moon
(One Louder, 1994)
What? Futurism and full-on surf guitar sci-fi, sonic assault.

Some bands meet at school or university, others because one member sticks a notice on a music shop wall, or on Facebook. The extra-terrestrials who make up Man…or Astro-man? became marooned on this planet in our time when a key piece of time-travel equipment failed. Since then the band have been engaged in a return mission to their own little corner of the cosmos, sometime in the future, and their only means of achieving their aim is to construct a sound-bridge to the future.

In practical terms this has involved Birdstuff (drums) Coco the Electric Monkey Wizard (bass) and Star Crunch (guitar and occasional vocals) donning costumes that owe much to trashy fifties and sixties sci-fi movies and television, turning the amplifiers up loud and unleashing a brand of surf-guitar assault with samples that manages to sound retro and forward looking in equal measure. Over the years others, with similarly exotic names, have come and gone from the band. Heavy on samples of hitherto forgotten shows and movies, the band's music trawls a seemingly endless supply of sound-bites of pedigree actors (like Peter Graves and Richard Baseheart) in early stinkers they'd sooner forget. The snippets of dialogue have their own unapologetic pulp glory and fit perfectly into a surf-guitar assault that combines speed and – apparently - endless invention. Coco the Electric Monkey Wizard anchors the operation with steady bass figures allowing for those moments when Star Crunch's speed and power break out to drive the rhythm forward, giving the usually frenetic pace of the music that extra nitro-boost.

Technically speaking, Your Weight on the Moon is a mini-album, but it's probably the most accessible release from a period of prolific Man…or Astro-man? operations. The band managed five albums, and a slew of singles between 1993 and 1997, along with touring. It was either exhaustion, or vital operations in constructing the all important sound bridge, that led them to send out a bunch of clones on tour in 1998, an experiment subsequently repeated with female clones!

For all the amusing self-mythologizing this is still a listening experience likely to grab you hard and hurl you round the room – metaphorically speaking at least. Man…or Astro-man? are insistent, in-your-face and generally one step ahead of the listener in terms of where the next idea is likely to come from and where, exactly, the lead guitar is taking that melody. Your Weight…also betrays some of the influences, other than the obvious Link Wray/Dick Dale school of ear-splitting surf guitarists. Their cover of the Rezillos "Destination Venus" is a massive nod to their trashy glam-rock roots. The glam/trash aesthetic is there big time in track titles including "Special Agent Conrad Uno," "Electrostatic Brain Field" and "Taser Guns Mean Big Fun." It's also worth noting that their singles include the brilliantly titled "Supersonic Toothbrush Helmet" and the albums boast Intravenous Television Continuum and Made from Technetium. John Peel loved them.

Charles Manson:
Lie
(Awareness, 1970)
What? Introspective and gentle folk-rock, from notorious mastermind of murder.

Lie isn't so much the banality of evil as the public face of a private monster. Manson's musical work is taken more seriously, and listened to more often than the recordings linked to other cult figures like Jim Jones and David Koresh. These demos betray their low-fidelity origins (Manson once remarked that most of the album was recorded on a tape machine that cost $7). Sound quality aside, this is still fairly listenable stabs at folk and psychedelic rock, with a handful of cuts that have gone on to have their own life. The stand out and opening track: "Look at Your Game Girl" – a choppy rhythmed acoustic ballad with lyrical twists that attack the dishonesty of the female subject of the song – has been covered by Guns 'n' Roses. "Cease to Exist" was reworked by the Beach Boys into "Never Learn not to Love me." Manson emerges as a witty, grimly humorous and tuneful singer with enough command of guitar chording to hold his demos together. This material was never intended for release in this form, so one continuing school of debate concerns how any of this might have sounded if Manson had ever secured a proper recording contract. "Arkansas" is a gritty country number with Manson managing something of a drawl in the delivery, "Ego," "Mechanical Man" and "Don't do Anything Illegal" have some chaotic creativity in their imagery and sound suggestive of the sparky psychedelic pop of Lothar and the Hand People or The Strawberry Alarm Clock. "Eyes of a Dreamer" hints at the troubadour quality of Jim Croce.

Of course, the album has gained appeal on the back of Manson's subsequent conviction, cult status as a criminal mastermind, and his role as the focus for a range of dissolute and rebellious minds fascinated by the cracked logic of the most rock 'n' roll of convicts. Sonically Lie can only hint at what might have been, though much of the hard critical discussion directed at Manson's music damns the man with faint praise, suggesting he'd never have made it anyway. Lie has appeared under many titles, and in a two-on-one CD coupled with The Manson Family Sings (on which the members of his "Family" performed his songs to raise money for their imprisoned leader). There are also quite a few recordings smuggled out of prison of Manson's more recent stream of consciousness performances inside. One such album rejoices in the – ironic – moniker of Live at San Quentin. Manson makes no money from sales of the sixties demos that make up Lie (under whatever title it might appear), a 2006 reissue of the sessions – complete with bonus tracks – was arranged with the artist royalties channelled to the family of Wojciech Frykowski; murdered by Manson Family.

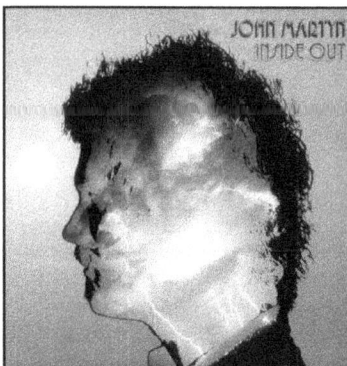

John Martyn:
Inside Out
(Island, 1973)
What? Innovative risk taker's most innovative and risk taking record.

Martyn's approach to music making saw few boundaries, a cynic might suggest he treated his career like he treated his body. He'd push the limits and count it a success if he survived. Always a hard act to define, Martyn started out in folk and soon threw in elements of jazz. By the time of his masterpiece Solid Air he had a trippy stoner sound and slurred vocal delivery that ran through most of his catalogue from that point onwards. Solid Air and One World (1977) tend to take the credit for their huge influence on trip-hop, and mainstream folk-rock, their ubiquitous presence as favoured soundtracks to lengthy smokes and romantic sessions, and their hosting of Martyn's "hits." However, for full-on fearlessness in forging ahead musically, they probably slot in behind this eclectic rag-bag.

Inside Out plays with the same palette used on Solid Air but pushes the envelope on experimentation. At the time Martyn described it as: "everything I ever wanted to do in music...my inside coming out," and said the collection was an exploration on the theme of love. Built from studio jams, and boasting a stellar cast of sidemen including Steve Winwood and bassist Danny Thompson, tracks fade in and fade out rather than starting and finishing, and the centrepiece is the sprawling "Outside In" which draws on a variety of styles and clocks in a shade shy of eight and half minutes. An eighteen minute improvisation on the same track would later appear on Martyn's Live at Leeds. The creative method that spawned Inside Out leaves a lot of lyrics feeling loose and unfocussed and the album packs a brace of instrumentals, one a traditional cover and the second, "Beverley," dedicated to his first wife. Despite not appearing on the record her presence is everywhere on Inside Out. From the mumbling lyrics about love on "Outside In" through the track that bears her name to the more revealing thoughts "If I ever took another woman/ I was in my need for you"("Ways to Cry") and "Getting very tired of crying/Though I'm laughing from the inside out/ Need your easiness around me/ Need you to tell me what it's all about" ("So Much in Love With You"). Inside Out is the sound of a man working away from his wife, often hopelessly adrift, and trying to hold it together. The different shades of sobriety, different moods and random creations in the jam sessions that make up the album give the whole thing the feel of being in the presence of an inebriated but highly compelling companion. Like a drunken night out, the really precious moments often go past in a blur and only reveal themselves later as you try to recall why they had such an impact. Unlike a drunken night out, Inside Out, is there to be replayed over and over again, gradually revealing its complex secrets.

Harpo Marx:
Harpo at Work
(Mercury, 1958)
What? Virtuoso outing from talented musician, not played for laughs.

Solo harp recordings and/or instrumental albums featuring the harp (as in the large-framed innards of a piano balanced on its side, not the harmonica "harp") as a lead instrument are never likely to be nailed-on best-sellers. A few curios like The Jazz Harpist have become cultish and – more recently – players like Joel Alexander have added abstract and meditative cover-art and a sense of stillness in the music to give the harp a steady appeal in the new age market. And then there are the likes of Joanna Newsome…

So, the highest profile harp albums and best available budgets to source good backing musicians were always likely to depend on some wild-card element in the deal. Step-forward Harpo Marx, as in the mute Marx brother much given to the biggest comedy pratfalls and most surreal visual Marx Brothers' movie moments (check out the scenes in which he pulls either a full-grown dog or a candle burning at both ends from his coat). Harpo's turns on the harp in the movies show his ability to play, but his handful of albums showcase a talent only hinted at on screen. Where the screen appearances – especially the earlier movies – showcase the visually impressive "glissando" waves over the strings, Harpo's instrumental albums aim for virtuosity and allow him to express a talent that always remained controversial in the music world. Harpo's son, writing on the official website explains it best: "when he sat down to play the harp, Harpo became Arthur. You can see it in his face. He's got that rapt, hypnotized quality to his expression…Dad took music really seriously."

The case against Harpo suggests he was self-taught, lacking the classical technique and reverence for his instrument and lucky to get a recording deal on the back of his film star fame. The case for Harpo starts with his albums and notes that his combination of classical and personal playing, and his appetite for any suitable material, makes for unique and characterful albums. Harpo's personal friendship with the likes of George Gershwin and his access to the session players working for MGM movies allowed him to get material and a sound quality that would guarantee listenability for his works.

Decades after their first release, Harpo's collections now offer that curious quality of effortless M-O-R schmaltz and a real sense of character that has fuelled the rediscovery of a range of exotica. He might lack the range of sound effects gathered by the likes of Les Baxter, but Harpo brings a totally different quality in his sense of timing and touch on the strings. His own site, and his die-hard fan base, have long heralded Harpo as a player who treated his melody line on the strings as a lead vocal, bringing enough originality in his sense of timing and touch on the strings to give his playing a distinctive voice. Those personal touches became more marked through Harpo's recording career making At Work, his final album, a good starting point to appreciate the man at his best.

Along with true standards like "My Blue Heaven" and "I Got Rhythm" there's a real loungecore curio in the one original "Harpo Woogie" and moments of effortless beauty in tracks like "Laura." The cover art on Harpo's records – misleadingly – presents him in comic poses. The man could talk as well, and once told his life story…but that came out in a book!

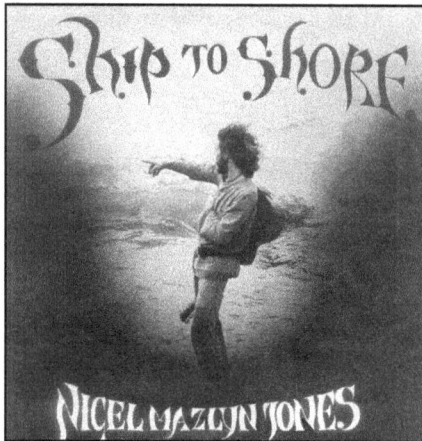

Nigel Mazlyn Jones:
Ship to Shore
(Isle of Light, 1976)
What? Unique work of sublime acoustic guitar and singular vision.

The years from the mid-sixties to mid-seventies saw ambitious folk musicians develop and hone the style that gained the name acid folk, whilst others undertook personal journeys into hitherto unknown territory for a music rooted in acoustic guitars and traditional ideas. The British folk scene was amongst the most vibrant and vivid on the planet and – by 1976 - it had spawned conspicuous success stories including Al Stewart's foray into a massive selling blend of jazzy AOR with Year of the Cat and John Martyn's weed soaked meandering into the use of tape delay and a host of other influences that started with Solid Air.

Whilst Nigel Mazlyn Jones would probably reel from close comparison with Martyn or Stewart they are useful touchstones here, if only to locate the peculiar genius of a man who has made a trademark of avoiding over-exposure. The lengthy workouts and Echolplex effects used by Martyn have some resonance on Ship to Shore. Martyn's deployment of electronic treatments on reworkings of traditional material like "Spencer the Rover" is a key to a sound that Mazlyn Jones made his own. Stewart's career turns have never lost sight of his essentially British qualities or his personal and slightly whimsical style. All of the above could be applied to Mazlyn Jones.

Ship to Shore places a varied set of original material at its heart, and features guitar playing – frequently reliant on harmonics, the differing tones of six and 12 string guitars, and extensive use of shades of production – to provide a sonic palette for Mazlyn Jones' heartfelt observations. Released in 1976, Ship to Shore was conceived and compiled throughout the seventies. Each perfectly crafted piece bears the marks of consistent refinement. The opening "A Singularly Fine Day" has been described by Mazlyn Jones as "a mantra for the hippies." With its epic references and deft guitar lines it feels much longer than the near five and half minute running time.

The following "Take Me Home" is around a minute longer, opening with fluid guitar and Mazlyn Jones' deepest and most conversational vocal of the album. By contrast, "How High the Moon" packs an effortlessly spacey guitar sound, a relatively simple melody and works perfectly over three and a half minutes. The epic title track reworks almost every guitar and production trick into a singular masterpiece worthy of any of the "legends" of British folk of the era.

Self-released material, a single-minded approach to steering his own career, an adherence to the original community values of the folk scene and following the music in opposition to jumping on any commercial bandwagon have all conspired to keep Mazlyn Jones' career on the very fringes of fame. Ship to Shore remains the perfect start point. Twenty first century reissues of the album now offer over 20 minutes of additional material, much of it as good as the cuts on the original album.

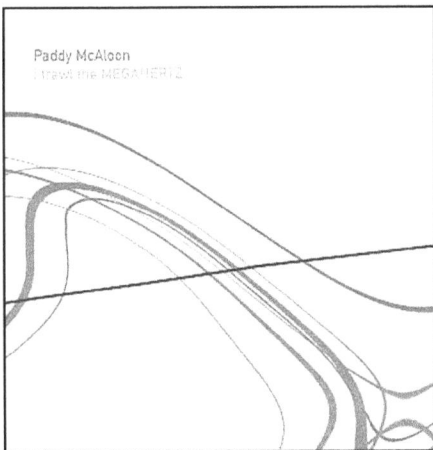

Paddy McAloon:
I Trawl the Megahertz
(Liberty, 2003)
What? Pop mastermind turns inward for inspiration.

Paddy McAloon's ability to turn out superior pop tunes for his band Prefab Sprout was already well established when the master-craftsman suffered a double detachment of his retinas in quick succession. Denied his usual ability to read or work, he became increasingly attached to radio listening and this album is a work inspired by that period.

Stylistically it's very hard to define. The opening 22 minute title-track is a plaintive and occasionally bleak work that collides the internal monologue styling of a challenging radio play with swirling semi-operatic music, shot through with pop instrumentation and modern production effects. Less a song and more of an experience, it sets the tone for eight other short pieces, mainly instrumental, but often packing the rising and falling cadences of conversation.

When – during the seventh track, "Sleeping Rough" – McAloon's familiar soft-edged and clearly enunciated vocals chime in with the line "I'll grow a long and silver beard and let it reach my knees" it's a moment that borders on shocking simply because his presence is everywhere in the listening experience, but revealing himself so completely seems a little out of character by this point. It also highlights some of the most distinctive qualities of his first solo album.

This is a very individual, almost eccentric, piece rich in its own sense of beauty and compromising very little to accepted notions of genre or radio friendly writing. This is McAloon's work and the man is congenitally incapable of writing a poor melody. So, it was always going to be very listenable. But this most demanding of his works, takes time to reveal itself.

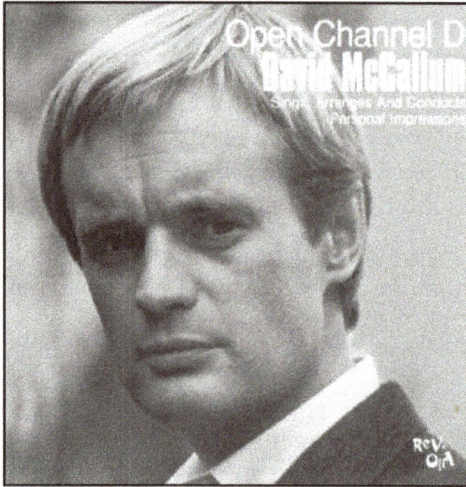

David McCallum:
Open Channel D
(Rev Ola, 1996)
What? Surprisingly under-stated performance from heart-throb actor.

Usually arriving somewhere between out and out novelty and over-blown surreal escapades into hitherto undreamt of depths of self-delusion, the albums produced by a string of actors: William Shatner, Leonard Nimoy etc. now earn plaudits they never sought in the first place.

David McCallum – whose role as Ilya Kuryakin in The Man From U.N.C.L.E. had turned him into a teenage idol, despite being 31 when he first appeared in the series – was soon on teenagers bedroom walls. McCallum's fame was duly rewarded with a recording contract. The first fruits were two singles covering the usual deep and meaningless meditations on life with a comedy slant. "Communication" actually staggered up to 32 in the UK singles charts, "In the Garden – Under the Tree" (McCallum's take on the doings of Adam and Eve), didn't match the performance. But in their wake came two albums that stand as genuine celebrity curios, for all the right reasons.

When MGM approached McCallum with the notion of turning him into a recording artist they probably failed to appreciate his genuine musical pedigree. His father – David McCallum Snr – was a high-profile classical musician who had played on "A Day in the Life" by The Beatles and may have been the man who first suggested Jimmy Page used a violin bow on a guitar.

Young David had inherited much of his father's talent and had studied classical composition at the Royal College of Music. He suggested to MGM that he arrange and conduct classical arrangements of modern pop music standards. This, with the odd McCallum original and one or two from fellow arranger H.B. Barnum, went on to make up Music…A Part Of Me and Music…A Bit More Of Me, both boasting a couple of dozen highly listenable arrangements.

McCallum wrote arrangements for woodwind and a quartet of French horns Barnum (who would later go on to work as musical director for The Osmonds), added a basic rock rhythm section and electric guitars.

Open Channel D gathers both early singles, their B-sides, and the two Music albums in their entirety, and it bops along like a slender beast. The singles are engaging, if highly-dated, celebrity tosh. But the two albums of prime M-O-R lounge greatness have – if anything – grown in their charm. Bouncier than cocktail jazz and more characterful than standard easy listening takes on hits already done to death, they bring out a mellow quality in classics like "Turn, Turn, Turn" and "(I Can't Get No) Satisfaction" and match them with McCallum and Barnum's deftly tuneful originals.

Granted, this is music made to burble agreeably in the background rather than grab you by the throat and throw you against the wall, but it's outstanding in its own niche and longer lasting than much of the celebrity froth of its era.

John Lennon McCullagh:
North South Divide
(359/Cherry Red, 2013)
What? New bottles, old medicine.

The involvement of prime scenester and stirrer Alan McGee in everything from the production to release of North South Divide always meant the album was going to be discussed on more than its musical merits. For all the credit earned as a major shaping presence in the music industry it is worth noting that Alan McGee's greatest successes in the market place – Oasis, Teenage Fanclub etc. – often had a massive retro-streak in their work. Something they retained whilst being hailed as future talents. With his Creation and Poptones labels both consigned to history McGee teamed up with Cherry Red in 2013, and opened the account of 359 Records with a trio of releases. McCullagh's album earned the all-important #1 listing in the catalogue.

A minimalist, almost skeletal, selection of acoustic guitar, vocal and sporadic spot-colour instrumentation, John Lennon McCullagh (his real name, incidentally) is presented on the press release as a youngster from Doncaster with a list of influences boasting Dylan (seen on stage nine times in quick succession during one tour), Paul Weller, Marc Bolan, Johnny Cash and Donovan. Jake Bugg is also name-checked on the press release, but he's a token 21st century reference in an old school litany of the great and good. Old school is certainly the way the music works.

The album comprises mainly acerbic, painfully honest and directly addressed communiqués in which McCullagh's raspy and expansive vocals fill most of the mix and control the melody lines. The highest and lowest notes are forsaken for a more conversational and emotive vocal style wherein the occasional blast of harmonica (early Dylan is clearly his preferred period) works as an extension of the vocal line. McCullagh punctuates the songs with rhythmic chops on acoustic guitar, proving particularly adept at hammering one effective bass note to emphasize a chord or provide percussive effect. The songs range from bitter polemics – "Rivers of Blood" (within which McCullagh feels "sick to the pit of my guts" and comments on political change in the UK over decades) – to the lilting "Ballad of a Blue Poet" with McCullagh's vocals duetting with solo violin and the song making a virtue of the trite rhyming of train/ rain by/cry. It sounds and feels personal, though there's a fairly obvious similarity to the opening line of melody/lyric from "The Ballad of Mr Henderson" and John Lennon's "I'm Only Sleeping."

North South Divide does have something to say about grim northern (British) realities and as a statement of faith in the simplest of musical masonry – guitar, original songs, solo vocal – it's a bold move with which to start a label. But all of the above ignores the main talking point that McGee and his Cherry Red backers knew was always going to attend North South Divide. At the time of release – October 2013 – John Lennon McCullagh was 15 years old. He wrote and sounded much older, and the shamelessly retro stylings of his debut album were always likely to give it the feel of maturity.

Hype aside; this is an assured and easily under-rated collection that survives the obvious nods to early Dylan sounds and a basic production to present an astonishingly mature collection of work.

Dion McGregor:
The Dream World of Dion McGregor
(Decca, 1964)
What? Quite literally, a stream of consciousness.

Dion McGregor was a respected and successful songwriter in 1964 when this album was released. His achievements included penning material for an up and coming singer called Barbara Striesand. On that score, McGregor had a significant creative talent. His other notable talent was hardly unique, but his proximity to the recording industry allowed him to get noticed and released. As Mojo's Weird Records blog, penned by Johnny Trunk, states: "By night, he was a confirmed somniloquist, speaking loudly and freely in his sleep." In response to this: "His frazzled roommate, Mike Barr, would wake at 7am, start the tape machine and then go back to bed. The mornings were when Dion's dream world would really come to life." McGregor's ramblings were circulated on bootleg tapes, becoming legendary and the subject of much discussion. So, it was a natural process that ten such ramblings were compiled onto an album. The resulting collection isn't exactly representative of McGregor's complete catalogue; the more sexually explicit and generally disturbing moments were left off the album. But, released into a market already showing affinity with beat poetry and the off-the-wall vocal ramblings of performers like Ken Nordine, The Dream World… stands out as a peculiar and very individual set of performances. "Circles" – basically a free-form rant about visualising a shape, that diverts into judgement on McGregor letting others down – offers up vocal cadences, rapid-fire imagery and a perfect balance of abstract idea and rooting in the real world. Frankly, it stands beside the best beat poetry and draws strength in doing so from the audible noises of traffic and street sounds outside McGregor's apartment. Other exercises in talking to himself show McGregor as obsessed with detail, highly articulate and prone to a level of circular logic that gradually allows the listener to get to know the man. "The Gift" – concerning a present and the misfortune for someone to be born the day before Christmas – shows most of these qualities. The characters peopling these rants are never put into context. So whether Vera and Vernon – who feature in "The Gift" – are real or imaginary isn't made clear. Two fairly short sides of vinyl is – probably – enough of this material. McGregor's strange subconscious world has the fairly-tale logic of good fantasy writing, and works best in these short, and sometimes very short, stories. The near seven minute epic of "The Operation" – based around a medical procedure but soon diverting into the Freudian sub-texts that seep from this album – has the ability to leave the less intent listener behind in its wake, McGregor even asks: "I wonder if they understood anything I was trying to get at" as he rambles his way through the medical epic.

Medicine Head:
Don't Stop the Dance
(Angel Air, 2005)
What? Lost album, lost band, lost opportunity…

John Peel loved them, signed them to his own label, produced their first recordings and commissioned sessions throughout their career. They repaid him with the only hit single ever enjoyed by the great man's Dandelion label. Medicine Head were a well-known and much-loved fixture on the seventies rock scene but time hasn't treated them kindly. Their four hit singles remain something of a footnote in a classic, and much chronicled, era for rock. Their claim to anything like long-term notoriety is almost terminally undermined by the fact this band didn't spend a single week on the album charts.

Some of the reasons are obvious. For most of their existence the band were a two piece, John Fiddler usually singing, playing guitar and banging a bass drum and cymbal with his feet whilst the harmonica/mouthbow/jew's harp and massive blonde afro of Peter Hope-Evans jigged along beside him. On stage they were seldom less than excellent, but since they were such a cheap act to stage they spent much of their career opening in big halls for other bands. Their live sound was skeletal and incendiary, their records sounded nothing like the gigs and the problem was complicated by the fact they spent a lot of time playing live to other band's crowds. The obvious solution, money to hire a bigger line-up, finally materialised on the back of the #3 single "One and One is One." An effortless piece of throwaway pop that resembled virtually nothing in their catalogue.

As a five piece they turned in the listenable and catchy Thru a Five (1974) before leaving Polydor Records. Thru a Five was a solid, if rushed, set, stymied by the fact it packed two hit singles already released. Medicine Head embarked on a much more ambitious set. The results produced some good, if under-promoted, singles before the whole project collapsed amidst management, record label and financial hassles that reduced the band to the original duo and obliged them to start again on a the modest Barn label. Despite a die-hard fan-base who still refuse to let go, obscurity duly beckoned.

It wasn't until 2005, thirty years late, that the remains of their lost album finally turned up on a commercial release. Don't Stop the Dance is blues-rock, but shot through with a strong sense of pop and frequently hinting at something quintessentially British and very old. It's also an unfinished album, the odd track, like "Lay Around" amounting to little more than a riff, an idea and a run-through. Elsewhere the quality that could have taken this band to the fleeting glories enjoyed by their contemporaries leaps from the speakers and suggests they were on the verge of delivering the album many believed possible. The title track packs a stonking five-part harmony, "Can't Live a Lie" is the kind of plaintive ballad that could have earned a charting cover version from the likes of Rod Stewart and "Part of the Play" and "Mama Come Out" maintain the soulful radio-friendly Medicine Head tradition and support the notion that – given an even break - Fiddler could knock-out hits in his sleep.

Whether the full realisation of this dream, and a charting album, would have been a bonus for Medicine Head remains a debatable point. Die-hard fans, and the original duo themselves, continue to cherish the stark beauty and infectious vibe best represented by their first Dandelion album: New Bottles Old Medicine. But in an era that saw clear blue water between chart singles and credible albums Medicine Head remain totally undervalued for their ability to turn in long players of lasting quality. This, their best shot at being mainstream without selling out, might well have taken them into a bigger league.

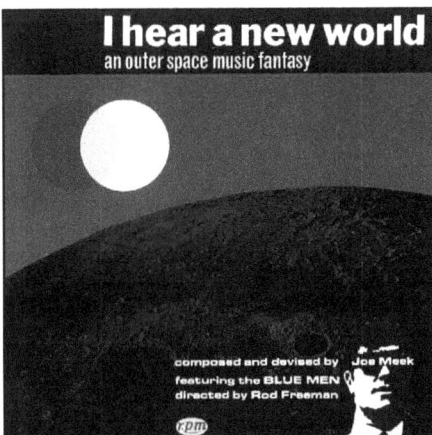

Joe Meek and the Blue Men:
I Hear a New World
(RPM, 1991)
What? Futuristic space fantasy; composed and recorded 1959.

A very British response to the epic instrumental-cum-narrative albums emerging from the United States in the fifties, I Hear a New World is also regarded by some as the most personal, elaborate and bold piece of work in Meek's mighty oeuvre. Only part of the work was released (on EP) in Meek's lifetime. The RPM release was the first time the 12 tracks and (almost) 33 minute work had been available in its entirety. A shuffle beat and (by Meek's standards) conventional vocals open the proceedings although Rod Freeman's refrain of "I hear a new world calling me" is echoed by high frequency – i.e. Chipmunk/Pinky and Perky – vocals. From this point onwards the vocal tracks are an exception. Such vocals as do appear are treated and tweaked to the point of adding novelty. The bulk of I Hear a New World features instrumental tracks saddled with Meekian names like: "Entry Of The Globbots," "Valley Of The Saroos," "Orbit Around The Moon" and "Valley of No Return." Meek's creative genius runs unfettered over the whole shebang as the worthy and willing skiffle band recruited as the house crew give his vision their full effort. The Blue Men – as they are called for the purposes of this album – provide the mainstay of a production in which Meek layers on the sound effects. A collision of novelty tricks, some straight out of the top drawer of his imagination, turns every track into a separate sonic realm and embellishes the concoction with his famed brand of lunatic pragmatism. So, when you hear bubbles coming up through water, that isn't a bought in sound effect, it is Meek and his engineer blowing bubbles through a straw. The attraction of this album is partly the knowledge that such atmospheric, haunting and attention grabbing work could be cobbled together by combining a skiffle band with random taping of the draining of a sink or banging milk bottles together. But, in the end, it is the fact that this short album breathes epic quality and provides the nearest thing available these days to a meeting with Meek, the shoestring-visionary. Meek's presence is there in his conception of the sequence of tracks as a complete work, and also in sleevenotes that provide a way in to the varied and vivid epic. For example, Meek's liner notes for the track "Magnetic Field" read: "This is a stretch of the Moon where there is a strange lack of gravity forcing everything to float three feet above the crust, which with a different magnetic field from the surface sets any article in some sections in vigorous motion, and at times everything is in rhythm".

Most of Meek's work is best heard as hit (and miss) singles and considered in the context of its time. I Hear A New World was welcomed with amazed and generally complementary reviews nearly a quarter of a century after Meek's death. It has gone on to earn a fitting place as a real "out-there" classic.

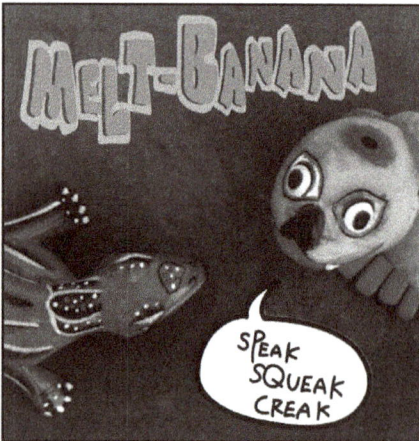

Melt Banana:
Squeak Squeak Creak
(NUX Organization, 1994)
What? Japanese hyper-speeding noiseniks set out the manifesto.

Melt Banana come from the same stable of arty insanity that produced acts like The Boredoms, and might also usefully be bracketed with boundary trashers like Lightning Bolt. All of which only matters if you are into pigeon holing in general. The whole point about Melt Banana is to savour the collision of noises coupled with moments of incredible musical dexterity. They are there to be experienced as much as listened to. If a song like "Rragg" clocks in at less than a minute and manages furious metal drumming, rapid-fire soloing and shouty vocals so fast you'd have to give it a second listen to begin to grasp what they are on about, then that – in a sound bite – is the Melt Banana manifesto. When the running time suggests "Smell the Medicine" is an epic by these standards, clocking in around two and half minutes, you won't be too surprised to find it starting with some ambient noises before morphing into the usual punky-prog noise assault, effectively cramming two different sound bites into one track. John Peel, predictably, loved them. Like other outsider acts of a similar vintage – The Boredoms, Napalm Death – Melt Banana achieve that classic revolutionary stance of always staying on the very margins whilst making clear progress all the while. Their albums vary the extent to which their constituent influences, ambient, grindcore, punk, electronic and, (no bull), classic pop are deployed in the mix. Squeak Squeak Creak is the opening long player, (okay, it clocks in a shade beyond 32 minutes, but you get the idea), in their searing noise-assault career, and still serves as a useful start point to any Melt Banana newbie. Oh yeah, and we hardly need to point out, any Melt Banana album comes highly recommended.

Melvins:
Colossus of Destiny
(Ipecac, 2001)
What? Colossal for sure. It's debateable if anyone was destined to listen to this.

A touchstone for post-rock extremity and something of an enfant/album terrible even amongst the alternative crowd. Colossus of Destiny is almost exactly an hour's recording from a single live show in December 1998, the album comprises two spontaneous and improvised tracks, both called "Untitled" the first of which clocks in at 59 minutes and 23 seconds, the second is there and gone in five seconds. For the most part, the album offers up a slow- tempo sludgathon of noodling from synthesiser, clattering drums and general noise assault. A few online sources gleefully report that audience members were prostrate and covering their ears during the performance. Quite believable given the random interjections of feedback and the sudden increases in volume that permeate the piece. It's rambling, unfocussed, apparently angry (given the insistent sense of attack rather than exploration) and timeless in that it fits no prevailing fashion trend then or now. As with all great outsider bands Melvins have their back-story and cultural reference points sturdily nailed down (Colossus of Destiny draws its name from a book within a book, after the character Arturo Bandini who appears in the book The Road to Los Angeles writes a book called Colossus of Destiny). On the basis of such reference points, the champions of Colossus of Destiny (the album) can claim it as a deep masterwork of nihilism, shot through with insightful and inspirational ideas. As a rite of passage for those hell-bent on nailing their own alternative credentials to the wall, Colossus of Destiny is right up there with the best. Superseded (maybe) by Lou Reed's Metal Machine Music. But it took Reed decades to put his unlistenable masterwork on stage. Remember, this is a live album, these guys – literally – lived this hour as they recorded it. Ultimately, the debate is really subjective and that may well be the point.

There is, if you choose to accept it, a narrative of sorts, provided by samples of porn sound, a nod to the band's relationship with pornster Gregory Dark. But whether they mean any more than the titular nod to the book within the book, is – once again – up to the listener. As blogger Nick Green puts it: "The totally-amazing-to-total-horseshit ratio depends on your taste—Melvins devotees tend to debate the merits of the band's recorded output with the sort of religious fervor that ninth graders in jazz band apply to Rush." And, that says most of what you need to know. If you want alternative credentials and that sense that you'll never be like everyone else, acquainting yourself with Colossus of Destiny via headphones, memorising exactly what sound emerges without warning after what other sound, and living with this unwieldy beast long enough to develop a deep-affection for its alternative glories, is highly recommended. For everyone else, it's on YouTube.

Ethel Merman:
The Ethel Merman Disco Album
(A&M, 1979)
What? Camp classic curio.

The original seven track vinyl of this album remains one of the most collectible and sought after sound-hound treasures of all. Not the fate its makers imagined or hoped for with an attempt at career rejuvenation for a Broadway legend 20 years past her last major success. Those unfamiliar with this late seventies disco curio really only need to know three things to fully appreciate why it enjoys its current reputation. Firstly, Ethel Merman, already in her seventies, recorded her vocals live, with a band playing; meaning she went for interpretation rather than perfectly timed and pitched vocals. Secondly, she heard no disco backing, only the kind of spirited showbiz band she had enjoyed on stage. The disco backing tracks were added later. Thirdly, Ethel's take on disco songs involved cutting 14 standards, seven of which - "Everything's Coming Up Roses," "I Get a Kick Out of You," "Something for the Boys," "Some People," "Alexander's Ragtime Band," "I Got Rhythm" and "They Say It's Wonderful" – make up the legendary 1979 vinyl edition.

The ensuing collision of styles and values has found two areas of die-hard appreciation. Firstly, this beast is an acknowledged camp classic, beloved by members of the gay community. Merman, like Bette Davies and other peers, already enjoyed a large following amongst the - then – mostly closet based gay community. The community's eventual emergence overground has helped to drag this album into continued cult appreciation. The other fans of the whole caper are those inexhaustible seekers of audio curiosities who treasure Ethel's vinyl as they also treasure the works of Tiny Tim and Wild Man Fischer.

The Ethel Merman Disco Album exists in a world so far beyond any meaningful judgements of good or bad that it remains untouchable and – probably – unrepeatable by any current collision of artist, material and producer. Basically, Disco Album works its own sweet magic for two reasons. Firstly, where the disco divas of the period – like Donna Summer – turned their considerable vocal talents to producing a melody line akin to a lead instrument to be layered over the top of a repetitive track, Ethel eschewed any rigid adherence to timing and pitch and instead produced a performance in which everyone else is clearly backing her. It is Ethel's character that assaults us from the speakers, and it is most certainly Ethel's album. She's not out of tune or out of time, but she is performing. The likes of Donna Summer, by contrast, are contributing a great performance to be part of the overall production. Secondly, Disco Album sticks out from the disco crowd because the classic songs of Sondheim, Berlin and Porter make it stick out. It's a crude analogy but one that – just about – describes the unique listening experience of The Ethel Merman Disco Album to say that the songs' transition from Ethel's first live take to the eventual dance mixes sees them pimped in a similar manner to a family saloon car re-emerging from a workshop with a fur lined interior, tombstone bass speakers and a headache inducing paint-job.

Olivier Messiaen:
Quatuor pour la fin du temps (aka Quartet for the End of Time)
(Classical work, 1940-41)
What? The end of time, in one room, inside one hour.

Covered and re-imagined sporadically since its inception we'll take a major liberty from the notion of an album here and simply highlight this 50 minute monster for string quartet as an album length work of truly ferocious intent. And, a visionary extravaganza that spends almost its entire length attempting to escape the confines of being a piece for four instruments in a chamber setting. To be fair, the conception of the piece almost demands the end results. Captured by the Germans and in transit to a prison camp, Messiaen met clarinetist Henri Akoka and showed him sketched ideas for a classical work. Eventually a quartet was developed and performed to 400 inmates, in the rain at Görlitz, (then in Germany, now Zgorzelec in Poland) in January 1941.

The quartet draws its inspiration from the Book of Revelation but it draws much of its power from two massive ideas intersecting. Firstly, the various instruments continually imitate other things and because the piece is for violin, cello, piano and clarinet there is scope for a variety of sounds. The gentle clarinet, imitating the song of a blackbird joined by the violin imitating a nightingale gives a pastoral flavour to the opening moments. By contrast, the entire quartet pounding away to imitate gongs much later is a complete contrast to the nature sounds of the first moments. The contrasting sounds, sense of strong narrative and changing moods are central to the strength of the whole quartet. The second major idea is more implicit. Mankind is powerless in the face of the end time and this has clear echoes of the powerlessness of prisoners and much of Europe before the rolling menace of the war instigated by Germany. An idea that clearly made sense to the first audience of prisoners.

The length of the work, the strong themes and changing moods in Quartet for the end of Time provide the kind of organic unity that became the rationale behind the best concept albums a generation later. Because it shares some superficialities with such progressive works, and some fairly clear good vs evil, life vs death reference points, Quartet for the end of Time has found an audience well beyond the time in which it was composed. It also continues to be heralded as an authoritative, cathartic and highly important classical work of the twentieth century.

Mrs Miller:
Mrs Miller's Greatest Hits
(Capitol, 1966)
What? Seminal "so bad it's good" collection.

Despite the claims of the title this is the first album by Elva (Mrs) Miller and, with 250,000 accredited sales, also her greatest long-playing hit. Gary Owens – who went on to work as announcer on Rowan and Martin's Laugh-In - contributed liner notes comparing Mrs Miller to Florence Foster Jenkins and praising: "one of the most interesting voices." For which read: out of tune, out of tempo, permanently capable of mangling a familiar melody out of shape and possessed of the car-crash brilliance that frequently turns vocal calamity into public spectacle. Like others mentioned in the same breath – Leona Anderson and Foster-Jenkins – part of the listenability here is in the unholy alliance of well-orchestrated backing, good quality production, the sense of technical understanding in the singer's approach and the final shambles of missed notes, inappropriate nuances and the inescapability of falling in the gutter every time the performance strives for the stars.

In this context Mrs Miller's Greatest Hits scores massively by sticking to the tried and tested formula for novelty-destruction-of-standards; packing in some currently fashionable material and some old favourites. Bear in mind Mrs Miller's Greatest Hits entered the market in the same period that saw the USA taking Staff Sergeant Barry Sadler and his "Ballad of the Green Berets" to its heart. In this world Mrs Miller was better able than Sadler to sustain a career because she spoke to a small audience of white middle Americans. Probably, like her, they were somewhere around sixty, packing a few pounds beyond a slim figure and worrying that the counter-culture was destroying a great nation. To these people Mrs Miller's heart – if not her vocal chords – was in the right place. But she also spoke to a wider audience of rock and pop fans who couldn't take Barry Sadler. To them Greatest Hits was comedy writ large and an affirmation of the fact that the originals be they The Beatles ("A Hard Day's Night") or even Nancy Sinatra ("These Boots are Made for Walking") packed their own mystical charm that defied mere imitation.

On cuts like "A Lover's Concerto" Mrs Miller's unique fusion of operatic warble, high-concept delivery and utter incomprehension of why the song mattered to a younger generation blend to perfection. Her differently abled vocal dynamics are further enhanced by "Gonna Be Like That" - written for the album and covering all her main vocal expressions and tics in one song – and by her inclusion of a precise and tinny whistling sound she achieved by sucking ice during the recording sessions. The presence of work as varied as "Downtown," "Chim Chim Cher-ee" and "Let's Hang On" ensure that no style or specific sound reduces the collection to monotony and complete kitsch classic status is assured.

Elva Miller died in 1997, having lived long enough to see her original collection of five albums released in the 1960s, gaining (ironic) appreciation as the CD reissues began to appear.

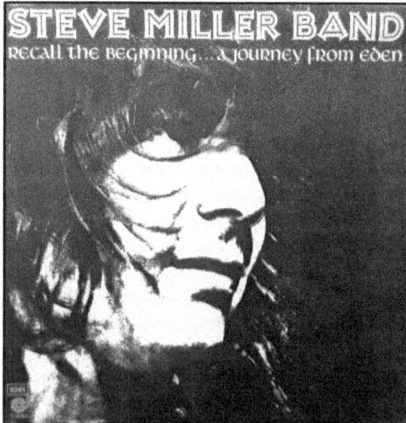

The Steve Miller Band: Recall the Beginning…A Journey From Eden
(Capitol, 1972)
What? The undeserving runt of a glittering litter.

S'cuse the indulgence here but…when one of those behind this book (Neil) wrote a Rough Guide to Rock entry on The Steve Miller Band he made the point that if every big-selling act beloved of the AOR market poured the same amount of craft and passion into their music as Steve Miller, the whole world would be a better place. That opinion still stands.

Miller's major selling hits – "The Joker," "Abracadabra" etc. – and massive albums like Fly Like an Eagle (1975) put him amongst the most impressive performers of his generation. His work rate in the early career years of late sixties to early seventies was up there with the most driven of acts, like ZZ Top, and his ability to craft cutting edge music from the basic blues/jazz/rock ingredients meant he could pull an audience from older and younger listeners; and always get played somewhere on radio.

Six albums in little more than two years produced against a suicidal schedule of live dates saw The Steve Miller Band deservedly build a reputation. Children of the Future (1968) and Sailor (1968) established a band who played stunningly, wrote from a number of different musical styles and frequently nailed the disparate sounds on albums that repaid close listening. Under the relentless workload the talent – notably Boz Scaggs and Ben Sidran – either jumped ship for a solo career, or simply jumped ship. Diminishing returns critically and commercially gradually set in and with Recall the Beginning… Miller faced his seventh Capitol album in less than five years in a totally different place to his first masterpiece.

What's wrong with Recall the Beginning… (which peaked at #109 on the US Billboard charts and bothered no other lists around the world) is easily explained. By this point Miller was close to jumping ship (label wise) and wasn't up for massively promoting this set on stage. So, it is way more complicated than the rocking and psych-laced efforts that preceded it. Recall the Beginning… is also an explosion of great playing and varied styles delivered by Miller and a "Steve Miller Band" that existed only in name. This was a studio-bound crew crafting a piece of work to perfection. Nobody expected to tour the resulting album. For all the portentous lyrical asides and excursions into prog keyboards or evocations of a concept album Recall the Beginning… appears to have little consistent intention beyond making an incredible showcase for the assembled talents.

In this vein it visits soul and funk in the opening instrumental fragment "Welcome" and the soulful stomper "Heal Your Heart" which could have easily come from one of his first albums. Recall the Beginning… is forward looking too. Side one's closer; "Somebody Somewhere Help Me" foreshadows the kind of muscular white soul that Hall and Oates would hone to massive commercial success a few years later. The two sides of original vinyl showcase two different styles. The first a solid band workout across different styles but all made of music that sounds like Steve Miller from his opening half dozen albums. The second a lusher and more conceptual sequence in keeping with the cosmic folk rock vibe of the early seventies. The four cuts on side two make up the real tour-de-force here: "Love's Riddle" layers strings around Miller's acoustic guitar and records his vocals as a near-whisper, in close to the mic. "Fandango" continues the mood before scattering into a bigger sound as the band all play strongly before two epic tracks combine the styles just heard. "Nothing Lasts" starts on fingerpicked guitar but gradually builds with the use of strings as Miller sings a duet with himself. "Journey From Eden" is the one track here compiled onto best ofs from the period. It subsequently appeared on Miller's three CD career retrospective. A mystic reverie of communing with nature and grieving Man's destruction of the environment, the song presents Miller's dream as a ray of hope for humankind with a simple ringing acoustic guitar motif to give emphasis and slowly chugging bass to push the song forward.

Because it journeys everywhere from cosmic folk to doo-wap Recall the Beginning… is not an easy listen end-to-end. It lacks the familiar hit to locate it in time, and swims uncomfortably between Miller's explosive first brace of albums and the cosmic AOR that would turn the likes of Fly Like an Eagle and Book of Dreams (1977) into multi-platinum sellers. But this generally unloved, moderately successful and seldom radio-played album packs enough of Miller's best to deserve more recognition.

Kylie Minogue:
Impossible Princess/Kylie Minogue
(Deconstruction/Mushroom, 1997)
What? Fullest flowering of indie identity from celebrated popette.

An attempt, apparently, by Mingoue at: "unleashing the core of myself and being totally truthful in my music." Impossible Princess resulted from an intense period of writing down ideas and lyrics, before Brothers in Rhythm, a house music duo comprising Steve Anderson and Dave Seaman, were taken on board as the main producers of a new album.

Impossible Princess marked the second and final flowering of Indie Kylie on the Deconstruction label. Ms Minogue's career had begun its worst period of commercial slippage, and Kylie herself had hung around with enough arty and alternative people to develop a sense of self-discovery and re-appraisal of her past. Add to this the ill health afflicting Deconstruction's head of A&R, Pete Hadfield, which kept him away from the sessions, and you have an unlikely bunch left to their own devices, working in unfamiliar ways (Kylie wrote almost all her own lyrics and sought to avoid the kind of trite couplets she'd previously managed to contribute to some songs), and all taking their reality checks from each other.

Impossible Princess, (re-named Kylie Minogue for some releases in deference to any apparent link to the recent death of Princess Diana), marked a commercial low point for Minogue. The death of Diana led to a hasty rescheduling of the original release which placed the album (pushed back to 1 November release) in a crowded Christmas market. The lead single, "Some Kind of Bliss," stalled at #22 in the UK charts. Critically, the album drew varied reviews, gaining mainly praise in the US, mainly scathing put-downs in the UK, and mixed reviews elsewhere. Australia bought it in huge quantities, America – where Minogue meant little – bought a few and her main market in the UK placed the album at #10 (six places lower than its predecessor).

Retrospectively Impossible Princess has the good and bad points you'd expect of any pop idol suddenly given freedom. It visits an array of styles, drags in credible collaboration (James Dean Bradfield of the Manics co-wrote "Some Kind of Bliss") and wears its identity crisis, literally, on its sleeve (the 3D cover allowed Kylie to move and represent the different elements of herself). The opening "Too Far" includes the thought "what I'd give for a deep breath inside, where the chaos has me captive." The closing "Dreams" performs an epic sweep of different pop styles inside four minutes and most of the album involves Kylie exploring her fractious relationship with past deeds and her own fame. It sounds nothing like David Cassidy's infamous concept piece The Higher They Climb, The Harder They Fall, but Impossible Princess is most certainly a similar fearlessly overachieving, rootless, potpourri of fleeting brilliance and car crash fascination. It's notable, probably, that both of the mentioned albums were made by giving creative control to actor/pop stars who had outgrown their teen audiences. Significant too, probably, because, like Cassidy before her, Ms Minogue fronts the whole thing with a sense of drama and gravitas, giving just enough torture to the vocals when we hit deeply personal territory.

The self-discovery rhetoric dried up pretty damn quick after EMI gave her a contract, a big pop sound and chart topping records in UK again. So, how much Impossible Princess marks a high watermark in expressing the inner Kylie remains a debateable point. She sure as hell looked convincing, scrubbed up in various guises for the attendant singles and even openly mocked her past in the "Did it Again" video. The shoot for the packaging photographs involved mild torture of poor Kylie, but she fronted that pretty well too. Then again, a cynical view might suggest it was all part of the act at the time and there were probably moments on the set of Neighbours when she genuinely believed she was a good car mechanic. One other curious point so many years later is the extent to which Impossible Princess conceived and recorded before the sessions for Madonna's monster Ray of Light had begun, resembles that album. The pair don't exactly map out the same territory, but the range of styles, dance/indie/pop collision in the production and sense of introspection channelled through the highs and lows of the music does give them a nodding acquaintance.

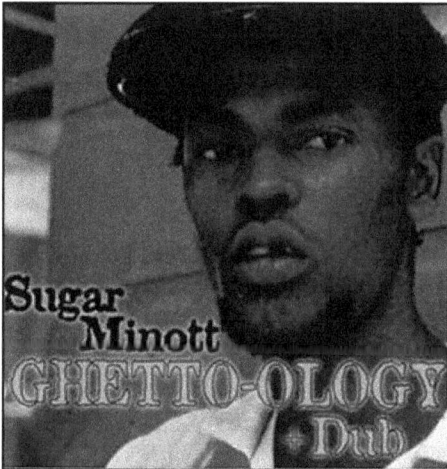

Sugar Minott:
Ghetto-ology
(Trojan, 1979)
What? A revolution of lovers.

Lincoln Barrington "Sugar" Minott is best remembered for a series of lovers rock hits in the 80s. On his death in 2010 the charting of tunes like "Good Thing Going" and his long-lasting UK popularity were the main focus of the obituaries that followed. This gentle but gritty little gem had fallen a long way off the radar by 2010. Although the album – Sugar's first self-produced set – pre-dates his UK chart career by little more than a year it exists in a different area politically. It also inhabits territory seldom trawled by most reggae artists, then or now. Technically speaking the production and instrumentation, along with the bonus on the current CD reissue of the entire album in dub form, puts this collection squarely in the Roots Reggae genre. But Sugar's light voice and the gentle rhythms and melodies look ahead to the successful lovers rock period to come. With no sense of any intended pun, the packing of a harsh political message in this soft approach sugars a fairly bitter pill and makes Ghetto-ology a strange record in the reggae canon.

Apart from the hopeful evangelical Rasta messages in songs like "Dreader than Dread" and "Never Gonna Give Jah Up" Ghetto-ology is a bleak protest record that takes few prisoners. "Africa is the Black Man's Home" is as uncompromising as it appears and the opening trio of "Man Hungry," "The People Got to Know" and "Walking Through the Ghetto" set up the whole message of poverty, politicisation and the need for change. All come with gentle refrains and the sense that if change isn't coming quickly, then Sugar – along with many others – has the strength and patience to wait it out. The title track, located halfway through the second side of the original vinyl release, wraps the whole collection up in a new philosophy and a sense that understanding the ways of the ghetto is complex but important work.

The rhythms seldom stride above a slow walking pace and Sugar's gentle vocals frequently stretch out the syllables to lay a simple and insistent melody over the bass and drums, making Ghetto-ology a strange presence amongst a slew of more strident reggae albums packing blatant songs of protest. It remains as angry as the punk releases that appeared at the same time, and as gentle as the lovers rock that would eventually give Sugar the respect and acclaim this collection should have earned.

Miranda Sex Garden:
Madra
(Mute, 1991)
What? If The Supremes had performed for James 1st?

There is no easy way to do justice to the bizarre career arc of Miranda Sex Garden (1990 – 2003) other than to point out that only one of the original trio (Katherine Blake) who performed on this album stayed the course to Carnival of Souls (2003). And, in that 13 year period the band went from a debut album covering original madrigals dating back to the sixteenth century to industrial, darkwave, ethereal and a wilfully dark and sexual blend of indie and alternative. To cover that in four albums and two EPs is to place yourself permanently in the midst of a terminal identity crisis. Should the definitive best of album ever emerge it is likely to sound like a sampler for an indie label keen to promote female artists.

So, let's talk madrigals. Madra is exactly what it claims to be: three young English female singers (Blake with Kelly McCusker and Joycelyn West) singing unaccompanied and presenting 25 beautifully enunciated and sparingly produced vocal performances culled mainly from material originally published in the seventeenth century. Music originally performed in royal residences and the homes of the landed gentry is here re-imagined for a 20th century audience with a reassuringly dark and aloof cover shot of the three with handwritten graphics in dark red. The only sonic nods to the gothic/indie market who were clearly part of the target audience is a willingness to blend the harmonies within the production in a manner befitting a modern record, and some brazen booting of the mix between channels on cuts like "Though Sweet Delightful Ladies" to give a sense of movement to the performance. On occasion the girls can't help themselves and almost let the odd consonant slip. All of which is a minor deviation from what they do for most of the duration. Stand upright, sing the madrigals as butter-wouldn't-melt young maidens should, and bring some sense of soul to music so old as to be virtually absent from any "popular" post-war tradition.

Taken on its own merits this is a true curio that keeps a straight face and keeps the quality level high. Taken in the context of a career that ended with dark gothic rock in the shape of Carnival of Souls this is a benchmark of a beginning for one of Britain's most wilfully opaque bands.

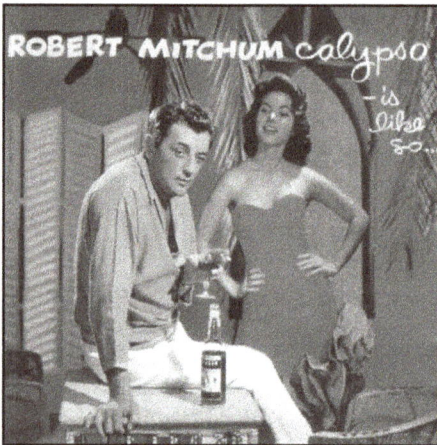

Robert Mitchum:
Calypso Is Like So
(Capital, 1957)
What? Celebrity tightrope walk safely straddles sublime and ridiculous.

The tonnage of execrable celebrity aural abominations over the years has blurred the fact that a few genuine gems of exotic charm, musical merit and/or excellent execution exist; many of them finding a slow but steady uptake of new fans. One of the foremost triumphs in this regard is – by common consent – Mitchum's calypso caper. The many and varied favourable reviews posted over the years tend to agree on the "charm" of the collection. Put simply, Calypso - Is Like So pulls its strongest winning trick because at no point does it take itself seriously. It's a flavourful and rollicking collection, fronted by Mitchum's – ahem – wandering accent, so cod-West Indian it's more tribute than travesty. Lyrically, there are tales of light philosophy ("Beauty is Only Skin-Deep"), augmented with cautionary tales and some local colour ("Coconut Water"). Musically, Mitchum's crew manage the same robust backing of steel drums and other local instruments that fuelled the first international calypso sounds by the likes of Mighty Sparrow. Mitchum may have been lucky to get in ahead of a generation of West Indian acts who played it dirty and authentic, but the lingering charm and popularity of his collection is also rooted in some inspired work and true musical merit.

The general absence of prominent guitar leads, ignored here in favour of brief banjo flurries, is positively forward thinking. So is the sense that this was rehearsed and recorded in enough of a rush to nail the feeling and avoid diluting the whole work with a pristine production. It isn't exactly low-fi, but Calypso - Is Like So does have the same warmth/ramshackle quality of early rockabilly. Indeed, the album's CD reissues generally come with the bonus of a couple of rockabilly cuts –veritable sore thumbs in their calypso company – that show Mitchum acquitting himself equally well in an American style. If the superficial observations of "Dance All Night" (basically middle-America's dropped jaw faced with the spectacle of a Caribbean carnival) have dated badly, the album more than compensates with the sense that very few celebrity novelties – with the notable exception of William Shatner and his ilk – have held their creative vision so well over the length of an entire album.

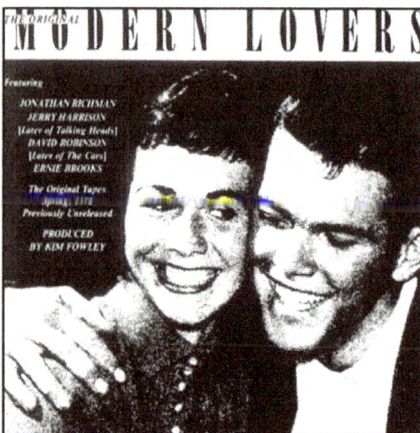

The Modern Lovers:
The Original Modern Lovers
(Bomp International, 1981)
What? A statement of pure rock 'n' roll in the teeth of pomp and introspection.

The Modern Lovers' career and that of their founder Jonathan Richman remains out of step with almost every prevailing trend at any given time. Separating Richman and the band is also difficult, and making sense of when this album was recorded has taxed producer Kim Fowley and Richman to the point of conflicting accounts appearing on the back cover. So, we'll establish what clarity we can and then consider why this particular Modern Lovers' album appears in this book.

Richman was always a singular visionary with a love of The Velvet Underground and Lothar and the Hand People. So his presence in Boston in the early seventies pushing a basic and scratchy brand of rock 'n' roll when James Taylor was the height of cool, progressive rock the height of ambition and Aerosmith the most-tipped local contenders, was always an act of optimism over reason. The band Richman eventually assembled included future Cars' drummer Dave Robinson and future Talking Heads' keyboardist Jerry Harrison. This line-up were the most like a proper band and the least like accompanyists to Richman ever assembled under The Modern Lovers' moniker. They would eventually produce The Modern Lovers album; a proto-punk masterpiece, referencing the Velvets, distilling garage band spirit to perfection and earning a ten star review from the British music paper Sounds (when the paper's top limit on reviews was five stars). The Modern Lovers is a focussed and pulsating effort, stuck in one room but referencing the entire human condition (assuming you're young). The Original Modern Lovers might best be regarded as the sketchbook for the subsequent master-work. For starters Original contains four of the nine songs that make up The Modern Lovers (including two versions of "Roadrunner"). All are recognisable – although "Girlfren" would later emerge as "Girl Friend" – and all possess the Velvets/garage band sound that would give the official first album such an impact. However, the seeds of Richman's wayward and idiosyncratic take on music are all over The Original Modern Lovers to the point that his subsequent swerves into childish lyrics and ultra low-fi recording make sense once you've heard how he was in 1972 (when at least some of this was recorded). The conflicting accounts on the back cover present this as the first complete Modern Lovers' session from 1972 containing the early versions of material on the first album (Fowley's account), or a ragbag of recordings that overlap with the legendary album and stretch from 1972 to 1973 (Richman's version). Either way, the indulgences and personal touches that were reined in when John Cale helmed their first album are given plenty of space here and it's a bizarre insight into how high-art and visceral rock 'n' roll combined to make this band – briefly – one of the hottest on earth. Both versions of "Roadrunner" romp along, play their two chord riff into a mantra and let Richman's dream-poetry about the simple joys of AM radio (when the big FM sound was already breaking America) work its magic. Nobody, but him (obviously), was saying "hello to the spirit of 1956" in 1972. "Astral Plane" – as Richman's sleeve notes point out – has an "effeminate and laboured" quality. Though this is dwarfed by "Don't Let Our Youth go to Waste" a painfully intimate acapella pean to a girlfriend in which Richman sings: "I could bleed in sympathy with you." It's that feminine side, still given free rein during the recordings of what were – essentially – demos that makes The Original Modern Lovers something of a car crash. At once compelling and yet so painfully intimate as to be uncomfortable. "Dance With Me" is driven by Harrison's strong organ chords and presents Richman as a seasoned traveller, just back from Europe but still desperate for assurance from his girl: "When you dance with me…look at me, and smile." Baring his soul so starkly over the sound of a garage band already demonstrating the power that anticipated punk, Richman captures angst as only the best lyricists can. The Original Modern Lovers is stronger on this quality than anything else he ever did because it lacks the swagger that came with more assured songs like "Pablo Picasso" and "Someone I Care About" on the official first album.

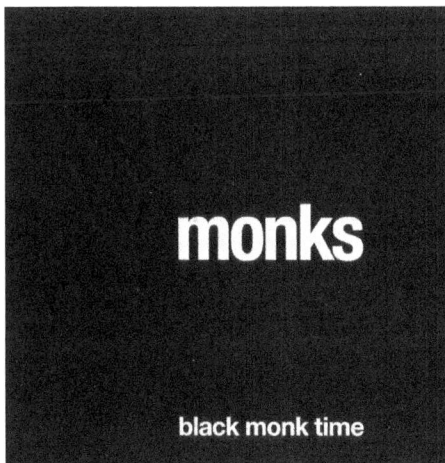

The Monks:
Black Monk Time
(Polydor, 1966)
What? Habits, haircuts and a half-hour hellish punk assault.

The Monks comprised ex-serviceman stationed at American bases in Germany. Their look was the standard habit, and tonsure (i.e. bald on top of the head) look of a monk. Their mid-sixties sound pulled the punk moves that would later be the bedrock of acts like The Stranglers. Julian Cope's Head Heritage site put it perfectly, the band and album were: "a gem born of isolation and the horrible deep-down knowledge that no-one is really listening to what your [sic] saying...as American rockers in a country that was desperate for the real thing. They wrote songs that would have been horribly mutilated by arrangers and producers had they been back in America. But there was no need for them to clean up their act, as the Beatles and others had had to do on returning home, for there were no artistic constraints in a country that liked the sound of beat music but had no idea about its lyric content."

Lyrically Black Monk Time is an angry and personal record. The opening "Monk Time" starts with; "Alright, my name's Gary, let's go...we don't like the army, what army? Who cares what army? Why do you kill all those kids over there in Vietnam?" Gary lost his brother in Vietnam, but the real point of the opening track is to get everyone onside. Within two minutes and 42 seconds "we're all Monks..." Elsewhere the levels of literacy required to get the meanings of the songs aren't that tough to master. The fleeting piece of glorious loud nonsense that is "Blast Off" simply counts down from ten to one and finishes with "Blast Off" and another in-your-face wonder "Complication" is there and gone in two minutes and 21 seconds, its 31 word lyric offering up the title four times, the word "constipation" once and a few other observations on mindless and moronic behaviour.

Musically this is punk, more shameless about its most moronic moments than many of the punks who would follow a decade later, and genuinely bitter and angry. What vocalist Gary Burger lacks in pyrotechnics he makes up in passion, and for the most part he is on a mission to unleash his anger. How many of the few subtleties in the lyrics communicated themselves to German audiences is debatable. But, the rapid tunes, fuzzed riffs and driving power of a sound packing both organ and electric banjo do have an immediacy that force themselves into your consciousness years after they were recorded. It's low-fi, but not hopelessly so. Early Stranglers or the rapid-fire live Doors playing "Break on Through" are good reference points, but – in the end – Black Monk Time is very much its own vision. Nihilistic, unrepentant, un-pretty and raw to the bone.

The Monkees:
Head
(RCA, 1968)
What? The audio equivalent of a few missing digits on the hand that had hitherto fed the "Prefab Four."

The Monkees' television show had been cancelled and the band's commercial fortunes were crashing and burning in the great tradition of pile them high-sell them quick pop sounds. But, The Monkees achieved the perfect kiss-off, artistically at least. The original quartet were all – just – on board, although Peter Tork would soon become the first to depart, meaning the remaining contract filling releases would see gradually depleting ranks before Davy and Micky, (still trading as The Monkees), closed the account with some forgettable sounds. Head, by contrast, continues to be celebrated because the sounds contained herein are – at their best – unforgettable, and The Monkees achieve something nobody considered possible when the band were hired. This is a proper group album, showcasing four disparate talents, taking genuine artistic risks, and frequently achieving its aims.

Considering that two of the four were hired from an acting background, and neither of the musicians (Mike and Peter), arrived with significant commercial or artistic success, Head is something of a fiery finale. Ostensibly the soundtrack to the surreal movie of the same name, Head still works without the visuals, largely because the production is inventive enough to give a vivid and visionary quality to some good songs.

The band apply a certain intelligence. Micky's major contribution – "The Porpoise Song" – is a Carole King/ Gerry Goffin tune given a Beach Boys' sound expansion and trippy vocal echo in The Monkees' own production. But this album features none of the sweet and reliable Boyce and Hart pop gems that formed the backbone of early Monkees' albums, and despite bringing in the odd song – Carole King and Toni Stern's "As we go Along" also appears and some of the sound mash filler tracks are credited outside the band – the real joy here is hearing the band step-up and deliver psychedelic pop to rank with the best contemporary efforts like The Notorious Byrd Brothers or The Turtles Present the Battle of the Bands.

Every Monkee gets his moments and it is unfair to single one out as a star when the clear intention is to show a band at work, proving themselves in the wake of a manufactured career. But…the real surprise package here is Peter Tork. His writing contributions had hitherto been less frequent and generally less critically favoured than those of Mike Nesmith. But, "Can You Dig it" and "Long Title: Do I Have to do This All Over Again" are absolute winners in a meaningful psychedelic-pop style, "Do I have to do This…" rocks out to some effect and both are thoughtfully positioned towards the end of the original sides on vinyl, where they segue ably into knockabout spoken word nonsense and snatches of music from the Head movie. Peter departed on this form and joined a band called Release who could have taken this sound forward but (ironically) released nothing. Elsewhere on Head: Mike's "Circle Sky" rips into your eardrums with more visceral attack than The Monkees were ever designed to display, and a battle is won.

Head's obvious weaknesses have dissolved with time. The manufactured career of The Monkees seems less of an issue in the current age (so the self-conscious moment in which the band savage their own image with a vocal parody of their original theme song seems less barbed and more fun today), so too the overall willingness to drop in sound effects, random musical interludes and the like. If anything, this sense of the songs emerging from every other scattered noise available helps Head to sound more modern and more complete than the wall-to-wall pop albums that marked the early Monkees' career, and topped charts around the world.

Hugo Montenegro: Bongos and Brass (Time, 1960)

What? Bizarre jazz exotica, epic soundtracks, beatnik percussion and a slew of sounds from crime movies.

Montenegro (1925–1981) has at least a footnote in musical history as a celebrated composer of film soundtracks. The Good, The Bad And The Ugly probably being his best known achievement. Cult appreciation attends this 1960 concoction that clearly made sense to Time Records, who bankrolled the whole affair. Amongst the champions of Bongos and Brass are Poison Ivy Rosarch and Lux Interior of The Cramps, who extol its unique charms in their chapter of Incredibly Strange Music Volume I and Björn Werkmann, host of the highly recommended ambientexotica.com, (a one-stop repository for information on the biggest wake up calls in easy listening). Björn notes: "The bongo craze and Hugo Montenegro never clicked together, making this album one of a kind in his discography." A fair point. But neither Björn Werkmann or this entry is insulting this strange collection. Far from it, the lack of Montenegro clicking with the bongo craze is the key to a series of standards and unlikely inclusions that make this one of the strangest slices of easy listening ever unleashed. Basically, this is a three way battle between a composer/arranger with epic intentions, the slapping and scraping sounds of a brief craze and musical material better suited to neither of the first two. The core of the album is comprised of a series of jazzy standards better suited to their original role in films or big band albums. "Slaughter On Tenth Avenue," is here along with brass heavy takes on Duke Ellington's "Take the 'A' Train" and Count Basie's "One O' Clock Jump." The Ellington cut opens the second side in a strangely subdued mood, reining in the brass and setting up prominent piano chords before dropping the bongos right in the middle of the mix. However, for sheer overreaching – the hell with it – ambition nothing here tops the opening "Hall of the Mountain King." We're talking Edvarg Grieg's classical masterpiece, here reimagined with a timpani rumbling away and rousing the crowd whilst the steady slapping of the bongos battles with rapier like bursts of brass. Just when things can't get crazier (Man!) the wild card arrives. As Björn Werkmann says: "sudden shifts into red-tinted Latin timbres round this wild ride off, making this tune the signature track of the LP." Another fair point. Bongos and Brass was reissued under the moniker of Montengro and Mayhem. An obvious attempt at belated sales on the back of Montenegro's name, long after the "bongo craze" had gone terminally cold. The retitle is fair summary of the album long collisions of the strange. This far after the event it sounds less like a fashionable cash in and more like a few people thrown together, totally unwilling to do something for the sake of fashion, and clubbing together to let their collective imaginations run wild. The production sounds dated but it's to the credit of everyone involved here that they used what audio trickery they had to conceive this whole piece as a series of separate sounds battling for control. The sudden swerves into sonic side streets (like dragging Grieg into "red-tinted Latin timbres") are what makes this album. Along with the way the various instruments are frequently set up to oppose and fight each other as the – fairly lengthy – cuts flow by.

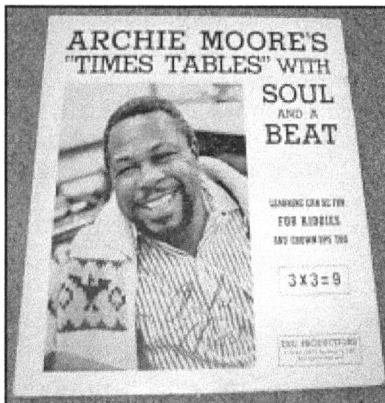

Archie Moore:
Times Table with Soul and a Beat
(ERU Productions, 1964)
What? Maths hits home, with soul.

Archie Moore's achievements in the boxing ring put him amongst the very best of all time. A reigning world champion (Light Heavyweight) for almost nine and a half years and a fighter who stepped above his weight twice to challenge creditably for the Heavyweight title, Moore boxed for over thirty years, winning over 130 bouts, a record in professional history. Whether this 28 minute attempt to educate youngsters into the ways of correct counting and calculation enhances the legend is less clear. The opening announcement describes Moore as – amongst other things – a "movie actor, humanitarian and politician" and suggests he helmed the album because most such recordings are "saturated with sameness and boredom." Further claiming "Archie has substituted these for soul and a beat."

Moore then appears to incredible applause (canned) and makes a short announcement before the main business starts. The announcer returns and talks us through the times tables with occasional clunky editing, and lots of music. Archie has already left the building, never to return. But the licks come thick and fast. Despite the editing clunkers there are fleeting passages of great guitar, a few familiar, and semi-familiar riffs (notably a strong steal of Bo Diddley's "I'm A Man") and a great deal of stuff that sounds like the outtakes from a Booker T and the M.G.s session, all of it quite listenable. A lot of it still listenable despite the endless intoning of "eight times eight is…"

Archie Moore's journey from teenage tearaway to feted figure intent on giving something back to his country and the black community makes Times Table… a worthy attempt to do good. This far down the historic line its relevance may have waned a little, but it remains a strange audio work, mixtape gold of the highest order and one of those thrift store (because this is aimed squarely at the US market) gems that keeps cropping up as a readily available mp3 on line. Reissue chances on CD remain negligible, in the opinion of the present authors.

John Moran:
The Manson Family: An Opera
(Point Music, 1992)
What? The mind of a mass-killer, pumped through your headphones.

"Hippie Cult Leader" Charles Manson is about as cool as mass killers get and his footnote in rock history is assured given Guns 'n' Roses cover of his work on their Spaghetti Incident album, the legend of his abortive attempts to become a Monkee and his own array of unofficially released recordings (one of which is covered elsewhere in this book). Of his erstwhile rocker compadres few have gone public with praise or attempted to prolong his legend in song, though Neil Young's "Revolution Blues" deserves some credit for exploring the nightmare visions of Charlie's mind. John Moran's master-work, on the other hand, pulls no punches and engages the whole insane world around Manson with a prolonged vengeance and a set of deft musical moves that bring the insanity to life. Conceived as an "opera" this is a work so rich in sampled sounds and studio trickery that its true performing arena is on disc, and into both your ears via good quality headphones. The lyrics are used sparingly, but with chilling effect. Over the 17 tracks and three acts a combination of vocal performances and musical styles paints the Manson story from murder, via the madness of life in Manson's "family," to the courtroom and his conviction. Central to the chilling insight into insanity is Moran's own performance as the mad/rapping/rambling/frenetic Manson, from the barely discernable logic of raps on womanhood to the cleverly lifted Mansonesque guitar licks on track 9 "Charles Manson (at Spahn's Movie Ranch)" Charlie is in the room, and it isn't easy listening. Elsewhere Iggy Pop brings an edgy growling gravitas to the role of Jack Lord "the Prosecutor" and the various nods to the influence of The Beatles music on Manson's mental state, stay just the right side of blatant lifting of the Fab Four's classic late sixties work.

It's demanding, maybe too demanding for one album, but the lyric sheet with the album contains all the spoken passages, and that helps the listener find a way in. The Manson Family is truly old-school in its demand that you dim the lights, slap on the headphones, take the lyrics in hand and do nothing else but LISTEN. In that regard it repays your attention by driving cars through your head, quite literally coming at you from a number of angles vocally, and packing in so many minute details (a lifted Manson lick here, hippie bongos there, subtle changes in vocal production to indicate someone has just been bundled into a car boot) that it doesn't sound exactly the same each time you hear it. The hairs might stand up on your neck for all the wrong reasons, but for a sense of the madness that continues to make Manson a compelling figure this recording probably beats any number of the fawning websites that have developed over the years.

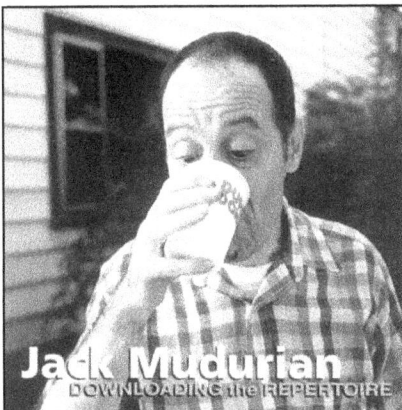

Jack Mudurian:
Downloading the Repertoire
(Arf Arf , 1996)
What? Pensioner points at traffic. Oh look; he's made an album!

An all time outsider music classic. The gist of this weird wonder is that Jack Mudurian – a Bostonian pensioner in the early eighties – said he knew, "as many songs as Sinatra." Jack would perform his songs in nursing home's talent shows and an employee, Dave Greenberger, challenged Jack to deliver on his claim to know so many songs. The resulting showdown took place on the back porch of Mudurian's home on a hot June afternoon. Greenberger brought basic recording equipment and the 47 minute, one-take, stunner of Downloading the Repertoire was the result. The low-fi quality and the presence of natural noises, like clearly audible birdsong, simply adds to the ramshackle glory of the performance. Mudurian matches his claim, in his own inimitable fashion. He certainly packs a set-list to rival Ol' Blue Eyes, but the unique and unpredictable twist on this album revolves around Mudurian's very singular performing style. The oldster delivers well over 100 songs, almost all of them reduced to fleeting snatches. He opens with "Chicago" stops dead after a few seconds to surge into "It's Been a Long Long Time" and proceeds to stumble unaccompanied through a slew of show-tunes, film soundtrack favourites and easy listening standards in his flat but well-modulated monotone. We don't get songs, we do get a few seconds of an introduction here, a snatch of the chorus from another tune there and sometimes a favourite couplet from a verse. At times it's an intimate and touching insight into an old man's fond memories of a bygone era when melody and clear diction counted for everything. At other times the sampled snatches of song come so quickly the whole endeavour stumbles straight into loony on the bus territory, especially when Mudurian's memory fails him to the point he repeats songs performed earlier in the set. For all this, the human jukebox certainly packs them in. And, the incomparable listening experience offers up some stone-gone classics including: "It's Only a Paper Moon," "My Bonnie," "I Wonder Who's Kissing Her Now?" "If You Knew Susie (Like I Know Susie)," "Over the Rainbow" and "When You Wish upon a Star."

The June recording date doesn't stop old Jack jumping into "Jingle Bells" and "Rudolph the Red Nosed Reindeer." Mudurian's master-work eventually secured a release on the aptly named Arf Arf Records, a home to several notable nut-job performers and very unique talents.

Os Mutantes:
A Divina Comedia Ou Ando Meio Desligado
(Polydor, 1970)
What? Blistering, genre-busting, brilliance from Brazil.

Difficult third albums come little easier than this purposeful plethora of confident cosmic rock. For those unfamiliar with languages outside English Os Mutantes are, literally, "The Mutants," and the album's title translates as: The Divine Comedy or I Am a Bit Disconnected. The absence of a question mark suggests Os Mutantes already know the answer. The collision of high-concept and playful pun in the title is a good entry point into the first album by the band to make a serious stab at psychedelic rock. The eighth track - "Chão de Estrelas" – is a Brazilian style ballad played (mainly) for laughs, elsewhere the album takes on life, the universe and everything and does its level best to combine some reference to Dante's vision with drug culture and musical dexterity. The band still work very much to their own agenda but Divina Comedia has one ear on the majestic and complex efforts of everyone from The Moody Blues to ELP. A move less about imitating the British masters and more about gauging the scale of what is possible over two sides of vinyl. On the other hand, the riff heavy opening of the album on "Ando meio desligado" soon gives way to psychedelia, a superbly rendered doo-wop segment in "Hey Boy" and a series of similarly fearless sprints into musical outposts. The perpetual identity crisis and burgeoning numbers of band personnel do make late sixties Mothers of Invention another obvious yardstick. It's the Mothers, rather than European psych rock, who are evoked with a jazzy ballad (complete with superbly controlled guitar solo) "Meu refrigerador Não Funciona." Apart from anything else, simply getting that worked up, and that eloquent musically, over a defective fridge is firmly in the tradition of Frank Zappa.

Like a few great psych cult albums, and some of the best audio comedy of the period from the likes of The Firesign Theatre, Divina Comedia is a gargantuan listen. It is not easily digested at one go and shot full of fragmentary moments of brilliance in any number of directions. "Preciso Urgentemente Encontrar Um Amigo" follows the doo wop excursion and brings in brilliant harmonies between Arnaldo Baptista and Rita Lee (who soars vocally through her turns on this album). Time and again you get the feeling Divina Comedia has been planned to tease out the complementary elements between tracks, like the very different but equally stunning vocals on "Hey Boy" and "Preciso Urgentemente Encontrar Um Amigo" and whilst you're listening to these subtleties there's always the black and white front/colour back dynamics of the packaging with all its visual references.

The album – too – uses light and shade to cultivate depth and detail. The third track, "Ave Lucifer," and penultimate track, "Haleluia" (an excursion into Electric Prune land with a funereal organ under-scoring the gentle intoning of the song's title), are both minimal and meditative stops on an overwhelming journey.

One label (prog, psych, jazz rock) isn't enough for Os Mutantes (who reformed in the 21st century) and, like their contemporaries The Mothers of Invention, they permanently pack the ability to celebrate and satirise in the same breath. Similarly, it's hard to say who their descendants are. The most insanely over-reaching moments of The Flaming Lips are – probably – as good a modern equivalent as any. But, Os Mutantes are rightly celebrated for being truly unique in an era when everyone claimed to be so. And, Divina Comedia ranks with their very best work.

National Lampoon: Radio Dinner
(Banana, 1972)
What? Seminal rock-comedy and the roots of Spinal Tap.

The National Lampoon now stands as a complex comedy brand, having evolved with its audience and with a close eye on the profits available from hit movies. In 1972 the troupe of young American comedy talent had their ears firmly fixed on the increasingly pompous outpourings of their rock-star contemporaries. This prompted a fistful of albums ravaging the rock elite and throwing in some political and popular cultural broadsides. A chief instigator in these activities, and the stand-out star on this collection, Christopher Guest, went on to hone this talent to perfection as one third of Spinal Tap.

Radio Dinner is a period piece from a time when drug culture was still an exciting new development and rock stars speaking out on social issues and raising money was still something of a novelty. So some of the comedy here – especially the savaging of George Harrison's concert for Bangla Desh and the material on Richard Nixon – only works if your knowledge of the time is exceptional. Political correctness has also changed the perception of some of Radio Dinner. It is debateable how many comedians today would risk the satire of the two Bangla Deshi comedians near the end of side two, let alone their "blue cholera…white cholera" gag. But, elsewhere Radio Dinner is chillingly good and still pertinent. It works partly because the targets are the big hitters and these targets have gone on to legend. "Magical Misery Tour" – basically an overblown send-up of Lennon's Plastic Ono Band period unburdening of himself - is amongst the best rock satires anyplace, anytime. With its cries of "genius is pain" and sideswipes at obsessive Beatle fans it hasn't dated badly. The spoof advert in which Bob Dylan (Christopher Guest) does a promotion for a Golden Protest compilation album pre-dates the record industry packaging the very same thing in the same way, and also predicts with uncanny accuracy the radio persona Bob would adopt in his Theme Time Radio Hour. The savaging of Joan Baez in full protest-mode with her refrain:

"pull the triggers niggers, we're with you all the way, just across the bay" is also spot-on and prescient in predicting the physical distance between some major rock stars and the struggles they support (though it's certainly a bit harsh on Ms Baez, who has been an honourable exception in that department).

As with other comedy records in this book – The Firesign Theatre and The Fugs – the above words come with a health warning. To describe and evaluate this stuff in print is partly to kill it. Full-on half of Radio Dinner is sidesplittingly funny despite its age. It works because it is played and performed to near-perfection, suggesting a certain amount of affection behind the savaging dished out.

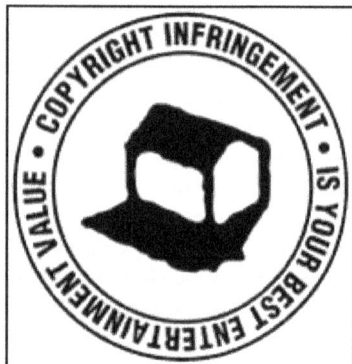

Negativeland:
Advertising Secrets
(Commissioned by New American Radio 1991)
What? Audio construct; informative, funny and mind-bending.

Sound artists as much as a proper band, Negativeland have worked as an audio alternativists since 1979. Releasing music, and a range of other sound recordings they have occasionally found themselves into trouble with some of those satirized, like U2. This clever, vicious and scathingly funny half hour is – as of this writing - available online from sites like ubu.com and features Negativeland doing what they do best. Cutting up, commenting, playing with form and showing themselves both masters of the things attacked, and inverately inventive in their own right.

The narrative/joke here is simple enough. The soundscape throws in a range of audio trickery and production effects to comment on the way advertising works. It uses every standard audio advertising tool in the act of destroying these tools. It employs genuine snippets of advertising in this act of destruction. Like the best satirists, Negativeland manage some act of celebration and make clear some admiration for the skills of the audio advertisers, even when they can't admire their cynical tricks. Advertising Secrets works on a number of levels. It informs, entertains, amuses and surprises. It also has such a tonnage of samples, twists and production trickery that it stands repeated listening. The point with much of the best Negativeland work is to get over a message of some importance, making the listening audience more critical as a result and showcasing innate skills in the art of creating sound collages and alternatives to standard narrative in sound. All of which sounds intellectual, but Negativeland are about the most fun a listener can have in a world sometimes inhabited by self-referential geeks. Though, an affinity with their left-wing and anti-establishment stance is probably important in enjoying their work.

Michael Nesmith:
The Prison
(Pacific Arts, 1974)
What? Novella and album combination = arty and ambitious launch for own arts project.

Described by All Music Guide as: "a quiet revolutionary occurrence" The Prison is a bold attempt to push creative barriers. Conceived as a combination of novella (supplied with the album) and long-playing record; the original edition of The Prison came housed in a presentation box and marked the first release of material from Nesmith's own Pacific Arts operation. Nesmith caused some confusion with live audiences by asking that rather than clap after he had performed the work people would simply leave quietly. But – in truth – the "quiet revolutionary" concept is a fair assessment of a work that has slowly become recognised as a significant achievement. The novella and song sequence are intended to be experienced simultaneously although The Prison is by no means as simple as a musical; wherein the story is supported by songs highlighting moments of narrative importance. It is more a case of songs and novella exploring a complex theme, and the concentration of the listener gradually revealing meditative elements and aspects of meaning. In this context a fragment from the novella gives some indication of the thrust of the narrative: "But there were no walls...anywhere...And yet the people in the prison moved around just as if there were."

Musically The Prison has appeared in different mixes. The original mix for vinyl has never been issued on CD. The mixes rely on a lavishly expanded acoustic guitar sound as the main accompaniment with synthesizer, (programmed) drums and other touches as required. The individual songs flow from one to the other with the fades and intros frequently remaining so indistinct that separating them for a specific purpose – like radio play – is clunky. The use of acoustic guitar across the album allows the chord sequences and guitar accompaniments to morph into one another like movements in a classical piece. The country roots of Nesmith's previous work are clear but the down-the-line country rock of his early seventies work is abandoned here for a sound that uses the different guitar tones as the backbone of a gentler approach, employing slower tempos than his work with the First National Band. Nesmith's perfectly controlled vocal rises and falls as the main melodic focus. All of which allows for the lyrics to be heard clearly, throughout, with the added bonus that all versions of The Prison print the words in full. The longer tracks, like "Dance Between the Raindrops" present the same combination of precise narrative and deeper meditative thought as the novella: "'Dance between the raindrops' where the last words that he said….But there is no way in, To where you already are, There is no way out, Of everywhere."

The Prison is a multimedia concept piece from an analogue and hard copy world. A world in which interactive approaches were generally, by definition, for works on the commercial margins. The first stirrings of the internet were still a decade away. Nesmith went on to play a major role in the development of pop video and dedicated television channels for videos and other creative ideas breaking the barriers between art forms. His songs have continued to explore the concept of living through a personal interpretation of your own experience, and in The Garden (1994) he revisited the concept of album and book, producing a strong companion piece to The Prison.

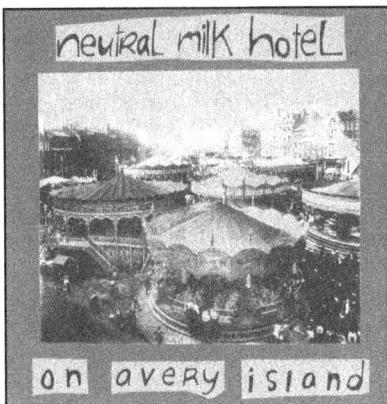

Neutral Milk Hotel:
On Avery Island
(Merge (US)/ Fire (UK), 1996)
What? Dense and definitionless work of depth and insight.

The mid-nineties saw a fair tonnage of bands willing to noodle away years of studio time whilst layered, confusing and sporadically brilliant masterpieces took shape. Neutral Milk Hotel earned respect in this company, shared a label with The Olivia Tremor Control and shared a fan-base with lovers of everything from late sixties dense psych to alternative and noise rock. Their second effort The Aeroplane Over the Sea gained many write ups and much attention, partly because it focussed much of its lyrical content on an exploration of the life and legacy of Anne Frank, and took her story into hitherto undreamt of sonic territory.

Avery Island remains a less revealing and less accessible affair, propelled for the most part by Jeff Mangum's songs and singular vision of using tensions evoked in chord sequences, snatches of lyric and the differing sounds of each track to eke out a sense of his personality and concerns. Avery Island isn't about to tell you what it's about, and – probably – isn't sure in the first place. It sets out to be an experience as much as a set of statements and uses blasts of feedback, layered guitars and sporadic breaks in the tension to take a listener on a journey. It gets as simple and spell-binding as three beautiful repeated acoustic chords on the fourth track: "A Baby for Pree." It gets as dense and ill-defined as the atonal – damn-near-a-quarter-of-an-hour – feedback-ridden noiseathon of "Pree Sisters Swallowing a Donkey's Eye," which closes the proceedings. This finale has some echoes of Lou Reed's unlistenable Metal Machine Music and it's probably deliberate that anyone listening right through to this point is given the user friendly option of jumping off before the noise-assault starts.

Even the most accessible moments betray a sense of self-loathing and confusion. The opening "Song Against Sex" is as opaque as anything here regarding what it really thinks. But, it does give up some dark thoughts: "why should I lay here naked, When it's just so far away from anything we could call love, And any love worth living for?" Grim, angsty, stuff, setting the tone for more lyrical fragments depicting a distance between singer and any reliable source of comfort or security. This dynamic plays out most compellingly in "Gardenhead/Leave me Alone" which welds two songs together, starts with a simplistic chord structure (albeit far from simple sound) and presents stream of consciousness lyrics that suddenly start to resolve themselves into a story of impossible love: "Leave me alone…this isn't the first time…the angels have slipped through our landslide and filled up our garden with snow." There follows a painful kiss off or goodbye to someone once cared about who is now loveable by: "the glory boys at your bedside."

Avery Island is intense, involved, better when repeated time and again, loner-bedroom-music. Much of the Neutral Milk catalogue serves well in this area. It is also a popular item in places where music production is taken seriously and studied. Indeed, on this evidence, Neutral Milk's variations and embellishment on the use of guitars, noise backing and the dramatic dynamic between standard melody and slabs of noise seems inexhaustible

nick nicely:
Psychotropia
(Tenth Planet, 2004)
What? Best moments of British wayward psych-pop genius.

nicely (who typically insists on lower case letters for his name) has all the credentials of a differently abled pop genius. For starters, he was brought up in the most normal of English settings but born in Greenland during a stop-over on a flight. Despite the 2004 release (vinyl only) and subsequent 2005 CD release with bonus tracks this album became instantly sought after because it finally offered up "Hilly Fields (1892)" (nicely's highly regarded and low-selling almost-hit single from 1982) and it's – previously unreleased – follow up "On the Coast."

Dripping psychedelic influences, dense layers of production and enough random attractions in the background to bear repeated listening; Pscyhotropic is an ecstatic vision of pop music as a beautiful dream. It's also a go-to collection for students of music production to explore various rumours that Kate Bush sings backing vocals (no! but the original single was on EMI and Bush is a touch-stone for nicely's take on popular music) and that "Hilly Fields…" features the first genuine scratching outside of hip-hop (true and it is a bizarre effect generated by moving tape reels, not vinyl records).

The striking thing about the entire collection is how well this complex, languid and slowly explosive psychedelic pop masterpiece hangs together. nicely skirted the fringes of music business for years after walking away from his original EMI contract. He finally made his next solo foray during the days of acid house and chilled dance. In retrospect his early recordings were prophetic where this music was concerned. So, the 2004 round up doesn't sound dated, and doesn't betray the twenty years spent recording material for one album. The singles are far and away the standouts, but every snatch of melody, lyric and looped backing sound adds to the belief that this tapestry of sound is pop at its most intense and sublime. Reviews elsewhere have name-checked Barrett era Floyd, and it is also worth considering the first Trashmonk album (presented in this book) as a companionable piece to Psychotropic, but – above all – this is one of those collections that starts by playing to its own rules, and seldom lets up in doing so.

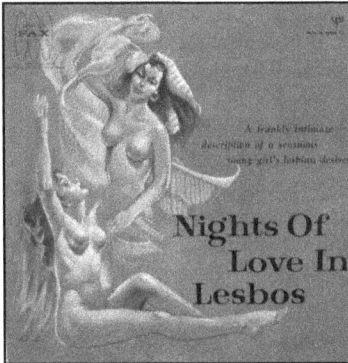

Nights of Love in Lesbos:
Nights of Love in Lesbos
(Fax, 1962)
What? Vintage Erotica.

Two sides of restrained and lightly artful erotica in the presciently named Fax label. This is ancient Greece as imagined with the same American slant that sees the primitive Wild Women of Wongo encounter the Men of Goona bathing and suggest: "Get out and we'll cook you a meal." Nights of Love is a skilfully woven collision between the writing of Pierre Louÿs (who is the inspiration for everything intoned here by our breathless narrator), the legend of Lesbos and an audio production crew intent on providing consistent spot colour with a piano, flute and a few sporadic shakes of a tambourine. "Ilona," narrates two separate stories of lesbian love, bringing a mischievous mirth to her sexual awakening as a lesbian and channelling a little of the spirit of Marilyn Monroe. This is light years from the deep down and dirty sleaze of Fornicating Female Freaks or the celebratory nymphomania of Flexi Sex, and Nights of Love is never better than when it turns the legendary tales of ancient Greece into high-class erotica for middle-American males. It's doubtful of any original lesbian on the Mediterranean isle said she would "douche" her breasts with milk, or referred to her girlfriend carrying "upon her face, the mark of my rounded nipple." Nights of Love was originally one of a series of recordings, but it has out-performed its stable mates by making it to cult/file swap status online and remains fairly easy to track down.

Jack Nitzsche:
St Giles Cripplegate
(Reprise, 1972)
What? Orchestral curio and commercial disaster. This may have been the best thing to happen to Nitzsche.

Nitzsche (1937-2000) carved a monumental career through the music business taking in many stops along the way from surf rock to major film soundtracks, including winning a Golden Globe and an Oscar. For sheer unique-sounding window-to-the-soul singularity he probably never topped St Giles Cripplegate. The origins of the album are simple enough. Having hired The London Symphony Orchestra to provide the backing orchestrations on cuts like "A Man Needs a Maid" from Neil Young's monster-selling Harvest Nitzsche found himself listening to an incredible sound with the orchestral instruments filling the air. On the back of one unused orchestral piece from the Harvest sessions Nitzsche cut a deal with Reprise to produce an entire album with the London Symphony Orchestra. The resulting album takes its name from the London church that housed the recordings and lines up six orchestral works; helpfully titled #1 - #6 and unhelpfully lined up out of sequence (6,4,2,3,1,5), because the numbers refer to the order in which they were recorded.

Long a favourite on radio shows fond of playing the curious and out-there St Giles Cripplegate was almost impossible to track down affordably on vinyl – given its withdrawl once the initial pressing was exhausted. The CD reissue finally appeared in 2006. By common agreement St Giles… often sounds good in fleeting bursts, occasionally sounds great and – over the duration – sounds like a series of chords, ideas and wonderful collisions of orchestral sound and perfect venue-acoustics. In short, it sounds like film music. After the commercial failure of this solo release Nitzshe still snagged the contract to score One Flew Over the Cuckoo's Nest; from which point he never looked back and spent much of his subsequent career looking at images on a screen and composing distinctive and critically acclaimed sounds to accompany them.

On the evidence of this singular selection Nitzsche's talent is for harmonies and striking effects in building and fading melodic ideas. Nitzsche clearly heard possibilities in sound where others heard snatches for main melody lines and had ideas about the subject of songs. Purists have – rightly – pointed out that the orchestra here are strangely slap-dash once or twice such that the performances could clearly have been improved. To others that spontaneous quality adds a little charm. Similar, arguably, to the way Nitzsche's orchestrations work with the loose vibe of the Stray Gators on Harvest. Those moments and Nitzsche's strong in the moment/less sure of the main theme orchestral pieces certainly set St Giles Cripplegate apart as a work that sounds and feels like very little in the classical or rock canons of its time.

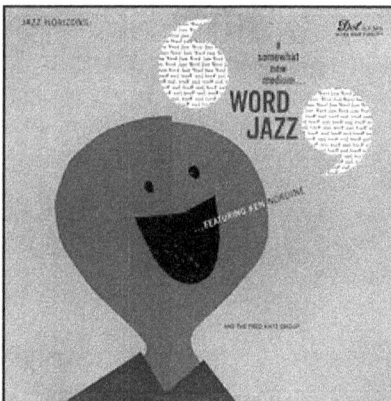

Ken Nordine:
Word Jazz
(Dot, 1957)
What? The beginning of a gloriously strange musical cul-de-sac.

Nordine's most celebrated album is probably Colours (1966) a blissfully strange slice of cod-psychedelic jazz in which his rich baritone raps over modern jazz; introducing and explaining the character (as in the personality) of different shades of colour. Nordine referred to this approach as "word jazz," turned himself into the world's leading exponent of the form, and achieved outsider music immortality; the least he deserves. He was already a highly paid and hugely well recognised voice-over artist when this creative route suggested itself to him and Word Jazz set out the manifesto he followed for decades afterwards. Recruiting the lively, adaptable and sympathetic (as in their playing style is sympathetic to Nordine's unorthodox front-man role), Fred Katz Group as backing musicians, Nordine raps a series of stories and vignettes, varying the contents from surreal to slapstick, and manages to provide the variety and quality to hold the unlikely caper together over the entire album length. Some of the jokes have dated. "The Vidiot" – for example – concerns itself with the imbecilic effect of too much television, and addiction to the form. It may be years ahead of its time, but the reference points have dated now. Not so "My Baby" a touching love story of complete mutual adoration with the punchline that the girl he shares his life with, and takes out to a club is – quite literally – his baby. Nordine ends the story with baby talk and ordering two glasses of warm milk.

Word Jazz feels like an experiment but succeeds so strongly that it – rightly – spawned a series of sequels and took Nordine's career into solid exotica territory. A world in which he remains revered. The fifties production; basically placing Nordine out front and reducing the band to a well-controlled sympathetic backing, also works well long after the event. Nordine's control over his instrument (i.e. that incredibly nuanced baritone speaking voice) is never less than excellent. Nordine went on to cut a marginal but hugely cultish figure working with – amongst others – H.P. Lovecraft (the band, not the author) and Tom Waits (who turned up to share vocal duties on Nordine's Devout Catalyst).

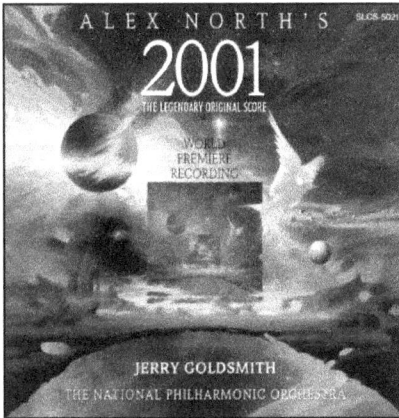

Alex North:
2001 The Legendary Original Score
(Varese Sarabande, 1993)
What? The best movie score that never made it to the screen?

North was originally commissioned to write the score for 2001 A Space Odyssey and the score known and loved around the world was never intended to achieve such legendary status. Initially, MGM studios were adamant the movie should have an original score and Alex North – with a CV that boasted Spartacus – appeared the ideal composer. Film director Stanley Kubrick was using pieces of assembled classical music in the rushes from his film and grew fond enough of some sequences to want his temporary soundracks retained. Alex North was eventually told to stop working on the music but it wasn't until he saw the completed movie that he realised none of his well-developed score had made the final cut.

The story of how the original score was finally given a full orchestral recording is included in an informative booklet along with detailed accounts of the links between North's original and the key scenes in the movie. An entertaining – if ultimately pointless – pastime for some music fans over the years has involved playing Pink Floyd's The Dark Side of the Moon whilst watching the opening minutes of The Wizard of Oz, in the misguided belief that the album is an undeclared soundtrack to the classic movie. A much more fruitful exercise is to take North's original score and play key tracks against their intended movie scenes.

Where the official soundtrack is an assembled work of popular orchestral works, like Also Sprach Zarathustra, and fringe works; like György Ligeti's vocal music, Alex North's take on the same task presents a space odyssey as Tchaikovsky might have heard it. Strident brass chords and the full orchestral sound are summoned throughout. Scenes including the famous moment of the apes eating meat and "Night Terrors" (the paranoid moments amongst the apes) are loud, epic, soundscapes propelled on strong thematic ideas. The docking in space – track 7 on the CD – is the first place where North and the official score appear to be clearly on the same page. Both present a slightly quirky and strangely beautiful take on the movements of vast tonnages of space hardware; but North clearly hears this in line with sixties notions of orchestral harmony. This scene in the final movie uses "The Blue Danube," a decision that was a hit with younger audiences but less successful with older film goers who couldn't divorce the popular waltz from other associations with the tune.

Equipped with Alex North's score there is little chance 2001 A Space Odyssey would have achieved the status it enjoyed with younger film goers; where it became something of a rite of passage to experience the movie whilst in some form of altered state. North draws most of his ideas from European classical music. Filters them through his own experience on epic movies and produces perfectly honed moments of brave, bold and monumental sound to theme a movie he clearly sees as a heroic quest in line with Hollywood's grandest epics. The official soundtrack assembled an array of appropriate music and sold massively on album. Like other soundtracks of its generation – Easy Rider and Zabrinske Point – it drew strength from the variety in the music and the willingness of the listening audience to recall the scenes as they heard the music.

North's music would never have worked that way. His take is more akin to John Williams' immense scoring for cosmic epics like Star Wars and Close Encounters of the Third Kind which would follow a decade later. North's work has a massive sound and big ideas throughout, much more thematic unity than the official soundtrack, and a constant sense of massive revelation and portent under-pinning the action.

Gary Numan:
Pure
(Eagle Rock, 2000)
What? "Cars" man mixes it with darkest-Depeche sounds.

Numan's critical standing took a turn for the better around the turn of the century largely because a tonnage of notable performers – like Trent Reznor – outed themselves as admirers of the man. Numan responded with his darkest and most challenging release. He impressed quite a few, especially in the USA, where his image wasn't hopelessly welded to an eighties electro-pop career. Pure is indeed a lumbering great black beast that doesn't so much assault you outright as bring itself up close, strike sporadically and generally rough you up. The beats are big, the keyboard washes more like slabs than stabs at notes and Numan's slightly metallic voice accrues a disturbing air because it performs its usual distant and observing role. The lyrics are – apparently - notes from personal nightmares. But, Gary retains enough focus to tell us rather than collapse under the emotional weight or hector his audience. There's no doubt that someone involved in producing Pure had paid attention to Depeche Mode's climb to major status in the USA and their "Personal Jesus" success is – arguably – referenced a bit too closely in "My Jesus." The tracks don't sound alike but both are made for alternative US radio play, albeit Gary's attack on Christianity appears more personal and focussed than Depeche Mode's ironic observations. The black front cover, black clothing on Gary, and crucifix pose on the front cover are also in there with the happening dark electronic sounds for a certain section of the US market. Lyrically he's bleak, personal and stridently anti-religious in places. Gary is also pushing an Emo envelope, especially on the title track: "I want to feel you touch my pain, I want to drown in your misery, Hey bitch, this is what you are, purified, sanctified, sacrificed." This from a track that opens with gentle keyboards, before dragging in the more industrial sounds. How much this is Gary (a man who has – apparently - enjoyed one of the longest and happiest showbiz marriages) and how much it is a serious attempt to update the image is never made clear. But Pure is a big beast of an album and even if it is part cynical career move it sounds like it cares about its messages, and it sounds like it hurts. That is certainly the case on the downbeat and nakedly honest "Little Invitro" and "A Prayer for the Unborn," both of which draw directly on a miscarriage suffered by Gemma – Gary's wife – and the couple's (then) unsuccessful attempts to conceive via IVF.

Critically Pure drew mixed responses (though in a British music press used to ripping Numan to shreds this could be counted as progress). Much of the pro/anti reviews divided depending whether people considered Numan to be ripping off the likes of Marilyn Manson and Trent Reznor or simply responding to their admiration of him. Pure is mainly dark industrial rock in keeping with its times. Grinding guitars and epic booming production are never far away and the album is careful to line up 11 cuts that run at radio friendly timings (nothing under two and a half minutes, nothing quite reaching six minutes). As such it is a more listenable and durable collection than much of the industrial rock of the turn of the century.

Laura Nyro:
Angel in the Dark
(Rounder, 2001)
What? Perfect parting shot to under-rated career.

Nyro (1947-1997) achieved much greater commercial success as a songwriter ("Stoned Soul Picnic," "And When I Die" etc.) than as a performer. Her small catalogue of original work is highly regarded for its ability to flit between soul, folk-rock, ballads and gospel. Her powerful and emotive voice was one of the most distinctive of her generation. Nyro retired from music to become a housewife aged 24, returned in the mid-seventies and continued a low key career until she died of ovarian cancer in 1997.

Angel in the Dark marks her final recordings. Cut – partly - for her personal satisfaction and nodding to no prevailing market trend, the album is 16 cuts of minimally arranged originals and covers. All place Nyro's powerful, rangy and perfectly controlled voice and soulful piano at the centre. When Frank Zappa was terminally ill it is reported he spent hours listening to the doo-wop records he had first loved in his teens. Nyro goes one better here and records some of the songs she loved – "Will You Still Love Me Tomorrow," "Ooh Baby Baby" and "Walk On By" – typically in slowed down arrangements with enough space around Nyro's voice to turn the simple lyrics to deep statements of emotion. Nyro's originals revisit the soulful-singer-songwriter style of her highly regarded early albums and "Angel in the Dark" – which opens this set – pits Nyro against a basic band with trumpet and tenor sax. "Gardenia Talk" is another stand-out Nyro original, located in the middle of the album.

Angel in the Dark is a strong collection, made stronger by rotating the faster, rockier, numbers with electric guitar and rhythm section around the solo performances; and also mixing the covers and originals to the point it feels like an intimate set in a small club. As a restatement of everything that made Laura Nyro a compelling artist, almost too good for the mass acclaim that found its way to her peers, it is a perfect signing off on an under-rated career.

Dr. Obscenity:
Suppressed Classics and Bawdy Parodies in American Music (Original, Uncensored Versions)
(RPE, 1978)
What? "Calling old ladies chicken-shit whores"

It's well known that many popular standards started life with different lyrics and different meanings. Blues songs especially had dirtier and more-earthy versions that named body parts and explicitly described sexual acts. Their writers and singers generally found a more receptive (for which read greater in number) audience and more accepting radio stations when the songs were cleaned up, and the explicit was made implicit; none of which stopped people playing and enjoying the original versions in live venues.

Suppressed Classics… sets out to redress the balance, lines up some of the obvious contenders: "Hallellujah I'm a Bum," "Stackolee" and "Frankie and Johnny" and plasters both sides of the vinyl sleeve in transcriptions of the lyrics, with the cuss words helpfully presented in red type. Sonically, it's a basic and very clean production based mainly on Dr. Obscentity's lightly lugubrious vocal, some sterling acoustic guitar work and the sparing use of louder instruments like drums and electric guitar. All the musicians – other than Dr. Obscenity – are identified by the names likely to be on their birth certificates and everyone turns in a solid, if somewhat restrained, performance. Some of the selections are better known on scratchy and rousing blues originals and the cleanliness of the Suppressed Classics sound does them few favours. The rhythm on "Sound Off" – literally the stomping of the performers – is another low-point, coming over as tinny and doing no favours to the filth on offer; if you're going to deliver a line like: "I don't know but I been told/Eskimo pussy is mighty cold" it's a hell of a lot more effective with a rough rabble of voices, or some tangible chaos evident in the background.

Dr. Obscenity's musicianship is flawless; taking in acoustic guitar, harmonica, mandolin, accordion and his skills here are a mixed blessing. There is a sense of the whole collection being the kind of studious work that collates and contains the originals; making clear why they mattered, but not always communicating the rawness and threat they once held. On the other hand the collection is made stronger for the academic nature of the digging that brought these originals together. The parodies – including "Let me Ball you Sweetheart" – add another dimension and some real humour. The final cut, all one minute and 17 seconds of "Beautiful Dreamer" opening with the lines: "Born in a whorehouse, raised as a slave/ Drinking and Fucking are all that I crave," is a chucklesome gem from which the line about calling old ladies "chicken-shit whores" also comes.

Carrol O'Connor and Jean Stapleton: Archie and Edith: Side by Side (RCA, 1973)
What? Celebrity tightrope walk between schmaltz and sublime.

O'Connor and Stapleton released a few albums on the back of their starring roles in All in the Family but this one is different to the others in that it starts with the premise that Archie and Edith Bunker find themselves at home, alone, for the evening and relive their lives with the help of a few songs played on the iconic piano in their front room. So, it's somewhere between full-blown concept/ musical idea and thinly veiled television cash in.

Incidentally – if you're reading this and wondering WTF we're on about - a brief catch up: All in the Family (1971-1979) was a massively successful US sitcom (the first show to take the main award as best television show for five years in a row). Based on the UK's longer-running Till Death us do Part, the show presents bigoted and garrulous cab driver Archie Bunker (O' Connor), and his wife Edith (Stapleton), living with their adult daughter and her layabout boyfriend. All in the Family was massive, partly, because it allowed hitherto taboo subjects for television comedy – homosexuality, rape etc. – to collide with Bunker's bigoted, shoot-from-the-hip opinions, presenting a picture of the best and worst of American attitudes and softening the social reality with an endless stream of great comedy set ups, decent gags and good performances from the lead actors.

Side by Side is an attempt to mine the same ground. Archie and Edith clearly care for each other, but their differences – especially in what each remembers of their lives – are never ignored. The notion of an evening in, reminiscing and using popular songs as a means to narrate their story, just about survives the demanding aspect of having to present the whole story with the two in character. Edith's awful – if well intentioned - singing was used for comic effect in the credit sequences of the show and O' Connor could interpret, but hardly get inside, a song. In truth Stapleton was a decent singer with stage appearances behind her and here she – just about – pulls off the trick of occasionally singing really well and passing off her ability to hold a note as if it were an accident for Edith. O' Connor has to drag up every bit of character acting he can to hold the interest as another scripted intro gives way to music rising in the background.

Nominally set in the Bunker's home, Side by Side has to call in strings and a professional musical arrangement to save itself because the duo and one piano would have been a dire option over 13 tracks, almost half of which are medleys of popular tunes. Stand outs – if such a term is appropriate here – include "I Remember it Well" (a playful romantic number about neither half of a couple being able to recall exactly how big events in their past took place). The production team behind the album also pull a useful trick by including "Oh Babe What Would you Say" and "Anything You Can Do (I Can Do Better);" the first well known at the time for an original sung in a characterful rather than technically brilliant way, the second a staple of so many live shows for kids it was already familiar as a song that worked, even when murdered by its singers. These choices, the acting, and the production – just about – save this album from celebrity audio hell; although the Golden Throats team saw fit to grab "I Remember it Well" for a compilation years ago. It's also merciful that the moments when O' Connor and Stapleton struggle to stay in character and/or deliver the vocal demanded by the tune – like "When I'm Sixty Four" or "They Can't Take That Away From me" – are truncated by including those songs in medleys.

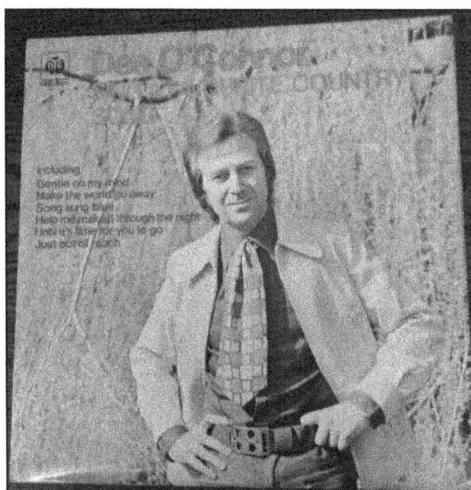

Des O'Connor: Sing a Favourite Country Song (Pye, 1973)

What? UK national institution meets US national institution; we'll give this one to the yanks!

If you're reading these words outside of the UK, or territories like Australia that have proven receptive to some British musical acts that have baffled the rest of humanity, it might be worth expending a sentence or two to explain Des O' Connor. A durable and improbably youthful light entertainer; O' Connor's career high points include a chart topping single "I Pretend" in 1968, a highly rated and very long-running chat show and another highly rated and long-running stint as a daytime television host. He has also turned his talent to comedy, and for many years was the butt of running jokes by comedy legends Morecambe and Wise regarding his inability to sing. Most countries in the west have some equivalent of Des O' Connor, and most struggle to export such creatures.

Sing a Favourite Country Song followed Sing a Favourite Song (1972). The earlier album had hauled itself up to #25 in the UK chart so turning out a country version made some sense. Four decades later it stands as an insight into a curious and very British fashion that broke out around this time. With rock and pop having won the battle for shelf-space in record shops and customer cash, those singers too set in their ways to update were stranded in a static no-man's land where rehashing their old hits could earn cash on the oldies circuit but any significant record sales would require a rethink at the record company. Bear in mind that pop careers were deemed to be so short at this time that Des's album came out around the same time The Bee Gees were reacting with horror at the serious suggestion they were ready to be pensioned off into cabaret and supper clubs.

Country music hadn't made a massive impact in the UK's record shops and even the greatest stars like Johnny Cash were playing to packed houses on the back of paltry British chart positions. For a handful of mature British acts country offered an attractive bolt hole. There were songs telling real stories, the genre placed the singer out front, often playing the role of an experienced narrator, the tempos were generally slow and steady and vocal performances could be characterful rather than impassioned. It would take a few decades for full-blown authentic country to grab enough market share in the UK to change the nation's perception. In that time a smattering of British talent – check out Vera Lynn's entry in this book if you've not done so already – would attempt to make a home in country.

Sing A Favourite Country Song is exactly what you would expect it to be. O' Connor croons his consummate professional way through a series of standards including: "Gentle on my Mind," "Song Sung Blue," "The Green Green Grass of Home" and "Sunday Morning Coming Down." His restrained croon never once threatens to drop itself to the level of a down home drawl and there's a sense that the tuneful session crew backing him have one eye on the clock and part of their mind on the pay-cheque. Instrumental skill is on show, instrumental brilliance by way of a memorable, song-stealing, lick never breaks out. Perhaps that is unfair to the members of Denny Wright's "Country Cream" who are all individually credited; the authors will publicly apologize to Denny and the boys as soon as the band are inducted into the Country Music Hall of Fame. We could blame the producer – a certain Des O' Connor – for not getting the best out of them, but that's hardly the point. Sing a Favourite Country Song was always intended to sound tuneful, pleasant, unthreatening and fit for a well-ordered front room.

It's doubtful if anyone saw that such recordings would eventually enjoy an ironic and kitsch appreciation but that's where Sing a Favourite Country Song really scores. For those unwilling to risk their ears over two sides and 14 cuts there's always the delight of surfing the internet for a look at the front cover. Des stands, resplendent in the sunshine, dressed – maybe – as a country singer as imagined by the clothing dept of British Home Stores: brown shirt, lovely wide tie sporting yellow squares, nice chunky belt and brown trousers, and a slightly off-white creation somewhere between a safari jacket and the kind of thing the more tragic youngsters were wearing in 1973 (assuming their mothers still bought their clothes). Throw in a stunning bouffant haircut and the kitsch factor of the cover is pushing the top of the scale.

As an insight into the way a small section of the British market imagined country music to work, it's hard to fault the time capsule offered by Sing a Favourite Country Song. As of this writing the CD reissue is still to appear.

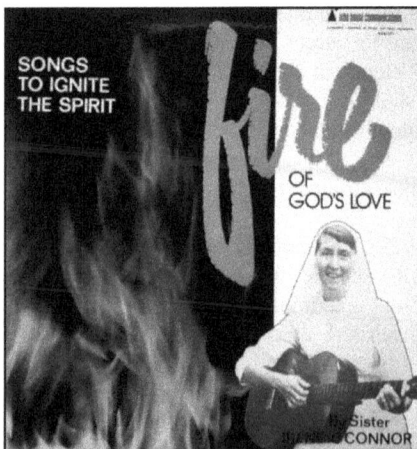

Sister Irene O'Connor:
Fire of God's Love: Songs to Ignite the Spirit
(Alba House, 1976)
What? Strangeness and spirituality in equal amounts on stunning seventies collection.

WFMU's blog is one of a number of online platforms that have brought this collection (little-heralded at the time) to a new audience. WMFU states: "Among the sea of sound-a-like private-pressed Catholic lps that came out in the 1960's and 1970's, Sister Irene O'Connor's 1976 album stands out with its primitive drum machine and spooky, echo-laden vocals...[the]

lp features several haunting and remarkable songs…In particular, the title track "Fire of God's Love" strikes me as so otherwordly and uniquely eerie that I wonder how far Sister Irene's O'Connor's seeming solipsism extended beyond music".

A perfect summary because the growing cult status of this album rests squarely on its outsider approach to production and performance, putting it in there with primitive classics like The Shaggs' Philosophy of the World. Some of the cuts are Christian/hymn standards including "The Great Mystery" and "Christ our King" whilst others are more secular and modern. Sister Irene approaches them with a strident acoustic guitar, very stiff wristed and precise. Her clear diction, high voice and love of a simple melody are wrapped in some highly odd elements. Primitive drum machine tracks underpin some of the work and elsewhere overdubs, harmonies and sporadic additional instruments are layered on. The presence of a strong male voice to duet on one track is also a vivid piece of spot colour. Whilst it sounds nothing like other "primitives," like The Shaggs, they remain a good reference point because the overall effect of Sister Irene's assembly of her varied elements is to give the album a feel of having everything on hand, and little idea of how everyone else uses the same tools. At worst it has that sense of worthiness that drips from some religious albums; desperately trying to have the same chops as their commercial cousins, but coming over as a pale imitation. At best – and a lot of Fire of God's Love falls into this territory – it has that sense of gleeful experimentation, and combining the unlikeliest of musical sounds to create something that sounds individual and ever so slightly "out there."

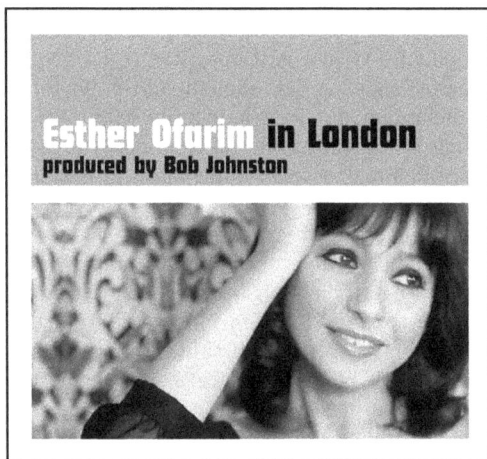

Esther Ofarim:
In London
(Bureau B, 2009)
What? High value pop with a very personal touch.

Ofarim's highest profile moment on the world stage involved a double act with her one-time husband Abi Ofarim and the massive novelty hit "Cinderalla Rockefella." But her pure and expertly pitched voice, along with her ability to imbue songs with a seemingly effortless sense of emotion, had long made her the subject of some attention from producers and others in the industry. When her failed marriage left her as a solo act one of the first to take advantage, musically, was Dylan producer Bob Johnson. In London features the best of their work. Ironically, given its title, this 2009 compilation is concocted mainly from Ofarim's self-titled 1972 album on Columbia and three bonus cuts from sessions in Nashville. These arrangements and performances make for a whole album showcasing the sound and sensibilities Johnson and Ofarim wanted. In its most predictable moments In London has an easy elegance, existing somewhere in a land between Scott Walker's highly ambitious pop efforts of the time and crossover middle of the road artistes who ventured into the works of singer-songwriters. It proved too restrained and slightly too mature for the mass market, but the performances have lasted well for two simple reasons. Firstly, Johnson's nous for the right arrangements puts an artistic strength and quality firmly at the heart of the work. Johnson actually stripped strings and other accompaniments off the final mixes to expose Esther's interpretations. The arrangements vary to keep each performance as a self-contained gem. Secondly, Ofarim and Johnson are smart enough to work to the songs and allow her to inhabit them so the pitfall of – say – turning in a version of "The First Time Ever I Saw Your Face" that sounds like a lesser take on Roberta Flack's classic is avoided. "Song of the French Partisan" – something of a call to revolution when covered by Joan Baez – is elegiac and heartfelt, and the varying of material from Bill Hawkins' "Gnostic Serenade" to Leonard Cohen's "Hey

That's No Way to Say Goodbye" gives the collection the feel of being an international work, before the market for such items had really established itself. Ofarim's most literal cover involves tackling "Morning Has Broken" in a version that strongly acknowledges Cat Stevens' hit arrangement. All Music Guide put it succinctly: "if it ain't Karen Carpenter it's not that far removed, really," and the press release from Bureau B heralded Bob Johnson's genius in uniting "apparently irreconcilable opposites." In London is hardly likely to change your life and probably won't oust Karen Carpenter, Joni Mitchell, Julia Holter or Francoise Hardy as your favourite female singer. But it belongs, in fleeting moments, in the company of all four of them.

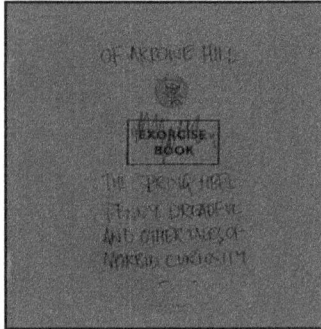

of Arrowe Hill:
The Spring Heel Penny Dreadful and Other Tales of Morbid Curiosity
(Must Destroy, 2003)
What? If the Victorians had skinned up a little more!

If one common element erupts from the random assorted of critical opinion directed at of Arrowe Hill (oAH) it's the fact that their fans often rely on juxtaposed examples when describing the breadth of the band's work and are reduced to the figurative possibilities of failure; basically, stating that words are never enough to do justice to Adam Easterbrook's songs or the band's variety of sound. Ace descriptive wordsmith Julian Cope opined oAH are best imagined if you: "heft several vats of raw Faust in the direction of post-Oasis Beatlemania." A fair enough start-point for a fusion of noise and songcraft that seldom seeks to resolve the argument. The whole point with oAH is the refusal to compromise on a love of drone and noise, often for its own sonic sake, an equal love of standard song-writing and melody, and the sense that any idea that makes sense in the moment is worth nailing for a track.

It leaves a sonic palette within which frequently brilliant word-play, often exemplified in song titles like: "Psychic Vampire Supply Teacher," "Dry-Eyed Ballad Of A Fink" and "Gadfly Adolescence" exist in a world in which anything from a Gallagher-esque crunching chord, a blues lick from the Muddy Waters catalogue or the most random of randomly sampled sounds rub shoulders in perfect balance. They don't sound like the Butthole Surfers but prime oAH, like Spring Heel Penny Dreadful, has some resemblance to works like Locust Abortion Technician in the cramming of disparate styles into a fragile but effective balance, the use of sound effects to break the brief moods and the sense of a short album feeling like an epic. All the more so since on songs like "Night Gallery Emissions" oAH will take the sound down to minimal; little more than a keyboard and looped noise/sound effects below the vocal.

Distinct oAH traits poured out here, and on other releases, also locate the band in a British tradition wherein the rapid-fire references – "'Bromide in my Ovaltine again" (from "Night Gallery Emissions") - and inescapable wit and wisdom reveal a work ethic underlying the wildest moments, and frequent diversions from the main musical path. There is a sense of oAH albums being built from constituent parts as much as planned and themed. Musical engineering that hints at a band in love with clever ideas and trusting in the intelligence of their audience to gradually peel away the noise and hooks to reveal the depth that lies beneath. Well, that and sometimes they keep a straight face and throw in a little dark humour. Spring Heel Penny Dreadful's best gag? Probably the five minutes of silence that leads to damn near another album's worth of bonus material culled from earlier singles and tracks donated to compilation albums.

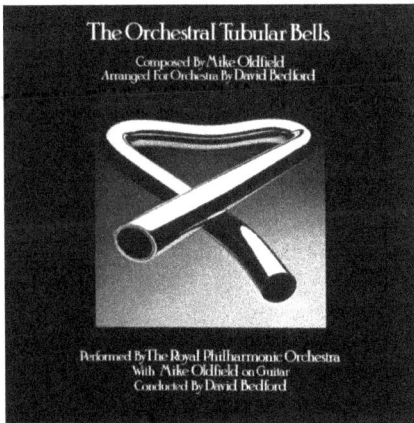

Mike Oldfield & David Bedford:
The Orchestral Tubular Bells
(Virgin, 1975)
What? Inescapably 70s sound, never likely to be rediscovered and labelled cool...but still timeless and strange.

It was such an obvious move that the existence of The Orchestral Tubular Bells shouldn't surprise anyone. For better or worse, Mike Oldfield's 20 million selling epic album opened the floodgates for elongated experimentation and the noodling output of a generation who – within a decade and a half - would lead us to a world in which anything of album length with slowly turning melodies and a host of overdubs would be labelled "new age" and a host of chin-stroking worthies would declare it deep. The Tubular Bells related bandwagon was well underway in 1974, Oldfield's second album Hergest Ridge had topped the charts and The Exorcist movie had adopted the first album for its soundtrack. So, getting David Bedford (the kind of hip classical composer dude who – like – hung out with arty prog rock types) to write up an orchestral score for Tubular Bells, before combining the Royal Albert Hall, the Royal Philharmonic Orchestra and live BBC 2 coverage of the whole caper, was always going to hit a lot of bases. Your dad could feel hip, the minority channel could hit a decent audience and a classical work sold to rock fans could keep the Bells brand earning a little longer.

Oldfield's own account in his autobiography makes clear that he hated the results, which came during a dark period in his life. Fame and fortune had sent him into a mental tailspin that would only resolve itself after he'd paid for a program of exegesis, wherein he could be locked in a room, bare his soul, hyperventilate, scream and generally make the kind of noises conspicuously absent on his rippling and thoughtful melodic works. So, critical opinion and the main player have consigned this curio to a space in time before punk drove a safety pin into the self-indulgent heart of the worst excesses of anything reeking remotely of progressive experimentation.

The one problem with all of the wisdom above is that – taken on its own merits – The Orchestral Tubular Bells is more than a melodic re-tread of familiar themes. Where a range of subsequent orchestral rock albums took songs and recreated the melodies this work is based on a composition within which the tones of various instruments and layering of a range of melodic patterns are, often, the point. It lacks the production effects of a well-worked album master-minded by a rock musician, but it replaces them with a work that employs a whole orchestra and emphasizes changes of pace and tone. Tubular Bells emerges as a muscular and ceaselessly inventive work, shorn of most of the glittering guitar lines, fader compressions and sudden changes of sound that made the original so memorable; it reveals the rhythmic structures and riffs that make up the background of the original. And, crucially, despite some obvious problems, it does stand up as a modern classical piece of some distinction. The one major problem is the clear disparity between the softer passages of strings and woodwind and the harder edged moments when the deeper strings sweep away everything in their path.

The one overdub – Oldfield adding some belated Spanish guitar – blends well with the electric guitar played in the original live recording by Steve Hillage and does serve as a timely reminder that this music draws most of its inspiration from rock.

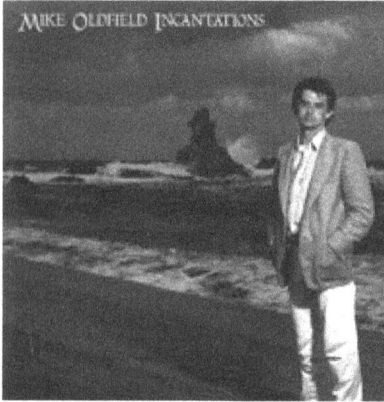

Mike Oldfield:
Incantations
(Virgin, 1978)
What? Seldom discussed, sparsely celebrated watershed album.

You could speak to 100 devotees of Mike Oldfield and not find one willing to claim Incantations as being close to his best work. Similarly, you could listen through the man's entire oeuvre and find very little to resemble Incantations. By common consent it is not the most listenable, not the most memorable and, by no means, the most accessible work the man has produced. So it may – just – belong in this book. In fact, Incantations shares qualities with a few other albums chronicled hereabouts. Like Yes' prog-monster Tales From Topographic Oceans this is an album frequently cited and dismissed in a sentence or two by someone who's seldom taken the trouble to pay attention all the way through. Like Ultramarine's Every Man and Woman this is a musical journey that passes and notices points of interest en-route. Like Les Baxter, Oldfield developed a sound and style that slowly evolved, becoming a byword for comfortable and unthreatening entertainment. So much so, that many people missed the moments when chances were taken.

Intentionally, or not, Incantations is truly one such moment. It remains one of the longest single works Oldfield has ever produced and its 1978 release came three years after his previous album. The double vinyl Incantations followed three compositions, each running around half its running time. In the period between his opening trio of albums, (which had taken him to worldwide fame and the establishment of a sound combining prog rock, roots influences and sensibilities that would eventually see him labelled a new age artist), Oldfield had fallen well down the critical radar. The dawn of punk rock had shredded the critical standing of many of his peers. Oldfield was consigned with the "boring old farts," although some punk musicians were older than 28 year old Mike Oldfield. Oldfield had faced down a few demons himself during this period, putting himself through the controversial and intense assertiveness programme known as Exegesis and disastrously marrying Diana D'Aubigny, sister of the leader of Exegesis.

A sense of personal restlessness and fleeting focus permeates Incantations. For starters, the album's title suggests an attempt to bring something about, where most other Oldfield albums are titled after a place, event, object or some other definite article. Incantations packs the familiar clear melodies, very treble heavy production sound and repetitive patterns of most of Oldfield's familiar seventies work but it also pulls two tricks most of his other albums avoid. Firstly, the instruments on show at any one time tend to be limited. Sounds appear as others slowly vanish, and Oldfield's trademark gradual building to orchestral conclusions is kept well in check; something that becomes noticeable over 73 minutes. So, Incantations sounds like a series of ensembles turning up, playing and walking away as others start. Secondly, the entire lengthy composition is built on a musical principal known as the circle of fifths; an effective if complex wander through musical mathematics that means Incantations slowly meanders through different musical keys, always feels like one complete composition and yet manages to sound hugely different if you drop the needle/shuffle your way to random moments several minutes apart. Add to the above that the production is simply louder and packing more attack than the trio of gentler albums that preceded it and Incantations comes over as an unsettled work trying desperately to present confidence and a sense of cohesion, but also a work desperately in search of balance. The purpose here is the journey, not the conclusion.

Lyrically, it's also a confusing affair. In the 12th minute of the second track Maddy Prior suddenly opens up into snatches of Henry Longfellow's Song of Hiawatha. Part four offers up a part of Ben Jonson's Ode to

Cynthia. What they have to do with Oldfield's personal journey from ground-breaking musical hermit to besuited/professional looking young man (as depicted on the Incantations cover) isn't by any means clear. Though Prior's mantra-like incantation of Longfellow's works (which appear out of sequence to the original text) is one of the most mesmerising musical passages of Incantations.

Incantations is played and produced to the highest standards. At times it hides itself to the point it can be mistaken for more listenable and less confused works but – given your full concentration over its complete length – Incantations is also a strangely unsettling piece, closer in some ways to experiments on the very edge of classical music and the deliberately disturbing works of some of popular music's more outré performers.

The Olivia Tremor Control:
Black Foliage
(Flydaddy/V2, 1999)
What? Complex, confusing, concrete/catchy collection.

A head-on collision between experimental effects, loops, improvisations on the same bass-line and some of the most inspired psychedelic pop of its generation, Black Foliage has been likened – with some justification – the The Beatles' White Album. A cursory listen makes the point about experiments. A few tracks – all called "Combinations" - erupt randomly and exit within seconds, the first clocking in around four seconds. Elsewhere the experiments, layering and indulgence go into mantra like indulgence with "The Bark and Below It" clocking in just short of 11 and a half minutes. These works sit in a psychedelic soup alongside some of the most insanely catchy psychedelic pop released in a generation. "The Sylvan Screen" – for example – packs the kind of sublime chorus best heard in the late sixties, throws in the kind of analogue style effects Mercury Rev were using at the time, and disintegrates into a fleeting sound collage before re-emerging into a perfect vocal harmony. "California Demise" – by contrast – is a gorgeous slice of west-coast guitar psych that also breaks down into layered effects and a trippy, repetitive middle eight before getting back into its insistent melody and a madly simple guitar outro. The fact that The Olivia Tremor Control repeatedly pull this old school/new school shtick and make the results sound so coherent is the reason Black Foliage – rather than its even more experimental cousin Dusk at Cubist Castle (1996) – tends to be cited as their finest hour, (their finest hour and nine minutes if you want to be pedantic).

The allusions to old school works of the first psychedelic generation are strong. For starters, Black Foliage is conceived as four sides (not a single CD) and the thematic elements are teased out gradually. Along with the "Combinations" fragments there are five songs called "Black Foliage (Animation)" each individually numbered, all drawing on the same bass line and all going somewhere different to each other. The "Combinations" and "(Animation)" pieces give a focus to the album.

When singled out and run consecutively the other tracks (mainly) make up a much shorter collection of brilliant psych-pop and present a totally different slant on Black Foliage (akin to the same stunt of pulling Lindsey Buckingham's tracks off Fleetwood Mac's Tusk and listening to a surprisingly good proto-indie band). So, like The White Album, Black Foliage continually teases with what else it could have been. It bears the scars of the years (1995-1998) of studio noodling that gradually allowed this monumental indulgence to take place and in "The Bark and Below It" Black Foliage – just about – delivers its own "Revolution 9."

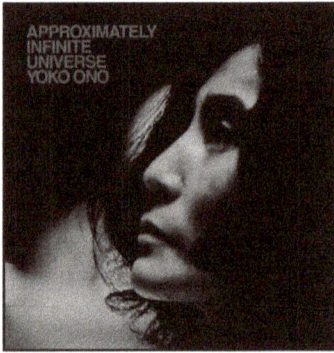

Yoko Ono:
Approximately Infinite Universe
(Apple 1973/ Rykodisc, 2004)
What? Much maligned songstress strays close to seminal work.

Music industry figures don't come more controversial, or railed against, than Yoko Ono. It remains a grim fact that much of the criticism levelled at Yoko's musical output comes from those who haven't listed to much of it. Few – for example – realise she was working at the experimental end of the music world before meeting John Lennon. Ono's art 'happenings' in New York brought her into contact with minimalist composers like Lamonte Young and John Cage. Her work was exhibited against a sound background, sometimes of her own devising. One exhibition featured the randomly timed and located sounds of a flushing toilet! So Yoko had stumbled on some of the makings of "Revolution 9" before John had seen the inside of a decent recording studio. Their joint albums drew fury from Beatle die-hards and derision from critics, By 1973 the music world had largely discarded Yoko, whilst they continued to hang on every word of John's lyrics. The couple recorded separate albums and – arguably – their respective 1973 efforts show her work standing the test of time better than his Mind Games.

Approaching 40 and every bit the mature artist Yoko concocted over an hour and half of varied, experimental and lively work. Approximately Infinite Universe would count as a "rock" album today. Then, its varied styles and random elements made it hard to categorise. The collection packs full-on proto-punk efforts with driving rhythms and nihilistic observations, like "I Feel Like Smashing my Face in a Clear Glass Window" but elsewhere the ethereal wash of "Shiranakatta (I Didn't Know)" takes us to territories the Cocteau Twins would later explore. The quiet, introspective "Looking Over From my Hotel Window," rubs shoulders with the raw emotional sparseness of mid-seventies Nico. Predictably Approximately Infinite Universe made a marginal – as peaking at #193 – impact on the US charts, and failed to trouble the listings in the UK. Decades later, the complex, ambitious and characterful work stands up well. If its sheer scale and range of influence make it a hard album to take at one sitting there is, always, the fruitful pastime of trawling through the 22 tracks (plus two bonus cuts on the Rykodisc reissued CD) and spotting the sounds others would later appropriate into their own work. An evening with a friend, and Yoko in the background, is likely to see the conversation interrupted with: "So that's where the B52s got the idea for that vocal sound" or "that bit sounds a lot like The Slits."

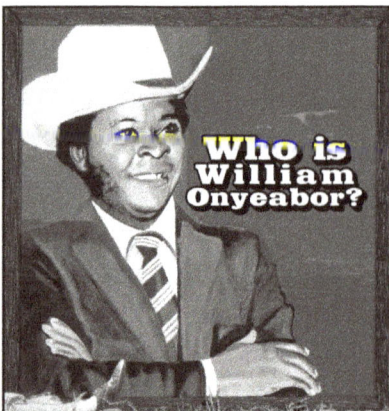

William Onyeabor:
Who is William Onyeabor?
(Luaka Bop, 2013)
What? African psych-funk, frequently low-fi, always different.

Onyeabor's career has that elusive Searching for Sugar Man feel about it. A self-contained artistic vision, honed and delivered to an adoring audience, lost to time only to be rediscovered long after the artist's prime. When his music was finally brought to a wider audience by the Luaka Bop label with their World Psychedelic Classics series, the man himself had, apparently, disowned the recordings from which Who is was culled. Reports suggested his born again Christianity had led him to refuse to discuss his eight self-released collections spanning the mid-seventies to mid- eighties. On first look and listen Who is presents some odd collisions. The grinning picture of the man on the front depicts him in a smart blue business suit, arms folded, with a loud striped tie, a broad grin and a Stetson. He looks like Nigeria's attempt at producing a middle-of-the-road country singer for the seventies. His lengthy, often low-fi, repetitive funk grooves reference James Brown. Onyeabor's righteous missives repeat their core messages, often anti-war incitements to unite and love one another. Of the nine tracks compiled here, three: "Good Name," "Something You Will Never Forget" and "Body and Soul" evidence Onyeabor's epic quality by running beyond ten minutes. The only thing that might have worked as a single, "Heaven and Hell," clocks in at just over four minutes. Onyeabor's work typically combines the massive funk intentions of James Brown, replete with repetitive female chorus and Onyeabor apparently channelling the lyrical message as a stream of consciousness. He veers between an understated, soulful style, counter-pointing against the bigger groove, and outbursts of emotion, typically arrived at after a lengthy pre-amble, including instrumental passages. The more awestruck listeners encountering this material in the twenty first century used phrases like "mind blowing" to describe the results. The present authors wouldn't go that far. The roots of this are fairly clear, the productions tend towards low-fi, often meaning the keyboards and guitars lack the breadth, rumbles and fat-fat sounds of Amercan equivalents. But Onyeabor has a strong sense of the African roots of his inspiration and the knack to keep the grooves hypnotically simple. When the fusion works it works brilliantly. The African licks, catchy hooks, and surges in and out of the different sections of "Atomic Bomb" are effortlessly captivating.

Opeth:
Watershed
(Roadrunner, 2008)
What? A metal master-class, in a smorgasbord stylee.

Opeth are one of those acts whose whole canon could usefully be included in a book like this. Formed in 1990 around singer/ guitarist Mikael Åkerfeldt the band boast a palette that draws from all areas of metal and combines classy production, seamless musical artistry and an approach to their craft that recognises no barriers within the metal genre. To put it simply, it's an old school/ new school mash up that works to perfection. The band have a loyal following but somewhat in the tradition of other major cult rock acts – Marillion, Jethro Tull, Napalm Death, Sunn 00 – this is a die-hard fan base, surrounded by a population that either doesn't get it, or doesn't want to get it.

Watershed earned critical plaudits around the world, notably finishing second to Metallica's Death Magnetic as Album of the Year in Metal Hammer. It also hit the top ten in Scandinavia (#7 in the band's native Sweden and #1 in Finland). The album managed a creditable #23 in the US and #34 in the UK. Higher chart positions than Opeth generally enjoy outside their home territory.

Musically Watershed delivers on an epic scale, even in the opening "Coil" the only track of a typical pop/ rock length here. The gentle acoustic ripples of "Coil" and Nathalie Lorichs's crystal clear diction give way to the death growl intonations of "Heir Apparent" and Opeth pull their winning gambit of segueing from AOR to death metal. The same trick permeates the album as it shifts moods, notably when the bludgeoning "Burden" dies in a pile of acoustic guitar, Åkerfeldt picking away as the instrument is being detuned.

Presented in words like this the collection may appear a series of stunts and tricks but the whole point of Opeth is that such unlikely musical manoeuvres under-pin a music so sure of its own destiny that they work artistically. By the time of this, their ninth long-player, they had a new line-up and a focus on their strengths that had attracted a fan-base including many whose tastes veered far away from heavy metal. Lyrically, Opeth do epic with an economy where the lyrical statements are concerned and a sense of the grandeur in their musical ambition. "Burden" concerns – well - carrying a burden, "Hex Omega" deals with a fractured relationship tearing lives apart etc. The words are their least adventurous element, but set against a background in which a delicate sequence of guitar notes can be crushed by an onrushing death growl and the drums sprinting from the speakers to explode inside your head, the simplest lyrical sentiments are often given an urgency and sense of the moment that makes them stronger and more real.

For all the extremes of their sound Opeth work because they have class, in spades. Watershed is up there with their best work.

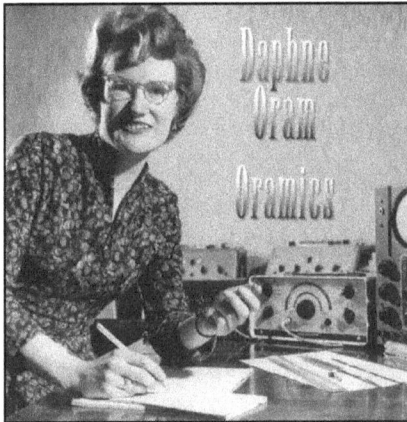

Daphne Oram:
Oramics
(Paradigm, 2007)
What? Cutting edge electronica from middle-aged English matronly type.

If you were to Google a photo of Daphne Oram you'd probably find yourself looking at one of a number of staged and quite formal portraits of a thin, bespectacled, intellectual looking woman; a solitary genius who worked in semi-rural surroundings, having left London for Kent in 1959. Oram's day job in this setting involved developing background sounds for television and radio, especially incidental music. Her tools were the (then) cutting edge electronic compressors, resistors and other varied gizmos that would eventually be boxed inside the first generation of synthesised instruments. Her success in this field (a very limited market in early sixties Britain which boasted little in the way of commercial radio and three main television channels) led to commissions for art installations, theatres and short films.

What sets her work apart, and makes the posthumous Oramics such a compelling listen is the distinctive sounds (like little else produced at the time) and Oram's deft application of tone, subtle changes in sound, narrative progression and the constant sense of focus and structure. In other words, everything, from the fragments to the longer pieces simply works to perfection by combining the best notions of classical composition and the most inventive approach to electronic sound. Sometimes the inspirations appear to be simple; individual tracks appear to be prompted by the sound of trickling water, the rhythm of a train or the sound of a finger run around the top of a wineglass. But Oram's brilliance is there in the ability to apply just the right amount of echo and make the music last exactly long enough. Each piece appears as a genuine composition without outstaying its welcome. Oramics also features Daphne Oram introducing herself and her work, making the entire compilation a greatest hits, with narration. This is a documenting one of the most singular and influential careers in electronic sound. Despite her apparent deference in the face of public interest, Daphne Oram coined the term "Oramics" herself and branded her work with her own name, turning herself into a cult hero years before such a notion was a short-cut to cool in the music industry. This was also years before Kraftwerk, a continent away from the early work of Silver Apples and light years away from a generation of (mainly male) bedroom geeks who would unleash a wave of electronic pop in the eighties. Fittingly, Oram's recorded archive is now the in care of a British university, available to influence and astound successive generations who – despite a vast tonnage of better tools - still struggle to touch her abilities. Oramics is the recommended starting point for anyone intent on following her journey.

Orchestral Manoeuvres in the Dark:
Dazzle Ships
(Telegraph, 1983)
What? "We wanted to be ABBA and Stockhausen:" Andy McCluskey

Orchestral Manoeuvres in the Dark's (OMD's) fourth album has never sat comfortably against anything else in their bulging and – largely – successful canon. Depending on your point of view this could be their most majestic and robust artistic statement or that difficult third album thoughtfully bumped one place down the running order. Dazzle Ships does neatly dissect itself into its constituent parts; it only struggles when it is considered as a complete album. Hugely successful and allowed their run of the new electronic gadgetry OMD spent part of their studio time sampling, editing and playing with sounds. Some of the resulting moments of musique concrète are confined to radio-friendly running times and provided with enough loops and repetitions to – at least – nod towards standard song writing. But, the band, thus far, had a very young audience and even the more accessible collage effects were alienating. So too the inclusion amongst the half-dozen poppier numbers of two songs - "The Romance of the Telescope" and "Of All the Things We've Made" – which were, basically, B-sides to earlier singles given a hefty makeover for Dazzle Ships, didn't help. Nor did "Radio Waves" a cut that had featured in the set of The Id (Andy McCluskey and Paul Humphreys' previous band); though "Radio Waves" – by general agreement – is one of the best songs on the collection. Those who bothered to investigate beyond the strong abstract lines of the front cover soon realised the title of the album and the cover design were a lift from Edward Wadsworth's Vorticist work "Dazzle-ships in Drydock at Liverpool". A nod – maybe – to OMD's Merseyside roots, but also a long distance from the pop audience they'd so successfully cultivated thus far. Critically the collision of pop and avant-garde drew generally savage reactions and the UK chart position of #5 owed much to the loyalty of their audience. Having sprinted for the top five Dazzle Ships didn't exactly linger at the top end of the charts. The album marked a widening of the gap between McCluskey and Humphreys that – eventually – saw a fracture in their working relationship for many years. Along with PiL's Flowers of Romance, Dazzle Ships ranks as one of the most challenging British chart albums of the decade. Unlike the Flowers… it has gradually enjoyed a major re-evaluation, something of a renaissance and a treasured place in the collections and inspirations of a generation – young at the time – who took its template and made their own musical journeys. So much so that the 25th anniversary edition, complete with bonus cuts, drew reviews largely at odds with the original slating.

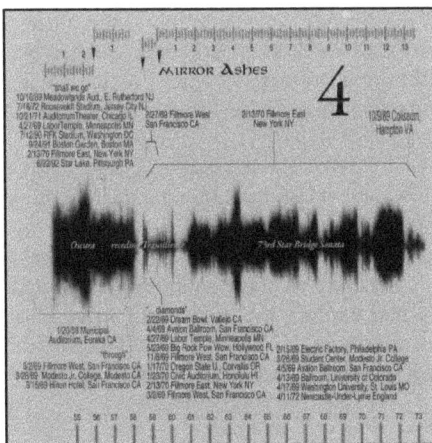

John Oswald:
Grayfolded
(Swell, 1994/1995)
What? A hundred minutes plus exploring inner space.

In the convoluted, contradictory and claim-ridden history of popular music's most mesmerising moments there has never been another composition like The Grateful Dead's "Dark Star." Generally absent from any high-profile list of the greatest rock anthems, largely ignored by the popular end of radio and covered only by those suicidal enough to compare themselves to true legends, "Dark Star" remains both a law, and a lore, unto itself. The story of how a two minute 44 second single that failed to trouble any chart became an expansive addition to classic live shows and, in turn, became the touchstone by which Dead directions and the innermost thoughts of band-members could be gauged, is available online if you want it.

"Dark Star" remains – to all intents and purposes – peerless. Any attempt to compare and contrast it with another composition of similar vintage might, just, help a novice grasp the complexity of the situation. But, it doesn't tell you what immersion in this most elusive of musical experiences might feel like. "Dark Star," like Tubular Bells, works best when experienced in its slowly unfolding entirety. And, like Tubular Bells, "Dark Star" exists in revisions and re-workings, all suggestive of the fact that its creators never saw any one performance as the final statement. Like Hawkwind's Space Ritual "Dark Star" is an event, and deeply cosmic, even if the space explored is inside the mind. And, like "Stairway to Heaven," "Smoke on the Water" and several other classics it has become a signature work of a band able to boast many career highs, and a defining work they never thought of as such when it was first created. Bear in mind, the first released version is a single! When the twenty first century BBC produced an ambitious and far-reaching history of classical music in the twentieth century one rock track seeped into the series. During a discussion of minimalism and other classical music that overlapped with rock in the late sixties The Sound and the Fury allowed a portion of "Dark Star" from the version on Live Dead to run underneath a voice over.

For the purposes of this discussion we need only establish three more things: firstly, "Dark Star" became such a legendary item in Dead sets that those in attendance would gain respect from their peers for having been lucky enough to have the experience. Secondly, "Dark Star" remained an unpredictable, randomly expanding monster and a focus for experimentation and the Dead's most daring and inventive moments throughout its tenure as part of their performances. Thirdly, despite a reticence about performing "Dark Star" that – sometimes – lasted years, the Dead had clocked up over 100 performances of their most distinctive work by 1993. At this point the Dead's Phil Lesh commissioned collage artist John Oswald to mix and explore these recordings with a view to creating one almighty composition based around varied performances of "Dark Star."

Grayfolded is the result. Over two CDs and just over one and three quarter hours of music portions of "Dark Star" performances recorded between 1968 and 1993 are mixed, faded, mashed and "folded" to produce an epic work of changing moods, spine tingling trills of guitar and solo moments of inspired invention from all the major personnel to have performed as part of the Dead in a quarter of a century. There are occasional moments of diversion that sound – by turns – like ambient music, hard rock and free-form experiments of jazz. The Dead's world was always differently abled, and in the case of Grayfolded an alternative logic applies such that the most accessible and typical moments are the longer tracks. The 17 minute sprawl of "In Revolving Ash Light" from the first CD is – probably – the closest a Grayfolded listener can now come to touching prime-period Dead in their "Dark Star" pomp. By contrast, the effortlessly sublime cascade of notes opening "Pouring Velvet" or the floating vocal harmony that is the fleeting fragment "Transilience" both capture and distil the essence of the Dead's ability to live in and explore a moment.

Grayfolded originally emerged as two separate releases in 1994 and 95 before being reissued in a deluxe double set complete with one of the most intelligent and reflective liner notes – an essay by musicologist Rob Bowman – in popular music history. The only work included in this book that may – just – claim some affinity with Grayfolded is Neil Young's manic mashing of stage sounds and assorted moments of crowd rapture, Arc. Both being attempts to capture and explore the essence of something fleeting and almost beyond comprehension. Arc amounts to an experiment, Grayfolded, by contrast, is more like a consolidation of the best elements of a unique musical journey by an uncompromising band.

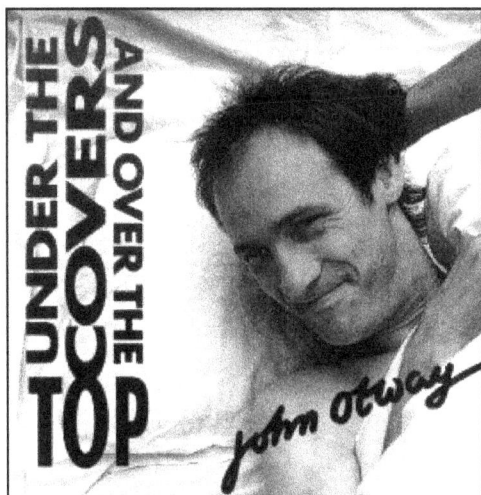

John Otway:
Under the Covers and Over the Top
(Otway, 1992)
What? Mirthful massacres of mighty hits.

It's doubtful if Otway's devoted legion of admirers, or even the man himself, would single out this collection as the best place to start any acquaintance. For those unaware of the antics of this perennial clown-prince of rock and pop it might be worth a (very) brief summary of greatest hits. Since the mid-seventies Otway has been a borderline-lunatic stage presence and inspirationally eccentric songwriter with a gift for surreal wordplay and in-your-face comedy in which the major joke is Otway's unceasing belief in his own right to stardom, and the transparent unsuitability of the man and his music for such a role. The big laughs along the way have come when – against all odds – his madcap-genius schemes have delivered (Otway achieved a top ten UK hit with "Bunsen Burner" largely by mobilising his fan-base to pre-order the CD and allowing anyone willing to turn up to Abbey Road to appear on a B-side demolition of "House of the Rising Sun;" thereby increasing their motivation to buy multiple copies). That scheme – however – is as nothing to the sheer brilliance of a scam in 1980 that saw Otway and his partner Wild Willy Barrett staying on campsites during a tour to reduce expenses, agreeing with venues that the gigs would be staged on the strength of the venues' bar takings; thereby dispensing with tickets for the tour, and obliging crowds to hand in copies of the single "DK 50-80." The song was duly hyped (with complete legality) into the lower reaches of the UK charts where an appearance on Top of the Pops was planned to ensure its continued climb. A technicians strike saw the show cancelled that week and a brilliant Otway idea crashed and burned as a result because the following week's tour dates (when the single's sales were expected to increase because of the Top of the Pops gig), were in smaller venues, accruing fewer singles sales and a resultant fall in chart position.

We digress; Otway's set has long relied on demolitions and bizarre re-inventions of popular standards; many now established crowd favourites as popular as originals like "Beware of the Flowers Cos I'm Sure They're Gonna Get You, Yeah." In 1992 Otway cut the most coherent album of his career and the only such release that has genuine cross-over appeal way beyond his fan-base. Under the Covers… is an atypical Otway compromise within which he allows the styles and sounds to vary as he covers a few numbers long-established in his set, and some others imported and destroyed in a variety of unfamiliar styles. All making the point about one thing he does superbly. Otway fans have long treasured a version of The Sweet's "Blockbuster" in which Otway uses a unique twin-necked guitar, (unique because each neck goes over a different shoulder and Otway plays with equal ham-fistedness both left and right handed guitar). That favourite and another seventies classic rocker – "You Ain't Seen Nothing Yet" – are played as standard rock with Otway's west country accent reducing their lyrics to borderline comedy. On "You Ain't Seen Nothing Yet" there is the added bonus of Attila the Stockbroker providing instant translation of the lyrics into German.

There is that Spike Jones sense of the participants lining up the standard songs and asking how – exactly – to spin each one into comedy gold. But, when Under the Covers… works, it pulls these stunts with confidence and timing; getting out of songs like "I Will Survive" and "I Am The Walrus" before the joke is exhausted. It's never better than the finale, a cod-northern British kitchen sink drama of "Space Oddity" wherein Otway intones the Bowie classic in a northern accent over the strains of a brass band: "Planet earth is blue and there's nowt I can do!" It brings the downmarket "tin can" references and personal drama of the original into a totally different focus.

Lucia Pamela:
Into Outer Space With Lucia Pamela
(Gulfstream, 1969)
What? Put it this way: All Music Guide claim this is the album Baby Jane (as played by Betty Davis) would have made.

Lucia Pamela (1904 – 2002) is in there with Florence Foster Jenkins and Mrs Miller as a classically trained car-crash of a vocalist who developed appeal partly on the basis of aiming for the stars, and falling in the gutter. There, however, any resemblance to the others ends because the creative vision behind this – her only long player – puts Lucia Pamela in another realm, literally. Into Outer Space…is a concept album claiming itself to be the tale of a journey beyond Earth. It also comes with a significant statement about the artist. From the liner notes: "The reason that Lucia is putting out this album is that everybody is asking and begging her to make a recording. Now they can have her in their homes to entertain them whenever they choose to do so and have her close to them at any time they want. Well, finally she is responding to their requests, and here is the first album from LUCIA PAMELA! So prepare yourselves for great entertainment."

We're not questioning the entertainment value. This is eccentricity writ so large as to beggar belief. Pamela claimed to have recorded this collection on the Moon: "The air is so thin everything sounds different up there." This is outsider music that has been likened to a mid-point between The Shaggs and Sun Ra. It is way more original than that. But, The Shaggs' untutored rampaging through standard song structures is a useful yardstick, so too Sun Ra's complete immersion in cosmic consciousness.

Sonically Into Outer Space is a thin sounding, overstuffed, clattering mess. Faced with a small studio, small budget and a massive idea Pamela and her crew didn't strip the sound or performance back. The ideas belong in space rock, the playing styles start somewhere in ragtime bands between the wars and throw in a grab bag of influences and flourishes as required. It's a dog's breakfast of random delights that has drawn superlatives from the high priests of outsider music. Irwin – Songs in the Key of Z – Chusid wrote: ""Imagine an LP of a peyote-soaked klezmer band, recorded with Joe Meek passed out at the console, wavering on your turntable between 31 and 35 rpm." R. J. Smith, writing in Los Angeles magazine stated the album was like: "a Dixieland band carrying boxes of silverware stumbling down a staircase."

Pamela's colourful biography claims contact with a cavalcade of musical connections, including classical greats. There is indeed a juxtaposition of classical instruments – clarinet and piano are to the fore – along with accordion, a range of percussion and some electronic contributions (widely claimed but never conclusively proven to be a Theramin). Pamela is more tuneful than Leona Anderson or Florence Foster Jenkins, but not much more so. She achieves this largely by aiming her well controlled combination of a little warble and a lot of rasp across melodies that stay well within her comfort zone. Lovers of off-key exotica will – however – be pleased to note some clanging failures here and there to hit the right note. Her album tells the story of her cosmic journey; remember she got to the Moon before Neil Armstrong and Buzz Aldrin; and found a place totally unlike anything they encountered in The Sea of Tranquillity. Like Walter Shumann's Exploring the Unknown: Lucia Pamela starts her cosmic journey locally. In her case in a place called Moontown; a utopian idyll in line with the most fantastic claims of 1950s UFO "contactees." A town in which she encounters, amongst other things: Animals, a taxless regime and an incredible ethnic diversity amongst the human inhabitants. Pamela's lyrics are more surreal fiction than science fiction. "Walking on the Moon" Her greatest hit – i.e. it got lots of response when Chusid played it on radio and was subsequently compiled when he started working on his Songs in the Key of Z albums – includes the lines: "As I was walking on the moon, I met a little cow-ow-ow, And this is what she said to me: Da-da da-da-da-da da-da, moo-moo-moo-moo moo-moo moo-moo-moo-moo!!!!" NASA sent twelve men to the same place soon afterwards. No bovine conversations were recorded!

The rest of the incredible journey is hinted at with a look at the titles that make up Into Outer Space: "Moontown/Walking on the Moon/Flip Flop Fly/Dear Me/You and Your Big Ideas/What to Do Is the Question/Hap-Hap-Happy Heart/Indian Alphabet Chant (A-I-Iddy-I-O-O-O)/Why? Because I Want To/In Love, In Love/I've Got a Song/ Blue Wind/In the Year 2,000!!!" The list also suggests – rightly – that Pamela's work has the same genius inanity that makes The Shaggs' lyrics so awe-inspiring. Pamela is clearly in love with the rhyming couplet, the sound of words in rhythmic patterns and the ability of description to capture the moment. For the most part, the moments captured belong in the colouring book for kids she also produced to celebrate this journey.

It is a debateable point whether Pamela's standing as one of the ultimate outsider artists would have been strengthened with more recordings (she was already in her mid-sixties when this album was released). It's also debateable whether acquainting yourself with her incredible life, and the claims she made about her many accomplishments and contacts, adds to the unique pleasure of listening end to end through this album. But it is beyond dispute that Into Outer Space... continues to trade on a reputation as one of the strangest long players ever recorded, anywhere (from Moontown to Motown).

Korla Pandit:
The Grand Moghul Suite
(Vita 1951)
What? Grandaddy of exotica; plays it like he means it.

This is one of those cases where a grasp of the artist's own biography adds masses to an appreciation of the music. The Grand Moghul Suite began life on a 10" album in 1951. One of a series of recorded keyboard works in which Pandit (1921-1998) performed lengthy compositions on piano and organ. Grand Moghul offers a big sounding, slightly ponderous, series of works all of which contribute to a lengthy suite, drawing on eastern percussive sounds and frequently availing itself of the most eastern sounding tones on the organ. With tracks like "Ode to a Desert Love" and "Procession of the Grand Moghul" this is light entertainment instrumental music at its most cinematic. The album varies moods and sounds with the clear intent of taking the listener on a journey. The occasional crash of a cymbal and gong adds an authentic flavour and anyone familiar with the dreamy eyes and vivid white turban of Pandit would – doubtless – feel an affinity with the man as his emotive instrumental pieces speak to them of his exotic past (the son of a Brahmin priest and French opera singer born in New Delhi).

Today the work is celebrated as one of the first great pieces of exotica, though such appreciation is considerably more ironic than it was in 1951. As exotica this is a flawless piece of high ambition, straight faced execution and glorious inauthenticity. The Grand Moghul Suite is about as Indian as a microwavable frozen curry, and Pandit's own story simply adds to the delight. Born John Roland Redd, Pandit's parentage boasted a French/black American lineage. His black skin saw him educated in a black school but its light tones allowed him to pass as Asian rather than African. Pandit wasn't his first pseudonym and his keyboard career saw him progress through supper clubs and radio until television and – fleetingly – film began loving his regal appearance and ability to stare blissfully into the camera as he played. In the days of static heavy cameras television ate up performing turns who could look interesting and do something vaguely clever as the camera maintained a fixed gaze for a few minutes. Pandit's party tricks included playing piano and organ simultaneously. Musically, many people bought the whole spurious biography and America took Pandit to its heart for a number of years. Though – in retrospect – it is quite telling that he lost one regular television booking when he was replaced by that other high-water mark of depth and classical authenticity: Liberace. Pandit's story packs enough twists and turns to be entertaining in its own right (one of the final significant things he did was to turn up, in person, in the Ed Wood movie). But his music stands as amongst the best and most enduring examples of exotica and The Grand Moghul Suite is – arguably – his most ambitious, and greatest, achievement.

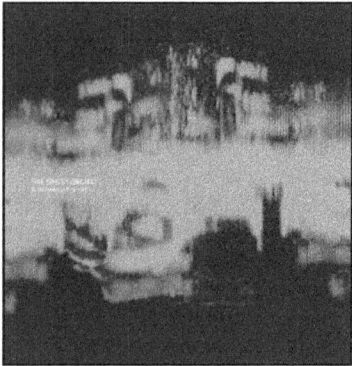

PARC (Parapsychic Acoustic Research Cooperative):
The Ghost Orchid
(PARC, 1999)
What? Dead or alive, that is the question.

There are occasional spoken word/factual recordings that so push the bounds of the listening experience that they make stranger sounds, and more memorable listening, than music. This bizarre collection is one case in point. Basically, what you get is an audio documentary on EVP (Electronic Voice Phenomena). For those not acquainted with EVP, these are disembodied voices collected from audio recordings on tape machines, and other electronic devices. Many people – like the dedicated research team who compiled this collection – take it as an item of faith that these voices represent attempts by the dead to contact the living. This album compiles examples and narrates the listener through the evidence. It charts some of the history and behaviour of EVP, discussing the research methods and – above all – lets the voices speak. It is a principle of research in this area that snippets are listened to repeatedly to reveal meanings. What you think you hear in the first run through may well sound clearer, and more convincing, by the third time. Because much of the album is made up of repeated snippets, and because much of what you hear offers up fleeting meanings at best, the whole collection can come off sounding like some massive electronic experiment that belongs somewhere in the more eclectic corners of public service radio. Indeed, a snatch of the album was played, along with other ghoulish delights, during a Halloween special on BBC Six Music's Stuart Maconie's Freakzone, where it fitted in to perfection. The jury remains out on whether any of this material represents the desperate attempt of any deceased person to break through to the world he or she once inhabited. Less questionable by far is the claim that a one-off encounter with the whole album played end to end will leave you with a listening experience you are likely to remember for a long time.

Parliament:
Osmium
(Invictus, 1970)
What? In the best democratic traditions of parliaments everywhere, a complete mishmash of conflicting opinions.

Osmium opened the albums account of one of the most influential soul/funk bands in history, and almost marked the end of that influential career. There are fleeting moments of Osmium when a casual listener would deny that the band have much soul influence, even hardened Parliament lovers have to take on board the blind alleys presented here. The album itself didn't threaten to derail their career, the main problem came from contractual issues that kept the band from releasing new product until 1974, by which point they were in the forefront of full-on funk and this curio was out of time, and off the radar. Osmium shows the same fearlessness about experimentation that has given rise to George Clinton's best and worst excesses. But, it also covers incredible ground. "Little Ole Country Boy" goes rampantly into red-neck territory with only Clinton's vocal pyrotechnics giving it a Parliament feel. The same track boasts pedal steel wails, a Jews' harp with heavy reverb and – no kidding – yodelling! "My Automobile" covers similar ground, and goes into spoken word territory as George and a female companion argue out a sticky love situation. However, for fearless strange-brewing these tracks are bested by "The Silent Boatman" which closed the original album. "Boatman" is a slow soul ballad that segues into bagpipes playing the melody from "The Skye Boat Song." Staggeringly, it drags soul from its constituent parts. And it is soul, rather than the awesome rhythmic funk assault of later Parliament, that rescues this ragbag of sounds from self-indulgence. So the incorporation of Pachobel's Canon (yes, really!) into "Oh Lord, Why Lord/Prayer" works beautifully as it floats between George's gritty vocal and the massed choir ranked around the melody. Elsewhere the Tamla licks, meaty hooks and Clinton's keyboard mastery manage, just about, to make the whole collection sound coherent. The massive chorus on "Livin the Life" and the funk rampage of "I Call my Baby Pussycat" and "Funky Woman" hint at the glories to come. The long marginalisation of Osmium has worked well for the handful of audio thrill-seekers who continue to chase it. Successive CD reissues haven't exactly skimped on the tonnage of bonus material, most of it as varied and bizarre as the original ten tracks. If you can snag one with the tracks culled from singles you can get "Hot Rod Mama" and the soulful political sloganeering of "Come in Out of the Rain," a track that takes Parliament into the rock/soul territory of Sly and the Family Stone. You are unlikely to be first to ask yourself why these gems weren't included on the original ten track album. Osmium was retitled as Rhenium and First Thangs for one reissue.

Harry Partch: Delusion of the Fury (Innova, 1999)
What? Signature work of Partcheon strangeness.

Partch (1901–1974) turned musical difference into a lifelong quest. Any of his major works would have qualified with ease for the current book and we could have included at least half a dozen without any need to apologise. That's the measure of how different most of Partch's major works are from the main body of twentieth century classical music, and from each other. The internet is awash with the information we're hinting at here. Suffice it to say at this point that Partch developed his own variant on notation scale, his own instruments to play a music only he appeared able to imagine and his own idiosyncratic notions of purity when it came to recording. Then there's his fondness for composing works that challenge the notion of roles within performance. Partch's classical musicians may well be required to become part of the stage action…Frank Zappa was mainstream in comparison.

Delusion of the Fury is as good a place as any to start. This 30th anniversary CD features the final major work of Partch's composing career, Delusion summarises some of the many things Partch did his way. Much of the work presents chords and competing sounds drawn from a broad cultural fabric. Information prepared for a 2013 live revival of the work highlights the main focus: "Based on Japanese and African myths, he develops a piece between dream and madness, that integrates all theatrical means, light, movement, and song with the extraordinary presence of his instruments in a theatre without a precise setting, where temporal layers overlap. A view of a culture that seems strange and yet familiar to us. Partch spreads out in all four directions a 'ritual net' that celebrates the reconciliation of the living with death and life."

In practical terms this amounts to a CD of resonances that challenge your perception of how instruments should sound, and how the story within a piece of music should develop. Passing moments betray the oriental and African influences, but Partch seldom sounds derivative because his instruments present tones and sonic ranges well beyond music heard in their time. A "sub-bass" instrument, christened the "marimba eroica," plays a starring role in Delusion intruding with incredible presence. There is a complex history relating to the recording of this work. Partch had a distrust of mechanical recording devices and the way their moving parts compromised the sounds he imagined. But, the original sound quality is excellent and the tonal subtleties of choir, percussion and drone instruments on a track like "Chorus of Shadows" do justice to Partch's contention that the sound was very much part of the message. Similarly, the use of echo and highly complex percussion on "A Son in Search of his Father's Face" is a triumph in the face of a very challenging task of turning a unique live work into a listenable album.

Ottilie Patterson with Chris Barber's Jazz Band:
That Patterson Girl
(Lake 2007)
What? Breathtaking blues, white, British girl singer.

Patterson (1932-2011) performed with the Chris Barber Jazz Band for a number of years. By common consent her best performances came in the late fifties. The band were the headline act in performance, and on the album covers. By the time CD compilers got around to gathering her best tracks Patterson was retired. Throat problems beset her career after the material on this CD (culled from 1955-63) was recorded and, despite a comeback in later years, she never regained the emotive power and vocal range she shows over these 23 well-chosen tracks. Patterson's contributions to shows and albums provided contrast to the other work performed by Barber's band. One positive result is there to enjoy on this album. She was obliged to try any and every aspect of jazz and blues. That Patterson Girl presents a consummate artiste with no noticeable weakness. At her most serious Ottilie is up there with Bessie Smith, showcasing a massive voice as the emotion runs raw in standards like "Beale Street Blues." A fair proportion of the work here has been interpreted by other singers, but Patterson more than holds her own, and frequently throws in an inflection or variation on timing that makes for a personal take on a particular song. She is as confident surging forward on "Weeping Willow Blues" as slowing things down for gospel tunes, especially when her own piano accompaniment contributes to a spell-binding "Heavenly Sunshine."

When the Barber band blew up a storm Ottilie would provide some humour with songs verging on novelty, like "I Wish I Could Shimmy Like my Sister Kate." A few of these also appear on That Patterson Girl. They show the rounded abilities of Ottilie Patterson. But the real gold here is the beauty and concentrated power Patterson brings to so much of the heart-rending blues material. At a time when UK talent was often regarded as a pale imitation of US originals Patterson's versions of songs like "Backwater Blues" were proof that Britain had at least one female singer amongst the world's best in jazz and blues.

Annette Peacock:
I'm the One
(RCA, 1972)
What? Soup of styles in experimental/psychedelic early outing for noted vocal talent.

Reviewing a reissue of this selection of strangeness for The Guardian in the present century John Fordham noted: "this seismically influential session [with its] synth-warped banshee vocals, morphed jazz ballads, Motown grooving and squelchy electronics were to touch many jazz and pop artists in [the seventies]." Peacock has been adopted and loved by more jazz fans than those of any other genre, but it's not for want of her trying to break barriers. I'm the One centres on her vocals. Deeper than most females and more likely to use changes in power and tone than to soar through a vast vocal range, Peacock challenged a lot of accepted vocal practice for 1972 by singing some of her lead lines through the – then – cutting edge Moog synthesiser. I'm the One throws a range of styles into the mix, offers up a notable cover of "Love me Tender" (think a reworking on the scale of John Cale's take on "Heartbreak Hotel") and showcases Peacock's voice as a lead instrument. A standard trick in this regard being the move she pulls on "Pony" whereby she begins singing before moving into a free-form, scatting and vocalising to mix her wails and melody lines over a looping jazz groove, like a trumpet. The arrangements frequently work as a spiralling and sonically loose base from which Peacock's vocals can soar before diving back to connect with a stray lick or specific beat. The unfolding of "Love me Tender" over almost four minutes is a particular case in point. A smoky and skeletal opening pits Peacock against a keyboard, she holds and twists notes as the backing grows to a generally jazzy groove, dives back in as the song threatens to turn into maudlin country, and then helms an emotional second half as the track melds the different sounds without ever making its mind up which direction to go. "Seven Days" is about as near to mainstream as I'm the One gets, with an impressive and exposed vocal over a slowly chording piano. But, even here some basic and highly effective electronic tones gradually weave their influence on the mood. "Blood" also starts with Peacock against one keyboard before morphing into a darkly demented attempt at a torch song.

By contrast, the title track earns its place by presenting such a range of sounds and styles that it touches on the places the rest of the album will subsequently explore. Despite its influence on other musicians at the time, and its role in providing Peacock with a calling card sufficiently strong to gain her guest slots and working arrangements with many others, I'm the One spent years languishing in RCA's vaults, unavailable and, apparently, unappreciated, until Peacock herself secured the rights and arranged a CD reissue in 2012.

Josh T. Pearson:
Last of the Country Gentlemen
(Mute, 2011)
What? Troubled American troubadour type sticks his Oar in.

Cut over a couple of days in Berlin, featuring seven (eight on the vinyl edition) newly written songs which had seen a few live appearances, and made up entirely of Pearson's musical efforts and the autobiographical lyrics pouring out his troubles, Last of the Country Gentlemen isn't exactly a country record and isn't that gentlemanly. Apart from anything else, Pearson's propensity for spilling intimacies might cause some consternation to those who identify themselves as the subject matter for his songs. This is a cynical, morose and troubled record in which the most striking tracks are the epic rambles: "Sweetheart I Ain't Your Christ" and "Honeymoon's Great! Wish you Were Here." Both run well past the ten minute mark. The inclusion of the epic title track is the one difference between vinyl and CD editions.

Pearson had barely recorded in the previous decade and had battled a drink problem for a lengthy period, before moving from his native Texas to Europe, falling in and out of love, and eventually pouring out the contents of the album. It is bare and basic, often relying on stop-start moments in songs, lengthy vocal diatribes against a backdrop of guitar chords that appear to be establishing their own time signature as they stumble along, and – lyrically speaking – the whole affair is a serious downer. At his lowest moments Pearson isn't so much a glass half empty merchant; he's prone to denying that glass was ever his in the first place. "When I said I'd give my life. I weren't talking suicide" ("Sweetheart I Ain't Your Christ"), "Woman when I've raised hell. You're gonna know it. There won't be a shadow of doubt…No pictures left hangin' only lonely unpainted halls" ("Woman When I've Raised Hell"). "I come from a long line of dreamers. Each one more tired than the one before" ("Country Dumb"). Pearson's lyrics are knowing observations of life's darker side, his voice is a lived-in drawl, his musical accompaniment is suitably minimal and never flashy.

The obvious comparison sonically and in mood is Skip Spence's legendary (sound of a man falling apart album) Oar. There's nothing psychedelic about Pearson's effort and – if anything – Last of the Country Gentlemen is even bleaker and more knowing than Spence's work. It scored massively in terms of critical plaudits on the basis of intense performances of the songs, its unsparing honesty and the consistency of quality achieved over the whole album.

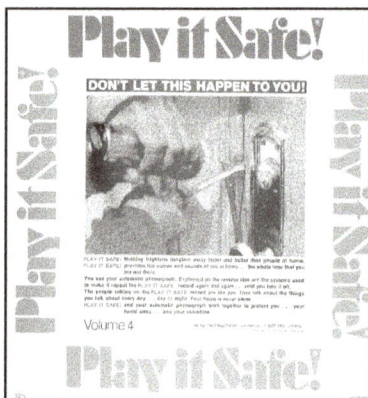

Penta Sales Corporation: Play it Safe Vol. 4 (Penta Sales Corp 1972)
What? Audio drama jaw dropper isn't what it seems!

As of this writing the entire 47 minutes and 45 seconds of this strange sortie through spoken word and sound effects resides as a free-to-download mp3 file, specifically as the download on January 10th 2007 of the 365 Days Project. Read this entry, then go online and get it, because, even in the 365 audio archive of oddities this is singular delight of seldom imitated niche market genius, or something like it. The best these words can do to replicate the experience is to describe and comment on the whole affair and leave you with the same problem faced by those encountering the recording unawares. Why, exactly, did the writers, producers and performers bother to do this?

On first listen Play it Safe is a vacuous audio drama, we encounter a couple who wander about their home, frequently exchange views, fall out a little, make up and discuss her mother, his underwear (which leaked in the wash), whether to pay a mechanic or let the husband try and fix the car himself etc. Doors slam, footsteps rattle around and the conversations are very middle-America circa 1972. Pea Hix, who comments on this recording for the 365 Days Project notes: "this is by far the best spoken word record I've ever heard. I usually like to play this record for people without telling them what it was intended for, to see if they can guess why anyone would buy it."

Have you got any inkling yet? Bizarrely the stereotypical middle-American chatter is the best clue, the "plot" is best ignored and if you listen to the entire piece you're missing the point completely. The intention of this record – and, presumably, volumes 1-3 of the same series – is to convince burglars, and anyone else intent on entering your property whilst you arc out, that someone is at home. Play it Safe... aims to present such a realistic recreation of normal household sounds that anyone chancing on a twenty or thirty second snatch of it through an open window, say, would skip past your property before vaulting your neighbour's wall, assuming, of course, that the neighbours had been thoughtless enough to go out leaving the house in darkness and the driveway empty. And also assuming the neighbours weren't smart enough to buy this album.

...Vol. 4 presents a couple prone to chatting about the price of women's hairdressing, slightly concerned about their weight and generally focussed on the standard fodder of the more forgettable scenes in soaps and sitcoms. Except, they're not prone to drama, or comedy on this evidence, just minor irritations and affirmations that they love each other really.

As a listening experience Pea Hix nails the fascination: "It's actors trying to sound as inconspicuously actor-ish as possible. Add to this the fact that, as per the instructions on the jacket, you're supposed to play it at a level where someone standing outside the house can hear that there's people talking inside without being able to make out what's being said, and to me that's a recipe for pure performance art!" The present authors can only concur, and suggest you investigate the download for yourself (vinyl copies are seldom sighted and a CD reissue has strangely failed to materialise). The cover artwork (also available online) coupled with more detailed discussions adds to the magic, and also makes clear the sincerity of this release. The original album came with instructions on how to arrange things so – in your absence – the album could repeat itself over and over on the turntable and your home could be rigged in such a way that the speakers would pump out the sound around the house.

Then again, you could save yourself the pseudo-roadie machinations and just buy, or borrow, a really bad-tempered dog.

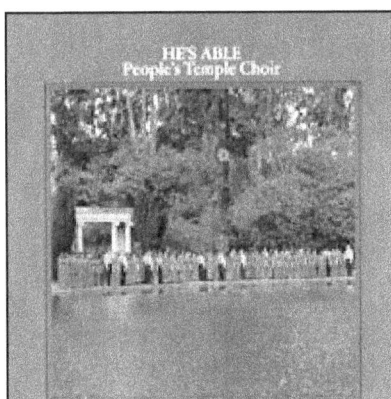

People's Temple Choir:
He's Able
(Grey Matter, 19??)
What? Possibly the most disturbing and distasteful audio artefact ever offered for commercial sale. So, it probably belongs in this book.

A bootleg offering up no official release date in its packaging He's Able starts out as a regular seventies gospel album, opening with a chirpy choir of children, offering up a spirited working of "Walk a Mile in My Shoes" – a much performed standard in Elvis' set at the time – and some competent if predictable musical chops. The guitars probably try too hard at times to infuse the whole show with a lurking sense of psychedelia and elsewhere the drumming is annoyingly busy, or a fraction too far ahead of the beat. The vocalists change, a few of the cuts emerge as characterful and sincere takes on seventies gospel and the high-spot in terms of hairs on the back of the neck soulful connection is an agreeably understated run through the old standard "Black Baby."

But let's not kid ourselves...nobody bought this bizarre twofer for the first album. That simply gave the CD reissue its title and – frankly – an excuse. The final track, album length in itself, is a little over 41 minutes of live recording. If you haven't sussed it yet this is the Jonestown massacre. The final sermon of the Reverend Jim Jones, recorded live in Guyana on 18 November 1978 and ending with the clearly audible screams of his followers dying after drinking Flavor Aid laced with a potent cocktail of drugs, including Cynanide. In all 918 people involved with the People's Temple died, including their charismatic, increasingly erratic, paranoid and rambling Elvis-alike leader: Jim Jones. Until 11 September 2001 this was the greatest loss of US civilian life at one place, at one time, by means other than natural disaster.

The convoluted story of how so many US citizens ended up in their own compound in Jonestown, Guyana, how their increasingly concerned relatives sought to extricate some of them, how Congressman Leo Ryan flew to Guyana to investigate and how his murder as he attempted to fly back with a handful of defectors promoted the mass suicide of the beleaguered group is well chronicled elsewhere. So, are the words on the "Death Tape" which forms the final track here: "Mass Suicide."

For the most part this sounds like the one-mic, low quality analogue cassette recording it is. Opening with some clearly audible frenzied staccato rantings from Jones, we get a couple of cuss words, some general shouting on the nature of love and a rousing call to arms combining a threat on anyone seeking to attack the People's Temple and an assertion: "I'll fight, I'll fight..."

The sound quality and thread of the story soon vanishes, unless you have a transcript, but the key moments in the ensuing drama do leap out. The fate of Congressman Leo Ryan is discussed, Jones stating that the plane taking Ryan and the defectors from Guyana will be downed when the pilot is shot by one of those on board. Jones' notion of "Revolutionary suicide" is the main point of debate and his voice prevails. One temple member, Christine Miller, tries to revive hope of the whole cohort fleeing to Russia; beyond American justice and influence. But, between 20 and 25 minutes another voice, Jim McElvane, persuades people differently.

Citing himself as a "therapist" McElvane discusses his work with past-life regressions and assures people that everyone recalling the moment of death in the therapy he carried out, experienced it as a moment of peace. A few minutes later an unidentified man announces "The Congressman has been murdered," Jones reiterates "The Congressman's dead" and the voices opposing revolutionary suicide vanish from the debate.

Surviving witnesses stated the first to die included the youngest, poisoned by their own mothers with Flavour Aid squirted from a syringe from which the needle had been removed. As the half hour mark approaches the gaps between speeches on the tape are clearly filled by the sounds of dying. Time matters, Jones and others figuring they have around 40 minutes before trouble arrives.

One unidentified woman urges everyone to "Hurry up." The tape had ran to a stop long before the majority of the deaths. But, what is recorded is enough to give a sense of the scale and nature of the tragedy that ensued. Above all else it is the chilling logic and efficiency of the mass suicide that overwhelms anyone hearing this horrific document. Jones' wisdom in the final minutes includes: "If everybody will relax.

The best thing you do to relax and you will have no problems. You'll have no problems with this thing if you just relax," and "I don't care how many screams you hear, I don't care how many anguished cries, death is a million times preferable to ten more days of this life. If you knew what was ahead of you – if you knew what was ahead of you, you'd be glad to be stepping over tonight."

Linda Perhacs:
Parallelograms
(Kapp, 1970)
What? A true psych-folk original.

Neglected to the point of complete critical and commercial indifference at birth, Parallelograms has spent over four decades slowly redeeming itself. In the process earning a reputation as an inventive, compelling, insightful and shimmeringly beautiful period piece. What it conspicuously lacks in terms of hit-single material and strident anthems it more than makes up for with an original and hard-to-imitate approach to songcraft and performance. Perhacs' main career was as a dental hygienist and – despite being resident in California – she existed at some distance from the hippie culture of the time. Her job did put her in contact with a slew of celebrities including composer Leonard Rosenman, which – in turn – led to the opportunity to make this album.

Her inspirations were similar to many hippie/singer-songwriters of her era and Parallelograms drips with a consciousness of nature and sense of expanding mental horizons. By Perhacs' own admission she had a vision of dancing lights (not drug-induced, you'll find online discussion linking Perhacs to the condition Synaesthesia within which sufferers perceive sensory input from one area in another realm, giving some of them the ability to "see" music). That may just be the key to the multi-layered acoustic guitar parts, overlaid voices and mantra-like choruses of Parallelograms' best cuts. Nothing here is less than very good, some of it remains so innovative it still sounds like nothing else you've ever heard. The CD reissues in the 21st century have brought some additional tracks and a welter of re-appraisals, making Parallelograms one of the go-to collections for a new generation of pscyh-folksters. And when hardened critics gush like the following, it's hard to ignore the achievements of this album: "It sits there on the shelf, a life's compendium, stunning in its beauty and the fact that no later albums can frame it in a historical context, or diminish its impact. Softer, less declamatory than Joan Baez, more daring than Joni Mitchell, Perhacs' songs are psychedelic on a daily, domestic basis." (That'll be the AllMusicGuide, then). Andy Beta of the L A Weekly sees "psychedelic on a daily, domestic basis" and raises you: "Imagine strolling through a hushed forest, only to have the humus break open and swallow you whole; such was the sensation of first hearing her uncanny, ruminative music. With a lovely, near-weightless whisper that conjures Karen Carpenter and British she-folk legend Vashti Bunyan, Perhacs gently moves with the acoustic guitar lines. But at crucial moments, drones and mystifying electronic effects appear, her voice suddenly deepens, and within arises a music of portent." We could go on, Perhacs current website offers you the option of spooling down – apparently – into infinity in a page of glowing reviews. But, we have another 499 albums to squeeze into this book. Though we should note that, against many expectations, Perhacs finally released a second album, The Soul of All Natural Things, in 2014.

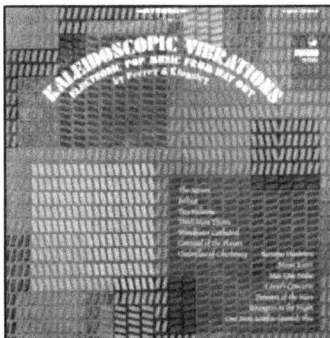

Perrey and Kingsley:
Kaleidoscopic Vibrations: Electronic Pop Music From Way Out.
(Vanguard, 1967)
What? Gloriously ecstatic ragbag of exotica.

Frenchman Jean Jacques Perrey (b.1929) and German Gershon Kingsley (b.1920) were already seasoned veterans of early electronica and had a working relationship dating back to 1955 when they unleashed this collection of cutting edge electronica on the world. It followed The In Sound From Way Out! (1966). Both albums showcasing a –then – cutting edge reliance on samples, keyboard loops and the presentation of electronica as a genre in its own right. Perrey and Kingsley both drew on slightly unusual personal backgrounds. Their relationship was further cemented with highly complementary skills: Perrey the inventive musician with melodic innovations forever at his fingertips, Kingsley the arranger and thinker who could see the wood whilst his colleague was busy planting more trees.

The pair's involvement with incidental music, commercials and – the mainly folk based – Vanguard Records provided the other tools required for their work. Basically, this duo got their hands on the Moog years before the rock elite adopted it as the defining instrument of progressive rock. Their studio-bound life gave them the patience and innate skills to hone solutions to most of the problems created by their fertile imaginations. In their working environment tape loops were – quite literally – loops of tape, sampling involved recording onto reel-to-reel machines and physically cutting the tapes. To this duo the kind of sonic trickery done by 21st century drop-down menus was generally achieved by musing over a cup of coffee before someone in the room said: "I know how we'll do it…"

Perrey and Kingsley's work was marketed with cod-psychedelic covers and the original pieces (in contrast to the obvious lifts from classical themes and the like) rejoiced in – apparently – hip titles like: "Jungle Blues from Jupiter." Where their 1966 effort was wall-to-wall with original material 1967's Kaleidoscopic Vibrations… pillaged contemporary and classic tunes to provide a cornucopia of film themes, classical reworkings and a few of the original turned on tunes that had been the complete focus of their first effort. Probably because it contains so many familiar musical reference points – like the theme from The Third Man – Kaleidoscopic Vibrations… has long since passed into exotica legend.

It most certainly isn't any-kind of early prog masterpiece. If nothing else, the wilful pillaging and reworking of anything the duo see fit to grab suggests an irrational love of their Moog and the possibilities of the studio. All of which is achieved at the expense of being down with any but the most marginalized of the kids. But the charm of the duo's work lies in this very fact. These are geeks who get that they are geeks. They feel love in their delight at transforming a tune into a speeded up, echoing or otherwise mangled nugget of electronica. As their work erupts from the speakers they're not stupid enough to believe for one second they have their fingers on any psychedelic pulse. They are – however – clever enough to see through some of the blissed out psychedelic bullshit for what it is and capable of fighting back with intelligence, imagination and experience. All of which – in print – makes this album sound like the kind of brittle and studied work of "proper" composers. It never veers too far into this territory and it is the life, exuberance and spirit of this album that continue to earn it radio play, and new fans. A note: this entry considers the original release of Kaleidoscopic Vibrations…The 1971 album Spotlight on the Moog - Kaleidoscopic Vibrations is exactly the same album, retitled, and more readily found today.

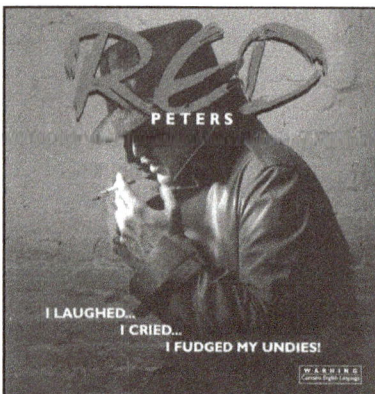

Red Peters:
I Laughed, I Cried, I Fudged my Undies
(Ugly Sisters, 1995)
What? Nudge-nudge comedy, the musical gags are pretty good too!

Red Peters (aka comedian Douglas Stevens) released a few comedy singles before unleashing this, his first album, in 1995. Stevens gives a consistent lounge singer delivery; supported by a tight band and ably embellished with faux vocal inflections to give just the right emphasis. He then throws in an album's worth of filthy gags, shredding the comfy longue-core feel with sideswipes at some obvious – and very American - targets. There's nothing too sophisticated in the puerile parade of lyrical smut and double entendre. In fact, the best gags are frequently the lowest. "How's Your Whole...Family?" doesn't look too promising with the lyrics printed on the page. Red's comic timing gets just the right emphasis on the phrase "How's your whole (hole!)…" from which point on you see the smut coming a mile off, but it is sing-along funny. "You Promised the Moon (But I Preferred Uranus)" is in the same comedy zone.

Like any good comedian Red varies the material and the album ties it all together with the spurious device of a host - Alan Pinchloaf – giving us some background on Peters, who is presented as a losing and embittered lounge singer so far down on his luck as to be performing a Tourettes benefit. The album also stumbles into varied musical territory. "The Two Gay Irishmen" is a hearty sideswipe at hearty Irish songs, and it mines an ancient gag about Patrick Fitzgerald and Gerald Fitzpatrick. This song also employs the phrase "fudge your undies" which has its own comic value presented in an Irish accent. The Chipmunks (as in the musical act) are almost beyond parody but "Holy Shit, It's Christmas" manages the trick of sending up and celebrating that great sound at the same time. Musically, this doesn't come close to the subtleties of Richard Cheese. Peters is primarily a comedian and entertainer for whom albums are a side-line. Cheese is closer to acts like The Bonzo Dog Band as a musical parody act. For all that, Peters can go hard. "Blow Me" with its vivid sexual description stands up alongside Cheese's takes on the likes of "People = Shit" as a perfect collision of lounge-core and an incessantly hard lyrical diatribe.

The on-going documentary commentary (complete with fart gags) and musical diversity keeps the album coherent. Those of a higher comic persuasion, and generally averse to smut, won't find anything here clever or funny. For others who find a spiritual home in this world there are karaoke mixes at the end of the album; offering you the chance to perform this filth the next time you find yourself in the company of others. Peters' reference points – musically, socially and career wise – are so strongly American that his recorded works have not exported too effectively. If you are reading this outside the US and think Peters' name rings some kind of bell it might be because, in an apparent accident, Peters farted in the presence of the Obama family on holiday in Martha's Vineyard in August 2011, causing one of the president's daughters some distress. Peters declared himself mortified and embarrassed by the events, but it did give him some international notoriety.

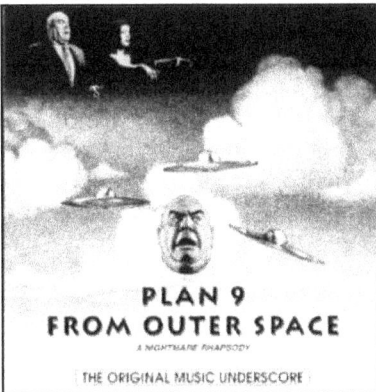

Plan 9 From Outer Space:
Original Sound Track
(Performance, 1994)
What? Like nothing on Earth…

If you are already familiar with the movie of Plan 9 From Outer Space and its creator Edward D. Wood Jr, it might make sense to skip to the second paragraph here. If not: Plan 9…became a certified cult-legend around the time the watching and owning of bad (as in truly brainless and inept) movies became fashionable in the late seventies. An originator of this pastime – Michael Medved – opened the floodgates by inviting movie fans to nominate the biggest stinker they'd ever encountered and Plan 9…duly took first place in the poll. This was some achievement because the runners up, Orca, the Airport sequels etc. were big budget recent releases known to many. Plan 9… is a late fifties sci-fi ultra-cheapie. The only conclusion that could be drawn was that whilst very few had seen Plan 9… all of those exposed had their senses so scrambled that the experience was etched in their collective psyches for all time. And it wasn't a good experience. Since this belated fame an army of the devoted, the amazed and the socially callous have gathered to celebrate this incredible movie and the other works of its creator Edward D. Wood, heroic war cameraman, transvestite and a movie maverick's movie maverick. A shorthand way to represent Ed Wood's talent is to reference Oscar Wilde. In terms of his achievements (and Plan 9… is simply the most celebrated in a small stable of stinkers) Wood may be in the gutter, but is he ever dreaming of the stars?!

The "soundtrack" here is exactly what it claims to be. Where other movies collect the songs and incidental music the Plan 9… soundtrack offers up everything the audience of the movie hears from beginning to end. Granted, it does lose a fair amount if you can't see the visuals. You miss the wooden acting, flapping scenery, recurring back-drops that serve as the inside of a UFO and an aircraft, the clunking continuity errors and the truly Ed Woodian device whereby the original star Bela Lugosi (who died a few days into filming) is replaced by an actor a few decades younger and a few inches taller, the whole cack-handed caper being cloaked (literally) because the stand-in spends his entire screen time walking about with a cape held across his face.

On the other hand…this soundtrack works as an ecstatic nightmare betraying some insight into why Ed Wood himself regarded it as his Citizen Kane. From the moment in the opening credits when television psychic Criswell says: "Future events such as these will affect you in the future" you don't doubt the dialogue's ability to ambush you with ineptitudes. Plot wise, simply listening to the movie doesn't discount too much of the story because the original title – Grave Robbers From Outer Space – appears in the over-dramatic opening announcements. From this point onwards the plot is easy enough to follow. Technically superior aliens have landed in middle-America and their plans for world domination depend in large part on re-animating the corpses in a nearby cemetery to act as their henchmen (and women) as planet Earth is made to succumb to their superior power. It helps the listener a lot that the aliens appear welded to typically American modes of speech and measuring their time in "earth days." Speaking of time, the entire soundtrack is conveniently contained on one disk since the original movie runs a shade under 70 minutes.

For the listener the utterly crude electronic effects and blatant filching of stock footage from the military work better when reduced to sound only, because nothing is complicated (other than the scientific logic behind the aliens' belief that Earth is endangering the Solar System). Wood was always a belt and braces guy when it came to story-telling, so seeing a flying saucer tended to go hand in hand with hearing a lowly-paid actor of limited talent gesturing at the sky and shouting: "flying saucer." Maybe Wood knew that one day his master-work would be released in audio-only form. Whatever the reason, following the twists and turns of Plan 9… doesn't greatly tax the listener deprived of the visuals. The listening experience is akin to the most vacuous and, yet, strangely inspired radio play you are ever likely to hear. Plan 9… remains a work so utterly sure of its right to exist that its worst moments are also its very best and any attempt at parody would be as doomed to failure as the aliens attempting to revive dead Americans are here.

Sidney Poitier:
Poitier Meets Plato
(Warner Brothers, 1964)
What? Greek philosophy, modern jazz and A' list acting talent combine to create mix-tape gold.

There isn't that much to say about this album once the constituent parts have been identified and described. Plato is amongst the greatest philosophical minds of all time; his works have remained in print, and under academic study for millennia. Fred Katz led a jazz ensemble with form where producing lively backing for bizarre spoken word recordings was concerned (Katz provides the musical accompaniments for much of Ken Nordine's most celebrated "word jazz" work). Poitier was on Hollywood's 'A' list in 1964: and probably the most prominent afro-American actor on the planet. Given the massive social changes relating to race (especially in the USA) during the period Poitier had been blessed/cursed with roles giving him moral high ground, emotional depths and massive character arcs within the narrative.

So, this curio made sense in the offices of Warner Brothers, who duly released it. Poitier Meets Plato might be something of a clunky title, but then the 1970 reissue went too far in the other direction and described itself as Journeys Inside the Mind. The concept easily survives the cack-handed conglomeration of its constituent parts and on cuts like "Our World is a Cave" (in which Plato discusses the changing experience of reality depending on how life is lived; effectively discussing becoming enlightened) Poitier's exemplary diction carries itself majestically over the backing. In 1964 there were obvious allegories to be charted between Plato's massive insights and the state of civil rights for all in the USA. To present day ears the album sounds dated, given its reliance on very clear diction and the meandering, but hardly slammin', jazz. But, the performances stand up. Greek rap might be a million miles from gangsta rap, but its 1960s incarnation continues to find new fans to the present day.

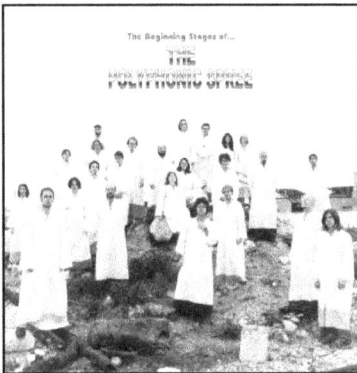

The Polyphonic Spree:
The Beginning Stages Of The Polyphonic Spree (Hollywood Records/ Good Records, 2002)
What? Blissful beginnings.

How – exactly – to categorise The Polyphonic Spree has taxed great minds in music criticism. So, we're not about to argue the point here. The nature of The Polyphonic Spree has partly been defined by events and sales figures, and each phase of their existence has been marked by an album, different in some essential way, from the music that preceded it. That dynamic applies to their debut which – on the admission of Polyphonic main man Tim DeLaughter – is partly a reaction to the drug death of his Tripping Daisy band-mate Wes Berggren. The grunge and noise elements of Tripping Daisy never threaten this hugely optimistic and determined drive to reach the sublime. Beginning Stages is a twenty first century embrace of the Age of Aquarius divided into sections. Each track name is preceded by the words Section 1, Section 2 etc. – and delivered by a massed choir clad in white robes with splashes of colour, and supported by instrumental backing that references soul, gospel, sunshine pop and indie. Conceived as a means of getting the band a deal, Beginning Stages navigates a path between retro-chic, knowingly ironic, insanely uncommercial and compellingly original. All of this is achieved with enough panache to embed its playful hooks and infectious sunshine into the listener's mind on first hearing. Reviews have considered the obvious influence of late-sixties Beach Boys or The Fifth Dimension, and compared the band to a whole raft of indie/psychedelic acts since, (all valid points), but it's the confidence of making this statement in 2002 that really makes The Polyphonic Spree stand out. Well, that and the closing 36 and a half minutes "Section 10 A Long Day" which takes on epic instrumental passages, throws in an impassioned statement of hopeful-longing and pretty-much nails the early Polyphonic manifesto with one line: "If the world could compromise another faith, I wanna be more than yesterday and somehow find a way to your new religion." A concept album in a closing track, that's, like, awesome!

Predictably they've never attempted a track as shamelessly elaborate since. But it has taken the world time to catch up with the majesty of The Polyphonic Spree. As the band's recording and touring budgets have obliged some reining in of the early explosion of creativity it is Beginning Stages that has paid them back more than any other album. In 2010 "Section 9 (Light & Day/Reach for the Sun)" was revealed as the most used track in UK advertising, having been adapted for a heavy-rotation commercial for the Sainsbury's supermarket chain.

The Portland Bike Ensemble/ The Levenshume Bicycle Orchestra:
Live at il Corral/ Spinning Priest
(Lost Frog, 2007)
What? On your bikes for a really strange ride.

It is worth a visit to Lost Frog's download division just to read their pithy liner notes. Regarding this release they state: "Transforming bicycle sounds into experimental music by two groups from the US and UK. PBE plays free improvised music on amplified bicycles, also LBO uses a specially adapted bicycle instrument, and plays mesmerising noise cycles from bicycles." The Portland bikers present a lengthy tone poem and experimental meander through sound effects drawn from every component to hand. "Free and improvised" might conjure up notions of rhythmic jazz, but this 25 minute plus cacophony is closer to a surreal soundscape concocted for a particularly gruesome indie horror flick. The tinny clanking and crude attempts to hold a rhythm are the light relief as grinding, groaning and scraping sounds erupt and clash in a lengthy battle. Disturbing, strangely cybernautic and an unrelenting outré audio feast of the most unapologetic kind.

Manchester's finest two-wheeled titans of sonic terrorism are in another realm. Their shorter (just shy of 11 minute) work sounds like a loose rehearsal for a post-punk ensemble located somewhere between Bowie's most impenetrable moments on Lodger and the slew of Mancunians who took Berlin Bowie's complete canon as the manifesto. Except that in this rehearsal the noises are generated as much from bicycle parts as traditional instruments and the aim is to hit the riff, rant unintelligibly, and let the resulting wall of sound be its own expression. If a really important point has to be made The Levenshume Bicycle Orchestra simply slow down, or speed up. The drums and cymbals get hit often and hard, marking the main changes in mood, and the end of the piece is a clattering melt down. Despite all of this Spinning Priest, just about, qualifies as a song.

The Portsmouth Sinfonia:
Plays the Popular Classics
(Transatlantic, 1974)
What? Orchestral epic fail; but that's the point.

Full-on orchestral massacres of well-known classical standards occur regularly, without intention, during rehearsals or accidental moments of performance. However, a group started by art students in England in 1970 set about making this catastrophic and random element the entire focus of their orchestral endeavours. Establishing an orchestra with the entrance requirement that nobody was allowed to be proficient on the instrument they played, they went on to recruit novices, non-musicians and a few genuine musical talents (who were obliged to play instruments they hadn't begun to master). Noted composer Gavin Bryars was one of the masterminds behind a project that produced – amongst other things - a hit single and a well-attended show at London's Royal Albert Hall. Brian Eno joined on clarinet and eventually took a role in producing the outfit.

Audiences, critics and the orchestra never appeared in agreement on whether this was one massive joke or a genuine experiment. With a repertoire based on the most popular of classical standards they couldn't go far wrong. Apart from anything else, every player in the orchestra, struggling to master his/her instrument would usually know at any one moment if they were supposed to go higher/lower louder/softer faster/slower. The resulting "sound clouds," as the entire orchestra simultaneously blasted out the right note and several other notes very close to the right note, along with sporadic bum notes and random mistakes, stopped listeners in their tracks on first hearing. The best representation of their peculiar genius is here in versions of the most hummable and best known works in the classical canon. The ritual dismemberment dished out to the likes of "Also Sprach Zarathustra," "The Blue Danube" and "The William Tell Overture" has the car crash fascination the originators of the orchestra sought. Indeed, "The William Tell Overture" and "The Blue Danbe" were twinned for a single that gained airplay, but few sales. Their one UK hit single came much later than this album, with a fusion of their finest hook-lines, sped up and put over a disco beat. The novelty tag never really escaped the orchestra, who haven't played live since 1979. But, their work is out there and is periodically revived. "Also Sprach Zarathustra" from this collection has become a massive internet meme; dubbed "orchestra fail."

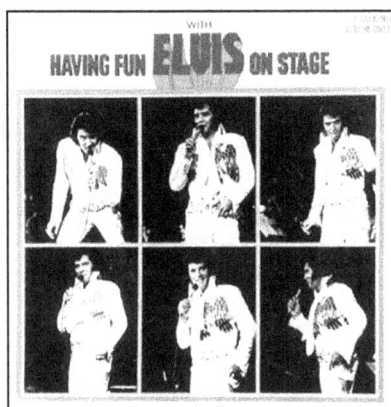

Elvis Presley:
Having Fun with Elvis on Stage
(Boxcar, 1974)
What? Fun! Did someone say…FUN?!!!

The All Music Guide prides itself on informative and largely objective appraisals of all forms of music so when they say:

"...apathy and ineptitude seems to be the only realistic explanations for this record's haphazard structure. Some have called 'Having Fun With Elvis' on Stage thoroughly unlistenable, but actually it's worse than that; hearing it is like witnessing an auto wreck that somehow ploughed into a carnival freak show, leaving onlookers at once too horrified and too baffled to turn away.'"

You know you are in serious trouble.

There is some logic to this record, but you won't figure it out from listening to the whole sorry affair. In 1973, having inked one of the worst deals for an artist in music history Elvis' manager, Colonel Tom Parker, was left with no control over any recorded music. With the guile and creativity he'd shown selling monster hot dogs at carnivals, basically taking a short sausage, sticking it out of either end of a long roll, and making it appear larger, the fake colonel hit on a top ruse. He owned none of Elvis' music, but Elvis' stage banter was a different affair. Forming his own Boxcar label, the Colonel unleashed 37 minutes and six seconds of rambling, poorly edited, largely incomprehensible spoken word recordings. A few fleeting hints of music survive, notably the "Well…" Introduction to "Heartbreak Hotel," but they just make the whole experience more frustrating.

Colonel Tom achieved his aim, creating an album he could sell directly to fans. He – eventually – obliged RCA to buy it and release it officially. But, this was an album Elvis hated with a passion. It remains one of the few legitimate Elvis recordings to stay unreleased on CD and it is worse by far than the infamous Elvis' Greatest Shit bootleg. Crucially, it didn't have to be this way. His school record showed little evidence of it but Elvis retained the capacity to be intelligent, witty and intensely deep-thinking. Graceland was packed with obscure tomes on the meaning of life, many annotated with Elvis' own observations. His wit onstage often involved responding to a fan, grabbing the moment and milking a joke. Edited and jumbled on this sorry slew of stolen moments the end results are baffling at best. Elvis could have cut an interesting spoken word album, but managing such an item was seemingly beyond the ambition of the man who remained proud to call himself Elvis' manager.

Presley's hatred for the album brought about a swift deletion in 1975. One unbelievable postscript: this album, containing not the slightest sniff of country music, hit number 9 on the Billboard Top Country Albums chart.

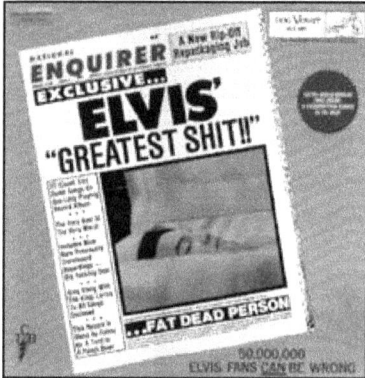

Elvis Presley:
Elvis' Greatest Shit
(Dog Vomit Records, 1983)
What? Regal stinkers from a right-royal catalogue.

Technically speaking this is a bootleg, although it remains more readily available than a lot of official releases. By bootleg standards it is also a rarity, since it is made up completely of stuff originally released officially. From the front cover picture of The King laid out in his open coffin, the concept of this mirthful muck-raking fest is obvious. Gather the most brainless and banal Elvis cuts, and celebrate the tack. The end result is akin to being locked in a toilet overnight and faced with the gormless wall scribbles that were funny for a couple of minutes. Most of the material comes from the least inspired soundtrack cuts of Elvis' movie career. Stripped of the context of the films songs like "There's No Room to Rhumba in a Sports Car" verge on the surreal. Especially when The King puts more effort into the performance than most of these stinkers ever warranted. Killer cuts on the vinyl release of this collection include: "Old Mac Donald," "Yoga Is As Yoga Does," "Song of the Shrimp," "The Fort Lauderdale Chamber of Commerce," and "The Bullfighter Was A Lady".

The track list offers a little hope, notably with the closing track, "Are You Lonesome Tonight?" but this reveals itself as the infamous 1977 live version, with Elvis reduced to hopeless laughter at the operatic wailing of one of his backing singers. The vinyl album ran to 23 tracks, a later CD release managed to add 14 other slices of regal stupidity including "Petunia the Gardener's Daughter" and "The Whiffenpoof Song". Imagine an Elvis tribute night, with the music department of CBeebies (or whichever childrens' television network is best known in your part of the world) penning the tunes.

Katie Price and Peter Andre:
A Whole New World
(K and P, 2006)
What? You know when some celebrity makes an album and you think it can't be that bad…

It didn't have to be like this. With most shameless celebrity related musical mush the rule is to hire some name production team, knock together a collection of up-tempo dancy ditties and keep the vocals down to a few whoops, warbles and the kind of interjections that fit perfectly with the beat, the one and only solo pop album of Victoria Beckham being a particularly accomplished example of how to do it. From the formation of their own label to release this assault on delicate sensibilities to the spewmongous snap of Katie 'Jordan' Price looking directly at the camera, and not at Peter Andre, this stinking selection of slaughtered standards says everything about the celebrity of the stars involved, and spews cynicism in your face. S'cuse the pun but, it's all front. K and P Records was – in reality - a thinly veiled segment of Sony BMG and these collected tracks celebrate the high-profile couple's love the way hastily printed t-shirts at Glastonbury in 2009 paid "tribute" to the cooling corpse that was once Michael Jackson.

For the most part this is a dozen dissections of ballads better known from emotive evocations by talented artists, two cases in point "Endless Love" and "Tonight I Celebrate my Love For You" exist in far superior versions, sung by soul stars with the vocal pyrotechnics to float above the instrumentation and turn their voices into finely crafted instruments. To Peter Andre's credit, he manages some of the above on the less demanding selections, but Jordan's contributions smack of studio trickery and suggest the infamous auto-tune technology combined with deft production decisions have been used to keep her listenable. Of course, if her lawyers are looking in, everything here is a personal opinion only, we may be wrong and – if so – we apologise.

The end result is a collection of great melodies and competent if unexciting production work that feels forever held back by the lack of a definitive vocal interpretation. Insipid re-workings of daytime radio classics like "Islands in the Stream" and "Don't Go Breaking My Heart" follow each other with grim insistence, making this an unrelentingly underwhelming experience. An experience akin to gorging forever on cake and sweets as your body cries out for something packing protein and vitamins. As a celebration of the plastic pair's (that's Peter and Jordan as the plastic pair, okay?) perfect love match this collection is probably the perfect memento, and like their love it enjoyed a brief high-profile before a longer career in the bargain bucket alongside the festering remains of the rest of yesterday's fashions. Their loyal fans raved with online reviews, others told it differently. One single star review on Amazon noting: "It is a brilliant CD. Just the right size to put my coffee mug on." One more single star review – which has greatly influenced this book's understanding of the album - opined: "I've waited for this ALL MY LIFE. I knew that perfection in music could be achieved. But who would have believed that it would have been achieved by a couple who are, to many people (not to me of course) a simple, overly muscled, lantern jawed twit and his hunch fronted attention junkie of a wife?" Another wag chiming in with: "I know they are both really talented and that them releasing a recording has nothing whatsoever to do with the fact that they are freakish to behold, but that isn't the point. It oozes sincerity and I am wholly convinced. They didn't use any session singers at all, it's so clearly all their own work. They are dead good. I hope they will be my new mummy and daddy after I grow out of my encopresis."* This collection briefly scraped a place in the UK top 20 albums.

Public Image Ltd:
The Flowers of Romance
(Virgin, 1981)
What? A truly out there album, a truly improbable hit.

Public Image Ltd (PiL)'s Flowers…lived up to the notion of a "difficult" third album. Difficult for the band because bassist and provider of the signature sounds on their awesome second outing Metal Box – Jah Wobble - had departed. Difficult for the audience because they didn't replace him and set off in a totally different musical direction. Internet write ups discuss Flowers… as one of the

* Encopresis: Involuntary faecal soiling, usually associated with those already toilet trained and often linked to psychological problems.

least commercial records ever released in a commercial context. True. Most of the standard rules are out of the window. John Lydon performs on instruments – like violin – for which he has no training. Samples of anything to hand – like a wristwatch – weave in and out and most of the "songs" stumble around the industrial noise/concrete poetry area. They're songs (probably) because Lydon's vocals fall into his familiar style and provide the one clear continuity from the Sex Pistols and early PiL albums, and because they got played on rock radio stations alongside other post-punk material. Almost everything on offer here is some variation on the theme of feedback loops, banging gathered from drums and a selection of objects, some never designed as percussive instruments, and guitar/synth material used to cold, concrete, sonic-effect. The "tunes" are mainly the vocal melodies. Most of what's left is sculpted sound. "Flowers of Romance" and "Banging the Door" both approach a skeletal punk style, the former hit the top 30 in the UK singles chart, but the likes of "Track 8" (second in the running order) take the collection into the kind of rhythmic territory later trodden by experimental dance music. Improbably, this collection reached #11 in the UK albums chart.

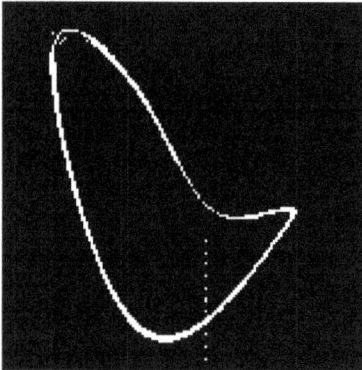

Quantum Dub Force: Assymetric
(Palm Pictures, 2001)
What? Other planes of dub.

One of those the-sound-is-the-whole-point albums: but an exceptionally good and often overlooked example of the form. Assymetric picks up where the likes of King Tubby made their mark, but takes on board the changing nature of early 21st century dance. The grooves and dubs are never less than widescreen and solid in their rhythm, but this is dub that remains mindful of trip-hop and everything that followed. As such, it is dub that varies, experiments (more than your average dub) and picks random sounds and samples from a wide array of possibilities. Fully half the tracks take basic reggae dub and paste on keyboards, snatches of melody and additional percussive effects. But, the dropping in of a well-modulated lead vocal on "Big Bang" and the fleeting ambient-techno intro of "9th Dimension" mean the collection keeps hinting at other spheres, and the limitless possibilities of dub.

Unusually – considering the company it keeps in this book – Assymetric is one collection that would work quietly in the background. You could read, eat, have sex and drive with Assymetric for company (though attempting all four at once isn't recommended). We'd respectfully suggest the collection is worthy of a place here because it packs the quality inherent in some of the best and most enduring instrumental releases, of retaining an accessible charm, but also providing the capacity to surprise after a few spins.

The dub rhythms, and lead parts, revolve around each other creating some tension. The individual sounds and licks sometimes reveal themselves best once the listener is familiar with the whole collection. The choral vocal and reverberating guitar lick of "Harmonic Collapse" provide one apparently simple combination that gradually gets inside your consciousness and begins to inhabit that space without any prompting.

Whether Quantum Dub Force would welcome comparisons with albums like Tubular Bells is an interesting question, but like such pervasive works; Assymetric has the potential to slowly grow in the listener's affections. It is also distinctive enough to stay there and conveniently cut into short enough tracks to be great mix-tape fodder.

Quintessence:
Indweller
(RCA, 1972)
What? "Bliss trip."

Quintessence recorded four and a half studio albums between 1969 and 1972 (filling half of their fourth outing Self with a live recording from the University of Exeter). Prog rockers to the last dying resonance of Raja Ram's floating flute solos, and highly influenced by jazz, the original six members all followed the Hindu faith. High spots of their early period included successive Glastonbury performances in 1970 and 1971, later immortalized in movie footage, and a slot on the 1971 concert for Bangla Desh at Kennington Oval where they shared billing with The Who, Mott the Hoople, Lindisfarne, Atomic Rooster, The Grease Band and America. Quintessence typically worked up album tracks with incessant jamming, emphasized the spiritual in their lyrics (which included chants) and employed massed percussion; incorporating contributions from local Hare Krishna devotees.

Faithful fans typically laud the trio of albums cut for Island Records between 1969 and 1971 (In Blissful Company, Quintessence and Dive Deep). By contrast Indweller remains regarded as a falling off in all ways. It ended a run in which the previous three releases had charted, marked a slimmed down line-up and relied on a reduced number of musical options compared to its predecessors. The band reduced to a quartet with departures, including that of founder-member and vocalist Shiva Shankar Jones, cut the guitar solos and songs in favour of looser chants and still, meditative, pieces. Raja Ram's flute is the main lead instrument here. Both sides of the original vinyl album open with a praise song/chant the first to Jesus, the second to guru Sai Baba. Fragmentary interludes of bliss "Butterfly Music" and "Portable Realm" form individual tracks and the penultimate track is the ambient and ultra-trippy "Bliss Trip." By the time of Indweller's release Britain was bathing in "T.Rexstacy" probably bemusing Quintessence members who'd rubbed shoulders with the hippie Marc Bolan when both acts were regular fixtures on the London underground scene. Fellow members of that club, Hawkwind, had also exploded overground with their thudding anthem "Silver Machine." Indweller was out of time when released and is terminally so today. As a loose, unhurried and blissful insight into a level of innocence impossible to recapture it does more than the proggier and more focussed quartet of Quintessence albums that preceded it. Indweller's trippier fragments anticipate the blissed out end of ambient techno, and bands like The Orb. The reinvention of some of the spirit kindled by the likes of Quintessence didn't occur until the late eighties, far too late for this album to find significant sales.

Sun Ra:
Cosmic Tones for Mental Therapy
(El Saturn, 1967)
What? Saturnian jazz maestro at his sublime best.

There are a few artists – Captain Beefheart, Frank Zappa, Harry Partch etc. – to whom we could have devoted entire sections of this book. Their musical careers having run parallel rather than within the conventional critical and commercial ideas of their time. Had we taken such a route it's likely that Sun Ra (1914-1993) would have got more entries than anyone else. Prodigious, prolific and a fringe act even by the standards of the most out-there divisions of jazz; Sun Ra never really belonged to society, let alone the music industry. Ra's life was marked by events that set him apart. He repeatedly talked of an experience when he was a young pianist in which – during a session of deep religious concentration – he had a mystical experience in which he saw through himself, and was transported to a planet he felt to be Saturn, where he met aliens and received wisdom and guidance regarding his life. One piece of guidance involved the centrality of music to his future. The exact date and location of the experience remains debateable. But, it was years ahead of the phase of UFO contactees and others who claim to have communed with other worlds. Ra fought the draft in World War 2, eventually serving jail time and being moved to duties in forestry. The man wasn't for marching to anyone's tune…even when his country was at war.

His incredible and eventful jazz journey is well chronicled. His monumental mound of recordings have proven as compelling to his fan base as do the works of Zappa, Beefheart and other individualists. We'll make an educated guess that many of those motivated to buy this book are already familiar with Sun Ra to some degree. The point of including Cosmic Tones for Mental Therapy is to show what it was that made the man so great. Recorded in 1963 this is a watershed work, even for the constantly changing Sun Ra. Comprising five pieces – "And Otherness," "Thither and Yon," "Adventure-Equation," "Moon Dance" and "Voice of Space" – Cosmic Tones… anticipates psychedelia, and funk, and provides a sketch for the experimental orchestral works Sun Ra would indulge in hereafter. "Adventure-Equation" finds echoes (no pun intended) in the early psychedelic journeys of Pink Floyd. A few splashes of sound gradually coalesce into tune driven by the organ before the sonic assaults gradually overwhelm the melody and the whole piece falls apart to leave space for a sax solo. "Moon Dance," by contrast, is a funky (bear in mind this is 1963!) groove overlaid by a war of percussion. George Clinton – who would subsequently claim to be a fellow diner with Sun Ra at "Out to Lunch" – would take these ideas and run with them a decade later. "Adventure Equation" pushes early sixties echo effects to their limit and brings reverberating percussion and flurries of sax into a space rock soundscape produced almost a decade before the same ideas found their perfect realisation in Hawkwind's apocalyptic Space Ritual. Cosmic Tones… however, is more than just a collection of flashes of genius that enabled other legends. As a single snapshot of a significant player in musical invention it is up there with his best work. It helps – immensely – in gauging Ra's talent to appreciate that this was recorded before pscychedelia, space rock or the mammoth funk of Funkadelic were even on the horizon. But Cosmic Tones… is a perfect junction for two-way traffic. If Pink Floyd, George Clinton etc. are your entry points, it is worth following Cosmic Tones… to those places in Sun Ra's catalogue that no-one else could ever reach.

The Railway Children:
Gentle Sound
(Ether, 2002)
What? Totally atypical of their early style, but – possibly - the best compilation they'll ever have.

Wigan's Railway Children emerged in the mid-eighties British indie scene and released their first mini-album on Manchester's Factory Records, making them label-mates with New Order. Within a year they'd jumped ship to Virgin and within another four years EMI had taken over Virgin and deemed the Railway Children surplus to requirements. Two years later Gary Newby (songwriter and lead vocals) was all that remained, but he kept the name for recording purposes. The above history matters because it makes it clear that this band of jangling guitars, classic guitar-pop melodies and vivid-vignette lyrics struggled for consistency. Their best work is spread around the catalogues of different companies. Factory got the insistent early guitar-pop. Their opening collection Reunion Wilderness (1987) is a glorious sounding piece of alternative indie-pop. Virgin groomed them for hits and were rewarded when "Every Beat of my Heart" hit #24 in the UK charts and topped the (then) new Modern Rock chart in the US. But Virgin put bigger beats and a radio friendly production behind them. So, played back to back, their fleeting career doesn't sound like the same band.

But, relocated to Japan, Gary Newby opened the 21st century with a masterful move to reclaim some of that legacy. Gentle Sound lines up a lot of the tracks originally recorded by the band. It favours their singles, throws in some new songs and brings a different sound. It's minimal. Drums and bass appear sporadically, percussion is sparing and the main interest in sound comes from shimmering acoustic guitar overdubs that often trade different licks off against each other from each speaker. Newby's acoustic rhythm guitar is central to the mix and his alternatively muscular and sparing work on this gives tone and colour. The production sound remains constant and everything is taken at a slower, more deliberate, tempo than the originals. What emerges is a canon of gorgeous love songs, compelling story songs, simple melodies and – above all – an argument that this band had a great songwriter at their heart. Proof of that final point comes in that, 15 years after some of these songs were first recorded, the stripped back new style, allows them to re-emerge sounding like mature and confident work.

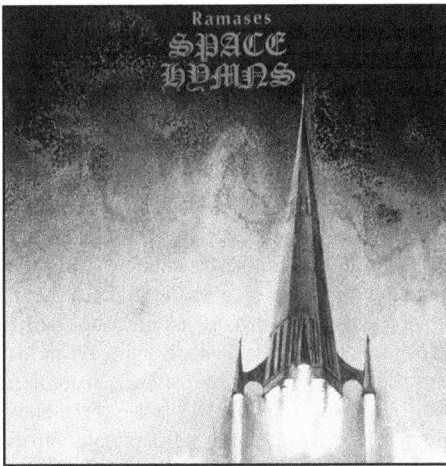

Ramases:
Space Hymns
(Vertigo, 1971)
What? Space rock of legend.

An album that has become something of a legend in those circles where rare records are discussed. Ramases' first full-length solo effort can't hope to match the hype, but it is still a stunning listen. It's also quite a story. Sheffield born Martin Raphael (who also used the name Barrington Frost) had a career history as an army PT instructor and central heating salesman, the latter in cold cold Scotland where central heating sales tended to generate decent profits. A vision came to him in his car that convinced him he was, in fact, a reincarnation of the Egyptian Pharaoh god Ramases. Consumed with a duty to spread this news and inform the world of the truth about the universe "Ramases" set about getting a recording contract and letting music be his medium. Two poor selling singles (now hugely collectable) followed before Vertigo signed the man, and his wife "Selket," to an album deal.

Space Hymns was the first of two long-players produced. Recorded in Strawberry Studios, Stockport and featuring the studio owners – later to become 10cc – as backing musicians, Space Hymns is early space-rock with a surprisingly clean production, and very catchy twists to most of the backing music. For all its cosmic pretentions it offers up a lot of traditional verse-chorus-verse material, touches on acoustic rock and brings in the impressive 10cc harmonies a couple of years before the band used them for their own lucrative ends. Lyrically the album explores the meaning of life and presents a vision of humanity in search of meaning. The liner notes state: "We are most probably existing on a molecule inside the material of, perhaps, a living thing in the next size up." The lyrics and cover art also flirt with the then popular theory that space travellers visited and guided the earth in the distant past. A quick glance at the cover appears to show a rocket blasting off from Earth. On closer inspection the "rocket" doubles as the top of a church steeple. The opening lyrical couplet: "The sun is fading from your city Life Child/From where I stand it ain't so pretty Life Child," sets the tone of mankind in crisis and redemption coming through a true understanding of our history and place in the universe. The strangest element is a rambling final section to the closing "Journey to the Inside" which features Ramases discussing his philosophy of inter-connection; "if you took a pill to get smaller and you... vanished... ... you get smaller and smaller and vanish inside that chair that you're sitting….." Whatever the truth of the message, the presence of 10cc as the backing band, and the Roger Dean cover art, have conspired to ensure this strange gem never quite falls off the radar. Its vision of the Earth as a living thing is well ahead of the new age movement a couple of decades later. Space Hymns and the subsequent Glass Top Coffin did little in terms of sales. Ramases is reported to have committed suicide whilst living in Felixstowe, Suffolk, in 1976.

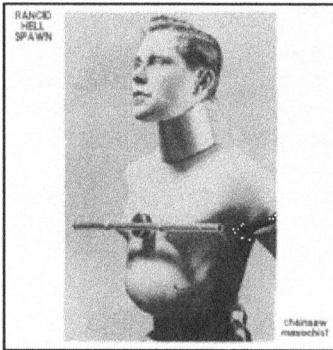

Rancid Hell Spawn:
Chainsaw Masochist
(Wrench Records, 1990)
What? More punk than punk itself.

An iconic moment in the history of British punk came at the end of the first Desperate Bicycles EP. Having cobbled together the recording budget the band ended their opening release with the incitement: "It was easy, it was cheap, go out and do it." Charlie Chainsaw who – to all intents and purposes – is Rancid Hell Spawn, took up the challenge, and - despite a lengthy mid-career hiatus with regard to recording – he's still at it. Hell Spawn songs are typically short, brutal, driven at warp speed and topped with a fizzing and fuzzed out covering of low-fi keyboard and feedback. Steve Wells, legendary NME scribe, once described the ensuing signature sound as "listening to Eddie Cochran while wearing a chemical warfare suit full of angry wasps." The lyrics remain inaudible and with other wilful noiseniks – like Lightning Bolt – Rancid Hell Spawn typically add to the mystery by writing great lyrics and inciting die-hard fans to make the effort to understand them by tempting them with titles suggesting intelligence, humour and a deep knowledge of life's absurdities. Every Hell Spawn album offers up brilliant titles and cut-price but gloriously sick graphics. Chainsaw Masochist - the outfit's second full-length outing – comes up with some corkers, including: "cirrhotic neurotic," "dead today, hip hip hooray," "my pet corpse," "stomach pump rock" and "listerine pissup." The latter, a meditation on the alcoholic content of a best-selling mouthwash. Charlie Chainsaw's modus operandi through the late eighties and into the nineties was to use a home portastudio, do all his own vocals and other instruments and only incur anything like a proper recording cost by paying a recording engineer to set workable levels on the cutting master. As such, Rancid Hell Spawn took the DIY ethic of the likes of Desperate Bicycles to previously uncharted levels of affordability. In the process they gave permission to another generation of bedroom bound anarchy hounds to unleash their own wares on the world. Hell Spawn's approach renders everything in the first wave of the band's existence (1988-1995) as one ubiquitous wall of buzzing noise to the point that only a die-hard presented with a few seconds each of "zombie girl" or "pigsty of love" – both included here - would be able to tell the pair apart with confidence. Chainsaw Masochist is an album that makes Desperate Bicycles sound like ELO.

?:
The Wit and Wisdom of Ronald Reagan
(Magic, 1981)
What? A concept album for those who hate concepts, and albums.

Released when Reagan's popularity, and infamy, were at their height, this vinyl album was briefly a celebrated novelty item. Apart from anything else, the joke, and attraction of the whole piece weren't exactly hard to grasp. Side one devoted itself to Reagan's wit, side two to his wisdom. Both played full LP length, both were exactly the same length in playing time and both were completely silent. Not exactly a subtle joke. It could be argued, though few bothered to press the point, that the essentially vacuous nature of the album, combined with a skilful packaging and selling, was the perfect comment on Reagan and his free market policies.

Years after his death Reagan has gradually been rehabilitated as a folksy and essentially well-meaning president whose vision of small government and freedom to achieve was quintessentially American. He remains revered in some quarters. However, like Margaret Thatcher, others continue to see Reagan as a divisive and uncaring figure who didn't get, or didn't want to get, the notion that the state might owe a duty of care to its less able citizens.

As a piece of Reagonistic opportunism it's hard to fault The Wit and Wisdom of Ronald Reagan. It's only a stupid idea until you see it in context and consider its success. Magic Records, who opened their account with this album and gave it the catalogue number Abra 1, was really a division of London's mighty and respected Stiff Records; punk and indie specialists with a stable that at various times included Elvis Costello, Nick Lowe and Madness. Their minimalist packaging for the Ronald Reagan album included a tasty one-liner on the back cover stating: "You may or may not hear something interesting on this record." Given the fairly obvious and open joke the album became briefly well-known and went on to shift a staggering 30,000 copies, knocking the album sales of some of the critical favourites on the indie scene into the shade. Taking into account the lack of any recording costs and cheap packaging this was good business.

Historically the album probably deserves a belated celebration alongside other tacky joke media of the period. As production costs of a range of media items fell against inflation the eighties became an era of celebrated novelty tack. Such items included M25 The Movie: basically a VHS tape of traffic on London's orbital road to nowhere. The internet took such ideas into hitherto undreamt of realms of the surreal and – at the same time – virtually killed the commercial potential of elaborate jokes such as this silent album.

Lou Reed:
Metal Machine Music
(RCA, 1975)
What? Unlistenable…well, that's the whole point, right?

Best known to British ears as the composer of "Perfect Day," Reed became an international rock star of some repute during the seventies. Rumours abounded suggesting his record company, RCA at this time, were in constant conflict with the star. Reed's die-hard audience kept buying his work but his record company pressured him for more commercial material, a fact that clearly annoyed Reed. How else could you explain Metal Machine Music? This legendary double set has defied most other explanations. Depending on where you're doing your research, it is "a series of random electronic bleeps and squawks," "an elaborate joke" or "four sides of white noise." Basically, it is four tracks of electronically generated sound. Legends abound suggesting that sides three and four are the first two sides played backwards, each track is from the same tape loop etc. Nobody in over thirty years - it seems - has had the strength to listen long enough to find the definitive answer.

One explanation for the whole caper is that Reed decided to stuff it to his long suffering record company once and for all, forcing them to write press releases lauding his talent and distribute the insane album. It was certainly seen as insanity at the time with some fans taking records back to the point-of-sale and complaining there was something wrong with them, and critics genuinely stumped for words. Reed subsequently moved labels and over the years Metal Machine Music has settled into a critical niche that has gained it a few champions. Reed himself claiming the work as existing in a tradition of avant-garde and classical work linked to the likes of John Cage. He has also explained its recording as the result of placing two guitars, detuned, played in front of amps and then left to sit in the resulting feedback. As the amps in question were large, stage, models the sound waves from the original playing built up a feedback loop, the loop vibrated the strings and the guitars, in-effect, played themselves.

Reed put together a trio who played small and largely well-received gigs in 2010 featuring music rooted in this most bizarre of his recordings. By this time a handful of champions of Metal Machine Music had emerged, some of whom had taken its ideas and run them in different directions. For all that, sales of this album remain miniscule, most of those in possession of a copy seldom play it and those who do play it frequently do so in short bursts. If anyone ever lovingly listens to this album; that person is a very rare individual indeed. It is entirely possible that some of those from management in RCA Records who endured the artistic battles with Reed still find their sleep disturbed by nightmares in which 'a series of random electronic bleeps and squawks' can be heard.

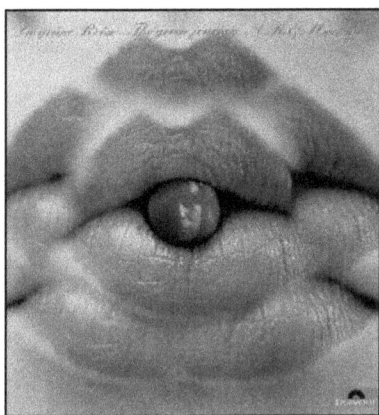

Achim Reichel/A.R & Machines: Die Grüne Reise (Polydor, 1971)
What? Kruatrockfreakout…seminal spacerock!

The German post-hippie sounds of the seventies sprinted off into many directions, sub-classical, jazzy, electronic and guitar-freakout. The music would go on to influence whole generations of bands in other territories and some cities – like Manchester – owe a lot of "their" sound to this work. But it took some brave, commercially-suicidal pioneers to kick-start the whole German movement. Their efforts were often so out-there, they've defied categorisation and shunned significant sales ever since. So, over four decades on, it's time to give Achim Reichel, AKA "A.R." his due as one man who shaped the music before anyone else even believed it possible.

Reichel is generally described as a composer, musician and producer, though his work has an almost visionary quality. An early career spent in fairly predictable German pop bands did nothing to warn the world of what was coming. A.R. and Machines' first outing is basically an avant-garde exploration of the cutting edge studio technology of its time. Heavy on sound effects, distorted guitars and voices used as drones, wails and looped sounds well back in the mix, it straddles the boundary of classical, experimental rock and "concrete poetry" with a wilful disdain for anything approaching a genre. At worst it is the ceaseless noodling of a clever kid who wants to play rather than settle down to anything like a proper job, at best it is insane and inspired in a truly glorious way. The po-faced conceit that calls the epic finale of the whole caper "Truth and Probability" is offset by the harking back to simpler melodic forms and the sounds that would inspire the first generation of electronic Krautrockers in "Cosmic Vibration."

The collection is dressed up in some self-conscious and portentous elements that haven't dated too well. The cover shot, a mouth wrapped around a green pea (with the pea displaying Reichel's reflected face), with a kaleidoscopic effect of another mouth surrounding it is very much a trick-lens/trippy photography statement of the time. Though it does – at least – focus the mind on the fact the title translates literally as The Green Journey or The Green Voyage. Track titles like "Globe", "Beautiful Babylon" and "A Book's Blues" also have a grandiose quality that doesn't necessarily warn the listener of what is coming. The most sympathetic critics, notably Julian Cope in his book Krautrocksampler, have heaped superlatives on Die Grüne Reise. Cope sees the work as: "the final result of a kind of higher awareness…" and Brian Eno's highly influential Another Green World gives a nod to the work in its title. Eno himself has cited it as an influence on his sound and ideas. There are few openly hostile "what kind of rubbish is this?" reviews online. One indication of the negative response the record continues to get is its consistently low profile despite its champions. The major reason for this may well be that short bursts of Die Grüne Reise can sound so wilfully uncommercial, and so much like random musical experiments, that few of those hearing it by accident bother to investigate much further. The album does have that impenetrable quality on first listening. It is less a single cohesive work and more akin to an attempt to make every possible idea explode in every possible direction, limited only by the studio technology of its time.

Reichel eventually honed his style into a less abrasive blend of psychedelic guitar and rhythms, moving somewhere into the space-rock territory also frequented by the likes of Steve Hillage. But, his early work, notably this first outing, continue to astound new listeners.

Terry Reid:
River
(Atlantic, 1973)
What? Loose and ludicrous, louche shuffle-along and/or long-lost masterpiece.

The second you start arguing a non-chart album cherished by a handful of fans is a "flawed masterpiece" you are in danger of opening the floodgates for others to make a passionate case for the forty minutes of moronic sound they've cherished for some totally subjective reason (losing their virginity as it played in the background, hearing it as they revised etc.) So, let's forget the potential masterpiece arguments and concentrate on Reid's seven track third solo effort. Rightly dubbed "a highly personal but uneven record" by All Music Guide, River was culled from a series of sessions that produced enough material for a few albums. The sessions took place in the UK and USA and touchstones for the resulting album could be cited from both sides of the Atlantic. The closing "Milestones" is a soaring yet strongly understated spiritual meander that suggests nothing more than Reid grabbing at David Crosby's "I'd Swear There Was Someone Here" and expanding that fragment to a full six-minute mini-epic. Elsewhere the choppy and expressive acoustic guitar work, jazzy timings and slurred vocals match John Martyn's Inside Out and Solid Air sounds from the same year.

If Reid is famous for one thing it's the fact that he was the first choice as vocalist in The New Yardbirds (AKA Led Zeppelin) and his blues shouting gets the occasional spotlight on River. In reality, this is the sound of a man escaping his contract with Mickie Most and running away from the row that resulted when Most set out to turn Reid into a rock balladeer, and Reid countered by suggesting he simply make the kind of loose, expressive and happening music his friends and contemporaries – Jimmy Page and Graham Nash – were involved in. River is – therefore – personal to the point the lyrics don't offer clarity (even when you've finally worked out what he's singing), the riffs ramble on beyond being obvious attention grabbers and every once in a while a lick will force its way forward from bass, keyboards or guitar to grab the moment and further erode any sense that radio play or massive sales were in the minds of anyone involved in making this album. Online discussion, and the informative sleevenotes that accompany the CD reissue, tend to concentrate on the feel of the whole piece. That feel – pretty much – is the point of River. Cliché or not, River is one of those elliptical efforts that nails a vibe, inhabits a room and slowly releases its charms. The sense of everyone jamming at once can be overwhelming on the first listen through the livelier efforts (not that anything really rocks here!) like "Things to Try." But, it's that quality above all others that allows River to re-emerge years after you last heard it and throw something at you that still surprises.

The Residents:
Commercial Album
(Pre Records, 1980)
What? Typical Residential Strangefest, in fun-size chunks.

The Residents self-referential strangeness has carved its own unique path in music and art since 1972. Apart from film soundtracks, DVDs and the like The Residents' recorded works tend to apply a totalitarian zeal to taking on and obliterating existing popular music classics. Or present themselves as complex and frequently impenetrable masterworks of wilful strangeness. Vocals are obscured, timing and rhythm moves to a different beat, and The Residents' sound overturns the role of melody against the sound of production. At times, the sound tends to drive the pieces forward and melody intrudes randomly to distract attention. Their seventies work was hugely influential on generations of electro geeks to follow.

1980's Commercial Album is – even by the standards of Shreeveport, Louisiana's wilful weirdos – a curious affair. Offering up 40 numbers, each – apparently - exactly one minute in length, it mimics complex masterworks in its conception and also presents the Residents' other beloved pastime of trashing pop sensibilities. A claim made on the liner notes suggests that each track should be played three times in succession to form a perfect pop song! In reality it is a series of simple compositions, played, often in jazz-timings, and concocted with layers of keyboard and other instrumental sounds that clash like the different sections of an orchestra in a discordant classical work. Because the whole collection is conceived in this way the big ideas behind the music ensure that its reliance on the recording technology and instruments of the period, when analogue was gradually surrendering to digital, doesn't date. It sounded on release, and continues to sound, like the pop radio of some still-to-be-discovered planet harbouring intelligent life. The album also packs some interesting collaborations and references. XTC's Andy Partridge sings lead on "Margaret Freeman." The heavily distorted – but still recognisable – faces of John Travolta and Barbara Striesand adorn the front cover whilst the back mainly presents the track titles in bold typeface. Titles like "Perfect Love," "Handful of Desire" and "When we Were Young" might suggest classic pop ideas but they rub shoulders here with "Die in Terror," "The Nameless Souls" and "My Work is so Behind" which come from another direction. As a final twist, something known to die-hards and radio programmers for years, and finally revealed with a CD reissue is that most of the titles are not 60 seconds long, typically they run a few seconds longer.

Ambrose Reynolds:
Greatest Hits
(Zulu, 1982)
What? Banging tunes!

Ambrose Reynolds isn't exactly a household name, though he has been around the music industry most of his adult life and boasts a CV including work with Pete Burns, a formative role in the first line-up of Frankie Goes to Hollywood and helping to found Pink Industry; an arty/experimental/punk outfit which lasted for five years in the eighties. During the Pink Industry years Reynolds released solo material on the Zulu label. His Wikipedia page describes a "tsunami" of product. With access to the – then – cutting edge sampling and production devices that were fuelling the development of electro music and more ideas than most acts would need in a career, Reynolds managed to crank out a few distinctly different items. None more so than Greatest Hits.

Longer than an EP and shorter than most albums, Greatest Hits duly delivers a meaning to the word "hits" usually associated with the mafia or military. In case you haven't sussed it yet, this is basically an album of recordings and news reports of famous assassinations, with banging guns and a few bangin' tunes thrown in for good measure. Over electro/dance mixes we get to relive the biggest hits of the post-war years. Martin Luther King, both Kennedy brothers and the Kent State University killings. A couple of other tracks include the thoughts and reflections on particular killings as recorded in interviews from Richard Nixon and Edward Kennedy.

Most of the musical tricks are archaic by today's standards but the hard-sounds of early electro work here to provide a brittle atmosphere in which to place the most pitiless of killings, and the shocked reactions of news commentators on the spot struggling to describe what they've just seen. It's not exactly a dance album, but the momentum of the rhythms and the minimal keyboard melodies give the whole collection a sense of movement, and stay just short of smothering the original recordings. Assembled in this way the tracks manage an ironic sense of re-inventing live assassination as the grimmest end of the entertainment business, and still leave the best known moments of the original live recordings with their chilling power to shock. If such a collection can ever have a highlight it is probably "Get the Gun" featuring the commentary in the hotel kitchen as shocked bystanders struggle to over-power Sirhan Sirhan who has just fatally wounded Robert Fitzgerald Kennedy. The cover art, a mock up of the Stars and Stripes with little handguns replacing the stars, is another twist that could be argued as a bleak artistic statement, a sick joke, or both. Greatest Hits is about as uneasy as listening gets.

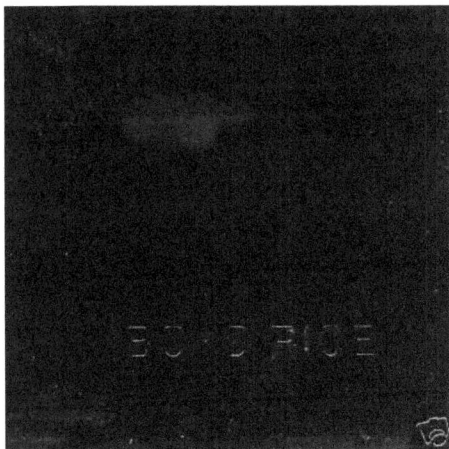

Boyd Rice:
The Black Album
(Own Label, 1977/ Mute, 1981)
What? Obtuse early electonica that has lasted very well.

Rice (b. 1956) is an American composer, artist in many fields and a practical joker whose more amusing moments have included his membership and public support for the religious group The Partridge Family Temple, and whose most mystifying have included photographs that have led some (wrongly) to be fooled into thinking him a fully-committed Nazi. There is a sense of Situationism (i.e. the predicament in which the audience find themselves is part of the point of the work) to most of Rice's highest profile moves. In a simple way, this early slice of electronica, his first album release, is just that beast. Both releases (Rice's initial private pressing and Mute's reissue) feature no information on the sleeve other than the artist's name. The label suggests the tracks are "playable at any speed" and the individual cuts have no names. Side one packs six anonymous sound loops, side two throws in another trio. Most are fast (even if you take the obvious 33 rpm option), repetitive exercises in electronic sound and the kind of classical/noodling-geek-with-computer trills that formed a lot of early electronica. The final cut is altogether slower, darker and mixed so quietly it verges into the kind of ambient territory Brian Eno was beginning to explore at the same time, though it ends with a wake up call of rapid sounds and a louder mix of a simple melody. By comparison with much that followed in Rice's work, and those working in the same area, The Black Album also has a simple and playful quality that makes it a refreshing listen years after the event.

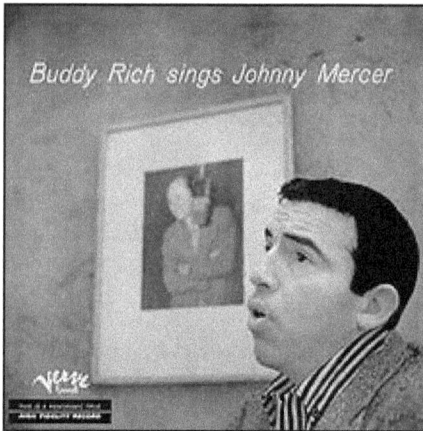

Buddy Rich:
Sings Johnny Mercer
(Verve, 1956)

What? Surprisingly soulful crooning from stupendous sticksman.

Rich (1917-1987) remains one of the greatest jazz drummers ever to have thumped a tub, but his legacy as a vocalist is all but forgotten. This 1956 collection is, arguably, his greatest foray in front of the kit. The material is, mainly, classic fodder better known in the repertoires of other notables. But Rich's willingness to take on "One for My Baby (and One More for the Road)" or "Skylark" is the key to a collection in which his character, sense of timing and innate feel for an arrangement allow him to triumph over two sides and 12 songs. Johnny Mercer's lyrics are key to this success, often presenting first person scenarios in which our narrator is looking at life, musing, and about to reveal some great insight. The longing of "One for My Baby..." suits Rich's vocals, if only because his limitations in range and tone make him a more believable inhabitant of the song's bittersweet mixture of love and longing than – say – Sinatra (who acts out a more Hollywood version of the same scene). "This Time the Dream's on Me" and "Blues in the Night" are other standouts as Rich's abilities to use the storylines to communicate his own depth of character gradually lull the listener into appreciating an all-round performer of real skill. The musical backing swings and stills itself to order. No band with Rich in the vicinity was ever likely to get off with less than the best performance. For a man approaching 40 on its release, Sings Johnny Mercer is also a record that betrays a world weariness and cynicism, albeit with a very humane sense that love may be worth the effort and rewards in life are what you earn. Musically, never less than highly accomplished, vocally, very characterful.

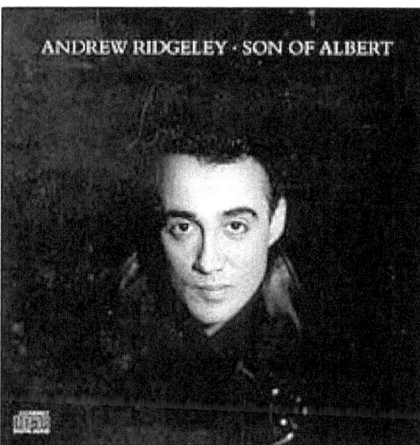

Andrew Ridgeley:
Son of Albert
(Columbia, 1990)

What? Cat in Hell's chance first solo venture from the half of Wham! that wasn't called George.

The CD copy of this release sitting on the desk as these words are typed tells a story. The original price tag (£10.99) is crossed out, a sale sticker appears underneath offering the release for £1.99 but beside that is a handwritten note saying: "Make an offer." Neil Nixon duly did, but can't recall exactly what was paid; only that the "offer" in question involved adding Son of Albert to a fistful of CDs purchased in the sale and agreeing to leave the shop with no change. In other words, it cost pennies. Frankly, there weren't high expectations for this one, either by the world when it was released or by Neil when he bought it.

Ridgeley had been perceived as the decoration in Wham! and his colleague George Michael was being steadily groomed for solo stardom by way of releasing solo material before Wham! split, being lauded in press releases for his song-writing talent and generally being moved towards a more adult audience and the promise of a vast tonnage of American dollars when that country – as was always the intention – bought copies of the Faith album by the truckload.

Wham! split in 1986, Ridgeley didn't exactly sprint from the starting gate where his solo career was concerned. Son of Albert duly suffered (topping out at #130 in the US Billboard charts). The album is a clear attempt to place Ridgeley amongst the rockier end of pop with hard guitars, a big sound and seven new songs (all boasting Ridgeley as co-writer) amongst the ten cuts. Ridgeley's songs typically open with an insistent beat and a lick or two, sprint like hell for the big chorus and repeat it in the hope they'll prove memorable. They also throw in some characterful turns. "Mexico" ends on a Latin section which segues into the insistent rock lick that opens "Big Machine." The two cover versions are also perfectly chosen to suggest the right things about Ridgeley. A nineties kick-ass cover of the Everley's "Price of Love" clearly has one ear on what made Bon Jovi's "Livin' on a Prayer" such a winner and covering Chic's "Hangin'" is another statement of Ridgeley's essential cool.

The album proved so unsuccessful and the returns from the first two singles so mediocre that the planned release of "Mexico" as the third single was scrapped. Ridgeley's solo efforts were always likely to be derided (Rolling Stone's review awarded Son of Albert half a star). We would go so far as to suggest it isn't that bad. Sure, it rocks away often to very little purpose and lacks a lead vocalist with the big pipes to focus the busy and cluttered backing, but it suggests Ridgeley's chops as a writer might have been under-rated, (one reason he's managed to avoid embarrassing celebrity comeback activities is the small fortune earned as a co-writer of songs like "Careless Whisper"), and it plods away so pleasantly in the background that nobody has seen fit to rip it from the CD tray whilst this entry was being written.

Billy Lee Riley:
Classic Recordings 1956-1960
(Bear Family, 1990)
What? "That boy sounds more like me than I do": Elvis.

You've certainly heard Riley's work, but probably his session efforts on behalf of artists like The Beach Boys and Dean Martin. Riley, and his band The Little Green Men, were the house band at Sun Studios. The situation did them few long-term favours as Sam Philips promoted Jerry Lee Lewis and others at their expense. Riley countered this by setting up his own label in the sixties, though ironically his third solo album saw him producing harmonica led instrumental covers of Beatle songs (ironic since he was in the first wave of rock 'n' roll that inspired them). We could pick that album as a case study in how cruel the business can be, or his Grammy nominated 1997 effort Hot Damn! But, to do justice to the inflammatory work that has inspired others to cover him the only fair assessment of Riley involves gathering the original Sun Records cuts as the basis for any decent collection. Bear Family's 49 track twofer is as much rock 'n' roll Riley as most people are likely to need. A 48 page booklet charts the twists and turns of a career that should be better known, and the first of the two CDs concerns itself with a chronological cull of sides cut between 1956 and 1960 by "The Cherokee Elvis." These 21 tracks amount to one of the best single CDs of original rock 'n' roll and blues cut by any artist of his generation. The collection includes cuts for the Rita and Brunswick labels along with classics like "Red Hot" and "Flying Saucers Rock 'n' Roll." It places blues alongside original rock 'n' roll. Some of the cuts might be novelty/space oriented but Riley and the Little Green Men rock with an insistent beat and a mix that always sounds alive. Riley's voice combines the edge of a manic shriek with perfect control of pitch and tone. He doesn't have the emotive authority of Elvis but he does bring a diction and sharpness that cuts through the most cluttered and chaotic rockin' moments.

Riley also wrote, or co-wrote, an impressive proportion of the best material here. "Rock With me Baby" and "Trouble Bound" – which formed his first single and open this collection – are both co-compositions. "Baby Please Don't Go" is solely composed by Riley and his skeletal version is a true stand out. Not so the few cuts that sprint too hard for novelty value. Brunswick signed Riley, who had become really unhappy with Sun Records, but "Rockin' on the Moon" is a throwaway sprint for "Stupid Cupid" style fame that does Riley few favours. Artist and label parted soon after this single. The second CD has alternative versions, re-produced originals and the kind of additional material completists regard as gold. It helps to build a portrait of an artist every bit as vital and talented as others who went on to legendary status, and that nails the value of this comprehensive collation of Riley's best early work. But the first CD is (almost) all killer, and that's where the curious should start.

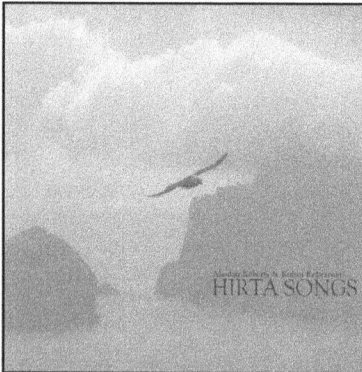

Alasdair Robinson and Robin Robertson:
Hirta Songs
(Stone Tape Recordings, 2013)
What? Heartfelt and heart breaking song cycle about a lost community.

A sympathetic and spell-binding collaboration between poet Robin Robertson and songwriter Alasdair Robinson. Hirta Songs started when Robertson visited St. Kilda (a group of western isles of Scotland, abandoned when a combination of dwindling population and a series of tragedies persuaded the inhabitants to leave). The resulting album charts a singular vision, Robertson's words are voiced mainly by Robinson, but the album's centrepiece, "Leaving St. Kilda," is a lengthy poem, with music, spoken by Robertson, using frugal description and a litany of details and evocative place names to chronicle a journey round the lost isles. Elsewhere the narrative strength of the songs grows with the sparing use of emotion in the details of a hard life in an unforgiving landscape. "Farewell to the Fowler" charts the true story of a St. Kildan man who fell hundreds of feet into the sea only to be buoyed aloft by the air trapped in the bodies of fifty sea birds he had collected before his fatal fall. Tales of tragedy unfold against a musical backing bearing witness to a place of a stark beauty. Evocative instrumental passages take over repeatedly. The slow teasing out of the inevitable move gradually reveals itself with each passing vignette. When the islands are abandoned the pragmatic, but harsh reality is told in simple images, like the drowning of the islands' dogs. Hirta, the largest of the isles in the St. Kilda group and the site of the largest community on the islands, gives the collection its name. The ensemble, occasionally including Robin Williamson, give haunting and economic beauty to every shifting pattern of sounds and the varied vocal performances deploy the spoken words and songs in a perfect sequence.

Rock 'N' Roll Allstars:
Red China Rocks
(B & C Records, 1972)
What? In the great tradition of communist China, you were never supposed to know the truth about this one.

In the company of the 499 other albums hereabouts this is probably one of the most unremarkable recordings on show. There's nothing particularly wrong about the 14 track romp through rock 'n' roll's glory moments. It's all played with enough guts to suggest this mob combine their rock 'n' roll revival/pub rock sensibilities with the passion and skill to deliver a decent set. They certainly don't let up in terms of picking the best songs and giving them their best shot. The good time album lines up and lays down a bumper 14 cuts. In order: "Slippin' And A Sliding," "Peggy Sue," "Slow Down," "Dixie Fried," "Folsom Prison Blues," "Blue Suede Shoes," "20 Flight Rock," "Long Tall Sally," "Rip It Up," "Bonie Maronie," "Shakin' All Over," "It Keeps Raining," "One Hand Loose," and "My Girl Josephine. Good calls. Some classics, a bit of Johnny Cash to show the range of skill, some well chosen lesser cuts – BIG respect for turning in a good take on the under-appreciated Fats Domino corker "My Girl Josephine."

And then there's the unique selling point of the whole collection. Let's face it. It's not every bunch of London-based chancers that got their shot at taking rock 'n' roll to communist China and reducing their rock 'n' roll starved population to a pulp by the end of the evening. Hell, it's not as if the Rock 'n' Roll Allstars were particularly stars in London, let alone Britain. So getting a tour of China, that was some popular movement right there, wasn't it?

Well, no, and when you appreciate why this otherwise unremarkable slab of sparky rock 'n' roll continues to enjoy cult status you also appreciate why it belongs in this book. It does have a certain tacky charm because the cover – featuring Chairman Mao's head grafted onto a fully adorned Teddy Boy, complete with brothel creeper shoes. The figure then pasted onto a section of a map of China – still sees action on websites that celebrate the worst dressed albums, ever. But that's as nothing to the conceit that conceived the confidence trick behind the whole caper. If you haven't sussed this yet, the Rock 'N' Roll Allstars never went anywhere near China. In fact, they never left Britain. According to some reports, they didn't even leave London. They did lay low for a while, pretend they'd toured China and punted this album onto the market as the proof of their labours. And, in the great tradition of hidden messages put there for discerning and die-hard fans, they revealed as much by cunningly adding the settlement of Tooting to the place names on the map of China adorning the cover of the album.

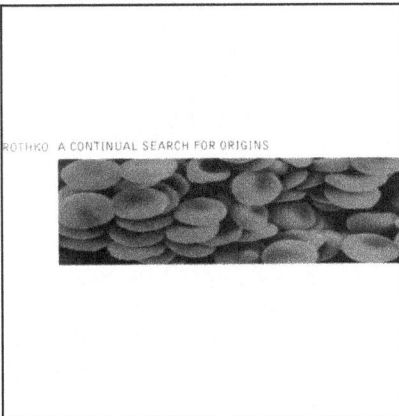

Rothko:
A Continual Search for Origins
(Too Pure, 2002)
What? Rueful and reflective ambient and alternative band. A bit keen on the old bass guitar!

Rothko (1997-2010) went through line-up changes and different labels to such an extent that their (slightly) changing music is probably the most consistent element of the band. By 2002 only Mark Beasley was still present from the founding trio. Rothko worked like a band, albums like A Continual Search... being reliant on a number of musicians. The borrowing of the surname of the famous abstract expressionist painter is some indication of where Rothko (the band) function. Rothko (painter) is best known for canvasses in which huge slabs of colour, frequently blurred and ragged at the edges, appear to float next to other colours. The contemplative qualities of the work are the point in both Rothkos. A Continual Search for Origins is mainly instrumental, mainly very slow and mainly built around resonations and echoes from extended bass guitar notes. To Rothko the bass is king, forming vibrating walls of sound, being mined for its different tones; especially its potential as a slowly played lead instrument, and being blended with keyboards, and with other bass guitars, to form the basis of works that skirt jazz, modern classical and post rock. Beyond these basic points musical labels are fairly pointless. Rothko are more appreciated for their unique recordings than as leaders in any genre.

A Continual Search… credits Mark Beasley and features him – personally - signing off on the liner notes. The other musicians are credited separately. Caroline Ross's restrained vocals and miniature lyric open the album effectively in "On the Day we Said Goodbye" but most of the 11 tracks here are instrumental, reflective and touched with a sense of over-arching melancholy. Things speed up occasionally and if there is any one track demonstrating the range of Rothko's talents it could be "I Sense You Fading Away" which starts with slow echoes, brings in background noise which gradually rises in the mix before a strident bass figure and drums kick it aside. Past the five minute mark the track subsides into ambient bass guitar and slowly fades to silence. Rothko's use of background noises is something of a trademark, confusing the unwary who may have their music on quietly into brief confusion as to whether what they're hearing is on the album or some random noise occurring outside.

Rothko generally contrived to sound unique to the point comparisons are limited in their use. Brian Eno and everything claiming to be ambient in his wake tells you something about the origins of A Continual Search… but not much. Like Morphine, Rothko have an ability to record and produce bass guitar sounds to bring every tinge and gradation of difference out; treating them with the care and attention generally afforded to more traditional lead instruments.

In the end Rothko's signature lies in the combination of these sounds and the blend achieved on every track that gives A Continual Search… its rueful and reflective quality. Typical Rothko flourishes include the intrusion of feedback in "To Other Horizons" or the finale "Words Melt Away" proving itself the most robust and combative piece on show after ten others have lulled you into a quiet contemplation.

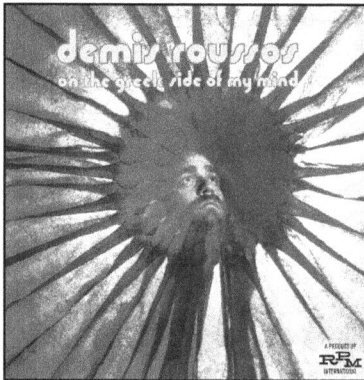

Demis Roussos:
On the Greek Side of My Mind
(Phillips, 1971)
What? Semi-prog, semi-spiritual identity crisis debut solo effort.

Better known in some territories as Fire and Ice Demis Roussos' first solo outing was recorded around the same time as Aphrodite's Child's magnum opus 666. Roussos' vocal chops had ably intoned 666's apocalyptic visions, soaring over the prog soundscapes of the band. Half a decade later, Roussos would be ensconced as the kaftan-coated king of a ubiquitous brand of listenable euro-pop, beloved of housewives, record shops and anyone remotely associated with his record label. The story of how the voice of an over-blown prog masterpiece became a licence to print middle-of-the-road money is partly told in a dozen widely varied songs here, because this collection makes clear the man had the visionary genius and varied vocal abilities to set his own agenda. Like his contemporaries, The Carpenters, he mined middle-of-the-road gold because he brought this creative talent to bear on radio friendly fodder and set a standard others would struggle to match.

On the Greek Side…/Fire and Ice continues to fascinate sound-hounds and lovers of exotica for two major reasons. Firstly: it is – stylistically – all over the place, secondly: when it sets off to go somewhere, it goes like hell. So it touches prog, it touches the winning pop sounds Roussos would trawl in later years but elsewhere it gets wonderfully strange. The original title track "On the Greek Side of My Mind" is a spoken word meditation on Roussos' heritage, resplendent with a chorus of monks and sounds of the sea. Elsewhere there are enough acoustic guitar trills and a slightly rougher edge to Roussos' voice on "End of the Line" as he aims for the lived-in end of the singer songwriter market. On the following cut "My Ship's A-Sailin'" we're into pseudo operatic wailing and the kind of performance that would fit snugly into an epic movie. All this, and we haven't mentioned the Greek instrumentation and rapid handclapping that turns up towards the end.

It's an album in the way a series of holiday snaps is an album, different destinations, different things to discover in each destination and our guide appears to be willing to go native wherever he touches down. The listening experience is softened by a lush production and superb playing (in the technical rather than explosive sense). The production, lavish by early seventies euro standards, also extends to some superb arrangements with bass instruments, soaring strings and a few other colourful touches arriving on cue to keep the interest. The arrangements – arguably – are bested by the masterful growing histrionics on the opening cut, "Fire and Ice." It would be a truly dedicated 21st century listener who'd slap on the headphones, prepare to concentrate, and live with this album from beginning to end. Such a person might well the kind of audio thrill-seeker motivated to buy this book!

Ssgt. Barry Sadler:
Ballads of the Green Berets
(RCA, 1966)
What? Jingoistic monster seller that wiped the floor with the Fab Four.

An album much derided as the aural equivalent of John Wayne's Green Berets movie, it's worth taking on board (assuming you live outside the USA) that the title track of this collection was the biggest selling single in its native country in 1966. And, the album also topped the US charts, shifting its first million copies in five weeks. So, technically speaking, this is a biggie. It's also a curiously quiet and restrained affair considering part of the motivation behind its release was to take on the long-hairs and anti-war brigade at their own game. So far as musical attack, righteous fury and taking the performance and production into the danger zone are concerned, Ballads of the Green Berets seems content to remain in the barracks. For the most part it is light country, balladry and light touches of other middle-America, with Sadler's high and perfectly controlled voice always presenting a clipped diction and the clearest of messages. The title track sets out its stall as it opens side one with the lines: "Fighting soldiers from the sky / Fearless men who jump and die," it might be an anthem of praise for the US military elite but we're seconds into the album and getting slaughtered in the service of your country has already reared its head. Indeed, the continuing interest in this period piece is very much down to its unapologetic jingoism and complete lack of irony with which it combines tales of heroism with the ever-present danger of death. Over a dozen very similar-sounding cuts Sadler takes a series of soldierly themes and tells a tale that proved immensely popular with middle-America. Armed conflict is noble, The Green Berets are an elite force of which the country should be proud, and the Vietnam War is a just conflict. There are references directly to Vietnam and the fifth cut is a paean to the city of Saigon, it is followed by "Salute to the Nurses" praising the medical staff who care for wounded soldiers. Elsewhere tracks like "I'm Watching the Raindrops Fall" (a meditation on the loneliness of the serving soldier and his simple longing for his sweetheart) and "The Soldier Has Come Home" (a chocolate box picture of the hero returning to his loving family) turn Ballads of the Green Berets into a revival of the Hollywood schmaltz that pervaded some movies about World War Two.

It's easy to be cynical, and cynicism and curiosity in this dated offering probably drove many of the sales when it finally earned a CD reissue, but it's worth noting a few other points. Sadler's album was a massive seller in 1966, and it predated the most strident anti-war outings by the hippie generation. It also came at a time when many in the USA felt the Vietnam War to be winnable (as in winnable by means of the US and South Vietnamese forces storming north and conquering opposing ground). This was years before the Tet Offensive that saw Vietcong soldiers attacking the very heart of the American military machine in Saigon, and well before revelations of atrocities like the My Lai massacre sullied the reputation of American forces. Sadler's simple and homely message didn't strike such a popular chord by then.

Sadler remains the most unlikely of musical heroes. His one album and its title track were massive, but his subsequent career was low key with only one other single making the top 30. Sadler's life also took some strange turns, he became a novelist writing (and subsequently giving his name to ghostwritten titles of) the Casca series of novels (based on the soldier who speared Christ on the cross and was destined to remain a soldier, trapped on Earth, until the second coming). He was also convicted of manslaughter after killing a love rival. Eventually Sadler – having relocated to Guatemala City - was shot in a robbery attempt, suffered brain damage and died of complications as a result.

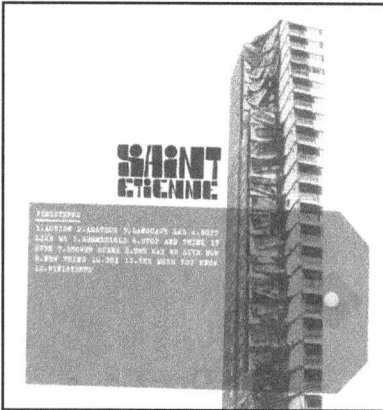

Saint Etienne:
Finisterre
(Mantra, 2002)
What? Conceptual genius from pop masters.

Saint Etienne's straddling of the pop charts and the higher echelons of artistic respect always sounded effortless. Finisterre marked something of an abrupt change for the band, spawned no singles that dented the UK top 40 and stalled well below #50 on the UK album charts. After a pair of lush productions and gracefully gliding albums of near perfect pop, Finisterre was also a strong return to varied styles of music and more challenging items, like spoken word links between the tracks. What it lacks in accessibility the album makes up for in accomplishment. To be appreciated in its full majesty Finisterre is best sampled along with the film of the same name. The album works in its own right but the lengthy instrumental passages on tracks like "The Way we Live Now" are very suggestive of the bustle and movement of a city. To hear these over the topographical documentary movie, with its shots of London life, is to appreciate that Finisterre is partly a love song to a city that has always inspired the band, and to the ability of pop songs to capture pieces of personal lives. The elliptical narration of Michael Jayson provides some guidance and quirky dark humour. "Our Father who art in Heaven, please stay there" precedes the harsh, electronic and slightly dark beats of "New Thing." The deep well of pop genius/insatiable love that fuels Bob Stanley and Pete Wiggs was never dredged with such relentless fury as it was on Finisterre, but Sarah Cracknell's vocals are also central to the magic here. Cracknell persists with the apparently unassuming sweetness she brings to much of the band's pop confections, but also shows herself adaptable, following a rap section in "Soft Like me" with a street girl indie vocal and, a couple of tracks later, giving it the breathy, sixties, slightly chanteuse feel on "Stop and Think it Over."

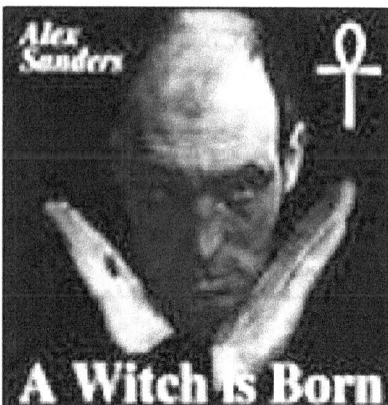

Alex Sanders:
A Witch is Born
(A & M, 1970)
What? The rite stuff.

Sanders (1926-1988) was one of the best known and most celebrated witches of his generation. A detailed Wikipedia page notes an associate stating Sanders never courted fame, but found himself unable to avoid it. He certainly had a choice about this work, released around the same time as the first Black Sabbath album and bought by those with a serious interest, and some of those for whom the Sabs and their ilk were their main point of contact with all things occult. A Witch is Born presents three tracks and three samples of witching lore. The main piece of business – "The Initiation" – features almost 25 minutes of ceremonial rite, serious ritualistic business carried out with due reverence and notable English accents. Janet Owen becomes a witch (and finally gets to speak around the 18 minute mark) as a detailed ceremony is reverently enacted with a permanent backing track of classical music. The same mixture appears on "The Legend of the Goddess" and "The Great Rite." Some of the classical music offered up is down-the-line Classic FM gold, and the well-modulated English voices, intoning rites and Wiccan lore, over classical favourites makes for surreal listening. The serious point of the recording is to present Wiccan rites as they take place. Stuart Farrar provides commentary on the main ritual as High Priest Sanders leads the rite that makes Janet Owen a witch.

Low key CD reissues have become available, reproducing the grainy black and white photographs, dark cover and copious sleeve-notes of the original album. In a world of extreme dark magic/magick of all forms A Witch is Born now presents a slightly staid, and very English take on the whole business and – like the Aliester Crowley recordings also chronicled in this book – does have a certain approachable charm.

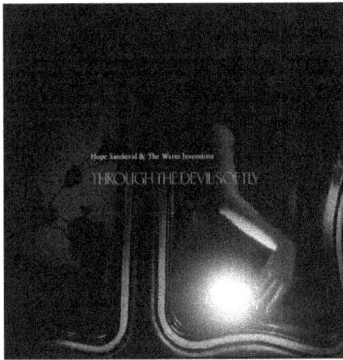

Hope Sandoval and the Warm Inventions: Through the Devil Softly
(Nettwerk, 2009)
What? Dark, ambient and ethereal may be the buzzwords from Hell, but this sounds great.

Sandoval is best known as the voice of Mazzy Star but two long-playing efforts away from the band Bavarian Fruit Bread (2001) and this collection allowed her to mine a slightly different seam of echoing vocal/ moody atmospheric music. It isn't that far from the best known work of Mazzy Star but does allow Sandoval and Colm Ó Cíosóig to bring in a range of percussion, change the time signatures and blend their dark and meandering melodies with percussive tones. All of this in a way that generally evokes mournfulness and melancholy. As with most of Mazzy Star's work and Warm Inventions' earlier release the reviews were both fawning and grasping at metaphors to put the music into some context. For some reviewers the album conjured up empty landscapes, dark clouds, the realities of an inescapable dream etc. It also – uniquely for Sandoval's solo albums – conjured up a place in the Billboard top 200 (#160).

Sandoval's work with Warm Inventions draws on slow country guitar styles, pedestrian percussion (generally given massive echo and blended with her voice which hovers between a whisper and understated following of a melody) and throws in elements of other music (a blues lick here, sudden shift of time signature there) to create work that shows the effort and craft applied to it.

Sandoval's vocals generally hover on the limit of intelligibility. It often seems like an intrusion to crank up the headphones to decipher what she is singing. So, Through the Devil Softly is less about the subject of its individual songs than it is about a journey through moods. A dim the lights, shut out the world meander that sets out to affect your mood, deliver minor missives of emotional intent, and leave a feeling of attachment between band and listener. You know you've been visited by a Warm Inventions album. Mark Powell – reviewing this for Drowned in Sound – noted: "an album whose drowsy currents you'll want to bob far away on, with no immediate concern over getting back." As good a comment on Warm Inventions music as you're likely to hear. Through the Devil Softly edges its way through different sounds – betraying the years it took to craft the collection – starting out on positively lively form by Sandoval's restrained standards with "Blanchard" which presents an insistent rising and falling melody, repetitive and effective electric guitar licks and what passes in this context for an anthemic chorus. The pace soon slows and some tracks – like

"Lady Jessica and Sam" – are verging on spoken word and the most minimally executed guitar licks. The closing "Satellite" pulls a beautifully effective trick of reining-in Sandoval's voice to the extent she appears to be singing through a tiny speaker on a radio.

Walter Schumann:
Exploring the Unknown
(RCA, 1955)
What? Space journey in sound, recorded before any human had been into space.

Schumann died tragically young after complications set in following one of the first generation of open heart surgeries in 1958. He left an impressive tonnage of easy listening and orchestral works; some recorded for theatre, film or television, and this bona-fide classic of exotica. Exploring the Unknown is a story album using spoken word over an orchestra to narrate the story of man's first journey into space. Technically speaking Schumann gets loads of the facts wrong – the journey begins on a numbered (not named) Pacific island, the rocket appears to be launched on behalf of mankind rather than any one nation etc. But, that's hardly the point. As Mickey McGowan – onetime curator of The Unknown Museum – put it when interviewed in Incredibly Strange Music: "Most of his records were glee club-like and true easy listening, but on this one he hit pay dirt. Amidst celestial choirs you hear the deep resonant voice of PAUL FREES narrating."

It is one hell of a journey. The full orchestra stays engaged for most of the time, their playing moving along with the story rather than repeating themes. Frees has the depth and emotive qualities to render the descriptions of scenes to perfection. The choir ooh and aaah celestially and as the first side draws to a close the journey moves on to Venus and to meditations about the feelings of "great insignificance" felt by humans in the void of space. At this point the choir strides in at march tempo with a lyric including: "There are new frontiers out in space…let's travel on to the new frontier." It's a message that likens space exploration to settling the wild west. This sentiment is expressed with Soviet precision and sensibility. When the mists of Venus finally subside: "We are looking at a woman; she is small and dainty…" and all the great elements of American science fiction are in place just before we venture into side two, encounter the friendly aliens and think as far as our minds will allow us to think into space. Exploring the Unknown has a period charm and kitsch quality, but it is a glorious example of its form and – for sheer ambition and creativity – it walks all over the less inspired and largely forgotten competition of its era. Unlike most of them, it has also enjoyed a CD reissue.

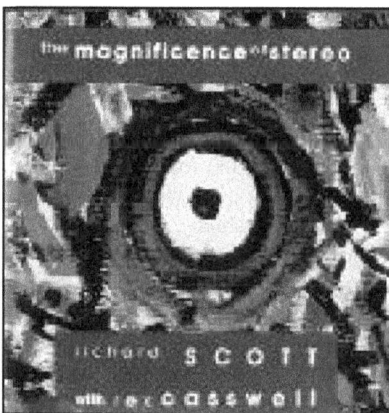

Richard Scott with Rex Casswell:
The Magnificence of Stereo
(Sruti, 1992)
What? Playful plunderphonics.

With the rest of the world going mad for sampling and computer technology Richard Scott and Rex Casswell set about thinking along the same lines and working with old school, analogue tools. The resulting "plunderphonic" creation is a conglomeration of cutting edge thinking and human charm that samples the great and the good but still sounds charcterful and creative in its own right. The "tools" here – as listed on Scott's web site – include:

"turntables, CDs, radio, ansaphone, sound FX, documentary recordings and cassette tape players through a little Radio Shack disco mixer." All of these sources recorded live onto DAT. Lacking the sampling technology available to big studios the various sources were played, the tracks planned and the recordings done as the resulting material was played live in the studio.

The preference for classical and experimental works over cutting edge rap or anything so contemporary is part of the reason The Magnificence of Stereo sounds like something created for BBC Radio Three (or a public service station/arts installation if you're reading this outside the UK). The Magnificence of Stereo packs some funny and playful titles – including: "Slug Talk," "Thorns That Sleep And Grow" (which relies heavily on a comic combination of "Every Time we Say Goodbye" and animal noises like a barking dog and mooing cow) and "Idiot Tube." It is happy to offer up fragments, "Slug Talk" is a fraction under two minutes and the closing and untitled track presents exactly one minute (of silence). Elsewhere there are lengthy sonic explorations like the 15 minute and 40 second "The Day Has Gone." The album can't make up its mind if it is any one thing artistically, although the attempt to push the barriers of sound and invention with its special set of tools and performance is really the point. Sonically it is miles away from the Moog experiments of 25 years before but in terms of attitude it might be worth imagining a windowless van containing the Monochrome Set, Durutti Column and The Aphex Twin pulling up and kidnapping Perrey and Kingsley before dragging them off to Hulme – where this collection was recorded – to give their vibe a big Doc Marten up the rear end. Richard Scott's description of "a kind of DJ mix gone far too far" is a fair assessment of the forward movement and live feel of the whole collection.

At its worst (which isn't to say it's bad music, just sometimes off at a tangent) The Magnificence of Stereo is still an interesting experiment, more personable and generally more enjoyable than much sampled and self-indulgent material of its age. At its best – on tracks like "Piracy" which features samples from Brian Eno's Ambient 1: Music for Airports – it is an assertive and self-confident, taking great ideas, blending them and running with their possibilities to create music of invention and character.

Screw Radio:
Talk Radio Violence
(SST, 1995)
What? Black Flag vs the great American public...we'll call it a draw.

Black Flag's Greg Ginn provides the guitar and bass, and the varied opinionated callers to talk radio provide the rants for a collaboration none could have planned. The idea is simple enough – Poindexter Stewart – the character creation and presenter of Screw Radio is credited with "vocal samples" – in other words the rants – and over 17 tracks America's knee jerk jabber is teased into bite sized chunks and turned into muscular and listenable rock tracks.

That – pretty much – is the point. It is less belligerent than Black Flag in full flight but – oddly – all the more disturbing because when it gets onto a subject like "That Crack Smokin' Mayor is Back" (track six), or "You Could be Like the Devil" (track 16), Talk Radio Violence is hanging between satire and celebration. The moral position of the makers of the album, the listeners and the origins of the opinions on each track constantly shifts. Consequently, as a product aimed at the market, Talk Radio Violence takes on a strange reality. Left unchecked, this is a portrait of a nation so keen to have its say that it's questionable if anyone is left to simply listen. The fact these samples have been turned – effectively - into rock songs means they're there to be listened to, but as listeners we're constantly caught between rocking along with Ginn, and reacting to nuggets of political, religious and personal opinion. This randomly assembled rockumentary asks as many questions as it answers, and that – probably – is the point. If the greatest nation on earth is going to hell in a handcart, is anyone left to save it? Taken seriously it's scary, treated as entertainment it has humour value beyond mere scripted comedy. As an insight into Ginn's motivation to create the music that made Black Flag such a force Talk Radio Violence also has something to say.

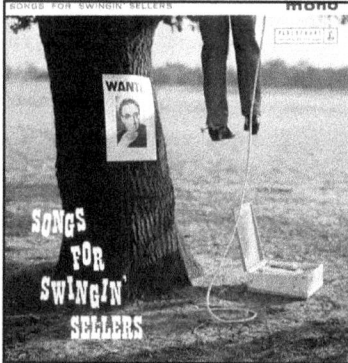

Peter Sellers:
Songs for Swinging Sellers
(Parlophone, 1959)
What? Short on songs, and not much here that swings.

Sellers acting career was decidedly high-profile by the late fifties and when a series of Songs for Swinging Sellers 7" EPs sold well Parlophone compiled a dozen of his best comedy skits onto one long-player. Once the opening "You Keep Me Swinging" has been dispensed with any pretence at big-band swing is over. For the most part this is a classic comedy album, helmed by the production skills of George Martin and aided by a few choice co-stars, notably British actress Irene Handl. One running feature is a cynicism about music and musicians. One skit features a racehorse owner discussing his stable of rock 'n' roll singers, suggesting he ditches any who can actually hold a tune and considering them more as bloodstock than talent. A similar attitude under-pins "Puttin' on the Smile," a vicious satire on Lonnie Donegan and skiffle stars in general. Whilst "Peter Sellers Sings Gershwin" is a fragmental finale in which he literally, sings the one name. The disdain for rock and pop gives the collection a focus, though it does sound more than a little bitter. It leaves Sellers using his substantial acting talents to create a work of subtlety and twists that stands repeated listening. Over half a century later some of it sounds very contemporary, especially the political interview in which the befuddled subject struggles to get in one reply as he is hounded by a journalist and an arts review that amounts to little more than meandering pretentious bilge from start to finish. The tape techniques allowing Sellers to appear as more than one character in some sketches were cutting edge at the time, and they are milked for full-effect. To a listening generation unfamiliar with his work the ideas still stand up. Most of the jokes are still funny, some of them are very funny and the more complicated ideas are given life by Martin's production which gets the balances right. Martin practices the same skills of creating a picture in sound that would later make his contributions central to The Beatles. The Beatles' famous fan club Christmas records certainly owe a debt to this album. However, Sellers is the undisputed star, adopting personae at will, making the unbelievable sound plausible for a few minutes and going at his subject with the utmost savagery when the joke demands it.

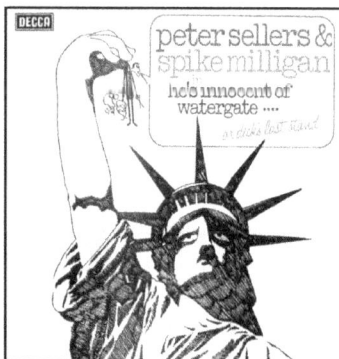

Peter Sellers and Spike Milligan:
He's Innocent of Watergate, or Dick's Last Stand
(Decca, 1974)
What? With "friends" like these, Richard Nixon didn't need enemies.

A lot of seventies LP comedy has finally found its way to CD reissue. This timely piece of period fun hasn't had a sniff of such rediscovery action. Clearly inspired by the existence (and denied existence) of White House tape recordings, Sellers and Milligan set off into surreal comic territory to concoct a musical and comedy revue in defence of Nixon.

Time hasn't been kind to some of the jokes, and the sheer strangeness of the whole piece is also a barrier to engaging with it today. Mr Fab, discussing the album on the Music for Maniacs blog nailed its otherness: "a gleeful and genuinely deranged mélange of vicious satire, relentless political incorrectness (in every possible sense of the word - you have been warned!), and sheer Dadaism."

In mundane terms that means Sellers in full vocal artistry flow, Milligan's retinue of silly voices and love of varied sound effects (including speeding up and slowing down of the tape) and an inexhaustible bag of tricks to keep the energy levels high. The gags are received rapturously by canned laughter, quite welcome in this context because the more off the wall flights of fancy need signposts to pinpoint the humour. The supporting cast is impressive, including June Whitfield and (go-to guy for gravitas American voices recorded in the UK) Ed Bishop.

True grasping of the interminable turns within the narrative would require some familiarity with the allegations and twists and turns of Richard Nixon's ongoing Watergate trauma to 1974. But the fart gags, heavy handed political incorrectness and deep deep cynical cruelty about politics and the security services are crystal clear to this day. He's Innocent hovers in some comedy netherworld between Derek and Clive and The Firesign Theatre, presenting two thirds of The Goons at their most politically satirical, and edgiest.

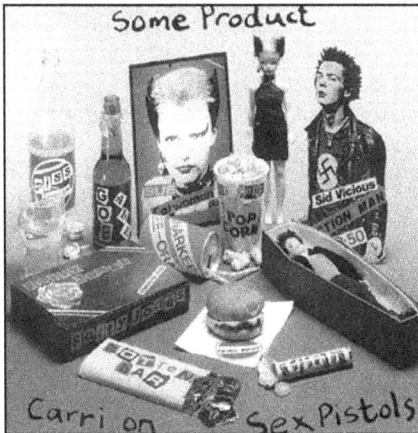

The Sex Pistols:
Carri On Sex Pistols: Some Product
(Virgin, 1978)
What? Ragbag compilation light on music, heavy on attitude.

The Pistols' fleeting career ended in acrimony and death, nothing of any significant worth was left in the vaults SO Carri On... filled the gap. A compilation cum mash-up of interviews and other spoken word items, like adverts, Carri On documents a band and time since distorted by history. Frankly, it remains blatant cashing in and was even sold as such, so it's wrong to see it as any kind of definitive statement, but it does give insights history has tended to overlook. Sid Vicious comes over as more thoughtful and intelligent than time has presented him, John/ny Rotten/Lydon remains as obtuse as ever and guitarist Steve Jones spends as much time as anyone batting off questions about what punk actually means.

The band get little further than the usual platitudes about honesty, slagging off pretty much every other band and identifying their targets as "grown ups," record companies and the like. But the insight into the personalities involved shows something of what punk was about. This is five working class youngsters (both bass players get a look in) partying hard in the eye of a storm. Jones' performance on "Big Tits" a track composed mainly of a US radio interview in which Jones consistently asks female callers about their breast size is don't give a shit/politically incorrect to a degree unthinkable today.

And the music makes fleeting appearances, with snatches of the handful of great singles the band made and – bizarrely – a crude attempt to mash the Pistols' music in with their Virgin stable-mate Mike Oldfield's classic Tubular Bells.

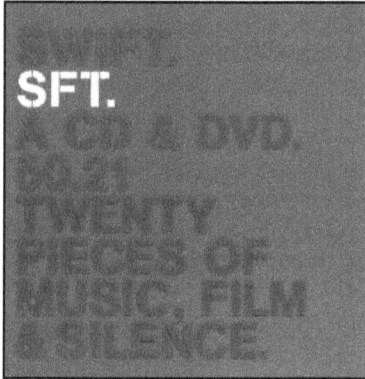

SFT:
Swift
(Mute, 2002)
What? "as if The Godfather Of Punk had been produced with great strictness by The Godfather Of Minimalism."

The Godfathers Of Punk/Minimalism quote above comes directly from the website of Simon Fisher Turner (aka SFT) and suggests that even his most challenging releases spring from demanding concepts in which he completely gets what he is doing. The question of whether others do get it, or could get it, is really the point of including Swift in this book. By his own admission, the most demanding work on Swift – "Sandstorm" – involves SFT producing: "gracefully floating, dappled piano and clarinets...it's apparent that Fisher Turner has eluded categorisation and set himself magnificently adrift." That – pretty much – is the point of a collection that takes the alternative approach of performers like Boyd Rice, includes a cover note asking listeners to play the whole album on shuffle (thereby creating new patterns, running orders and meanings) and also asks listeners to play the work both quietly and loud. Fisher-Turner's eclectic stagger through the music industry includes touch-downs as a would-be pop star supported by Jonathan King (and once written up in Disc and Music Echo as Britain's answer to David Cassidy), a period as press officer for Cherry Red Records (which led in-turn to) a stint in The The. He has also served as film composer, worked under a number of names (John Peel was especially fond of his work as The King of Luxembourg) and enjoyed a residency working on art installation projects and in academia. We'll leave aside his acting career for the moment. Swift is a useful entry point into this vastness if only because it distils some of Fisher Turner's best qualities. The pieces all evoke an atmosphere and Fisher Turner's abilities with individual instruments, arrangements and atmospherics are at their best evocative of Brian Eno and Eno's collaborations with David Byrne. Like those works there is generally a hint of the music created providing a doorway to a complex reality wherein different rules of reality are applied. Fisher Turner also works brilliantly in producing ostensibly simple tunes but developing complex and compelling dynamics between competing sounds; so much so that the claims on his site to producing music of "valour" are totally justified. Even the slow works, built of keyboard figures, lengthy tones and vocal interjections are fearless in following their own journey. "Colourfaker" – a suggestively haunting piece built of single military drum, cornet and minimal keyboard wash – being a good example of the form. The unrepentant otherness of Swift is both its greatest strength, and weakness. At best this collection packs the same argument to be taken on its own merits as collections by The Aphex Twin. It isn't derivative, it imagines music as a place and reality as much as any set of rules and it exists so completely in this world as to make its own case. At worst, it demands that listeners make the effort to move into Swift's reality before the gems of insight and emotional impact are truly revealed.

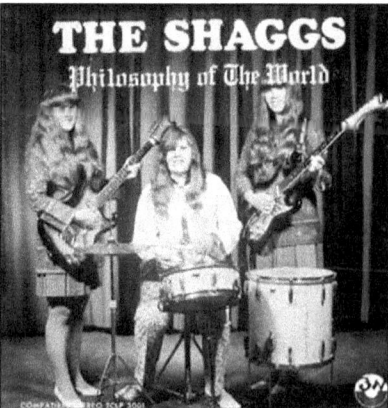

The Shaggs:
Philosophy of the World
(Third World, 1969)
What? One of the all-time greats of outsider music.

First released to widespread indifference in 1969 Philosophy of the World has long been recognised as one of the most gloriously strange recordings ever produced, and a cornerstone work for any claims regarding the merits of outsider music. Outsider music is typically identified because its main performers eschew traditional ways of composing or performing on instruments, achieve a greater control over their creative vision as a result and – at their best – produce work that teaches and inspires others.

Rant over.

Consider the following: when recording engineers working on Philosophy of the World heard The Shaggs stop and retake a song after making a mistake they were amazed. To the engineers the music sounded so slap-dash and amateurish they had no idea how The Shaggs could spot a mistake. By contrast fans of Philosophy of the World included Frank Zappa and Kurt Cobain (who listed it as #5 amongst his favourite albums).

Kitted out with supermarket instruments The Shaggs – sisters Dorothy "Dot," Betty and Helen Wiggen, with some involvement from sister Rachel – pound their way through a little more than half an hour's worth of original tunes. Traditional song structures of verse-chorus-verse are ignored in favour of a mass cavalcade of voices telling breathless stories and the usual complementary use of instruments is ditched in favour of everything appearing to be clamouring for attention all the time. Add to this that the songs typically speed up and slow down with the singing and the overall effect is something akin to recording the first crude run through of a normal band attempting a tune, before pressing the results onto vinyl and then using a finger to speed up and slow down the record as it plays. Shaggs' vocals are lower than most girl groups and appear happy to stay in that area. Shaggs' lyrics typically take on domestic and down-home observation of the world and settle comfortably on the knife edge between triteness and depth.

"Things I Wonder" opens with: "There are many things I wonder/There are many things I don't/It seems as though the things I wonder most/Are the things I never find out/I wonder about the stars above/I wonder about the birds that fly…" And, The Shaggs were good God-fearing American girls at a time when the counter-culture drove many into rebellious ideas and away from God. The closing track, "We Have a Saviour" spells it out: "Why does the world go unholy?/ Why does everyone fight more and more?/Don't they know we have a saviour?/All we have to do is believe and pray/ Why must we go unheathen?"

The Shaggs' story went on spawn a stage musical. The tale of how a group of sisters from Fremont, New Hampshire came to record an album that stunned and divided musicians and critics is compelling. The slow trickle of cult fandom for the band has been fuelled by sporadic reissues of Philosophy of the World some of which incorporate the tracks for a second (aborted) album which was ditched when their father (also their mentor) died suddenly. You can go online to find discussions of typical melodic intervals in Shaggs' songs and some dissection of just what it is that makes their music so compellingly unique. All very good, and recommended if you're the type likely to devour every entry in this book. But, nothing beats a serious listen to the whole of their first album.

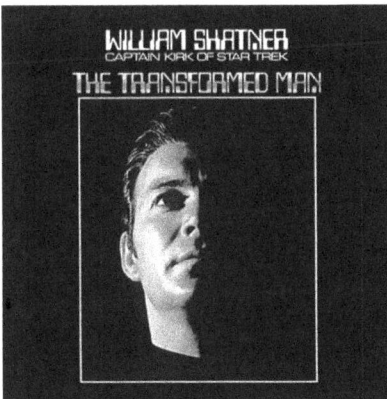

William Shatner:
The Transformed Man
(Decca, 1968)
What? The blue touchpaper that lit up a sparkling musical career.

The Wikipedia has a page devoted to Shatner's musical career. None of which would have been possible unless the curious magic of The Transformed Man had worked its way into popular culture. Shatner's more recent works have been more knowing in their ability to balance the over-emotive acting out of lyrics against a musical backdrop, and the involvement of Ben Folds in helming Has Been (2004) with its glorious covers of works like Pulp's "Common People" was a clear attempt to rekindle what is great about The Transformed Man. However, it is the fact this greatness – by common consent – frequently courts unintended comedy that makes The Transformed Man the quintessential Shatner collection; probably one of the defining outsider albums of all time.

Shatner narrates and acts his way through a mind-bending assortment of classic work. The album opens with a crowd pleaser from "King Henry the Fifth," a useful warm up for the extract from Hamlet that marks the fifth performance. Elsewhere the two most often played tracks on radio – "Mr Tambourine Man" and "Lucy in the Sky With Diamonds" – see Shatner acting out the wild-eyed wonder of the newly turned on, and give The Transformed Man its down-with-the-kids moments. The musical backing, especially the moments of dramatic tension produced by an orchestra, add to the sense of overblown theatricality.The grouping of tracks together to form dramatic counter-points is also a self-important master-stroke/monumental clanger. The only stand-alone track, "The Transformed Man," closes the proceedings, presenting itself in three movements and mapping out: "earthly ureality-transitional awareness-contract with divinity." Bear in mind Sgt Pepper made fewer claims and Brian Wilson only aspired to write his "teenage symphonies to God." The Transformed Man, by contrast, seeks to get inside the divine and allow Shatner to method-act himself into this position before intoning it to his listeners. It's a big ask, a big sound and a collection of musical works that has seldom been equalled for the scale of its reach and its willingness to push back boundaries. For that alone The Transformed Man is likely to remain revered and remembered well into the future.

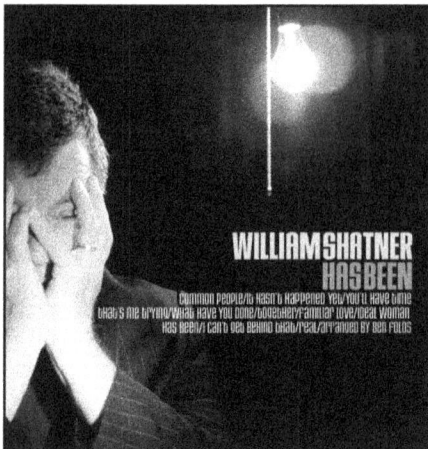

William Shatner:
Has Been
(Shout Factory/Sony, 2004)
What? A seamless synergy of irony, inspiration and the incredible.

To William Shatner's credit he embraced the ironic appreciation poured onto The Transformed Man and developed enough self-knowledge to bring about an incredible transformation in his musical fortunes. The happy collaborative work on Has Been resulted from contact with Ben Folds, with whom Shatner was scheduled to appear onstage, and a phone call offering Shatner a new album deal. The combination of a tolerant label wanting only more Shatner product, Folds' expert musical direction and inspired input from Shatner himself makes Has Been something of a tour-de-force. Albeit, a varied, strange and demanding example of the form. Folds' comments in the liner notes identify Shatner as "an extremely intuitive musical orator" and, near-enough, warn you that the varied gems on offer here will veer in several directions.

Shatner co-writes eight of the 11 tracks, mainly with Folds but also with occasional help from Lemon Jelly and Henry Rollins. Each Shatner original offers a vignette wherein the man can act out a character part, either as himself or in some imagined life. Shatner is smart enough to take on board reference points well outside his usual realm. On the gloriously overblown "You'll Have Time" Shatner borders insane gallows humour, challenging the notion that anyone ever has time to do the things they plan in life and name-checking a litany of the fallen, including JFK and Joey Ramone. Has Been, just about, qualifies as a rock album, or muscular indie version of the form, and Folds' deft arrangements, the incorporation of a range of influences and Shatner's ability to vary the vocal styles make it a more sympathetic and nuanced work than The Transformed Man.

Shatner's one solo composition, "What Have you Done," is an ambitious nugget involving a post-traumatic retelling of a failed attempt to pull a suicidal love out of deep water. It is followed by the amiable and upbeat "Together," the one co-composition with Lemon Jelly. The variety, sequencing and elements of musical surprise work repeatedly to make Has Been a lively work that stands repeated listening, revealing its finer touches once the listener is familiar with its basic shape.

To Shatner's credit he deploys restraint and acting craft here in a manner The Transformed Man suggests would have been impossible. The cocktail jazzy "Familiar Love" is self-knowing kitsch of the highest order, the title track a blistering broadside at critics – Shatner pointing out a has been was somebody once, and might well be again – and the closing "Real" is a remarkably honest exploration of the curious existence of a star with a public image and his own private awareness of how far his real personality is from his public persona. The "hit" – Shatner's reworking of Pulp's "Common People" – is the best known piece on offer here and greatly enjoyed by the masses if the YouTube figures are anything to go by, but it is only one facet of an accomplished 21st century reinvention of a true one-off amongst recording stars.

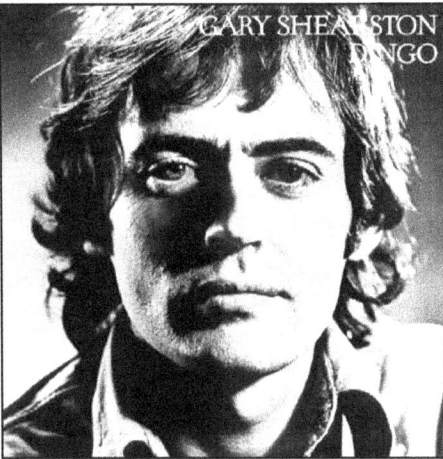

Gary Shearston: Dingo (Charisma, 1974)

What? Singer-songwriter tour-de-force which had the misfortune to spawn a major hit that was a cover version.

It's doubtful whether Gary Shearston (1939-2013) would see misfortune in Dingo. The album marked a critical and commercial high-point for the singer-songwriter, spawning a hit cover of Cole Porter's "I Get a Kick out of You" that made Shearston the first Australian artist to simultaneously hit the top ten in the UK and Australia. It also allowed him studio time with a budget lavish enough to add strings, complex percussion and a rich sound when required. He was a label-mate of Genesis, after all. Having been a star in his native land, seen his songs covered by the likes of Peter, Paul and Mary and spent years on the fringes of a breakthrough in the USA, Shearston finally had significant solo success. However, Dingo didn't chart and didn't mark the beginning of a lengthy high-profile career.

Dingo is a contemplative, occasionally lush and very mature affair, lining up eight originals and ending both of its five track sides on the original vinyl with covers of age-old standards. "I Get a Kick…" rounds off the first side, the second ends with "Without a Song." The cover versions were the singles, probably because they were always a shoo-in for some airplay but they're misrepresentative of the main thrust of the album. Shearston's originals explore his Australian roots, triumph and tragedy in personal relationships, and really take flight with a contemplative gem like "Witnessing," one of those rare life, the universe and everything efforts that still manages to sound understated, wise and listenable. It is moments like the beautiful keyboard solo on "Witnessing" and the highly effective and achingly stark percussion on "Aborigine" that push Dingo out of seventies singer-songwriter predictability and into territory that would later become fertile ground for hit artists looking to build critical respect and sustainable careers. Described this way Dingo is too easily reduced to another item worthy of CD reissue (which still awaits outside Australia as of this writing), but it's the emotional and personal nature of the collection that really shines through and makes this an enduring and assured collection that, if anything, sounds more assured and impressive so many years after its first release.

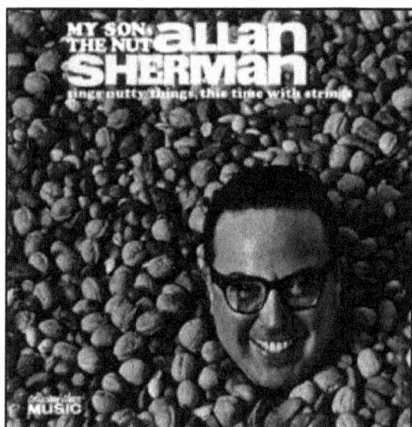

Alan Sherman:
My Son, the Nut
(Warner Brothers, 1963)
What? Prime-period long-player from massively successful satirist.

Allan Sherman (1924-1973) remains one of the most successful satire and parody artists in the history of popular music. Born Allan Copelon, he slogged his way through comedy writing and other forms of show-business; often looking for the main chance on the back of taking the biggest hits around – like the musical My Fair Lady – and giving them a massive Jewish makeover. If the ideas were obvious enough (mining comedy gold from every social more and cultural misunderstanding) it took a long time for the right format to emerge. His venture into comedy recording came when a lucrative television job dried up and My Son, the Folk Singer (1962) opened the account for a series of comedy albums providing Jewish parody re-workings of popular hits. Popular legend has it that Sherman's fans included JFK. The president was, apparently, witnessed singing "Sarah Jackman" – Sherman's Jewish makeover of "Frere Jacques."

Early period Sherman's basic tools were simple enough. Musical remakes so close to the original their opening notes would be familiar to audiences – and often fool them into believing they heard the real thing – before a Jewish accent, Jewish cultural reference points and some decent Jewish jokes appeared in the lyrics. It's a formula that has worked with variations as the source of humour for the likes of Weird Al Yankovic. But, Sherman's first album hit the top of the charts and became a popular staple on radio. By 1963 this style had expanded into producing his own original work in popular styles; but not necessarily re-working existing songs.

My Son, the Nut stayed on top of the charts for two months and spawned the massive single "Hello Muddah, Hello Fadduh," – which, incidentally, name-checks a certain "Leonard Skinner" – and featured a big orchestral sound and a few diversions from the purely Jewish gags. The album opens with the strains of "The Battle Hymn of the Republic" – although this is in the context of a song about the French revolution. It soon morphs into a Latin-based rant about the performance of Louis XVI as monarch. The album hits several popular American themes. "Automation" takes a side-swipe at labour saving inventions (Sherman spends some of the song considering whether his wife is better replaced by the robot "the 503"), "Here's to the Crabgrass" is a witty examination of suburban life that mocks so gently that suburbanites could almost feel admired, and the closing live recorded monologue with orchestra, "Hail to Thee, Fat Person," is all the funnier because Sherman's rotund form is the butt of the joke and he presents weight gain as a public service: "when I was a child my mother said to me; clean the plate; because children are starving in Europe, so I would clean the plate…they kept starving and I got fat!"

Sherman's career continued at a high profile – albeit to diminishing returns – until his death, aged 48, in 1973. To 21st century ears his work is mainstream and settles comfortably on the thin line of being inventive enough to stay funny after a first listen, and confident enough to address the comedy basics of day-to-day living with strong characters and original ideas. The onus at the time was on the largest audience numbers, so Sherman was already moving away from wall-to-wall Jewish comedy in 1963 (though the Jewish angle is still the single strongest source of jokes here). A modern day Sherman would face massive challenges – not least finding a common demographic likely to see humour in such obvious and everyday subjects – but the original still packs gags that work.

Judee Sill:
Heart Food
(Asylum, 1973)
What? Finest food for the heart.

Sill's self-titled debut album was the first long player released by the Asylum label and her work represented the highest art and furthest reaching ambitions of folk rock. Sill's troubled past included spells of serious drug addiction and work as a prostitute, but also an affinity with gospel music (some of which she'd come to appreciate whilst playing church organ in reform school), and classical arrangements. All of these elements, along with a sense of making music to transcend the moment and express something of the whole human condition, inform that first album and Heart Food. The nine song collection is culled from material, some dating back to the late sixties some composed during the sessions, that finds a perfect fusion of Sill's disparate influences and expresses depths of emotion and insights into character sufficient to terrify lesser songwriters. The final song, "The Donor," features a hugely complex and perfectly realised choral arrangement and "The Kiss" combines a similar idea with a lyric rich in Christian imagery. Sill's lyrical trademarks include stories of relationships told with symbolism, metaphors and the awareness of the fragility in human interactions. This comes with an outward looking perspective and none of the self-regarding fragility of the narcissistic contingent amongst some singer/songwriters of her generation.

Sill's two studio albums suggest strongly that music, as in the conglomeration of words, arrangements, tunes and production, was the goal for her. There is rich meaning in the gospel, choral and classical nuances, just as there are genuine depths in her lyrics. She remains fully in control on Heart Food, writing and arranging the orchestral and vocal parts. Sill's music gives up its secrets slowly, she never achieved a hit single. But the relationship with her most devoted listeners is strong and enduring. A review on Pitchfork.com notes of "The Kiss": "If ever there was a song that lived up to the glorious, simultaneous heartbreaking and mending I might expect from a symphony to God, it's this. Sill once again plays piano (and in fact did all the orchestral and vocal arrangements herself), using another unbelievably gorgeous chord progression, taking advantage of pedal notes and resolving cadences in much the same way as Bach did, and uses her lone, double-tracked vocal to deliver a melody that arrests me no matter how many times I hear it." Heart Food presents nine songs as good as this, a double CD reissue in 2006 presented both Asylum albums, along with an equal amount of outtakes and unreleased songs.

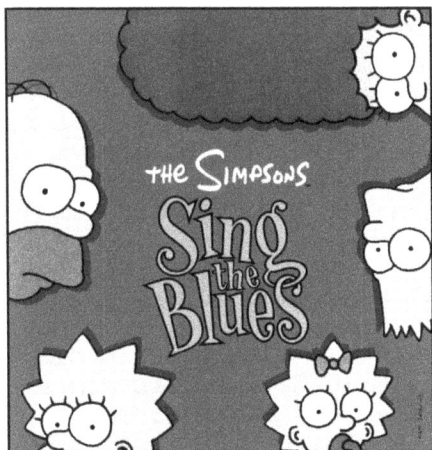

The Simpsons:
Sing the Blues
(Geffen, 1990)
What? Like all the best jokes…it's packed with truth.

Released in 1990, and boasting the chart-topping "Do the Bartman" Sing the Blues is still thought by many to be little more than a cash in, the musical equivalent of the plastic figurines and t-shirts that have kept Simpson's coffers well stuffed for years. It's way better than that. For starters they cover Chuck Berry, Billie Holiday and Randy Newman, rope in a – then – uncredited Michael Jackson to co-write "Do the

Bartman" get the talents of DJ Jazzy Jeff writing "Deep Deep Trouble" and boast session guests including Eagle Joe Walsh and jazz piano legend Dr John. Though for sheer blues credibility the appearance of B.B. King is probably the trump card. Superstar sessions of a similar ilk have crashed and burned in the past, but this stellar collection is held together by the same vision that sees Springfield's most celebrated family for what they are: the voices of ordinary America, living out a national vision in their local lives. Where the television show lifts celebrated scenes from epic movies and tackles global themes Sing the Blues starts with a really clever idea to pull a similar stunt. The blues might be the music of the oppressed black poor of long ago but The Simpson's take on the music is very wide, if it's about them and their lives it is the blues…even if Michael Jackson co-wrote it and it sounds for all the world like comedy dance-pop. They lift the spirit of the blues, and mash it up with the music of everyone.

So we get Simpson's characters voicing classics. For all its comedy value Homer's take on "Born Under a Bad Sign" has a sense of genuine pain. He was born (sorry, invented) to sing: "If it wasn't for bad luck, I wouldn't have no luck at all." A similar genius mixture of character and message pits the put-upon genius of Lisa Simpson with Billie Holiday's "God Bless the Child." Originally a song of loss and longing it is reinvented as a perfect fit for Lisa's right-on views and loneliness. The variety of characters, songs and styles gives the album the same breadth offered up by the television show and it is only the likes of "Sibling Rivalry" – a Bart/Lisa duet - late on in the proceedings, that drop below the full-on genius, mainly because this track, more than the others, betrays some of the novelty cash-in possibilities which formed a part of the original thinking behind The Simpsons Sing the Blues. Elsewhere, the album works because everyone – writers, actors, star musical help – all deliver the goods like they mean it, and sound like they had fun. And it's to their credit they put in the work to make a damn good album and it's to the eternal credit of the management behind The Simpsons and this record that they opted to make a collection of original cuts, featuring virtually nothing that had already been used in the show.

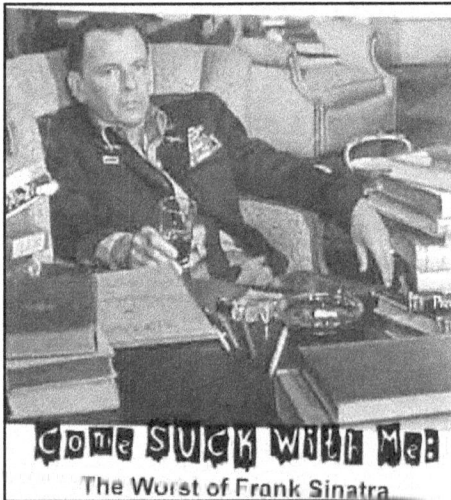

Come SUCK WiTh Me
The Worst of Frank Sinatra

Frank Sinatra: Come Suck With Me (Bootleg, 2013)
What? Old Blue Eyes' posthumous stab at the action enjoyed by Elvis' Greatest Shit.

Credited to a pair of compilers, known as Windy and MadJon, this fifteen strong stinkerthon is a shining example of a favoured online party game of sound hounds. Sinatra might have regarded himself as The Chairman of the Board, but every manager makes mistakes, and this is the proof. Where Elvis' Greatest Shit is a cornucopian crap-fest Come Suck With Me is more a melange of misjudgements, adding up to a comedy of errors. Sinatra was highly conscious of his status and standing. Gay Talese's classic magazine article "Frank Sinatra has a Cold" is recommended for anyone intent on getting a snapshot of the character behind the classy recordings.

Come Suck With Me betrays its secrets readily. Some of the stink here arises from Frank sprinting for a hit market. "Everybody's Twistin'" stabs unconvincingly at a dance craze and the disco version of "All or Nothing" has the same clunky, car crash, fascination that makes Ethel Merman's Disco Album a cult classic. Elsewhere Frank duets with a dog "Mama Will Bark" (this one complete with the couplet: "I shall never see, a canine lovely as thee"), and gets, kinda, trippy on the highly ill-advised "Feelin' Kinda Sunday" and "Life's a Trippy Thing" (these two with daughter Nancy). Sinatra is only "High on life" and "hooked on something new" in his hippie phase, but it still sounds far from convincing. Next to the forays far beyond the Board's usual territory the covers of "You are the Sunshine of my Life" and "Bad Bad Leroy Brown" are more ill-fitting than off the rails, but they're dodgy enough to merit their place here. Nothing here sounds as downright odd as Bing Crosby's demolition of "Hey Jude" but the worst cover versions do approach that territory, and when Frank repeats the mantra "light my fire" at the end of covering Stevie Wonder we're in rambling mid-life crisis territory for a very uncomfortable moment.

Most of Come Suck With Me is readily available on official releases, though they'd come at a cost these days since these cuts are the ones least favoured with reissue and compilation slots. The disco version of "All or Nothing," for example, was considered so bad at the time (1977) it remained in the vaults, finally seeing release on a boxed set in 1995. What Bono thinks of his duet with Frank making this bottom 15 is anyone's guess.

Bernie Sizzey:
Hippie Heaven
(berniesizzey.bandcamp.com 2013)
What? Prolific outsider puts hippie soul on the line.

A lengthy consideration of Sizzey's career on the Music for Maniacs site provides the following introduction: "Meet Bernie Sizzey (aka Bernie aka Solitaire): mental patient, transvestite, drug user, coprophiliac, and, more importantly, singer/guitarist/ keyboardist/ lo-fi home recorder and songwriter for 30 years now of everything from instrumental ambient space-rock, to unrepentant lysergic trip-outs, to confessional ballads detailing his life in catchy, upbeat songs that are never feeling sorry for themselves. He hasn't been dealt the best hand in life, but you won't hear him complain. (Well, unless maybe he runs out of pot.)"

So, as with many acts presented in these pages, you could start almost anywhere in Sizzey's oeuvre. We chose to start with Hippie Heaven for three pragmatic reasons:

1 – it is long and varied, 2 – it was a very recent release when this book was being compiled. 3 – Everything he does well appears on Hippie Heaven at some point.

Self-produced and self-released, Sizzey has been reliant on friends in a nearby arts centre in Colchester, Essex, for support. Bandcamp has given him an outlet for a hugely prolific output. A cruel appraisal of his work might present him as a street-drinking Syd Barrett (Lee Ashcroft who sought out Sizzey and raised his profile was told he could be found behind a local theatre drinking Special Brew). Sizzey is a hippie in the most general sense. Lengthy keyboard passages, introspective musings, the sense that intoxication is central to some of the headspaces explored in his music and an honest vulnerability all inform his work. The Barrett comparison is worthy because Sizzey has the ability to make an epic statement from simple elements and a permanent sense of otherness in all his creativity. There is also a dark humour on tracks like the lovelorn but self-aware "Rock 'n' Roll Brothel" and "Lady Dub." Sizzey's prominent Essex accent pervades a lot of the vocals. He fronts songs by way of narration as well as singing and has fun with different aspects of the frontman position from song to song. Sometimes Sizzey is confessional and honest, at others he's playing a character. As with most great outsiders there's method in the maddest moments and an innate cunning even when the music steers itself into meltdown. Sizzey commented to Lee Ashcroft who facilitated his move to bandcamp: "I've been loved. I've learned how to communicate." Sizzey's work continues to search for communication, and empathy, which is why it goes beyond mere song writing into becoming the clearest expression of a frequently confused mind. Sizzey's work has become more complex and ambitious over time the early recordings, as Solitaire, are starker and more consistently confessional.

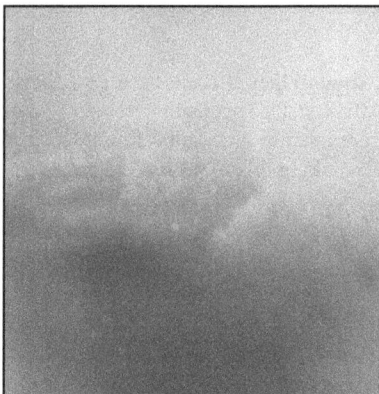

Richard Skelton:
Landings
(Sustain-Release, 2009)
What? A requiem.

Recorded over a period of four years, Landings is dedicated to Skelton's wife - Louise – who died in 2004. A self-produced work composed with much emphasis on slowly drawn bowing of the violin and fragmentary guitar arpeggios, the recording exists somewhere between modern classical and ambient works. The violin figures climb but never soar and the insistent background drone never overwhelms but lingers like fog, or grief. A near-contemporary of The Durutti Column's Someone Else's Party (also examined in this book), Landings remains distinctive because – despite the different tracks and titles – this is clearly one complete work and Skelton's work as visual artist and writer puts Landings into a wider context of works in which the original album is part of "an ongoing series of texts, recordings, artworks and editions." In this context Skelton has frequently despatched recordings with additional items, like twigs; found in the landscape. His work in all its incarnations draws on the patterns and rhythms of nature. On Landings – with its packaging art featuring photographs of misty Pennine landscapes – the sense is of grieving, loss and the slow irresistible power of nature to heal. Comparisons have been made to Brian Eno's Ambient 4: On Land though Skelton's work is much more emotive and considerably stronger in the way its slowly unfurling rhythmic structure apes both the human body and elements of nature, like wind.

Landings is an ambient work as much as it belongs in any category. It draws on the same few instruments throughout, presents tracks that resemble each other and provide a thematic unity and, crucially in this regard, it works exceptionally well at low volume, providing a presence and guiding the mood of the listener. However, to log it as ambient is to miss the way this music works as part of a deep and personal emotional journey, and how well that fact is communicated within the music.

Sleep:
Dopesmoker
(TeePee, 2003)
What? A song!

There's a moment at the start of the gloriously loose and shambolic live double CD by Neil Young and Crazy Horse – Year of the Horse – in which a member of the audience shouts: "they all sound the same" and Young deadpans an instant retort: "it's all one song." That – in a thought – is where Dopesmoker starts. The long and convoluted history of this riff-oblivion sludge-fest is available online if you're that bothered. The story will lead you to discover that Dopesmoker is the fourth unleashing (both official and unofficial and not always offering the same mix or material) of a master-work conceived when these sultans of stoner-rock spent years working on one almighty song. The other thing worth knowing is that the release on TeePee came about after the famously tolerant Earache Records and London Records had allowed the band, and the rights to this material, to pass through their hands. Taken in bursts of a few seconds Dopesmoker sounds exactly as you would expect. Slow pounding saggy slacker rhythm with a ragged endless riff roaring over the top. Critically Dopesmoker was lauded as a ground-breaking, hypnotic and fearless work; a finely honed masterpiece that becomes more compelling over time. Then again, most of those writing were people who'd acquired the whole thing for free. Appreciating the attempt and execution is one thing, living with the album as part of your own lifestyle choices is another.

As the absolute zenith of stoner/slacker/dope rock Dopesmoker IS damn near peerless. It has riffs (well, one hell of a riff that – like – varies a bit), it has vocals (though it pulls the Eraserhead trick of setting the dark dark mood and lulling you in so when you finally hear a voice after eight and a half minutes, the moment is shocking), it has attitude, it has highly understated class and it isn't about to apologise when it continues surging and mugging your eardrums well past the one hour mark. As an exercise in sonic excess Dopesmoker also surpasses most of the competition. Though, frankly, the Melvins' Colossus of Destiny could probably take it in a fight. Beyond which, words are fairly futile. Dopesmoker is an experience. More a case of because we can than because it fits a market. This much dope, this much space on a CD, this heavy with the sound is pretty much the point. And, it matters that it took – like – four years to perfect it. Dopesmoker stands as the kind of behemoth of an album best described in similes. This is a national anthem for a country in which the annual athletics championships involve a shuffle from the stoner's couch to the sweet shop because the munchies have got you bad (the winner of said sprint is the last one still smoking when the others are gorging chocolate). Dopesmoker is a Catcher in the Rye of an album; if Salinger's book-long sulk represents the best mind that never left grade-school then Dopesmoker is what happens when the best minds reject thinking in its conventional forms. Dopesmoker has been reissued in the recent past in a mix louder than the originals.

Sleepytime Gorilla Museum: Grand Opening and Closing (Seeland, 2001)
What? Dadaism kicks ass!

Sleepytime Gorilla Museum (SGM) have rotated personnel and changed styles to such a degree that it would take up a fair tonnage of space here to attempt to cover their history, and what it is – exactly – that makes them unique. Describing this, their first album, is probably a better way to try and tell the story. Then again, we might just mention that this band may well be the only rock outfit in history to perform their first gig to an audience that comprised one banana slug.

There's enough noise-assault rock on show on Grand Opening and Closing to make SGM safely a "rock" band. There's enough variety, noise, samples and sheer lunacy for its own sake to put the band comfortably into the "alternative" and "experimental" brackets. Then there's their habit of performing part of what they do on instruments of their own invention. Beyond that, the band claim – with evidence – a path of inspiration going back to Dadaist art. But, that claim also casts into doubt the veracity of many claims about what they are doing and why.

Grand Opening and Closing spends a lot of time being loud, rapid and overwhelming but it also throws in a bombardment of sound references, ideas and jokes to the point you're never in much doubt about the intelligence behind the whole project. "1997 (Tonight we're Gonna Party Like it's…)" being a good example. Way more than a sideswipe at Prince, the sound explodes from the speakers, manages to mimic an emergency siren without polluting the notion of an insistent hard-as-hell punk/rock sound and still slows down towards the end for some instrumental brilliance. "Sleep is Wrong" is a bludgeoning opener with which to start any album and SGM can still take the sound somewhere else completely; especially on "Sunflower" with its opening Tibetan chime and stumbling minimalist/acoustic vibe. With tracks like "Sunflower" there's always a sense that SGM would be afraid to be this sensitive and this beautiful for too long, but it's the fact that the band pack this capacity in the first place that gives their music – and this album – such a compelling tension.

If the greatest romantics are those who present as the greatest cynics on the surface, then the intractable otherness of most of SGM's debut album hides a love of the very thing they destroy before our ears. And, their ability to savage it and re-create it in the same moment is the heart of strong and complex debut album.

Sly and the Family Stone:
Small Talk
(Epic, 1974)
What? Mostly, tender and intimate offering from seminal king of psychedelic soul.

Sly and the Family Stone played at Woodstock, pioneered a blend of soul, rock and psychedelia that – briefly – placed them amongst the most cutting-edge acts on the planet and produced a series of hits including "Family Affair" and "There's a Riot Goin' On" that influenced an entire generation of musicians. The route from soul and blues to MOBO would – probably – sound different without them. By the mid-seventies Sly Stone was settled and had become a father. Any confusion about the meaning of the title of Small Talk is quickly cleared up with a look at the front cover on which Sly's family – i.e. Sly, wife Karen Silva and new born son Sylvester Jr. – appear in a blissful portrait. The title track which opens the proceedings is a loose soul groove with (genuine) baby talk and Sly mumble-singing in a playful conversation with the new born. The riots and freaky jams are over in favour of sweeter soul and the addition of violinist Sid Page to Sly's roster of musicians takes the sound somewhere The Family Stone had never been, and would never go again. But on "Say You Will" Page's eloquent violin creates a beautiful emotive calm. Small Talk is a strange and patchy collection – indeed that's the whole point of putting it here – but it delivers monumentally with two killer singles. "Time for Livin'" is an up-beat soul-funk groove that duly delivered with a position on the American charts and "Loose Booty" is the one moment of playful lunacy/out-there invention that looks back to classic Sly Stone jaw-droppers of the past. Over a solid and insistent up-tempo funk groove the band repeatedly chant the names: "Shadrach, Meshach, Abednego." "Loose Groove" gives way to two slower soul numbers: "Holdin'On" and "Wishful Thinkin,'" the latter being one of the mellowest and most soulful items in the entire Sly Stone catalogue. Two of the closing tracks take us into gospel and the most confused and atypical Sly and the Family Stone album is done. Small Talk is a genuine oddity because – unlike the occasional ragbag in the catalogues of other acts – it always sounds like the band. Sly's trademark vocals are a solid presence and when the band kick-in they really couldn't be anyone else. The contentment (which would be short-lived; Sly and Karen were divorced before he released another album), seeps through much of the music but the singles show the band in full – classic – force. And, they are still capable of throwing in the odd random firework; particularly by way of the biblical name-checking chant on "Loose Booty."

Commercially Small Talk is also a watershed hitting #15 on the US charts but marking the end of high places for Sly's albums.

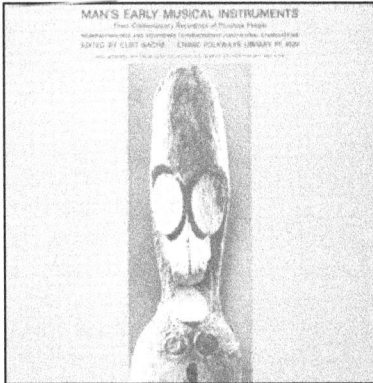

Smithsonian Folkways:
Man's Early Instruments
(Smithsonian Folkways, 2012)
What? Solo sounds of instrumental relics.

Smithsonian Folkways is the recording arm of the Smithsonian Institute and it is right to credit this release to them as the line-up of tracks, and this album's presence amongst a series of historic recordings, shows off their curatorship of a priceless archive. Smithsonian Folkways is a not for profit operation, so anyone venturing money to buy this collection is contributing to a project within which more of the same can be made available. Man's Early Instruments might be the creative concept behind the album, but it is also a literal description of the contents. The album is a reissue of a 1956 compilation researched by German musicologist Curt Sachs. Sachs' work as co–creator of the Sachs–Hornbostel system of musical instrument classification, underpins the presentation of recordings, many offering samples of singular sounds, seldom heard in isolation. The cuts are arranged in groups, including percussion, membranophones (skin–sounders), strings etc. Some earlier tracks (i.e. those on what is now the first of two CDs) present the featured instruments as a lead in a short ensemble piece. So, for example, the pan pipes track has percussion behind the pipes. But, it is only the final cuts that blend the varied sounds into ensemble and orchestral varieties. The fifties recording still allows a sound quality that presents the unique tones of each instrument and the obvious twenty first century useage of the ensuing tracks as mix-tape material is one reason to check out the snatches of everything from log drums to nose flutes. Heard back to back the varied sounds soon exhaust the audio palate, but sampled in bursts, or thrown into mixes with other sounds, this is a deep well of audio delights.

The Space Lady:
The Space Lady's Greatest Hits
(Night School, 2013)
What? Slow shimmering space-rock of a highly individualistic hue.

The Space Lady aka Susan Dietrich aka Suzy Sounds performed on the street in the 1970s. She earned money fronting original songs and highly individualistic cover versions of the more cosmic end of the pop canon of the time, her main audiences being passers-by in Boston and San Francisco. Most of her recordings both sound their age, and transcend it. There's no mistaking the classic sounds of a seventies Casio keyboard or the simple echo and rhythm effects employed. But The Space Lady also brought a dreamy delivery, a slow somnambulant air to her navigation of pop standards and – unusually for the time – a full embracement of child-like innocence even when performing songs like "Ballroom Blitz" that often used the accessibility of pop to inject a sense of underlying darkness. There were original songs in her set, generally written by her (then) husband, but the occasional compiling of her work into other areas – like her inclusion on Songs in the Key of Z and the 365 Days Project – has tended to favour the covers.

The Space Lady's sound and personal story are exotic to the point of being almost a cliché. The tale of how an attack from a drunk led to the destruction of her accordion, originally her instrument of choice, her growing up near Roswell just after the infamous (alleged) UFO crash and then the bizarre space helmet worn as she performed...you get the idea. Everything you need to know is available online or in the liner notes for this album.

Until Night School unleashed this collection the only available albums were long out of stock privately released cassettes or very scarce CDs. The CD Greatest Hits (with a vinyl issue that sold out rapidly) allowed for a cherry picking of the best moments in a stop-start campaign of outsider music gold, and also marked a return to the public domain for the performer who had semi-retired in 1999 to look after her parents. Along with the originals – which tend to explore the same sonic and lyrical territory as her favoured cover versions – we get a distillation of pop nuggets, most of which are tackled ably, and lulled into a blissful state as the more nuanced corners of their melodies are stripped back and The Space Lady's keyboard wash paints a pastel shade over the proceedings. If there is a bench-mark work here and/or a greatest hit it is probably her – fairly reverent – take on "I Had Too Much to Dream Last Night" but "Fly Like an Eagle" and "Showdown" (as in the ELO song) aren't that far behind. The cosmic end of pop is definitely the favoured territory but "Born to be Wild" belongs more readily here than you might think, such is the power of a Space Lady makeover. Her own languid gems like "Synthesize Me" – with its slow rhyming of synthesizer, energergizer etc. - are the perfect companions to the covers of the hits.

Sparklehorse: Vivadixiesubmarinetransmissionplot (Parlophone, 1995)
What? Savage and beautiful, intensely personal and hugely accessible.

If people know one thing about Sparklehorse/ Mark Linkous it is that he committed suicide. Sadly, that one fact might stand in the way of the appreciation of a small but engaging catalogue of four albums and a few other cuts that form a body of work few others could touch for consistent quality. Born in Virginia in 1962, Linkous was already a music industry veteran with a creditable pedigree when he formed Sparklehorse. This mid-nineties offering opened the account and represents – arguably – the most accessible of a quartet of albums. Dragging in indie, punk, country and folk influences Sparklehorse were at the forefront of a sound and eclecticism that would become almost obligatory for singer/songwriters in the ensuing decade. But in terms of the ability to set a mood, bring the hairs on the neck up and then over-ride the whole effect with an effortless riff or lyrical aside, few could touch Linkous, (despite performing as a band Sparklehorse was – essentially – his creative vision from start to finish).

Vivadixie...packs everything you need to know about Linkous into 16 cuts, the resonant and understated opener "Homecoming Queen" starts with an improbably simple and echoing riff, never gets above walking pace and intones a mordant mantra of a vocal that manages to sound passionate and hopelessly resigned. Even the rapid guitar assaults like "Some Day I Will Treat You Good" perfectly nail the slacker sentiments along with their corking riffs. In those moments Linkous' very personal genius to sound emotionally involved and distant at the same time comes perfectly to the fore. Sparklehorse always had the feel of sounding like the inner turmoil of an outwardly resigned character. Lyrically the tone ranges from slacker-rock to the totally surreal, some references in titles and lines offer jumbled word-play as wilfully dense and impenetrable as anything in the Tom Waits or Captain Beefheart catalogues. Musically Waits and Radiohead have been cited as points of comparison with elements of the Sparklehorse sound, along with the generation of sonically experimental songwriters that included Linkous. The subsequent Good Morning Spider was a supremely dark effort, mostly written before a brush with death and released afterwards, it proved the commercial high point of the band, the bleak It's a Wonderful Life and understatedly lush Dreamt for Light Years in the Belly of a Mountain both hit the lower end of the British charts and all maintained the quality and vision first unleashed on Vivadixiesubmarinetransmissionplot.

Alexander Spence:
Oar
(Columbia, 1969)
What? "one of the most harrowing documents of pain and confusion ever made." Rob Brunner: Entertainment Weekly

It is ironic that the telling quote above should come from Entertainment Weekly. Whatever else you might say about Oar – and millions of words have been devoted in print, online and conversation over this deep trawl of a dark psychosis – it is not generally linked with any traditional notion of entertainment. Oar's reputation grew in the years after its release and the 1991 and 1999 CD reissues brought the strange, psychedelic sounds to a new generation. Since when the entire album has tended to be regarded as a single work and linked inextricably to Spence's fragile mental health. Oar marked Spence's first work after emerging from psychiatric care (having been put there after LSD trips and his own demons had combined to prompt him to attack fellow members of Moby Grape with a fire axe). Oar's songs include material written on the inside and its stark, rambling, occasionally incoherent quality is cemented because much of the material on the original album was – in Spence's mind – a demo recording. The muddy and inconsistent quality of the sound and the habit of songs to taper off and fall apart rather than end clearly is central to the way the album has been perceived. So too the random bursts of humour in songs like "Dixie Peach Promenade (Yin and Yang)" in which Spence jokily sets out in search of missing elements in his life: "I could use some yin for my yang, that would make everything alright." Spence's deep voice is mixed up front on songs like "Cripple Creek," making the album feel all the more personal and obliging the listener to react to Spence as much as the music. "Diana" starts with Spence rasping for breath and, apparently, pouring a stream of consciousness into the lyrics. The involvement with the singer, and his obvious troubles, is beyond comfortable.

Lyrically there are dark visions and the sporadic appearance of demonic characters. Predictably, Roky Erickson, Syd Barrett and other celebrated drug/madness casualties have been invoked in discussions of Oar. The comparisons – both sonically and in terms of the creative vision here – hold water. But, Oar remains its own missive of madness, possessing a unique value, largely because it has that chaotic and unfinished demo quality. Barrett, Erickson and the rest were often able to craft something – however bizarre – before decisions were made over what to release. Oar is the sound of Spence, in the room with you, trying to reason his way out of the worst mental crisis of his life, and it demands attention even when it isn't focussed because you're never quite clear whether he's talking to you, himself, or some other presence only he can perceive.

The clichés describe the album as "dark" and "scary" and Oar is most certainly both of these in large amount. It's also a blueprint for other works of darkness and fear and a vindication of the power of music – however fragmentary – to provide a gateway into the most impenetrable recesses of a troubled mind. For those willing to truly engage with Spence, his music and his history there is also the inescapable question of whether the Oar he intended to make – probably a full sounding, more vibrant work closer to early Moby Grape – would have been any artistic improvement on this work. "War in Peace" – for example – layers psychedelic guitars and even lifts directly from "Sunshine of Your Love" in a manner that suggests Spence envisioned it as an incendiary piece of guitar driven psych.

An album of cover versions of the original songs – More Oar (1999) - set about reimagining Spence's vision. The fact Tom Waits, Robert Plant, Beck and Mudhoney all wanted a piece of More Oar tells you everything you need to know about the inspiration Oar has provided to a range of other musicians. So does the presence in this book of a few works – notably Josh T. Pearson's Last of the Country Gentlemen – that summon up the spirit of this seminal album.

Spirit: Future Games:
A Magical Kahauna Dream
(Mercury 1977)
What? Sci-fi dreaming in the age of punk!

Credited to hippie-experimental-jazz-rockers Spirit this collection is largely a solo album from their lead guitarist/ vocalist Randy California. Recorded after a shambolic ending to a gig that saw keyboardist John Locke storm offstage and the band implode in the aftermath, Future Games is so free-form and experimental it has alienated some otherwise loyal Spirit fans. Given that Spirit was always up for a meander away from the mainstream that is some indication of how far away from a standard rock album Future Games is.

The "recording" of Future Games was something of a diversion from the usual way of making an album at the time, it might be more accurate to say the concoction of song-fragments, CB chatter, Star Trek dialogue and other found sounds was "assembled." California's guitar and vocal run through the 21 tracks, forming the main current in a meandering journey that delivers on the notion of a magical dream. If this caper makes any sense it is in the subconscious, though some of the longer songs work in their own right and – true to his heritage as a Hendrix acolyte and sometime collaborator – California also throws in Spirit's take on "All Along the Watchtower."

The varied delights include wall to wall samples trawling chat between truckers and seminal Star Trek moments, the recurrence of some melodic fragments at different times during the album and ideas that trawl the depths of the mind. At other times there are specific references to everything from the bombing of Hiroshima to Kermit the Frog. Future Games is a strange dot on the face of late seventies music. Hopelessly hippified and about ten years out of time from one angle, it is positively prophetic in its random qualities and manages to anticipate the experimental end of dance music, no mean feat since it was released when dance pioneers were just getting to grips with the elongated grooves offered by the 12" single.

Future Games tanked in terms of sales, marked the end of Spirit's recording contract with Mercury. The band – still touring – never entered a studio again with Mercury money and closed their albums account with a live set. The album's fades in and out of tracks rendered it practically useless for most mainstream radio although the BBC's John Peel gave it a blast, playing an entire side on his show, sandwiched between the emerging punk sounds in the UK at the time. It also divided the band's fan-base, one stinging criticism, the poor quality of the sound on a great many of the tracks, has certainly blunted the ongoing appeal of Future Games. But the album remains a strange and truly unique listen from one of the most eclectic acts of their time.

Spock's Beard:
V
(InsideOutMusic, 2000)
What? Prime 21st century prog from prime exponents of the form

LA's Spock's Beard have carved a lengthy and impressive furrow over 20 years of uncompromisingly intelligent and high-achieving music. For want of any other label they get referred to as a progressive rock band but it's nowhere near that simple. The difficulty of fitting them easily into anything from a radio playlist to a short car journey has probably been to the detriment of sales and benefit of a die-hard audience who continue to regard Spock's Beard as their band, and nobody else's. Their fifth outing, V came eight years into their career - (ten years and five albums later they returned to form and called an album X) – and V is probably as good a place as any for the uninitiated to start. "Progressive" gives some insight into the sound of Spock's Beard but doesn't say much about what they're about. V displays their finest qualities and features both of founding brothers, Neal and Alan Morse. Neal departed in 2002. Spock's Beard are progressive in as much as they owe a massive debt to the likes of Genesis and Yes (especially in believing high-points of lyrical drama work best when succeeded by massive washes of keyboard and lengthy soloing). However, deft vocal harmonies, a nod to the big AOR metal sounds favoured by American radio, and a fondness for fleeting moments akin to country rock, all form part of the mix. Then there's their habit of spinning out tracks to twenty minutes and beyond. A band capable of wrestling Rush under the table for longevity, and contriving to sound different if you fast forward to random moments in lengthy tracks might best be described as epic rock.

V is up there with their best epic works and also highly listenable for all of its (almost) 63 minutes. The opening "At the End of the Day" is a tempo changing but essentially simple (well; by Spock's Beard standards it's simple) exploration of the dynamics of a relationship. The centre of the album packs four hook-laden and (just about) radio friendly numbers, especially "Revelation" (which clearly has one ear cocked to 1980s Yes) and the closer "The Great Nothing" is a 27 minute (life, the universe…) epic complete with visits to a number of virtuoso instrumental diversions and sub-headings on the lyrics to help the listener keep track of exactly where in the dense story they are. Never fashionable and never knowingly undersold for instrumental skill or epic ideas, Spock's Beard are behemothian to the seventh vocal harmony track that doubtless lurks at the very edge of the mix seven minutes and seven seconds into the seventh track on one or other of their epic albums.

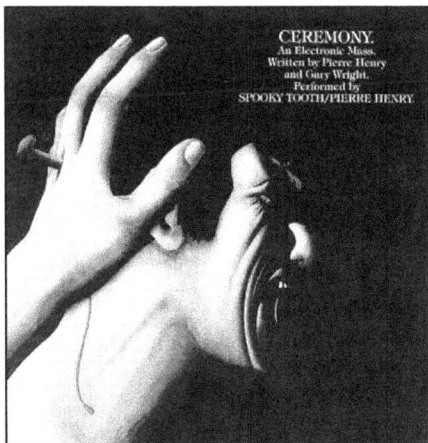

Spooky Tooth with Pierre Henry:
Ceremony
(Island, 1969)
What? A church service, but not like anyone you've ever been to.

Start with a head-on collision between blues based proggers (with their roots in Cumbria) and avante garde French soundster Pierre Henry, throw in an overblown cover almost beyond satire (a screaming young bloke with a nail through his hand) and focus all of this around a progressive notion of a church service. Ceremony offers up Dark Side of the Moon levels of ambition without the hooks, hits or borderline moments of pop or humour.

Its worst moments are less collaboration than they are collision, with the constituent parts scattered in the vicinity. The conception of the album wasn't matched by the working method. Such histories as appear online generally suggest that Henry conceived the notion of applying his "musique concrete" with the work of a rock band, at this point the "band" involved remained to be identified. Spooky Tooth, force of nature blues proggers with the ability to flit between bestial levels of riffage and inspirational flurries of melody and songcraft, eventually took on the role. By all accounts Tooth's ranks were divided on the caper with keyboardist Gary Wright the main champion, and – therefore – responsible for the bulk of the band's compositional input. Crucially, the band and Henry didn't work together throughout the project. Wright's music was quickly recorded by Tooth and passed to Henry who – ahem – embellished the final results with his unique touches. The results, predictably, are akin to very little else recorded then, or since.

It was a watershed for Tooth for the wrong reasons, poor sales, musical differences that eventually resulted in Wright's departure, and the stalling of a momentum they'd built up in the wake of the impressive Spooky Two album. Ceremony's detractors, who remain visible in cyberspace, damn it as a convoluted work of histrionic highs that makes for the uneasiest of listens. Predictably, there are also convinced champions out there who see it differently.

For the uninitiated a few touchstones might be helpful. Ceremony is not a religious work in any accepted sense, more a rock/avante garde/generally wild imagining of the key points of a high church service. It's a lot harder and more extreme than The Electric Prunes foray into the same territory, easily as complex (though a lot less tuneful) than Deep Purple's Concerto for Group and Orchestra and might find its closest sonic relative in Jack Nitzsche's St Giles Cripplegate.

The two works share an immense sound and the ability to be stunning in the moment, and confusing in the long run. Nitzsche set out to explore the sonic possibilities of an orchestra and a recording venue, Tooth and Henry explore the outer limits of rock/"musique concrete." At their best, they make sounds that perfectly meld the constituent parts, "Offering" – by far the shortest piece here – has a catchy gothic feel, a solid Tooth/Sabs riff and panting noises around a sterling Mike Harrison vocal. The book-ending tracks also work impressively. The opening "Have Mercy" offers up primal Spooky Tooth, touching their expertise with the standard blues and morphing into harder, more frantic, rock, whilst the closing "Hosanna" showcases the best moments of Luther Grosvenor's guitar soloing on the album.

Ultimately Ceremony can't escape its experimental conception. "Offering" might show the constituent parts coming together well but at other moments they are pulling in different directions. Tooth riffing and rocking a storm, but somewhat on autopilot and directionless, and Henry more intruding than accompanying.

The less successful moments of Yoko Ono and Lennon's collaborations have the same feel as "Credo" wherein a cracking piece of Tooth's portentous prog-blues finds itself invaded by random – as in someone intoning "baaaah" – vocalisations. "Confession" presents another instance of industrial Henry noises rubbing up against a band stuck very much in a rock groove. Ceremony's pure curio value continues to mark it as an essential listen, if not always an essential love, for sound hounds intent on finding the strangest collaborations around. Considered in that context, it remains a singular piece, unlikely to disappoint.

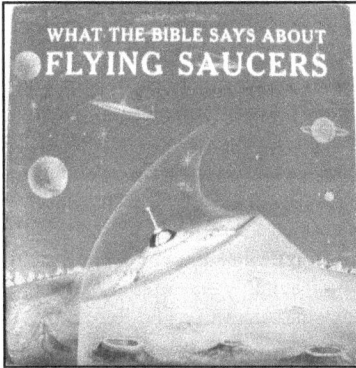

Rev O.W. "Bud" Spriggs:
What the Bible Says About Flying Saucers
(World Wide Records, 1966?)
What? End times sermons, delivered with alacrity and passion.

Known as "the 'Chaplin of Hell," a title he received from the Mayor and City Council of Hell, Michigan (all explained in the liner notes), Spriggs combined a new age sensibility and embracement of the UFO phenomenon with a fire and brimstone take on Christianity. The resulting long playing record finds Spriggs' philosophy played out over three lengthy tracks and two sides of vinyl. The opening cut amounts to a sermon running almost 20 minutes and expounding a belief that modern saucer sightings and the biblical prophesies of Ezekiel are describing the same thing. Spriggs is a forceful speaker bringing the argument into a lucid focus, there's a halfway decent gag towards the start suggesting any man married 13 years is well acquainted with flying saucers. Conspiracy experts will also spot one notable howler when he refers to a UFO author as Major Keyhole (not Donald Keyhoe) but elsewhere the argument is delivered with the sincere passion and fervour of one waiting for the end time to occur in his own life.

The 365 days project – which rediscovered this gem and made it widely available in 2007 – asks you to: "Try and imagine that Fox Mulder was a conservative 1960's preacher instead of an FBI Agent. One day he records a Religious spoken word LP which shared his view on the biblical connection to UFOs." This is cosmic consciousness shot through with a right-leaning morality. Spriggs sees the breakdown of law and order, the   civil rights movement and emerging hippie culture as evidence of his beloved country entering the end times. On the second track he interviews Sergeant Snider, a police officer who recounts an intense and lengthy UFO sighting and on the final track Spriggs prepares us all for the coming of the end with a pragmatic vision of America's end times, as aircraft fall from the sky, the righteous simply vanish from their neighbourhoods and everyone finally cottons on to the wisdom of the message on this album (Spriggs doesn't actually predict everyone will have heard the album…but you get the general idea).

The album bears no release date but Officer Snider references his sighting early in 1966 and American losses in Vietnam are also referenced, making the staid portrait and gaudy fifties artwork of What the Bible Says… something of a throwback by the late sixties. For a spoken world album this remains something of a rarity. A compelling enough listen from end to end to justify its twenty first century revival and an unquestionably heartfelt vision, Spriggs is self-aware to the point of avoiding the ranting "madman" fate of some who have ventured into the UFO/conspiracy territory.

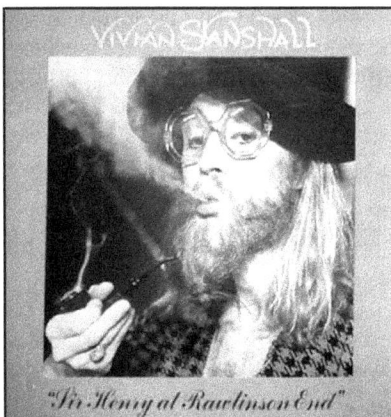

Vivian Stanshall:
Sir Henry at Rawlinson End
(Charisma, 1978)
What? A beguiling and very English comic-eccentricity.

Stanshall is best remembered as lead singer (if that concept made any sense in the context of such an outfit) of the Bonzo Dog Doo-Dah Band, British masters of the comedic popular song. However, his solo career from the early seventies took him into some singular and surreal territory; never more so than when he gave vent to the menagerie of characters that inhabited his fertile and, sporadically, disturbed mind. The fictitious fermentations of Rawlinson End (an English country house that would have been at home in a Monty Python sketch) under-pin this spoken-word tour de force. Stanshall, inhabits the voices and enlists musical help from an impressive coterie, including Steve Winwood, for occasional songs which punctuate the action. Having established in the opening words that Rawlinson End is "English as tuppence, changing yet changeless as canal water, nestling in green nowhere, armoured and effete, bold flag-bearer, lotus-fed Miss Havishambling opsimath and eremite, feudal still, reactionary... "Stanshall proceeds with a series of comic vignettes; telling the stories of Sir Henry Rawlinson (a true throwback of the English aristocracy) and the characters with whom he collides. Following the story is easier on the second or third run through since the vivid details and Stanshall's gift for mimicking accents and intonations often distract from the – suitably – rambling narrative. Jokes are layered on jokes with literary flourishes introducing most events. Characters like Old Scrotum the Wrinkled Retainer erupt at will from Stanshall's imagination.

Major jokes are introduced and explored. Sir Henry attempts to shoot-down a passing hang-glider with his pistol, but proves so drunk he ends up venting his fury on a couple of out of work actors working as cleaners under the name of Nice and Tidy. One-liners abound, "Silent as a smelly one, Hubert entered the room" and the drink-sodden Sir Henry is a comic creation of genius: "If I had all the money I'd spent on drink, I'd spend it on drink." The songs punctuate the end of each scene, drawing from early twentieth century stylings and earlier elements, so whilst the album had greatest sales amongst rock fans, there's nothing remotely rockish about it. Sir Henry eventually spawned a full-length movie, with Trevor Howard playing the main character. However, the album continues to stand on its own merits, rubbing shoulders with the likes of The Firesign Theatre amongst the cherished few comedy recordings that stand repeated listening.

Stark Reality:
The Stark Reality Discovers Hoagy Carmichael's Music Shop
(Stones Throw, 1970)
What? The most-ambitious and out-there kids' music you're likely to hear.

Boston's Stark Reality contrived to make one of the best-known slow burning, long-tail sellers in music history. Their masterwork is constructed from the unlikeliest of elements. The band always appeared too complex to jump any bandwagon, combining jazz, rock and fusion sounds with a few other oddments and favouring improvisation over a standard live show or well-rehearsed studio recordings. Throw into the mix that this band comprised mainly music students from Berklee College of Music and you have a recipe for noodling self-indulgence likely to please a handful of fans just like themselves. The wild card in creating this outsider music gem was television producer Hoagy Bix Charmichael, son of the great Hoagy Charmichael. Hoagy Jr. had the idea of allowing the band to cover, (for which read re-imagine and rework in ways Hoagy Sr. couldn't have conceived), a children's album from 1958 entitled Hoagy Carmichael's Havin' a Party.

Music Shop was far from a success on initial release but its strange magic slowly worked its way around a handful of DJs, gradually becoming a cult favourite, changing hands for vast sums on the original vinyl and – in the 21st century – getting compiled, reissued and finally given the celebration it deserved.

It works, wonderfully, because the fluid and free passages of jazz/fusion/rock let rip in lengthy cuts before the simple melodies and inspired lyrics of Hoagy Sr. arrive to save the proceedings from indulgence. To Hoagy Sr's credit the original tunes and lyrics are well-crafted, don't speak down to children and possess enough sense of their own self-worth to stand a mauling on this scale. To The Stark Reality's credit they let rip in free-abandon but still rein it all in when a chorus or reminder of the fact we're here to explain music to children is required. To Hoagy Jr's credit this collision of material and musicians is truly inspired and it took a visionary to see the potential. So composer, band and facilitator all contribute to a concoction that is way more than the sum of its considerable parts.

Psychedelia and its offshoots frequently flirted with the innocence of childhood, often courting disaster in the process. Children's music has often aimed to be hip, again, frequently courting disaster in the process. Once in a lifetime a game changer like The Stark Reality Discovers Hoagy Carmichael's Music Shop comes along and shows everyone how it should be done.

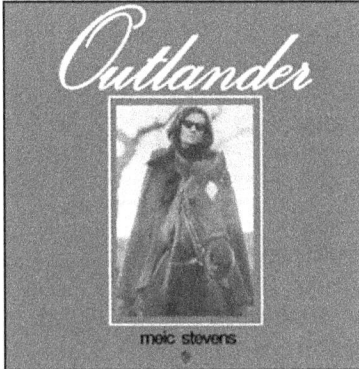

Meic Stevens:
Outlander
(Warners, 1970)
What? Psyche-folk classic/rarity.

The "Welsh Bob Dylan" tag has been something of a mixed blessing for Meic Stevens and his reputation, but it's useful here because it gives some sense of why this album, and Stevens' prolific output matters. Following a late sixties nervous breakdown Stevens set about rethinking his promising musical career and made a ground-breaking decision to base himself, his recording and much of his song-writing firmly in Wales. Above all, Stevens decided to be true to himself and to be ambitious for his art. Outlander which started this quest is – therefore – something of an aberration because it appeared on a major label and because of the English lyrics on some of the cuts, most of what followed in Stevens' career is sung entirely in Welsh.

The album matters here firstly because it stands as a genuine classic of psych-folk, dripping in layered acoustic guitars, boasting some well-played sitar and wall-to-wall with meditative lyrics looking inward at love and outward at politics. The Indian influences are strong enough to make the likes of Davy Graham useful comparisons, whilst the loose rhythmic approach to some work and the feel-good vibe permeating most of the tracks makes David Crosby's If I Could Only Remember my Name another useful touchstone. A track like Ghostown which opens with gentle acoustic chords and settles into an agreeable groove driven gently with drums is typical of the core of the album.

The album's longest and most complex track – "Yorric" – has the epic quality of classic Incredible String Band. None of which means Outlander is a copycat work. It belongs in the company name-checked here but it's also a statement of intent from a musician who soon broke from his major label contract by mutual consent, to devote himself to very personal work, mostly performed in his native language.

On this evidence, another and more lucrative career may well have been beckoning if Stevens had been willing to rein in the things that make Outlander a deep and very meaningful record. Musical histories cite him – rightly – as an influence on the likes of the Super Furry Animals and Gorky's Zygotic Mynci, but all the company he keeps in this write up simply help to locate the mix of influences and good vibes of a record that was right with the spirit of its times, but also manages to sound timeless. A 21st century CD reissue offers up a generous nine bonus cuts, mainly alternative versions and out-takes but also "Blue Sheep" a 1970 B-side.

Stinky Picnic:
Peacecful and Quiet
(Bandcamp, 2012)
What? Male/female age-gap Aussie outsiders.

Outsiderdom incarnate from Aussie duo employing some of the least promising elements. The duo of Mat (various instruments/inventive use of loop pedals) and Indigo/Indi (most lead vocals/most improvising of lyrics and vocalisations) inhabit an alternative/semi-psychedelic universe of scary monsters, stinky experiences and maximum milking of minimal musical effects. A decent riff and feedback laden vocal will do for a song, a nice sound, decent groove and bright idea is also enough. "Number Language" is concocted from Indigo singing up the numbers: "One, two, three…" as Mat replies with varied, but similar licks. For the most part it is gleeful, knockabout, infectious fun infused with a sense of two musicians playing for the love of their collective sound.

The twist here is the ages of the two performers, specifically the fact that this, the band's second album, came out soon after Indi's fourth birthday. Given the potential for a father and daughter act to be a twee indulgence, a pointless exercise in self-loving and/or simply abysmal, Peaceful and Quiet is little short of a revelation. Its main strengths come from Mat's accomplished touch on creating twisted sounds from the most basic elements, for example: using little more than clanking, echo and drone effects on "Meow." Indi, by contrast, is sparky, inventive and possessed of a mile-wide attitude. Her concerns may be communicating with her mother ("I'm a Bear Mummy"), her ability to count ("Number Language"), food ("Strudels"), and the usual concerns of kids ("Noisybums (part 2)"), but these come with humour, and a blatant love for her work. Stinky Picnic work because the sheer love of making this music pours from the speakers, and in their musical language with each other the pair each reference their own ground and meet perfectly in the middle.

If Mat's territory is alternative/indie/psychedelic material he's happy to use the production sounds from there to jumble up handclaps and a simple riff on "Noisybums (Part 2)" to create kiddie music, with attitude. Indi does what children do, singing, chanting, shouting and making up stories on the spot, all the while clearly loving the opportunity to treat studio trickery like the products of a toy shop. "Tortoro" is little more than a catchy riff, slowly ramped up with additional touches as Indi gradually rises to the challenge and riffs (vocally) in response to the music. Whether this is the best kids' music around or the most defiantly indie act in Australia is beside the point, Stinky Picnic make outsider music sound like the most normal, unconditionally loving, activity available in the home, and that is life affirming for any listener.

Karlheinz Stockhausen:
Helicopter Quartet
(Naive Montaigne, 2000)
What? You thought prog-rock was up itself, well, we'll go up…in helicopters!

Modern classical music has often seated itself unsteadily on a fence with brilliance on one side and barking-mad bloody-minded insanity on the other. According to the pre-performance hype this most eccentric of works came about when Karlheinz Stockhausen, (arguably best known as being the only classical musician pictured on The Beatles' Sgt Pepper cover), had a dream of musicians flying through the air. Whatever the inspiration, this work performed in 1995 in Amsterdam remains the only classical piece with parts for four helicopter pilots and a crucial role for airborne sound technicians. The bizarre and hypnotic nature of the whole caper is certainly improved when you realise that the first section "Ignition of the Turbines" takes on board the sound qualities and rhythms generated by the choppers. Thereafter the string quartet play a piece composed to bring about a perfect union of the individual stringed instruments and the insistent thrums, whirrs and swishing sounds generated by the four helicopters. The entire work meanders and builds impressively, and most certainly packs its moments of melodic invention. The finale is best viewed on the DVD as listening alone fails to convey the majestic sight of the four helicopters rising in unison whilst the music builds to a climax.

In the end it's hard to escape the notion that this is a hugely eccentric idea taken to performance because nobody was totally sure if it was brilliant or barking. Cost wise alone the performance of this quartet flicks the finger to preening rock pretenders like Pink Floyd who have – to date – only managed to get an inflatable pig trundling along a wire above the massed crowds. It's also an implicit snub to major stars fond of the tired old tactic of arriving for their festival topping appearance by chopper, and never once considering incorporating that chopper in their art. Consider for a moment that this little quartet is one smidgeon of a 29 hour grand work, incorporating seven full-length operas, and you get a brief glimpse into the insanity, grand ambition and orgasms of ecstasy that appeared to be the norm on planet Stockhausen. The man himself died in 2007, his reputation as a true pioneer of the magnificent and absurd remains intact.

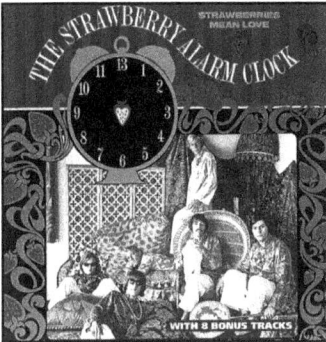

Strawberry Alarm Clock: Strawberries Mean Love (Big Beat, 1992)
What? A one band, one compilation version of Nuggets.

California's The Strawberry Alarm Clock (SAC) are justly famed for "Incense and Peppermints," a sixties hit periodically revived whenever the like of an Austin Powers movie needs the perfect period sound. There are loads of bands that could claim with some justification that a hit ruined their careers by misguiding the public about their true worth. Strawberries Mean Love is as good an argument as you are likely to hear that this group belong with the likes of Medicine Head (also included in this book) as under-appreciated for the breadth of their achievement.

Strawberries Mean Love is a British compilation but it packs more music – and slightly greater diversity – than US collections devoted to the band. SAC devotees typically hold their Wake Up...It's Tomorrow (1968) album as the watershed in terms of truly appreciating the band. "Incense and Peppermints" and its attendant album had established the band as prime psychedelic popsters, knockabout funny, better than bubblegum, but primarily an outfit with an eye on the charts.

Wake up... is well represented on this collection and marks the place SAC truly carved their own niche. They could hit a heavy(ish) groove, throw in some keyboard wizardly and pioneer a sound that would see their last days before their first split (there have been long gaps and periodic reformations since) marked by a tour on which the fledgling Lynyrd Skynyrd were the support act. If we are to believe those who have subsequently come to champion the band, SAC located themselves more effectively in the ground between Blue Cheer style acid rock, Doors style improvisation and the psychedelic pop of the late sixties charts, and did a more effective job of making this territory work musically, than most of their peers. It is important to qualify this opinion because Wake up... also marked a dramatic collapse in the band's commercial fortunes from which they never recovered, and it was far from a happy experience for SAC. The extensive sleeve notes on Strawberries Mean Love do address the way Wake up... was something of a mish-mash. Guided beyond question by the band's own creative vision it does – never-the-less – feature material that was more the vision of the production team on the album than of the band, and also contains un-credited session players.

SAC also veered – briefly – into novelty song territory and put in an appearance, complete with original music in the iconic psychedelic move Psych-Out. So, their creative genius was often filtered through the vision of others and their resulting catalogue packs the range and diversity of a decent compilation album from the period. The 21 tracks on Strawberries Mean Love offer up the hit, better album cuts from the later work, "Pretty Song" from Psych-Out, a Trashmen style throwback novelty song (complete with quacking duck noises) "The Birdman of Alkatrash" and "Small Package" (a harmony-ridden curio wherein the SAC monumentally rip off the Beach Boys' "California Girls"). The album's 1992 release in the UK saw it launched into a market where indie-bands were trawling the same territory. In the world prepared to love Teenage Fanclub, Velvet Crush and Pooh Sticks Strawberries Mean Love made sense and found friends.

Styx:
The Serpent is Rising
(Wooden Nickel, 1973)
What? "As Bad as This."

The point of listening to, and considering, this record so long after the event is to make up your own mind with regard to a reputation, probably little deserved, as "one of the worst recorded and produced" albums "in the history of music." It isn't, but that opinion comes from Dennis DeYoung, who sang, played, wrote and produced some of its most notable moments.

DeYoung's mythical pretensions and big ideas are writ large in "The Grove of Eglantine" and "Jonas Psalter," both of which have a prog leaning and hard(ish) rock vibe. DeYoung's distaste for the record and its subsequent commercial tanking (barely scratching the Billboard top 200 and shifting less than 100,000 copies in 40 years, despite Styx' subsequent major success), appears primarily down to the ongoing identity crisis that stalks The Serpent is Rising. From the cranking guitars and theatrical bombast on "Winner Takes All" to the catchy hooks on half the album, Serpent is a sprint for the increasingly formulaic FM rock market, and the major fan bases that would give the likes of Queen monumental sales in the US. Elsewhere, however, ham-handed prog ideas and some ill-thought out tacking on give the album a truly bizarre finale as the cod-electro "Krakatoa" subsides into just over two minutes of Handel's "Hallelujah Chorus."

As any serious rivals to (the then massive) ELP Styx are befuddled behemoths at best. The first side ends with a "hidden track," a true novelty in 1973. The track in question is a cod-calypso of scatological delights called "Plexiglass Toilet," hidden after another song; "As Bad as This."

"Plexiglass Toilet" remains by far the most atypical and jaw dropping cut in the Styx canon and is a worthy inclusion on the twenty first century bootleg Polluting the Mainstream, a collection of brainstorms from some of the best sellers of all time (also considered in this book). Wherever albums are still consumed from beginning to end, The Serpent is Rising stands as a strange collection of oddly assembled delights.

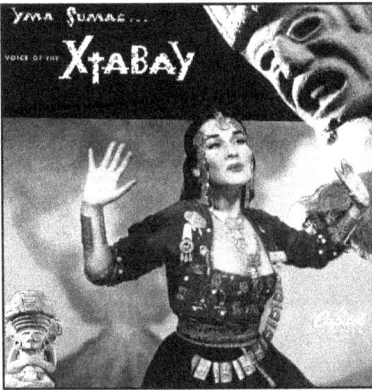

Yma Sumac:
Voice of the Xtabay
(Capitol, 1950)
What? Primal exotica from a queen of the genre.

Sumac's (1922-2008) incredible vocal range; south American roots and characterful vision of her music made her a titan of exotica before the form existed. Her opening album for Capitol Records still ranks as one of the best exotica collections ever unleashed on the record buying public; it's only shortcoming being that the 10" original LP only packed eight tracks (though the CD reissues currently doing the rounds generally surround the original album with much more music and still come in very affordably). Voice of the Xtabay was produced and composed by another easy-listening and exotica titan, Les Baxter. It presents Sumac as a phenomenal vocal power, set amongst Latin American arrangements and instruments. Sumac's subsequent releases included standard ballads and pop songs all of which were arranged to suit her four octave vocal range. Her popularity continually relied on her interpretive skills, striking looks and the notion that her music was infused with the Latin influence that pervades Voice of the Xtabay. This is south America as imagined by Hollywood; a cinematic sound rich in peripheral detail and full of events: additional percussion here, a striking note held after the backing fill has abated there, and songs arranged for Sumac to start on a low note and conclude on a massive outburst in the middle of her range. It is also a strangely enduring and exotic collection that has dated less badly than those that followed because it makes virtually no effort to fit a prevailing early fifties trend. The winning trick is the varying of tempos and the arranging of the original eight tracks to provide a guided tour of south American music stop-overs. The third track "Accla Taqui (Chant of the Chosen Maidens)" packs the steady chanting rhythm it promises, "Chaladas (Dance of the Moon Festival)" is clearly a dance number. The extent to which these cuts are genuine Peruvian music drawing on a long tradition and the extent to which they are Hollywood reinventions isn't really the point. Sumac appeared in the film Secret of the Incas (1954) which featured two of the songs included here and that seamless blend of performer, roots and manufactured image is really the point of Voice of the Xtabay. The evocative music and the ability of Sumac's strong and perfectly controlled voice have kept this music current and appearing in the least predictable places. "Ataypura" – the second cut here – turns up in The Big Lebowski. Voice of the Xtabay is almost the perfect exotica product from the titles – including: "Virgin of the Sun God (Taita Inty)," "Lure of the Unknown Love (Xtabay)" and "Dance of the Winds (Wayra)" - it promises the exotic, supports it with vivid cover art (just the right side of gaudy), and satisfies on the back of a casual listen. Any short blast of Sumac's voice always exposes the instant drama she can conjure and the sheer size of her vocal talent. The fact that these vocal vistas promise a full landscape and all play themselves out inside three and a half minutes is all the more impressive.

Donna Summer:
Back Off Boogaloo
(Columbia River, 1999)
What? Not so much what might have been as what was never likely to be!

The death of Donna Summer (1948-2012) prompted an outpouring of admiration for a massive vocal talent. Summer's best known hits involve her expressive, wide-ranging and intriguing vocals being layered over single-minded and visionary productions. If you wanted someone to live the sound rather than front it, Summer had the chops to spare. Any one of "McArthur Park," "State of Independence," "Love to Love you Baby" or "I Feel Love" would have been enough to make a singer deserving of significant attention on her death. Summer's best singles are an embarrassment of riches, her compilations and original albums from 1976 onwards generally offer up other great performances, even if the original songs aren't always so good, and her filmed live performances are generally good enough to justify her highly respected status.

Back Off Boogaloo – by contrast – is recommended if you are one of those sound-hounds who likes to put the whole picture together. As an insight into where Summer's recording career started, it has a certain curio value. All you need to know about the quality of most of the nine cuts is explained when you track the way these songs have been hawked by budget labels under different titles. Seven of the cuts here are workmanlike, slightly muddy sounding, offshoots of soul with a jazzy touch. All recorded in Germany, before the fateful collision with Georgio Moroder. This is a decent voice striving like hell to give identity to an anonymous production. The points made without any debate are that Summer could dignify work worthy of derision and her contribution to her greatest hits should – therefore – be respected. She worked well with the best producers, but she could turn the worst productions into acceptable sound. Four of the cuts here are inconsequential stabs at different styles. A pedestrian cover of "Na Na Hey Hey (Kiss Him Goodbye)" doesn't lift many spirits but there are a couple of genuine curios to be enjoyed.

It is something of a review cliché to cite one or two songs as "worth the price of admission," when reviewers get music for free. But – since these bargain basement Summer tracks have seen a range of releases – the resulting CDs do shift online for next to nothing, plus postage of course. If we're talking about that combination as the price of admission, then Summer's covers of War's "They Can't Take Away the Music" and Ringo Starr's "Back Off Boogaloo" are truly worth a punt. She started off fronting a psychedelic rock band and performing in the musical Hair, and had grown up on gospel music, so Summer could interpret this material with ease. The War cover drags a soulful vocal into a song produced by a musically brilliant band without an obvious lead singer. "Back Off Boogaloo" (which some would suggest bears the hallmarks of Marc Bolan's – ahem – influence in the writing) was made for Ringo's lugubrious vocal. Summer, by contrast, gets anthemic, loud and big sounding to turn it into a roller-coasting chant. Had a costly production and some decent song-writing taken her in the directions suggested by either of these cuts she would have been great, and the world would never have seen her slut-dropping, caressing the mic stand and turning the relentless cold electro backing of "I Feel Love" into the seventies sex anthem.

Sunn 0))):
Flight of the Behemoth
(Southern Lord, 2002)
What? Where droning on changes perceptions.

Surely it's obvious – unless you opened this book at random and happened upon these very words – some of those included here are terminal outsiders and the purpose of including one of their releases is simply to draw attention to the fact they exist. So it is with Sunn 0))); (the tripled closing bracket being a reference to their sound). Sunn 0))) specialise in metal/thrash with the added twist that tempos are typically as slow as the most mordant classical music and the use of reverb and super-slow riffs frequently reduces the music to drones and ambient approaches (i.e. the guitar chords resonate in a ")))" fashion). They're also fond of guitar tunings that emphasize all of these qualities and take their sound slightly further away from standard metal. Categorising something that is – arguably – new age with a new edge, remains impossible to the point that the band – built around the original duo who formed in Seattle in 1998 -

are as likely to turn up somewhere like BBC Six Music's Freak Zone as on a standard heavy metal radio show.

Flight of the Behemoth – Sunn 0)))'s second album-length outing – offers up enough variety and experiment to catch the band at their best, and show the journeys and migrations that make up their usual movements. The five tracks include four mini-epics and – sat in the middle of the running order – the five minute 54 second "Bow 1." Japanese producer/artist Merzbow mixed "Bow 1" and the following "Bow 2" giving them a slightly richer and warmer sound than the other material. Merzbow and Sunn 0))) also collaborated on a massive mauling of Metallica's "For Whom the Bell Tolls" – christened "F.W.T.B.T," referencing little more than the basic riffs of the original, and placed last in the five tracks.

Stylistically, the entire album is uncompromising, the monster drones wander like mammoth beasts. If there's any specific meaning it revolves around creating the sound, lengthy and slow as it gradually builds. The opening brace of tracks: "Mocking Solemnity" and "Death Becomes You" have the epic and grim suggestions of classic metal. The heaviness of sound and suggestion of flight in the album's title are key to what Sunn 0))) continue to do best (albeit in a fairly esoteric field) and for the uninitiated this is probably as good a place as any to start.

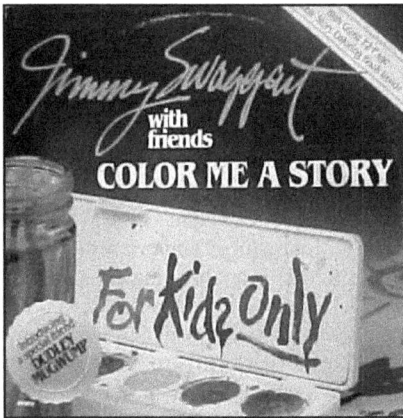

Jimmy Swaggart with Friends: Color me a Story (Jim Records, 1980)
What? Infamous preacher brings Jesus to the little ones.

Jimmy Swaggart survived the career crisis in 1988 that saw the evangelist break down sobbing in front of an audience of 7000 people in Baton Rouge and a worldwide news television audience, since supplemented by countless internet hits, to confess to consorting regularly with a prostitute [*]. His marriage and career hung in the balance, though he recovered to lead ministries and reclaim a place amongst the elite of evangelism. However, he remains famous outside the Christian community for the scandal and that, in turn, has ensured this children's record a place amongst the more cultish and celebrated such product.

It is a bizarre listen, supported with a high end production (or what passed for a high end production on a 1980 gospel album). This ensures the live audience of children, Swaggart himself and his prat falling comedy sidekick Dudley Mugwump are all audible and the listener can follow the twists and turns of the action. Swaggart whips up the young crowd, who clearly love Jesus from the outset. Mugwump's off-key singing provokes genuine hilarity (well, the kids love him) and the two sides of the album present a well-paced selection of songs, guests and on programme messages about racial equality, Christian values and how to live a good life. Swaggart has a real touch as a children's entertainer, witness the misunderstanding about whether the "Whopper" biblical giant Goliath was the same as a Burger King Whopper, and the genuine peals of laughter from the kids. It isn't exactly the most original gag, but Jim's comic timing milks it for more effect than it deserves.

An anonymous respondent to the "The Other Side of Music" blogspot noted: "just listened to these stories again…I had small children at the time Jimmy did these and my children listened to them over and over."

* EDITOR'S NOTE: Amusingly Swaggart is cousin to legendary rocker Jerry Lee Lewis. Cue great balls of fire jokes.

Color me a Story has the quality to withstand repeated listening, it also has the self-righteous/with the spirit fervour to attract a certain car crash fascination amongst the curious who know what followed eight years later.

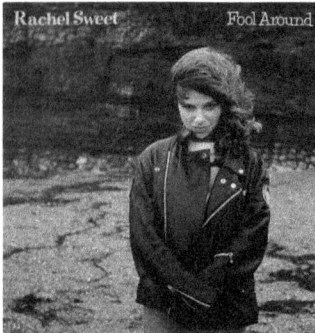

Rachel Sweet:
Fool Around
(Stiff, 1978)
What? Varied and sporadically cutting edge pop confection.

The laddish motto of the London label: "If it ain't Stiff, it ain't worth a fuck" nailed their macho/beery and independent take on punk firmly to floor. Most of the belated reverence for the label lies with its discovery and launching of Elvis Costello, Ian Dury and Madness. Lost in this potted history is the early career of Akron poppette Rachel Sweet. Given the laddishness of the label, the picture of the diminutive teenage songstress, with the improbably leather-lunged delivery, pouting against a lamppost on the back-cover could be read the wrong way. But this album is a genuine attempt to do something decent by their new signing. Sweet's natural forte was radio friendly pop/country/rock fodder where her varied range and deft control of her vocal pyrotechnics allowed her to inhabit a song to powerful effect. For most of her small catalogue she sings ahead of her tender years and carries the illusion convincingly. Fool Around – by contrast – sees her searching for an identity, and comes over sounding like a compilation album of girl singers. But, it packs enough varied gems to be worth a listen, long after the event. Central to the success of the venture is the pairing of Sweet with a few songs by Liam Sternberg, who produced the kind of quirky and differently abled pop songs that allowed Sweet to put her considerable talents in the centre of the mix, where she frequently pulled off the trick of sounding simultaneously like she meant it, and she was being ironic, "Girl with a Synthesizer" being one wonderful example; a rowdy slice of country 'n' pop in praise of a female master of early electronica. Sweet does sterling work bringing emotion and genuine empathy to Elvis Costello's tear-jerker "Stranger in the House" and Del Shannon's "I go to Pieces," packs a punky edge on Sternberg's "Cuckoo Clock" and totally commands the alternative and wistful Sternberg gem "It's so Different Here." The latter being the kind of "pop" song that could grace a Black Box Recorder or Saint Etienne album without embarrassment. The attempted big hit that might have kept her career in this vein – a commanding and incendiary take on the standard "B-A-B-Y"- didn't set the charts alight (just scraping the top 40 in the UK) and Sweet went off in a more mainstream direction, signed to CBS and sold a few more records than she had on Stiff. So Fool Around stands as a one-off. Note, the album came with different covers and – infuriatingly – different tracks in different territories. "Girl with a Synthesizer" was one casualty of these cuts, so if you're buying a physical copy in whatever format it's offered, check before you buy, or cut out the guesswork and opt for Cherry Red's 2014 twofer collecting all Ms Sweet's Stiff cuts.

Margaret Leng Tan:
Art of the Toy Piano
(Point/ Universal Classics, 1997)
What? Pretty much what it claims to be: the toy piano raised to the level of art.

There is ample material online about the composers and other performers who have – from time to time – dabbled with the toy piano, i.e.: an instrument designed primarily to acquaint children with the rudiments of the piano keyboard. With its high-tone, limited octave range and small stature, this is an instrument unwieldy in larger adult hands. When musicians and composers like John Cage have approached the instrument they have often focussed their compositions in one area of its performance. Therefore, the work for toy piano available on record is frequently a very varied collection of maverick notions and not necessarily representative of the way the instrument itself is best used.

Margaret Leng Tan is one of the few virtuoso performers on the instrument and this – one of two CDs focussing on the art of the toy piano – ranks alongside collections like Thomas Bloch's exploration of the glass harmonica as a strange and strangely beautiful listen. The success of this album allowed Tan to claim, rightly, to be the first performing virtuoso toy piano player. "Eleanor Rigby" (second in the running order) marks one end of the range of work and references the likes of Perrey and Kingsley's reworkings of ubiquitous pop hits, whilst Tan's own hard work in transcribing and adapting classical works and ragtime pieces gives Art of the Toy Piano enough breadth to keep the surprises and sublime moments coming to the final "Gymnopedie Three" (which works incredibly well). The spirit of minimalist keyboard composers like Cage and Satie is never far away but it is to Tan's credit that she pushes beyond these limits and brings a sense of artistry and creative interpretation to the final results.

It is occasionally out of tune and often reliant on the clunky percussive sound the toy piano generates. There are also sporadic appearances of other childrens' instruments: melodica, toy accordion and crude drum effects. Art of the Toy Piano works hard to win the battle to be taken seriously. Beethoven nestles next to Klucevsek and makes it obvious that everything from the mood of each piece, to its age, was considered in producing a sequence that would work. By She Herself Alone: The Art of the Toy Piano 2 (2010) Tan was covering a piece by Ross Bolletor and performing on a ruined toy piano.

Tater Totz:
Alien Sleestacks from Brazil
(Giant, 1988)
What? Yoko's children, play it strange, and throw in some laughs!

Tater Totz turned in a trio of albums, and drew members from White Flag and the Three O'Clock. This prime slice of late-eighties alternative music, bursting with references to other sounds, kicked off their long-playing career and set out the stall for what followed. It, just about, qualifies as rock but packs so much experimental, random and elongated noodling that a better insight is to suggest the collection simply heads off in different directions as it sees fit but – by virtue of the guitar/bass/drums core – keeps coming back to rock. The second side gives a decent rock grunt and some superb slide guitar to a rollicking cover of Yoko Ono's "Don't Worry Kyoko (Mummy's Just Looking for her Hand in the Snow")" and the cover art, including a depiction of a black-clad Yoko in the her famous pose with grapefruit, says everything about Tater Totz' inspiration. Yoko's avant-garde take on popular music is referenced throughout most of the collection.

The album's most accessible cut and only significant attempt at anything playable on radio, a snappy cover of The Beatles' "I've Just Seen a Face" with Danny Bonaduce (yeah, him, really!) on vocals, can be read as a reference to the collision of avant-garde and popular that saw the Lennon/Ono partnership carve a unique swathe through half a decade of sixties/seventies music. Most of the first side places Bonaduce's fleeting appearance in a colliding mix of pop and sound-art. "Give Peace a Chance" and a surprisingly reverent re-working of "Tomorrow Never Knows" appear, the former in a bizarre mash-up with Queen's "We Will Rock You." Danny Bonaduce's appearance is preceded by a snatch of the "na, na, na…" vocal refrain from "I

Think I Love You" by The Partridge Family. The Totz' love of cult heroes was cemented when former Runaway Cherie Currie turned up to sing on their second album.

Aïcha Tachinwite:
Aïcha Tachinwite
(Awesome Tapes from Africa, 2014)
What? Moroccan disco diva on top form.

The Awesome Tapes from Africa label is a wonderful throwback, and an act of musical curatorship that verges on the life affirming. Still working as a cassette (with attendant downloads) label well into the 21st century, Awesome Tapes... set out to find and release the African music that pushes boundaries. Masterminded by Brian Shimkovitz, and run from his New York bedroom, Awesome Tapes has the kind of personal slant that makes for a roster of music like no other. Shimkovitz has a love for the kind of African sounds that sacrifice little of their native tradition but consume influences from elsewhere and recycle them ravenously. The resulting mashes make for music of real character. Most Awesome Tapes material involves literal reissues, though the label also compiles works by particular artists.

Aïcha Tachinwite wails with a sharp diction and impressive command of the melody line. A few overdubs allow her to answer her own questions and sweep from one speaker to the other as her eponymous collection covers four lengthy disco workouts, the third one referencing a classic disco riff and her final cut opening on a plaintive melody, and strong Moroccan feel, leaving Aïcha with acres of space at the front of the mix to share her feelings with the listener. A loose groove with flutes and light electric guitar riff kicks in and she wails the perfect sweep to take us into the faster tempo. The opening two cuts (side one if you're being pedantic about the cassette format) are more predictable old school disco/Moroccan pop mashes.

As a cultural repository, informed by musical traditions and steered by a creative intelligence, Awesome Tapes From Africa is a sparkling breaker in a sea of musical cynicism. The label is worthy of investigation. This particular album stands as an accessible start to embracing Awesome Tapes' best moves.

The Creed Taylor Orchestra:
Panic the Son of Shock
(ABC-Paramount, 1959)
What? Cinematic sounds of a superior nature.

Taylor was one of a number of music industry figures who saw the advent of stereo sound and the increasing popularity of long-playing records as an opportunity to experiment and produce an entertainment experience. Much of Taylor's notoriety in the music business comes from his time spent running record labels and overseeing the best recordings of artists like George Benson but on Shock (1958) and Panic the Son of Shock Taylor's creative vision is behind a combination of light and narrative jazz orchestrations and inserted sound effects and dialogue that leave the separate tracks sounding like snatches of soundtrack from dramatic movies. It's deliberately hammy to the point that the couple in "Alpine Honeymoon" set the scene by discussing exactly where they are...you know it won't end well and the track is all the better because Jack (as in the newly wed husband) simply laughs as his wife desperately asks him if he can hang on to the rope. Taylor leaves it, literally, on a cliff hanger. That is typical of a series of sonic sketches that are confident enough to avoid the standard beginning-middle-end structure of songs. Taylor is celebrating the narrative possibilities of samples and music so the point of "The Fastest Gun" is to set up the gunfight, build up the tension and leave the listener wanting more (the track ends before a shot is fired).

There are others chronicled within this book – like Joe Meek and David Holmes – who have created long-players reliant on the narrative qualities of music and the vivid imaginations of their listeners. In Creed Taylor's case the playfulness of frequently setting a listener up before leaving at the moment of impact is a trademark that sets his work apart. It's also a very good advert for the skills of the much maligned A&R man, Taylor ditched his full-time trumpet playing career when he became head of A&R at Bethlehem Records in 1954 and works like Panic... combine a creative vision with a rock-solid sense of niche market and fashion trends. By the time he began creating works like Panic... Taylor was in a position to oversee the signing of talent, and capable of understanding what would work within a budget. That – probably – is why the clearer focus of Panic just edges it over the earlier Shock despite Panic... playing safe by announcing itself as the "son of" Shock. No matter, the pair have been available for some time packed onto the same CD reissue.

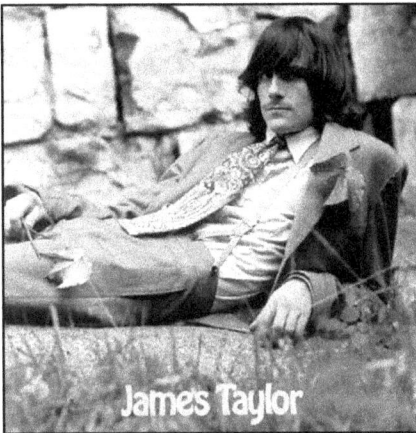

James Taylor:
James Taylor
(Apple, 1968)
What? Nothing like the hits; dark, fragile and strangely British.

Taylor has been such a fixture of the folk-rock mainstream that his easy style, gentle delivery and homely songs are part of the furniture at soft rock and album oriented radio stations the world over. The blueprint for a winning sound, and the source of some stage favourites like "Fire and Rain" and "Sweet Baby James" was his monster-selling Sweet Baby James album which opened his account for Warner Brothers. Even at the height of his fame it was possible to meet people who believed Sweet Baby James was his first album.

In fact, Taylor's first long-player was recorded in London for The Beatles' Apple label, and it sounds very little like the hits. It also opens a window to a different side of Taylor's life, and a story that has eluded his casual fans over the years. Much of Taylor's best work contains an awareness of life's more fragile elements and the need to grab at happiness. His cover of Carole King's "You've Got a Friend" fits into this category, also "Sweet Baby James," written for his newly born nephew. From the late seventies onwards songs like "Secret O' Life" and "Line 'em Up" took this viewpoint into the lives of other characters. The notions that life constantly threatens to overwhelm you, that dark experiences constantly lurk in the background and that happiness, and sanity, might be elusive permeate almost every song on James Taylor. A fact made more understandable when you realise that the album was recorded soon after Taylor spent time in a psychiatric ward.

Raw and honest lyrics on James Taylor record this fact. "Knocking Round the Zoo" with its lengthy howling screams tackles his time on the inside, but it is the more personal songs hinting at fragile friendships and lingering self-doubt that make James Taylor an uncompromising listen. Even the moments of hope provided by "Something in the Way She Moves" and "Sunshine Sunshine" have lines suggesting any hopefulness could be shattered in seconds. Production wise this is a very English record, tinny and sparing on the bass, lacking drums on most tracks and annoyingly mixing them to the side on most occasions they do appear, James Taylor is probably a little over-fussy sound wise. Though the presence of fleeting and varied musical interludes, offering up a solo harp, a brass section and a harpsichord between tracks is engaging and gives James Taylor a sense of being a very personal record.

If the precision and radio friendly production resembling the gentler moments of The Eagles are a touchstone for most of James Taylor's best-known work the James Taylor album belongs in a different world. Closer, arguably, to an American Nick Drake.

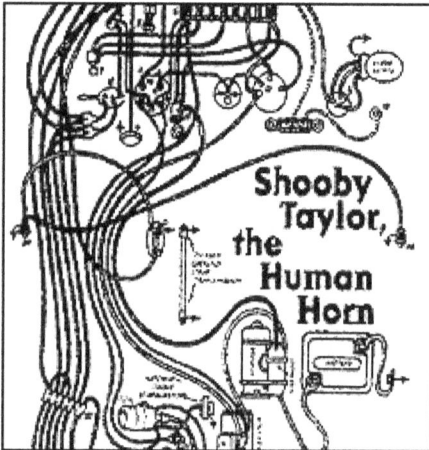

Shooby Taylor: The Human Horn (shoobytaylor.com)
What? The most singular and strange scat singing you'll here.

Technically speaking, Shooby Taylor (1929-2003) never made a solo album. For years his family, friends and Absolutely Kosher Records have been working to get official releases from a hoard of 50 tracks. That's the gold Shooby's small but dedicated fan-base are holding out for. In the meantime, Shooby Taylor: The Human Horn is a pretty good substitute. Turned to mp3 from an original cassette tape, the sound isn't exactly studio quality and there's a certain one-dimensional feel to an album's worth of material most of which features Shooby scat singing over a lively keyboard backing. But that's the nit-picking over. There's a reason that Shooby's work was compiled by Irwin Chusid onto the Songs in the Key of Z series and championed on his radio show. Chusid's show and compilation both being an acknowledged home for the strange and differently abled in music.

As the Wikipedia succinctly put it: "He is noted for his highly idiosyncratic scat style, using sounds and syllables quite unlike those used by other scat singers." A fair point and one supported by the brief clip of Shooby on stage at the Apollo Theatre (the only known film of Shooby). The clip is brief because he'd barely begun his act before being booed off. Fascination with Shooby begins with the sounds incorporated in his scat technique. A few crowd pleasing touches like "tiddly" a low and resonant "brawwww" and an impressively high "twee" are common sounds along with inventive and extended arpreggios in which Shooby riffs at will up and down a scale; occasionally whilst seemingly oblivious to where the musical backing is heading. It's a style that turns a standard like "Who's Sorry Now" into a unique study in scat technique as Shooby - apparently – speaks in tongues for a couple of minutes. The first and most striking element of Shooby's scat sound is the sheer scale of what's attempted. He dominates most of the cuts currently available, singing constantly, smothering the backing and sounding for all the world like an unapologetic ambassador from another world. Never more so than when he scats over a simple recording of "How Great Thou Art" rapid-firing his way through a series of "slay-doobly-la-la-braw-wheee!!!" phrases as the original recording rises and falls in its usual places.

The fact that some of his best work involves crashing the recordings of others and laying his unique patter over the top is central to the frustrations of those trying to bring Shooby to the world on CD. For fairly understandable reasons some of those whose work has been ravaged by Shooby's inventive accompaniment are reticent about licensing the results for commercial sale. In the meantime there are 14 tracks, plus some additional material, available at shoobytaylor.com and both volumes of Songs in the Key of Z feature Shooby (specifically offering the same versions of "Stout Hearted Men" and "Lift Every Voice and Sing" that are available at shoobytaylor.com).

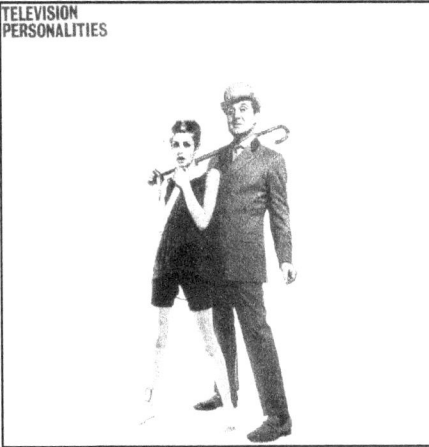

Television Personalities:
And Don't the Kids Just Love it
(Rough Trade, 1981)
What? Posh punksters get the mix of DIY charm and sixties throwback just right.

Given that the core of this band found each other at the London Oratory the formation of Television Personalities is verging on the likes of Genesis coming out of Charterhouse School. Perhaps it was having London's major museums as next door neighbours, but one element of the distinct Television Personalities genius was their ability to pillage the past, reinvent it for their present day audience and still leave the whole lot sounding like something unique and characterful. They'd knocked out some notable singles under other names before this album launched them firmly into the post-punk market.

From the cover picture of Twiggy and Patrick (John Steed) Macnee it was obvious the band had a sense of classic style to go with the DIY ethic of their sparky low-fi music. Released appropriately on indie-titans Rough Trade. And Don't the Kids... manages 14 tracks of bittersweet lyrical barbs, shot through with some good jokes and supported with a skeletal combo of chunky guitars, solid rhythm and just enough spot colour touches from elsewhere to make this the audio equivalent of the kind of fanzines that circulated at the time.

One obvious touchstone is very early Pink Floyd (i.e. those fleeting days when Syd Barrett's ravings were in check and the band thought it useful to ramp up and riff, even when their lyrics were spiralling out of the Solar System). If a listener needed any more clues to this influence Dan Tracey's stand-out "I Know Where Syd Barrett Lives" duly makes things crystal clear. A delightful, if slightly delirious, hymn to Syd, suggesting Dan Treacey is in the habit of dropping into the Floydster's home in Cambridge for "Sunday tea...sausages and beans". It's nonesense, of course, but glorious, bright pop nonsense. Dan Treacey's vocals manage a shy, introspective quality and cut through the limited production with a sense of character and identity that gives the collection a sense of its own personality. For every knock-off formulaic piece of cynical punk like "Parties in Chelsea" (basically a been-there/done-it account of a series of non-events), there are allusions to other targets, like Dorian Gray and Look Back in Anger that betray the true intellectual standing of the band; but still sound insistent, fresh and true to the indie ethic.

Lyrically the album still stands out from a slew of such quick turn-around, low-budget material produced by every chancer and his dog around the same time. Musically, perhaps its greatest achievement is to vary the basic punk ingredients to such an extent that the changes in pace, minimal additions of other instruments and the switch from fast to slow numbers still makes this one of the few collections of its era and ilk that withstands being lined up and played end to end without the need for skipping or shuffling. And, it has one truly sublime moment that stands in its own right for all time, as the twee tune and innocently bedazzled vocals of "I Know Where Syd Barrett..." fade we are left with a gleefully chirping chorus of birdlife, they sing merrily in a happy "hello trees, hello sky" stylee for a few seconds, setting a true hippie mood before Treacey's final shout of "Oh, shut up" brings it all to a rapid halt.

This Heat:
·This Heat
(Piano, 1979)
What? Post-punk, progsters debut transcends their time; or another highly influential/low-selling Peel favourite.

It is widely believed by some that punk had to happen because prog-rock had vanished so far up its own rear-end as to have nothing left to say that anyone would understand. A fair point, but prog's best ideas were often about sonic advancement, playing with sounds, audience perceptions and breaking barriers of song and compositional structures. So, nobody ever said you had to sound massive to be progressive. As early as 1976 the trio This Heat were experimenting with taped effects, adding in their (multi) instrumental talents and crafting a bleak, uncompromising and occasionally atonal sound that threw the affordable low-fi stylings of punk in with themes of political awareness and intelligent crafting of their music. Their eponymous debut album in September 1979 loaded "The Fall of Saigon" and "Diet of Worms" into the track list along with form-as-purpose missives like "24 Track Loop" and "Music Like Escaping Gas."

This Heat may have a credible claim to being Britain's best attempt at matching the first Velvet Underground release. The drone moments of both releases bear some sonic resemblance but the main overlap is in the way both eponymous albums sold desperately low quantities at the time but went on to influence whole swathes of the ground-breaking music that followed.

This Heat breaks most of the rules that applied in 1979. The album opens and closes on sounds imprinted into the run-in and run-out grooves and after the opening fragment "Testcard" – which is expanded in the final track – This Heat offers up the two longest cuts "Horizontal Hold" and "Not Waving." The former sets up the basic sonic palette, keyboards towards the centre, analogue sound generation, some standard instruments but basically a reliance on experimental/sound wash noises to build each track, and lead instruments used in unusual ways. "Horizontal Hold" offers up a keyboard solo so slow and mournful as to be both a mood-setter for the whole (almost) seven minutes of the cut and also a scathing comment on the keyboard bombast that (by 1979) had become a by-word for prog excesses. When "Not Waving" finally delivers a lead vocal (not exactly a traditional, perfectly pitched, radio friendly vocal), This Heat delivers another slap to the senses, akin to the first shuddering surprise when more than ten minutes into Eraserhead we finally hear the line: "Are you Henry?"

David Lynch's ground-breaking low-budget horror-noir has nothing – officially – to do with This Heat but it is a useful touchstone in many ways. This Heat is a smart and knowing record that references a lot of what has gone before, sticks to being influenced and seldom steals anything directly, turns the low-fi into a virtue, never forgets for one second that playing with the audiences perceptions can be riveting and ambles through the sublime, haunting and challenging in a way that always keeps the tension simmering, even when – apparently – there isn't much going on.

In this context the layered loops of "24 Track Loop" are as much a statement as the way "Diet of Worms" plays with a title drawn from history but delivers little more than minimal electronica designed to leave the audience wondering if they are listening to composed sounds or the sampled noises of buzzing in high-voltage electric lines. This Heat was never designed to be radio friendly and if it falls down massively – other than in the limited production budget – it may simply be too ready to put an inappropriate combination of title and sound out there. It's clearly an album celebrating possibilities and experiments and – therefore –

more about the journey than the eventual destination. A review on Julian Cope's Head Heritage site meaningfully compared This Heat to the sounds you might hear if you accidentally picked up radio broadcasts on the fillings in your teeth. Probably the most apt comment made amongst the impressive tonnage of positive assessments of the album.

Jens Thomas and Verneri Pohjola:
Speed of Grace: A Tribute to AC/DC
(Act, 2012)
What? For those about to noodle in a minimalist, darkly, ambient-jazzy way; we salute you!

It's not like the world is short of radical reinventions of a celebrated musical canon mashed/re-imagined/murdered into another style. So, to stand out, you have to be special, right? This book would like to make such a case for Speed of Grace. The idea is fairly simple. Thomas (a noted jazz pianist with a history of experimentation) and Pohjola unite to rework one of the rawest and most in your face catalogues of any major act as an exercise in dark minimalist sounds and gently intoned spoken word. Led by the acoustic trills and sparing chord work of Thomas, and supported with basic percussion, sparing keyboards, other elements of musical spot-colour and spoken word/gently sung snatches of lyrics that verge into whispers, the album takes on AC/DC in a way the originators of these rock anthems probably never imagined. And they don't skimp on the classics: "T.N.T," "For Those About to Rock" "Hells Bells" and "Highway to Hell" are all here.

The genius that – just about – makes this compelling listening is the appreciation that AC/DC's power lies in the collision of basic – often brutal – elements, and the same dynamics can work in an understated way. In fact, the lack of an obvious strong melody (because we're deprived of Bon Scott/Brian Johnson's strident vocals and Angus Young's inflammatory guitar-lines) is part of the strength. Shorn of their main focus, the tunes emerge as insistent and repetitive musical works that benefit from the application of tone and colour provided on this album. Never better than when "Highway to Hell" is reworked as desperate/demented plea or when "The Jack," originally a laddish anthem directed at a VD ridden girl, emerges as a sensitive and intimate little gem.

Thomas performs Speed of Grace live, and if you're unable to get to a gig, there's always YouTube to give you a taste of this very singular collision of catalogue and performer.

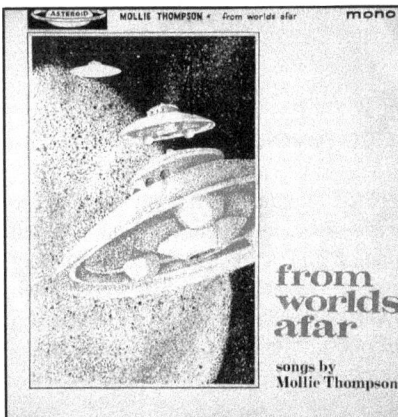

Mollie Thompson:
From Worlds Afar
(Asteroid, 1966)
What? One of the most out-there (literally) albums of the sixties.

There's plenty written about cosmic consciousness and the like from the mid-sixties onwards but nowhere near enough written about this privately pressed album of singer-songwriter space-exploration. But, amongst the few who have come into contact with this work – including Jello Biafra and some of those involved with WFMU Radio – there's almost universal astonishment at what they have found. By far the most insightful write-up of From Worlds Afar appears in Flying Saucery: A Social History of UFOlogy (2007) where one of the book's co-authors, Andy Roberts, actually made it his business to interview Mollie Thompson.

Thompson had been fascinated by UFOs and stories of aliens for a few years when – in 1963 – she met legendary UFO contactee George Adamski, and was told "the brothers" (as in alien intelligence in contact with Adamski) had "work" for her. By her own admission: "words and music began to drop into my mind." The combination of words and music led to Mollie performing in front of audiences interested in paranormal phenomena and – eventually – to a private pressing of her songs. Ten cuts of Mollie and her acoustic guitar make up From Worlds Afar. Lyrically it is a combination of material about UFOs and aliens and some general works dealing with raised consciousness. Some of the words map out standard conspiracy theory ideas: "Those flying saucers whisking through the skies…government departments just hide their eyes/ And call them meteors" ("The Cock-eyed Song"). Elsewhere the songs are more uplifting: "The third wise man is a baby, the future looks bright in his eyes/ For his brothers will be from the planets, and his teachers will drop from the skies" ("Three Wise Men").

Musically From Worlds Afar doesn't push too many barriers. The acoustic guitar is nylon strung, Mollie's favoured style of accompaniment wouldn't have been out of place round a camp fire or in a church youth club and the songs are typical story-line with a message folk tunes. It's the strange messages and the notion that this charming low-budget oddity is in some way being fed to Mollie directly by a higher intelligence that is the main point of interest. Her sleeve notes include: "The words and music came into my head, though I am neither a writer nor a composer, so I think I can say that this record is the result of 'inspiration' – a word which to me simply means 'breathing in.'" Mollie – as discussed when Andy Roberts interviewed her in 2005 – recorded her songs in the belief a major consciousness raising event was imminent on Christmas Day 1967. She gradually become disillusioned and drifted away from the community celebrating UFOs.

But she remained willing to discuss her involvement and left an album that – despite a distribution network almost totally reliant on those in the UFO community at the time - has continued to accrue a following ever since. Songs like "Space Talk" envision a world in which Earth is part of a galactic community and in the closing "Think Big Thoughts," in her own words on the sleeve, Mollie notes: "This last song is the golden key to all tomorrows – a 'do-it-yourself-handbook.' Thoughts are such powerful things for they shape the world in which we live. The world which my inner eyes view is peopled with a race of human angels. They will have a dictionary in which you cannot find such words as hate, fear, poverty or disease – tomorrow's earth will even have forgotten what these unlovely concepts were." Easily as cosmic – then – as her peers – long-haired and popping every conceivable stimulant, at the same time. The authors of this book managed to contact Andy Roberts, but not Mollie Thompson. Roberts' attempts to bring about a CD reissue have – to date – been scuppered by an inability to get hold of the original copyright holder of the album. Keep trying Andy.

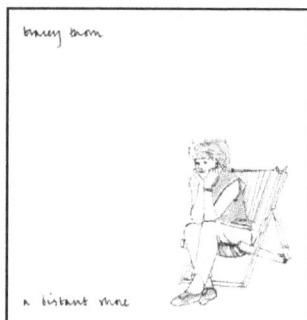

Tracy Thorne:
A Distant Shore
(Rough Trade, 1982)
What? A very understated little revolution.

Recorded for £138 and running a mere 23 minutes A Distant Shore is the most unlikely of game-changing albums. But, its fragile and understated beauty continues to captivate an audience and work its magic in making others believe the simple combination of vocal, guitar and well-crafted words and tunes can be the most powerful musical armoury of all. Seven originals and an effortlessly beautiful cover of The Velvet Underground's "Femme Fatale" make up A Distant Shore and the album marks Thorne's transition from the lively but wilfully shambolic Marine Girls to the more restrained and assured sounds of Everything but the Girl.

A Distant Shore is one of those unfussy creations that quietly changes the rules as it lulls the listener. Singer-songwriters were something of an anachronism in 1982 and low-low budgets were for the smelly die-hards intent on proving punk wasn't dead. The Human League – all bright videos and ironic knowing in their re-invention of pop - were the gold standard for alternative acts with an edge on mainstream success. Those intent on singing their own songs with a guitar were well advised to boast a punchy band behind them. In an age that spurned introspection, and valued acquisitive ambition, Thorne's lyrics were also at odds with most of the new pretenders. Even The Smiths' honesty and vulnerability came cloaked in the bleakest humour. Thorne makes a virtue of all the things others shunned: "Still trying to get over my small town ways, But still so much a part of me is my past disgrace" she sings on the opening "Small Town Girl," bringing the emotional baggage into view. It's to A Distant Shore's credit that it wears this baggage and Thorne's clear intelligence so lightly, aiming to craft the thoughtful treasures that are the real prize here. A Distant Shore may go inside itself for material but it is the journey that is the point. The album remains unafraid of open endings; accepting the learning process and capturing the moments that count. "Plain Sailing" – the shortest cut here – made the biggest impact when released as a single, Thorne opining she is "old enough now to know there's no such thing" and pulling the same trick in the final moments in "Too Happy" when she identifies the need to destroy a love that is threatening to overwhelm before ending on: "then I realise I love you more, but is that what we go through it for?"

Built on unpretentious guitar, solo vocal and the most sparing of overdubs: A Distant Shore floats somewhere between Nick Drake's Pink Moon and Bon Iver's For Emma Forever Ago. Nobody expected its climb to #2 in the UK Indie chart. It went on to inspire a generation of bedroom songwriters and it continues to captivate new listeners.

Throbbing Gristle:
DoA: Third and Final Report
(Industrial, 1978)
What? Industrial-noise nightmares on wax.

Arguably the nearest thing to a masterwork produced by an act who always set themselves up as the alternative voice. Gristle's anti-commercial stance tended to explode with so many ideas even their most ardent admirers struggled to stay in touch. With DoA, for example, one batch of 1000 albums was cut with false track pressings, a glance at the grooves would indicate the album contained 16 tracks of equal length, fooling people into dropping the needle in the wrong place. DoA packs more diversity and character than the full-on sonic assaults of some of their other material mainly because it offers four solo tracks. Not that Gristle would ever go into commercial territory; a fact proven here by the inclusion of a 16 second version of "United" one of their more popular tracks, the original ran for just over four minutes, the DoA version is the original, simply sped up to become incomprehensible.

For all that DoA contains the dark-synth tones, disembodied vocals and slow pulsing rhythms of "Hamburger Lady." A stark and ambitious piece that runs the risk of being labelled a "hit." The origins of the track – inspired by a story of a burns victim's hideous injuries – appear on the sleeve, along with general background information on the album. Some of the solo work is surprisingly tender and personal, Cosey Fanni Tutti's "Hometime" uses delays, echoes, piano sounds and a little girl's voice to produce a short concrete poem and Genesis P. Orridge's solo offering "Weeping" collides four violins, production effects and a vocal line reminiscent of Brian Eno on very malevolent form.

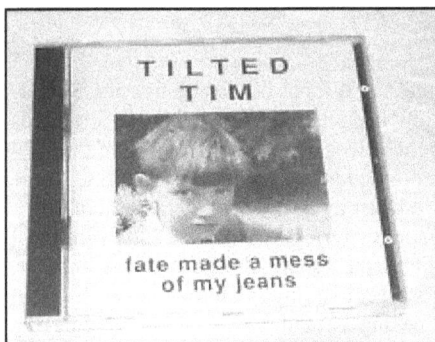

Tilted Tim:
Fate Made a Mess of my Jeans
(Flagrak, 1992)
What? The authentic voice of early 90s indie Britain…well, one of the authentic voices…

In the days just before the internet, Indie music had progressed past low-fi tape experiments to produce a generation with access to Portastudios and the means to burn CDs of the resulting music. Whilst the music press discovered and championed a range of clones and mavericks with attitude and – often – the complete works of Joy Division and the Velvet Underground on hand, a few others had an altogether different vision. One such was Tilted Tim and his work stands as a fleeting insight into a breed of home-grown legends-in-the-living-room visionaries who were there and gone so quickly that many missed them. In simple terms Fate Made a Mess of my Jeans is what happens when a normal(ish) bloke from Harrow gets his hands on the means to make an album, ropes in a few mates and has no need to impress a record company or adhere to anything approaching a fashion trend. It is shamelessly in love with melody, clearly taking something from late sixties McCartney songs and the slower moments in the XTC catalogue. The rhythms are precise, the chords clear and always on the beat, the lyrics always audible and the vision…personal, nakedly ambitious, whimsical, witty and seldom threatening, even when it's supposed to sound threatening. Imagine Badly Drawn Boy's twin brother who buys all his clothes in Marks and Spencer's and holds down a professional job on the side.

The one thing that leaps out of the speakers two decades down the line is that this is an album that sounds like very little else and marches to a beat entirely of its own. It is standard guitar/ keyboard/bass/drums rock/pop, heavier on acoustic guitar than many and very fond of muscular strumming as a means of pushing the song forward. You get proper chord progressions, clear melodies and – usually – Tim chiming in behind himself on a backing vocal, to emphasise the catchy and important moments. At worst it's people who couldn't dream of getting a deal living their own dream because they've saved the cash. Tim's busiest backing musicians delight in the names of "Superstar" Bob Green and Dave Spiggy Miller. Lyrically he opens with boundless ambition: "There is nothing I won't do/ In my quest to reach the top/ To be the king of heap/ To be the cream of the crop" ("Hi I'm Tilted"), soon we're into kiss-off territory with a barbed lyrical bullet: "You say mudslinger/I say archaeologist" ("My New Career") and briefly into the deepest ennui "Building/Isolation/Nothing here seems real/Never knowing how to feel/ So what's the point in trying?" ("Nightfall"). Ultimately this is a very English curio, hopelessly out of kilter with the grunge-ridden, dance obsessions fashions of its time and far too clean cut to have a hope against the – then - emerging Brit-pop. Fate Made a Mess… wears its home-grown origins like a badge of pride. Despite the black and white cover shot of its creator as a child, it packs a determined punch. Not strident, but certainly sure of itself, and fiercely unashamed, the album is – if nothing else – authentic, and more independent in its thinking and vision than most of the competition who delighted in being called "Indie."

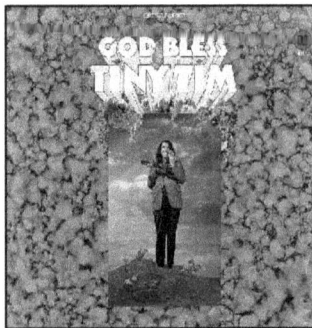

Tiny Tim:
God Bless Tiny Tim
(Reprise, 1968)
What? Fabulous freak show in full flight.

"Tiny" Tim was a giant of a man best known for playing a ukulele and singing in a high-pitched voice. His repertoire of choice was old Vaudeville numbers and the film score songs that most resembled old Vaudeville. His moment of glory in 1968 coincided with the head audience around the freakier end of hippie sounds extending their love to a handful of the most eccentric and wilfully out there acts. Wild Man Fischer was another beneficiary of such a following. Balancing Tim's strangeness with the need to create a listenable long player was never likely to be easy but God Bless is an object lesson in how to get it right. None of the main players could have known at the time that by snagging Richard Perry as producer they'd got one guy who could create a vision for the project that would hold it all together. The sound varies just enough to give Tim a range of situations to display his art. This same sound stays close enough to a standard production of Tim's varied vocals and ukulele, respectfully keeping the man at the centre of his album. Perry's short CV at the time included production duties for early Captain Beefheart. Within half a decade Perry would be performing, arguably, his greatest feat of managing the sound that took Ringo to the top of the US album charts.

The next master stroke is allowing Tim to MC his own show, "Welcome to my Dream" opens the album and allows him to talk directly to the listeners, "Tip Toe Through the Tulips With Me" (Tim's one genuine hit) follows, and from here on Tim's observations on life, his sporadic chats to the listener and the style and sound shift just enough to keep things inventive. Finally, much of the material is well chosen. Tim, despite his long hair, was never a hippie. But, occasionally, there are flights of imaginative fancy that take him and acid consciousness, briefly, into the same space. "The Other Side" muses on the melting polar ice caps (this is 1968, BTW!) at which point Tim's blissfully accepting approach suggests we'll all have "a swimming time." This song is followed by the gleefully over the top "Ever Since you Told me you Loved me (I'm a Nut)." Basically a stagey tune, but opened with manic laughter and a few vague acid rock noises.

The notion that anyone would repeatedly listen to God Bless, then or now, seems fanciful, but it is listenable. Much of its robust strangeness stands up very well decades after it first saw release, and the varied attempts to capture and focus Tiny Tim that followed this never again achieved such sustained quality. God Bless Tiny Tim (and Richard Perry).

Julie Tippetts and Martin Archer: Tales of FiNiN (Discus, 2011)
What? Epic journey acted out over ceaselessly inventive soundscape.

Several entries in the present book include the thought that any dip into the catalogue of a particular act – Half Man Half Biscuit, Captain Beefheart etc. – will produce something of interest to the uninitiated. Where a true polymath like Martin Archer is concerned, locating such a catalogue, or – indeed – any defining style, is more difficult. But Archer, the guiding intelligence behind Discus Records, and a self-taught musician of stunning virtuosity, has made a particular strength of producing self-contained works, each boasting a particular and unique vision. Discus Records suggests "jazz, free improvisation, contemporary classical music, electronica, and cutting edge rock music are all present within his work" and Archer's live audiences can expect: "improvised and composed elements…raw material from various studio recordings recombined and reprocessed in real time using laptop technology."

Tales of FiNiN uses all of the above and more in varied combinations, over two lengthy CDs and throws in a sterling vocal performance from Julie Tippetts, who contributes the lyrics/story and varies between singing and speaking as she acts out a journey. The "tales" of the title cover a classic hero's quest narrative, presenting moments of forward movement and self-doubt and ending with a track titled "Atonement/The

Way Back." Musically, Archer helms a soundscape that pushes the narrative forward, permanently suggests the journey is as much inside as outside the mind and still manages to create a work in which each track wouldn't sound out of place, in isolation, in some programme in the more eclectic corner of music radio.

Any attempt at categorising such a theatrical and varied work is all but pointless, but it is worth noting that Tippetts (aka Julie Driscoll) contributes massively with her ability to inhabit the varying moods and challenges of the journey. The lyrics – printed in their entirety – are helpful, but this is a performance that truly demands your undivided attention, preferably with headphones and dimmed lights, to reveal all its secrets. Such exposure to the album may well convince you Archer's self-proclaimed status as a "unique inhabitant of the school of English maverick composers" is no idle boast.

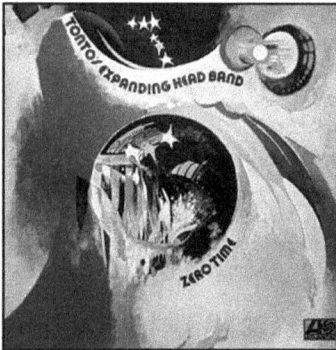

Tonto's Expanding Headband:
Zero Time
(Embryo, 1971)
What? The sound that made Stevie (and a few others) wonder.

S'cuse us ripping the Wikipedia but the following information matters: " TONTO is an acronym for "The Original New Timbral Orchestra," the first, and still the largest, multitimbral polyphonic analog synthesizer in the world, designed and constructed over several years by Malcolm Cecil. TONTO started as a Moog modular synthesizer Series III owned by record producer Robert Margouleff. Later a second Moog III was added, then four Oberheim SEMs, two ARP 2600s, modules from Serge with Moog-like panels, EMS, Roland, Yamaha, etc. plus several custom modules designed by Serge Tcherepnin and Cecil himself - who has an electrical engineering background. Later, digital sound-generation circuitry and a collection of sequencers were added, along with MIDI control. All of this is housed in an instantly-recognizable semi-circle of huge curving wooden cabinets, twenty feet in diameter and six feet tall."

In other words, what you hear on this and its sister release It's About Time (1974) is a collision of geekdom, cutting edge imagination and technology, all of it now doubling as a snapshot of musical history. Cecil and Margouleff had big dreams, but never lost sight of the beauty and voice of the music they wanted to make. Key to this vision was the need to keep each note with a different tone quality, the way an acoustic instrument would deliver it. The uniqueness of the instrumentation created by Tonto's Expanding Headband and the way subsequent electronics went in a totally digital direction has frozen their work in time (though the likes of Zero 7 have made serious efforts to revive something of their feel). Zero Time is the manifesto and, arguably, their finest work. Each side of the original vinyl lines up a series of effervescent electronic works with non-specific titles: "Cybernaut," "Jetsex," "Timewhys," "Aurora," "Riversong" and "Tama." Collectively they inhabit the kind of space that early Tangerine Dream and a few others aimed for. There are classical pretensions, a sense of open-minded exploration of new realities and a nod here and there to the emerging progressive sounds in rock.

Tonto remain special in this company because their music always offered a warm, organic quality and brought a soulful sensibility to sounds others were already taking into colder and more abstract directions. The band's output tailed off partly because their vision and very human qualities were called into action in helping others to produce albums. The duo are, for example, credited with co-production work on every Stevie Wonder album from Music of My Mind to Fulfillingness' First Finale. Zero Time still sounds innovative today. Its offspring include countless bedroom computer/keyboard wizards. But the instrumentation and sound achieved here were imagined and brought into being for the purpose of creating the kind of music you hear on Tonto recordings. That breadth of ambition, and the seamless links between instrument, creators and the eventual sounds make Zero Time a very special work.

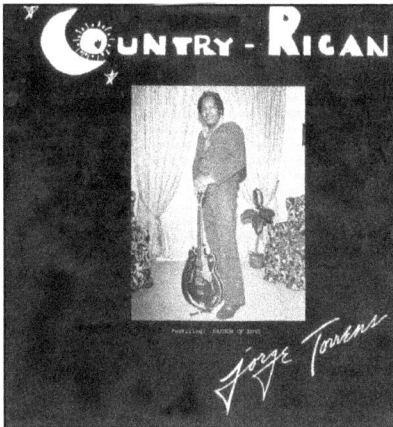

Jorge Torrens:
Country Rican
(1976)
What? Country standards slaughtered.

Another source of download delight, mirthful file swapping and some mystery. This little known 1976 vinyl album is easily summarised. Listening, in this case, is everything. Torrens turns in a set of, mainly, standard material over simple drums and bass, guitar. A sweeping ostentatious steel guitar is the main wild card in the pack. The mix stays solid where the backing band are concerned, honing a sound that leaves yer man Torrens out front, channelling a mumble-heavy Elvis vibe and swerving into a nasal and highly Spanish twang when the melody lines go too high for his King impression. Throw in a sense of a rushed project, and some lyrics learned phonetically, and you have a piece veering towards unintended comedy, frequently in those moments Torrens intends as the most serious. "Yesterday the dead is gone" doesn't appear in the original lyrics of "Help me Make it Through the Night," "Your Cheatin' Heart" was made for a more maudlin sense of loss than Torrens seems to appreciate and the strangulated semi-yodel that besets Torrens in the middle of "Spanish Eyes" might just fool a pet lover into believing a treasured animal was suffering somewhere in the house. The set here would easily have passed muster as live entertainment where beers and South American food were consumed in the mid-seventies. But it is cruelty and/or comedy to expose these thin productions and eccentric interpretations to a generation used to hearing Autotuned vocals and fat sounds, even on the tightest recording budgets. Torrens sounds for all the world like a politically incorrect comedy stereotype of a Latin singer. He isn't. To be fair, the female backing chorus and lead guitar throw in some moments of inspiration, notably on Torrens ill-advised rendering of the blues standard "Summertime."

Torsofuck:
Erotic Diarrhoea Fantasy
(Goregiastic, 2004)
What? Full-on goregrind meets full underwear.

Clearly some see erotic potential where the rest of us just see the need to use Immodium and the strongest biological washing agents. The revolving line up and low key fortunes of Finnish goregrind gods Torsofuck took a swift upturn when the band managed to produce cover art work, a title and lyrics so shamelessly sick they stood out, even in the feast of fetishism and full-on shock tactics seen at the extreme end of the metal business. If goregrind has passed you by it is worth noting that the music typically combines the growling vocal pyrotechnics of thrash or death metal with a fascination for horror imagery and sampled sounds from horror movies. Goregrinders generally pack a sense of humour with the sensual assaults so it's best not to take to heart Torsofuck's cover art of snogging oriental youngsters, apparently sitting in the fetid results of her faecal incontinence. Similarly the song titles and lyrics are worth a chuckle, lining up nine sonic sledgehammers in just over 30 minutes, Torsofuck offer up:

- Mutilated For Sexual Purposes,
- Erotic Diarrhoea Fantasy,
- Fistfucking Her Decomposed Cadaver,
- Worm Infested Anal,
- Raped by Elephants,
- Pussy Mutilation,
- Snuffed Freak,
- Four Legged Whore,

and

- Cannibal.

The title track details an orgy so filthy it would be likely to attract flies from miles around, it ends with the puzzling: 'Suddenly I woke up, it was only a dream But why was I covered with diarrhoea?'

Dunno Pal, but your mum is sure to be mad when she strips the bed!

Elsewhere there's comic book fun aplenty with lines like: 'Extremely huge load of elephant sperm filled my throat,' (Raped by Elephants) and 'What a perfect sight to see/ Decomposed dead bitch' (Worm Infested Anal). These – bear in mind – are the milder lines in a stupendous sicko-fest that sees sexual potential where others smell waste and decay. They could use the excuse of "consenting adults" but most of the sexual partners described in song died before the action started. Others are dumb animals. Both forms of unions offer the same obvious compensations. Apart from anything else, a date night is always likely to be cheap. Just as well when the chance of earning cash via radio plays or massive CD sales is virtually non-existent.

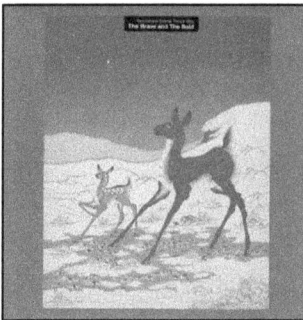

Tortoise and Bonnie 'Prince' Billy: The Brave and the Bold
(Domino, 2006)
What? A covers album from two great song-writing acts.

The world is full of covers albums but this one still packs a punch, an inconsistent one, but a punch for sure. Post-rock pioneers Tortoise know their soundscapes inside out, Bonnie "Prince" Billy has an eclectic history of vivid and individual songs of his own. His vocals, Tortoise' musicianship and a slew of tracks strongly identified from well-known performances elsewhere make for strange and sometimes compelling listening. At its best this album reinvents material to the point it sounds like their own originals, the best example – arguably – a melancholy and hugely under-stated re-imagining of Bruce Springsteen's "Thunder Road." Stripped of the original bravado it's a view of America more often seen in low-budget independent movies. By contrast the harsh sounding and deliberately clunky re-working of Elton John's "Daniel" strips the original soul and casts the song as a basic hit-by-numbers piece of formula pop. The Brave and the Bold works because it is brave and bold in seeking out song-choices fainter hearts wouldn't dare touch. Often these are songs of passion and individuality strongly identified with their original creators. The musical distance between Richard Thompson's "Calvary Cross" and Devo's "That's Pep" could be measured in light years, but their respective covers on this collection work equally well, and stand up so strongly that any knowledge of the originals tends to inform the listener rather than distract them. It's not an easy listen, reviews (both press and public) were mixed, but in a world awash with needless cover versions, this is a brave and bold attempt to make a distinctive album.

Tortura:
The Sounds of Pain and Pleasure
(Bondage Records, 1965)
What? Nightmares on whacks.

There are probably only two things we need to note about this collection. Firstly, it is what it appears to be, an album's worth of the sounds of dominatrix action, whipping, moaning, screaming and crying. All of this tastefully arranged in 21 short tracks with variations to suit your taste, moaning man, moaning woman, whipping and pain, whipping and pleasure…All very user friendly and none of it requiring any great expertise to understand what's going on. There's a little bit of music. In fact there's some musical merit to the cheery jazz piano that accompanies the female moaning and sharp inhalations of the lady being beaten on track 21. But this is a bondage album, pure and simple. Singing along to The Sounds of Pain and Pleasure isn't like singing along to the more musical efforts that make up most of this book.

Secondly, since the CD reissue hasn't begun to rear its head in rumour columns anywhere we've noticed, we should mention that #129 of the 365 Days Project (9th May 2007), offers the whole downloadable album. Ironically, a position that sees it nestling next to the long playing effort by Dame Barbara Cartland, the irony is surely intentional, so BIG RESPECT to WFMU who arranged that! Mixtape gold, maybe, but only if you know your audience intimately.

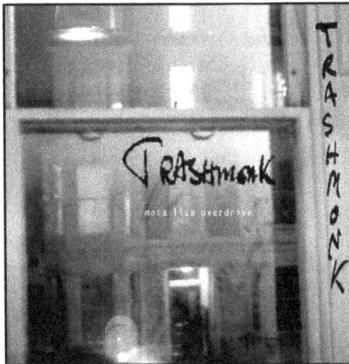

Trashmonk:
Mona Lisa Overdrive
(Creation, 1999)
What? Ambient, indie, psych slew of strangeness and deep emotion.

For "Ambient, indie…" read, basically, very good, very varied and, ultimately, very individual. The same description laid out above could be shorthand for self-indulgent formless shite of the worst kind. Nick Laird Clowes aka Trashmonk has worked in and around the music industry as a member of The Dream Academy, composer and consultant on film soundtracks and lyricist contributing to Pink Floyd's The Division Bell in 1994. This, to date the only album in the guise of Trashmonk, has been released twice in slightly different guises, a 2001 reissue offering additional tracks and a lengthy period of silence in the bonus "Mr Karma" leading to a hidden ending. Mona Lisa Overdrive is mostly, a slow somnambulant stroll. Laird Clowes sings through a heavily treated vocal mix putting a distance between his lyrics and the listener, and presenting a character clearly dealing with emotional troubles, and slowly revealing his feelings. The opening "Girl I Used to Know" sets the tone, with a pedestrian beginning before the bulk of the instrumentation arrives after two minutes. The album exists in a dark musical netherland, drawing on a range of sounds. "Girl I Used to Know" employs a mournful and strangely effective banjo. The subsequent "Polygamy" is a shuffling but insistent cousin of Primal Scream's more soulful moments and the softer outings, like the closing "On the Way Home", are quiet and introspective to the point of being wilfully impenetrable. To listen hard and grasp their meanings is only to discover they never intended to reach out to you in the first place. Mona Lisa Overdrive is a beautifully crafted collection that survives the magpie mentality of grasping at every available sound as required. The variety extends to a jarring insistent drumming and Arabic style female wailing vocal on

"N.W.O." The album's success relies on the strong sense that Trashmonk remains in control and intent on channelling his, often, dark and sombre sensibilities. Online reviewers have referenced The Blue Nile, Spiritualized, Nick Drake and The Beatles. A hard listen to Mona Lisa Overdrive would easily reveal the passages each reviewer had in mind. Similarly, an exploration of titles and lyrics would reveal the album shares a title with a William Gibson book. All of these points give the work some context, but Mona Lisa Overdrive has a mordant beauty of its own.

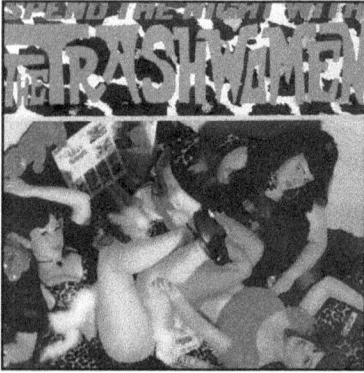

The Trashwomen:
Spend the Night With The Trashwomen
(Estrus, 1993)
What? Sublime she-surf guitar assault.

Latter day surfniks were not exactly in short supply in the 1990s, some of those not already convinced to give the genre a go soon jumped aboard the bandwagon when the Pulp Fiction soundtrack put the sounds back in the charts. Much 90s surf rocks along credibly but betrays its modern lineage with the odd pulled punch musically and a smoother production than the original analogue heroes of this world could have dreamed of. The Trashwomen escape that trap, and a few others, with the brutally short and blissfully brainless debut collection. Superficially the fact an all-girl group did this was of fleeting interest. So, having mentioned that, let's talk about an incendiary album.

There are several reasons why Spend the Night With… simply works. Combining covers with originals, surf trash with three chord thrash punk was always likely to be a winner. Having drawn on two genres that benefit from minimal budgets and maximum energy The Trashwomen set about creating work in the spirit of The Trashmen (if you hadn't sussed the origin of the name it's worth noting that this lot originally formed for a gig which involved playing a set of Trashmen covers).

The Trashmen, and their ilk, are a perfect touchstone for an album that assaults your eardrums, beats you up and clears off just as you register what's going on. Like the trashier end of the sixties, Spend the Night With The Trashwomen forever threatens to fall apart but just holds together its varied elements long enough to hit the target. The dirt-cheap production doesn't do the shrieking and – occasionally – tuneless vocals any favours, but since a lot of what matters vocally is down to repeated choruses and phrases the damage is minimal. The best surf combines the moronic and sublime and in this department The Trashwomen have the perfect combination. Tina Lucchesi (drums) and Danielle Pimm (bass) had barely mastered the basics when this album was cut and their thud,thud/thud again backing makes this a stomper to rank with anything produced at the time.

Their luck in securing the superlative fret skills of guitarist Elka Zolot is the one element that takes Spend the Night With… into the stratosphere. Zolot's ability to curl a riff over the thumping backing and find the right flick of a note between vocals ties everything here together. She's as adept with punk as she is strutting out front in a surf guitar instrumental and prime-period Dick Dale or Link Wray are comparisons worth making when she lets rip in their style. Her deft delivery of "Peter Gunn" is a standout here, whilst a cover of The Starfire's "Space Needle" suggests the trio did their homework well. Insistent, incendiary and inspired riffs spill often enough from the speakers to give The Trashwomen a toe-hold on cult status – something helped with their own self-mythologizing on a track like Zolot's "I'm Trash." The woeful obscurity that befell this, their first and best release, makes it all the more worthwhile if you do manage to track it down.

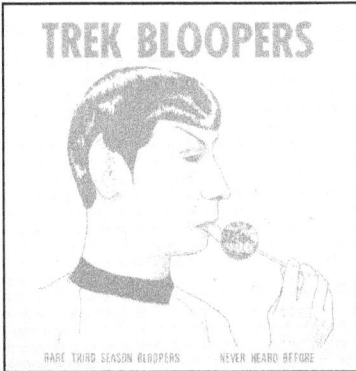

Trek Bloopers
(Blue Bear Bootleg, 197?)
What? Beam me up Scotty, I just fucked up my lines!

This undated bootleg of missed cues, forgotten lines and other on-set calamities appears to date from the early seventies. Obviously, these are original recordings of Kirk, Spock, Scotty and their mates attempting to boldly go into a nailed first take. That much is clear from the familiar voices, audio tracks referencing the scene numbers and dialogue familiar to trekkies. Indeed, for real trekkies this is double gold, a rare insight into the production process and a unique chance to hear some original lines and intonations that never made it to the final cuts. Track 24 on the original side two, for example, amounts to two slightly differing runs through the line: "You must accept the reality, you are insane Dr Lester" locating it squarely in the episode Turnabout Intruder, (#24 from series three if you want to be that anal), in which Captain Kirk's body is taken over by an insane scientist, Janice Lester (cue major acting opportunity for William Shatner!).

For the most part the bloopers on offer amount to snatches of dialogue, occasional corpsing and some mild swearing when things go wrong. Occasionally the actors nail a decent performance only to be interrupted by direction and told to "cut" or try things a different way. As mix tape gold this is hard to beat, though as a listening experience it remains bitty and fairly random. The original reel to reel tapes were apparently retrieved from a skip so the album's compilers had only what could be snatched. Anyone intent on using the album to deepen an understanding of the original Star Trek series would be well advised to acquaint themselves with the aforementioned Turnabout Intruder as well as Whom Gods Destroy, The Way To Eden, and Let This Be Your Last Battlefield. All 58 bloopers come from one of these episodes and all episodes from the final series.

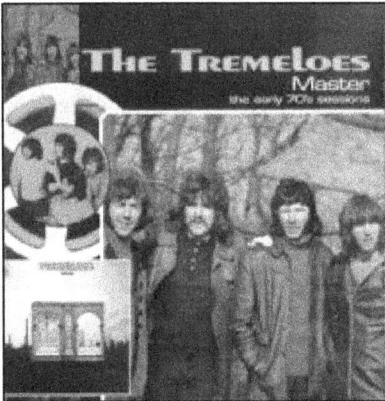

The Tremeloes:
Master
(CBS, 1970)
What? Overlooked pop classic and/or legendary suicide note by British pop institution.

To be brutally honest this one probably doesn't live up to the over-blown billing it has enjoyed in rock legend over the years. But it is worth investigation for all that. If casual music fans know anything about this collection they recall that the band followed up the one big hit single it contains, "Me and My Life," with an interview for Melody Maker in which they indicated they were about to leave their cheery pop sound for more challenging musical climes. In the course of the interview they branded their audience – mainly of nice teenage girls, little given to massive drug binges or large-scale promiscuity – as, depending on the version of the story you believe: "silly suckers," or "morons." This was 1970, the hippie caravan had come and, largely, gone but prog-rock, heavy-rock and a range of other highly serious avenues were opening up. Having parted company with Brian Poole, their one-time leader, "Me and My Life" had given The Tremeloes their ninth UK top twenty hit, but the band were frustrated.

They wanted the respect that came with "rock" and the Melody Maker interview was the first salvo in the battle to convince everyone they had the musical chops to live alongside the best. Lyrically Master makes a lot of the right noises, exploring the depths of a relationship, the way the world is etc. and generally coming off as concerned and in touch, though the lighter idealism of say – Graham Nash – is a better reference point than the full-on revolution of John Lennon.

Musically Master is a different animal. It probably tries too hard to visit every station on the line of rock credibility and the overall effect is more of a showcase than any coherent collection making a statement. When it works, it works well. "Boola Boola" is a glorious piece of jump-about instrumental nonsense driven forward by some impressive psych-rhythm guitar. "Before I Sleep" is a pristine little gem reflecting on impending fatherhood – the child about to be born, incidentally, turned out to be Chesney Hawkes! The obligatory, (well, for the time it was obligatory), hint at madness comes with "Willow Tree" easily the most intense musical interlude that ends with manic laughter, leading to the final track, and the only big hit on offer "Me and My Life." In the end, some punches are pulled, even "Willow Tree" clocks in at a Tremeloe-like and radio friendly three and half minutes. And the band can't help themselves for the most part, frequently layering their heavy sounds on top of cheerfully choppy guitars and verse-chorus-verse structures. But they can play, and the musicianship, electric and acoustic, stands up well without the aid of any session help. Not that anyone much cared at the time. Their old fans deserted them in droves, the rock crowd had never rated them and saw no reason to try. Master didn't trouble the charts and its closing track proved to be the band's final foray into the UK top 20.

Like The Turtles' Battle of the Bands or David Cassidy's The Higher They Climb…this is a collection that ends up showing you how much stylistic ground one act can cover. It may not have too much to say that will change your life, but the way it says it is worth a listen.

Trio:
Trio
(Mercury, 1981)
What? Understated avant-pop gets seriously under-rated because of novelty hit.

Trio's wilfully moronic "Da Da Da" is one of those instantly recognisable hits that became so ubiquitous that it obscured pretty much everything else its creators achieved. Trio's second album; and the one that shifted a few copies in the wake of "Da Da Da" is a stripped down slice of alternative avant-pop that communicates humour, hellishly good ideas and a willingness to challenge most accepted wisdom on how to make great pop music. You'll know after 30 seconds if you're on board with their thinking. A brilliantly alternative guitar solo (i.e. it's short, technically poor and you get the feeling throughout they know what they're doing) heralds the opening "Achtung Achtung" where it is joined by a megaphone-howled "Achtung, Achtung." What would have been the prelude to a progressive epic in other hands then stumbles to a halt and you realise that guitar/shouted warning combo is the whole track. "Ja Ja Ja" follows, setting up the sound that will see us through most of the album. Guitar, vocal and drums, tunes so minimal as make a virtue of shifting sounds between the two main instruments and vocal and a production that leaves in the rough edges and forces the resulting clatters and buzzing up front as part of the experience. "Ja Ja Ja" – like most of the album – uses German lyrics, and minimal ones at that, though it does break into English towards the end. The repeated mantras, best demonstrated by the punky twists of "Ja Ja Ja" are discussed in a rave review of the album on Julian Cope's Head Heritage site wherein it is concluded: "German is the best language for minimalist chanting." To most English-hearing/speaking ears it's a vital point because that is how Trio will be experienced.

Trio hit their highest profile around the same time as Laurie Anderson's "O Superman" was a hit and whilst the two acts sound very unalike there are worthwhile comparisons to be made. Both produced a form of pop that included within itself a challenge to everything pop stood for. They both did this at a time of some identity crisis for music (with pop and rock markets busy trying to figure out what they stood for in the wake of new wave and the emerging electro scene), and both acts produced a music that worked on its own terms but still sounded alternative and challenging despite employing a lot of standard pop and rock structures.

In Trio's case this philosophy is writ large over the 14 tracks of the album. It's Krautrock in the reliance on electronic sound, repetition and sonic collisions between a few instruments rather than instrumental skill. It's pop in the insanely simple tunes, effortlessly catchy lyrical lines and its repeated attempts to distract you with novelty and grab your attention. But, it's also hellishly clever in taking this pop approach and applying it to something so monumentally minimal that it mocks itself as it goes. The cover – worth a Google if you've never seen it – is a cardboard square with scrawled titles. So, all told, this is punk attitude, even when it sounds nothing like punk.

Trio works its way manfully through the complicated dynamics above and adds to the impact by sequencing the tracks to deliver a few massive surprises towards the end; all of which appear perfectly designed to kick any sense of complacency out of the listener. Three tracks into side two "Nur Ein Traum" packs an incendiary blues riff (where the fuck did that come from?!) and explains itself (mainly) in English so it's easy to figure out the title means "Just A Dream." Later on the band cover Lee Dorsey's "Ya Ya" sticking within their accustomed clanking/ low-fi world but bringing enough loose soul into the arrangement to suggest they have the chops to break out anytime they see fit.

Trio walks that novelty/ we're clever and just messing line so expertly that the entire collection often has that differently abled and sporadically explosive confidence of an art school performance. In that context the band are somewhere within the same mindset as Laurie Anderson and Joe Dolce (no, seriously, he was taking the piss, he's a respected artist with a nut-case sense of humour). Though, you'll hear very little on Trio that sounds like Laurie Anderson, Dolce or many other products of art school. You will hear an ending to side two in which the band finish "Danger Is" by screaming madly, suggesting – maybe – they're only in the studio because humanity needs protecting from them, before a closing half-minute fragment (echoing the opening fragment) features a live recording from the end of the gig with the name "Trio" being howled out to an appreciative crowd to the tune of "The Banana Boat Song." As a complicating factor the "Da Da Da" hit was added to some pressings of the album (making it blindingly obvious that their cover of "Ya Ya" is pretty-much a dry run for the hit), and "Da Da Da" also found its way onto copies of Bye Bye (1983) or – as the third album was called in the USA: Trio & Error. Confused? You will be. But just take the message that these capers suggest Mercury Records' staff – confronted with albums like Trio and the unlikely world wide hit single – spent office time looking at each other and thinking: "what the hell do we do with these guys?"

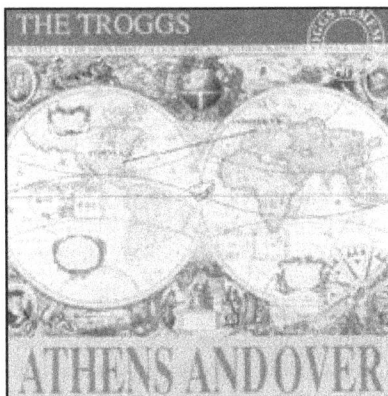

The Troggs:
Athens Andover
(Rhino, 1992)
What? Perfect synthesis of masters and pupils?

The question posed by the "perfect synthesis" point is who (Troggs or REM), are the masters? Truthfully nobody is in charge, everyone mucks in, and the "band" here amounts to eight people and a bit of additional help. The worst thing about this collaboration, from the point of view of it getting the due recognition it deserves, is that it is a really good album. Some collaborations, for example Metallica mixing it with Lou Reed on Lulu, find egos colliding and the resultant collision damage forming moments of spectacular success and failure. Others simply see people going through the motions. REM and The Troggs, basically, get on, do the job superbly and produce a glorious halfway house of a collection showcasing the talents of all concerned. The Troggs inspired REM (who duly covered "Love is All Around" and stuck it on a B-side). The two combined to produce a classic old school line up of decent songs, varying sounds, perfect sequencing and much merit. This is three quarters of REM, plus touring REMster Peter Holsapple, plus The Troggs. Produced as REM entered their high-profile pomp and Britpop rediscovered the sixties, Athens Andover seemed slightly out of time. More understated and down to earth than REM and not as brash or blatantly chart driven as Britpop, the album earned respect rather than rapture. It's way better than that. For starters, REM get a great sound and The Troggs' are showcased perfectly. Each additional instrument and tweak of the sound supports the individual songs and Reg Presley, in particular, emerges as a singer of character. His lived in voice, and unfussy fronting of a tight band gives Athens Andover a companionable and experienced feel, more chummy than world weary, and all-the-better because it offers insights without attempting to explain the world. The notable stand out, "Nowhere Road," is written by the three REMs and Holsapple, but The Troggs' contributions, notably Presley's "Together," "Suspicious" and "Don't you Know" aren't far behind. The original 11 songs were reissued with an impressive tonnage of outtakes later but the one merit of the initial release is its perfect positioning, halfway between classic, nail 'em and move on, Troggs' albums and REM's well realised but essentially commercial late eighties/early nineties collections.

Athens Andover is, therefore, a classic piece of rock/pop produced by masters of the art. It belongs in no time, and sounds good up against any original collection by a good, old school, guitar/drums/bass/voice band. It may be credited to The Troggs, but Athens Andover showcases the brand of inspiration, vision, sweat and professionalism that underpins the best of REM too.

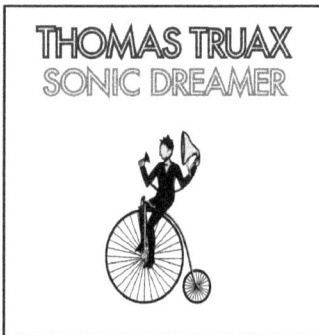

Thomas Truax:
Sonic Dreamer
(Psycho Teddy, 2010)
What? If Beck didn't give a toss about his record sales...

A compatriot of Beck from the early days of the anti-folk movement in the 1990s, Thomas Truax was raised in the USA but moved to the UK in the 21st century and has carved a truly unique niche in the singer songwriter/outsider music market. Truax (pronounced Troo-aks) is one of those hard to categorise artists who tends to make sense when, and only when, heard over a long playing work or watched throughout a performance. Writing and performing songs is the basis of his act but that simple observation does little to explain why he is truly unique amongst his peers.

Truax' approach to the sonic possibilities of his art has taken a very personal route. Some songwriters take on the costs of a backing band, others strip down their sound to perform solo. Truax has forged a middle ground in which he has invented his own instruments to provide very particular sounds. His most useful invention is, arguably, The Hornicator a contraption crafted from the horn of an old gramophone and played with a ringed finger to provide a clicking beat, and fingers to create a bass-drum thud. Having started with the lowest technology, Truax then builds tracks on stage by looping Hornicator beats through a pedal and layering more sounds on top.

The simplest implements, including rubber bands, have also provided backing sounds for Truax' songs. The end result on albums like Sonic Dreamer is a music that leaves every track sounding like a well-crafted and highly individual sonic adventure. In this context Truax might be more at home at a craft festival or arts fair than in the modest concert halls he plays to his devoted fan base.

What he has lost in his quest is any sense of having a single winning sound, or well-honed and definitive style. What he has gained is the ability to produce albums that burst with ideas and tend to sound fresh on repeated listening. Sonic Dreamer is probably as accessible and – though the word tends not to be used in discussing Truax – commercial sounding as he will ever get. He certainly skims a range of styles over 11 tracks, the insistence and energy of "Beehive Heart" showcases his own unique percussive styles, "It Always Rains on Sundays" is a glorious piece of whimsy about copping a sickie and brooding over a break-up with your girl. There's surreal comedy in "The Cannibals Have Captured Nicole Kidman," the title track is an instrumental showcase of dazzling variety and the low-key "Lonely Taxi" shows he can mix it with the best tear-jerking songwriters.

The Twiggs:
20,000 Leaves Under the Tree
(Solipsist, 1994)
What? Criminally neglected Cumbrian psych-pop power trio

For all that the early to mid-nineties get bracketed as Britpop's time it is worth remembering that other sounds and styles hung in there very strongly. Psychedelia painted a massive stripe through Britpop's pillaging of the rock roots laid down by The Who, the early Beatles and The Kinks. Madchester maintained itself with a vengeance too and if The Happy Mondays had long forgotten what day of the week it was The Charlatans had a heady collision of recycled sixties ideas and their very own mix of dance, pop and rock. The NME could generally be found praising the slightest squeak from Teenage Fanclub and there was always Kula Shaker…oft derided but radio friendly unit shifters of the highest order.

So basically, you couldn't go wrong with the right roots back then. Well, you could if you were The Twiggs. Cumbria's finest wrote an album's worth of effortlessly catchy tunes, toured in support of Echo and the Bunnymen and generally impressed the people who saw them. The trio made enough noise for a four-piece and managed to recycle the roots that had made others into household names into a series of songs that came over as fresh, ambitious, insistent and – basically – winning.

They earned Radio One plays and the NME certainly got it with 20,000 Leaves Under the Tree invoking the name of the mighty Big Star in discussing The Twiggs' strengths. It is a fair point, the album opens with "Fast Number One" and within the first minute we're into a halt in the verse, a shimmering guitar chord and the kind of rising and falling melody line that makes Big Star a timeless listen. Lyrically the Twiggs collided bright psychedelic visions with the hint of something northern, very assured and faintly cynical. Musically they nailed a handful of winning influences, threw in a sense of a band absolutely unafraid of its own inventiveness and turned in a first album to be proud of. "Fly So Hard" drives ahead with a punk insistence and takes the brakes off for an improbably simple vocal refrain, "Beaming In" escapes into fully-fledged psychedelia and comes back totally sure of itself, "California Rain" pulls the northern English ironically dreaming of America trick to perfection.

The fact that 20,000 Leaves…now rests in obscurity and lives in only a few hundred memories is another tragedy, if only because this band so obviously had it. Their Cumbrian origins didn't help and Solipsist Records were based in the heaving home of media opportunities that is Galashiels, in the Scottish Borders. But blaming the locals for trying their best isn't really the point here.

A decade later MySpace and YouTube would have given this band a better chance. As a footnote to this story a decade later the world did wake up to a band with similar ideas and similar talent. British Sea Power had chosen to make their home in Brighton, though the band draws some of its membership from Kendal, Cumbria…very close to Twiggland.

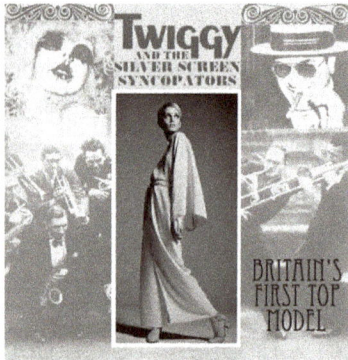

Twiggy and the Silver Screen Syncopaters: Twiggy and the Girlfriends
(Ember, 1972)
What? Very thin concept, variable results.

S'cuse the blatant plug here but…during a production get together for Miskin Radio's Strange Fruit show this album was playing. Neil Nixon was weighing up which of the two single B-sides might be used on the show. A discussion ensued about the twenty first century fashion for ageing artists to get out there and play "classic" albums from end to end. Neil wondered aloud what would happen if artists of that vintage were obliged to get out there and play end to end sets of the albums they wished they'd never made, and the public had never bought? Would anyone show up, and, if so, would they listen without prejudice or just throw things at the stage?

Respect to this collection which prompted that debate. It hasn't prompted much other respect or debate. Record Collector magazine, commenting on a CD reissue under the title of Britain's First Top Model, stated: "what we have here are the four sides she cut for Ember to cash in on her sudden worldwide fame back in '66/67, and the remaining eight cues are trad/Boyfriend-style ragtimey Charleston numbers that were composed for the subsequent Ember cash-in album following the success of said film… Her career as a model was far more fabulous."

In other words, it's likely that the limited sales enjoyed by the original collection included a few where feckless punters mistook this flagrant cash in for the genuine soundtrack album to her movie, The Boyfriend. That soundtrack preceded this album. By the time the CD reissue appeared there was a cover concept, about Twiggy being a star model, that bore no relation to the bulk of the music.

Having duly lambasted the recording career of a British national treasure, the least we can do is redress the balance in two areas. Firstly, Twiggy does have some feel for music and her subsequent re-emergence in the mid-seventies betrayed her love of singer/songwriter work (her daughter was named after Carly Simon). Two albums worth of material showed her ably acquitting herself at material lodged somewhere on the borderlands of folk rock and straight country.

She's also managed dance/pop and show tune recordings with some distinction. Secondly, the original pop songs on this particular collection are worthy curios with odd tempos, slightly strange melodies and an engagingly befuddled performance from the star herself. She, apparently, dislikes the results, but they do have the kind of faux, unintended, outsider charm displayed by a few other recordings in this book.

As an end to end listening experience this album is a strangely schizoid experience that does no favours to any of the participants. Its twenty first century relaunch under the spurious guise of representing Twiggy's place in history, simply deepens the hole, prepared for profits from a cynical cash in, already excavated in 1972.

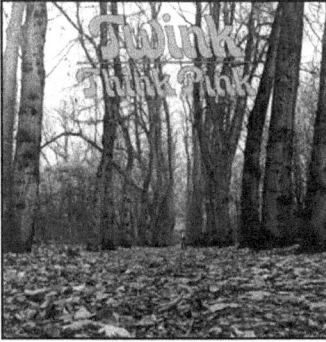

Twink:
Think Pink
(Polydor (UK)/ Sire (US), 1970)
What? "probably the last high-water mark of old-school psychedelia the moment before it gave up the ghost" – The Seth Man, posting on Julian Cope's site: Head Heritage/ "Spacey but piercing psychedelia" – Jello Biafra

Another of those period pieces overlooked on release and subsequently accorded cult status on the back of an uncompromising artistic vision. Well, that, or this star-studded effort – various Pink Fairies and Deviants and Steve Peregrine Took of Tyrannosaurus Rex – is such an obvious drug fest that most people now listening wish they'd been in the room when it, like, went down, Man! Think Pink comfortably visits both extremes of opinion above, packing enough in terms of songs and – just about – coherent vision to suggest everyone had some kind of plan. There is enough quality in the production to give the oddest flurries strong expression and enough random diversions of snatched conversation and strange effects (like a backward sitar) to make Think Pink a unique listen. The opening brace "The Coming of the Other One" and "Ten Thousand Words Inside a Cardboard Box" (the latter a Twink song previously released by The Aquarian Age) are damn near perfect. The opener using layered effects and spoken words to intone some sense of insanity and "Ten Thousand Words…" storming in with a killer tune to make it clear the madness is accompanied by good music. Three years later Pink Floyd's Dark Side of the Moon would pull a similar stunt at the start. From which point on Think Pink covers the trippy gamut and seldom lets the quality slip. "Rock and Roll the Joint," a two and a half minute chug along through some basic blues/acid rock moves probably in praise of whatever – ahem – large cigarette was being passed around at that very moment, is about as bad as it gets. Think Pink stops well short of 40 minutes and delivers at least two other genuine psych showstoppers in "Tiptoe on the Highest Hill" and "Suicide." The first of which is a gentle gem that builds its blissful mood to perfection, the second a style-changing slice of psych pop/rock sitting in the centre of side two that switches codes so readily as to mock any notions of being able to pigeonhole the album. The contrast between these and the throwaway material, like a barely coherent attempt to tell the classic story of the three little pigs, is part of the period charm of the whole piece. Think Pink goes far enough into madness and drug-fuelled cul-de-sacs as to come over as the real deal, and ventures frequently enough into brilliant songs as to be – fleetingly – awesome. That well known Amazon customer "a reviewer" asserts of "Tiptoe on the Highest Hill:" "all we can do is allow ourselves to be transported by the musical waves that wash over us. Perhaps this is even THE BEST SONG OF ALL TIME - tall order, I know, but just possibly, this is it." That is not an opinion typically shared by most music fans or critics still respected for their opinions, but Think Pink still enjoys rabid devotion and sporadic reissues (a UK reissue appeared in 2013).

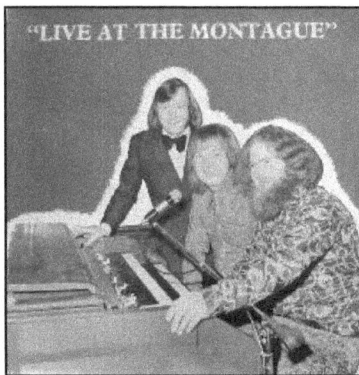

The Two Petes:
Live at the Montague Arms
(Private Release, 1981)
What? Pub rock (veering from prog to novelty), unique in almost every way possible.

We could bang on about this, but, in truth the glory for finding and sharing this gem belongs entirely to Scott Taylor who thought to offer it to the 365 Days Project where – as of this writing – it sits at #195 in the 2007 list (July 14th). Scott's accompanying description has been filleted to provide the following outline: "a friend insisted that I accompany him to a pub in New Cross, South East London, to see a duo called The Two Pete's. Comprising a blind keyboard player with more synths than Rick Wakeman and a drummer with a kit matched in scale only by his beard, my friend assured me that The Two Pete's launched themselves at popular classics with such individuality and gusto that a good night out was guaranteed...Recorded before the drinkers and ably supported by a selection of guest singers drawn from the crowd, the performances veer from the wayward to the excruciating to the downright bizarre. However, the warmth and the enthusiasm of all concerned is self evident...I have a particular fondness for the good kicking meted out to Macarthur Park - the helpful addition of a Prog Rock style synth solo and a segue into Popcorn surely improve on the original."

The present authors would add that "Nobody's Child" within which Pete on keyboard and vocals channels Otis Redding and Pete on drums appears, fleetingly, to think he is Carl Palmer is another mash of merit, whilst the inclusion of two minutes and 21 seconds of "The Yodelling Song" takes the menagerie of musical styles into territory seldom charted by similar pub rockers. A seven and a half minute "Bee Gees Medley" is another highly dramatic highlight, keyboard/vocal Pete, apparently convinced he is dying in the New York Mining Disaster before both Petes engineer a short, funereal, ending. The closest the set comes to a reverent cover is when a female singer joins the pair to reprise the unaccompanied arrangement of "After the Goldrush" made into a UK hit by the band Prelude. Pete and Pete harmonise with minimal embellishment and show their softer side to good effect.

The internet was surely made for such rediscoveries, we salute those who made this one possible.

Ultramarine:
Every Man and Woman is a Star
(Rough Trade, 1992)
What? Fictional canoe journey re-imagined as ambient, electro dream.

Paul Hammond and Ian Cooper make up the British electro/dance combo Ultramarine, purveyors of a pristine and vivid brand of dance sounds throughout most of the 90s, and sporadically active since then. Ultramarine specialise in magpie-like raids on musical genres during which they sample the sounds that make each style unique before recycling them in largely instrumental albums. Their works typically sparkle with production effects and shimmering keyboard passages. Their real genius is the combination of characterful production sounds, and the sampling of material that shows an affinity with the production work of several unsung producers of the past.

Every Man and Woman...which was released twice, a 12 track version in 1991 on Brianiac Records and the 14 track Rough Trade version the following year, is – arguably – their masterwork. To call this dance is to miss the point, Every Man and Woman... packs insistent and looping rhythms but overlays them with the unlikeliest of samples and sets up the kind of ambience that will have you dancing in your chair, assuming you're using this as background music as you go about work. Some of the samples here trawl very unlikely territory for ambient/dance. The Eagles' opening bass-figure from "One of These Nights" intrudes at one point and folk-rock in the form of the jangling guitar refrain from "Rainy Day" from the first America album is also at the centre of another track. There are solid drum tracks throughout but the acoustic instruments, lilting keyboard melodies and the mass of samples dating back to analogue productions and warm intimate recording sounds give the album its character.

The band mentioned the "curious woody production" sound of early America in an interview at the time and also indicated Every Man and Woman… described an imaginary canoe journey downstream. That concept and a fleeting prose fragment in the packaging notes about a blissful night drinking with Dewey, (presumably Dewey Bunnell; one third of the early America linc-up), set up the feel of a warm summer, slowly flowing water and a pace dictated as much by nature as the pre-set programming of Ultramarine's studio technology. The title comes from a phrase originally coined by Aleister Crowley and featured in his The Book of the Law.

Every Man and Woman… is a conundrum of construction, UK dance colliding with folk-rock, beats and rhythms colliding with nature, and above all a sense of soulfulness and bliss emerging from the unlikeliest corner of the early nineties music industry.

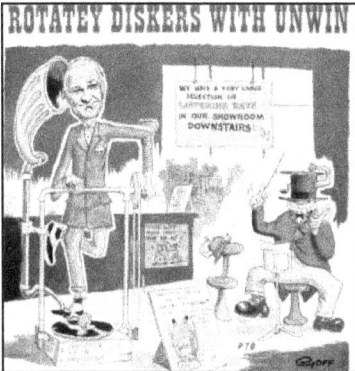

Stanley Unwin:
Rotatey Diskers
(Pye 1961/Spectrum, 2008)
What? Hi-de-Fido, artycraft and the populode of the musicolly, oh yes!

"Professor" Stanley Unwin was born in South Africa but established himself as one of the great comedy eccentrics of the twentieth century. Best-known to music fans for his spoken word contributions to the Small Faces' Ogden's Nut Gone Flake, Unwin's stock-in trade was to present lectures, interviews and the like in the spoken language of "Unwinese," a mangled, rhythmic and semi-penetrable version of English that frequently reduced key facts in his diatribes to vivid and surreal descriptions. Elvis Presley, for example, is described on Rotatey Diskers as "wasp-waist and swivel hippy." His only full-length original album released in 1961 combines some original monologues with three live tracks (which formed the second side of the original vinyl album). Basically, Stanley talks up a storm. The first side has the cleverer wordplay and each track shows signs of careful scripting, even if the hesitant delivery and basic production flatten a little of the comedy, but the trio of tracks that close the whole caper are a different experience. Recorded live at London's Astor Club, the "Professor" (which he wasn't, incidentally) holds forth on music and, in the final segment, answers questions from his live audience. This is the real gem, showing that Unwin's ability to invent this stuff in the moment and go where the laughs suggested he should go, was innate and his comic timing was natural. For all the dated subject matter ("What do you think of Elvis Presley?" "Will Frank Sinatra last?") the jokes and good-natured mirth of the night still hold up decades later.

Like all good comedy, Unwin's work packs authority and sense, even in the moments when both seem to have deserted the proceedings. Stan was 50 in the year of Rotatey Diskers' first release and his experience shows in the command he holds over the live audience. One of the best moments comes with the discussion of musical rhythms, having described a basic rhythm with a blast of surreal wordplay to rival his very best moments he points out to the man who asked him a question that the reply might seem a little obtuse, and just lets the moment hang. It's something of a revelation if only because it shows that behind the rabid eccentricity there lurked an intelligence capable of grasping all aspects of comedy, even the deadpan.

Stanley was also more media savvy than the image suggested. His discovery as an entertainer came when an ad-hoc broadcast he made whilst testing radio equipment was played to BBC producers. After a few pieces on radio Stanley's big break came when he had to fill in for an ailing Frankie Howerd on a live radio broadcast. Radio guest spots, television appearances and cameos in films all gave him a solid focus on the craft of comedy and by the time he cut Rotatey Diskers Unwin was a well-loved national figure, with an instantly identifiable style. He lived until 2002, though his work-rate gradually tailed off as he grew older.

His style hasn't so much dated as disappeared, probably because doing what he does on this album and making it sound so natural is a skill nobody else has managed to master half as well as Stanley.

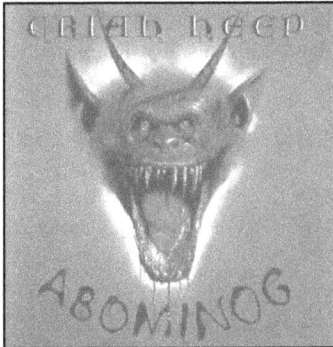

Uriah Heep:
Aboming
(Bronze, 1982)
What? Behold…The Resurrection!

The history of Uriah Heep has enough Spinal Tap moments to make for a good movie in its own right. The oft-derided UK prog/metallers are frequently reduced to a footnote by rock historians and critics. However a string of chart albums – notably in the UK and US – showed the band had the staying power and fan appeal many doubted. Their major problem throughout much of their early life had been finding the right niche. Heep albums could – by turns – sound like fully-fledged prog-rock, Zep-alike metal or well- crafted pop with harmonies. Basically, they rocked, and that was always the point, but the keyboards, operatic vocals and excursions into other forms of song-writing meant the focus tended to blur.

The changes in the music industry as the seventies turned to the eighties did Heep few favours. Their popularity in Germany and other bastions of traditional rock was the only consolation as the band fell apart and their stock sank, apparently without hope. By 1982 there was a band in name only and it had one member, founder/guitarist Mick Box. By his own admission; "I locked myself in my flat for two days and drank myself senseless in complete self-pity. But I somehow managed to pull myself together and consider my options." One option clearly on the table was to end Uriah Heep and send Box out as a guitar hero fronting The Mick Box Band. But the Heep mainman decided to have one more stab at keeping his band alive. Former Heep drummer Lee Kerslake had been a founding member of Ozzy Osbourne's Blizzard of Oz and had put a solid driving beat behind Ozzy's two opening solo albums. Box rang him, Kerslake brought in bassist Bob Daisley – who'd worked on the Ozzy albums as well – and the nucleus of a new line-up was in place. John Sinclair's keyboards and Pete Goalby's vocals completed the band.

The resulting Abominog broke several of the unwritten rules in the Heep book, half composed of cover versions, straight down the line in one style and clearly in touch with changes in the world rather than self-regarding, it was a surprise to critics and something of a surprise to the band when it began to generate hits. "That's the Way it is" hit #25 on the US rock charts, Heep's best placing ever on that list. Above all, Abominog is Box and Kerslake's album. Box blazes away on guitar in the emerging "hair metal" style, blitzing into a solo, changing voice occasionally, making his point and getting out whilst the listener is still thinking ahead to where he might go next. Kerslake's drumming clearly draws on his work with Ozzy Osbourne, always pushing the beat along, solid, unfussy, assured and packing the power to fill out the whole sound. Abominog rocks hard, and consistently, and sounds for most of the ten tracks that make up the original album like a band ten years their junior raised and schooled on US metal. Heep had played their own part in creating a world in which AC/DC's Back in Black was the template, Ozzy Osbourne was the king and short in-your-face metal anthems of Motley Crue were the manifesto. Abominog doesn't get its hands dirty enough to engage with all of these touchstones, but it belongs in their world and it sounds like solid eighties metal from its first note to its last.

It also revived a brand that was dead in the metal water. Given their reputation Heep would never be the critical or commercial darlings of the new decade, but when Glasnost opened up eastern Europe to western rock Heep played a major Russian gig, alongside PiL and Big Country. It was Heep's set that prompted the crowd riot, through nothing other than the sheer power of their music. That set was fuelled with the sound that started on Abominog and – for once – the music world looked on and marvelled. Heep continue to sell out arenas in those territories to this day.

U.S. Girls:
Gem
(Fat Cat, 2012)
What? Abrasive sound-artist goes mainstream and avoids sell-out, shocker!

Meghan Remy – who to all intents and purposes is U.S. Girls – started out in 2007 with an aural assault of an act based on old school reel-to-reel technology, percussive mixes that audiences felt as well as heard and vocal performances that pushed singing into the areas charted by Yoko Ono and those who have followed. The short journey in time to 2012's Gem took in a range of different sounds until Kraak (2011) began pillaging samples rather than just percussive mixes, and Gem completed the journey to radio playable sounds.

Percussion tracks remain at the heart of the U.S. Girls sound but producer Slim Twig helped Meghan fashion a sound that always suggested experiments, but ditched the most discordant banging and ear-jarring vocals. Songs like "North on 45" still use Remy's vocals as a sound effect as much as a lead instrument. Singing over stark piano chords and shuffling programmed percussion, her vocals are given enough echo and space to inhabit the whole sound; affecting the mood with her timbre as much as the story in the words. "Jack" pushes this particular envelope harder, with a drone-athon vocal that hints at the pleading teen-pop vocals of female pop singers and takes that particular notion to an extreme. At times it has a T.Rex (as in the British band) feel in the vocal warble, descending melody on the chorus and the rock 'n' roll influenced guitars.

Gem has a solid retro feel lacking on earlier U.S. Girls releases; evoking glam rock in its big drums, simple bass lines and slabs of guitar. "Slim Baby" is the star of this particular department of Gem, packing a Glitter Band thud (note: US readers may not be aware that imitating Gary Glitter borders on commercial suicide in the UK where the man's convictions for sex crimes involving children has made him a national disgrace – so Gem's venture into this territory made it a startling listen to some in the UK). "Work From Home" is one of a number of short pop-song cuts that builds the simple keyboard/drums package into such rhythmic insistence that early U.S. Girls are suggested, even if the sound is miles away from those challenging early tracks. It's also notable – and appropriate – that "I Don't Have a Mind of my Own," which thrashes away to open the album is the most like early U.S. Girls of any cut here.

As an exercise in selling in without compromising the ability to surprise, invent, challenge and comment Gem is up there with the works of acts like The Flaming Lips.

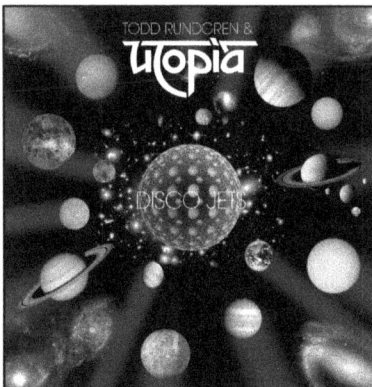

Utopia:
Disco Jets
(Esoteric, 2012)
What? "Great lost album" that was never really great, or lost.

Widely claimed to be recorded in 1976 Disco Jets finally saw a release in its own right in 2012. Whilst some claimed it as a great lost album that isn't totally the case. The whole album had been available officially since 2001 as part of a Lost Albums and Demos release and bootleg copies had circulated for many years before that. Rundgren himself has been unable to pinpoint exactly when Disco Jets was recorded and its main fascination over the years for his die-hard fan base has been its somewhat ramshackle quality and the fact it sounds like little else in Todd Rundgren/Utopia's varied and frequently experimental canon.

Rundgren's vagueness may well be down to the fact Disco Jets doesn't sound all that much like a finished album and its inconsistent lapses into disco, funk and prog sounds suggest a series of experiments and one-offs. Considering the hugely complex and somewhat po-faced progressive material Utopia released in the seventies Disco Jets' inclusion of the Star Trek theme and the full-on novelty "Cosmic Convoy" (basically a rip-off of C.W. McCall's country hit "Convoy" but set in space!) is out of character. Indeed, "Cosmic Convoy" is – more or less – a distant cousin of novelty tracks like The Firm's "Star Trekkin." Disco Jets has vocals, but not proper lead vocals. There are treated speech tracks in "Cosmic Convoy" and tracks like "Black Hole" incorporate shouts from the band. But basically, this is an instrumental record, packing short tracks for the most part ("Black Hole" despite the epic title and its instant sprint into prog-noodling still checks out after three and a quarter minutes) and presents a vision of Disco as imagined by fiercely intelligent musicians with instrumental talent to burn and an over-riding sense that all of the message should be in the music. In other words, there's little sense here of disco as the add-on to emerging gay culture or any other social scene. However, for all its geek-chic chops and its provisional quality Disco Jets is at its best when it (frequently) descends into knockabout fun, jokey melodies and shameless instrumental noodling for its own sake. Tracks like "Time Warp" (NOT the Rocky Horror classic; this is a sparky slice of jazz rock with a disco beat), and "Pet Rock" (named in honour of a passing fad) are pretty much where its childish and chuckling heart lies.

Dino Valente:
Dino Valente
(Epic, 1968)
What? Meandering and mainly mournful. Sole solo effort from Quicksilver mainstay.

Valente's work with The Quicksilver Messenger Service marks some of the greatest achievements of psychedelic rock and the San Francisco bay area sound. Valente's life was marked by a certain amount of self-mythologizing, and a lot of collaboration with others so this – his only solo album – is the closest his recording career takes us to the elusive man himself. In truth, Dino Valente (album) doesn't take you that close to Dino Valente (man). It does, however, provide some elliptical insights and a look into the process that allowed Valente to craft the songs that contributed massively to the San Francisco sound. A fairly obvious yardstick is the much more celebrated Oar by Alexander "Skip" Spence. Like Oar, Dino's solo effort has the intimate feel of work that verges on a collection of demos. For the most part Dino Valente is based on one lead vocal and one – twelve string - guitar, the stark sound being drenched in enough echo to make the guitar sound like a room full of sound and take the nasal edge off Valente's unaccompanied voice. Lyrically, this is also an intimate exploration of relationships, moods and the minor crises of life. Melodically it has a repetition and uniformity that makes much of Dino Valente sound like a lengthy exploration of particular period in the singer's life. So, it gives up its secrets slowly and with great reluctance, but frequently feels like a visit from a confused but cherished friend.

Oddly, we are soon into the most atypical cut – "Time" – with Dino accompanied by percussion and harpsichord. On this and a few other cuts Valente begins to explore the lengthy psych folk with odd time signatures that would – briefly – become the trademark territory of Tim Buckley. "Something New" – a lengthy piece with a jazzy feel – moves strongly into this area and "Listen to me" is a doomier piece along the same lines. Lyrically much of Dino Valente is personal, emotional and – apparently – directed at people and situations we can only guess at. "Listen to me" offers: "Listen to me girl and go find your mind, it's been so long runnin' babe and it's high flyin," and "Tomorrow" provides: "And baby we're just passing, we're only passing through, and it's lasting, as long as I can love you."

Time and again the lyrics hit on a momentary feeling or unresolved personal issue, giving Dino Valente an uncommercial but highly personal slant. The spirited "Tomorrow" which gets animated and packs something akin to a decent hook is about as radio friendly as Valente manages. But, this is a long way short of the soaring, insistent, power of Quicksilver at their best. Dino Valente is – probably – as honest and open as the man ever wanted to be, and as a portrait of a writer coming directly from the heart and focussing his work entirely on the things felt in a given moment, it is in the same territory as Spence and Buckley sr.

Van Der Graaf Generator: Pawn Hearts (Charisma, 1971)

What? "truly minging combinations of Brecht and primal scream therapy. This was rock'n'roll only because no other category would fit": Julian Cope

This book acknowledges the massive contribution made to promoting the strange and marginalised in music by Julian Cope's Head Heritage website, a repository of online reviews relating to sounds as eclectic and strange as those found between these covers. Cope's work in curating the menagerie is a service to humanity. The Copester retains some of his strongest praise for this particular three track prog excursion and doesn't so much write a review as provide an academic assessment of a work uncontainable within any one musical genre. Even "prog" is too narrow, and Cope's assessment that Pawn Hearts is rock by default is the best place to start.

A number of critics have been reduced to using the figurative possibilities of failure in the face of the massive slabs of sound, orchestral referenced rock arrangements and Peter Hamill's cod-operatic performance. In other words, their reviews make it clear they can't tell you what this is, they can only describe what they have found and leave you to marvel at the fact it exists at all. Attempting to make conclusive statements here is dangerous. The articulate Cope ably uses "extremely everything" and "fucking well weird" as the opening gambit in his assessment.

Pawn Hearts is best summed up by a later Cope comment: "punks in a prog-rock style." Fleeting snatches of the album have the prog hallmarks of difficult time signatures, needlessly complex noodling (often-apparently-for its own sake), on a variety of instruments, lyrics challenging enough to oblige repeated listenings and thumbing through a few large and pictureless books before sense emerges, and a few moments so singular and surprising they can ambush you long after you've stopped listening, erupting in your mind during idle moments. Beware, this is well heavy shit. It's not punkish by virtue of any short songs, rapid guitar chords or pogoable beats. It's punk because all of the prog traits above are deployed to assault your senses and question everything you know about music. VDGG come not to entertain, they come to point out the vacuity and pointlessness of much that passes for entertainment. In the great artistic tradition, they won't point the way. They'll go somewhere remote, and make a case for you to follow.

The remote places visited on Pawn Hearts are called "Lemmings," "Man-erg" and "A Plague of Lighthouse

Keepers," the final of which runs 23 minutes and amounts to a suite, not a mere song. As Pawn Hearts unleashes its multi-layered magic you will hear Peter Hammill adopt two different singing voices, performing a duet with himself (fitting since so much of the lyrical content appears to be an exploration of his own complex inner space). Incredibly, you'll also hear David Jackson perform a duet on saxophones, blowing two at once in a cacophony of focussed fury that manages to generate a melody and sonic assault – quite literally – in the same breath.

There are moments of strange beauty, notably when Hammill and the luminous keyboard are thrown to the fore in "Man-erg," and moments of furious solo expression on sax, keyboard and guitar. Two things conspicuous by their absence are hummable and catchy tunes and any sense that VDGG have the remotest intention of sounding like anyone else. "Lemmings" resembles a few of their contemporaries, All Music Guide cite Gentle Giant, but that's only because a few other bands dared some of the same journey as VDGG. One defining trait of Pawn Hearts is its ability to sound nothing like the highest profile and most progressive indulgences of the same period. Pawn Hearts rubs shoulders with Hawkwind's Space Ritual or ELP's Pictures at an Exhibition only because it sees ambition and refusal to compromise as central to making work of any value. King Crimson's discordant and dissonant vibe may be in the same territory as Pawn Hearts but, once again, you'd never mistake a few seconds of this for prime prog period Crimson. Pawn Hearts also presents a band with four front men, so Hugh Banton (keyboards) and Guy Evans (percussion) are integral to everything here. Lyrically the work is challenging, but the music matches every twist and turn of the narrative, and the narratives start in stark contemplation before taking the kind of turns that still leave die-hard fans arguing in cyberspace about the real meaning. The songs open with: "I stood alone upon the highest cliff-top" ("Lemmings"), "The killer lives inside me; yes, I can feel him move," ("Man-erg") and "Still waiting for my saviour, storms tear me limb from limb" ("A Plague of Lighthouse Keepers"). Incidentally, not everything here is as convoluted and penetrating as it seems, the title of the album resulted from a David Jackson spoonerism, when the saxophonist attempted to explain he was on his way to the studio to record some "horn parts."

A word of warning should be added beyond this point. Original vinyl issues in some territories included the insanely catchy and very un-Pawn Hearts-like "Theme One" on side one, and twenty first century CD reissues have attempted to restore the original idea of Pawn Hearts as VDGG's Ummagumma, a single album's worth of band material coupled with individual tracks and some reworked tracks from earlier outings. These moves make for a good, extended, listen but also dilute the dark intensity of the three tracks discussed here.

The Velvet Illusions:
The Velvet Illusions
(Tune In, 2011)
What? Tune in, turn on…but you know there's no drugs allowed, right?

The Velvet Illusions tread a strange middle ground part-Monkees, part Seeds (as in legendary US garage-psyclsters). Formed in Washington State in 1966, the band were aged between 14 and 17 and (for reasons explained on the very welcome liner notes with this CD) ended up sponsored by Vox (as in amplifier and musical instrument company). Changing line-ups and the usual band shenanigans predictably played their part but the Velvet Illusions cut five singles in under two years, changing styles slightly but turning out ten sides of prime garage rock with nods to the likes of The Seeds. Given their youth, and its impact on their ability to play venues that sold alcohol, the anti-drugs message of some the songs wasn't such a bad idea. "Acid Head" (a put-down on drug casualties) and "She Was the Only Girl" (an angsty melodrama; boy-meets-girl, boy-gets-girl, girl cheats, rips him off and dies, but he still loves her, and manages to tell the whole story in two and half minutes of prime garage-rock) made up the first single. Acid Head (the album) collates the Velvet Illusions' complete catalogue. The styles and sounds change slightly with the second single "I'm Coming Home Los Angeles"/ "Town of Fools" coming in with more clarity and melody. There are a handful of true garage-gems here "The Stereo Song" (penultimate B-side), and the final single "Mini Shimmy"/ "Hippy Town" being particular toe-tappers, and "Velvet Illusions" (a mid-period theme song with at least a nod to The Monkees) being another stand-out. It took until 2011 for the entire oeuvre to find its way onto an album with the lengthy sleeve notes this under-appreciated footnote to sixties USA garage rock truly deserve. Their anti-drug stance is a curio but it's the old clichés that matter here; the band have spirit, fire, drive...

Ana Vidovic:
Guitar Recital
(Naxos, 2000)
What? Prize winning performance, in a series of such works.

This is a vivid and varied collection of superbly interpreted works on the solo classical guitar, offering no overdubs and no additional accompaniment. With all due respects to Ms Vidovic, the point of including this one collection is to highlight a small but captivating corner of the classical market. The Naxos Laureate series typically showcases competition winning classical musicians, towards the start of their careers, presenting collections of skilfully chosen works to showcase the particular talents of the soloist. Consequently, the resulting CDs tend to avoid the more predictable corners of showcase classical CDs within which the works of one composer are presented, or a high-profile solo performer is accompanied by other talents to present a definitive interpretation of some piece. All this, and their other USP is a low retail price! Ana Vidovic brings incredible dexterity, notable power and a certain understated flashiness to her fretwork as she tackles works by, amongst others, Bach and Ponce. The opening Bach Prelude is a veritable rip through a piece many guitarists treat as a walk around a beautiful melody. Over the whole album Vidovic wrings some notable crescendos and variations of volume from six nylon strings and one soundbox. Frankly, there's a certain calculation in selecting this particular collection for this book. Amongst the Naxos Laureate titles the guitar works are a standout, and amongst the guitarists Ana Vidovic is, arguably, the rockingest act on show. It's light years from The Great Kat, but she has the same fiery fluency as the foul-mouthed femme star of guitar shred, just a very different way of channelling it.

Vitamin String Quartet:
The Gay Wedding Collection
(Vitamin, 2008)
What? Compilation curio from insanely prolific recording institution.

LA's Vitamin String Quartet may well be one of the most prolific recording acts currently active. With a catalogue boasting well over 250 original albums the outfit specialise in quartet reworkings of all types of pop music. Their repertoire boasting mainly pure quartet work and mainly cover versions; although some of their original compositions have crept onto their releases since 2009. There are also moments of an instrument other than those in the string quartet appearing on a track.

The mainstays of the quartet's output are CD long collections of greatest hits by acts not normally associated with classical or chamber sounds. Bjork, Deftones, System of a Down, Green Day, Muse, Linkin Park, The Mars Volta and AC/DC have all had their best known tracks adapted by the VSQ. Along the way, the quartet have also taken to producing compilations for a range of events, like weddings. Their collections include music for a gothic wedding and this touching 14 tracker for couples of the same sex. Culled from collections as varied as their tributes to Emmylou Harris, Shirley Bassey and The Smiths, The Gay Wedding Collection ambles along at a reassuringly slow pace, presenting simple and instantly catchy versions of the familiar: like The Smith's "There is a Light That Never Goes Out," and the very familiar: like Queen's "You're my Best Friend" and Madonna's "Like a Prayer." Sonically, the VSQ manage to get some contrast into the sound, often by following a bass part of counter melody from the original at the expense of covering all the nuances and licks of the original lead instruments. They also score heavily for keeping the arrangements simple, familiar and short. Their covers typically visit the main points of melodic reference, pay respect to the verse, chorus, verse structures and politely vanish into the background before outstaying their welcome. The Gay Wedding Collection drops in on some openly gay artists: Sylvester and Elton John, favours female acts over males: Emmylou Harris, Etta James, Sade, Diana Krall, Madonna, Dusty Springfield, Celine Dion, Mariah Carey and Shirley Bassey are all covered, and culls its selections from fifty years of the best tunes – apparently - favoured by same sex couples.

Bespoke string quartet collections for specific weddings are a limited field and – given their prolific output – it's doubtful if anyone will ever dislodge the VSQ from their predominance in providing CDs to this market.

Vulcan Freedom Fighters:
Stardate Unknown
(Alien Communication, 2006)
What? It's post-rock Jim, but not as we know it.

The idea is simple and done to death by generations of low-fi chancers. Plug in, riff up, throw in a few samples and indulge yourselves. Few, however, have turned out an hour of gleeful, laugh-out-loud, shamelessly inventive, hook-laden rifforama to match Stardate Unknown. As of this writing much of the entire masterwork was freely available as an unpaid download, suitable for beaming in on demand.

Vulcan Freedom Fighters describe it thus: " ambient space rock, techno overtures and stoner-based riff rock with sound FX and dialogue from the original (Star Trek) series." The 23 album cuts line up titles like: "Romulan Divide," "Spock's Deceit" and "Klingon Advance." Most tracks owe a blatant debt to a plot-line from the original Star Trek series and three or four listens down the line even casual Trekkies are likely to identify the episode(s) involved and find themselves able to picture the action.

Musically VFF don't do one genre when a couple of dozen will suffice, but the effect of throwing in every good idea on hand is to blend a music that surprises repeatedly. The whole "out-there" quality of the complete work hints at psychedelia, but surf guitar sounds, blues harp wails and a multi-layered sound rich in samples keep the whole thing teetering between genres, and grabbing at the listener's ears for the duration.

Produced exactly 40 years after the first broadcast of the first episode of the first Star Trek series, Stardate

Unknown is a more reverent tribute than it appears to be on first listening. It's a fitting one too. With its cheerfully cheesy sensibilities, willingness to reach for the most ambitious target on a shoestring budget and its sense of being at once familiar and, yet, slightly strange and very much in its own world, it has that early Star Trek feel. Anorak Trekkies can play spot the sample, but for most listeners VFF are simply a musical trip worth boldly going on.

Scott Walker:
Bish Bosch
(4AD, 2012)
What? You thought third albums were supposed to be difficult; try fourteenth albums.

In 2013 The Rolling Stones prepared for their Glastonbury debut, and a return to Hyde Park after 44 years. Mick Jagger mused in a promotional interview that being a rock singer was intellectually undemanding. So, he had probably lost touch with the career of his near contemporary Scott Walker, then. Walker's wayward ramble from pop god, desired and desirable crafter of definitive interpretations of other's works and respected writer, to cutting edge composer of material mocking the very notion of "popular" music has involved a hell of a lot of thought, invention and experiment. In another life, he'd be a professor. His solo works from the eighties onward have been highly sporadic, bemusing and bedazzling in equal amount, and have slowly carved a niche almost beyond criticism. It's an interesting, though ultimately futile, enquiry to speculate how the world might regard him if his career had started with the wilfully weird Climate of Hunter (1984).

One thing, however, is certain; the approval rating for Bish Bosch was sky high. In general it was deemed challenging, difficult, sprawling and powerful; even those who couldn't begin to comprehend the work could – at least – appreciate its ambition. Apart from anything else, the fact that a man so far down the career road as Scott Walker was prepared to put out 73 minutes of the most complex music was life-affirming. Whatever else Bish Bosch tells you there is no doubt Walker believes in the power of his songs and in the album as a means of conveying them. All of which is only old school nonsense until you hear the end results. Bish Bosch pits the starkest of percussive tracks – sometimes little more than hand held simple percussion treated with enough echo to suggest bare walls and the most basic surroundings – against slabs of melody instruments; once again typically delivered as waves of sound and reverberation. If you pay attention to the patterns established by the instruments there are – just about – standard verses, choruses and song structures. Well, some of the time anyway. Walker's voice retains most of its power, sense of torture and enough vibrato to present a picture of a man in touch with his demons and willing to conduct a conversation. Somewhere in the middle of these elements, typically built into lengthy tracks and adorned with complex open-ended lyrical flights, you can – if your perception takes you in that direction – just about tease out a story from the whole collection.

To make sense of anything here is to believe yourself capable of surviving in Walker's world, a place where the seven minutes and 46 seconds of the closing "The Day the 'Conducator' Died (An Xmas Song)" pits the kind of inane replies required of computer dating with coruscating self-analysis and still manages to offer up lyrical couplets so deceptively simple they pass you by before coshing you senseless with a line like: "The mad dogs swarming from her groin." Indeed, tracks four and five don't even offer a titular clue as to their contents; clocking in at around half an hour between them "SDSS1416+13B (Zercon, A Flagpole Sitter)" and. "Epizootics!" provide the dark heart of this impenetrable masterpiece. If you're inclined to sample Scott online before indulging in the whole disc, you'll know from a fleeting acquaintance with that pair whether you'll survive almost an hour and a quarter in this strange land. So, Mick Jagger thinks his profession intellectually undemanding, eh?

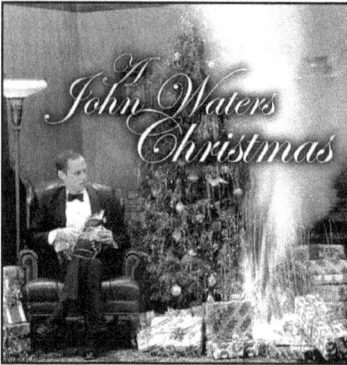

John Waters (Compiler):
A John Waters Christmas
(New Line, 2004)
What? Waters sits surrounded by gifts on the cover, the raging fire in the room is about to spread to the Christmas tree.

Technically speaking this is a various artists compilation, but it is Waters' creative vision. His masterful act of curatorship here matches the kitsch collisions of tacky cultural items that give his movies their signature identity. Most of the twelve tracks on offer had languished in obscurity. A quarter of the acts, Tiny Tim, Little Eva and Alvin and the Chipmunks, had enjoyed chart success to some degree. But, the real gold here is the revival of genuine cult treasures like Akim and Teddy Vann's "Santa Clause is a Black Man" (a child's tale of witnessing a black Santa). The cheerfulness and knock about fun of most of the album allows in the bare faced vitriol of Rudolph and the Gang's Christmas-hating country rant "Here Comes Fatty Claus" ("Here comes fatty with his sack of shit and all them stinking reindeer"). It's the listener's choice whether this belligerent broadside is scarier than "Happy Birthday Jesus (A Child's Prayer)" by Little Cindy, a po-faced peon to the joys of a fundamentalist festive season. But the real message here is that Waters' tasteful touch provides the perfect alternative to inanely happy Christmas albums.

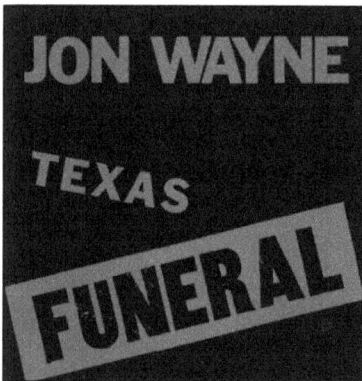

Jon Wayne:
Texas Funeral
(Hybrid 1985/ Cargo 1992/ Third Man, 2010)
What? Rambling low-fi, cow-punk, redneck, gorm-fest; Jack White loves it!

Cultish country comes little crazier than this. Described in a review on Julian Cope's Head Heritage site as: "A hideous, drunken, sloppy mess that grafts the musicality of Merle Haggard etc. onto a very loose/chaotic California punk sound," Texas Funeral packs a few mysteries, the most pressing of which is are we laughing at Jon Wayne, or with him? Lyrically the album never leaves Texas or the redneck mindset and the whole set has the feel of one of very long drunken evening, starting with some focus on the opening "But I've Got Texas" and "Texas Funeral." The punky rhythms of the opening cut, and the cod-Never Mind the Bollocks mock up of the front cover show one clear influence on Wayne. The morose tale of departing girlfriends pissing on the carpet and the death of his drunken dad in the title track bring in the comi/tragedy elements and the rest of the set tries to reconcile the two. Some of the tracks are little more than doodles. Lyrically it gets less focussed and more surreal as the proceedings wind on, though mentions of Texas run through the whole caper as wide and reliable as…well…the Rio Grande. The CD reissue added slightly to the surreal comedy with the bonus of the utterly strange "Apple Schnapps" and "One Hundred And Fifty-One Owl Caricatures."

Studio chatter, false starts and the sense of a singer hopelessly trapped in his Texan ways recur throughout. The tracks come and go in rapid succession as we get lists of animals he likes to shoot, a lengthy digest of those who done him wrong and – finally – a closer devoted entirely to "Studio Chatter" in which Wayne's dilemma of whether to try a commercial record or simply tell it like it is gets explored. If this is an elaborate joke then it's in the Idiot Abroad variety of Karl Pilkington's broadcasting career, wherein our main character chooses to remain wilfully befuddled for our entertainment. Vocally Wayne is more an intoner than a singer and the low-fi vocal, low-rent instrumental sounds on offer give the whole set the cheap DIY ethic of the mid-eighties. The release of a CD version by Jack White's Third Man label in 2010 shows the lasting impact of this unique take on country. At its best moments Texas Funeral touches on a manifesto that the early White Stripes adopted and adapted, and for that alone, this album has a small claim on lasting glory.

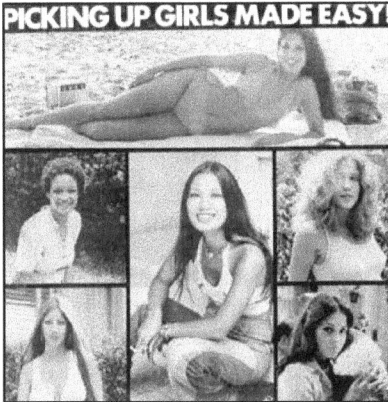

Eric Weber (narrator):
Picking up Girls Made Easy
(Symphony Press, 1975)
What? Seriously strong cheese from a less health-conscious time.

Googling the cover or liner notes for the eight cheesy chunks on offer here offers a deep end immersion in seventies culture. The liner notes suggest Weber – who also wrote a best-selling book on the subject and was a chat show regular - will: "teach you a whole new system for picking up girls -- a system that is so complete and so absolutely foolproof you'll soon be picking up girls automatically!!!" (note the triple exclamation marks). Also note that this album will show you: "Picking up girls can be as easy as opening a beer!" and you've got some insight into the market for the vinyl master class in smooth seduction. The opening minutes discuss "choosing your chick carefully" and present the first of eight acted out scenarios. In the opening scene our hopeful hitter on women is surrounded by southern girls sporting "Tex-a-size titties." Are you still reading? The present authors would respectfully suggest that your imagination may well be right in guessing the rest of the contents and that such enjoyment as you can gain from this album (which is available by way of pirated mp3 files all over the internet) is ironic. Picking up Girls Made Easy doesn't begin to imagine present-day notions of political correctness, or show any level of self-awareness that suggests it is played for laughs. The young actors, especially the girls, hired to bring reality to Weber's typical scenarios of pick up, acquit themselves fairly well, though the lack of sound effects or other backing betrays the limited budget underpinning the whole effort. Then again, the cynicism of that is as nothing to the suggested lies and deceit (including inventing an imaginary sister) that takes our hero "Frank" into helping a girl to buy blouses, or helps another hero "Jeff" to blag his way into a girl's life by way of lying his ignorant ass off about a love of ballet.

Scott Weiland:
The Most Wonderful Time of the Year
(Softdrive/Atlantic, 2011)
What? Stone Temple Pilot slurs through festive classics.

There is a fairly robust defence available online for this collection, most of which revolves around the notion that Weiland is acting out a Bowie phase, playing a character and creating a new identity as he inhabits this role. Weiland's work as leader of the Stone Temple Pilots, singer with Velvet Revolver, and high-profile survivor of a fairly public and stupendously large drug problem would lend some credence to this case. Part therapy, part experiment, The Most Wonderful Time of the Year might have some merit. However, it has long been a staple of the likes of the Music for Maniacs site and other online homes of debate regarding the biggest career mistakes and calamities of notable musicians.

The Most Wonderful Time is what you might imagine. Weiland ditches the ear-splitting backing in favour of a full orchestra and throws out the self-penned insights into personal demons in favour of the syrupiest standards available to celebrate twelve days of loved up family time. These include: "White Christmas," "The Most Wonderful Time of the Year," "Silent Night" and "White Christmas." He croons, as in really croons, and brings a studied mixture of slurs and eccentric intonations into the mix. For the most part the sound is the standard Bing/Blue Eyes set up with the orchestra rising, falling and emphasising the main points, with much space left centrally for the singer to display his art. Weiland definitely does that, but how convincing this is remains a subject of some division to listeners. It certainly lacks Bowie's straight faced assurance displayed when crooning along with Bing. But it does produce the odd surprise "O Holy Night" references reggae and "Silent Night" has a keyboard generated rhythm track that drags it towards some eighties kitsch/home-made vibe.

Weiland isn't a big band singer, and struggles sometimes to decide if this is ironic or rehabilitating his connection with simple pleasures. The results certainly make for a strange listen, though this is a listenable album that sequences and varies its treasures with a sense of purpose. Because the classic Elvis/Frank/Bing approach informs so much thinking on the age-old Christmas album formula, it is hard to listen to Weiland without some sense of this template clouding your judgement. In that regard, he has made over the formula with skilful nods to the odd sound or slight of production that make the collection his own.

But how much of Scott Weiland is in here remains a hard question to answer.

Mae West: Mae West on the Air: Rare Recordings 1934-1960 (Sandy Hook, 1985)
What? "I may be divine; but I ain't no angel"

West (1893-1980) ranks as one of the most controversial film stars of a highly censored generation. Her genius – apart from being insanely funny on screen and in front of a live audience – was her ability to mine sexual innuendo and present a comically cougarish sexuality that hinted at everything and spelled out nothing. As her brand of highly camp and highly suggestive comedy waned in the light of more realistic and sexually explicit movie content West increased her output of audio recordings. On record, she is best known for spirited and highly camp versions of standard songs; notably a rollicking cover of "Great Balls of Fire." Some of her recordings did very well commercially but such items were always a trade-off between the demands of a song and the (usually impossible) job of containing her massive character inside the running time of a pop single. It's also true that Mae was more an interpreter who acted her way through songs than any kind of technically impressive singer.

This collection – by contrast – gathers the audio work – and a television show with Red Skelton - she did brilliantly. Culled from five appearances; Mae West on the Air sees a number of Hollywood actors and recording stars – Skelton, Dean Martin, Perry Como and Duke Ellington – playing the straight man to Mae's lurid jokes and sassy one-liners. The results are variable but the three longest cuts here – two from Perry Como's radio show and one from Red Skelton's television show – have Mae on unstoppable form. The plot lines of the little vignettes acted out are paper thin, and the scripted banter between Mae and her male hosts never misses an obvious gag, but Mae's comic timing is perfect and the two meetings with Perry Como have him playing the ultra-straight man to her sexually rapacious force of nature. Written down, the gags are passable. Heard on disc they come alive. "Which are you" she asks the reserved Perry; "perfect or gentleman?" Perry bemoans the lack of his usual trio of backing singers as a duet beckons, Mae thinks it no great problem because: "I've taken the place of three women before." Acting out their own version of Romeo and Juliet Como points out: "Shakespeare kept the two lovers apart." West responds: "well, would you rather do it his way or mine?"

The interplay between the two is exceptional as Como sings "I'm in the Mood for Love" West butts in repeatedly.

> Como: "I'm in the mood for love"
> West: "Who isn't?"
> Como: "Simply because you're near."
> West: "That's reason enough"
> Como: "I'm in the mood for love…"
> West: "You've got a one track mind, but you're on the right track"

There's a fair degree of predictable Hollywood schmaltz, Mae is – by turns – promoting a live show and her autobiography and the two excerpts from Como's radio shows come with advertising for Chesterfield cigarettes. But – as a prime example of what Mae West did better than anyone else – this is a better insight than her camp and novelty ridden retreads of popular songs.

When People Were Shorter and Lived Near the Water:
Bobby
(Shimmy Disc, 1989)
What? Not so much a covers album as a complete re-write of an under-appreciated catalogue.

The words "experimental psychedelic-rock band" can cover a multitude of sins. Some of the most inspired sounds and most self-indulgent rubbish have come from this end of the music industry. Exactly where New York's When People Were Shorter and Lived Near the Water fit into this collection is anyone's guess, but for sheer chutzpah the band deserve some credit. Their albums account opened with this stunning collection of 15 covers of Bobby Goldsboro's best known efforts, almost all of them twisted through punk guitars, some studio trickery and the kind of full-throated vocal assault usually found in the more extreme ends of the music market. For the uninitiated Goldsboro is best known as a light, if slightly maudlin, US pop-ballad merchant. Sonically the production and performance owe something to grunge, even if the music often doesn't fall into this category. Such historic tributes as have been penned to this very singular band have often questioned whether Bobby and the subsequent Porgy (made up of re-treads of songs from the Porgy and Bess musical) were affectionate tributes or deliberate hatchet jobs. The question is probably too simplistic, a listen to When People's demolition/re-invention of a tender ballad like "Watching Scotty Grow" demonstrates this is more a case of musicians with a totally different take on the original setting themselves the task of re-creating the song as if it were theirs to start with. A conceit on their part so ambitious it explains why cultish DJs like John Peel loved them, and their album sales were limited.

Gregory Whitehead:
Pressures of the Unspeakable
(ABC Broadcasts, 1992)
What? Sublime sound artist produces signature work.

Gregory Whitehead's works include writing, directing and some of the most imaginative sound art available online. Sites like ubu.com host the work of Whitehead and his ilk. Much of Whitehead's best material – certainly around the period in which Pressures of the Unspeakable was produced – revolves around a cod-academic presentation of a subject, twisted through a creative maze, re-emerging as a more insightful commentary because it has dragged the listener through a thought process. A couple of shorter works from the same early nineties phase - "Principia Schizophonica" (wherein the resulting noises allow listeners to hear a discussion of mental illness and experience random mental voices) and "How To Pronounce 'Prosthesis'" (wherein a language lesson is developed through random vocal noises to the point that it sounds like a collision between lesson and the random thoughts of a struggling student) – explore this concept and appear on ubu.com. Both of these were released on 7" single and credited to Vicekopf. Assuming you wanted to sample Whitehead's stock-in trade, they might be the best place to start.

Pressures of the Unspeakable – by contrast – is a lengthy, interactive work based on screaming. Whitehead explores the sounds and purpose of screaming, but is constantly interrupted by members of the (Australian) public, from a child presenting an end of a hard day in year six scream, to people with their own specialised screams and a man discussing a number of screams taken from videos, including porn tapes. The work therefore has serious points to make about screaming, also manages to take the listener through the torment that produces screams, and adds sound effects, music and a sense of organisation such that its existence as both entertainment and art is established. Write ups on Whitehead describe his work as playful, inventive and provocative. His roots in theatre and improvisational music are generally fairly evident. That is certainly so in this 40 minute production that benefits from the unexpected twists and turns, and Whitehead's willingness to play the straight man/presenter as the madness erupts around him. Whitehead's theatrical roots provide a source of both mirth and narrative strength in his best works. Like Del Close – also discussed in this book – Whitehead grasps the concept of anchoring the drama by giving others the space to perform. In Pressures of the Unspeakable the high-points of this po-faced comedy come with the narrator – apparently – producing a genuine female childbirth scream and his pedantic categorisation of different kinds of screaming, calmly presented with interruptions from ear-splitting howls.

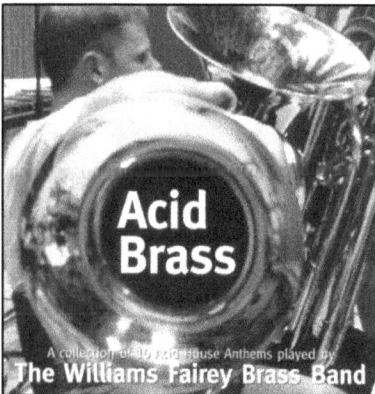

Williams Fairey Brass Band:
Acid Brass
(Maxi, 1997)
What? Bangin' tunes, brassy sounds.

As early as 1997 the notion of some unlikely musical outfit tackling a catalogue of songs that seemed to exist in a different universe had already been done to death. Orchestral punk covers were readily available and complicated tribute bands like the Joshua Trio (U2 coverists with a down-home bluegrass style) had become a fixture of the music industry. To make an unlikely marriage work beyond the point of novelty value you needed a good idea. And the Williams Fairey Brass Band hit pay-dirt with Acid Brass.

The idea is simple enough, take a slew of early rave tunes, rework them for a brass band, crank it up LOUD and record the results in front of an audience prepared to respond with loud clapping. The genius in this case is the match of the originals and the act and the sense that the audience are loving every second.

Early rave worked on solid rhythms, massive slabs of sound and looped melody and vocal lines floating in the spaces between the monumental chunks of bass, keyboard and drums. The same dynamics in a totally different context have been the mainstay of a good brass band for years. Brass bands pit the low notes of tubas against the high end of the horns, and then throw in percussion and the optional use of chimes to take keyboard parts. The best bands tend to pack a posse of players into each section, making for a BIG sound built from the various slabs.

These tunes and this act collide head on and catch fire from the opening notes of "Can U Dance." The collection works as a whole and packs no obvious weak moments. Stand out choices in a stand out set are, arguably, the rocking cover of A Guy Called Gerald's "Voodoo Ray," if only because the Williams Fairy crew get remarkably close to the dark brooding supernatural sense of the original, "Pacific 202" in which 808 State's light melodic touches are translated with real feeling and the stone-gone classic that is "What Time Is Love" which loses none of its banging insistence and gains a hairs-on-back-of-the-hand quality as the brass riffs build towards the finale.

It is most certainly a novelty item, and a week playing this stuff wall-to-wall in the car would probably start to drag. But, for all that, Acid Brass trashes most of the random collisions of unlikely act and classic material out there and certainly bears some repeated listening.

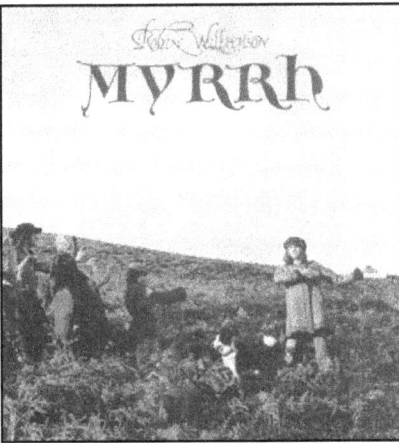

Robin Williamson:
Myrrh
(Island, 1972)
What? Simple and very singular first solo effort from Incredible String man.

For all their idealism and synonymity with the highest ideas of the counter culture The Incredible String Band spent much of their time together as a brittle duo with the seeds of their own break-up sprouting just below the surface. The first incarnation of the band finally parted company as their commercial fortunes tanked badly in 1974. But Robin Williamson and Mike Heron had already started working out their personal frustrations before then with solo efforts that showed their different characters. Heron's more standard rock and pop leanings took him towards greater use of a rhythm section and work more of a more radio friendly nature than the ISB had ever attempted. Williamson's first outing contains ten tracks of introspective and feeling laden folk material with a heavy use of heritage instruments, some nods to ethnic sounds from outside the western mainstream, effective use of strings and a strong central role for his nasal and highly enunciated vocals.

Myrrh also nods lyrically towards an eastern philosophy and songs like "Strings in the Air" bring a still drone-scape of sounds together with simple observations of scenes and a sense of understanding. Musically Myrrh has gathered a following because of the way its "odd instrumentation and serpentine melodicism… fuel standout tracks" (All Music Guide), a fair point and the album is frequently as layered and mannered in its delivery as the classic 5000 Spirits… and Hangman's Beautiful Daughter period String Band material. But occasionally it allows a simpler approach to melody and lyric and in "Dark Eyed Lady" it packs a gorgeous, vivid and uncharacteristically direct Williamson original; fuelled by a gently picked acoustic guitar and soulful vocal.

In its free use of flute, mandolin and Jew's harp Myrrh was already backward looking in 1972. In its complexity and willingness to court depth over accessibility it stands with the likes of Davy Graham and the many items in The Strawbs' catalogue that see the band labelled as progressive. But this is very much Williamson's world, from the arrangements – built around his distinctive vocals – to the visions of the world in his lyrics, Myrrh is clearly a solo album.

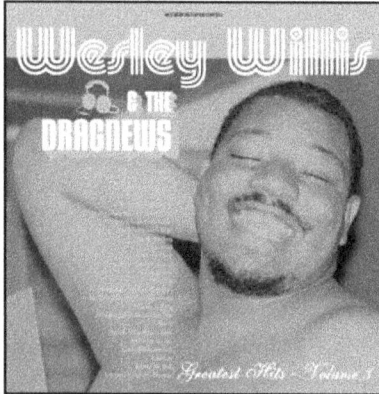

Wesley Willis:
Greatest Hits Volume 3
(Alternative Tentacles, 2008)
What? Suitably representative selection from "savant-garde" star.

Troubled by crippling bouts of schizophrenia and deep-paranoia, Willis (1963-2003) was forever an outsider from Chicago society. His massively prolific career produced many albums, typically boasting over 20 tracks each, and his celebrity began to rise with the first of his Greatest Hits collections, released by Alternative Tentacles in 1995. The compilations continued, including reissues, into the 21st century.

Having fronted a punk band - The Wesley Willis Fiasco – wherein Willis howled obscenities and barely coherent rants at anything troubling him, the man already had a taste for taking on his enemies in song. A subsequent solo career saw Willis thumping out chords on a Technics keybord (he would obsessively trade his models up as new versions were introduced), adding programmed beats and intoning some rant on a familiar theme. Issues of choice in Willis' songs are his clashes with minor authority (bus drivers and the like) acts of gross-out transgression (this album includes "Suck a Pit Bull's Dick" and "Suck a Polar Bear's Dick") and commentary on fast-food, crime and other musical acts (some of whom he had opened for). Lyrically, Willis often half-talked his way through a verse, delivering minutiae before getting to a chorus in which he sang loudly and barely in tune, repeating the song title. His prolific song-writing has confused many because some of his songs repeat phrases, and ideas – for example, stating the "crowd roared like a lion" in his songs praising other musical acts.

Interest in Willis includes those who find hope in the way music and visual art allowed a man with severe psychiatric issues and other medical problems to make a reasonable living. But Willis is inescapably a freak-show and the line between social callousness in appreciating his work and genuine curiosity is, near enough, invisible. Particularly so since many of these songs were performed in front of roaring and appreciative crowds; who loudly cheered the worst obscenities. Willis' own twisted logic also found expression in these ideas. On "I'm the Daddy of Rock 'n' Roll" – included on this 25 track compilation – he explains that his worst lyrical rants are intended to drive away and disgust the demons he experienced plaguing his life during episodes he described as "hell rides." Incidentally, by demons, he meant demons, Willis is sparing with metaphors in his song-writing.

Any good Willis compilation will give a flavour of the man's standard style and themes. The first Greatest Hits album has the bonus of "Rock 'n' Roll McDonalds" – probably his best known song – but Vol. 3 – arguably – bests it on the basis of greater gross outs, a bit more insight into Willis and some half-way decent social commentary; notably in "My Mother Smokes Crack Rocks." Willis sings about God in "I Love God" and celebrates Oprah Winfrey and Tom Petty and the Heartbreakers in song, he gets gross, likes to shout or sing "ass" and "motherfucker," and frequently reworks the theme of out of tune, repeated and simple chorus lines. For all this, he still emerges as someone capable – briefly – of grappling the demons out of the picture to the point he can reveal himself.

The question of whether we laugh with, or at, Wesley Willis will never be resolved, but the question of where to start investigating his music probably begins with the greatest hits compilations, and this may well be the best of them all.

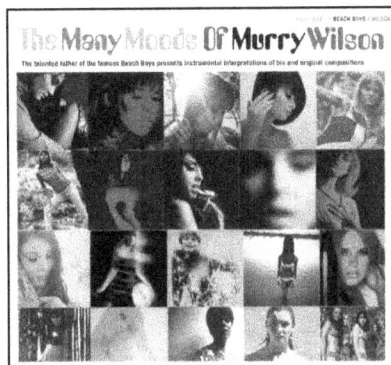

Murry Wilson:
The Many Moods of Murry Wilson
(Capitol, 1967)
What? Beach Boy dad falls short of teenage symphonies to God.

Most detailed histories of the Beach Boys paint Murry Wilson – dad of Brian, Carl and Dennis Wilson and Mike Love's uncle – as a domineering monster driving the boys hard, deeply jealous of the massive talent in Brian and frequently over playing his own influence on the band. Comparison is possible because – in 1967 – Murry made his own album, released on the same Capitol label that was home to his boys. The Many Moods of... presented a selection of photographs of young women on the cover and a varied array of music over the two sides and half hour running time. Short, lively if hardly distinctive M-O-R tunes, with standard easy listening arrangements follow each other. The many moods translate more into many different ideas. Some of the "moods" started life in other minds. The standout tune, by some degree, is a cover of Brian's "The Warmth of the Sun" and Al Jardine contributes the spirited and lightly catchy "Italia" – an instrumental he composed before joining The Beach Boys.

The liner notes present an all-inclusive philosophy: "in keeping with Murry Wilson's philosophy that new talent should be heard, several of the songs included in this album are those of new songwriters: "The Happy Song" and "The Plumber's Song" by Eck Kynor, a 40-year old plumber, who's been writing only a short period of time; "Islands In The Sky" by 20-year old Rick Henn; "Broken Heart" by lifetime friend, George Kizanis."

Whether the inclusion of two songs by a hitherto undiscovered plumber would have been in keeping with Capitol Records' usual quality control procedures, or whether George Kizanis would have got one of his tunes released on a major label album had he lacked Murry's friendship is another question. Even Murry's wife – and the mother of three Beach Boys – Audree Wilson is afforded a co-composing credit on "Betty's Waltz;" one minute and 49 seconds of a waltz tune that plays with harmony but does achieve the liner-note claim of sounding "like one melody."

The Many Moods... is – by common consent – well produced, of some minor interest because of the Al Jardine original and the marginal involvement of Brian Wilson on "Italia". It is similar sonically to much of the vast tonnage of easy listening and M-O-R material America produced in industrial quantities around this time. Mood wise it isn't that varied. In any case, Murry's "many moods" are limited to his composing four of the 12 cuts and co-composing "Betty's Waltz." The album didn't shift massive quantities or show much of the visionary producing and arranging qualities that had – by 1967 – become Brian Wilson's forte.

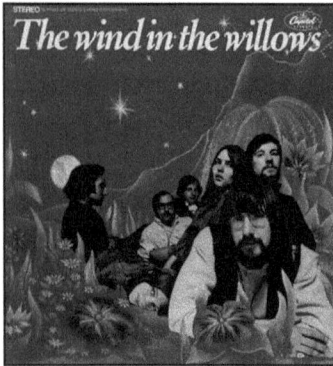

The Wind in the Willows:
The Wind in the Willows
(Capitol, 1968)
What? Oft-scorned slice of psychedelia.

The current authors would argue the one thing this album has lacked since 1968 is a fair hearing from all and sundry.

The steady slew of major-label late-sixties psychedelia meant The Wind in the Willows sounded right for its era, but faced the stiffest competition. Having edged its way to a US chart position of #195 this, the band's first and only officially released outing, sank without trace, only to be reissued for totally different reasons just over a decade later. By the time of the reissue the Wind in the Willows' female second vocalist and finger-cymbal queen – a certain Debbie Harry – had become much better known for fronting another outfit. Prior to any sniff of a reissue she had slammed her former band as: "a pretty awful baroque folk-rock band," and described their sound as "depressing listening."

Blondie era Debbie Harry might well have been the worst possible ambassador for the band. Blondie always had a knowingly ironic twist about them and The Wind in the Willows take on simple sincerity and total acceptance of the sixties, hello trees, hello sky, hippiedom had to be disowned if she was going to stay cool. Reviews of the reissue frequently slammed it as second rate psychedelia.

In fact The Wind in the Willows is a dreamy, if unfocussed, stumble through the main stations on the more lightweight hippie tour. Introspective at times, cosmically conscious at others, it never gets rabidly politically angry but it is certainly out to turn you on. Largely acoustic (though the band's one national tour presented a show that started with a reading from Kenneth Grahame's The Wind in the Willows and finished with full-on electric rock), the album veers from sunshine pop to gloriously pretentious spoken word intonations on the eight and a half minute epic "There is But One Truth Daddy." The epic cut offers up flute, sitar, slow hand-drums and a tale that collides Grahame and acid consciousness in a blissful union perfect for 1968, and belonging nowhere else.

The Wind in the Willows' seven members included a handful with formal musical education. Guitarist/ vocalist Paul Klein – their nominal leader – presides over a lush take on the hippie dream existing sonically – at different times – somewhere between The Doors' more restrained moments, Brian Wilson's most vivid brainstorms, the more tripped out moments of The Mamas and the Papas and – fleetingly – into the brief bliss-trips found on The Monkees' or Spanky and our Gang's albums.

Debbie Harry fronts a lovely piece of psych-pop in "Djini Judy" (though it ends with a crude cymbal crash), and tracks like "Moments Spent" and "The Friendly Lion" are passable attempts to marry the shameless love children vibe with hooks and radio friendly mixes, all in the hope of a hit single.

This late in the day nobody is about to present a credible argument that The Wind in the Willows is any major rival to the era's acknowledged masterpieces. But when albums by The Music Emporium, The Dragons and a few other overlooked combos of the time continue to get belated recognition The Wind in the Willows is surely worth a listen, if only because its shameless innocence and superb rendering of a sound so much of its time make it one of the purest examples of tree-hugging hippiedom ever committed to album.

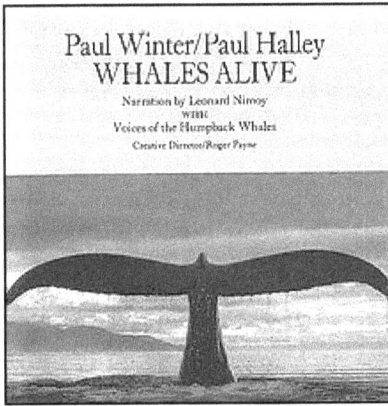

Paul Winter/Paul Halley:
Whales Alive
(Living, 1987)
What? New age noodlings, real whale songs and…Leonard Nimoy.

With all due respects to the visionary musicians who conceived and played this, Whales Alive continues to derive some of its cult appeal from the occasional presence of Leonard Nimoy as narrator. Nimoy's earnest intoning helms a piece of floating new ageism wherein genuine recordings of whale songs are mixed and melded with sparing melodies, mainly on sax and pipe organ. The biggest cliché in the book when it comes to describing new age music is the word ethereal. But to leave it out of this entry would be to ignore the very essence of what Whales Alive seeks to achieve. Why else conceive "Concerto for Whale and Organ," which makes up track five here? Nimoy's interest in the project was awakened through his work on Star Trek IV: The Voyage Home (the plot of which incorporates whales), and his contribution to the liner notes includes: "There is an amazing majesty in these creatures, a gentleness in the presence of great power…" Musically, Whales Alive is aiming for that combination of strength in simplicity, and effortless majesty. A piece like "Turning" which opens on Nimoy's narration and slowly gives way to a gentle combination of keyboard and sparing sax takes this concept in a spiritual direction, whilst the aforementioned "Concerto…" is aiming for an epic depiction of the whale. If the titles appear overtly portentous, and the closing "The Voyage Home" is surely a blatant attempt to hit the bottomless market for Star Trek merchandise in all its forms, then Whales Alive stands out in the abundant new age genre as a work that might usefully be described as compelling and inventive.

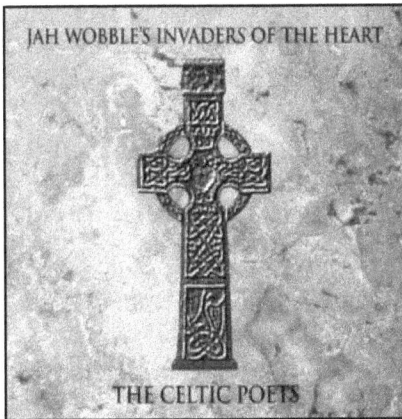

Jah Wobble's Invaders of the Heart:
The Celtic Poets
(Hertz, 1997)
What? The Celtic Dub Foundation.

Wobble's many and varied musical escapades make him the umpteenth act for whom we can say: almost any solo album could have made this book. The Celtic Poets amounts to a determined diversion, even in his diverse career. To call Wobble, (born John Joseph Wardle), a bass player is an understatement. Wobble's most acclaimed solo work tends to place his bass guitar centrally and weave a soundscape and overarching creative vision into a long player. Considering the resulting output of solo work it is safe to say two things. Firstly, Wobble is one artist who has shown unwavering belief in the album as am effective vehicle for his talents. Secondly, Wobble's works bear similarities to each other, but generally manage to achieve their own individual voice. When you set out to produce Chinese or Japanese dub, (both allocated a Wobble album), you are already in very select company.

The Celtic Poets followed a work focussed on the poetry of William Blake. It lines up soundscapes and varied moods and tempos and places five "Celtic" poems in settings that collide world music, traditional Irish sounds and Wobble's fluid bass. Two of the poems are originals by Shane, (Pogues/Popes), MacGowan, the others by Brendan Kennelly, Louis MacNeice and Freidrich Ruckert. Thematically the words are linked by issues of life and death, MacGowan's opening poem concerns thoughts on the potato famine in Ireland, Kennelly's "A Man I Knew" concerns a man thinking about his own burial. Dubliner's singer Ronnie Drew voices the words, his ragged and lived-in tones providing effortless gravitas and his Irish accent strong throughout. But the themes, and music, soon veer into abstract territory. "Bagpipe Music," predictably, meanders away into a fusion of bass and bagpipes.

"Market Rasen" and "Thames" are both instrumentals, the first pitting a fifties style hip-jazz trumpet against a sitar, the second a slow, meandering meditation on the mighty river, clocking in just over sixteen and half minutes. Wobble bosses both these pieces effortlessly, conjuring enough variety from his bass to play the role of a lead guitarist when required. Wobble's work remains eclectic to the point that picking a best album is futile. The Celtic Poets shows him at his best and offers his signature trick of making the oddest musical combinations sound effective.

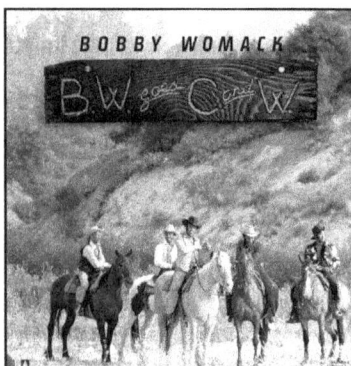

Bobby Womack:
B.W. Goes C and W
(United Artists, 1976)
What? Down the line country from a towering soul man.

Womack lobbied hard for the right to make the album that cost him his contract with United Artists and alienated a fan-base that had steadily grown through the seventies. That's not to say B.W. Goes C and W is a bad album. It's well played, packed with the usual heartfelt original material Womack has always been able to knock out and – despite what a few dismissive online comments would have you believe – it's also pretty soulful. In its better cuts – like the opener "Don't Make this the Last Date" – we have a few Womack trademarks: spoken intro, tasteful strings, the rough-edged vocals and Bobby gradually working himself into a bit of a frenzy as the emotion overtakes him. Granted, there's the unfamiliar pedal-steel in there and a country swing underneath the soulful vocal.

Thankfully United Artists nixed Womack's original idea of an album title: Step Aside, Charley Pride, Give Another Nigger a Try but nothing convinced the public to embrace the new sound. The running time – a shade shy of 28 minutes – didn't help and in the US (always Womack's main market) radio formatting was already shaping into the niche markets that locate Bobby Womack well inside the soul arena.

Womack's increasingly wayward ways were another complication; he subsequently discussed major drug use, and the death of his infant son as elements that made the late seventies a nadir in his career. B.W. Goes… didn't get remotely close to generating a hit song, or decent sales, Womack's contract was offloaded to Columbia; who wouldn't consider a move like this. Pedal steels in the mix and horses on the front cover were never again a noticeable feature of Womack's career.

Having said this, Womack grew up with country, the presence of Womack and other family members on horseback on the cover makes it clear this is a personal record and the ten cuts prove, at least, he can write a country tune without too much trouble and cover the likes of "Behind Closed Doors" with some sense of why they are meaningful songs. Ultimately, B.W. Goes C and W at least proves itself better than some of the more unlikely stumbles into Nashville. It isn't down there with Dame Vera Lynn's visit to the same territory, probably finding allies in Jonathan Richman's album long visit to the same ground or Neil Young's mid-eighties experiment Old Ways in that it still sounds like the same guy, just in a very very country style.

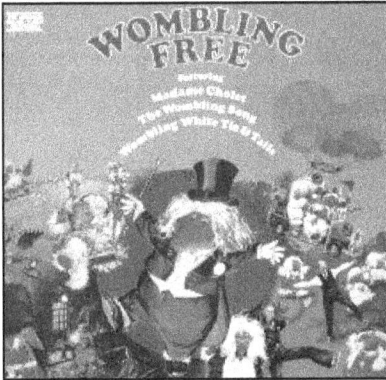

The Wombles:
Wombling Free
(CBS, 1978)
What? The last long-playing trip to Wimbledon Common.

There was little life left in the Wombles' recording career when this particular expiring horse was led out for its final long-playing flogging of the seventies. To put the furry funsters' musical career in context it should be remembered that they were – briefly – a major chart power in Britain. 1974 was glam rock's grandest moment, with Bolan and Slade just slipping but Mud, Suzi Quatro and Alvin Stardust all storming to the top position. During one of British pop's silliest years, the 7" single experienced a sales bonanza. It was The Wombles who shifted more units than anyone else, pumping five fun-filled musical delights into the charts. The problem – as with most novelty acts – was always going to be their staying power.

By the time The Wombles' movie Wombling Free was unleashed on cinemas the burst bubble of their record sales had fallen to little more than a damp puddle on the ground. The Wombles hadn't had a chart single hit in over two years and the tell-tale signs of contractual obligation were everywhere. The greatest hits album actually preceded this release. Wombling Free (the movie) made some sense. If you couldn't persuade the kiddies to keep buying chirpy pop ditties on vinyl singles you could – at least – herd them into cinemas with the added bonus that most Wombles fans were so young they'd need at least one mum/dad/grandparent or big-sibling to mind them, and pay for a seat whilst doing so. Seeing the little furry litter-lifters on the big screen was a new experience. Hearing them on another album, wasn't new.

But some credit is due to Mike Batt and the production team behind The Wombles' hit career. In its own very understated and utterly British way, this little oddity is Wimbledon Common's answer to The Monkees' career-destroying magnum-opus, Head. Since the main point of Wombling Free (the movie) was to put life-sized costumed actors in place of the television animation and make everything, from story-line to set, BIGGER, the soundtrack album responded with a slew of sound-bites that collided Batt's pop-sensibilities with a sound-palette that smacked of the range and diversity of a well-appointed jingle factory. The incidental music, shorn of the visuals of the movie, comes over as a series of simple, slightly surreal and frequently inventive little vignettes that stand up surprisingly well so far down the line. New versions of "The Wombling Song" and "Wombling White Tie and Tails" bookend the first side of the vinyl album and 19 seconds of the national anthem close the whole caper, but elsewhere the point is to create little sound-scapes to support film scenes. With Batt's typically clean and uncluttered production these fleeting incidental delights offer up everything from "The Creation of the World" (basically a mini-epic; imagine a Sooty puppet composing and conducting the theme to 2001 A Space Odyssey) to "Under the Hills and Far Away" (a Scots flavoured collision of accordion and bag pipe).

A bewildering array of instruments and moods crowd the short running time of the album, and exposure to any given minute of the instrumental stuff could unleash a sound sample fit to drop anywhere from an indie album to the experimental end of dance. Batt's jingle-factory approach to his work, combined with a the free-spirit he was able to bring to this collection does offer up some really odd glories. There is none stranger than the two minute 44 second concoction that is "Edinburgh Rock," apparently the music of Cairngorm McWomble. This collision of blues-harp, glam rock backing and Scots instrumentation rocks out with an insistent vengeance.

Wombling Free remains a quaint, strange and very British listen. The album packs the added bonus of the listener not having to watch Bonnie Langford's well...Langfordesque performance in the actual movie.

Chris Wood:
Trespasser
(RUF, 2007)
What? Articulate, old school and highly relevant in the twenty first century.

A complete throwback to the days when strident messages and personal tales, told in folk songs, were an incitement to action. Chris Wood's slow, deliberate and sparse tale telling unfolds a message questioning the right of any elite to own and control the lives of others. By his own admission in the liner notes Trespasser collects songs "about enclosure in some form or another. Spiritual, geographical, cultural, legislative, chronological, imaginative." The style, instrumentation and message is old school acoustic folk, the production makes few accommodations to twenty first century sounds and so the odd intrusion of a modern expression feels like an aberration. The narrator of "The Cottager's Reply" refuses to see his home in cash value terms and talks disdainfully to the potential purchaser about the history the home holds. The reference to the would-be buyer's "4x4" jars in the lyric, as does a later reference to a "plasma screen" in "Riches on the Bold." The songs take as long as they need, "England in Ribbons" clocks in at exactly 11 minutes and the liner notes discuss differing concepts of time with regard to the mummers play and "the deep and wondrous melting" together of tragic time and resurrective time.

Trespasser teases out recurring themes. Though it would be an overstatement to regard it as any kind of song cycle, two songs set up a dynamic informing the whole album. The opening "Summerfield Avenue" presents domestic life held within a home and looks at the way growing up means becoming accustomed to limitations. "Mad John" slowly meanders over a brass backing and winsome acoustic guitar to explore the way the fencing in of his home gradually brought about the mental decline and incarceration in an asylum of the poet John Clare. Sung from the point of view of an observer there's a metaphor for the message of the album in the line: "Mad John, they made a trespasser out of you." Trespasser is more resigned than righteously angry, but the short sightedness of surrendering social good for private greed is there in music that refuses to pander to radio friendly notions of folk and in the stories unfolding in the vivid vignettes. Trespasser was a worthy album of the year in the BBC Radio 2 Folk Awards of 2009.

Peter Wyngarde:
Peter Wyngarde
(RCA, 1970)
What? "Sex on a stick" British television hero Jason King unzips a genuine jaw-dropper, of an album.

A true one-off, collecting vocal arrangements of new and traditional material and spoken word/dramatic pieces. Peter Wyngarde has few precedents and its closest living relative might be William Shatner's Transformed Man curio from the same period. After a loud musical burst our host – Wyngarde – welcomes us in, points out the lights haven't fused, he's simply happier in candlelight, we can have a drink. He has "started on champagne." It promises to be a fun, romantic evening but things soon take a turn for the worse. In fact, that turn is now the main reason the collection has been restricted to one low-key reissue under the title When Sex Rears its Inquisitive Head. Skip to the next entry now if you're easily offended. Track three, "Rape," is an absolute stunner of out-there incomprehensibility, opening with sexual noises and unmistakable female screams it involves Wyngarde adopting a range of foreign accents as he explores the differing international experience of rape. If (as appears to the be case) it's intended as a joke it is all the more incomprehensible in the 21st century because its running theme involves explaining rape in the context of the most facile of national stereotypes: the French shrug it off like any other scandal, its rare in Russia because it's so cold… you get the idea. If this is a joke then we're expected to believe that sexual assault exists somewhere in the same territory as inadvertently injuring a member of the opposite sex through any other careless or misunderstood act. Well, maybe that attitude passed muster in some quarters in 1970, if you're of that persuasion today those behind this book respectfully suggest you go online and acquaint yourself with the way the sexually predatory instincts of Jimmy Savile and television presenter Stuart Hall eventually collided with reality.

"Rape" sets a tone in which apparent sophistication in the form of Wyngarde flexing his acting muscles goes alongside momentary outbursts of sleaze and surreal comedy. The ages old standard "Widdecombe Fair" keeps some strange company here with "Hippie and the Skinhead" – arguably – matching "Rape" for high-strangeness as Wyngarde presents the extremes of fashion consciousness of the time and intones a tale of the two in cultural collision. His acting skills see him flit effortlessly from working class London to sophisticated English accent as the album unfolds and the production moves with him. It certainly bears repeated listening on the basis of packing occasional tricks and asides that escape you on first hearing but Peter Wyngarde also begs the question of who all this effort was supposed to impress. It remains so far outside any popular style and leaves other pieces of the same period like Shatner's Transformed Man and Richard Harris A Tramp Shining looking coherent and positively mainstream by comparison.

XXX Maniak:
Harvesting the Cunt Nectar
(Red Candle, 2004)
What? Brief and break-neck romp through celebrated goregrind atrocity.

First off the usual, "if you're easily offended calm yourself with the entries on Vera Lynn and Bing Crosby" warning. Still here? Right. So, the opening seconds – almost inaudible – feature two slacker dudes sparking up a smoke, mumbling a little, and then one asks: "So is that the first time you fucked a dead girl?!..." Cue 20 odd (like really odd) minutes of relentless porn goregrind, played for the sickest of laughs, boasting stomach churning song titles and driven forward by computer programmed drums resembling a battle. Guitars explode rather than riff and singing only breaks out when they can't be bothered to grunt, shout or scream. Fair enough, this is what goregrind is about. XXX Maniak's back-story – apparently formed from two former label bosses, pro gamblers, strip club owners, and pornography producers – might not stand the hardest scrutiny and the duo both trade under more than one name Jason Sidote (AKA Anthony West) and Matt Moore (AKA Michael Yale), but that's also par for the goregrind course. The lyrics are hard/impossible to make out; though the opening spoken word items on tracks like "Skeleton Toucher" are helpful. So are the graphic song titles including: "Sprayed by Cans of Shit," "Buying a DVD Player (Then Raping You with My Old VHS Tapes)," "Priest in the Preschool" and "Baptized in Semen and Steel." Lyrically it doesn't matter beyond the titles in many cases; the one about buying a DVD player only runs for 16 seconds, though "Baptized in Semen and Steel" is a stonking 50 second epic.

The lurid (and superbly executed) cover design is likely to appeal to anyone prone to enjoying the grossest of splatter movies and for the most part Harvesting the Cunt Nectar delivers on the promise of the gory cover art and gross-out song titles. Listed in some places as an EP (probably because of the short running time) it still packs thirty odd (as in strangely odd) maniak missives into its truncated time and feels like a bigger undertaking than it is because the spoken samples from B-movies, porn tapes and the like give it a slightly epic quality.

Yes:
Tales from Topographic Oceans
(Atlantic, 1973)
What? Because it's there, and this book is what it is.

Some albums become touchstones or shorthand references for an entire genre and if ever an album were used and abused in arguments on the merits of progressive rock then that album is Yes' first double set and – arguably – their most shamelessly out-there recording. Its presence in this list is down entirely to one thing. In the years we spent tinkering with this book we found it hard to find anyone, other than a die-hard Yes fan of the first generation, who would admit to having actually listened to this thing from end to end. We did – however – finds loads of people with strong opinions on what was right and wrong with it. The "wrong" arguments greatly outweighed the champions of this sprawling, and mystifying, masterwork but the most obvious thing of all was how few people listened to this much discussed waxing. Apart from anything else, we found very few people who could quote track titles or a running order of the four pieces that make up Topographic Oceans.

Basically this is the "classic" Yes line-up Anderson-Wakeman-Squire-Howe and White, giving it large and complicated. Passages that would have made useful solos on their previous outings are here expanded to the length of songs, dropped into side-long (this was initially four sides of vinyl) compositions and wrapped around lyrics so elliptical as to make Finnegan's Wake appear as an elementary reader. If the reference to a James Joyce novel appears pretentious in this context then avoid Topographic Oceans like the plague because the thing that makes it a truly hard listen is the way Jon Anderson's lyrics take flight, leave the Earth, and barely approach intelligible for the duration. Much more meditations than simple stories, tracks like the opener: "The Revealing Science of God," have been likened to ever-opening flowers, presenting their delights only to those prepared to seize the stillness within the chaos. The album opens with the couplet: "Dawn of light lying between silence and sold sources/ Chased amid fusions of wonder, in moments hardly seen, forgotten…"

It isn't exactly Tamla Motown, though those defending Topographic Oceans would argue that grasping the soul within the whole piece is the key to truly getting it. If it makes any sense at all then Topographic Oceans is an ecstatic and fabulous trawl through heightened levels of consciousness and its meaning reveals itself as each lyrical observation leads you to the same mental revelations, whilst the frequently intense musical assault reveals astonishing moments of sublime melody and fleeting stillness, even within the polyrhythmic complexity and virtuoso passages from each player. Well, either that or it's so far up its own anus that the whole caper has actually reached the brain. It is certainly true that many of the extended musical passages do smack of a band who know how well they can play and resolutely insist on making the rest of us aware of this. What matters in this context is that the assembled musicians frequently achieve this technical perfection whilst also playing with a level of soul and passion frequently overlooked by those commenting on Topographic Oceans.

Yes never again attempted anything quite so obtuse and whilst portions of Topographic Oceans went down well with the faithful as the band toured, it is also true that during an extended solo piece that didn't include him keyboardist Rick Wakeman was once known to order a curry to be delivered to the stage so he could remain there and eat it until his contribution was called for again.

Beyond the comments above it is probably pointless to try and make sense of this album by throwing words at paper. Topographic Oceans does truly seize a moment in musical history, probably better than any other album lumped into the same early seventies prog-rock bag, and for that reason alone it makes sense to seek it out, rather than reading about it and pontificating.

Neil Young:
Arc
(Reprise, 1991)
What? Grunge-rock Wagner.

The crusty Canadian curmudgeon has driven critics and record companies to distraction on several occasions during his career, however, this 35 minute, ermmm, composition is easily the single strangest piece of audio in his bulging catalogue. It's probably worth a brief round-up of Young's greatest non-hits before we get to Arc, because to truly grasp the majesty of this monster a familiarity with his wayward ways is essential. Young had long had a reputation for wilfulness and singularity amongst his peers but the first global manifestation of this quality came in 1973 when he followed Harvest – the biggest selling album on the planet in 1972 – with Journey Through the Past, a ragbag soundtrack to a virtually incomprehensible movie. Young's status as a soft-rock superstar was mightily compromised and his record company were greatly relieved when he recorded Human Highway, an album firmly in the Harvest style. At a pre-release listening party for the new title a greatly inebriated Young played a tape of a roughshod and rambling series of songs and promptly decided to ditch Human Highway in favour of this bleak alternative; titled Tonight's the Night. All of this precedes his simmering stand-off with Geffen Records (where artist and label came to trading legal communications regarding the extent to which Young's output represented the work expected the "major artist" Geffen's financial outlay expected him to be). That story is book in itself. The point to note here is that his departure from Geffen marked no departure from his habit of "following the music," wherever it might lead.

In 1990 it led to a fuzzed out firestorm of a tour with proto-grunge pioneers Sonic Youth in support and most of Young's then current Ragged Glory album on the set list, along with barnstormers like "Rockin' in the Free World" and "Like a Hurricane." The feedback and riff-fest led to Young being dubbed the "Godfather of grunge," a fair title considering the obvious musical debt the likes of Nirvana owed to the man. Apart from anything else, the new movement had embraced Young's anti-fashion combi of ripped jeans and lived-in lumberjack shirts as a uniform.

Typically, Young wouldn't simply accept the accolade. It fired him to heights of feedback and fury fit to drive noise abatement campaigners to suicide. The whole caper kicked off when Young chanced on the idea of filming his stage performances and editing out the beginnings and ends of songs to create some weird alternative to a concert movie, highlighting the very bits audiences usually discount. The movie remains a figment of Young's ever-fertile imagination but his conversations with Sonic Youth front-man Thurston Moore did hatch an altogether different slant on the same idea. Young had his footage of the Ragged Glory tour, with audio collected via the mic on his portable onstage camera, and he set about messing with the soundtrack, encouraged by Moore. The results were christened Arc and originally released as an extra disc in a very limited bonus edition of his tinnitus inducing live double CD Weld. A single disc edition of the impenetrable opus duly followed. Arc is a "compilation composition" basically a series of looped samples taking in the onstage noise, feedback-laden finales of songs and other random sounds. The looping serves to give the 35 minute single track some sense of pace and structure, but it's hard going and those who take most delight in easy listening of any kind are best advised to avoid it. The whole piece does bear a passing resemblance to Lou Reed's infamous Metal Machine Music. It also counts as a bizarre low-fi masterwork, given its ungainly combination of massive sounds and recording reliance on the single mic on Young's video camera. Critically the best summary is probably to say the jury is out, permanently, because Arc was never "in" to start with. So it is fitting we leave the last word to one of Amazon's best known reviewers, a certain, A Customer.

"Where to start? Well, this could be called a sound collage I guess, with bits of noise, feedback and crashing cymbals welded together to make a half an hour long mess that you will only ever listen to once- unless you are in a psychiatric hospital (which I am- we listen to it all the time here)."

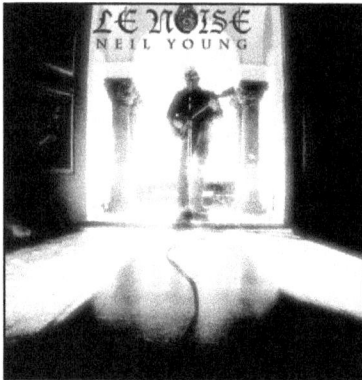

Neil Young:
Le Noise
(Reprise, 2010)
What? "I said solo…they said acoustic"

He isn't going gently into that goodnight. This album, near enough, marked Young's 65th birthday and arrived on the back of his celebrated Twisted Road solo trek across the USA. Young had conceived the tour, his first since a marathon two-year haul around the world, as an intimate and solo affair. Buoyed up by the early dates on his world tour there were critics and fans hoping he'd repeat the crowd-pleasing interlude in which he'd dusted off and performed long-neglected standards, stripped to their basic acoustic beauty.

That wasn't quite what he had in mind. Promoted under the slogan: "I said solo…They said acoustic," Twisted Road might more usefully have been dubbed Twisted Roadmap. Young's new obsession was obviously based around challenging the very notion of the respective sounds of solo acoustic and electric guitar. Live he combined a few new tracks destined for Le Noise with some familiar pieces presented in an entirely unfamiliar way. For starters, he turned accepted wisdom in terms of the sonic possibilities of his guitar playing on its head. Delicate acoustic numbers were cranked up to filling-rattling fury and still performed as if he was playing to someone three feet away. Full-on rockers were turned down, reducing crowd pleasing riffs to pleasant and repetitive melodic snatches. As the tour progressed he explored the possibilities of this approach, gradually building the blueprint for the new album.

Fired up from the successful experiment – once they got used to the idea critics and audiences came down massively on Young's side – Young and producer Daniel Lanois set about translating the vision to a full-length set of new songs. The title of the album may refer to the fact it plays with expectations and sounds as much as it delivers proper songs. Then again, with Young's insatiable love of surprises and straight-faced jokes the title is also a pun on the pronunciation of the French-Canadian producer's surname.

Le Noise delivers on its creative vision, though not on hook-lines, radio friendly melodies or the full-on driving rock that has garnered Young most respect. The one acoustic track here – "Peaceful Valley Boulevard" – a haunting lament for the loss of nature, is arguably the stand out. As the album's most acccssible lyrical statement it is also a key to the working of the rest of the set. Melodic figures recur, walls of sound rise and decay and looped snatches of guitar and vocal fade in and out around the main thrust of each song. Most are held together with lyrics that pledge allegiance to a feeling or faith, and the album comprises an expression of the art and passion that have remained at the heart of Young's relentlessly restless quest to follow the music.

More an album for a darkened room than a car journey, Le Noise does beg one almighty question. Just how many of his contemporaries could attempt this and pull it off?

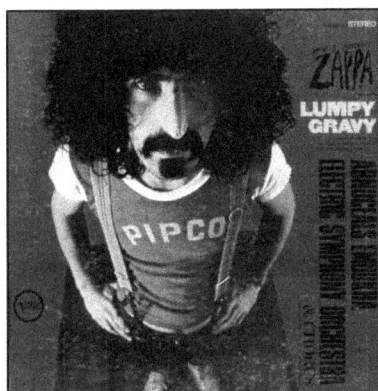

Frank Zappa:
Lumpy Gravy
(Verve, 1968)
What? 1st solo outing for visionary artist.

It is unlikely that most of you motivated to venture into this book will need much introduction to Frank Zappa (1940-1993). Zappa's massive career skirted the fringes of rock (by way of jazz, classical and a few ventures into other styles) but this early warning in the form of his first solo album showed his intention to create cutting edge works of modern classical music fit to leave most of his regular fans bemused. It took the world a long time to catch up; though the most accessible results are now easily sampled on the compilation Strictly Genteel.

Lumpy Gravy originally saw a release in 1967 but a lawsuit – in which Zappa's record company took exception to his conducting an earlier recording of the work for Capitol Records – forced a new and longer edition featuring two lengthy works of musique concrète (using elements of the original orchestral score for Lumpy Gravy) placed alongside some spoken word pieces and surf music.

It sounds haphazard and provisional on first listening, a perception only strengthened by the fact Zappa substantially re-edited the work in 1984, (not released until the Lumpy Money box set in 2009).

The orchestral passages shift time-signatures and sonic qualities often enough to confuse on first listening. The spoken word passages – notably a surreal conversation involving the question: "how do you get your bathwater so black?" to which the answer seems to be suffering from paranoia – add to elliptical quality. Zappa continued to experiment with these "talking strings" spoken word items; involving people having conversations next to a grand piano with raised lid. The strings would resonate with the voices adding a low key harmonic quality to the recording. He also stated that Lumpy Gravy – as in the 1968 version – could be edited in different ways and still emerge as a complete work.

That, ultimately, is the key here. Impenetrable as it appears, Lumpy Gravy sets the scene for the complex time signatures, intense orchestral pieces and the combination of musique concrète and modern classical composition that would increasingly pre-occupy Zappa in his later years. It is – quite literally – years ahead of the classical experiments of the first generation of progressive rockers and some of those working on the – then – cutting edge keyboard instruments like the Moog. Lumpy Gravy is also funny (both strange and ho-ho) in its little meanders into spoken word territory and use of typical Zappa titles like: "Very Distraughtening," "White Ugliness" and "Take Your Clothes Off" and remains a vibrant and explosive work.

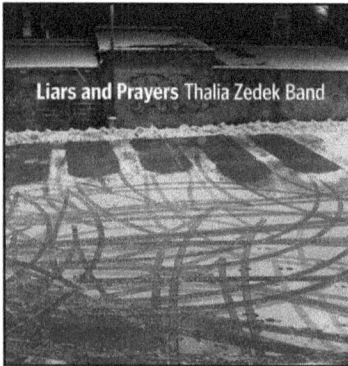

Thalia Zedek:
Liars and Prayers
(Thrill Jockey, 2008)
What? Noise rocker employs full sound for experiment with commercially minded release.

Zedek had fronted creditable noise rock bands, like Come, and collaborated with others before, belatedly, heading out on her own. Her first releases mined the same territory as she had covered within bands, but the fuller sound and more accentuated hooks of Liars and Prayers marked a serious effort to harness this power in a more radio friendly format. Less a sell out and more an attempt to wrestle notions of commerciality squarely into her corner, Liars and Prayers has the feel of a battle – akin, arguably to Lydia Lunch colliding her avant-garde sensibilities with standard song craft on Smoke in a Darkened Room.

Zedek's voice is a rasping, lived in, instrument of real character and her influences clearly reference the masters of the very personal song, she once covered Leonard Cohen's "Dance me to the End of Love" in definitive style. On Liars and Prayers she spreads this over a range of styles, the opening "Next Exit" starts with gentle country backing, allowing Zedek's vocal to work its way slowly in. Most of the songs here are long, narrative affairs. The styles vary, the sequence of songs keeps changing the mood, and Zedek emerges as a writer/performer of incredible strength and personality. "Next Exit" slowly builds to the emotive point: "There are no half measures/Only the lost and the winners." By contrast, "Body Memory" is a straight in your face rocker with a hint of Patti Smith/P J Harvey. "Begin to Exhume" takes her back to the noise rock of old but still sits well within this varied collection, supported by a sympathetic backing band. Described in isolation each song lends itself to comparisons. It's beyond doubt that the more personal and enduring writers in this territory, from Patti Smith to Neil Young, are an influence. Liars and Prayers climbs beyond the influences to show a reflective, focussed and multi-faceted talent taking on the mainstream and doing it her way. If there's a significant weakness here All Music Guide may well have nailed it, the: "unflagging intensity is almost overwhelming." Liars and Prayers needs time and attention, but it repays both.

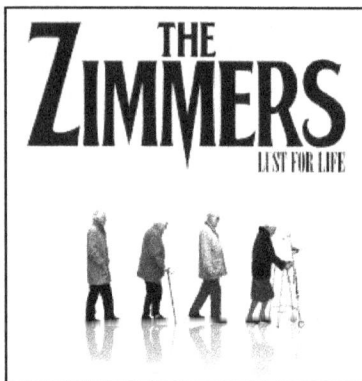

The Zimmers:
Lust for Life
(Shameless/BBC, 2008)
What? Rock of aged.

A novelty act for sure, but one with a point. The Zimmers (Est. 2007) are a British band made up entirely of pensioners and generally believed to have the oldest members of any band in the world. Since their inception, death has – predictably – claimed a few of their number, including Joan Bonham (mother of the Led Zeppelin drum legend), but they continue, and the core of their repertoire remains available on this disc. The centre of the Zimmers* appeal is a combination of lively and loud rock production sounds and, session musicians who sound like they're on it most of the time, a catalogue drawn from the most anthemic and opinionated rock and pop cuts and a lingering sense of pathos as the words generally associated with young performers and composers are moved in this context to comment on the lives of the elderly. A television documentary and subsequent publicity made it clear that The Zimmers exist partly as a means for lonely elderly people – including care home residents and those living alone in high-rise accommodation – to get involved in purposeful activity. Add to this mix the availability of enough studio trickery to get the harmonies of an essentially amateur group spot on and you have the recipe that made Lust for Life a steady seller and allowed this novelty act to place their own version of "My Generation" in the UK singles chart.

Lust for Life lines up classics from fifty years of rock and pop including full-on AOR bombast (Queen's "We Will Rock You"), edgy if catchy anthems: "Lust for Life," "My Generation," "Fight for Your Right to Party" and "Firestarter," and some poignant re-workings of tender and reflective material: "Let it Be," "Tears in Heaven" and "What the World Needs Now is Love." There are 13 assorted tracks, varying lead singers and different production styles on the album, ending – perhaps predictably – with The Zimmers' take on "My Way" before the collection serves up a 14th cut, the Capt. Fandango mix of "My Generation."

It's to the credit of the producers that the backings may have been tidied up in the studio but some of the lead vocals allow in the occasional flatness and the performances that betray the age of the singers and give a sense of their speaking voices intruding. Never more so than on "Old and Wise" (a re-working of a US #21 hit for the Alan Parsons Project, originally sung by Colin Blundstone), which is transformed by The Zimmers into a truly strange beast. In keeping its forward looking lyric intact and putting a croaking older vocal in place of Blundstone's high-ranged beauty "Old and Wise" works as a reflection on the fact that the combination of age and wisdom may come so late that the wisdom brings with it a reflection on mortality.

*For those resident in some territories the name might translate literally as The Walkers. The band were named in honour of the mobile-towel-rail-alike walking aids generally used by the elderly and infirm. In Britain, and one or two other territories, these aids are popularly known as Zimmer Frames; the generic name having arisen from the role of Zimmer Holdings in manufacturing and supplying said items.

Zola Jesus:
Versions
(Sacred Bones, 2013)
What? Industrial meets Diamanda Galas vocalisings over a classical backdrop.

With its roots in an invitation for Nika Roza Danilova (AKA Zola Jesus) to perform at the Guggenheim Museum Versions is an hypnotic and strangely effective combination of the electronic music that had (hitherto) been the usp of the Zola Jesus brand, stark industrial stylings provided by JG Thirlwell (Foetus) – invited by Danilova to join the performance – and a string quartet, brought in to back Danilova's vocals. The results do credit to all concerned. Thirlwell's arrangements are hesitant, painstaking and fragile, Danilova's vocals touch on a range of moods from conversational and troubled on "Avalanche (Slow)" to assertive and unapproachable on "Fall Back;" (the only cut here that was previously unreleased).

The Guggenheim performance was received with rapture by many. The consensus of critical opinion suggesting that her songs - stripped of most electronics and supported with strings instead – had space to breathe and communicate. Versions sounds nothing like Nirvana's stint on MTV Unplugged but, like that set, it presents the brooding and turbulence at the heart of a sound and artistic vision, and thereby allows a wider public to appreciate why the artist has such a dedicated following. Zola Jesus had never before attempted anything as still and focussed as the versions here of "Night" and "Collapse."

It's strange to think that the odd discordant note or jarring tone might be reassuring. But, Versions packs a few such moments, which serve as reminders of how pristine Zola Jesus' studio recordings sound. Versions – by contrast – surrenders almost nothing of the uncompromising and artistically vibrant studio work but still moves itself into a place from which it can reach a wide audience. If the string-backed ballads of every artist packed the integrity of the slower cuts here, the whole world would be a better place.

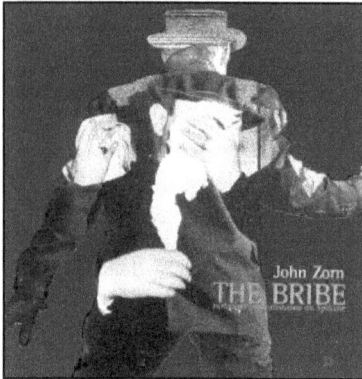

John Zorn:
The Bribe
(Tzadik, 1998)
What? Free thinking jazz genius plays unaccustomed supporting role.

Zorn belongs with some of those perennial outsiders chronicled here. Like Sun Ra, Hawkwind and Captain Beefheart Zorn is represented by an atypical work in this book because we're assuming many of those motivated to wander into these pages will have some familiarity with the man and his myriad works. Indeed – like Sun Ra – almost all of Zorn's long-playing releases could have passed muster with regard to inclusion in this book. The Bribe is formed of three long pieces – sub-divided into sections – originally composed as a backing track for radio drama, and subsequently used in a similar capacity on stage. Zorn's immense discography of works featuring his searing sax skills and multi-instrumental talents contains few works like this. For the most part Zorn is a born musical story-teller; much of his work taking strong sounds and lead lines and pushing them at warp speed to improbable destinations. The Bribe is a fluid ensemble composition with improvisations and much sympathetic playing. The original music was – after all - intended to run behind the speeches of actors.

This is music that would add to such a performance, but it also stands on its own merits. Short tracks like "The Big Freeze" romp along resolutely. This may be pedestrian by Zorn's standards but it is still a long way from ethereal or ambient music. The Bribe emerges as an unapologetic and strange beast. This is background music of quality and distinction which rewards repeated listens by revealing a deft lick here, a brilliant shift of percussion there, and always a strong sense of where the overall sound is going. This is an album of sympathies. Sympathy with the original intention of the piece as accompaniment to a performance and also sympathy between the septet performing the music. The presence of piano and organ gives endless melodic possibilities to the musical themes and turntablist Christian Marclay opens up a range of arbitrary elements that work well to bring humour, and surprise. Zorn's best work is intense and uncompromising; making him as much an acquired taste as many of the singular artists featured in this book. The Bribe is one of the odd exceptions in Zorn's catalogue; that works for a range of tastes.

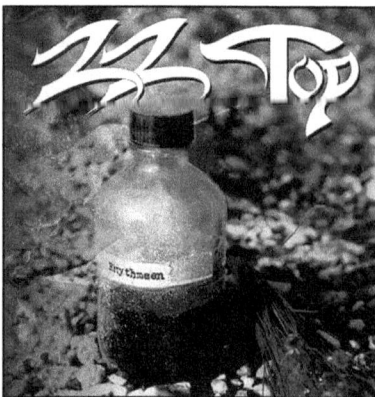

ZZ Top:
Rhythmeen
(RCA, 1996)
What? Grunt, grind, sputter…good ol' boys go blues again.

Top's ascendency to the heights of rock stardom was achieved on the back of hard work and clever marketing. But, alongside the route one assault on the top of the rock mountain Top always had the problem of holding in some qualities that didn't necessarily sit well together.

Initially a bar-blues band with the ability to reduce most small venues to swirling sweat-pits, the band's fame grew through some audacious live stunts; such as the stage appearance of a live steer during their massive tour behind the Tejas album in the mid-seventies.

MTV and the surreal comedy of the videos for hits like "Sharp Dressed Man" was the making of ZZ Top in commercial terms, their blues base still remained but the hard sheen on the guitar sound, synth drums and the playing of their nudge-nudge humour for mainstream laughs diluted some of the qualities that had earned them a hard-core fan-base. When the Eliminator album topped 10 million sales and the subsequent Afterburner, Recycler and Antennae mined the same formula to decreasing, but still massive, returns, it seemed like Top had the faders pre-set to "radio friendly" with every visit to the studio.

Their second outing for RCA Records was a stunning about-turn. So called, apparently, because it packs mean rhythms Rhythmeen is sludgier, more ragged, more shamelessly down in the gutter with its jokes and – above all – more unashamedly blues than anything in their catalogue. It polarised critics, most of whom responded with lukewarm reviews, and marked the end of the band as a rock-solid cert for top 10 chart positions. In the USA no ZZ Top album in over 15 years had failed to dent the top 20, Rhythmeen stalled at 29. In the UK they'd had four top 10 albums in a row, until Rhythmeen stopped dead at 32. Strangely Finland, a territory that hadn't bought their albums in massive quantities before, loved it and gave them a #3 chart position.

Having balanced the sexual elements in their humour with the needs of a mainstream audience, and matched their dyed-in-the-blues power-trio chops with the need to knock out ear-catching hit-riffs, Top had thrown the manual away and returned as full-on evangelists for Texan eccentricity and the darker side of the blues. In terms of laugh-out-loud Top humour "Zipper Job" – a celebration of sex-change surgery - probably shades it, "Vincent Price Blues" collides a falling vocal line, surreal images and a low-down-sludgy riff, and tracks like "Humbucking Part 2" are so thick with riffs and growls they are more like late-night howls at the moon than simple rock songs. The one serious punt at a catchy single "What's Up With That?" sits a little uneasily towards the start of the lengthy album.

Musically, they pulled it off because the band – by this point marking 26 years with no line-up changes – were as tight as ever, and the growl and grind came over a solid driving rhythm that gave the most incomprehensible moments a sense of direction. If it wasn't exactly commercial suicide (the ticket sales for Top gigs continue to hold up well), it was certainly a watershed moment, a clear statement of the capabilities of the band and a shameless standing up for the essence of craziness that had made them a compelling act from the start.

Various Artists:
African Scream Contest: Raw and Psychedelic Afro Sounds from Benin & Togo
(Analog Africa, 2008)
What? Fusion, freakout and a seamless dredging of the darkest depths of psychedelia.

The sparing release schedule on the Analog Africa label is one indication of the quality of each release. So much so that, frankly, the present authors would recommend any of the opening dozen releases on that label. Scream Contest is, therefore, included here partly because it's a genuine revelation and partly because it ably demonstrates what the label does to perfection. Aiming their collecting efforts at cultural melting pots, Analog Africa gather hitherto overlooked sounds released mainly on labels long since lost to history and by artists generally unknown even by the world music community. The detailed liner notes (44 pages including 16 interviews) that accompany Scream Contest put a creditable argument together explaining why Benin and Togo – located near to Ghana and Nigeria – managed to keep their own traditions alive, embrace a strong French influence, take on board James Brown and channel a little Voodoo (which began in Benin). How much of the resulting 14 track collection is genuinely psychedelic remains questionable. Most of the music on offer blends some combination of local beats (frequently complex polyrhythmic material, often spread over a lengthy track) with the influences mentioned above.

This material pre-dates any significant understanding of the market for world music, and lots of it stumbles into a territory recognisable as an offshoot of jazz fusion (albeit with no sense that those making this music were imitating anyone in the USA). All of the above is channelled through a combination of standard rock instrumentation augmented by local instruments. The tracks generally feel as if they were written by people playing live, the grooves are insistent and effective and a lot of the production surprisingly good. Gabo Brown & Orchestre Poly-Rythmo nail a groove from the opening seconds of "It´s a Vanity," the James Brown influence is clear but their own stamp on the proceedings gets stronger as the track develops. So too, Orchestre Super Jheevs des Paillotes' "Ye Nan Lon An" which hits a blend of mind expanding pscyh/funk/ African and mixes it to devastating effect. The vast majority of the cuts do not present their lyrics in English and most of the material is so long, and so groove based, that it can't have been aimed at lucrative export markets. When Les Volcans de la Capital's "Oya Ka Jojo" feels a shade too short after 13 minutes, you know you have a rare, and wonderful, compilation on your hands.

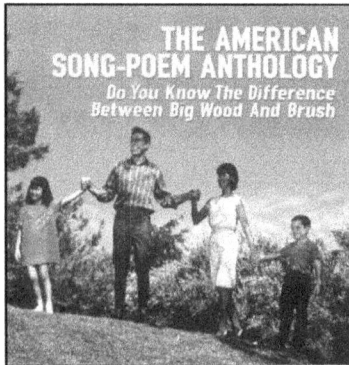

Various Artists:
The American Song-Poem Collection: Do You Know the Difference Between Bigwood and Brush?
(Setanta, 2003)
What? "A gold mine of mix-tape material:" All Music Guide

The birth of this material is well recorded online so we'll keep this outline basic and get to the music. Song-poems resulted when recording studios offered the general public the chance to send in their original words and pay cash – generally between $75 and $400 – to have their ideas turned into proper studio recordings. The USA was the world leader in this industry which flourished in the 1960s and 70s and was killed off by improved home-recording equipment. Effectively vanity publishing for songwriters; the song-poem industry was also notorious for its willingness to take on board any and every insane rant or nonsensical rhyme and record it quickly. Quality control was often limited to a solid assessment of whether the customer could pay; from which point a record – however bizarre – would be made.

Such works have long been the quarry of a particular breed of collector and the growth of interest in outsider music has made compilations of the best/most bizarre recordings bankable. Bigwood and Brush is about as good as it has ever got in this department. A varied trawl of triumphs of songwriting hope over reality, offering up 28 conversation stoppers. The first and most important thing to note is that the musicians here, lowly paid and little regarded at the time, play, sing and embellish out of their skins to make silk purses from putrifying sow's ears. On most of the tracks here they are the real stars and seasoned campaigners in this war against irredeemably crass lyrics like Rod (aka Rodd) Keith have – rightfully – become highly regarded by afficionados of the avant-garde. (See the entry on a Keith's album I Died Today elsewhere in this book).

Keith's genius extends to a soprano (as in he's singing a female part) virtuoso lead vocal on "I'm Just the Other Woman (Remake)." As a vision of a nation in love with its own (frequently misguided) dreams Bigwood and Brush throws a new light on history. "Richard Nixon" and "Jimmy Carter Says Yes" sit side-by-side in the running order, both taking campaign hyperbole at face value and anticipating their subjects would eventually rank alongside Abraham Lincoln as part of the national myth. Minor obsessions also make for compelling listening with one song in praise of "Convertibles and Headbands," Bobbi Blake's "I Like Yellow Things" and the madly percussive beat-poem "Beat of the Traps" (basically a hymn to the joys of drumming) all providing the mix-tape gold described by All Music Guide.

Sonically the production is lacking in breadth and studio trickery, but the musical talent hired by the hour were generally experts at squeezing the last drop of fi from low-fi conditions. Consequently, Bigwood and Brush frequently achieves a B-movie charm to the point that your imagination and sympathies stretch to what is being attempted, not what you actually hear. The compilation is also well ordered, rotating the cod-country, big ballads and attempts at pop novelty on a regular basis and bringing in enough insanity, inspiration and hokey-charm to make the album a great listen. The changing dynamic between the original lyricists and the hired hands contributes to the variety on offer; never more so than with the closing track. Probably placed at the end to allow those of delicate sensibility to rip the CD from the tray after hearing their favourites, Ramsey Kearney's rendition of "Blind Man's Penis (Peace and Love)" with its refrain of: "A blind man's penis is erect because he's blind, it's erect because he's blind" and its drug-fuelled ramble about aliens and getting "high…on LSD" does suggest that some of those paying up to hear their lyrics turned into 7" singles did so in the full anticipation of creating music like nothing else they could buy. Whether the songwriters are laughing at the session hacks, or vice versa, is hardly the point with a song like "Blind Man's Penis (Peace and Love)." This closing cut is probably a rare case of customer and service industry both hearing exactly what they expected to hear.

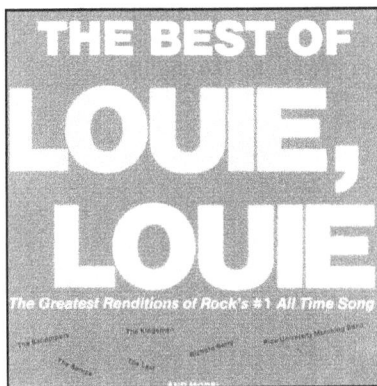

Various Artists:
Best of Louie Louie
(Rhino, 1990)
What? Two great chords, ten great cuts!

The gleefully moronic 1955 rock 'n' roll standard covered by ten different artists, including The Kingsmen's 1963 hit version and a cover version by original composer Richard Berry. Sadly it lacks Motorhead's apocalyptic rendering of the song, but the ten tracks pack enough variety and strangeness to make end to end listening of the compilation a unique experience. In order you hear: The Rice University Marching Owl Band, Richard Berry (NOT the original), Rockin' Robin Roberts, The Sonics, The Sandpipers (a latin and loungecore version), The Kingsmen, The Last, Eddie and the Subtitles, Les Dantz & his Orchestra (basically imagining Chic produced Bowie covering the song) and The Impossibles. The original and exceedingly hard to find vinyl version omits Eddie and the Subtitles but offers Black Flag's assault on a song they clearly love. "Louie Louie" emerges from the maulings as a malleable wonder, capable of enabling the creatively gifted and creatively challenged in equal amounts. The notion of any version being better than the others doesn't compute in this company. By the time you reach Les Dantz, the blatant steal from Bowie's hit is a welcome variant on the grinding chords. Repeated exposure to the album (not recommended unless you're hardened to audio strangeness in its varied forms) does scramble your senses to the point that identifying novelty and artistic sincerity becomes impossible. How, for example, do you regard the closing cut by The Impossibles? A gleeful fragment of choral singing which collides the vocal refrain from the trash rock classic with the melody from Handel's "Hallelujah Chorus."

Various Artists:
C86
(NME, 1986)
What? Indie on fire.

The British music paper NME had been giving away free cassette tapes for some time by 1986. The C86 compilation followed a similar C81 concept five years earlier. The C81 became notable for giving the first high-profile exposure to Aztec Camera and Scritti Politti, but in terms of lasting impact C86, probably, shades it, and earns a place here. Lining up a litany of little known bands, C86 nails a vision of the UK alive with ramshackle pop mavericks united by a love of loud guitars, reinventions of classic pop structures and individual ideas clamouring for attention. The strength of the C86 is its trawling of a range of established and dedicated independent labels. Along with the predictable operations like Creation, C86 takes tracks from the likes of Probe Plus (home of Half Man Half Biscuit) Head Records and Ron Johnson Records.

Most of C86 is guitar music, steeped in the classic pop verse/chorus approach and focussing the songs around a clear narrative. But the strength of the album is in the variety of sounds. Bogshed and Stump sit side by side on the first side of the tape, each bringing an indie guitar pop meets Beefheart vibe. Elsewhere some highly individual voices, including Bobby Gillespie of Primal Scream (who open the collection) and David Gedge of The Wedding Present (who close it), get their first high profile outings. And hard to pigeonhole acts, like Fuzzbox, bring a sense of breadth to the indie ethic. As a vision of the under-belly of Thatcher's Britain, a place alive with creativity, ideas and a sense of celebrating the moment, C86 is a powerful document. It amounted to a manifesto at the time, spurring on a generation of musicians and contributing to the subsequent Madchester and Britpop explosions. Cherry Red's 2013 five disc line up, Scared to Get Happy, provides a view of the whole decade of indie in Britain. But this collection is the best snapshot of a glorious moment of that party at its height. Note: the compilation CD86 is a two CD set, reverently created by Bob Stanley and compiled in honour of the C86, it's great, it has some of the same acts and some of the same tracks, and it's way longer, but it isn't this one. To further complicate this issue Cherry Red released the original C86 in 2014, with additional CDs of similar material.

Various Artists:
Cambodian Psych Out
(Defective, 2006)
What? Impressive beat boom and proto psych, lost to political brutality.

The heartbreaking fact leaping from 14 tracks of sweet pop, lively psychedelia and much south Asian flavouring is that the artists, and ideas, that drove an explosive pop industry, are almost all lost. Only three of the cuts here are attributed to anyone, and those are all credited to Cambodia's queen of pre Pol Pot chart pop, Ros Serey Sothea, aka Srei Sothear. Unearthing this work and compiling it has become a painstaking passion for a few die-hards (it's worth a visit to the Bodega Pop website to see how this phenomenon has found other Cambodian work, and treasures from other countries). Cambodian Psych Out presents a trashy and, occasionally, transcendental pop scene where throwaway charms of true tacky genius like "Go-Go Dance" rubbed chart places up against Sothea's impassioned pop balladry and Asian flavoured remakes of American garage band pop.

The collection really comes alive when all of the above mash into a three minute wonder like "Enjoy Now While You're Young" which has everything: rapid fire guitar, strident low budget organ chords, a clear and confident vocal and (tellingly) crackles from the original vinyl. Compared to the countless deaths of the killing fields it is a minor issue that the world lost a generation of musicians, a pop scene in Cambodia (and most of the master tapes). But this album is a worthy requiem for the nameless talents captured when they were carefree and loving their chance to shine.

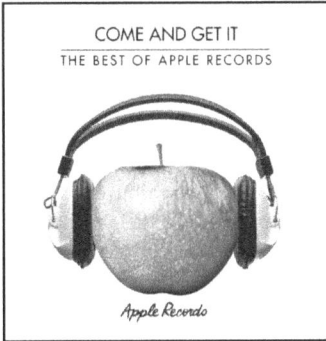

COME AND GET IT
THE BEST OF APPLE RECORDS

Apple Records

Various Artists:
Come and Get it: The Best of Apple Records
(Apple, 2010)
What? Sublime and ridiculous in equal measure. A record company gone mad…in a good way.

The Beatles' own label was both maligned and celebrated for a whimsical signing policy that made little commercial sense but produced the occasional nugget of genius that seemed to justify all the idiosyncrasies. Come and Get it lines up a series of Apple singles, packing one UK #1 hit, at least one other stone-gone sixties pop classic, some other hits, a slew of eclectic and under-rated curios and some random material that leaves you wondering what – exactly – the Fab Four were thinking some of the time. Mary Hopkin's beautifully sweet "Those Were The Days" deservedly tops the running order, just as it once took up lengthy residence at the top of the British charts. Badfinger's ultra-catchy "Day After Day" closes the show. In-between we get a raging and contradictory stable of acts. Come and Get it is years ahead of its time in the ethnic mix on offer. Hot Chocolate – chart fixtures of the 70s – turn up here with a patois-riddled take on "Give Peace a Chance" and sound unrecognisable as the act that would go on to record "You Sexy Thing." Reggae pioneer Doris Troy rubs shoulders with Billy Preston, whose take on "My Sweet Lord" takes no prisoners and actually preceded George Harrison's hit version. In fact, Harrison emerges with some credit from the compilation, masterminding the Radha Krsna Temple's "Govinda" and helming the soulful version of his own "Try Some, Buy Some" by Ronnie Spector. The inclusion of James Taylor's "Carolina on my Mind," recorded before he'd become a fixture in every student bedsit, shows Apple's A&R policy had some promise. Though the presence of the Black Dyke Mills Band and the gormless novelty of "The King of Fuh" (where the main interest is the variations they can get into the lyrics on the theme of Fuh-King) by Brute Force also suggest Apple put some commercially hopeless singles out, simply because they could.

With a whopping 21 singles on offer, Come and Get it probably pays off best when downloaded and savoured sparingly. But for those willing to stack it up end to end and shut out all other distractions this is a vision of The Beatles unavailable elsewhere and a vision of a record company few others would be able to contemplate.

DEATH DEALERS

Various Artists:
Death Dealers
(Nasty, 1995)
What? Total trashfest of crucial killer cuts!

Rejoicing in the catalogue number Nightstalk 1 this home-tape turned vinyl album is a concept piece based around a fairly simple idea. Gather eight low-fi trash-rock takes about murder and drop genuine news reports and interviews with the real murderers between the tracks. It's gruesome fun/ needlessly sick depending on your taste. The selected cuts are the kind that were already known to compilers of works like Wavy Gravy by the mid-nineties and the interviews were also a regular feature on privately traded cassette tapes and photocopied fanzines. But the compiling talents behind Death Dealers have still done a good job of gathering the great stuff. John Wayne Gacy, Charles Manson and Jeffrey Dahmer appear in interviews, the killer cuts include two by Eddie Noak (including the awesome "Psycho" which also appears on Wavy Gravy) and the fast, furious and gleefully psychopathic paean of praise to Ed Gein, "Grind Her Up" by The Uncalled 4: "Grind her up…put her heart in the refrigerator, if you want to save it for later."

Cheap cash ins on genuine crimes include Red River Dave's "California Hippie Murders," "Gacy's Place" by The Mentally Ill and the stupendously overblown theatricality of the "The Tower" (as in going up the water tower for the purposes of shooting passers-by) by Johnny Legend. The recording quality wasn't great on the originals and suffers again slightly here from being copied. The low-fi experience is taken to the limit by the poor quality of some of the interviews and the loud music/quiet interviews dynamic doesn't lend itself to living easily with this collection playing in the background, but it's still a chilling and very unusual listen. Above all, it's the collision of bad taste celebrations and the matter-of-fact nature of some of the anti-heroes who appear that give the whole album a sense of tension. More-or-less the final word is given to serial killer/ cannibal Jeffrey Dahmer who discusses his crimes with no more emotional involvement than some other person chatting away about job choices: "I was branching out, that's when the cannibalism started…at first it was curiosity then it became compulsive."

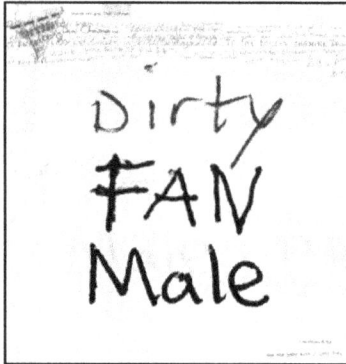

Various Artists:
Dirty Fan Male
(Trunk Records, 2005)
What? Wankers; The Album.

"Dear Mistress Louise, I am a pervert…,"and so begins a listening experience so hard to categorise that it's probably best just to state what is going on here and let your imagination do the rest. This album of the stage show of the on-going project compiles a slew of sexually charged communications sent directly to high-profile glamour models of the 1990s. The frequently incoherent, surreal and sometimes sad missives spill the inner lives of the correspondents and reveal virtually nothing about the girls they adore. A local Elvis-alike has had his head kicked in on a monumental scale, but remains unrepentant because there is a girl willing to get her ample charms out for the cameras and give him a reason to live. So it goes.

Jonny Trunk (head honcho of Trunk Records) had the inspiration for the project when he began reading the fanmail of his glamour model sister, Eve Vorley, and the nous to deputise his friend Wisbey to provide the back-bone of the recording with a series of letters read out in a cod-Cary Grant style. The sporadic musical accompaniment gradually ratchets itself up to the point of some letters re-appearing as full-blown musical numbers. Letters, read and sung, rely on pastiche performances, aping popular styles of musicians and actors (Cary Grant's is simply the most prominent such style), so – for example – a lurid little rant that starts with the request "I Want to Hold Your Hand" is fittingly performed in a McCartneyesque piano style complete with needlessly over-done soul stylings towards the end. The Dirty Fan Male show ran to packed houses on the Edinburgh Fringe for a few years where live audiences could marvel at missives like the following: "In 95 I had a vivid dream that I am to have a mystical experience. My name will change to Don Male and lead an important campaign. I become London Male my Active Force is PowerDon. My dreams tell me to make preparations." Our software tells us some of that is ungrammatical…but that is part of the unique charm of Dirty Fan Male, and its parade of doodles from the dregs of the Daily Sport's readership. Incidentally, PowerDon was still living at home when he wrote to Donna Ewin.

This relic from the pre-internet porn days packs a period charm and sense of introspective isolation in which fantasies had to be elaborate and creative because – back then - there wasn't any Serbian housewife waiting on the other end of a broadband connection to respond in real time to the tosser directing her machinations.

"PS: Penis, cock, willy dong…."

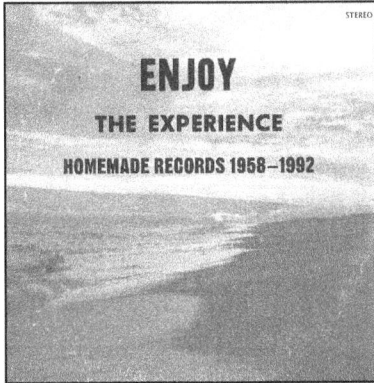

Various Artists:
Enjoy the Experience: Homemade Records 1958-1992
(Now Again, 2013)
What?   Hokum, Hell and high points: but it's anyone's guess which is which.

The internet has opened the floodgates for rediscovery of every local hero and wannabe with a record still languishing in a junk shop. WFMU and a few others, (including one of the authors of this book), have a habit of inflicting this stuff on radio listeners. Music for Maniacs and a number of like-minded blogs also see fit to share it. A few other compilations, like the Song Poem Collection listed in this book have scratched the surface. But this two-dozen cut twofer is one of the most user-friendly trawls of random assaults on stardom from the golden age of home record production you are ever likely to find. Notions of best/worst talent/scary should be left at the door, because Enjoy the Experience is as much an assault on the senses as it is artistic statement. There are several ways into understanding the whole lot. The obvious entrance doors involve starting with the self-identifying wannabes (i.e. spotting the guy who thinks he is Jim Morrison), alternatively see this collection as the unfiltered outpourings of the American dream, where everyone has a shot.

Many of the acts aren't greatly troubled by the acceptability of their message and some are absurdly talented but blatantly in the wrong time period. The Invaders' pumping and jazzy "Spacing Out" is an unapologetic barnstormer of an instrumental, worthy of a hit, but probably released in the wrong year, by the wrong people. By contrast, Ray Torksy's upbeat toe tapper, "666," is an outrageous mash up supper club singer and lyrics heralding the imminent arrival of the Book of Revelations upon the Earth. On balance, The Sillhouttes' psych-jazz-with-fuzz-guitar-and-flute "Lunar Invasion" may be a better soundtrack for any forthcoming apocalypse.

A few wannabes are, literally, paying tribute. Though whether Elton John would regard the nine minute medley of his best works provided by Silk and Silver as reverent or repugnant is up for discussion. Elton John's backing tracks have never sunk as low as the basic percussion accompanying "Rocket Man" in this mix. The sound quality is, predictably, variable, and some of the playing more enthusiastic than accomplished. But the compilers have done an admirable job of sorting the items that betray their ambitions despite the resulting sounds. Clearly, many of those on show believe in their own dreams, even if history and our own ears now suggest depressing levels of delusional thinking. Stephen David Heitkotter isn't Jimi Hendrix and "Cadillac Woman" isn't "Purple Haze" but you just know that during the guitar strangling he believed some power was pouring through him. Enough power, certainly, to help him ignore the fact his "drummer" was bashing a pair of bin lids with hammers. The compilers also deserve credit for finding the perfect fragments to open and close the festivities, two mix-tape friendly gems, one by The Muzzy Band and the other by Vinny Roma, celebrate the act of creating music for your friends, and the joy to be had. Like they say on the cover of the admirably well-informed liner notes: "Enjoy…"

Various Artists: Faith:
A Message From the Spirits
(Soul Jazz Records, 1996)
What? Around the world in eight faiths.

There isn't exactly a shortage of religious recordings for any of the world's main faiths. But this collection still achieves a certain distinction because it sets off with a simple idea of chronicling the sounds, mainly musical, of the world's leading faiths. The copious liner notes give insight into each of the tracks. Faith visits around eight different faith groups (depending on how separately you regard "Christian" from the Greek Orthodox version of the same thing and how interchangeable you consider the various groups of Buddhists to be). The album also pits some vehement English language Christian preaching against mantra like chants from other religions, varies field recordings, including recordings made in the street, with studio recordings and lines up the 15 track collection in such a way as to provide variety of sound, mood and intensity of worship from one track to the next. Faith has the ear of a documentarian for the interesting and eclectic, and the good sense to trust in the response and intelligence of the listener. It is never better than when it follows the outpourings of Evangelist Sheila from a US radio broadcast with Voodoo drumming from Haiti. As an insight into a multi-cultural world praying and playing with equal passion and irreconcilable beliefs, Faith is a powerful testament. To any secular listener, it is also a potential source of eclectic mix tape gold.

Various Artists:
Elvis Impersonator Blues
(Helvis, 1995)
What? Unauthorised tribute and major work of Elvisology.

The first – and to date only – long-player unleashed on Helvis Records, Elvis Impersonator Blues compiles a series of high-strangeness and heartfelt tributes to The King. Appropriately perhaps, it only saw availability on vinyl and it wears its – ahem – independent release fairly prominently on its sleeve with gleefully gaudy artwork. One side of the label features an apparently unconcerned young Elvis smiling as the fires of Hell rage behind him. The low profile of most of the performers leaves even the most knowledgeable fan at something of a loss. But, once you've heard a gem like B.F. Snow's "Elvis is a Legend" you won't quickly forget it. In any case, by the time you're a few tracks into the fun Elvis Impersonator Blues may well have worked its very special magic of convincing you that this is the sound of 24/7 radio in the world in which everything is Elvis and the individual acts on show here are way less important than combined love they bring as they fall before the power of The King. That point is ably made by the presence of an otherwise unidentified track called "Let's Lock" (basically an Asian rehash of "Jailhouse Rock" that can't make its mind up if it's in English or the language of the singer). Side two opens with an introduction from a DJ identified as "SaucerElvis" and the cultural explosion of tributes here is further enhanced by – arguably – the greatest of all the fawning gems on offer with both sides of Peter Singh's glorious single "Rockin' with the Sikh"/ "Elvis I'm on the Phone." Singh, a resident of Wales who performed an Elvis tribute with a Las Vegas Elvis suit whilst also wearing his turban, opens his A'-side with a genius-ridden lyrical gem: "I don't smoke dope, I don't drink bourbon, all I wanna do, is shake my turban."

Utterly classic! For the most part the album is rock 'n' roll, in the widest sense. Some of it low-fi and much of it played with more passion than skill, though the presence of Cramps Lux Interior and Poison Ivy discussing whether Elvis is still alive does change the pace in the middle of side one.

Various Artists:
Flappers, Vamps and Sweet Young Thing
(Asv, 1990)
What? It wasn't just Mae West, then.

The years 1924 to 1931 aren't greatly regarded as a classic rock 'n' roll period but a certain amount of decadence and hedonism did give them that kind of edge. The genius of this compilation is to chronicle that period with a focus on female vocalists and characterful performances; some of which hint at the underground scene of the time. That's never clearer than when Ruth Etting sings Irving Berlin's "It All Belongs to Me" and keeps the gender roles true to the original lyrics (i.e. she addresses the song to another woman). The Brox Sister's take on "Red Hot Mamma" is a similar article. Elsewhere the 20 tracks on offer are sequenced well enough to keep changing moods. These moods range from slow and sentimental, to blue-tinged jazz and a selection of standard sugary ballads. Though even these betray some character and personality; Gertrude Lawrence – for example – giving it some grunting and glottal stopping towards the end of "Do, Do, Do" in an ever-so-slightly suggestive way.

The productions show their age, and the work on offer here is variable to the point that listening from one end to the other guarantees you'll react differently depending on where you are in the running order. But this is an historical document if only because it is a window on a party generation who shared more with current self-obsessions than we might realise. In their own way a few of these songs are as much about sex, drugs and flap 'n' roll as work produced decades later.

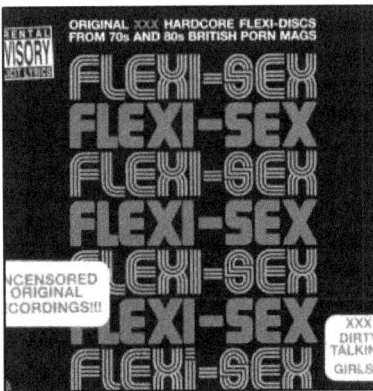

Various Artists:
Flexi-Sex
(Trunk, 2003)
What? Pint-sized parcels of pornucopia.

Subtitled: "Original XXX Hardcore Flexi-Discs From 70s and 80s British Porn Mags," it isn't hard to figure out the creative vision that brought the contents of this album into existence. The porn models pinned together with staples in the mag pour their public identities into breathless accounts of their hard-wired horniness and insatiable desire to please their men. The objects of their lust are normal blokes, their fantasies involve a lot of exposure, posturing and pleasuring, and they are up for anything and everything you (as in ordinary bloke buying the magazine) might want. The snatches of music betray the crudely tacked together production and the surface noise betrays the collation of this collection from the original cover mounted flexi-discs. Seven of the nine cuts are variations on a well-meaning model giving it her best shot at imaginative fantasy. "Rosie and Nobby" involves our heroine intoning in a strong Geordie accent. Geordies come from Newcastle (that's a working class hotbed of traditional manliness in northern England, assuming you're reading this in some other country). Rosie is a reader's wife. Predictably, then, the "reader" to whom she's married, loves nothing better than to watch her in action in their home with some other stud, and Rosie likes her men "boozy" (assuming any women are still reading this entry at this point, we're only reporting the truth of this record, we struggle to believe Rosie's fantasy as literal truth).

The finale, rightfully saved to last, is Mary Millington's narration of a sexual encounter with the kind of person forming the original audience for the flexi-discs. Britain's pint-sized porn queen packed a deal of acting talent in her diminutive frame. She manages to inhabit her fantasy to a more convincing level than her peers on the CD. The production values are slightly better too.

The internet long ago rendered this pantomime pornucopia as passé. You could, just about, construct an argument suggesting this compilation amounts to an insightful, oral, history. Though, frankly, it's easier to conclude with the thought that this is an unusual listen, worthy of its place in this book.

Various Artists:
The Girls are at it Again: UK Beat Girls 1964-1969 –
(Universal, 2009)
What? Many-mooded pop compilation packed with forgotten glories.

One of those vault-scraping sessions that was truly worth the sweat. The Girls… gathers twenty varied tracks from UK pop singles, four of which started life as B-sides.

The collection tells a story of girl-pop as a repository of personal thoughts and emotional scenes; cutting a swathe through sixties fashions. Considering the time-period chronicled it is remarkable how little psychedelia, or even its freak-beat offshoot, intrudes. The Girls… offers banging beat-pop, some soulful sounds and soul searching thoughts; and a lot of catchy and convincing hooks. From the rain-soaked street scene with a popette in the picture to the domestic dramas played out in the lyrics; this is a vision of black and white Britain, working class, austere and dreaming of love.

Most of The Girls… is made up of love songs. You can seize the moment: "So Little Time" by Diana Dors; believe hopefully: "I'm Gonna Marry The Boy" by Danielle or regret and learn: "Love Made A Fool Of Me" by The Carolines. A few acts went on to much bigger things though the early pop works of Lesley Duncan and Kiki Dee gathered here don't bear that much resemblance to their acoustic and introspective successes of the seventies. The compilers worked hard here and the net is spread fairly wide to catch the best sounds. Never more so than Australian Lori Balmer (who cut "Four Faces West" for Polydor UK in 1968).

The fact this B-side by a hopeful imported artist makes the cut whilst (presumably) a stack of less inspired tracks by better known artists were rejected says everything about The Girls… The Diana Dors cut is a spirited classic. By no means the best singer in any technical sense in this company, Dors grabs the lyric and – by the sounds of it – the man she's singing to by the throat, and demands a result.

This collection is a vision of a rain-soaked country slapping on the make-up and a new pair of kinky boots for a night's partying followed – possibly – by love, or something like it. It is beat-pop, more Mod than any other fashion style and soulful; though not necessarily soul, music.

Various Artists:
Golden Throats: The Great Celebrity Sing Off
(Rhino, 1988)
What? NOT the original as claimed but – arguably – the best.

It is claimed elsewhere that this collection – running a shade under 40 minutes - is the start of the craze for kitsch "celebrities make bad records so let's compile their worst moments and laugh ourselves sick," compilations. Technically, no, there are bad record compilations, fairly heavy on celebrity abominations, that precede this. In any case, the existence of collectors of this stuff was known for years and a handful of DJs – Dr Demento in the USA and Kenny Everett in the UK to name a couple – made a habit of pouring this stuff into their airtime. Kenny Everett's World's Worst Record Show collection dug out a few celeb cuts and…

Anyway, this is a still amongst the best of the bunch, even if – largely – it's playing by its own rules. For starters, Golden Throats heads (appropriately) straight for the jugular, pulling in some bankers and opening up with one of the biggies: Leonard Nimoy's variable accent supported with perfunctory session backing in an uncalled for massacre/interpretation of "Proud Mary." A genuine "stick to the day job" moment if ever such a thing existed on record. Nimoy, his Star Trek captain: William Shatner, and actor Sebastian Cabot each contribute two tracks to the 14 on offer. Shatner's The Transformed Man is a box of delights when presented to the Golden Throats compilers and Sebastian Cabot's dramatic reinterpretations as he speaks his way through Bob Dylan lyrics are a similar find. What Golden Throats does better than the competition is find the gold, mine the seam to perfection and line up the resulting nuggets with some sense of providing a sequence that simply works when played in the original order. Nimoy's cuts are far enough away from each other, and blissfully short enough, for his welcome never to wear out. And the spot-colour is provided by the sublime sounds of Mae West rocking her way through "Twist and Shout" and Noel Harrison's oh-so English/oh so wonderfully unaware of the original take on "A Whiter Shade of Pale." Obviously, production quality varies, the amount of musical talent on offer is similarly variable from track to track, and the one real consistency appears to be the heavy presence of songs backed by session musicians who nailed it and got the hell out of there quickly enough to preserve what little sanity they had left. All the better to leave the front of the stage to the actors, then. It's true that these days the world is wall-to-wall with lesser imitations of this little cul-de-sac in the compiler's art. And, also true that Golden Throats deserves respect in this company for maintaining the quality. This original was followed with a second volume pulling – more of less – the same stunt before a third collection put its focus firmly on country/folk rock and a fourth instalment mined the rich seam of celebrity massacres of Beatles' tunes.

Various Artists:
Great Lost Elektra Singles Volume 1
(Elektra, 2005)
What? Ten tuneful brainstorms!

There's a blindingly brilliant box set celebrating the work of Elektra Records, a label that at its very best – Love, The Doors – broke artistic barriers, and did so with impressive album sales and chart singles. It took several abortive early sixties attempts to hone an awareness of the singles market, an area in which the label remained very ambivalent until their more psychedelic acts pioneered a brand of incendiary and innovative chart fodder that was seldom equalled, let alone bettered, in its own time. The Great Lost works here might not, exactly, achieve trade description levels of matching the claims on the cover. Some of this work never totally fell off the radar and some of it – frankly – is great only the minds that conceived it. Over ten tracks this compilation tells the stories of maverick talents, hopelessly over-achieving acts who poured brilliance onto one side of 7" vinyl, and two embryonic talents who matured in tangential ways to their early outings. The two sides of The Beefeaters that open the collection catch a hopeful bunch of tunesmiths turning out catchy pop in shameless homage to the British invasion of the USA in the early sixties. It's good, if slightly anonymous, stuff rendered riveting when you realise David Crosby, Gene Clarke and Roger McGuinn are the front line of the band. For full-on curio value it's a toss-up between Judy Collins' rendition of "I'll Keep it With Mine" and David Ackles' "La Route a Chicago." Collins presents a workmanlike stab at folk rock with bright production flourishes, and makes the best of a song the sleeve notes rightly admit is "flat." It remains worth investigating on the basis that it's one of the least known covers of an obscure Bob Dylan song. Ackles' French reworking of his own "The Road to Cairo" is a wonderfully overblown epic ballad, aiming for Scott Walker's signature territory, when Walker himself was still a cuddly pop star. Some flaming blues from Paul Butterfield, the insanely ambitious folk rockers Eclection (some of whom found fame elsewhere) and a brace of cuts from Stalk-Forrest Group (basically an early version of the band subsequently known and loved as Blue Oyster Cult) also give the collection moments of wonder. As a validation of a label occasionally tortured by the level of its ambition this package is a short and riveting insight into a side of sixties music seldom heard, or bought, at the time.

Various Artists:
I am the Center: Private Issue New Age Music In America 1950-1990
(Light in the Attic, 2013)
What? A revelation, across 20 tracks and two discs.

The world isn't short of compilation albums claiming to provide "the definitive," "the ultimate" or that "change your life" experience. To be fair, the hyperbole that accompanied this twofer scouring of the fringes of new age music wasn't that overblown, Light in the Attic's website simply advised you should: "Forget everything you know, or think you know, about new age, a genre that has become one of the defining musical-archaeological explorations of the past decade." It further promised: "I Am The Center…is the first major anthology to survey the golden age of new age and reveal the unbelievable truth about the genre." It is debateable how much of the music on offer packs an unbelievable truth of any kind, hearing in this case, is - probably – believing. But, there is a serious truth to be gleaned once you have availed yourself of the shortest items – a dozen of which are packed onto the first CD – and the longer items – eight of which make up the second CD. It is that a range of serious minded and totally sincere experiments in mathematical music, raising spiritual consciousness and exploring inner space were out there long before "new age" became a byword for soporific, somnambulant soirees through a few chords and a snatch of melody. I Am The Center is also a celebration of the compiler's art and one album that defies most downloading under-mining because it offers up music still unavailable via the usual pirate haunts.

By rotating the styles, providing copious information in the accompanying booklet and digging deep into privately issued and little known recordings, the compilation charts the roots of a new age music, digging up the material that was outside of any well-known movement of its time and frequently produced with little or no hope of significant commercial success.

Sure, it noodles, shimmers, drones on and – depending on your opinion – vanishes somewhere in the vicinity of its own naval on several occasions. But the collection is also an informative and insightful companion to the ideas and passions that kicked off one of the most derided of all musical genres and – on that basis alone – it remains as a challenge to the argument that every nuance of new ageism should be consigned to the bin. The spiritual explorations are here in bite sized chunks – "Gongs In The Rain" by Nesta Kerin Crain offering up pretty much what you'd expect from the title – and there are a few "names" – including an early Laraaji cut. For sheer curio value it's hard to top the opening cut featuring the piano music of Thomas de Hartmann, produced in association with spiritual guru G.I. Gurdjieff. The second CD offers up the visionaries and dyed-in-the-new-age hard cases for whom spiritual experience was/is indivisible from every note they play, presenting some complete pieces and others extracted from full-length works. The goodly – 11 minutes plus – selection from "Tien Fu: Heavens Gate" by Aeoliah is typical of the latter, taking this collection into the realm of a group of artists who re-christened themselves in line with a spiritual calling and set about inhabiting a musical territory one realm above the most trance-line moments in the Steve Hillage and Tangerine Dream catalogues. There are also a few moments of strange familiarity that drag these serial non-conformists into the mainstream. We'd defy anyone to listen hard to the slowly changing background chords in Larkin's "Two Souls Dance" (from 1984) and not be at least slightly reminded of 10cc's "I'm Not in Love."

It is beyond the remit of the present authors to decide whether Light in the Attic's claims to have produced a case to recognize this music as "great American folk art" are proven over the twenty tracks. But, I Am The Center is a high-quality gem in a very muddy musical area.

Various Artists:
Incredibly Strange Music Volume II
(Asphodel, 1995)
What? Extreme exotica and assorted aural abominations.

The rise of exotica and loungecore music in the later years of the last century owed a lot to a brace of Incredibly Strange Music books written by Vivian Vale and Andrea Jung. The pair met and interviewed key figures, like "word jazz" performer Ken Nordine and exotica fiends like Lux Interior and Poisy Ivy Rosarch of The Cramps. With the books the pair were involved in compiling two CDs of the same music and this – the second volume – edges it as a recommended listen. Its 17 cuts make it four tracks longer than Volume I and the variation of artists takes it to stranger territory than its companion. Basically, Incredibly Strange Music Volume II trawls novelty records, early stereo and electronic keyboard experiments and the strangest cuts available in the jazz/ easy listening market. Much of the material is made more exotic by its age and its – usually – feeble attempt to have jumped some fleeting bandwagon long since passed. So, Myrtle K Hilo's flat and hopelessly spirited attempt at the standard "A Lover's Prayer" is made all the more riveting when you see her larger than life figure, ukulele in hand, stood in front of her taxi cab on the cover of her 1967 album The Singing Cab Driver. Big hitters, like Ken Nordine, appear: "Flesh," "Green," and "Yellow" are all culled from his classic Colors album. Novelty-esque early synth pioneers like Hot Butter and Jean Jacques Perry give some inane and up tempo jollity to the proceedings and the quality is enhanced with cuts from Eden Ahbez' Eden's Island and Les Baxter's "Terror" from The Passions. The variety of – apparently – serious music, blatant low-cost novelty, sound pioneers and some famed paint-peelers from the museum of the strange – like Lucia Pamela's "Walking on the Moon" – is the key to the listenability of this collection. The fascination with exotica, and its free availability from a series of specialist labels and sites has come a long way since Incredibly Strange Music Volume II. Many of the cuts here are easily obtainable on reissues of the original albums that spawned them. But as a primer for the whole genre, this collection still cuts it.

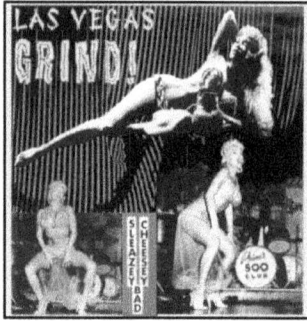

Various Artists:
Las Vegas Grind 3
(Crypt, 1999)
What; Sweaty sleazathon wall to wall with transcendental trash.

Crypt Records' Las Vegas Grind series culls cuts from long-forgotten low-fi/low budget sessions. The nominal reason for the series is the belief that this music sound-tracked the gyrations of showgirls and exotic dancers at the seedier end of 50s/60s Vegas' life. Well, either that or it's a shameless excuse for the presence of such girls on the front covers of most of the series. The number of times each of these cuts featured in such action isn't chronicled. Nor – for most of the Las Vegas Grind series – are the particulars of acts, many of whom signed short-term deals at best, relied on fluid collections of musicians (frequently fuelled by their own fluid intake) and knocked out these colourful gems in record time. Rockabilly, surf-guitar jazz and the odd fleeting Latin influence under-pin this collection of 30 (mainly) killer cuts. A few of the numbers offered here have escaped their humble origins to enjoy some celebrity. The Rhythm Kings' drum-heavy "Don't Sweat the Small Stuff" has been sampled a few times and the Four Instants' "Bogatini," was given a massive going over to re-emerge within Bentley Rhythm Ace's "The Return of the Hardcore Jumble Carbootechnodisco Roadshow." There are some classic novelty items: Pete Roberts' chuckle-heavy "Ho Ho Rock 'n' Roll" has also seen action as part of the Wavy Gravy collection, whilst Chaino's "The Chase" and "Rockin' Bongos" both throw restraint out of the door to bring a smile with their riffs (the chase also offering up horror grunts and howls with real B-movie charm).

In the end, this compilation, and its small army of Las Vegas Grind siblings, succeeds because it trawls the trash with an ear for presenting a complete collection. For every throwaway novelty with a title like "First Rhapsody for Knives, Forks and Spoons" there's an insistent rocker like Jimmy Oliver's "The Sneak." On most of what is offered up there a sense of a bunch otherwise anonymous musicians with little to lose by going for it. One of the 30 tracks here exceeds three minutes (and that only by one second), and most offer up licks and solos by way a mercifully short blast of sax, surf guitar or drums. Most are cut with the levels up high and little attempt to give any hi-fidelity balance to the end results. Conceived as B-sides, hopeful stabs at a novelty hit or throwaway DJ fodder, the Las Vegas Grind cuts are an insight into a musical world it would be nigh-on impossible to revive in an age of digital production and retro-chic. Hailed by All Music Guide as: "a worthwhile collection of novelty, garage, and surf artefacts," We'd go one further and say this is "the most worthwhile" of the Las Vegas Grind series.

Various Artists:
Listen to the Banned
(Academy Sound and Vision, 1984)
What? You want a double entendre? We'll give you one!

The concept is simple, the results variable, the collection, amiable, in a slightly smutty sort of way. Basically, Listen to the Banned compiles audio filth of an innocent era, going back so far that wall-to-wall radio play and ownership of music playing devices was in its infancy, and many of the original fans of the music on offer were accustomed to seeing the stuff performed live, or playing the songs themselves on a piano. This latter point matters because – for all the focus on sex and sexual practice here – the messages are carried in what they don't say. Some of the cuts have lasted better than others so Mae West's "A Guy What Takes His Time" and George Formby's "With my Little Ukulele in My Hand" are still widely available online where the facial expressions, like George's cheeky winks, say all you need to know. The true genius of the compiler here is exercised in gathering work from both sides of the Atlantic and taking it for granted the twentieth century listening audience will do the work to make sense of it all. It's the quality of the original banned record that matters more than anything, so Cliff Edwards' (AKA "Ukulele Ike") glorious "I'm a Bear in a Lady's Boudoir" might be shot-through with references to "grid-iron" football (and therefore incomprehensible to some listeners outside the USA), but the message is clear. He might lack the heroic athleticism of college football players but his athletic performances in close proximity with young women are more enjoyable and equally impressive. Some of the names here are well remembered, Billy Cotton and his Band (UK staples of early radio and television) open the proceedings, Formby and West follow from which point some the tracks are slightly more obscure, but the double entendres flow thick and fast. Along the way Sophie Tucker and Jimmy Rogers appear. For the most part these are low-fi, early recordings (everything on offer was recorded in the 20s and 30s), put through early eighties digital equipment, so at times it's tinny and the lack of quality on the source recordings shows through. But, it's great fun, still widely available and as definitive a collection of this stuff as you're likely to find on one disc.

Various Artists:
Mindexpanders Vol 1
(Past & Present, 2009)
What? Less is more trawl of psych strangeness.

The Past & Present label have trawled the limits of psychedelia and compilations like their Psychedelic Salvage Company twofer have helped push the limits of what, exactly, such music might be. The Mindexpanders series, by contrast, is a snapshot of one element of this music, eked out over five compilations. The company's website spells out the manifesto: "In Search of the Orgiastic Flashtastic Psychspastic Groove. Classic compilation of groovy instrumentals from around the world that will flip your top. All the usual exploito moves that cover a wide spectrum of music, with sitars, twangy guitars, horns, and even a steel drum track that will bring a warm glow to your day…Artists include: Los Diablos, Jokers, Jim Sullivan Sound, Dave Myers Effect, Guy Pedersen & Son Grand Orchestre, Blue Phantom, Emmanuel Brun, Crazy Elephant, Sound Of Lane, Morgans, Horror Charly, Le Apollo & La Danse Cosmique, Rowdies, Sun Rock Rodeo Roundup, Lord Sitar, and Clubman."

In plain English that means virtually nobody who would qualify as a household name and a range of sounds from fully-fledged freakouts to stuff little more dangerous than The Shadows after a few sherbets. The act of compilation and curatorship extends to thoughtful liner notes making it clear just how deeply the well was trawled. Les Diablos are Peruvian, Emmanuel Brun is French etc. For all this, the provenance of a few acts on the Mindexpanders discs, like Horror Charly on this one, still escapes the compilers. The true genius of this mix, and the others in the series, is the flitting from mood to mood and the window on the changing pop world provided by focussing closely on material that was generally a frippery. Such tracks were frequently recorded by session musicians for soundtracks aiming to be hip, and/or foreign acts hoping for a sniff of UK sales. A few of the novelties stand up well. Lord Sitar (aka session legend Big Jim Sullivan) twangs the nuts off "Have you Seen Your Mother Baby." Some of the obscurities also leap out. Sun Rock Rodeo Roundup's "Afternoon Breakdown" is a particular fuzzed out and freaksome delight. For those wanting more obscure fodder still, the same label offers a stack of similar releases (including two box sets of five albums each) featuring the same fodder but all concentrated on sitar led tunes.

Various Artists:
Napalm Death You Suffer Tribute Compilation
(Sirona, 2011)
What? A second of thrash sparks an epic of sonic experimentation.

Released on the first Napalm Death album, "You Suffer" represented something of an anti-song. A single second of thrash crashing and "urghh" vocals. It became a crowd pleaser on stage and – coupled with a similar track from the Electro Hippies – earned interest from the likes of The Guinness Book of Records when put out on a 7" single, the shortest ever such release. In 2011 98 cover versions of the alternative gem were lined up to make one of the most unique of tribute albums. For the most part the participants are woefully obscure alternativists, hell-bent on pushing the sonic envelope well beyond the sounds and styles that might guarantee airplay. But, what makes the compilation so compelling is the way so many of the acts have taken "You Suffer" as a manifesto for attitude, rather than attempted any literal noise assault/straight cover. So the album careers its way through snatches, and epic re-workings, most of which attempt some collision of sounds to generate drama, each helpfully re-titling their cover with a bracketed second title. The playing of the whole collection from end to end is – therefore - something of a stagger through a sonic gallery. Along the way A1976C's: "You Suffer (Sickbrain)" sets out to destroy your eardrums with distortions and atonality, Bangkai Angsa's; "You Suffer (Njuk Ngopo)" starts with a childish "La, la, la" vocal, hurls thrash crashing over the top and drags the little kiddies back into the mix before it finishes well inside a minute. Contraband's: "You Suffer (Trisectrix Of Daath)" by contrast, is an ambient epic, a shade over 11 minutes of dark electronic sounds, slowly shifting. Some of the acts are clearly on board for the laughs as much as the sonic possibilities, Awesome Bin Laden make an impressive noise, but -probably – more of a statement with their name and Gay Napalm Death's "You Suffer (Butt Guys)," is there and gone fleetingly, but – sort of – makes a point too. The thought of anyone dimming the lights, settling into an armchair and letting the speakers bathe them in this collection is farcical. But, lining up the tracks in alphabetical order of acts does allow the surprises and strange delights to ambush you, creating some dramatic tension if you let the whole thing play. Without warning you may find yourself confronted with Pollux's: "You Suffer (Vocal Drone Version)" which - pretty much – imagines a collision of ambient trash and Gregorian chant, or – for sheer comedy value - Sicx's: "You Suffer (In Sexual Intercourse)" which drops samples of the original "You Suffer" in as a backdrop to the noises of sex.

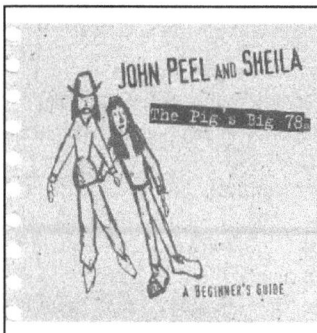

Various Artists:
The Pig's Big 78s
(Trikont, 2006)
What? A random vision of past delights.

Towards the end of his BBC career John Peel's show offered up truly random delights with "the Pig's big 78," basically Peel's wife Sheila – dubbed "the Pig" for her snorting laugh – presented a 78 rpm disc from a very varied selection found/offered to the programme. Some of the works were so old and obscure their origins proved impossible to trace, others came in foreign languages and all conceivable styles, often presenting a vision of an entertainment world lost to living memory. Two years after Peel's death Trikont Records issued a representative selection. Ranging from an unknown act singing an unknown song in Cantonese, to music hall comedy – like Billy Williams' song about the comedy/embarrassment potential of someone losing their trousers. The collection also took in seminal early blues and a collection of orchestral and dance band performances. This is a rag bag of the early and mid-twentieth century in musical action. At times it truly rocks out, Peanuts Wilson's "Cast Iron Arm" is one of few tracks here that would have made it to Peel's program with or without the Pig's themed slot. But Big 78s works wonderfully because it spins out from Peel's usual eclectic selection to take in twee and tuneful curiosities no radio station of any significant profile is likely to touch. Freddy Dosh's impressions of dogs, world record-breaking cars and domestic appliances, for example, belongs in a radio world long since gone. Inescapably low-fi, and packed with the random quality you'd expect from grabbing a fistful of charity shop records without looking first, Big 78s remains more unique than most compilations.

Various Artists: Polluting the Mainstream
(Bootleg, 2012)
What? What were they thinking?

Along with Elvis' Greatest Shit and Sinatra's Come Suck With Me this is a celebration of the party game/bootleg/mix tape genius allowing fans to select their own dream compilation for reasons the original artists would never endorse. The concept is simple enough, big selling artists and those famous for mainstream affiliations, caught at their most inventive and unhinged, and compiled to provide amusement for those less inclined to buy their records. Those behind this particular fun fest chose to do it in 2012 and put the results online. 23 tunes, from toe tappers to total meltdowns, lining up like so:

1. Chicago: "Free Form Guitar"
2. Donovan: "The Intergalactic Laxative"
3. The Eagles: "The Greeks Don't Want No Freaks"
4. Fleetwood Mac: "Somebody's Gonna Get Their Head Kicked In"
5. Frank Sinatra: "Reflections On The Future In 3 Tenses" excerpt (by Gordon Jenkins)
6. Hall & Oates: "Alley Katz"
7. Heart: "Hit Single"
8. Debbie Harry: "In Just Spring"
9. James Brown: "The Future Shock Of The World"
10. Marie Osmond: "Karawane"
11. The Police: "Mother"
12. Nirvana: "Montage of Heck Part 1"
13. Nirvana: "Montage of Heck Part 2"
14. Prince: "Bob George"
15. Buddy Holly: "Slippin' And Slidin' (sped-up version #1)"
16. Styx: "Plexiglass Toilet"
17. Joey Ramone: "The Wonderful Widow of Eighteen Springs"
18. Toto: "Robot Fight"
19. Van Halen: "Strung Out"
20. Willie Nelson: "Cowboys are Frequently Secretly Fond of Each Other"
21. Abba: "Intermezzo no.1"
22. Alice In Chains: "Love Song"
23. Cat Stevens: "Was Dog a Doughnut?"

The stunners? Well, the freakout free form guitar from Chicago Transit Authority (aka Chicago), is fully out there somewhere beyond Glenn Branca and other guitar/noise pioneers, and it runs to almost seven minutes. A few years later, in another reality, the remnants of this outfit recorded "If you Leave me Now" and conquered the world with a classic of easy listening soft rock. Sometimes the radio friendly types freaking out make it so easy to mock. The Eagles' "The Greeks Don't Want no Freaks" was never well-advised and Donovan's "The Intergalactic Laxative" (a comedy cut from the Cosmic Wheels album about the problems of going to the toilet in space) are just asking to be scraped into this company and Cat Stevens' early electro outing "Was Dog a Doughnut" isn't far behind. Sinatra, by contrast, is beyond novelty and somewhere into surreal on a cut where everyone but him appears to have a different creative vision. He rhymes "Hades" with "Ladies" during the only moment when he takes control of a cosmic calamity.

The real sport here, if you're that bothered, would be to gather this stuff, let it lie in one folder for long enough to forget who, exactly, is performing and play it blind, trying to guess as you go. Heart's "Hit Single," basically spoken word and sound effect strangeness, would probably defeat you, as it defeated their fans. Pinky and Perky', sorry Buddy Holly, performing "Slippin' and a Slidin'" is fairly obvious. But The Police, Styx, Debbie Harry and a few others here step so far out their accustomed realities as to present themselves as something totally unfamiliar. For complete anoraks/geeks there's a wealth of time to be spent compiling your own response to this bag of brainstorms. There's also much fun to be had searching out the evidence of what these people thought they were doing. Hall and Oates, for example, employed the legendary guitar of Robert Fripp in the act of performing one of the most bizarre one-off new wave excursions ever heard from musicians of their generation. If any inclusion here is unjust it must be ABBA, who always had the chops to move into pseudo classical territory. Their classical excursion is accomplished and well produced, delivering a sound many knew them to be capable of developing. You could also make cases for Willie Nelson or Donovan. Both, on the evidence here, were self-aware and intentionally ironic, or confrontational. Nelson's tirade against the homophobia in cowboy culture is bravery bordering on suicidal: "inside every cowboy there's a lady that'd love to slip out!"

Enjoy!

Various Artists:
The Rise and Fall of Paramount Records, Volume One (1917-1927)
(Third Man, 2013)
What? A matchless musical museum.

When is an album not an album? Maybe when it arrives in an oak cabinet boasting two large books, half a dozen vinyl albums, and attendant USB stick packed with 800 tracks. This isn't cheap, or freely available. It is indisputably both an event and a perfectly packaged piece of cultural history. It's also something of a labour of love for compiler Jack White. The set chronicles the work of Paramount Records, and their archive of blues recordings and other slices of – mainly forgotten – American music from the earliest years of recording in the United States. Blues legends like Blind Blake and Blind Lemon Jefferson are here with their earliest recordings but the point of the collection is to gather everything: novelty acts, one-off performers lost to even the most devoted archivists and every scratchy note released in the first ten years of a legendary label. Paramount Records habitually lost money and was – in any case – a secondary activity for a Wisconsin furniture business with an interest in cabinets and phonographs, amongst other things. Paramount trawled the talent where they could find it, taking in blues and country, and regarded the likes of Sweet Papa Stovepipe, The Beal Street Sheiks and Ida Cox as, potentially, as important as any other performer. For all its high-end presentation case and digital cleaning up, The Rise and Fall... revives that open mindedness to reveal an

America alive with accents, ideas and a the belief in the transformative power of music, certainly with regard to its ability to focus an emotion and present it to others. The other vital element to this collection comes because Paramount, faced with the need to find some means of making profitable recordings, actively entered the then contentious "race records" market, i.e. they made an issue of recording black artists and marketing them to a black audience. In hindsight, they helped to create history, back then they were simply chancing any means of making money.

The Paramount Records project in total covers the years to 1932, when the Great Depression obliged Paramount and many others to stop recording. The label finally folded in 1935. This collection, offering as it does more of the performers genuinely lost to archivists and available only via their recordings, is the most revealing and eclectic. There's a certain irony that some of the America's least profitable performers of the early twentieth century now find their efforts offered up on coloured vinyl with gold leaf trimmings in the presentation package. But this is cultural history and the reverence shown – however belated – is both sincere and fitting. Jack White put it perfectly in discussing the price tag of this release with Rolling Stone: "somebody sent me that recent Beatles box set of their vinyl albums, and that was $350. We were like, 'Fuck it. Those are just records. Think of what we're trying to do.'"

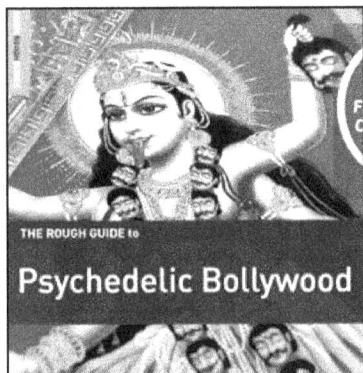

THE ROUGH GUIDE to
Psychedelic Bollywood

Various Artists:
The Rough Guide To Psychedelic Bollywood (World Music Network,) 2013
What? Less a tour guide, more a celebration of transcendental strangeness.

A glib summary might suggest the contents of this double package amount to Bollywood on Acid. Not far wrong in some cases, wildly inaccurate when applied to the whole compilation. The true fascination of The Rough Guide to Psychedelic Bollywood is akin to the experience of those dedicated scientists colliding beams of protons deep underground on the Franco-Swiss border. Their particle accelerator causes collisions resulting in random trails veering off in unpredictable directions. The collision of ultra-staid... Indian film industry, with its ritualised courtship and repetitive plots, and the trappings of the most hedonistic elements of sixties and seventies culture is here represented in some very strange sounds. "Psychedelic" in this context covers everything strange. The entry point is probably Asha Bhosle's admirably giddy rendering of 'Dum Maro Dum,' a benchmark song from Hare Rama Hare Krishna, a film about a young woman led astray into a world of drugs that plums Reefer Madness levels of over-acting and simplifying the evils of drug culture. The moments when the song flips instantly from indulgent thoughts to religious mantra count as psychedelic on their strangeness value alone.

The Rough Guide to Psychedelic Bollywood is inescapably a museum of the strange. There never was a core set of rules by which Bollywood might co-operate with swinging London or Haight-Ashbury, or judge its psychedelic winners from the other pretenders. So the vocal pyrotechnics (okay, yodelling) of Kishore Kumar are as meaningful a response to the wish to be western as the incendiary soundscapes and accomplished rhythmic palette of Kalynanji Anandji (who isn't one guy but actually a pair of brothers). Anandji isn't so much pure psychedelic as a very Indian response to America's seventies Blaxploitation soundtracks and the ambitious grooves of masters like James Brown. But, in this random and insanely inventive company the two Anandji cuts are little nuggets of genius, so too the oh so east meets west treat of R.D. Burman's "Freak Out Music" instrumental. The bonus second album of this set collects some of the more experimental and unrestrained moments of Burman's phenomenally productive career as Bollywood's senior purveyor of soundtrack perfection.

The tensions in this collection never truly vanish, most tracks betray moments in which the eastern flavours dominate, and other moments when blatant western percussion or a trippy guitar riff hogs the headphones. There is also a consistent sense of craftsmanship at work on music typically cranked out in rapid order to feed an insanely productive industry, and an insatiable market. It is anyone's guess which moments here the original creators regard as art, and which as artifice. But, as collections of the sonically strange and sometimes surreal go, this one ranks with the best.

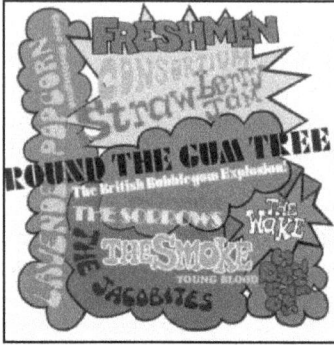

Various Artists:
Round the Gum Tree: The British Bubblegum Explosion
(Castle, 2004)
What? Muscular makeover for sugary American pop sound.

It's debateable whether Britain ever really did Bubblegum (an annoyingly catchy, incessantly upbeat derivative of pop based squarely on the singles market and a pre-teen audience). It's highly debatable whether the British acts veering into Bubblegum territory ever amounted to an "explosion" and it's certainly questionable whether The Real McCoy, an Irish showband would qualify as part of a "British," explosion. For the truly trivia obsessed it should be noted that The Real McCoy on this compilation were hitless in the UK and are nothing to do with a German dance act of the same name who charted in the 90's, rant over!

Spread over 30 tracks (three by The Real McCoy), and almost an hour and a quarter, Round the Gum Tree tells a little known story of late sixties British music. There are three things happening repeatedly in this compilation, each rotating around the others to provide a compelling and oddly powerful listen. Firstly, a few hopeful and overlooked British and Irish chancers are hopping madly on a stalled bandwagon in the hope of getting hits. Their works identify themselves by being reverent covers of US originals with as much of an American accent as the acts can muster. The Real McCoy (as a showband, covers were their trade) bookend this collection with "Round the Gum Tree" and "Quick Joey Small." Their first cover being a superior reworking of a song by Fire and the second a cover of a genuine US Bubblegum hit. Elsewhere the tireless Geno Washington just about emerges with his credibility intact from "Feeling So Good (Skooby Doo)" and Des Lee and Miami have a decent crack at "Goody Goody Gumdrops".

The second thing happening in large amount involves British pop bands, already schooled in live performance, honing a muscular blend of Bubblegum. Where their US counterparts generally ground their works out in studios and thought of the session fees there's a sense with The Tremeloes' "Sunshine Games" or The Arrows' "Mercy Mercy" of decent musicians more attuned to knocking out these gems and thinking about female fans, and potential fame. The latter is clear enough in the early work of Status Quo – "Ice in the Sun" is, rightly, included along with a determined reworking of "Green Tambourine" – and acts like The Sorrows. The third element, and probably the main reason to devour this collection for most readers of this book, is the presence of a great many acts who saw Bubblegum as one element in a vibrant psychedelic pop scene and used it as an excuse to stretch their creative ideas into radio friendly running times. In some cases, notably The Smoke's "Girl in the Park" we catch the attempted hits of acts now better regarded for their rock credentials. But given the presence here of freakbeat, and fleeting moments of full-blooded psychedelic fantasy, Round the Gum Tree is a glaring spotlight on some hitherto neglected jewels of the British pop crown. The detailed sleeve notes do a decent job of filling in the basic details regarding The Nevadas – check out the stunning psychedelic guitar break in "Gimme Gimme Good Lovin'" – and The Scrugg, their "Lavender Popcorn" is another standout. There are loads here worthy of rediscovery. The breathless, upbeat and effortlessly good "Cynthia Serenity" by The Consortium started life as a B-side. That says something about the amount good music aiming itself, usually without result, at the late sixties British charts.

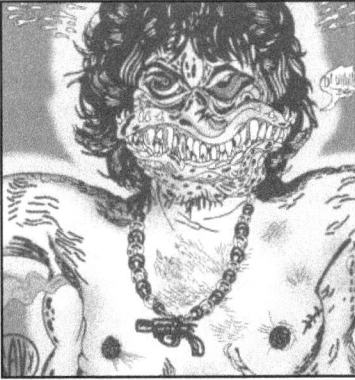

Various Artists:
Savage Pencil Presents
(EMI, 1999)
What? Eclectic compilation from very individual talent.

From the appearance of his first dark and vicious cartoons in the British music paper Sounds during the punk era Edwin Pouncey/ AKA Savage Pencil has been a fixture on the fringes of the music world and a focus for an audience who have appreciated his demented visions and unique talent. As with most cult heroes he packs a track record littered with work that has remained in the minds of those who saw it and a CV that might usefully be described as "varied." This album came about through a somewhat haphazard collision of EMI Records running a "Songbooks" project involving notable music figures compiling albums and Savage Pencil having unused work involving one of his strangest creations, Dead Duck.

That story, and the text for four chilling spoken word tracks, listed as "Bad Thort" items on the album, all feature in a lavishly illustrated and generous booklet. The 19 track compilation also packs another Savage Pencil original in "The Antiquack" a piercing assault of electric guitar skirting the borderlands of atonality and sequenced to open the proceedings. From this point we get a who's who of cult heroes and strange soundtracks, with the emphasis on unique and highly individual instrumental performers. Duke Ellington and a couple of cuts from Sun Ra and his Arkestra throw some strong jazz shapes, acoustic guitarist John Fahey and Faust also appear, the latter in the 12 minute epic "Krautrock." Most of the vocal tracks are packed to the dying seconds with some sense of eccentricity although the presence of UK folk idols Shirley and Dolly Collins and the sweet vocal machinations of Surf's Up era Beach Boys deliver a change in pace and tone halfway through.

Above everything else this is an artefact that drags the listener into the strange and hugely surreal world of Savage Pencil and makes for repeated and intense listening. The visuals in the accompanying book include some – well – savage reworkings of classic images including a Jim Morrison portrait and the cover illustration from A Clockwork Orange. Musically it is a superbly sequenced journey through some dark landscapes, worlds packed with the strange but very tangible quality of otherness. In such company the Beach Boys' "Til I Die" offers up its full sense of foreboding, and the bizarre spoken word "Bad Thort" tracks act like vivid stop signs on a dark journey through the subconscious.

Various Artists:
Savoy Wars
(Savoy Records, 1994)
What? In the alternative reality in which the Britain's miner's strike of the eighties defeated Margaret Thatcher's government, the charts sound like this.

This is a revolutionary manifesto dispensed in ten chunks of the most activist, cerebral, pop imaginable. Culled from the releases of Savoy Records between 1986 and 1990, Savoy Wars charts the period from The Smiths' exultant The Queen is Dead to the unstoppable rise of The Stone Roses and Happy Mondays via an aggressive Mancunian combination of dance pop and recycled classic revolutionary ideas. Savoy set themselves up as guardians of a subversive spirit, pouring their creative efforts into a combination of re-imagined pop standards and taking massive liberties in terms of combining singer and unlikely material. The extensive liner notes drip self-aggrandizing rhetoric. The album duly gathered a few fawning reviews.

It sounds less revolutionary in retrospect partly because others have picked up similar ideas and run a lot further since 1990, and partly because some of Savoy's regular targets for abuse, like high-ranking "God's cop" James Anderton, are now consigned to history. Like many revolutionaries, Savoy worked with the tools available. P. J. Proby, dissolute and, apparently, bordering deranged provides vocals for half the cuts here, including a rambling and positively scary "Hardcore: M97002." A 15 minute hardcore dance wonder that claimed on its original packaging to be a duet between Proby and Madonna. He opens with the observation that there's no such thing as rape when you're "wearing a Superman cape." The second you hear the female lead vocal it obviously isn't Ms Ciccone and that dynamic does infect some of the album. Savoy clearly had a great time dreaming up their epistles to undermine the music industry, but they're not everyone's ideas of a joke, or revolution. And some work way better than the others.

With Proby they hit gold. The further he falls into his cups the more he channels plain darkness and an almost primal pop singing power. His covers of "In the Air Tonight," "Sign O the Times" and Springsteen's "I'm on Fire" are fat sounding reclamations of popular song as a means of stopping time. The Irish separatist standard "The Old Fenian Gun" is also trusted to Proby. It's a great sound, but, grates against the other Proby covers. Elsewhere, the liner notes detail the way Kingsize Taylor, sixties pop almost-made-it turned hardcore eighties cynic, turned down Savoy. The label responded by signing Bobby Thompson, who sang with Taylor's band. His lengthy tirade fronting a monumental cover of Iggy and the Stooges' "Raw Power" certainly reimagines the track for a northern dance-floor of the eighties, but it's never certain whether Thompson has a clue what's going on.

The obvious comparison here is with the KLF/JAMMS' situationist slaughter of the pop ethic. Savoy's stock-in trade of assembling the pieces and recording the results has a certain hit or miss quality. When it works, which it does fully half of the time, it is pop as a genuine force, fit to incite action and threaten the centres of power. To achieve that on the back of a package of songs, many of them cover versions turned into the manic visions of the brains behind a record label, is some feat.

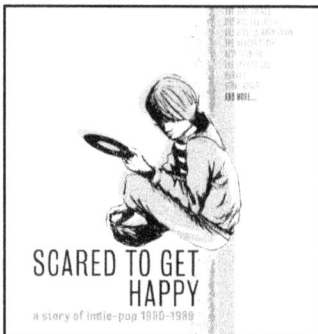

SCARED TO GET
HAPPY
a story of indie-pop 1980-1989

Various Artists:
Scared to Get Happy (A Story Of Indie Pop 1980-1989)
(Cherry Red, 2013)
What? Forty years later and thousands of miles away; the collection that tries to do for 80s UK indie what Nuggets did for US 60s garage bands.

The press release for Scared to Get Happy cited the legendary Nuggets compilation of 1972, the collection that launched dozens of imitations and made the point that anyone with the persistence to collect largely forgotten records, and sort the visionaries out from the rightly forgotten, might just have a story to tell. For all these outlandish claims, the sheer scale and diversity on offer here suggests Cherry Red have the right idea. Nuggets made the point that amongst the throwaway novelty and three chord wonders of the US garage scene there were some underappreciated masters of their art, and there was a time when every street appeared to play host to a would-be genius with a fuzztone amp and killer riff. Spread over 134 tracks, culled from the coolest of UK indie labels of the eighties (including: Creation, Factory, Cherry Red, Rough Trade, Zoo, Kitchenware, Vindaloo and Red Rhino) Scared to Get Happy spills a story of young pretenders crawling from the remains of punk, many of them listening to a previous generation of Beatles/Searchers/Troggs pop with harmonies, and all of them convinced they can get played on the radio and sell records. Like Nuggets this is a stronger compilation for the absence of the titans of the scene. Hits from The Smiths or New Order would only have distracted from the unheralded gems on offer here. And there is certainly a story to tell. For many of these acts BBC Radio One's John Peel show was a spiritual home and the big-hair, big-sound rock/pop of the eighties was the enemy. Their individual songs grow in this company and the specific talents of each act inform the story of the decade. The Fire Engines resplendently catchy and riff-heavy "Candyskin" makes an early statement about jangling guitars and the sheer infectious power of a good tune, Prefab Sprout follow soon after on the – roughly chronological – first CD "Lions in my own Garden (Exit Someone)" colliding indie/DIY sensibilities with a Beatlesque influence that would have been heresy a few years before.

There are big(ish) names here. The collection includes early efforts from Primal Scream and The Stone Roses, whilst James and The Boo Radleys (who had major British success bit didn't export so well) are also on hand. But, to see these in the context of a collection that also boasts cult favourites like Bradford's "Skin Storm" along with works by the likes of Jesse Garon and the Desperados, The Mighty Lemon Drops, The Pooh Sticks and Grab Grab The Haddock, is to see that a part of 1980s Britain was a vibrant world of local heroes, low-fi visionaries and individuals magnificently welded to their own pop dreams. The chronological ordering makes some sense of this but by the late eighties the notion of making music for the times was breaking down on an industrial scale. Madchester's dance scene began to pillage the late sixties for inspiration, and drugs, and others took their own roads away from the mainstream. To sit down and listen through five CDs of this is to gorge yourself to the point where the last morsels cease to be pleasurable. Set on shuffle and dipped into sporadically, Scared to get Happy is that rarity, a compilation capable of delivering on an ambitious promise. Its sonic resemblance to Nuggets isn't that strong but it does look at one country and one period of time to tell a story in music. And many of the 134 tunes on offer are absolute winners.

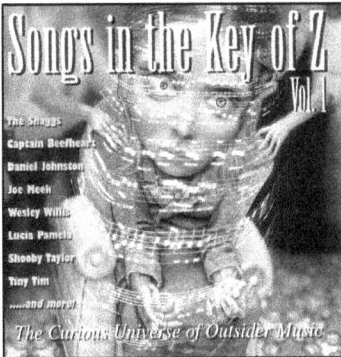

Various Artists:
Songs in the Key of Z
(Gammon, 2002)
What? A manifesto.

There is enough defining and claiming of "Outsider Music" online these days to allow the casual researcher to start with the Wikipedia page, navigate to specialist sites dealing with one area – like Exotica – and keep digging for the rest of their natural lives without ever running out of new sounds. Music well outside the mainstream has always been with us, but making sense of it, and herding this particular band of sonic cats into any coherent group remains a tough job. For a long time collecting and discussing such sounds was the province of a handful of people who knew little of each other's existence. Fanzines, and the internet gradually brought the community together and…well, you wouldn't be reading this book unless someone other than those involved in writing it had seen the commercial potential, rant over!

Irwin Chusid can take credit for putting outsider music into some sensible order and making a clear case for its merits. More than anyone else in this area his work in compiling, finding and explaining has given the rest of the community some basis for their arguments. His book Songs in the Key of Z is highly recommended (on the basis that if you're dipping into this book you'll doubtless love that one). Chusid also compiled two Songs in the Key of Z CDs.

The whole point about outsider music is that it has to be experienced, rather than read about and discussed. So, Songs in the Key of Z is as good a start point as you're ever likely to find. Touching all bases from the eccentric genius to the performers in danger of children pointing and laughing at them, Songs in the Key of Z includes: The Shaggs' "Philosophy of the World," a decent sized sample of Jack Mudurian's "Downloading the Repertoire." Shooby Taylor's "Stout-Hearted Men," and outsider gold from the likes of Wesley Willis, Tiny Tim and The Legendary Stardust Cowboy. Offering up 20 cuts, as much of the outsider range of styles as you can cover on one CD, and flawless quality control in the selection, this is as good a primer as you're likely to find on one disc. Particularly so because the real nuggets here are a few genuinely hard to find gems like Eilert Pilarm's – ahem – very individual interpretation of "Jailhouse Rock."

Various Artists:
Songs in the Key of Z Volume 2
(Gammon, 2002)
What? Proof there is substance to the manifesto.

Having made the point with the Songs in the Key of Z book and the first CD Irwin Chusid underlined it with this collection. Pretty much the same idea, pretty much the same experience with a variety of the diverse, different and downright insane. Volume 2 is conspicuously shorter on names with some previous clout in terms of music sales, focussing instead on those artists who have gone on to become celebrated cult stars of the whole outsider genre. So Shooby Taylor opens the proceedings with "Lift Ev'ry Voice and Sing," opening his song with the observation: "Blacks, let's not forget where we came from…" The pure eccentricity count is fairly high in the 17 cuts on offer but a few – like The Space Lady's ethereal float through "I Had Too Much to Dream Last Night" – double as sublime and under-appreciated moments of genius. By contrast, Wayne's paean to his big breasted companion "Deep Bosom Woman" is a show/ conversation stopper for entirely different reasons.

As with the discussion about Volume 1 of the same collection there isn't that much point in going on in print about this compilation. Hearing this ragbag of the rough, rabid and really under-appreciated is the whole point. Volumes 1 and 2 were subsequently combined into one release and – frankly – if you're motivated to read the book in front of you, you're unlikely to be disappointed by anything on Songs in the Key of Z.

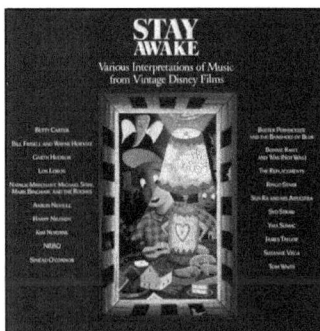

Various Artists:
Stay Awake
(A&M, 1988)
What? Disney's darker side.

Like many of the most effective compilations this collection works – big time – because the idea behind it is simple and brilliant. Released in the late eighties, almost the nadir for creativity and chance taking amongst the rock elite, Stay Awake rounds up a collection of big names (like Tom Waits) who'd forged reputations with a very individual talent, some reliable "character" performers (like Ringo Starr) and a few of those enjoying a briefly higher than usual career peak (like Aaron Neville). Collectively these talents and a host of high-profile backing musicians tackle some of the most noted material in the Disney songbook. Production wise it's standard AOR fayre with enough space for the various stars to throw in some inspired licks.

The results are never less than interesting and, occasionally, spell-binding. The stroke of genius to set the whole escapade alight is the realisation that most of the performers are characterful and capable of telling a great story and most of the songs have a strong story inside. Songs once featured as statements of melancholy, regret or personality for characters in a Disney film serve as comments on the lives of the performers. When they work, they sound like the perfect synthesis of the star and song. For sheer shameless immersion in the childlike mentality of the original it's hard to top Buster Poindexter (aka former New York Doll David Johansen) with his Tom Waits alike take on the Seven Dwarves marching song "Heigh Ho." Bonnie Raitt's maudlin and soulful take on "Baby Mine" was a radio hit on both sides of the Atlantic and if Ringo Starr turned in a better studio performance in the 80s than the lugubrious lament of "When You Wish upon a Star" it remains unreleased. Unlikely collaborations, Herb Albert joins Ringo on "When You Wish…" and the presence of talents as varied as Suzanne Vega and word-jazz eccentric Ken Nordine, ensure that each new track packs a surprise and the standard never drops.

Recorded in an era that often grasped the moment and tried too hard to stay fashionable, this overlooked collection remains blissfully timeless.

Various Artists:
Strong Love - Songs Of Gay Liberation 1972-81
(Chapter Music, 2012)
What? Big gay hearts.

A, fittingly, rainbow collection of, sometimes, strident and refreshingly varied polemics dedicated to campaigning for gay rights. Strong Love shows the gay rights movement as a broad church of folk, soul, new wave and most other variants on popular music over almost a decade. The sequencing pits the gently assertive Charlie Murphy next to the Blaxploitation groove of Blackberri and tours a number of musical outposts thereafter. The American theme of the collection is mediated by one notable British piece, Tom Robinson's "Good to be Gay," a genuine curio, a calypso reworking of his UK hit "Glad to be Gay." Much of the 15 track line up on Strong Love started life on poorly financed, or private, releases. Consequently, much of the Strong Love story unfolds like the varied songs in a musical, the narrative is clear, we know these campaigners eventually achieved many of their goals, and the songs punctuate the historical narrative. For sheer curio value Smokey's "Strong Love" with its disco/glam groove and lowly seductive vocal is a notable stand out, and one of a few tracks here that hints at the vibrant club scene supporting gay culture at the time. These touches of colour, and the cathartic humour of Lavender Country's "Cryin' These Cocksucking Tears," achieve as much as one CD can do in chronicling an underground culture, and focussing the messages swapped by means of cherished musical missives. In retrospect this is an articulate, enthralling and vibrant argument. So much so, that the album works as an alternative history of the period, whatever your sexual orientation.

Various Artists:
Trojan X-Rated Box Set
(Sanctuary, 2002)
What? Full-on filth with fantastic riddim'!

Covering near enough a decade of crucial reggae cuts (1966-1975) X-Rated trawls the top tracks in a vast-tonnage of material that never made it overground. Reggae's rise to global prominence owed much to the UK's Trojan label (which struggled in the USA partly because of the ubiquity of Trojan as the name of a brand of condom). Whilst Bob Marley and a number of other acts achieved international status, and owed something to Trojan in the process, there was also a strong demand for nudge-nudge playful sexy fun amongst reggae listeners. Trojan produced much of the best material in this area and a number of artists – like Max Romeo – achieved cult status as a result. Some of the rhythms and gags get recycled but it's no bad thing to give the 50 tracks here some sense of continuity. Derrick Morgan's "Horse Race (aka My Dickie)" rubs up hard against Matador and Fay's "Sex Grand National" – both reliant on the short running time and increasing tension of a horse race as a metaphor for sex. Elsewhere, the collection ends on a classic cover, The Fabulous Five's version of Benny Bell's "Shaving Cream." A number of cuts use a basic reggae rhythm as the backdrop to male/female conversations straight out of a crass sex comedy. Anyone bothered about political correctness or po-faced about issues of equality would probably hate some of X-Rated with a passion. Of the stars on show it is Max Romeo – who offers "Wet Dream," "Play With Your Pussy" and "Sexy Sadie" – who probably shades it as a genius of explicit comedy letching. But, this is a celebration of a label and style of sex comedy both lost to history. So the variety of the fifty filthsome fusillades of fun here is really the point.

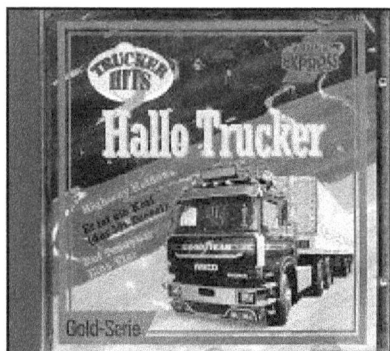

Various Artists:
Trucker Hits 3: Hallo Trucker
(Ariola Express, 1990)
What? Krautcountrysampler

Country and western travels well. Better in fact than many steeped in the sounds of Nashville give it credit for. Many nations have their own sound and traditions, especially in Europe, where "country 'n' Irish" thrives in the west and the former Soviet lands have their own regional traditions way to the east. The distance between these outposts is – roughly – that between east and west coasts of the USA, the distance in country traditions is far greater than seen in the USA. Located conveniently between the two, Germany has a strong, manly, beer drinkin'/meat eatin' mentality that has supported acts like Tom Astor (a home grown straight down the line country talent with an impressive discography).

Hallo Trucker compiles an albums' worth of Astor cuts, and adds some additional tracks by the likes of Jonny Hill. It is country – as in straight traditional country with nary a sniff of anything Gram Parsons and his followers did to the form – and it is very German. The pace steps up to rapid guitar picking now and again. But, much of the time the twanging, vocal harmonies and bass and drums are turned down to allow Astor to tell a story.

This is a world of trucking, marital fidelity and the standard country and western scenario of the little guy with the big dilemma, all sung in German. For sheer curio value there's nothing to top Jonny Hill's German cover of Red Sovine's tear-jerking classic "Teddy Bear" and for a literal translation of American country values to Europe there's nothing to top Astor's anthemic "Meine Antwort ist die Große Autobahn" ("My Answer is the Great Highway").

Nurembourg will never be Nashville and some of the interest in a compilation like this will always be in the imitation-is-the-best-form-of-flattery vibe that pervades when session players and limited budgets bring about pale imitations of an original sound. But, as a document of how much a tradition means when moved thousands of miles and applied to another country it is too easy to disregard Hallo Trucker. Once the novelty of hearing pedestrian (but highly competent) country tunes picked out behind a German lead vocal has abated, it is clear that any country with trucks, an ethic of hard work and at least part of its identity tied up in the notion of men being men, has a right to country music. The Germans – and in particular, Tom Astor - do it their way.

Various Artists:
Wavy Gravy
(Beware, 2005)
What? Transcendental trashathon, oft imitated, seldom equalled

Firstly: a word of warning. The title and compilation have appeared in various guises over the years. The identity of the original compiler and the identity and origin of the some of the material appears hopelessly lost in time, and even the most knowledgeable fan-driven websites admit defeat trying to identify everything on offer. It's a safe bet that some of the original performers – if they are still alive - remain blissfully unaware their work is available in this form. In its various incarnations Wavy Gravy has been a home for the low-fi trash of the late fifties and early sixties American teen culture. Gormless jokes, half-cocked and incomprehensible dance crazes and the occasional two chord teen-pop wonders rub shoulders with radio announcements and the soundtracks for film trailers. As a vision of a country obsessed with novelty to the point of emotional disfunction Wavy Gravy probably belongs in the Sociology department of every leading university, ready to be unearthed with the statement: "If you thought early sixties America was like Mad Men…"

The only well-known songs here "Bo Diddley" and "Wild Thing" appear in budget rehashes that make the originals sound like carefully crafted gems. Hambone Hunter's bizarre "Bacon Fat" may well be the most pointless and moronic dance craze record ever unleashed and some of the "jokes" on offer push the boundaries of taste to breaking point. For sheer insensitivity it's hard to decide whether Moses Longpiece or Eddie Noack shade the competition. Longpiece's "Slide Her Under the Door" reworks an old joke, the singer waxing over his love for his girl only to be told she has been run over by "a great big steamroller." He replies, "with tears in my eyes…I'm taking a shower…slide her under the door." Noack's tale is a Norman Bates story, a litany of those he has slaughtered, as told to the one person who will always forgive him, his mother. His mother's ongoing silence every time he asks: "Do you think I'm psycho Mama?" is both ominous and shamelessly tasteless.

Half a century or more since this trash-fest was competing for teenagers' hard argued dollars it is genuinely hard to separate the intentional jokes from the half-baked attempts to start a craze or shock an audience. But, Wavy Gravy in its various incarnations, continues to win fans and astound listeners.

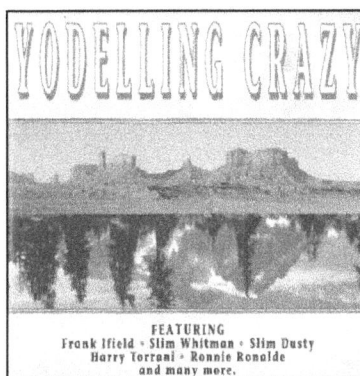

Various Artists:
Yodelling Crazy
(EMI, 1991)
What? From the Alps to Arizona and from the twenties to the nineties. Definitive yodelling.

A single CD best of covering a myriad of musical styles and the varied vocabulary of yodelling, from European folk music, through novelty pop vocal stylings to the mournful and morose howling of American country at its most inconsolable. Yodelling Crazy sets itself an ambitious task and presents 26 tracks to chart yodelling lore in all its forms. Oddly, the one clanger is – arguably – the 1991 remix of Frank Ifield's 1962 hit "She Taught me How to Yodel." Reworking early sixties novelty for the fleeting pop fashion sounds of 1991 has the proverbial sore thumb appearance when it fronts a collection of such companions as Tex Morton's "Big Rock Candy Mountains," an insanely upbeat and hyper-stylised piece of country with cod-opera and enough varied vocal improvisations to leave the standard religious speaking in tongues sound like a staid weather forecast.

The strength of Yodelling Crazy is its willingness to rank Tex Morton alongside Suzy Bogguss – an emerging country talent in 1991 – and still find space for clichéd classics like "Lonely Goatherd" and "The Runaway Train." Country schmaltz is well represented with Roy Rogers' "Night Guard" and Smokey Dawson's "Happy go Lucky Cowhand" representing the Hollywood cowboy angle. Also on hand are a couple of syrupy Slim Whitman tracks: "There's a Rainbow in Every Teardrop" and "Chimebells."

Yodelling Crazy is an exploration rather than any kind of definitive history – Jimmy Rodgers is nowhere to be heard and the presence of two cuts each by Frank Ifield and Slim Whitman over-plays their contributions to yodelling history – but in this context the exotica of Heino and the historic curio of Andreany, (a French music hall act nicknamed "The Yodelling Tramp" who remains so obscure the copious sleeve-notes can't find that much to say with any certainty), makes perfect sense.

Yodelling Crazy pushes an acquired taste to its sonic limits and is best used sparingly and/or as some flavouring for a varied mix-tape sequence. In the wrong circumstances this is a room-clearer. It could, with repeated use, probably prove effective in forcing a confession from a taciturn criminal suspect. But for those who can stand the heat – and we're guessing such creatures are the most likely readers of this book – Yodelling Crazy is also a little treasure chest of the strange and singular.

Where to Next?

Hopefully you were so taken by something you read here to start searching the site of a specific record company, a particular artist or the schedule of a radio station to put more of that music into your life. Somewhere out there in cyberspace the authors of this book are probably lining up alongside you to buy music, express opinions or consume the latest blog post from someone equally addicted to seeking out new sounds. One place regularly visited in this regard is the Music for Maniacs blog site, which has the kind of community feel that leaves you feeling supported, and never alone (important if you're the sort that would read this book down to the final section!)

Fittingly, then, we'll give them the last word in our book.

A series of office machines set up to play "Bohemian Rhapsody"...an entire album of "disco polka"...hip-hop instrumentals sampled entirely from animal sound effects...how can such things be?! An audio anomaly such as these is rarely considered to be "real" music by mainstream audiences, or even by those who fancy themselves "alternative." Anything that doesn't neatly fit into the accepted categories of jazz, rock, country/ folkloric, classical, even avant-garde, are dismissed as novelties.

In 2004, I started the blog Music For Maniacs to celebrate what these musics that fall in between culture's sofa cushions are really about: imagination. Artists/crackpots/visionaries who won't (can't?) accept the notion that music is a merely a handful of templates to be dutifully filled in by "professionals." We cover music that is often of no known genre, or a crazy conglomeration of multiple genres, whether by design, or thru an outsider's intuition. Music that is sometimes considered uncool, obsolete, or, dare I say, funny! It doesn't sound like anything in particular, and it's certainly not just random noise. It's simply what everyone else is not doing. You may already be a Maniac.

-Mr Fab

Gonzo
Books

There is still such a thing as alternative Publishing

robert calvert
centigrade 232

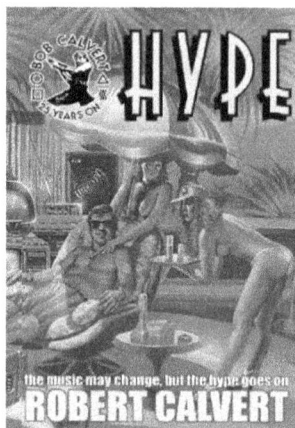

HYPE
ROBERT CALVERT 25 YEARS ON
the music may change, but the hype goes on
ROBERT CALVERT

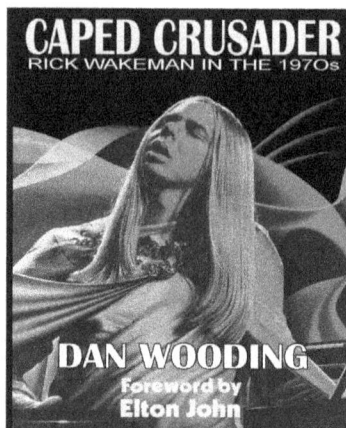

CAPED CRUSADER
RICK WAKEMAN IN THE 1970s
DAN WOODING
Foreword by
Elton John

Robert Newton Calvert: Born 9 March 1945, Died 14 August 1988 after suffering a heart attack. Contributed poetry, lyrics and vocals to legendary space rock band Hawkwind intermittently on five of their most critically acclaimed albums, including Space Ritual (1973), Quark, Strangeness & Charm (1977) and Hawklords (1978). He also recorded a number of solo albums in the mid 1970s. CENTIGRADE 232 was Robert Calvert's first collection of poems.

Hype   'And now, for all you speeding street smarties out there, the one you've all been waiting for, the one that'll pierce your laid back ears, decoke your sinuses, cut clean thru the schlook rock, MOR/crossover, techno flash mind mush. It's the new Number One with a bullet … with a bullet … It's Tom, Supernova, Mahler with a pan galactic biggie …' And the Hype goes on. And on. Hype, an amphetamine hit of a story by Hawkwind collaborator Robert Calvert. Who's been there and made it back again. The debriefing session starts here.

Rick Wakeman is the world's most unusual rock star, a genius who has pushed back the barriers of electronic rock. He has had some of the world's top orchestras perform his music, has owned eight Rolls Royces at one time, and has broken all the rules of composing and horrified his tutors at the Royal College of Music. Yet he has delighted his millions of fans. This frank book, authorised by Wakeman himself, tells the moving tale of his larger than life career.

"So many books, so little time."
Frank Zappa

THE NINE HENRYS
By Peter McAdam

TERRY DENE: BRITAIN'S FIRST ROCK & ROLL REBEL
DAN WOODING

King Squealer
MAURICE O'MAHONEY WITH DAN WOODING

There are nine Henrys, pur
ported to be the world's
first cloned cartoon charac
ter. They live in a strange
lo fi domestic surrealist
world peopled by talking
rock buns and elephants on
wobbly stilts.

They mooch around in their
minimalist universe suffer
ing from an existential
crisis with some genetically
modified humour thrown in.

Marty Wilde on Terry Dene: "Whatever
happened to Terry becomes a great deal
more comprehensible as you read of the
callous way in which he was treated by
people who should have known better
many of whom, frankly, will never know
better of the sad little shadows of
the past who eased themselves into
Terry's life, took everything they
could get and, when it seemed that all
was lost, quietly left him … Dan Wood
ing's book tells it all."

Rick Wakeman: "There have
always been certain 'careers'
that have fascinated the
public, newspapers, and the
media in general. Such
include musicians, actors,
sportsmen, police, and not
surprisingly, the people who
give the police their employ
ment: The criminal. For the
man in the street, all these
careers have one thing in
common: they are seemingly
beyond both his reach and,
in many cases, understanding
and as such, his only associ
ation can be through the
media of newspapers or tele
vision. The police, however,
will always require the ser
vices of the grass, the
squealer, the snitch, (call
him what you will), in order
to assist in their investiga
tions and arrests; and amaz
ingly, this is the area that
seldom gets written about."

"Outside of a dog, a book is
man's best friend. Inside of a
dog it's too dark to read."
Groucho Marx

LUNAR NOTES
ZOOT HORN ROLLO'S CAPTAIN BEEFHEART EXPERIENCE

BILL HARKLEROAD
with BILLY JAMES

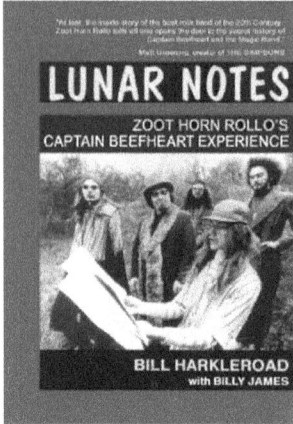

Bill Harkleroad joined Captain Beef heart's Magic Band at a time when they were changing from a straight ahead blues band into something completely dif ferent. Through the vision of Don Van Vliet (Captain Beefheart) they created a new form of music which many at the time considered atonal and difficult, but which over the years has continued to exert a powerful influence. Beefheart re christened Harkleroad as Zoot Horn Rollo, and they embarked on recording one of the classic rock albums of all time Trout Mask Replica - a work of unequalled daring and inventiveness.

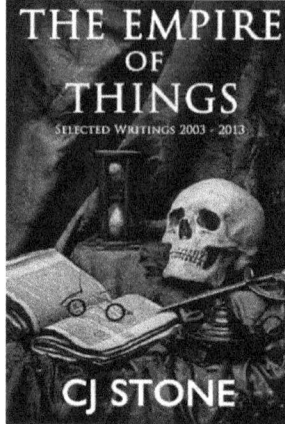

THE EMPIRE OF THINGS
SELECTED WRITINGS 2003 - 2013

CJ STONE

Politics, paganism and …. Vlad the Impaler. Selected stories from CJ Stone from 2003 to the present. Meet Ivor Coles, a British Tommy killed in action in September 1915, lost, and then found again. Visit Mothers Club in Erdington, the best psyche delic music club in the UK in the '60s. Celebrate Robin Hood's Day and find out what a huckle duckle is. Travel to Stonehenge at the Summer Solstice and carouse with the hippies. Find out what a Ranter is, and why CJ Stone thinks that he's one. Take LSD with Dr Lilly, the psychedelic scientist. Meet a headless soldier or the ghost of Elvis Presley in Gabalfa, Cardiff. Journey to Whitstable, to New York, to Malta and to Transylvania, and to many other places, real and imagined, polit ical and spiritual, transcendent and mundane. As The Independent says, Chris is "The best guide to the underground since Charon ferried dead souls across the Styx."

The Time of Feasting

mick farren

This is is the first in the highly acclaimed vampire novels of the late Mick Farren. Victor Renquist, a surprisingly urbane and likable leader of a colony of vampires which has existed for centuries in New York is faced with both admin istrative and emotional prob lems. And when you are a vampire, administration is not a thing which one takes lightly.

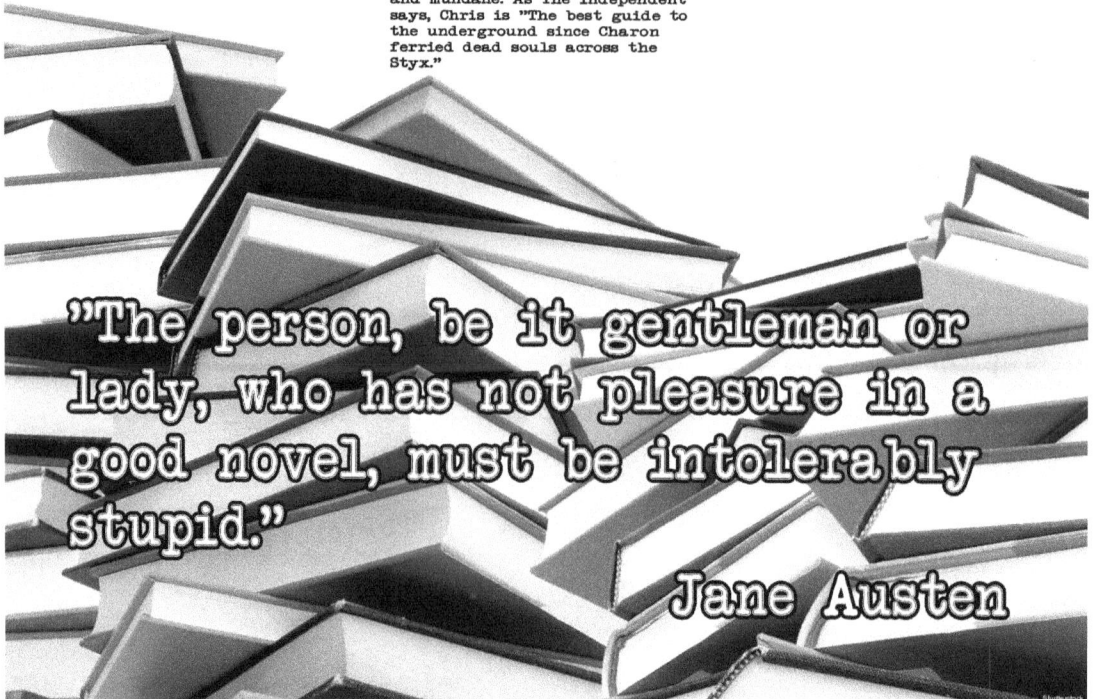

"The person, be it gentleman or lady, who has not pleasure in a good novel, must be intolerably stupid."

Jane Austen

www.ingramcontent.com/pod-product-compliance
Lightning Source LLC
Chambersburg PA
CBHW081422090426
42740CB00017B/3153